한국 인권문제

미국 반응 및 동향 2

한국 인권문제

미국 반응 및 동향 2

한국학술정보

| 머리말

일제 강점기 독립운동과 병행되었던 한국의 인권운동은 해방이 되었음에도 큰 결실을 보지 못했다. 1950년대 반공을 앞세운 이승만 정부와 한국전쟁, 역시 경제발전과 반공을 내세우다 유신 체제에 이르렀던 박정희 정권, 쿠데타로 집권한 1980년대 전두환 정권까지, 한국의 인권은 이를 보장해야 할 국가와 정부에 의해 도리어 억압받고 침해되었다. 이런 배경상 근대 한국의 인권운동은 반독재, 민주화운동과 결을 같이했고, 대체로 국외에 본부를 둔 인권 단체나 정치로부터 상대적으로 자유로운 종교 단체에 의해 주도되곤 했다. 이는 1980년 5 · 18광주민주화운동을 계기로 보다 근적인 변혁을 요구하는 형태로 조직화되었고, 그 활동 영역도 정치를 넘어 노동자, 농민, 빈민 등으로 확대되었다. 이들이 없었다면 한국은 1987년 군부 독재 종식하고 절차적 민주주의를 도입할 수 없었을 것이다. 민주화 이후에도 수많은 어려움이 있었지만, 한국의 인권운동은 점차 전문적이고 독립된 운동으로 분화되며 더 많은 이들의 참여를 이끌어냈고, 지금까지 많은 결실을 맺을 수 있었다.

본 총서는 1980년대 중반부터 1990년대 초반까지, 외교부에서 작성하여 30여 년간 유지했던 한국 인권문제와 관련한 국내외 자료를 담고 있다. 6월 항쟁이 일어나고 민주화 선언이 이뤄지는 등 한국 인권운동에 많은 변화가 있었던 시기다. 당시 인권문제와 관련한 국내외 사안들, 각종 사건에 대한 미국과 우방국, 유엔의 반응, 최초의 한국 인권보고서 제출과 아동의 권리에 관한 협약 과정, 유엔인권위원회 활동, 기타 민주화 관련 자료 등 총 18권으로 구성되었다. 전체 분량은 약 9천여 쪽에 이른다.

2024년 3월

한국학술정보(주)

| 일러두기

· 본 총서에 실린 자료는 2022년 4월과 2023년 4월에 각각 공개한 외교문서 4,827권, 76만 여 쪽 가운데 일부를 발췌한 것이다.

· 각 권의 제목과 순서는 공개된 원본을 최대한 반영하였으나, 주제에 따라 일부는 적절히 변경하였다.

· 원본 자료는 A4 판형에 맞게 축소하거나 원본 비율을 유지한 채 A4 페이지 안에 삽입 하였다. 또한 현재 시점에선 공개되지 않아 '공란'이란 표기만 있는 페이지 역시 그대로 실었다.

· 외교부가 공개한 문서 각 권의 첫 페이지에는 '정리 보존 문서 목록'이란 이름으로 기록물 종류, 일자, 명칭, 간단한 내용 등의 정보가 수록되어 있으며, 이를 기준으로 0001번부터 번호가 매겨져 있다. 이는 삭제하지 않고 총서에 그대로 수록하였다.

· 보고서 내용에 관한 더 자세한 정보가 필요하다면, 외교부가 온라인상에 제공하는 『대한 민국 외교사료요약집』 1991년과 1992년 자료를 참조할 수 있다.

| 차례

정 리 보 존 문 서 목 록

기록물종류	일반공문서철	등록번호	21358	등록일자	1994-10-04
분류번호	701	국가코드	US	보존기간	영구
명 칭	김근태 사건 관련 미국 반응, 1985-86				
생 산 과	북미과	생산년도	1985~1986	담당그룹	북미국
내용목차					

0001

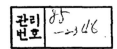
외 무 부 착 신 전 보
지 급

번 호 : USW-4581   일 시 : 510111848   종 별 :

수 신 : 장관 (미북)

발 신 : 주미대사

제 목 : 국내문제에 대한 국무성의 관심

1. ISOM 국무성 한국과장은 금 10.11(금) 오전 당관 김삼훈참사관에게 국내문제와 관련 아래와같은 미측의 관심을 조심스럽게 전달해옴.

가. 김근태에 대한 한국경찰의 가혹행위가 한국내 신문에 보도 되었는바 미국내 언론에의 파급을 우려하면서 우방국으로서 미국의 관심을 표명하는 바임.

나. 앞으로 발간될 국무성의 인권보고서에서 한국내 인권문제가 작년보다 나쁘게 반영될가능성 을 우려하지 않을수 없음.

다. 상기는 양국관계를 더욱 원만히 유지 발전해나가자는 취지임을 이해해 주기바라며, 주한미대사관 측도 이와같은 취지를 외무부에 전달할것임.

2. 김참사관은 사건의 내용을 알지못하나 종종 언론의 보도내용이 사실과 거리가 있는 경우가 많이 있는것으로 안다고 답하고 미측 관심은 본국정부에 전달하겠다고 하였음.

(대사 류병현)

재 분류 (19   )
예고 86.6.30일반·

0002

통 화 요 록

일   시 : 85.10.4(금) 10:30-10:35

송 학 자 : Dunlop 주한 미대사관 참사관

수 학 자 : 박건우 미주국장

통 화 내용

참사관 : 귀하가 콜롬비아 대사로 발령이 난 신문 보도를
보았는데, 우선 이를 축하함.

국 장 : 축하 감사함. 오늘 신임 국장인 장선섭 대사가
귀국하였는데 2-3일내에 국장 업무 인수 인계가
정식으로 있을 예정임.

참사관 : 금일 클리브랜드 공사가 주뉴질랜드 대사로 임명
되었음을 백악관으로부터 공식 통보 받았음.
클리브랜드 공사는 앞으로 6주 내에 서울을 출발할
예정인데, 후임 공사는 상금 미확정이나 David
Lambertson 현 주호주 공사가 부임할 것이 거의
확실시 되고 있음.

워커대사가 미리 박국장께 얘기를 해 주라고
한 사항인데, 이 기회를 빌어 좀 어려운 얘기를
한마디 덧붙이고자 함.

0003

다름 아니라 김근 태라는 대학생이 9.4-9.20간
한국 경찰로 부터 심한 고문을 받았다는 얘기가
변호인들로 부터 나왔는데, 이런 사실이 미언론에
보도될 가능성이 있는 것으로 듣고 있음.

대사관으로 서는 비록 한국인에 대한 일이지만,
이러한 일이 사실이라면 고문 행위에 대해 유감의
뜻을 표명하고자 하며, 이사실이 미언론에 보도
되지 않기를 바라는 바임.

국 장 : 사실 여부를 알아 보겠음.   끝.

0004

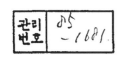

외 무 부 착신전보

관리번호 85-1681

번 호 : USW-4489
일 시 : 510081701
종 별 :

수 신 : 장관 (미북,정문)

발 신 : 주 미 대사대리

제 목 : 국무성 보도지침

연: USW(F)-761

국무성 한국과는 10.7. 정오 브리핑시 연호 NYT 지 보도관련 질문에 대비 하기 보도지침을 작성하였으나 질문이 없어 사용치 않았다함.

Q: DO YOU HAVE ANY COMMENT ON REPORTS THAT SOUTH KOREAN GOVERNMENT HAS BEGUN A CRACKDOWN ON DISSIDENTS ?

A: WE BELIEVE THAT KOREA HAS MADE A POLITICAL PROGRESS OVER THE PAST FEW YEARS, ALTHOUGH, AS DEPARTMENT OFFICIALS HAVE STATED ON SEVERAL OCCASIONS, THERE HAVE BEEN SOME STEPS IN RECENT MONTHS WHICH WE REGARD AS INCONSISTENT WITH THE REAL PROGRESS THAT HAS BEEN MADE.

WE CONTINUE TO ENCOURAGE POLITICAL PROGRESS AND TO URGE MODERATION AND DIALOGUE ON ALL PARTIES.

Q: DO YOU HAVE ANY COMMENT ON THE REPORT THAT SENIOR KOREAN JOURNALISTS WERE BE ATEN RECENTLY BY KOREAN INTELLIGENCE OF FICIALS ?

A: WE ARE AWARE OF CREDIBLE REPORTS SUCH AN INCIDENT OCCURRED. WE HAVE MADE KNO WN TO THE KOREAN GOVERNMENT OUR CONCERN ABOUT THIS DEPLORABLE INCIDENT.

(공사 한탁채)

예고문: 1985.12.31. 까지

0005

√ 미주국 차관실 1차보 정문국 청와대 안 기

PAGE 1

85.10.09 11:48
외신 2과 통제관

한국 다시 반정부 인사에 대한 탄압 시작

- 뉴욕 타임즈 (85.10.7) -

전두환 대통령의 권위주의 정부는 지난 몇달동안 정치범을
체포 · 기소 · 심지어는 고문까지 함으로써 반체제 인사에 대한
탄압을 다시 시작하였다.

관계 공무원은 한국이 아직 1년전부터 실시해온 "자유화"의
원칙을 포기하지 않았다고 주장하였으나, 한국주재 외교관과 국제
정세 전문가들은 한국이 반정부 인사에 대한 유화정책에서 강경
대책으로 급선회하였음에 틀림없다고 말했다.

전대통령의 정적들은 전대통령이 5년전 군사 쿠데타로 정권을
잡은 직후와 같은 탄압정책으로 되돌아 갈것을 우려한다고 말했다.

아마 최근의 강경조치의 가장 전형적인것은 좌익 급진파
학생으로 판결된 대학생에게 특수 재교육 훈련을 시키려는 법안
(학원 안정법)이라 할수 있다.

(6개월간의 지도)

이 법안은 일반재판 규정이 적용되지 않는다. 변호사와
교수의 합동위원회에서, 소요 학생들이 합법적인 정치행위에

- 1 -

0006

대하여도 6개월간의 지도교육을 받아야 하는 지의 여부가 결정된다.

손재석 문교부장관은 "학생들은 정치문제에 참여해서는 안되며 열심히 공부함으로써 장래를 준비하여야 한다."고 했다.

그러나 이 법안에 대한 반응은 성난파도와 같았다. 제1야당(신민당)은 이법안을 악법이라고 비난하면서 이의 철폐를 위하여 국회에서 투쟁할것을 다짐했으며 반정부 인사들은 이 재교육장을 몇몇 공산국가에서나 볼수있는 "재교육 캠프"에 비유했다. 광주지방의 한 청년은 이에대한 반대데모를 하다가 희생됐다.

집권당인 민정당내에서도 이에대한 불만이 있어 두 명의 반대자 - 그중 1명은 원내총무임 - 가 지위를 박탈당했다.

(법안은 철회됐으나 무효과 된것은 아니다)

예기치못한 거센 반대로 인하여 정부는 곧 이법안을 철회하였다. 그러나 손장관은 이법안이 폐지된것은 아니며 이번 가을에 학생들의 소요가 확대된다면 이법안은 다시 도입될 것이라고 했다.

- 2 -

0007

그러나 소요학생만이 정부의 목표 대상은 아니었다. 8월말 동아일보 사의 2명의 중견 논설위원과 1명의 기자가 구속되어 KCIA 의 후신인 안전기획부 요원에 의하여 구타를 당했다. 그들은 외교적으로 민감한 내용을 발표한후 체포되었던 것이며 이사건은 모든 언론인에게 하나의 경고로 인식되었다.

금년 여름에 정부는 삼민투 라는 학생단체를 용공단체로 낙인을 찍었으며 가입학생을 체포하거나 훈방하였다. 13명이 국가보안법 위반혐의로 기소되었으며 이들은 사형선고를 받을 가능성도 있다.

(학생들 간첩혐의로 기소)

22명의 또 다른 학생이 이번달(10월)에 체포되어 북한의 간첩망과 연결되어 있다는 혐의로 기소되었다.

금년 8월、 5일동안 경찰은 한국의 가장 저명한 반정부 인사인 김대중을 가택연금시켜 신민당 집회에 참가하는 것을 막았다.

8월 문교부는 지방교육위원회에게 "선동적"인 기사를 기고한 15명의 초、중、고등학교 교사를 해임하도록 지시했다. 수백권의 서적과 다른 발간물들이 반체제적이라는 이유로 출판금지 되었다.

- 3 -

0008

문교부는 한국에서 가장 존경받는 이현재서울 대학 총장을, 그가 7명의 선동학생을 제명하지 않았다는 이유로, 해임시켰다.

소요학생에 대하여 관대한 판결을 내렸던 3명의 판사가 서울에서 지방으로 전보 발령되었다.

가장 최근의 일로, 2명의 야당 국회의원이 2주일전에 고려 대학에서 데모를 선동했다는 이유로 기소된바 있다.

(반복되는 강약의 대응책)

오랜 세월동안 한국의 정부는 정적에 대한 관용이 큰 적은 한번도 없었지만, 강, 약의 정책을 주기적으로 적용해 왔다. 이러한 경향은 전대통령체제 하에서도 마찬가지로 계속되고 있다.

전대통령이 1980년 정권을 잡았을 때 계엄령을 실시하고 반대 인사를 체포하고 수백명의 정치인의 정치활동을 금지시켜 사실상 자신이나 자신의 정책에 대한 비판을 봉쇄하였다.

그러나 지난 2년동안 이러한 통제중 일부는 없어졌다. 경찰이 학원에서 철수 되었으며, 학교 당국이 데모가 통제할수 없다고 통보할 경우에만 경찰을 투입하겠다고 관계 공무원은

- 4 -

0009

말했다. 그러나 최근 경찰은 다시 학생데모를 진압하기 위하여
학교 내로 들어왔다.

전대통령이 정권을 잡은후 직업을 잃었던 대학교수 언론인들은
작년 복직이 허용되었고 제명학생은 다시 복교되었다.

정치활동이 규제되었던 정치인도 점차로 복권되었다.

(야당의 득실)

작년 1월 많은 야당 인사들이 신민당을 결성하였는데 이당은
온건했던 과거의 야당에 비하여 강경한 성격을 가졌다.
신민당은 불과 수주후의 국회의원 선거에서 놀랄만큼 많은 의석을
차지하게 되었다.

그러나 이선거가 한국의 힘의 균형을 변경시키지는 못하였다.
기본적으로 국회는 도장찍는 장소정도 밖에는 되지 못했다.
그러나 그 성격은 변하게 되었다. 야당은 변화를 요구하게 되었고
전대통령은 기꺼이 언론에 많은 비판을 허용하게 되었다.

이번주, 450만 달러의 부채가 있는 한국은 IBRD 와 IMF 를
주최했으며, 서울에서 내년에는 아세아 게임이, 88년에는 올림픽이
개최될 예정이다. 따라서 국내의 안정이 필수적이라는 것이 많은

- 5 -

0010

많은 한국인들의 공통된 의견이다.

김대중은 "전대통령이 한국정치를 계속할 능력이 없기 때문에 온건적인 방법으로 정치할 만큼 자신이 있는 것이 아니다" 라고 말했다.

반정부 활동을 하는 어떤목사는 현정부가 공포에 사로잡혀 있다고 말했다.

(반정부 행위의 집결점)

만일 전대통령이 학원안정법을 계속 밀고 나간다면 분산되어 있는 반대세력을 집결시키는 결과만을 초래할 것이라고 어떤 전문가는 분석했다.

학원안정법은 학생을 투옥시키거나 제명시키는 것이 아니고 재교육을 시킴으로써 그들을 적절히 지도하고 보호하는 취지를 가지고 있다는 것이 정부의 입장이다.

그러나 평소 상당히 현정부에 우호적인 사람들까지도 이러한 주장을 받아들이지 않았다.

- 6 -

0011

리처드 워커 주한미대사 역시 비록 우회적이기는 하지만 그 법안을 비난한 사람중 하나였다.

지난 광복절(8.15)에 그는 "국민들의 의견까지 정부가 지배한다는 것은 비합법적이다" 라고 말했다.

- 7 -

0012

번 호 : USW(F) - 761   1000-600

수 신 : 장관 (미북)   발 신 : 주미대사

제 목 : 미국 국내정세 <2매>

THE NEW YORK TIMES, MONDAY, OCTOBER 7, 1985   A11

After Pause, Seoul Renews

Crackdown on Dissent

By CLYDE HABERMAN
Special to The New York Times

SEOUL, South Korea — The authoritarian Government of President Chun Doo Hwan has begun a new crackdown on dissidents, with a long string of political arrests, indictments, dismissals and even beatings in the last few months.

Officials insist they have not abandoned "liberalization" policies begun more than a year ago. Nevertheless, foreign diplomats and political analysts say the Government has clearly swung toward a hard line after a period in which it seemed to show a greater tolerance for dissent.

Opponents of President Chun say they fear he may tighten controls still further and possibly even go back to the harsh policies that characterized his Government after he seized power in a military coup five years ago.

Perhaps the most graphic symbol of the latest crackdown is a bill that was crafted in early August to create special "reorientation" centers for South Korean college students judged to be left-wing radicals.

Six Months of 'Guidance'

The detention centers were to operate outside the normal judicial system. Committees of lawyers and professors would determine whether students should be sent away for up to six months of "guidance and enlightenment" on acceptable political behavior.

"Students should not be active in politics," Education Minister Sohn Jae Suk said in an interview. "They should study and prepare themselves for the future."

But the reaction against the proposal was angry and swift.

The chief political opposition party denounced the bill as an "evil law" and pledged to fight against it in the National Assembly. Dissident activists likened the reorientation centers to the "re-education camps" set up in some Communist countries. One young man in the southwestern city of Kwangju immolated himself in protest.

Even members of Mr. Chun's ruling Democratic Justice Party were unhappy. Two prominent critics, one of them the party's legislative floor leader, were replaced.

Bill Withdrawn, but Not Dead

Because of the unexpectedly harsh criticism, the Government soon withdrew the legislation. But officials say the proposal is not dead, and Mr. Sohn warns that it will be reintroduced if student protests surge again this fall.

Demonstrators are not the only Government targets, however.

At the end of August, two senior editors and a reporter for the newspaper Dong-A Ilbo were detained and beaten by officers of the National Security Planning Agency, formerly known as the Korean Central Intelligence Agency. They were picked up after publication of an article the Government considered "diplomatically sensitive." The incident was widely interpreted as a warning to all journalists.

During the summer, the Government branded a student group called Sammintu as pro-Communist, and arrested or charged 56 of its members. Thirteen were charged with violating the severe National Security Law. If convicted they could be sentenced to death.

Students Accused of Spying

Twenty-two other people, most of them students, were arrested this month and accused of belonging to two North Korean espionage rings. Separate raids led to the the arrest of 66 others in June.

For five days in August, the police put South Korea's best-known dissident politician, Kim Dae Jung, under house arrest to keep him from attending a convention of the main opposition party.

In August, Mr. Sohn's ministry ordered local education boards to dismiss 15 elementary- and high-school teachers for writing "seditious" magazine articles. Hundreds of books and other publications have been banned as sub-

0013

versive.

7) The Education Ministry also removed Lee Hyu Jae as president of Seoul National University, South Korea's most prestigious, after he refused to expel seven student activists.

8) Three judges regarded as too "soft" on demonstrators were transferred from Seoul to provincial posts.

9) In the most recent incident, two opposition members of the National Assembly were indicted two weeks ago on charges of inciting anti-Government demonstrators at Korea University.

Alternating Toughness

For many years successive South Korean governments have alternated between relatively hard and soft policies toward political opponents, although tolerance for dissent has never been high, even in the best of times. That tendency has continued under President Chun.

When he seized control in 1980, he imposed martial law, arresting dissidents, banning hundreds of politicians and virtually forbidding any criticism of him or his policies. Over the last two years, however, some of the more stringent controls had been lifted.

Officials withdrew police officers from campuses, which are traditional havens of protest, and announced that they would return only if school administrators said demonstrations were out of control. Recently, however, the police have begun again to enter campuses to stop student protests.

University professors and journalists who had been forced out of their jobs soon after Mr. Chun took over were permitted to go back last year. Ousted college students were readmitted.

Gradually, blacklisted politicians were reinstated.

Gains by Opposition Party

Last January many of them formed the New Korea Democratic Party, a hard-line opposition force compared with its relatively tame predecessors. Only a few weeks after it came into existence the party won a surprisingly large number of seats in National Assembly elections.

The elections did not alter the true balance of power in South Korea; essentially, the legislature remains a rubber-stamp body. But its character changed. An emboldened opposition has turned it into a forum for demands for change, and Mr. Chun seems willing to allow many critical comments to appear in the regulated press.

But lately, hard-liners seem to have won out once more in the Blue House, the official presidential residence. Now, Mr. Chun seems prepared to allow criticism if it stays in the National Assembly.

Mr. Chun's critics say his policies toward dissidents keep changing because his main interest is finding ways to keep things quiet as he approaches several critical deadlines.

This week South Korea, which has a $45 billion foreign debt, is acting as host to a meeting of the World Bank and the International Monetary Fund. Next year, the Asia Games will be held in Seoul, and in 1988 the Olympic Games are to take place here. Domestic tranquillity, or the appearance of it, is essential, many South Koreans say.

"Chun has continuously failed to control South Korean politics," Kim Dae Jung said. "So now he is not confident enough to deal with our politics in a moderate way."

A Protestant clergyman put it more bluntly. "I think the Government is panicking," he said.

Rallying Point for Opposition

If Mr. Chun chooses to press the Campus Stabilization Bill, some analysts feel he could create a rallying point for disparate opposition camps.

The Government position is that the proposed law is "lenient" because it provides for reorientation, not jail or expulsion. It is "designed not to control and punish students subject to its provisions but to properly guide and protect them," an official statement said.

But even usually sympathetic people reject this argument. Among those who attacked the legislation, albeit obliquely, was the United States Ambassador, Richard L. Walker.

In remarks made in mid-August, on the anniversary of Korea's liberation from Japan in 1945, the Ambassador said, "The opinions of men are not a legitimate subject for rule by civil government."

761-2

0014

외 무 부

착 신 전 보

번 호 : USW-4616　　　일 시 : 510151846　　　종 별 : 긴급

수 신 : 장관 (미북)

발 신 : 주 미 대사

제 목 : SHERMAN 부차관보 면담예정

연 : USW-4581

1. 당관 한공사는 국무성 요청에의거 명 10.16(수) 오전 WILLIAM SHERMAN 부차관

보를 면담예정임.

2. 면담 요청목적은 국내문제(학생 구타사건)에대한 외교적 관심 전달인것으로 탐문

되고 있는바 특별히 지시하실사항 있으면 하시바람.

(대사 류병현)

예고 : 85.12.31. 일반

0015

ㄴ 미주국　차관실　1차보　청와대　안기　2차보

발 신 전 보

관리번호 05 - 2380

번 호: WUS-3484 일시: 101618시 45   전보종별: 긴 급

수 신: 주 미 대사·총영사

발 신: 장 관 (미북)

제 목: Sherman 부차관보 면담

대 : USW- 4616(3), USW-4581(2)

1. 대호 면담시 Sherman 부차관보와 면담시 언급사항을
청취함과 동시에 미측 관심사항을 파악 보고바람.

2. 동 면담시 대호 (2) 김근태 문제가 거론될 경우 다음 사항을
설명바람. 동건 관계기관에 조회한바,

가. 김근태는 현재 국가보안법 위반 혐의로 수사당국에서
조사중이며 동인에 대한 고문관계 보도는 전혀 사실 무근임.

나. 동인은 현재 기소 단계에 있는 바, 재판과정에서
구체적인 범죄사실과 함께 진상이 밝혀질것임.

2. 동 면담분위기를 보아가면서 상기와 같은 아측 국내 문제에
대하여 미측이 일일이 문제시하는 것을 삼가하여 주기를
바라는 아측의 동향을 적절히 전달바람. (차관)

예고 : 85.12.31. 일반

0016

앙고재	85년 10월 1일	북미 과	기안자	과장		국장	제1차관보	차 관	장 관	발신시간:
								전결	후열	

외신과	접수자	과 장

통 화 요 록
----

1. 통화일시 : 1985.10.16, 14:30
2. 통 화 자 : 이정빈 비서관
3. 수 화 자 : 장선섭 미주국장
4. 통화내용 :

    가. 김근태건에 관하여 안기부측에 문의한바(손 차장 및
        1국장) 동인은 보안법 위반으로 현재 관계당국에서
        조사중이며 보도된 고문 운운은 사실무근임.

    나. 현재 기소단계에 있어 조사 진행중이며 재판결과 범죄
        사실이 밝혀질것임.　　끝.

공람	북미과 85년 10월 17일	담 당	과 장	심의관	국 장

0017

외 무 부　　착신전보

원본

번 호 : USW-4643　　일 시 : 510161840　　종 별 : 지급

수 신 : 장관 (미북)

발 신 : 주미대사

제 목 : SHERMAN 부차관보 면담

대 : WUS-3484

연 : USW-4581

당관 한공사는 금 10.16(수) 오전 국무성 요청에의거 WILLIAM SHERMAN 동아태 담당 부차관보를 면담한바 아래 보고함. (김삼훈 참사관 및 DAVID STRAUB 한국 과 담당관 배석)

1. SHERMAN 부차관보 언급요지

가. 금일 면담 요청은 많기 매우 어려운 문제즉 한국의 최근 국내문제에 대한 미측 의 관심을 전달하고자 하는것임. 국무성은 매우 신빙성있는 보고를 접수하였는바, 동 아일보 기자 구타 및 김근태에 대한 고문행위에 관한것임.

나. 워커대사가 서울에서 외무부와 총리실에 이미 관심을 전달한것이나. 금일 다시 한번 월포비츠 차관보와 본인의 관심을 한국측에 전달하고자함.

타. 미국은 제 5 공화국 수립이후 한국내 인권상황이 현저히 개선되었다고 믿고 있 고 또한 지난 수년간 공개적으로 또는 사적으로 한국의 인권문제와 정치발전 문제를 지지해왔으며, 여사한 상황이 계속되기를 희망하고 있음.

라. 그러나 최근의 발전은 지금까지 쌓아올린 한국의 국제적 이미지를 손상 시키고, 현금의 심정을 반영하는 국무성 인권보고서가 작년보다 악화될 가능성이 있음을 지적 하지 않을수 없음.

마. 의회나 일반 여론을 우려하지 않을수 없으며, 행정부로 하여금 한국정부를 강력 히 지지하는데 있어서 어려운 입장에 처하게 할 것임을 걱정하는 바임.

0018

✓ 미주국　차관실　1차보　청와대　총리실　안기　장운국

85.10.17 11:10
외신 2과 통제관

2. 한공사 언급요지

가. 전대통령 각하 취임이후 현저히 개선된 여건을 우리 모두 높이 평가하여야 할것이며, 북한의 위협하에 있는 한국이 처한 안보적 특수여건을 깊이 이해해야함.

(나) 김근태는 국가보안법 위반사범이며, 고문주장은 사실무근이고, 조만간 관계법에 따라 기소되고 재판을 하는 과정에서 그진상이 소상히 밝혀질것임.

(다) 국내문제인 만큼 아국의 관계법규에 따라 의법처리 될것인바, 우방국의 과도한 관심표시가 한국의 정치발전에 어려움을 줄 가능성도 배제할수 없음.

3. 셔먼 부차관보는 한공사의 언급에 대해 아래와 같이 추가 언급함.

가. 한국정부의 주장근거는 어느정도 이해하지만, 실정법의 적법한 적용을 운위하는 것이 아니라, 법에따른 처리과정에서 발생하는 문제점에 대한 관심을 전달하는 것임.

나. 거듭 말하지만, 대외적으로 널리알려진 신체적 가혹행위에 대해서는 미국내 여론의 공격에 대해 미정부로서 이를 방어하고 응호할 형편에 있지 못하다는 것임을 이해바람.

(대사 류병현)

예고 : 1986.6.30. 일반

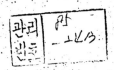

번 호: USW-4682   일 시: 51017 1830

수 신: 장 관 (미북)

발 신: 주 미 대사

제 목: 하원외무위 동향

연: USW-4568

금 10.17. 장재룡 참사관은 하원 외무위 아태소위 STANLEY
ROTH 수석 전문위원과 오찬을 같이 하고 작일의 월포비츠 차관보 브리핑
내용 및 외무위의 최근 관심사중 아국 관련 사항등을 탐문한바 동인의 언급
요지를 아래 보고함.

1. 외무위로서는 남북대화의 진전에 큰관심을 갖고 있는바, 한국이 지금
까지의 전진적이고 적극적인 자세를 견지하여 계속 북한측을 유도 함으로써
무언가 긍정적인 진전이 있기를 기대함.   작 10.16. 월포비츠 차관보
의 브리핑시에도 한국관련 사항으로는 남북대화 관계가 거론되었으며 동 차관
보는 주로 북한의 성실성에 대한 깊은 의구심을 표명하였음. (동 브리핑은
비공개로 진행된 만큼 자세한 이야기는 할수 없으나, 주로 마이크로네시아
독립문제, 비율빈 사태, 호주, 뉴질랜드 문제등이 논의되었으며 한국관련
사항중 남북대화 관계는 시간관계상 깊이 있게 다루지 못하였다함)

2. 지난 10.7. 자 NYT 보도 관련, 한국의 인권현황에 대해서도
관심을 갖고 있음. 따라서 이에관한 아태소위 청문회 개최 문제도 검토한바
있으나, 현 단계에서는 역시한 공개적 APPROACH 보다는 동 보도내
용에 대한 한국 정부의 적절한 해명과 입장 청취를 위하여 솔라즈 소위원장
명의의 주미대사앞 서한발송을 계획중임.

3. 라성 소재 KTE-TV 의 보도자세를 위요한 최근의 논란과 관련,

관광신	의전실	아프리카국	정부과	청와대	재무부	보안사
차관실	아주국	국기국	감사관	총리실	재험위	노동부
1차보	기주국	경제국	공보관	안기부	체육부	PAGE 1 -
2차보	미주국	통상국	의전실	법무부	SLOOC	
기획실	중동국	영교국	상황실	상공부	국방부	

85.10.18.

0020

미국내 반정부 인사측으로부터 상세한 자료제공과 함께 의회의 관심촉구가
있었으나 본건은 정책사항이 아닌만큼 사법절차에 의하여 해명될 문제로 생각
하고 있음.

(대사무방현)

보고필: 의기 '86, 6.30.. 일반
      정남

AGE : 2 -

종 별: 지 급

번 호: USW-468ɜ̌   일 시: 51017 1832

수 신: 장 관 (해기 , 미북 , 정문 , 기정)

발 신: 주 미 대사

제 목: 한국에 관한 인권 보고 (자료응신)

1. NYT 뉴욕본사 OP.ED 페이지 ASSIST. EDITOR 인 KENDALL WILLS 는 전화로 당관 공보관에게 " 한국에서는 23 명의 정치범이 고문 (TOTURE) 등 고초를 겪고 있다 " 는 내용의 AMNESTY INT'L 의 인권에관한 보고서에 관해 기사를 쓸예정이라 면서 이에관한 반응이나 논평을 요청하여 온바 " 그러한 보고서가 언제 RELEASE 되었는가 ?(동인은 며칠전 URGENT ACTION LE TTER 272/85 및 275/85 로 배포되었다고 답함) 고 반문 하고 둥보고서 내용에 관해 아직 아는바 없어 반응이나 논평을 할수가 없다 . 그러나 한국에는 정치범이 없다고 답변함.

2. 당관은 위보고서 내용입수 보고 위계인바 PRESS GUIDANCE 등 지침 지급 회시바람. (대사류병현)

보존기간 은 1986. 6. 30 .. 까지

외 무 부   착 신 전 보

번 호 : USW-4698   입 시 : 510181517   종 별 :

수 신 : 장 관 (영재 미북)

발 신 : 주 미 대 사

제 목 : 민통연합 시위

보안법 위반사범인 김근태 고문설과 관련 금 10.18 상오 11:30 부터 약 1시간동안 당지 민통연합 한국인권문제연구소 및 한국내 인권문제 북미연합회 공동 주관으로 교민 약15명이 국무성 앞에서 항의 시위를 가진후 자진해산함.

(총영사-문동석)

예고 : 85.12.31까지

0023

영고국   차관실   1 차보   미주국   청와대   안 기

PAGE   1

85.10.19   09:09
외신 2과   통제관

외 무 부 착신전보

번 호 : USW-4697　　　　일 시 : 510181420　　　종 별

수 신 : 장 관 (국연,미북,해기)

발 신 : 주 미 대사

제 목 : 국제사면협회 연례보고서

연: USW-4683

1. 국제사면 협회 85년도 연례보고서는 아국 관련 사항을 4페이지분으로 계재하고 있는바 주로 양심범 구속문제 및 구속자들에대한 가혹행위 문제를 다루고 있으며 당지의 동 협회 사무실은 김근태 양동화등에 대한 별도 REPORT 를 배포하였음

2. 동 자료는 금 10.18 정파편 송부함.

(대사 류병현)

예고:85.12.31까지 .

국기국　차관실　1 차보　미주국　청와대　안 기　문공부

0024

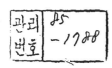
관리 번호 85 -1788

주 미 대 사 관

미국(정) 700 - 360   1985. 10. 18.

수 신 : 장 관

참 조 : 국제기구조약국장, 미주국장 (사본:문공부 해외공보관장)

제 목 : 국제사면협회 연례보고서

　　　　　연 : U S W - 4697

　　　　연호 자료를 별첨 송부 합니다.

첨 부 : 1. 동 보고서 각 1부.

　　　　　2. 별도 report 각 1부.　　끝.

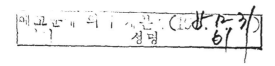

　　　　　　　주 　 미 　 대 　  사

0025

외 무 부	결재		
접수 인기 1985.10.2	지시사항		
처리 관련 제590			
주무과			
담당가			
		년 월 일 까지 시행할 것	

0026

URGENT ACTION   amnesty international   URGENT ACTION

UA office • P.O. Box 1270 • Nederland, CO 80466 1270 • 303 440 0913   International Secretariat • 1 Easton Street • London WC1X 8DJ England

UA   275/85   TORTURE/LEGAL CONCERN   2 OCTOBER 1985
REPUBLIC OF KOREA (SOUTH KOREA): KIM KEUN-TAE

AMNESTY INTERNATIONAL HAS RECEIVED REPORTS THAT KIM KEUN-TAE, AGED 39, FORMER
CHAIRPERSON OF THE NATIONAL YOUTH ALLIANCE (NYAD), WAS TORTURED DURING
INTERROGATION BY THE ANTI-COMMUNIST BUREAU OF THE NATIONAL POLICE. HE IS
REPORTED TO HAVE BEEN TAKEN INTO CUSTODY ON 4 SEPTEMBER 1985 AND DENIED ACCESS
TO A LAWYER OR HIS RELATIVES UNTIL 26 SEPTEMBER 1985. HE IS REPORTED TO HAVE
BEEN GIVEN ELECTRIC SHOCKS, SUBJECTED TO SUFOCATION WITH WATER AND DENIED
ADEQUATE FOOD AND SLEEP. ON 26 SEPTEMBER 1985 HE IS REPORTED TO HAVE BEEN
TRANSFERRED FROM THE INTERROGATION CENTRE OF THE ANTI-COMMUNIST BUREAU OF THE
NATIONAL POLICE IN THE NAMYOUNGDONG AREA OF SEOUL TO SEOUL PRISON. IT IS
BELIEVED THAT HE IS FACING CHARGES UNDER THE NATIONAL SECURITY LAW, BUT
DETAILS ARE AS YET UNKNOWN.

KIM KEUN-TAE STUDIED ECONOMICS AT SEOUL NATIONAL UNIVERSITY WHERE HE WAS A
STUDENT LEADER FROM 1965 UNTIL 1971, WHEN HE WENT INTO HIDING TO ESCAPE ARREST
AFTER AN ANTI-GOVERNMENT DEMONSTRATION IN OPPOSITION TO FORMER PRESIDENT PARK
CHUNG-HEE'S ONE-MAN RULE AND IN SUPPORT OF OPPOSITION POLITICIAN KIM DAE-JUNG.
LATER ON KIM KEUN-TAE BECAME INVOLVED WITH LABOUR ISSUES.

KIM KEUN-TAE PLAYED A MAJOR ROLE IN SETTING UP THE NATIONAL YOUTH ALLIANCE FOR
DEMOCRACY IN SEPTEMBER 1983. THE ALLIANCE'S STATED OBJECTIVES INCLUDE THE
ESTABLISHMENT OF A DEMOCRATIC POLITICAL SYSTEM IN SOUTH KOREA, BETTER WAGES
FOR WORKERS AND THE UNIFICATION OF NORTH AND SOUTH KOREA. THE ALLIANCE HAS
ORGANIZED DEMONSTRATIONS, DISTRIBUTED LEAFLETS AND GENERALLY TRIED TO
PUBLICIZE ITS VIEWS.

SINCE THE ESTABLISHMENT OF THE ALLIANCE KIM KEUN-TAE HAS BEEN DETAINED ON
SEVERAL OCCASIONS FOR HIS NON-VIOLENT POLITICAL ACTIVITIES. IN SEPTEMBER 1983
HE WAS INTERROGATED FOR ONE WEEK BY THE AGENCY FOR NATIONAL SECURITY PLANNING
ABOUT THE ESTABLISHMENT OF THE ALLIANCE BUT WAS RELEASED WITHOUT CHARGE. IN
MID-MARCH 1984 HE WAS HELD FOR THREE DAYS IN A POLICE STATION, WHERE HE WAS
REPORTED TO HAVE BEEN BEATEN, IN CONNECTION WITH THE PUBLICATION OF THE
ALLIANCE'S JOURNAL. IN EARLY NOVEMBER 1984 A COURT SENTENCED HIM TO THREE
DAYS' DETENTION FOR PREPARING AND DISTRIBUTING LEAFLETS. HE WAS AGAIN ARRESTED
ON 9 MAY 1985 AND SENTENCED TO 10 DAYS' DETENTION FOR ALLEGEDLY SPREADING
GROUNDLESS RUMOURS ABOUT THE KWANGJU INCIDENT OF MAY 1980.

AMNESTY INTERNATIONAL IS CONCERNED THAT KIM KEUN-TAE MAY NOW BE DETAINED FOR
THE PEACEFUL EXPRESSION OF HIS POLITICAL VIEWS.

0027

Amnesty International is an independent worldwide movement working for the international protection of human rights. It seeks the release of men and women detained anywhere because of their beliefs, color, sex, ethnic origin, language or religious creed, provided they have not used or advocated violence. These are termed prisoners of conscience. It works for fair and prompt trials for all political prisoners and works on behalf of such people detained without charge or trial. It opposes the death penalty and torture or other cruel, inhuman or degrading treatment or punishment of all prisoners without reservation.

URGENT ACTION

amnesty international

URGENT ACTION

UA office • P.O. Box 1270 • Nederland, CO 80466-1270 • 303 440 0913

International Secretariat • 1 Easton Street • London WC1X 8DJ England

UA 272/85   Fear of Torture/Legal Concern   1 October 1985
Republic of Korea (South Korea):
Yang Dong-hwa, aged 27   Kim Song-man, aged 28
Hwang Dae-kwon, aged 30   Ahn Sang-gun, aged 35
Dr (Ms) Lee Chin-suk, aged 35   and 17 others

On 9 September 1985 the South Korean Army Security Command and the National
Agency for Security Planning announced the arrest of two groups of alleged
espionage agents working for the Democratic People's Republic of Korea (North
Korea) for allegedly instigating anti-government protests and other activitaes
against the government. Yang Dong-hwa, Kim Song-man, Hwang Dae-kwon, are all
South Koreans who studied at Western Illinois University in the USA between
1982 and 1984. Yangdong-hwa and Kim Song-man are alleged to have been
recruited while studying in the USA. They are accused of leading a group of 20
epople who carried out espionage and anti-state activities in South Korea for
a North Korean agent resident in the USA. Ahn Sang-gun, formerly resident in
Frankfurt, West Germany, where he edited a Korean-language paper, and Dr Lee
Chin-suk, an assistant professor at Taegu University who studied for a
doctorate in sociology in Frankfurt from 1979 to December 1984, are alleged to
have been recruited as North Korean agents while living in West Germany.

All 22 people face charges under the National Security Law, which provides
penalties for activities related to an "anti-government organization". Those
convicted of leading such groups can be sentenced to a term of life
imprisonment or the death penalty.

Amnesty International is concerned that some, possibly all, of the defendants
may have been arrested for the non-violent exercise of their rights to freedom
of expression and association. It appears that those charged in connection
with activities undertaken while they lived in the USA or West Germany were
known to hold views critical of the South Korean government.

Amnesty International is currently working for the release of a number of
prisoners convicted on the same charges under similar circumstances, such
actions are thought to be designed to deter Koreans from engaging in political
activities critical of the government while overseas, and to discredit
opposition activities at home. Students have been in the forefront of
opposition to the present South Korean government, and that protests have
escalated since the university year began in March 1985.

In addition, Amnesty International is concerned that these prisoners may be
subjected to mental or physical duress while they are under investigation.
Amnesty International received frequent reports that political suspects are
ill-treated after their arrest to force them to sign 'confessions' that are
used in court to secure their conviction, although both torture and the use of
statements obtained under duress as evidence in court are prohibited by the
1980 Constitution.

0028

외 무 부   착신전보
지급

번 호 : USW-4715   일 시 : 510181951   종 별 : 지급

수 신 : 장 관 (미북)

발 신 : 주 미 대사

제 목 : 국무성 정오 브리핑

1. 금 10.18. 국무성 정오 브리핑시 최근 국내사태 관련, 질의응답이 있었음.   KALB
   대변인은 한국내 고문 주장설에 대한 미국입장을 문의한데 대하여 하기 요지 답변
   함.

가. 미국은 최근 3 명의 한국 언론인이 공안당국 요원으로부터 구타당했다는 신빙성
있는 보도를 알고있으며, 이에대하여 한국정부에 관심을 표명하였음.

나. 또한 미국은 얼마전에 있었던 청년운동가에 대한 고문 사건과 함께 최근 일련의
사태에 대하여도 관심을 전달한바 있음.

다. 한국은 그간 완전해금 조치를 단행했고 금년 2 월 역사상 가장 자유민주적인 선
거를 치루었으며 모든 교수 및 일부 언론인들의 복직을 허용하였음.

라. 그러나 국무성이 수차 밝힌바와같이 우리로서는 이제까지 이루어진 진정한 발전
과는 상치되는것으로 보여지는 일련의 유감된 조치가 최근 있었음.

마. 미국은 계속하여 정치발전이 이루어지고 모든 당사자간의 화합과 대화가 있기를
촉구함.

2. 동 보도지침 작성은 국제사면협회가 발표한 자료 및 이에대한 NYT 기자의 관
심표명 (USW-4683, 4697 참조), 그리고 금 10.18. 11:30 부터 약 1 시간동안 있었
던 아국교포의 국무성앞 데모 (USW-4698 참조) 정보등이 계기가된것으로 보이는
바, ISOM 국무성 한국과장은 대외 공개 대변인 만큼 동 지침 작성에 있어서 고심
한 것이 사실이며, 일부 내용은 이를 전적으로 부인하는 경우 오히려 문제를 확대할
가능성이 있음을 고려하지 않을수 없었다는 언급이 있었음.(보도지침 작성 사실을

√ 미주국   차관실   1 차보   청와대   총리실   안 기   정통속   0029

금일 정오경 사전 통보받았으며, 오후 실제 질문이 있어 답변하였다는 사실도 추가 통보받았음.)

3. 준비한 보도지침중 일부는 사용하지 않았는바, 실제 있었던 질의응답과 한국과가 준비한 보도 지침을 별첨 타전함.

첨부:

1. 질의응답 내용

2. 준비한 보도지침.

(대사 류병현)

예고문 1985. 12. 31. 일반

USW-4718 로 계속

0030

2

외 무 부 착 신 전 보

번 호 : USW-4718　　　일 시 : 510182001　　　종 별 :

수 신 :

발 신 :

제 목 : USW-4715 의 계속

(별첨1) 실제 질의응답내용

Q: THERE HAVE BEEN QUITE A FEW REPORTS OVER THE LAST FEW WEEKS OF ALLEGATIONS OF TORTURE IN SOUTH KOREA. DO YOU HAVE ANY COMMENT ON THOSE ALLEGATIONS ? ARE T HEY CONSISTENT WITH THE AMERICAN VIEW OF WHERE THE CHUN GOVERNMENT SHOULD BE GOI NG ?

MR. KALB: UH-

Q: DOES THE UNITED STATES APPRECIATE THE CRACKDOWN AGAINST DISSIDENTS?

MR. KALB: UH-- WE ARE AWARE OF CREDIBLE REPORTS THAT THREE KOREAN JOURNALISTSWE RE BEATEN RECENTLY BY KOREAN SECURITY OFFICIALS AND WE HAVE MADE KNOWN TO THE KO REAN GOVERNMENT OUR CONCERN ABOUT THIS DEPLORABLE INCIDENT. WE ALSO ARE AWARE TH AT A YOUTH ACTIVIST WAS SUBJECTED TO TORTURE RECENTLY. WE HAVE MADE KNOWN TO THE KOREAN GOVERNMENT OUR SERIOUS CONCERN, AS I SAID A MOMENT AGO, ABOUT THIS DEPLO RABLE INCIDENT AS WELL, AND ON YOUR BROADER QUESTION ABOUT CRACKDOWNS, LET ME SA Y THIS, IF I MAY, MIKE. WE BELIEVE THAT IN GENERAL KOREA HAS MADE POLITICAL PROG RESS OVER THE PAST FEW YEARS. IN 1984, EARLY 85, THE KOREAN GOVERNMENT COMPLETEL Y LIFTED THE POLITICAL BAND THAT HAD ORIGINALLY APPLIED TO 567 POLITIC IANS. IN FEBRUARY, 1985, KOREA EXPERIENCED ONE OF THE MOST DEMOCRATIC ELECTIONS IN ITS HI STORY. DURING THE CAMPAIGN, CA NDIDATES WERE FREE TO CRITICIZE THE GOVERNMENT IN FRONT OF LARGE RALLIES. AS A RESULT OF THE ELECTION, NEW PARTIES SUPPORTED BY L EADING OPPOSITION POLITICIANS BECAME THE LARGEST OPPOSITION PARTY. ALL THE PROFE

- -

0031

SSORS AND SOME JOURNALISTS WHO HAD LOST THEIR JOBS FOR POLITICAL REASONS WERE AL
LOWED TO RETURN TO THEIR POSITIONS.

ON THE OTHER HAND, AS DEPARTMENT OFFICIALS HAVE STATED ON SEVERAL OCCASIONS, TH
ERE HAVE BEEN SOME REGRETTABLE STEPS IN RECENT MONTHS WHICH WE REGARD AS INCONSI
STENT WITH THE REAL PROGRESS THAT HAS BEEN MADE. WE CONTINUE TO ENCOURAGE POLITI
CAL PROGRESS AND TO URGE MODERATION AND DIALOGUE ON ALL PARTIES.

USW-4719 로 계속

외 무 부   착 신 전 보

번 호 : USW-4719   일 시 : 510182001   종 별 :

수 신 :

발 신 :

제 목 : USW-4715 의 계속

(별첨2) 한국과가 준비한 보도지침

Q: DO YOU HAVE ANY COMMENT ON THE CHARGES MADE BY THE DOMONSTRATORS NOW OUTSI

DE THE DEPARTMENT THAT SENIOR KOREAN JOURNALISTS WERE BEATEN RECENTLY BY KOREAN

SECURITY OFFICIALS?

A:-- WE ARE AWARE OF CREDIBLE REPORTS THAT THREE KOREAN JOURNALISTS WERE BEATEN

RECENTLY BY KOREAN SECURITY OFFICIALS. WE HAVE MADE KNOWN TO THE KOREAN GOVERN

MENT OUR CONCERN ABOUT THIS DEPLORABLE INCIDENT.

Q: DO YOU HAVE ANY COMMENT ON THE CHARGES MADE BY THE DEMONSTRATORS NOW OUTSIDE

THE DEPARTMENT THAT A YOUTH ACTIVIST (KIM KUN TAE) WAS TORTURED RECENTLY BY THE

KOREAN POLICE ?

A: -- WE ARE AWARE OF CREDIBLE REPORTS THAT YOUTH ACTIVIST KIM KUN TAE WAS SUBJ

ECTED TO TORTURE RECENTLY. WE HAVE MADE KNOWN TO THE KOREAN GOVERNMENT OUR SERI

OUS CONCERN ABOUT THIS DEPLORABLE INCIDENT.

Q: DO YOU HAVE ANY COMMENT ON REPORTS THAT THE SOUTH KOREAN GOVERNMENT HAS BEGU

N A GENERAL CRACKDOWN ON DISSIDENTS ?

A: -- WE BELIEVE THAT, IN GENERAL, KOREA HAS MADE PLITICAL PROGRESS OVER THE PA

ST FEW YEARS. IN 1984 AND EARLY 1985 THE KOREAN GOVERNMENT COMPLETELY LIFTED THE

POLITICAL BAN THAT HAD ORIGINALLY APPLIED TO 567 POLITICIANS. IN FEBRUARY 1985

KOREA EXPERIENCED ONE OF THE MOST DEMOCRATIC ELECTIONS IN ITS HISTORY DURING THE

CAMPAIGN, CANDIDATES WERE FREE TO CRITICIZE THE GOVERNMENT IN FRONT OF LARGE RA

0033

LLIES. AS A RESULT OF THE ELECTION, A NEW PARTY SUPPORTED BY LEADING OPPOSITION POLITICIANS BECAME THE LARGEST OPPOSITION PARTY. ALL THE PROFESSORS AND SOME JOURNALISTS WHO HAD LOST THEIR JOBS FOR POLITICAL REASONS WERE ALLOWED TO RETURN TO THEIR POSITIONS. ON THE OTHER HAND, AS DEPARTMENT OFFICIALS HAVE STATED ON SEVERAL OCCASIONS, THERE HAVE BEEN SOME REGRETTABLE STEPS IN RECENT MONTHS WHICH WE REGARD AS INCONSISTENT WITH THE REAL PROGRESS THAT HAS BEEN MADE. WE CONTINUE TO ENCOURAGE POLITICAL PROGRESS AND TO URGE MODERATION AND DIALOGUE ON ALL PARTIES

Q: WHAT WAS THE KOREAN GOVERNMENT'S RESPONSE TO OUR REPRESENTATIONS CONCERNING THE BEATING OF THE JOURNALISTS AND THE TORTURE OF THE YOUTH ACTIVIST ?

A: -- THESE WERE HIGH-LEVEL DIPLOMATIC EXCHANGES. IT WOULD UNDERCUT THE VERY EFFECTIVENESS OF THE REPRESENTATIONS IF THEY WERE MADE PUBLIC. END

발 신 전 보

WUN-1687

번 호: WUS-3533 일 시: 1701/1230   전보종별: 지 급

수 신: 주 미   대사·(총영사)   (행장 사본: 차관, 주위인대표의장위)

발 신: 장 관 (미북)

제 목: 국무성 대변인 브리핑

연 : WUS-3484

대 : USW-4643(1), USW-4715(2)

1. 외신 보도에 의하면 Bernard Kalb 국무성 대변인의
브리핑과 관련,
10.18 기자들에게 한국 인권 문 제에 관해 공개적 논평을 한 것으로
국무성이
알려지고 있는 바, 대호 2항 아측 희망 전달에도 불구하고 국 내
언급
문 제에 대해 공개적으로 계속 거론 하는 것은 한·미 우호 관계에
비추어 결코 바람직 하지 못함을 국무성측에 재차 전달 바람.

적절히

(제1차 관보)

2. 동건 AP 및 REUTER

0035

앙 고 재	35 년 10 월 1 일	미 과	기안자	과 장	심의관	국 장	제1차관보 전체	차 관	장 관	발신시간 :		
										외신과	접수자	과 장

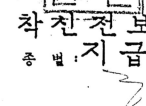

관리
번호 <del>85
ㅡ45X</del>

외 무 부

착 신 전 보
지 급

번 호 : USW-4730   일 시 : 51021 1743   종 별 :

수 신 : 장 관(미북,영재)사본:주유연대사(중계필)

발 신 : 주 미 대사

제 목 : 반정부 시위

연: USW-4698

1. 당지 소위 민통연합 소속 간부로부터 파악한바에 의하면 연호,김근태 고문설과
관련한 시위를 앞으로 국무성앞에서 약1개월간 계속할 계획이라는바,동 시위는 3인조
로 구성,2인은 프라카드를 들고,1인은 전단을 배포할것이라함(금21일에도 동시위가
있었음)

2. 민통연합측은 국무총리 워싱톤 체재기간중에는 1회에 한하여 상기 국무성앞 시위
의 규모를 확대(50명목표)할 계획이라하며 현재로서는 여타장소 (숙소또는 공항등)에
서의 시위는 계획치않고 있으나 앞으로 동 시위의 규모와 횟수가 추가,확대될 가능성
도 있다고함.

3. 당관은 동 시위가 확대되지않도록(특히 국무총리 당지 체재기간중)노력중에 있음
(대사 류병현)

예고:85.12.31일반

0036

√ 미주국   차관실   1 차보   2 차보   영교국   청와대   안 기   고안시

PAGE   1

85.10.22   09:43
외신 2과   통제관

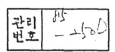

외 무 부 착 신 전 보

번 호 : USW-4847   일 시 : 510281603   종 별 :

수 신 : 장 관 (미북, 영재)

발 신 : 주 미 대사

제 목 : 민통연합 강연회

연 : USW-4698, 4730

 김근태 고문설과 관련, 당지 민통연합, 목요기도회 및 한국인권 문제 연구소는 85.
10.25. 20:00 당지 수도장로교회 (담당 박승화 목사)에서 80 여명의 교민참석하에 지
금한국에서는 --- 제하 반 정부 집회를 갖고 김근태부인의 육성 녹음테이프를 청취하
고 CDP 소속 이신범 및 당지 민통연합 사무총장 심기섭의 강연을 들었음.
(총영사 문동석)

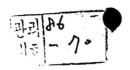

협 조 문	응신기일 198 . .

분류기호 및 문서번호	아일 700-31	제목 민청련 전의장 김근태 수사관련 대책

수 신	미주국장, 정보분화국장	발신일자 : 1986 . 1 . 9 .
	영사교민국장	

　　1. 86.1.7 안기부에서 신민당-일사회당간 교류문제 및 민청련 전의장 김근태 수사와 관련한 대책회의가 개최되었는 바, (동북아1과장 참석) 그중 귀국소관 사항인 김근태 수사관련 대책회의 자료(안기부 작성)를 별첨 송부합니다.

　　2. 상기 김근태 수사관련 대책회의 결과 당부 요조치 사항을 아래 통보하오니 귀국에서 필요한 조치를 취하여 주시기 바랍니다.

　　　　　　　　- 아 -

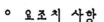

　° 요조치 사항

　　- 문제교포(재미) 심기섭, 이신범, 정동채의 여권기간 만료시 연장 불허

　　　· 심기섭 : 88.12.30 만료

　　　· 이신범 : 88.12.31 만료

　　　· 정동채 : 87.11.30 만료

　　- 재미 반한단체에서 한국인 문제와 관련, 방미 초청 예정(86. 3)인 재야 인물 출국 불허조치

　　　· 이부영, 임채정, 예춘호, 양순직, 박종태등

　　　　　　　　/ 계속 /　　　　　0038

1205 - 8 A
1981. 12. 1 승인

190mm×268mm (인쇄용지 (2급) 60g/m²)
가 33 - 41 1984. 10. 10.

- 상기 문제교포의 비위 취약자료 수집, 교포
  사회내 고립화 및 이간 유도
- 미국을 비롯한 우방정부 및 인권단체, 교포
  사회에 대한 홍보 강화.   끝.

첨부 : 상기자료 1부.

아   주   국   장

0039

┌───┐
│ ──── 民靑聯　前議長　金槿泰 ────   │
│   │
│ 捜査　方法　是非　關聯動向　및　對策方案   │
└───┘

1986 . 1 . 7 .

0040

1. 槪　　況

○ 不法團体인　民靑聯　前議長　<u>金槿泰</u>는　國家保安法　違反
等으로　<u>拘束起訴</u>（85.10.25）되어　現在　1審　公判中

```
─────────────＜主　要　嫌　疑＞─────────────

△ 85.3　同團体를　民族民主革命理論에　따른　反帝・
反파쇼 鬪爭　標傍　利敵團体化

△ 85.1～85.3　<u>民靑聯會員</u>　等에게　北傀　對南革命
路線에　同調하는　〃民族民主主義革命〃理論　伝播

△ 美文化院　占拠籠城　및　大宇어패럴　籠城事件　等
背後操縱
```

○ 이와　關聯　金槿泰는　12.19　1審公判時　警察調査期間中
拷問　및　苛酷行爲를　받았다고　主張,　<u>在野・宗敎・拘束者</u>
家族　等이　聯合鬪爭을　展開

○ 特히　<u>海外問題僑胞, 人權團体　및　政界　等에　歪曲 伝播</u>
<u>國益을　沮害하고　있어　對策講究　必要</u>

-1-

0041

2. 關聯動向

✓ 拘束者家族	○ 85.9.26 金槿泰 妻 印在謹은 檢察廳 복도에서 送致되는 金槿泰를 接觸後 各界에 歪曲 伝播 ○ 印在謹·崔貞順(李乙鎬妻)·李起淵(延聖洙妻) 等은 隨時 　△ 搜査方法 是非 各種 声明書 發表 및 　　民民聯 等과 連繫 籠城 　△ 木曜祈禱會 및 梨大, 서울大 示威現場 參席 　　金槿泰 搜査方法 事例 發表 　△ 在美 反政府人物 李信範, 沈基燮 等에게 　　金槿泰 關聯動向 歪曲 伝播 　△ 12.3 NCC人權委 事務室에서 派韓 AI 　　調査要員 〃웨슬리 그릭〃 等 接觸, 　　金槿泰 搜査方法 歪曲 說明
✓ 擔當弁護人團	○ 85.10.2 洪性宇 等 弁護人團은 裁判部에 金槿泰의 〃身体鑑定証拠 保全〃 申請 　※ 10.15 擔當裁判部에서 棄却 ○ 金槿泰 面會時 拷問事例 陳述토록 煽動 ○ 12.19 1審公判時 裁判部에 拷問檢証 申請 　※ 12.30 大韓弁協 人權委에서는 金槿泰가 　　調査過程에서 拷問 等 人權侵害를 받았다 　　면서 擔當警察 8名 告訴

0042

-2-

48　한국 인권문제 미국 반응 및 동향 2

民 推 協	○ 金大中・金泳三은 民推協 指導委 및 常任 運營委 等 合同會議 主宰코 同事件關聯 声明書 發表 (10.2, 10.19) ○ 太倫基 等 13名으로 〃緊急對策委〃 構成 (10.10), 声明書 發表 (12.21)
民民聯 等 問題團体	○ 9.27 NCC는 東京아시아基督教會議에 同事件 通報 ○ 10.17 民民聯 文益煥 等 問題圈 代表 12名 은 NCC 小會議室에서 〃共同對策委〃 構成 ○ 10.18 教協人權委는 아시아教協에 金槿泰・ 李乙鎬 關聯事項 電文發送 ○ 10.29 在野・教界・民推協・新韓黨 等이 聯合, 〃搜査方法 是非 共同對策委〃結成, 記者會見 ○ 11.14 民民聯 美NCC 國際赦免委에 伝播 ○ 12.26 NCC에서 人權消息을 通해 同事件 內容 揭載 配布
海外反韓勢力	○ 民青聯 美國本部에서 △ 10.15 同事件關聯 声明書 配布 △ 10.19 〃民主化運動 消息 2号〃를 通해 歪曲 伝播 ○ 李信範(美 亜細亜 政策開發委 委員, KT追從者) 沈基燮(在美 民民聯 事務總長)等 反政府 人物들은 △ NYT・WP・WSJ 等 言論에 同事件 資料 提供 (10.15)

0043

△ 美下院議員 6名에게 歎願要請書翰 發送
（10.16）

△ 런던所在 國際赦免委 및 獨逸人權團體에
關聯資料 發送（10.17）

△ 金權泰 寬容 歎願呼訴文 1万4,000枚
美全域 社會團體 및 宗教團體에 配布
（10.21）

△ 金權泰 妻 印在謹 肉声録音테이프 公開 및
金權泰 救命 5万名 署名運動 展開（10.25）

△ 金權泰 法廷陳述 英訳配布 및 美國務省에
伝達（86.1.5）

※ 李信範은 86.3 韓國人權問題세미나
開催 및 유럽 6個國 巡訪時 同事件
伝播 企図

○ 海外 反韓僑胞 30余名 美國務省 앞에서
同事件 非難 示威（10.18）

※ 美教協 및 國際人權委 弁護士協會로 부터
支援을 받은 ″피카트″弁護士 1.9 ～
1.11間 來韓 金權泰 公判傍聽 및
拘束者家族 接触 豫定

※ 國際人權弁護士協會 總務 ″개미 영″
1.23頃 訪韓 金權泰 公判 傍聽 豫定

0044

-4-

3. 予想 問題點

　　○　拘束者家族, 問題圈團体와　連繫, 金槿泰　救命運動　展開

　　　　△　救命運動　憑藉, 對政府油印物　配布, 籠城, 示威　展開

　　　　△　金槿泰　釋放　署名運動　展開

　　　　△　國內外　人權團体에　救命支援　要請

　　○　搜査方法　是非, 意図的　公判　妨害　恣行

　　　　△　公判進行　遲延　誘導, 公判日程　蹉跌　招來

　　　　△　辯護人團, 公判時　政治宣伝場化　誘導

　　　　△　公判廷內에서　集團　騷乱, 公判妨害

　　　　△　公判進行　狀況　錄取, 油印物化　國內外에　伝播

　　○　在野問題圈團体, 對政府鬪爭　擴散　劃策

　　　　△　搜査方法　是非로　在野　問題圈　結束　企図

　　　　△　新学期　学園街　煽動, 改憲　鬪爭으로　變質　誘導

　　○　海外　反韓勢力과　連繫, 國益　沮害　　　　　0045

　　　　△　國外　問題僑胞　連繫, 外國　言論　및　機關에　事件眞相
　　　　　　歪曲　伝播

　　　　△　問題僑胞　主動, 僑胞社會　煽動으로　籠城, 示威　等　展開

　　　　△　國外　人權團体　및　朝野에　人權問題　圍繞, 救命運動　및
　　　　　　對韓政策　圧力　誘導

　　　　△　國外　人權團体　所属　辯護士　等을　通한　國際人權問題　輿論化

-5-

4. 對處方案

가. 基本方向

○ 捜査方法 是非를 名分으로 한 在野運動圈의 改憲鬪爭
  変質 企図, 徹底 封鎖

○ 拘束者家族 動向監視 强化 및 必要時 遮断措置

○ 公判時 緻密한 事前對策樹立 物議素地 除去

○ 海外 反韓勢力의 不純活動 最大限 牽制

○ 人權問題關聯 海外弘報 强化

나. 細部對策

對策	關聯事項	有關機關

捜査方法
是非關聯
行事 瓦解
	○ 拘束者家族 및 在野 問題團体의
	  人權問題 關聯行事 一切 不許
	○ 强行時 行事主動者 隔離·遮断措置
	○ 人權問題關聯 油印物 製作 等 關聯者
	  依法措置
		警 察
		檢 察
		安企部

拘束者家族
徹底管理
	○ 管轄警察署長 責任下에 拘束者家族에
	  對해 月2回以上 說得 및 警告措置
	  와 함께 1:1 密着監視 並行
		警 察
		安企部

0046

-6-

對　策	關　聯　事　項	有關機關
	○ 所謂 〝民主化運動 家族實踐協議會〟 等 拘束者家族團体 瓦解工作 推進 ○ 金權泰 救命關聯 集團行動 徵候捕捉 時 初動段階에서 瓦解	
在野問題人物 不純 活動 強力措置	○ 過激 問題人物 犯法行爲時 採証資料 確保後 依法措置 ○ 集會示威 等 集團行動時 徹底 沮止 ○ 記者會見時 參席者 事前 遮断 等으로 瓦解 ○ 學園街 連繫集團行動 煽動時 強硬 依法措置 ※ 改憲鬪爭으로의 変質은 絶對 不容	警　察 檢　察 安企部
<u>公判對策樹立</u> <u>徹底 對処</u>	○ 公判日程遵守，2月中 1審宣告 完結 ○ 金權泰에 對해서는 <u>重刑（7年以上）</u> 宣告誘導 ○ 訴訟指揮權 確立으로 法廷秩序 最大限 維持 ○ 警備強化로 問題人物出入遮断 및 隔離 ○ 傍聽券 嚴格制限發付 및 出入者 檢索強化 ○ 言論縮小報道 調整 ※ <u>美國人辯護士（〝피카트〟및〝애미·영〟）傍聽不許</u>	檢　察 文公部 安企部 2라공2 1.9

0047

對　策	關　聯　事　項	有關機關
海外　反韓 勢力　活動 徹底　封鎖	郵檢强化　및　空港湾　出入　問題 人物에　對한　徹底한　檢索으로　不純 物品（油印物，錄音테이프　等）　押收 問題僑胞，沈基燮，李信範，鄭東彩 非違　脆弱資料　蒐集，僑胞社會內 孤立化　및　離間誘導 → 제끼（거주여권 말소 ※　不純活動　關聯事項　採證，帰國時 　　依法措置 居住　旅券期間　満了時　旅券　延長 不許 　　－　沈基燮：88.12.30 　　－　李信範：88.12.31 　　－　鄭東彩：87.11.30 제끼 ○ 反韓　團体에서　韓國人權問題와　關聯 訪美　招請予定（86.3月）인　在野 人物　出國　不許　措置（李富榮，민민련 林採正，芮春浩，楊淳稙，朴鍾泰　等） ○ 美國을　비롯한　友邦政府　및　人權 團体　僑胞社會에　對한　弘報　强化	外務部 法務部 文公部 安企部 ← 반한인물에대한 　견제의행요로〉

0048

85. 10. 4 자 AP 보도

W214

R

SOUTH KOREA-TORTURE

RA

28

DISSIDENT GROUP CHARGES TORTURE BY GOVERNMENT

SEOUL, SOUTH KOREA (AP) - AN OPPOSITION GROUP, HEADED BY TWO DISSIDENT LEADERS KIM DAE-JUNG AND KIM YOUNG-SAM, FRIDAY ACCUSED POLICE OF HAVING TORTURED STUDENTS, WORKERS AND OTHER DISSIDENTS ARRESTED ON POLITICAL CHARGES.

THE COUNCIL FOR PROMOTION OF DEMOCRACY IN A STATEMENT DEMANDED THE GOVERNMENT TELL THE TRUTH CONCERNING ''THE UNDEMOCRATIC AND IMMORAL ACTS'' AND SEVERLY PUNISH THOSE INVOLVED.

THE STATEMENT QUOTED FAMILY MEMBERS AND FRIENDS AS SAYING THAT POLICE INVESTIGATORS TORTURED THE ARRESTED DISSIDENTS WITH WATER, POWDER OF HOT PEPPER, ELECTRICITY AND BEATINGS.

THE COUNCIL SAID THAT IT WILL CARRY OUT A CAMPAIGN WITH THE MAIN OPPOSITION NEW KOREA DEMOCRATIC PARTY AND OTHER OPPOSITION FORCES TO SEEK AN END TO WHAT IT CALLED SUCH INHUMANE ACTS.

THE STATEMENT DID NOT SAY HOW MANY PEOPLE IT CLAIMED HAD BEEN TORTURED BUT SAID THEY INCLUDED TWO WELL-PUBLICIZED ACTIVISTS - HOE IN-HOE AND KIM KUN-TAE.

HO, A STUDENT AT KOREA UNIVERSITY, WAS ARRESTED A MONTH AGO ON CHARGES OF VIOLATING THE LAW OF ASSEMBLY AND DEMONSTRATION. HE HEADED THE SAMMIN STRUGGLE COMMITTEE WHICH WAS INVOLVED IN THE OCCUPATION LAST MAY OF A DOWNTOWN U.S. GOVERNMENT LIBRARY BY A GROUP OF WHAT THE GOVERNMENT CALLED LEFTIST RADICAL STUDENTS.

THE STUDENTS DEMANDED AN AMERICAN APOLOGY FOR THE MOVEMENT OF KOREAN TROOPS TO SUPPRESS REBELS IN KWANGJU SOUTH OF HERE IN MAY 1980. A TOTAL OF 191 PEOPLE WERE KILLED DURING THE RIOTING, ACCORDING TO AN OFFICIAL COUNT.

KIM, FORMER CHAIRMAN OF THE YOUTH ALLIANCE FOR DEMOCRATIZATION MOVEMENT, WAS ARRESTED LAST MONTH ON CHARGES OF VIOLATING THE NATIONAL SECURITY LAW.

A GROUP OF LAWYERS DEFENDING KIM HAS ASKED A COURT TO SECURE PHOTOGRAPHIC EVIDENCE ON THE SIGNS OF ALLEGED TORTURE OF HIM FOR USE LATER DURING TRIAL, ACCORDING TO ONE OF THE LAWYERS.

NO GOVERNMENT COMMENT WAS IMMEDIATELY AVAILABLE ON THE ALLEGED TORTURES.

END

AP-NY-10-04-85 0952GMT

0049

0050

(별첨 2)   85. 10. 4. 東亞

保安法 위반혐의로 구속된 金槿泰씨

「고문흔적」증거보전 신청

변호인 "발뒤꿈치등에 심한상처"

국가보안법위반혐의로 구속된 前민청련의장 金槿泰씨 (38·서울구치소수감 중)의 변호인단 8명은 4일 「金씨가 경찰조사과정에서 가혹한 고문을 받았다」고 주 장、金씨의 신체에 남아있는 고문흔적에 대한 증거보전을 청구、이날 서울 형사지법에 냈다.

李敦明변호사등 변호인단 이 이날 신청서에 따르면 金씨 는 지난 9월4일부터 같은 달 20일까지 치안본부대공 분실에서 조사를 받으면서 전기고문·물고문등 10여차 례에 걸친 가혹한 고문을 받 아 발뒤꿈치등에 심한 상처 가 남아있었다는 것이다.

金씨의 변호인단은 「경찰조사당시 받은 육체적 고문과 공 포감등이 검찰조사과정에까 지 계속될 것이 명백하다」 고 주장하면서 金씨의 신체 에 대한 사진촬영과 의사의 진단등 고문흔적을 보전 해달라고 신청했다.

변호단은 「金씨의 고문관련 상처가 자연치유돼 없어지거 나 계속된 고문으로 가중돼 사용할수 없을 것」이라고 주장했 다.

金씨는 국가보안법위반혐의 로 지난 9월 7일 경찰에 구 속돼 같은달 26일 검찰에 송 치됐으며 구체적인 혐의사실 은 알려지지 않고있다.

0051

김근태 사건 관련 미국 반응, 1985-86   57

한국정부 강압정책으로 전환

- Clyde Haberman특파원 기고 -

1. 전대통령은 지난 1년이상의 기간동안 점진적인 자율화, 민주화 조치를 실시해 왔음.

2. 그러나 최근 몇달 전부터 정치범을 체포, 기소, 고문까지 함으로써 반정부 인사에 대한 탄압을 재개하고 있는바, 이러한 정책변화는 다음과 같은 사례에서 잘 나타나고 있음.

   가. 데모 참가학생들에 대한 6개월간의 강제교육 실시를 목적으로 하는 학원 안정법안 제정 추구 (동 법안은 현재 내외의 심한 반발에 부딪혀 제출 보류중)

   나. 안기부요원의 동아일보사 언론인 3명에 대한 구타

   다. '삼민투'를 용공단체로 규정

   라. 22명의 학생을 간첩혐의로 기소

   마. 김대중의 가택연금

   바. 선동적 기사 기고 교사 15명 해고

   사. 서울대 이현재 총장이 데모주동 학생을 제적시키지 않았다는 이유로 해임

   아. 데모학생에 대한 미온적인 판결로 담당판사가 지방 전보 발령

0052

자. 고려대 학생 선동혐의로 야당 국회의원 2명등 기소

3. 현정권이 학원안정법과 같은 강압정책을 계속 실시할 경우
   현재 분산되어 있는 반대세력을 집결시키는 결과만을 초래할
   것으로 분석

0053

미국무성 Kalb 대변인의 기지 브리핑시 질의응답 내용

Q : There have been quite a few reports over the last few weeks of allegations of torture in South Korea. Do you have any comment on those allegations ? Are they consistent with the American view of where the Chun's Government should be going ?

A : Uh -

Q : Does the United States appreciate the crackdown against dissidents ?

A : Uh-- We are aware of credible reports that three Korean journalists were beaten recently by Korean security officials and we have made known to the Korean government our concern about this deplorable incident. We also are aware that a youth activist was subjected to torture recently.

0054

We have made known to the Korean government our serious concern. As I said a moment
ago, about this deplorable incident as well,
and on your broader question about crackdowns,
let me say this, If I may, Mike. We believe
that in general Korea has made political
progress over the past few years.

In 1984, early 85, the Korean government
completely lifted the political ban that had
originally applied to 567 politicians.

In February, 1985, Korea experienced one
of the most democratic elections in its
history. During the campaign, candidates
were free to criticize the government in front
of large rallies.

As a result of the election, new parties
supported by leading opposition politicians
became the largest opposition party. All
the professors and some journalists who had
lost their jobs for political reasons were
allowed to return to their positions.

0055

On the other hand, as department officials
have stated on several occasions, there have
been some regrettable steps in recent months
which we regard as inconsistent with the real
progress that has been made.

We continue to encourage political
progress and to urge moderation and dialogue
on all parties.

0056

(별첨 5) 김근태 관련사항

통 학 요 록
----

1. 통학일시 : 1985.10.16(수) 18:00

2. 송 화 자 : 안기부 북미과장

3. 수 화 자 : 이호진 서기관

4. 통화내용 : 김근태 관련 사항을 아래와 같이 통보함.

가. 김근태 인적사항

　　○ 본　　적 : ████████

　　○ 주　　소 : 경기도 부천시 역곡동 일두아파트
　　　　　　　　 1동 111호

　　○ 생년월일 : 47.2.24(당 38세)

나. 김근태 특이사항

　　○ 친형제중 월북자 3명

　　○ 친척 10여명이 6.25동란중 부역(북측 인사에 적극
　　　 협조 제공)

다. 관련상황

　　○ 본명은 83.9 "민주화운동 청년연합"을 조직, 불온
　　　 유인물인 "민주화의 길"을 90여회 발간, 배포하고
　　　 20여차례나 반정부 시위활동을 선동한바 있음.

0057

o 본명은 국가보안법 위반으로 9.5-26일간 경찰에서
  합법절차에 의거 조사후 검찰에 송치되어, 현재
  조사중이며 기소되어 공정한 재판을 받을 예정임.

o 10.4일자 동아일보는 김근태에 대한 고문행위를
  운운하고 있으나 상기 조사 과정에서 가혹행위는
  없었으며 수사 절차상 있을수도 없는일임. 끝.

0058

국내 인권문제 관련 대책 회의 자료

1. 상황

가. 재미 반체제 인물(심기섭, 이신범등)들은 국내 반체제 인물들과 연계하에 김근태 사건 및 동아일보 기자 연행 사건등과 관련, 고문설 및 용공 조작설을 미국 정계, 국제사면위등 국내외에 유포, 아국 정부에 대한 압력 행사 요청 및 국내 불안 조성을 기도하고 있음.

나. 국내외 반체제 인물들의 활동에 오도된 미국무성 및 국제 사면위등은 사실 무근인 고문설등을 근거로 아국의 인권상황에 대해 관심과 우려를 표명하면서 시정을 요구하고 있음.

2. 대책

가. 기본방침

(1) 정부, 국회, 재외공관, 사회단체 및 여론 지도층 인사들이 능동적으로 인권 관련, 홍보활동을 전개함.

(2) 홍보논리

° 아국이 호전적인 북괴와 대치하고 있는 특수한 안보 상황에도 불구하고, 제5공화국 정부는 출범이래 과감한 각종 자유화 조치를 취함으로써 인권문제 개선을 위한 노력을 해 왔음.

° 금번 김근태의 고문설 및 용공 조작설은 사실 무근으로, 수사결과 김근태는 "민족 민주주의 혁명"이론을 근거로 "민중연합 정권" 수립을 위하여 "민청연"을 주도, **0059**

1

학생·노동자 연대투쟁을 배후에서 조종하였음이 밝혀졌음.

o "민청연"을 배후 지원, 현 정권 타도를 목표로 활동중인 재야 운동권 세력은 견위 투쟁 전열이 붕괴된데다 수사 진전에 따라 자신들의 배후 추궁에 대한 불안감을 느끼고 "고문,용공 조작"이라는 허구적 주장을 유포하고 있는바, 이들은 다음과 같은 목적을 가지고 있음.

    - 구속자외 투쟁의식 고취

    - 대내외 여론 환기

o 또한 재야 반체제 인사들은 정치 외적인 인권문제를 잇슈로 재야 운동권 단체와 연계, 개헌 투쟁의 발판을 구축하기 위해 금번 사건을 악용하고 있음.

o 해외 반체제 인물들은 국내 반체제 인물들과 연계하여 국내정세 불안 조성을 위해 악의적인 고문설을 유포, 세계여론을 오도하고 있음.

    나. 세부 대책

       (1) 국내대책

대 상	대 책
언론기관	o 문공부 명외로 해명 자료를 작성 배포, 진상 보도토록 유도
여론지도층	o 정부인사들을 중심으로 각계 지도층 인사들과 수시 간담회등을 개최, 정부의 인권상황 개선 노력을 설명하고 여론을 지도토록 유도
오염가능성 있는 운동권 인물	o 정부인사 및 유력인사들이 개별적인 접촉을 갖고 설득 활동 견지

2

0060

(2) 국외대책

대 상	대 책
미 국무성	o 국무성 인권보고서 작성(매년 2월)에 대비, 문공부 명의의 해명 자료 작성, 미 국무성에 전달 o 국무성 인권국 요원과의 접촉강화, 설득활동 전개
주한미대사관	o 외무부는 국내 반체제 인물들의 일방적 주장과 유언비어를 근거로 주한 미대사관이 무책임한 보고를 국무성에 제출한 사실에 유감을 표명하고, 상호 이해증진을 위해 대화체제를 강화
미 의회	o 대한 비판활동 가담 의원 및 지한파 의원들에게 문공부 명의의 해명자료 제공 o 상, 하원 외무위 소속 의원 및 전문위원들에 대한 대한인식 고취 및 접촉활동 전개 * 미 의회는 85.11.1-86.1.3간 휴회중
미 언론	o 해외공보관을 통한 기자 및 편집진 접촉 순화활동 강화 o 유력인사(미국인 및 교포)를 이용한 독자투고를 통하여 정부입장 해명
국제사면위등 단체	o 정부정책에 호응하는 단체들로 하여금 한국인권 관계 보고서 작성, 배포 * 국제인권 옹호 한국연맹(회장: 김연준 한양대 총장), 한국 기독교 고역자 협의회(회장: 조문경 목사)등
교포 사회	o 국내언론 해외지사: 정부입장 홍보기사 게재토록 문공부가 조종 o 순수 교포언론: 해명자료 제공, 협조 유도 o 공관장, 공보관 주도외 주기적인 교민간담회 개최, 정부입장 설명 o 평통위원등 지도급 교포들의 정부 홍보 요원화

0061

끝.

85. 11. 9

0062

목   차

0063

1. 국내외 반체제 인물동향

  가. 재미 반체제 인물(심기섭, 이신범등)들은 국내 반체제 인물들과 연계하에
     김근태(38세, 민주화운동 청년연합 전 의장, 9.7 구속)사건 및 동아일보
     기자 연행사건(8.24 중공기 불시착 보도 관련 연행 조사)등과 관련,
     고문설 및 용공 조작설을 미국 정계, 국제사면위등 국내외에 유포

  나. 국내외 반체제 인물들은 다음과 같은 활동을 통해 아국 정부에 대한
     영향력 행사 및 국내 불안 조성을 기도하고 있음.

해외 반체제 인물동향	○ 10.1부터 미 인권단체, 런던소재 국제사면위, 미 국무성, 미 의회 및 노동단체등에 고문 관련, 허위자료 작성 유포
	○ 10.18부터 국무성 앞에서 간헐적으로 인권시위 전개
	○ 10.15 NYT 기자회견을 비롯한 각종 언론기관에 관련 자료 배포
	○ 10.25 워싱톤에서 한국내 고문 폭로 반한집회 개최("레이건" 대통령 앞 서신 발송)
	○ 10.26부터 10만명 서명 운동 전개 및 아국정부에 대한 압력 행사를 요청하는 14,000통 서한 발송
	○ 85.11 김근태등의 재판 참관을 위한 미국 변호사 방한 비용 모금운동 전개
국내 반체제 인물동향	○ 10.17 문익환등 29명, 구속인사 고문 행위 비난 연좌 데모 및 성명서 발표
	○ 10.19 김대중, 김영삼등 김근태 고문 관련, 비난 기자회견

0C64

1

	○ *11.4* 김대중 및 54명의 신민당 국회의원, 카톨릭 신부, 인권 운동가등은 "고문 및 용공 조작 저지 대책위원회"를 구성, 한국정부 고문행위 조사단 파견을 UN 에 요청하고, 메세지를 UN 인권위, 국제사면위, 국제법률가 위원회에 발송
	* 86.2 유엔 인권위원회 전체회의가 개최될 예정이나, 85.8 개최된 유엔 인권 소위원회 의제 채택에서 한국 인권문제가 기각되었으므로 아국 문제가 거론될 가능성은 희박함.

2. 미국반응

국내외 반체제 인물들의 활동에 오도된 미 국무성과 사회단체들은 왜곡된 고문설등을 근거로 아국에 대해 하기와 같이 관심과 우려를 표명하면서 시정을 요구하고 있음.

국무성	○ *10.16* "셔먼" 부차관보는 주미대사관 한탁체 공사에게 동아일보 기자 구타 및 김근태에 대한 고문 행위와 관련하여 제5공화국 수립이래 인권 상황이 현저히 개선되었다고 믿고 지지하여 왔으나, 최근의 사태 발전은 현재까지의 한국의 국제적 이미지를 손상시키고 있어 미 행정부가 한국정부를 강력히 지지하기 어려운 입장에 처하게 될 것이라고 언급
	○ *10.18* "칼브" 대변인은 국무성 정오 브리핑시 답변을 통해 한국 언론인 3명과 운동권 청년들의 고문 문제에 대한 미국 정부의 우려를 한국측에 표명했다고 언급
	○ 주한 미대사관은 본국 훈령(*10.22*)에 따라 국내 고문 사례 24건에 대한 조사 보고서를 작성, 보고

0065

2

언 론	○ 10.20자 "뉴욕 타임스", 10.30자 "볼티모어선"등 유력 언론들은 한국 정부의 고문설을 보도하면서, 이에 대한 미 국무성의 반응을 기사화 ○ AP 등 유력 통신도 유사 내용 보도 ○ 신한민보, 세계신보등 반정부 교포 신문에서 비판기사 게재

기 타	○ 10.25 뉴욕 세계 성직자 연합 교회 위원회 "폴 그레고리", 대통령 각하 앞 서한 발송
	  - 수감자들에 대한 고문행위는 세계속의 한국 이미지를 흐리게 하고 있음.
	  - 특히 김근태, 허인회, 이을호에 대한 고문에 항의함.
	  - 동명들의 변호사와 가족들이 면회할 수 있도록 보장해 줄 것을 요청함.
	
	○ 11.7 뉴욕소재 New School for Social Research 경제학부 교직원 대표 "졸베르그" 교수, 아국 법무부장관 앞 서한 발송
	  - 한국 정부가 본고 학생인 황대권을 구속한데 대해 심히 우려하고 있으며, 동 학생과 구속된 21명에 대한 혐의 내용과 증거를 밝혀 줄 것을 요구함.
	  - 우리는 동명들이 자신의 의사를 비폭력적으로 표시했다고 믿는바, 이들을 무조건 석방해 줄 것을 촉구함.
	
	○ 카나다 성공회 "스코트" 및 "옥스만" 목사도 대통령 각하 앞 10.24자 전문을 통해 김근태 사건, 동아일보 기자 사건등에 대한 고문 중지 및 언론 자유를 촉구

0066

3

3. 유럽지역 반응   -

국제사면위	○ 10.8 발표한 85년 연례 인권 보고서에 "시위 진압 경찰의 폭력 사용에 대한 많은 보고를 받았으며, 학생 시위 증가에 따른 단기 구금 사례가 증가하고 있다"고 지적
	
	○ 10.10 국가보안법 위반자 이광용에 대한 사면 탄원서를 주불 아국 대사관에 전달
	  - 이광용 및 관련자 5명의 즉각적 석방 요구
	  - 이광용 고문 사실에 대한 조사 및 가족, 변호사의 고도소 방문 허용 요청
	
	○ 10.3~10.14간 조사국 "그릭" 부국장은 아국 인권문제 조사차 방한(동명은 11월말~12월 초순 까지 재방한 예정)
	
	○ 10.24 런던 "헌 힐" 감리교회에서 아국 인권문제와 관련한 영사회 개최(1975년 당시 아국 인권 상황을 그린 "주님의 해")

언론 및 기타	○ 10.17, 10.19, 11.4 AFP, REUTER 등 유력 통신은 서울발 기사로 고문행위에 대한 국내 반체제 인사들의 비난(공동성명 발표) 발언등을 보도 ○ 10.23~26 서전 노총간부 "노오링"의 1명, 대우 어페럴 사건 진상 조사차 방한, 섬유노조 관계인사 접촉

0067

4

4. 대책

가. 기본방침

(1) 정부, 국회, 재외공관, 사회단체및 여론 지도층 인사들이
능동적으로 인권 관련, 홍보활동을 전개함.

(2) 홍보 논리

o 세계에서 유례를 찾아 볼 수 없는 호전적인 공산집단인 북괴와
대치하고 있는 특수적 안보 상황에도 불구하고, 제5공화국
정부는 출범이래 다음과 같은 과감한 자유화 조치를 취하였음.

- 정치 규제 해금

- 학원 자율화

- 각종 사면, 복권, 복학등 조치 계속

- 광주사태 관련자들에 대한 전원 사면등

o 금번 김근태의 고문설 및 용공 조작설은 사실 무근임.

o 김근태는 이을호("민청연"정책 부실장)의 "민족, 민주주의 혁명"
이론 지원을 받아 "민중연합 정권" 수립을 위하여 문제 제적생들의
집단인 "민청연"(민주화 운동 청년연합)을 주도하였으며,

o 또한 "삼민투", "깃발", "서울대 민추위", "위장 취업 노조 투쟁"으로
이어지는 학원소요 및 각종 노동분쟁등 학생·노동자 연대투쟁을
배후에서 조종하였음.

o "민청연"의 활동 방향을 제시하고, 자금 지원을 하면서 현 정권
타도를 궁극적 목표로 활동중인 재야 운동권 세력들은 전위
투쟁 전열이 붕괴된데다 수사 진전에 따라 자신들의 배후 주종에
대한 불안감을 느끼고 이를 모면하고 기도를 은폐, 합리화 시키기
위해 분명히 밝혀진 사실마저도 부인하고,"고문, 용공조작"이라는
허구적인 주장을 유포하고 있는바, 이들은 다음과 같은 목적을 갖고 있음.

- 구속자의 투쟁의식을 고취

0068

5

- 대내외의 여론 환기로 정부를 궁지에 몰아 넣으려는 발악적인 자구 행위

o 또한 재야 반체제 인사들은 고문이라는 정치 외적인 인권문제를 잇슈로 재야 운동권 단체와 연계, 개헌 투쟁의 발판을 구축하기 위해 이번 사건을 악용하고 있음.

o 해외 반체제 인물들도 국내정세 불안조성을 목적으로 국내 반체제 인물들과의 긴밀한 연계하에 악의적인 고문설등을 유포, 미 행정부, 언론계 및 세계 각종 인권단체들의 여론을 오도하고 있음.

나. 세부 대책

(1) 국내대책

대　상	대　　　책
언론기관	o 문공부 명의로 해명 자료를 작성 배포, 진상을 보도토록 유도함.
여론지도층	o 정부인사, 유력인사들을 중심으로 여론 지도층에 있는 각계 각층의 인사들과 수시 간담회등을 개최하여 정부의 인권상황 개선 노력등을 설명하고 여론을 지도토록 유도함.
오염가능성 있는 운동권 인물	o 정부인사 및 유력인사들이 개별적인 접촉을 갖고 설득 활동 전개

0069

6

(2) 국외대책

대 상	대 책
미 국무성	◦ 미 국무성의 인권보고서 작성(매년 2월)에 대비, 문공부 명의의 해명 자료를 작성, 주미대사관으로 하여금 전달 ◦ 인권국 요원과의 빈번한 접촉을 통한 설득 전개
주한 미대사관	◦ 외무부는 국내 반체제 인물들의 일방적 주장 및 유언비어를 근거로 주한 미대사관이 무책임한 보고를 국무성에 제출한 사실에 유감을 표명하고, 상호 이해 증진을 위해 주한 미대사관 측과 대화체제를 강화
미 의회	◦ 대한 비판활동 가담 의원 및 지한파 의원들에게 문공부 명의의 해명 자료 제공 ◦ 상·하원 외무위 소속 의원 및 전문 위원들에 대한 대한인식 고취 및 접촉활동 전개 * 미 의회는 85.11.1-86.1.3간 휴회기간으로 현재로서는 인권문제에 대한 직접적인 비난 활동은 없으나, 국무성의 인권보고서가 제출될시 조직적 비난 활동 전개가 예상됨.
미국 언론	◦ 해외 공보관을 통한 언론계 유관 기자 및 편집진 접촉, 순화 활동 강화 ◦ 미국 및 교포 유력인사를 이용한 독자 투고를 통하여 정부 입장 해명

0070

7

국제사면위등 단체	○ 국제 인권 옹호 한국연맹(회장: 김연준 한양대 총장), 한국 기독교 교역자 협의회(회장: 조문경 목사)등 정부 정책에 호응하는 단체들로 하여금 한국 인권관계 보고서를 작성, 배포함.
교포사회	○ 국내 언론 해외지사에 대해서는 기획 기사등을 통하여 정부 입장을 홍보하는 기사를 수시 보도하도록 문공부등이 조종 ○ 순수 교포 언론에 대해서는 해명 자료를 제공하고 협조를 유도함. ○ 공관장, 공보관 주도의 주기적인 교민간담회를 개최, 정부 입장 설명 ○ 평통 위원등 지도급 교포들의 정부 홍보 요원화

첨부: 1. 국내 인권문제 파급 경로

2. 국내 인권문제 관련, 해외 동향 및 반응. 끝.

0071

8

6

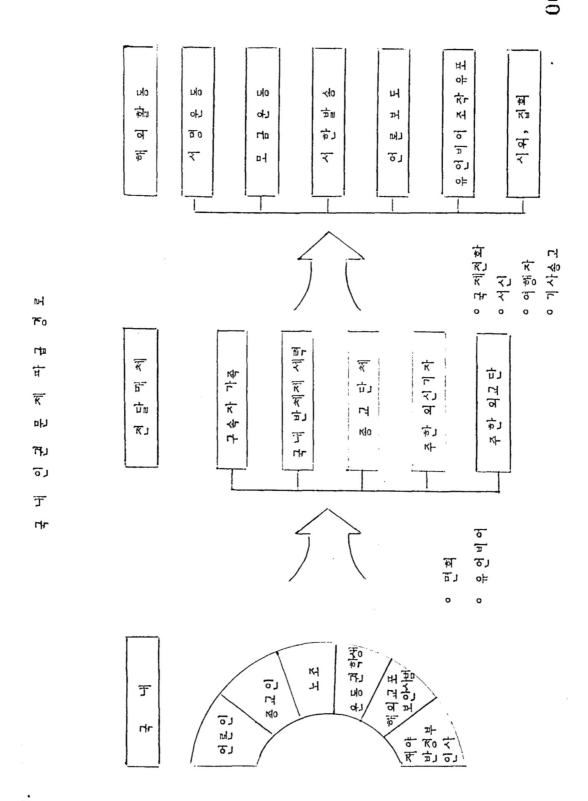

대북방송선전활동 흐름도

참고 1.

첨부 2.

최근 국내 인권문제 관련, 해외동향 및 반응

1. 미국무성

일 시	내 용
10.11	○ "아이숍" 한국과장은 주미대사관 김삼훈 참사관에게 다음과 같이 미측 관심 전달 - 김근태 관련, 한국 경찰의 가혹행위가 한국 신문에 보도되었는 바, 미국내 언론에의 파급을 우려하며, 우방국으로서 관심을 표명함. - 국무성 인권보고서에 작년보다 나쁘게 반영될 가능성을 우려함. - 이는 양국 관계를 더욱 원만히 유지 발전해 나가자는 취지임을 이해 바라며, 주한 미대사관도 이와 같은 취지를 한국 외무부에 전달할 것임.
10.16	○ "서면" 부차관보는 주미대사관 한탁채 공사에게 다음과 같이 언급 - 미 국무성은 동아일보 기자 구타 및 김근태에 대한 고문행위와 관련한 신빙성 있는 보고를 접했음. - 미국은 제5공화국 수립 이래, 한국내 인권상황이 현저히 개선되었다고 믿고, 이를 지지하여 왔는 바 최근 사태 발전은 지금까지 쌓아올린 한국의 국제적 이미지를 손상시키고 있어 국무성 인권보고서 작성시 작년보다 악화될 가능성이 있음. - 신체적 가혹행위가 대외적으로 널리 알려질 경우, 미국내 여론을 악화시켜 미 행정부는 한국정부를 강력히 지지하기 어려운 입장에 처하게 될 것임. ○ 이국은 상기 발언과 관련, 다음과 같이 답변 (3국이 1국과 협조, 외무부에 제공) - 조사과정에서 가혹행위는 없었으며, 수사절차상 있을수도 없음. - 현재 기소단계에 있는 바, 재판에서 진상이 밝혀 질 것임. 0073

10

10.18		○ "칼브" 대변인, 정오 브리핑시 기자 질문에 다음과 같이 답변
		- 미국은 언론인 3명과 운동권 청년들의 고문문제에 대한 미국 정부의 우려를 한국측에 표명하였음.
		- 미국은 최근 수년간 한국이 이룩한 정치발전이 계속되기를 바라며, 이를 위해 모든 당사자간에 화합과 대화가 있기를 촉구함.

나. 언론

일 자	신문명	내 용
10.10	신한민보 (라 성)	○ "민주학생, 시민 80명 심한 고문 당하고 있다" 제하 - 서울 남영동 소재, 대공수사반 사무실에는 대부분 학생들인 80여명의 민주 인사들이 지난 8월부터 심한 고문을 당하고 있음. - 민청연 진 의장 김근태씨 부인은 9.27 서울형사 지법에 들렀을때 남편이 알아볼수 없을 정도로 구타, 고문을 당하여 상처를 입고 있음을 목격하였음. - 김씨는 부인에게 80여명이 매일 7시간씩 10일동안 고문을 받았으며, 심문관으로 부터 전기 고문이나 통닭구이 고문을 당했다고 알려 주었음.
10.17	REUTER (서울발)	○ "문익환"등 반체제 인사들, 구속인사에 대한 경찰의 고문 행위 비난" - 문익환등 29명의 반체제 인사들은 구속인사 석방을 요구하는 3일간의 연좌 데모후 성명서를 발표

0074

11

		－ 자신들은 고문 행위에 대한 전국적인 투쟁을 전개할 것이라고 밝히고, 경찰이 민청연 수명에 대해 야만적인 고문을 자행했다고 주장
10.19	AP/ AFP (서울 발)	○ 반체제 및 야당 지도자들, 당국의 반체제 인사 고문행위 비난 － 김대중, 김영삼등 반체제 인사들의 공동 명의로 발표한 성명에서 민청연 전 의장 김근태가 심문 과정에서 구타, 전기 및 물 고문등 난폭한 처우 받았다고 지적 － 한편 공동 기자 회견에 참석할 계획이던 김대중은 10.19 오전 가택연금 상태에 있음.
10.19	REUTER (워싱톤 발)	○ 재미 반한단체 신문, 한국의 고문행위 주장 ○ 반한 한국인들 10여명, 국무성 밖에서 시위
10.19	AP (워싱톤 발)	○ 미 국무성은 10.18 "버나드 칼브" 대변인을 통해 한국외 고문설에 우려를 표명
10.19	VOA 방송	○ 미 국무성의 한국내 인권 유린 실태 지적과 관련한 "칼브" 대변인의 논평 내용 보도
10.20	NYT	○ "한국 반체제 인사 고문" 제하 － 국제사면위는 지난 9월 한국외 정치범 23명이 유죄판결에 이용될 자백서에 서명을 강요 당했다는 보고를 받았다고 밝혔음. － "칼브" 국무성 대변인은 10.18 미국정부는 한국외 언론인 3명과 청년활동가 1명이 고문을 당했다는 보고를 받고 미국 정부의 우려를 한국측에 전달했다고 밝혔음.

0075

12

10.21	영국, Financial Times	○ "미국, 한국의 고문행위 항의 지지" 제하로 아래 내용의 기사 게재 - 미 정부는 한국정부의 고문행위에 대한 서울에서의 항의를 공식 지지하였음. - 안기부는 8월 동아일보 기자 3명을 구금, 구타하였음. - 학생운동가 김근태는 경찰에 의해 전기 고문 및 고추 가루 고문을 받았음.
10.26	세계신보 (뉴욕)	○ "죽음의 공포에 객인 민주 이상"제하, 심기섭의 학생들에 대한 고문사례 기고문 게재
10.26	서독 Süddeutsche Zeitung	○ "독재정권은 수세에 있다" 제하로 아래 내용의 기사 게재 - 한국 정부는 한국을 자유민주 체제라고 선전하고 있으나, 아직도 언론 검열과 고문을 자행하고 있음. - 안기부는 8.30 동아일보 기자 3명을 구금, 고문하였음.
11.4	REUTER (서울발)	○ 한국 야당 및 재야세력, 정부측 고문행위 조사를 위한 조사단 파견을 UN에 요청 - 김대중 및 54명의 신민당 국회의원, 카톨릭 신부, 인권운동가들은 11.4 한국 정부의 고문행위 조사를 위한 조사단 파견을 유엔에 요청 - 이들이 작성한 메세지는 UN 인권위, "런던"의 국제 사면위 및 국제법률가 위원회에 발송되었다고 야당의 한 대변인이 밝혔음.
10.30	"발티모어 선"	○ 사설에서 김근태 고문 관련, 한국정부가 88올림픽 및 86 아시안 게임을 앞두고, 고문등의 행동을 범하는 우를 저지르고 있음.

0076

13

다. 재미교포

일 시	관 련 동 향
10. 1	° 재미 반정부 인물 이신범(정책개발 연구소 연구원)은 미국 인권단체 American Committee for Human Rights 회장인 Johnathan Fine 및 America's Watch 대표 자들과 회동 - 민청연 전 회장 김근태에 대한 고문문제를 항의키로 결정 - 10.1 당일 "런던" 소재 Amnesty Int'l 본부에 동조를 요청함. - 주장내용 (9.27 남영동-치안본부 수사실의 통칭-에서 김근태를 전기 및 물 고문과 발바닥 고문을 자행)
10. 15	° 재미 반정부 인물 심기섭(38세, 김대중 추종, "민통연합" 사무총장)은 김근태 가족(처와 부)의 자필 진정서를 번역, 뉴욕에서 NYT 지와 기자회견
10. 16	° 심기섭, 이신범을 중심으로 한 반정부 인물은 김근태 고문 관련, 자료를 - 미 하원 비공식 인권기구인 Congressional Human Rights Caucus 에 배포 * CHRC : 약 140명의 의원 회원을 가진 하원의원 비공식 기구로서 "에드워드 포터"(공화, 일리노이), "톰 란토스" (민주, 캘리포니아)가 공동 의장임. - "런던" 소재 Amnsty Int'l 및 독일 인권단체에 관련자료 송부
10. 17	° 심기섭, 이신범등 김근태 고문 관련, 미 국무성 한국과 방문 면담
10. 18	° 민통연합, 한국 인권문제 연구소 및 한국내 인권문제 북미연합회 공동 주관으로 국무성 앞에서 항의시위(10.18기점으로 한달간 계속 예정) - 참석인원: 심기섭, 박벽선등 약 15명 - 구호내용: 한국내 고문중지, 전OO 퇴진, 군사독재 지원 중단

0077

14

10.21	° 심기섭, 이신범, 미국 관련기관에 지원 요청 　- 미국 전역 사회단체, 종교 계등에 김근태등에 대한 관용조치 　　탄원을 호소하는 호소문 14,000매 발송 (10.21부터 계속) 　- 미 노동 총연맹 산업별 회의 산하 12개 직능 노조가 미 경제 　　요로로 하여금 대한 압력을 가하도록 협조 요청 (10.21이후 추진)
10.23	° 심기섭, 시카고 강연차 워싱톤 출발
10.25	° 한국내 고문 폭로 교포집회 개최 　- 장　　소: 워싱톤 시내 수도 장로교회 　- 참석인원: 40여명 　- 폭로내용: 김근태 처의 고문진상 폭로 테이프 공개, 이신범의 　　　　　　 증언 (나는 이렇게 고문 당했다) 심기섭의 현 정권 　　　　　　 음모 폭로 (전 정권 음모 분석) 　- 집회중 소위 민주화를 위한 모금 운동 전개 　- 주최측은 레이건 대통령 앞 호소문을 서한 형식으로 채택 발송
10.26	° 심기섭은 뉴욕 민청연 사무실에서 한국 정세 긴급 보고 대회를 　개최하고 다음과 같이 활동 　- 참석인원: 10여명 (김경재, 임병규, 이돈만등) 　- 심기섭은 운동권 학생에 대한 고문사례 발표 　- 결의사항: 고문방지 서명운동을 전 미국적으로 전개키로 결의 　　　　　　 (10만명 서명 목표)
11. 6	° 심기섭이 주동이 되어 10만명 서명운동 전개중
11.14 (예정)	° 상항, University of California / Berkeley 　한국학생회 산하 　그룹 "호롱"은 심기섭을 초청, 11.14 강연회 실시 예정

0078

15

라. 국제사면위 동향

일 자	내　용
10. 8	° 국제사면위, '85년례 인권보고서 발표 (세계 123개국에 대한 국가별 인권침해 사례 발표) (남·북한 관련사항) - 북괴는 인권 관련, 정보 수집원이 차단되어 있어 북괴의 인권 실태 파악은 매우 어려움. - 사면위는 최근 한국정부의 고문 행위에 대한 보고서를 받아 보질 못했으나, 시위 진압 경찰의 폭력사용에 대해서는 많은 보고를 받고 있음. - 국제사면위 조사단이 84.10.3~14간 한국을 방문, 관계당국 및 인권 피해자들을 접촉하였음. - 한국은 84년 하반기부터 학생시위가 증가, 이에 비례 단기 구금 사례가 증가하고 있음. - 한국정부는 84.1~5월간 약 200명의 학생들을 석방하였음.
10.10	° 국제사면위 불란서 지부, 국가보안법 위반자 이광용에 대한 사면 탄원서를 주불 아 공관에 발송 (탄원서 요지) - 이광용 및 관련자 5명의 즉각적 석방 요구 - 이광용 고문 사실에 대한 조사 실시 - 가족, 변호사의 교도소 방문 허용

0079

16

10.14	○ 국제사면위 사무총장 T. Hamuarerg 주영 공관에 조사단의 아국 입국 비자 발급 신청
	  - 조사단: 국제사면위 조사국 부국장 Gryk
	  - 방한 희망시기: 85.10월 중순
	  - 목적
	    최근 국내 학원시위 및 노사 분규사건 피고인 재판 방청 및
	    담당 검사 면담
	○ 국제사면위는 동 비자 발급신청시 주영 대사에게 아래 사항도 요청
	  - 85.7 대구교도소 수감 복역수 구타사건에 대한 관계 당국의
	    수사 진행 결과 통보
	＊ 사면위 조사단 Gryk 은 84.10.3-10.14간 아국 인권문제 조사차 방한

10.24	○ 국제사면위 영국지부 런던분회, 런던 Herne Hill 감리교회에서 국제사면위 회원 50여명 참석하에 아국 인권문제와 관련한 영사회 개최
	  - 영화명: Anno Dominai (주님의 해)
	  - 동 영화는 1975년 당시 아국의 인권상황을 배경으로 제작된 영화임.

11.8	○ "그릭크" 국제사면위 부국장은 10.30 영국 주재 아 대사관에 입국사증 발급을 요구, 11.5 동 사증을 수령
	  - 동명 일행은 11월 말에서 12월 초순 까지 10여일간 방한할 것을 계획중
	  - 동 일행은 방한중 아국 정부 입장도 청취하기 위해 정부 주선 인사들과도 면담하겠다고 언급

0080

17

마. 기타 단체

일 자	내 용
10.22	° "스트라스불그" 개최, 유럽 외회 '84 세계인권보고서 결의안 토의시 북괴외 공개처형 및 언론통제 비난 결의안 채택 — 아국은 세계인권 침해 사례국에서 제외
10.23-26	° 서전 노총간부 "노오링"외 1명, 대우 어패럴 사건 진상 조사차 국내 입국, 섬유 노조 관계인사 접촉
10.24	° 카나다 "클라우딘 옥스만" 목사, 대통령 각하 앞 항의 전문방송 — 김근태, 허인회, 이올호등 정치범에 대한 고문중지 바람.
10.24	° 토론토, 카나다 성공회 "스코트" 목사는 하기 내용외 전문을 대통령 각하 앞으로 발송했음을 서울, 한국 기독교 교회 협의회에 타전 — 카나다 성공회는 남영동 소재 치안본부 대공분실에서 학생들에게 행해지고 있는 고문에 대해 심히 우려하는 바임. — 우리는 각하께서 투옥과 고문외 공포가 없는 언론과 표현외 자유를 허용할 것을 촉구함.
10.25	° 뉴욕, 세계 성직자 연합교회 위원회 "폴 그레고리"는 전 대통령 각하 앞 하기 요지 서한 발송 — 수감자들에 대한 고문행위는 세계속의 한국 이미지를 흐리게 하고 있음. — 특히 김근태, 허인회, 이올호등에 대한 고문에 항의하는 바이며, — 동명들외 변호사와 가족들이 면회할 수 있도록 보장해 줄 것을 요청함.

0081

18

11. 7	° 뉴욕, Ncw School for Social Research 경제학부 교직원
	대표 "쥴 베르그" 교수는 한국 법무부 장관 앞 체포 학생 석방을
	요구하는 하기 전문 발송
	- 학문의 자유를 보호하고 인권 개선에 전념하고 있는 우리
	교수 일동은 한국정부가 본교 학생인 황대권을 구속한데 대해
	심히 우려하고 있으며, 동 학생과 구속된 다른 21명에 대한
	혐의 내용과 증거를 밝혀 줄 것을 요구하는 바임.
	- 또 우리는 구속된 사람들이 자신의 의사를 비폭력적으로
	표시했기 때문에 그들을 무조건 석방해 줄 것을 촉구하는 바임.

0082

19

관리
번호 86
-135P

主 미 대 사 관

미국(정)700- 160   1986. 6. 3.

수신 : 장 관

참조 : 미주국장, 영사교민국장

제목 : 미국 변호사협회의 법정 방청

        연 : USW - 2720

        연호 American Bar Association 측의 서한을 별첨
송부합니다.

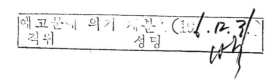

첨부 : 동 서한 1부. 끝.

주   미   대

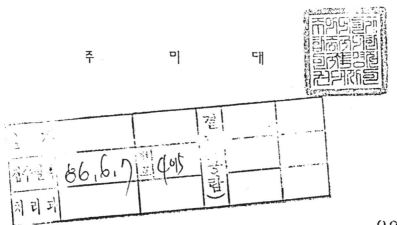

0083

American Bar Association

1985-1986

CHAIRPERSON
Abner J. Mikva
U.S. Court of Appeals
U.S. Court House, Rm. 3800
3rd & Constitution, NW
Washington, DC 20001
202/535-3375

CHAIRPERSON-ELECT
Sara-Ann Determan
815 Connecticut Avenue, NW
5th Floor
Washington, DC 20006
202/331-4588
ABA/net: ABA2735

VICE-CHAIRPERSON
Philip A. Lacovara
1201 Pennsylvania Avenue, NW
Suite 300
Washington, DC 20004
202/626-6262
ABA/net: ABA2930

SECRETARY
Clifford D. Stromberg
815 Connecticut Avenue, NW
5th Floor
Washington, DC 20006
202/331-4699
ABA/net: ABA2932

RECORDING SECRETARY
William L. Robinson
1400 Eye Street, NW
Suite 400
Washington, DC 20005
202/371-1212

IMMEDIATE PAST
CHAIRPERSON
J. David Ellwanger
555 Franklin Street
3rd Floor
San Francisco, CA 94102
415/561-8260
ABA/net: ABA4396

SECTION DELEGATE
Martha W. Barnett
P.O. Drawer 810
Tallahassee, FL 32302
904/224-7000
ABA/net: ABA353

COUNCIL MEMBERS
Mark I. Harrison
Phoeniz, AZ
ABA/net: ABA1375

James M. Nabrit III
New York, NY

Janet R. Studley
Washington, DC

Randolph W. Thrower
Atlanta, GA

Robert T. Coulter
Washington, DC
ABA/net: ABA2765

Richard K. Donahue
Lowell, MA
ABA/net: ABA1035

Robert F. Drinan
Washington, DC

Ellen Mercer Fallon
Montpelier, VT

Michael Franck
Lansing, MI
ABA/net: ABA1119

Betty Southard Murphy
Washington, DC

Ronald L. Plesser
Washington, DC

Samuel L. Williams
Los Angeles, CA

LAW STUDENT DIVISION
LIAISON
Ari D. Levine
Hoboken, NJ

YOUNG LAWYERS DIVISION
LIAISON
Mark I. Schickman
San Francisco, CA

BOARD OF GOVERNORS
LIAISON
Samuel S. Smith
Miami Beach, FL
ABA/net: ABA271

STAFF DIRECTOR
Steven G. Raikin
Washington, DC
ABA/net: ABA339

SECTION ADMINISTRATOR
J. Wade Carey
Washington, DC

May 30, 1986

Ambassador Kim Kyong Won
Embassy of the Republic of Korea
2370 Massachusetts Avenue, N.W.
Washington, D.C.   20008

Mr. Lee Sun Jin
First Secretary, Political Section
Embassy of the Republic of Korea
2370 Massachusetts Avenue, N.W.
Washington, D.C.   20008

RE: Request for expedited issuance of
visas to Messrs. Samuel Heins, Eugene
Thomas, Jerome Cohen and Jack Greenberg
to attend legal proceedings concerning
Mr. Kim Keun-Tae in the Republic of Korea
and request for assurance from your
Government that they will be permitted to
observe all public proceedings in this
case

Dear Ambassador Kim and First Secretary Lee:

On behalf of the American Bar Association (ABA)
and its over 320,000 member lawyers, and on behalf of
ABA President William W. Falsgraf, this is to
respectfully request that you assist us by expediting
the ABA's request that your Government issue visas to
four American lawyers, Samuel Heins, Eugene Thomas,
Jerome Cohen and Jack Greenberg, for the specific
purpose of their observing legal proceedings in the
Republic of Korea concerning Mr. Kim Keun-Tae, under
the auspices of the ABA International Human Rights
Trial Observers Project. Because of our
understanding that the next hearings in Mr. Kim's
case will be held on June 5 and 12, 1986, we
respectfully request that you issue the requested
visas as soon as possible. We also respectfully
request that you obtain on our behalf an assurance
from your Government that our representatives will be
permitted to observe any portion of these legal
proceedings which are open to the public.

To expedite the issuance of visas, I am
delivering this letter to you today in the hope that
you will immediately wire your Government for

SECTION OF INDIVIDUAL RIGHTS AND RESPONSIBILITIES

0084

1800 M STREET, NW, WASHINGTON, DC 20036 • (202) 331-2279 • ABA/net: ABA339

instructions with regard to this matter in advance of the time
you receive the completed visa applications of our
representatives. The completed visa application of Mr. Heins
will be delivered to your embassy on Monday, June 2nd. A xerox
copy of his draft application and passport is attached. Mr.
Greenberg is currently in Japan and holds a Korean "multiple
re-entry visa." In Mr. Greenberg's case, we ask that your
Government authorize the use of his multiple re-entry visa for
the specific purpose of attending these legal proceedings. We
will deliver to you next week the visa applications of Messrs.
Thomas and Cohen as soon as they are completed.

The attached memorandum of credential from ABA President
Falsgraf to the aforementioned American lawyers specifies the
limited purposes of their proposed trip to your country. It
would be our intention to send no more than one or two ABA
observers at a time to observe these legal proceedings. Visas
are requested for all four lawyers, since their availability
will depend upon the actual dates on which the various
anticipated hearings in Mr. Kim's case are held.

Please be assured that our representatives are under strict
instructions to in no way interfere with the legal proceedings
they witness, but rather to passively observe the proceedings
and to report what they see and hear to the President of the
ABA. This is an educational project, designed to help
enlighten American lawyers about legal processes in various
countries around the world. So far, in the past two years, the
Governments of South Africa, Yugoslavia and Liberia have all
extended full cooperation by inviting ABA representatives to
observe legal proceedings in their countries. In this way, we
seek to foster greater understanding among American lawyers
about the judicial systems of other nations.

Thank you very much for your cooperation in this matter.
Please do not hesitate to contact me if I can provide you with
any further information.

Sincerely,

Steven G. Raikin
Staff Director

Enclosures
1528P

0085

AMERICAN BAR ASSOCIATION

OFFICE OF THE PRESIDENT
WILLIAM W. FALSGRAF
AMERICAN BAR CENTER
750 N. LAKE SHORE DRIVE
CHICAGO, ILLINOIS 60611
TELEPHONE: 312/988-5100
ABA/NET: ABA007

PLEASE REPLY TO:
1800 M STREET, N. W.
WASHINGTON, D. C. 20036

MEMORANDUM

TO: Eugene Thomas
       Samuel Heins
       Jack Greenberg
       Jerome Cohen

FROM: William W. Falsgraf
       President
       American Bar Association

RE: Official authorization to be the representatives of the
       American Bar Association to observe legal proceedings
       concerning Mr. Kim Keun-Tae in South Korea

DATE: May 23, 1986

I hereby designate you as the official representatives of
the American Bar Association (ABA) and its over 320,000 member
lawyers as observers at the appellate proceedings in South
Korea concering Mr. Kim Keun-Tae. You may give copies of this
memorandum of credential to any appropriate South Korean or
American government officials or others in South Korea to
request their cooperation and assistance regarding your
responsibilities as a trial observer on behalf of the ABA.

Your mission is part of the ABA International Human Rights
Trial Observers Project, administered by the ABA Section of
Individual Rights and Responsibilities, which has been
authorized by the Board of Governors of the ABA. The purpose
of this project is to promote fairness in judicial proceedings,
and thereby fulfill Goal VIII of the American Bar Association
by encouraging adherence to the rule of law throughout the
world by sending prominent American lawyers and jurists
overseas to observe political trials with significant human
rights implications. Your mission is also in furtherance of
the resolution adopted by the ABA House of Delegates on
February 25, 1975, reaffirming our Association's support for
the rule of law in the international community and its
recognition of the need for an independent judiciary and for
the independence of lawyers as essential elements in
maintaining the rule of law.

OC86

Among the objects of your mission are the following:

1) To make known to the court, to the authorities of South Korea, to the prosecutors, defense counsel and the defendants in these cases, and to the general public the interest and concern of the American legal profession and the American Bar Association in the trials in question;

2) To communicate to the court, by your presence as an observer, the importance of affording the accused fair trials consistent with recognized international legal norms;

3) To obtain information about the conduct of the trials, the nature of the case against the accused and the laws under which they are being tried; and

4) To collect more general background information concerning the circumstances leading to the trial.

The primary concern of our Association is for the maintenance of the rule of law and the elements necessary to sustain it. On behalf of the American Bar Association, I thank you for volunteering for this important mission, and I look forward personally to receiving your report.

cc: The Honorable George Shultz
     U.S. Secretary of State
     U.S. Department of State
     Washington, D.C. 20520

WWF:sgr
0281j

0087

공 란

공   란

공　　　란

공   란

공   란

외 무 부

관리
번호 86
     -1345

번 호 : USW-2741   일 시 : 606032000   종 별 : 지급

수 신 : 장관 (미북,영사,법무부)

발 신 : 주 미 대사

제 목 : 미국 변호사협회 (ABA) 법정방청

대 : WUS-2227

연 : USW-2720

1.금 6.3.(화)   ABA   측에 대호 2 항 내용을 설명하였던바,   ABA   측은 당관의
신속한 협조에 사의를 표한다고 하면서,   방청권 발급권한자인 금번 항소심 재판장과
직접접촉 하고저하니 동 재판장의 성명 및 연락처를 알려줄것을 요청하였음.

2. 금일 ABA   측 추가 통보에 의하면 연호 입국예정자 4명중   EUGENE THOMAS
및   SAMUEL HEINS 2 명만 방한 예정이라는바, 그중   EUGENE THOMAS   는 차기   ABA
회장 (오는 8 월 취임) 이라함. 이에 비추어   ABA   측으로서는 동 조직의 권
위와   THOMAS   차기회장의 비중에 비추어 쉽사리 입국을 포기할것으로 보이지 않으
며, 당관으로서도 신중히 대처해야할 것으로 사료되는바,   외국인의 방청을 억제함이
바람직하다는 대호 통보에 따른 당관 의견을 참고로 보고하오니 본건 다각적으로 검
토후 동 결과를 지급 회시바라며,   최소한 재판장의 성명 및 연락처는 명일 (6.4.)
중 회보바람.

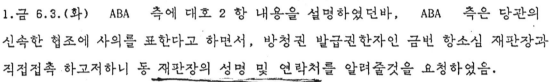

가   ABA   측이 요청하는대로 방청권 발급권자인 재판장의 성명, 연락처를 제공하
고,   ABA   측이 재판장을 접촉해 오는 경우 재판장이 외국인을 방청케할 의도가
없음을 눈명히 답변해 주거나 또는 서면요청의 경우 이를 묵살하는 방안

나. 외무부가 재판장과 접촉한 결과, 재판장은 외국인의 방청을 허락할 의도가 없음
을 알려왔다고 당관이 통보하는 방안 (이경우에도 ABA   요청이 있으므로 재판장
의 성명, 연락처는 알려주어야 할것으로 사료되며,   ABA   측이 직접 재판장과 연락,
재확인 할것에 사전대비해야 할것임)

0093

미주국   차관실   1 차보   2 차보   영교국   청와대   안 기   법무부

다. 기타 본부가 판단하는 가장 적절한 방안

3. ABA 측은 방청의 사전 보장여부와는 관계없이 명 6.4.(수) 중 당관에 사증 발급을 신청하겠다는 의사를 표명해 오고 있는바, 허가여부에 대한 본부입장 회시바람. 당관으로서는 사증발급 자체를 거부하는 경우 복잡한 문제를 야기할 우려가 있다고 판단되므로, 일단 사증 (9-4) 은 발급하되 동재판의 방청을 보장하는것이 아니라는점을 분명히 하는것이 좋을것으로 사료됨.

4. 방청권 배부 및 입수절차를 당관의 참고로 알려주시기 바람.

(대사 김경원-차관)

예고 : 1986.12.31. 일반

발 신 전 보

번 호 : WUS-2259   일 시 : 60605 1820   전보종별 : 지 급

수 신 : 주   미   대사·총영사

발 신 : 장   관 (미북)

제 목 : 미변호사협회 (ABA) 법정 방청

대 : USW-2741

연 : WUS-2227

1. 김근태사건 항소심 재판장은 한대현 부장 판사이며 연락처는 서울 중구 서소문동 37번지 서울 고등법원 형사 5부임.

~~2. ABA 측의 방청요청에 대하여는 동건이 사법부의 권한에 속하는 문제라는 연호입장을 고수하여, ABA 측으로 하여금 재판부와 직접접촉토록 유도하기 바람.~~

~~2.~~ 관계부서에 의하면, 김근태사건 항소심의 예정된 6.5 공판이 변호인측의 기피신청으로 연기됨에 따라 6.12 공판도 연기가 불가피할 것으로 예상된다 하며, 이경우 빠르면 동 항소심 공판은 6.19이후로 재조정될 것이라 함. ~~른 참고바람~~ ~~동 사실을 귀관에서 ABA 측에 통보할 경우 재판 방청허가가 사법부의 권한에 속하는 문제라는 아측입장에 ABA 측이 의구심을 가지게 될 가능성이 있는바, 동 사실은 귀관의 참고로만 하기 바람.~~

0095

3. 대호 보고 대로 ABA 측이 6.4 사증발급 신청을 해 왔는지 여부 지급 보고 바람. (차관 이상옥)

보안
통제 [서명]

앙고재	86년 6월 5일	북미2과	기안자	과 장	국 장	차 관	장 관	외신과	접수자	통 제
			[서명]	[서명]	[서명]	[서명]			[서명]	

~~보고~~ 예 ~~원~~ 시 : 86.12.31. 일반
~~특위~~ 성립

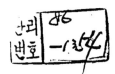

통 화 요 록
----

1. 통화일시 : 1986.6.4 (수) 15:50

2. 송 화 자 : John Miller 주한미대사관 정무과 1등서기관

3. 수 화 자 : 이양 북미과장

4. 통화내용 :

서기관 : 미국 변호사협회 (ABA) 대표 일행이 김근태사건
항소심 공판방청을 위해 방한을 희망하고 있음.
동 단체는 지난번 방한한 Amy Young 이 속한
Int'l Human Rights Law Group 이나 Asia Watch
등 인권단체와는 다른 보수적 성격의 전국적인 규모의
권위있는 변호사협회로서 미국 내에서 대단한 영향력을
행사하고 있으며, 소속회원이 200,000명에 이르고 있음.

　　　동 협회의 비중이나 성격을 감안할때 공판방청 및
사증 발급이 바람직할 것으로 보이는바, 이에대한 귀정부의
입장을 알려주시기 바람.

　　　ABA 같은 영향력있는 단체 대표들에게 방청을
허용함으로써 한국에서 공개재판(fair trial) 이
보장되고 있으며, 또한 고문에 대한 외부의 의구심을
지워버릴수 있는 좋은 기회가 될것으로 생각함.
동건에 관해서는 ABA 측에서 이미 주미한국대사관과
접촉한바 있음.

공람	86년6월4일 북미과	담당	과장	심의관	국장	차관보	차관	장관
		거	多	2			h次	

0096

과　장 : ABA 측의 방청요청에 관해서는 워싱턴으로부터 보고를
　　　　받았으며、 동 요청에 대해 다음요지로 회신하였음.

　　　　ㅇ 김근태 사건의 항소심 공판은 공개될 예정임.

　　　　ㅇ 공개재판시 법정규모에 비하여 방청희망자가 과다할
　　　　　경우 법정질서 유지를 위하여 방청석수에 해당하는
　　　　　방청권을 발행하는 바、 동 방청권 발행은 재판장
　　　　　(사법부)의 권한이므로 행정부에서 관여할수 없음.

　　　서기관 : 잘 알겠음.　　끝.

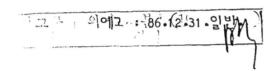

0097

외 무 부

착신전보

번 호 : USW-2786   일 시 : 60605 1811   종 별 :

수 신 : 장 관(미북)

발 신 : 주 미 대사

제 목 : ABA 법정 방청

대 : WUS-2259

1. ABA 측은 당지시간 금 6.5.(목) 오후 현재까지 비자신청을 하지 않았음.

2. ABA 측 담당관이 부재중 임으로 금일 현재 대호 재판장 성명, 연락처등을 통보치 않았음을 참고로 보고함.

(대사 김경원-차관)

예고 예고원거 1986.12.619 일반
성명

0098

미주국   차관실   1 차보   청와대   안 기

PAGE   1   86.06.06 15:47
                                            외신 2과 통제관

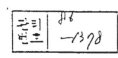

의　무　부

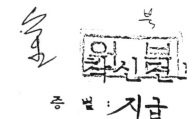

번　호 :　　　　　　일　시 :　　　　　증　별 : 지급
수　신 :
발　신 :
제　목 :

USW-2808　60606　1650　　　장관（미북, 영사, 법무부）, , 주미대
사, , 미국변호사 협회원 사증신청, , 연：USW-2720, 2741, , 대：WU
S-2227, , 1연호관련, 금 6.6（금）오후 미변호사협회측은 당관 영사관
에 아래 2인에 대한 입국사증을 신청하여왔는바, 사증발급여부를 당지시간 6
.9（월）09：00 까지 회시바람（하기2인중 1인은 당초 6.7（토）서
울향발예정이었다고함）, , MR.EUGENE C.THOMAS, , MR.SAMU
EL D. HEINS, , 2.사증발급신청서상의 입국목적란에, , TO OBS
ERVE LEGAL PROCEEDINGS CONCERNING THE CA
SE OF MR. KIM KEUN-TAE AS A REPRESENTATI
VE OF THE AMERICAN BAR ASSOCIATION 으로 기재
한것과관련, 동변호사협회측에서는 입국사증 발급이 재판방청을 허가하는것은아니
라는것을 주지하고있다고하면서, 입국후 법원측에 방청허가를 신청할것이라고부연
하였음（대사 김경원-국장）, , 예고86.12.31.일반

0099

미주, 차관, 1차보, 2차보, 영교, 법무부, 안기）

PAGE　1

의신 2과　통제관

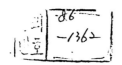

번 호: USW-2816   일 시: 60606 1814

수 신: 장관 (미북, 영사, 법무부)

발 신: 주미대사

제 목: ABA 법정방청

연:USW-2786

대:WUS-2259

1.금 6.6 ABA 측에 재판장 성명 및 연락처를 제공하고 공관 연기 사실을 통보하였음.

2. ABA 측은 주한미대사관을 통하여 재판장을 알고 있었으나 공관 연기사실은 알지못하고 있었다고하면서, 국무성으로 부터 주한 미대사관측이 서울 외무부 및 항소심 재판부측과의 접촉한결과를 다음과같이 통보받았다함.

가.외무부측은 김근태 항소심이 공개되나, 외국인 방청여부는 재판부가 결정 할것이라고 답변하면서, ABA 측 방한인사에 대한 비자발급에는 문제가 없을 것으로본다고 하였음.

나.한편, 재판장측(ABA 측 표현에 의하면 CHIEF SECRETARY TO THE JUDGE)과 접촉한결과, 방청권 발부문제 관련 OUTRIGHT REFUSAL 을 하지않고, ABA 대표단이 서울에서 직접 신청할때 그때가서 방청권 발급여부를 결정할 것이며 사전 보장할수 있는 문제가 아니라고 답하였다 함. (ABA 측은 이를 방청권 획득 가능성이 있는것으로 해석하고 있었음)

3.국무성 한국과에 의하면 ABA 측은 주한미대사관을 통하여 한태연 판사및 한국 변호인 협회 회장앞으로 메시지를 발송, 이미 전달되었다함.

4. SAMUEL HEINS 및 EUGENE THOMAS 양인 비자 신

- PAGE: 1 -

0100

청서금일 접수하였는바, 별전 보고하겠음 (대사 김경원 -)

예고: 86 . . . 2 (3) . . .

배부처	장관실	의전실	아프리카국	총무과	청와대	재무부	보안사
	차관실		국	국기국	감사관	총리실	해협위	문공부
	1차	미주국 O	경제국	공보관	안기부	체육부	
	2차	구주국	정문국	외연원	법무부	SLOOC	
	기획실	중동국	영교국	상황실	상공부	국방부	

- PAGE: 2 -

`0101`

```
┌──────────────────────────────────────┐
│                                        │
│     최근 아국 인권문제 관련 참고자료      │
│                                        │
└──────────────────────────────────────┘
```

1985. 11.

미   주   국

고재	85 미대 인수	담 당	과 장	심의관	국 장	차관보	차 관	장 관
		한	정					

0102

최근 아국 인권관련 주요동향

10.2   국제사면협회, 김근태 고문에 관한 별도보고서
        배포
        - 동인에 대한 정부관계 당국의 전기 및
          물고문, 급식중단등 주장

10.4   AP 통신, 민추협의 고문관련 성명발표 보도
        - 김근태 및 허인회등 정부 비판인사에 대한
          고문 가해 주장 (별첨 1)

10.4   동아일보, 김근태 고문관련 보도
        - 김의 변호인, 김의 발뒤꿈치 상처를 이유로
          고문흔적 증거 보전 신청 (별첨 2)

10.4   Dunlop 주한미대사관 참사관, 박건우 국장과
        통화
        - 9.4-9간 김근태에 대한 심한고문 가해사실이
          미언론에 보도될 가능성 언급
        - 사실일 경우 고문행위에 대한 유감표명

10.7   뉴욕 타임즈 최근 한국 인권관련 보도
        (별첨 3)

0103

10.11   Isom 미국무성 한국과장、김삼훈 참사관 면담시
        언급
        - 한국 신문지상의 김근태 관련 가혹행위 보도가
          미국내 언론 파급 우려
        - 금년도 국무성 인권보고서의 아국부분 개악
          가능성 시사

10.16   본부、Sherman 부차관보 면담시 지침 훈령
        - 고문관계 보도는 사실무근이며 재판과정에서
          진상이 밝혀질것임.
        - 미측이 아국 국내문제에 관해 일일이 문제시
          하는 것을 삼가해야 할것임.

10.16   Sherman 국무성 부차관보、주미공사 초치후
        동아일보 기자 구타사건과 김근태 고문사건에
        대한 유감표시
        - 최근 상황은 한국의 국제적 이미지 손상
        - 대외적으로 널리 알려진 신체적 가혹행위에
          대해서는 미행정부가 한국정부를 방어하고
          옹호할 입장이 아님

10.16   서울 형사지법、김근태 변호인의 고문증거 보전
        신청기각

                                                0104

10.17   주미대사, 10.7자 N.Y.T. 보도관련 Solarz
         하원 아·태소위원장의 항의서한 작성 움직임
         보고

10.18   Kalb 국무성 대변인, 아국 인권문제에 대한
         기자 브리핑 (별첨 4)
         - 최근 3명의 한국언론인이 공안요원으로 부터
           구타당한 사실에 관해 한국정부에 우려표명
         - 아울러 청년운동가(김근태)에 대한 고문
           사건과 함께 일련의 사태에 관해서도 우려
           전달
         - 이러한 상황은 그간 한국정부가 이룩한 정치
           발전과 상치

10.18   국무성 대변인 브리핑과 관련한 본부입장 훈령
         - 국무성이 국내문제에 대해 공개적으로 계속
           거론하는것은 한·미 우호관계에 비추어 결코
           바람직하지 못함.

10.18   교민 15명, 국무성 앞에서 항의 시위

10.21-25 민통연합, 국무성 앞에서 시위 및 반정부 집회

0105

35. 10. 4자 AP 보도

SOUTH KOREA-TORTURE

RA

28

DISSIDENT GROUP CHARGES TORTURE BY GOVERNMENT

SEOUL, SOUTH KOREA (AP) - AN OPPOSITION GROUP, HEADED BY TWO DISSIDENT LEADERS KIM DAE-JUNG AND KIM YOUNG-SAM, FRIDAY ACCUSED POLICE OF HAVING TORTURED STUDENTS, WORKERS AND OTHER DISSIDENTS ARRESTED ON POLITICAL CHARGES.

THE COUNCIL FOR PROMOTION OF DEMOCRACY IN A STATEMENT DEMANDED THE GOVERNMENT TELL THE TRUTH CONCERNING ''THE UNDEMOCRATIC AND IMMORAL ACTS'' AND SEVERLY PUNISH THOSE INVOLVED.

THE STATEMENT QUOTED FAMILY MEMBERS AND FRIENDS AS SAYING THAT POLICE INVESTIGATORS TORTURED THE ARRESTED DISSIDENTS WITH WATER, POWDER OF HOT PEPPER, ELECTRICITY AND BEATINGS.

THE COUNCIL SAID THAT IT WILL CARRY OUT A CAMPAIGN WITH THE MAIN OPPOSITION NEW KOREA DEMOCRATIC PARTY AND OTHER OPPOSITION FORCES TO SEEK AN END TO WHAT IT CALLED SUCH INHUMANE ACTS.

THE STATEMENT DID NOT SAY HOW MANY PEOPLE IT CLAIMED HAD BEEN TORTURED BUT SAID THEY INCLUDED TWO WELL-PUBLICIZED ACTIVISTS - HOE IN-HOE AND KIM KUN-TAE.

HO, A STUDENT AT KOREA UNIVERSITY, WAS ARRESTED A MONTH AGO ON CHARGES OF VIOLATING THE LAW OF ASSEMBLY AND DEMONSTRATION. HE HEADED THE SAMMIN STRUGGLE COMMITTEE WHICH WAS INVOLVED IN THE OCCUPATION LAST MAY OF A DOWNTOWN U.S. GOVERNMENT LIBRARY BY A GROUP OF WHAT THE GOVERNMENT CALLED LEFTIST RADICAL STUDENTS.

THE STUDENTS DEMANDED AN AMERICAN APOLOGY FOR THE MOVEMENT OF KOREAN TROOPS TO SUPPRESS REBELS IN KWANGJU SOUTH OF HERE IN MAY 1980. A TOTAL OF 191 PEOPLE WERE KILLED DURING THE RIOTING, ACCORDING TO AN OFFICIAL COUNT.

KIM, FORMER CHAIRMAN OF THE YOUTH ALLIANCE FOR DEMOCRATIZATION MOVEMENT, WAS ARRESTED LAST MONTH ON CHARGES OF VIOLATING THE NATIONAL SECURITY LAW.

A GROUP OF LAWYERS DEFENDING KIM HAS ASKED A COURT TO SECURE PHOTOGRAPHIC EVIDENCE ON THE SIGNS OF ALLEGED TORTURE OF HIM FOR USE LATER DURING TRIAL, ACCORDING TO ONE OF THE LAWYERS.

NO GOVERNMENT COMMENT WAS IMMEDIATELY AVAILABLE ON THE ALLEGED TORTURES.

END

AP-NY-10-04-85 0952GMT

0106

(별첨 2)

85. 10. 4. 東亞

保安法 위반혐의로 구속된 金槿泰씨

「고문흔적」증거보전 신청

변호인 "발뒤꿈치 등에 심한 상처"

국가보안법위반혐의로 구속돼 같은달 26일 검찰에 송치됐으며 구체적인 혐의사실은 알려지지 않고있다.

국가보안법위반혐의로 구속, 송치된 전민청련의 장 金槿泰씨(38·서울구치소수감중)의 변호인단 8명은 4일 「金씨가 경찰조사 과정에서 가혹한 고문을 받았다」고 주장, 金씨의 신체에 남아있는 고문흔적에 대한 증거보전을 서울형사지법에 신청했다.

변호인단은 신청서에서 「발뒤꿈치 등에 심한 상처가 남아있다」는 것이다.

변호인단은 「경찰조사단계에서, 받은 육체적 고문과 공포감이 경찰조사과정에서 지속될 것」이 명백하다고 주장하면서 金씨의 신체에 대한 사진촬영과 의사의 감정을 통해 고문흔적을 보전해달라고 신청했다.

변호인단은 「수사기관이 열릴때까지 기다릴 경우 고문상처가 자연치유돼 증거로 사용할 수 없다」고 주장했다.

金씨가 국가보안법위반의 혐의로 경찰에 구속된 지난 9월4일부터 같은달 20일까지 치안본부대공수사반에서 조사를 받으면서 10여차례에 걸친 고문 가혹행위를 받았으며 전기고문 물고문등, 고문을 받은

0107

(별첨3) 85.10.7자 뉴욕 타임즈 기사

한국정부 강압정책으로 전환

- Clyde Haberman특파원 기고 -

1. 전대통령은 지난 1년이상의 기간동안 점진적인 자율화、
   민주화 조치를 실시해 왔음·

2. 그러나 최근 몇달 전부터 정치범을 체포、기소、고문까지
   함으로써 반정부 인사에 대한 탄압을 재개하고 있는 바、
   이러한 정책변화는 다음과 같은 사례에서 잘 나타나고 있음·

   가· 데모 참가학생들에 대한 6개월간의 강제교육 실시를
       목적으로 하는 학원 안정법안 제정 추구
       (동 법안은 현재 내외의 심한 반발에 부딪혀 제출
       보류중)

   나· 안기부 요원의 동아일보사 언론인 3명에 대한 구타

   다· '삼민투'를 용공단체로 규정

   라· 22명의 학생을 간첩혐의로 기소

   마· 김대중의 가택연금

   바· 선동적 기사 기고 교사 15명 해고

   사· 서울대 이현재 총장이 데모주동 학생을 제적시키지
       않았다는 이유로 해임

   아· 데모학생에 대한 미온적인 판결로 담당판사가 지방
       전보 발령

0108

자. 고려대 학생 선동혐의로 야당 국회의원 2명등 기소

3. 현정권이 학원안정법과 같은 강압정책을 계속 실시할 경우
   현재 분산되어 있는 반대세력을 집결시키는 결과만을 초래할
   것으로 분석

0109

미국무성 Kalb 대변인의 기자 브리핑시 질의응답 내용

Q : There have been quite a few reports over the last few weeks of allegations of torture in South Korea.   Do you have any comment on those allegations ?   Are they consistent with the American view of where the Chun Government should be going ?

A : Uh -

Q : Does the United States appreciate the crackdown against dissidents ?

A : Uh-- We are aware of credible reports that three Korean journalists were beaten recently by Korean security officials and we have made known to the Korean government our concern about this deplorable incident.   We also are aware that a youth activist was subjected to torture recently.

0110

We have made known to the Korean government our serious concern.   As I said a moment
ago, about this deplorable incident as well,
and on your broader question about crackdowns,
let me say this, If I may, Mike.   We believe
that in general Korea has made political
progress over the past few years.

In 1984, early 85, the Korean government
completely lifted the political ban that had
originally applied to 567 politicians.

In February, 1985, Korea experienced one
of the most democratic elections in its
history.   During the campaign, candidates
were free to criticize the government in front
of large rallies.

As a result of the election, new parties
supported by leading opposition politicians
became the largest opposition party.   All
the professors and some journalists who had
lost their jobs for political reasons were
allowed to return to their positions.

0111

On the other hand, as department officials
have stated on several occasions, there have
been some regrettable steps in recent months
which we regard as inconsistent with the real
progress that has been made.

We continue to encourage political
progress and to urge moderation and dialogue
on all parties.

0112

(별첨 5) 김근태 관련사항

통 화 요 록
----

1. 통화일시 : 1975.10.16(수) 18:00

2. 송 화 자 : 안기부 북미과장

3. 수 화 자 : 이호진 서기관

4. 통화내용 : 김근태 관련 사항을 아래와 같이 통보함.

   가. 김근태 인적사항

   　　○ 본　　적 : ██████████████

   　　○ 주　　소 : 경기도 부천시 역곡동 일두아파트
   　　　　　　　　　　1동 111호

   　　○ 생년월일 : 47.2.24(당 38세)

   나. 김근태 특이사항

   　　○ 친형제중 월북자　3명

   　　○ 친척 10여명이 6.25동란중 부역(북측 인사에 적극
   　　　　협조 제공)

   다. 관련상항

   　　○ 본명은 83.9 "민주화운동 청년연합"을 조직, 불온
   　　　　유인물인 "민주화의 길"을 90여회 발간, 배포하고
   　　　　20여차례나 반정부 시위활동을 선동한바 있음.

0113

o 본명은 국가보안법 위반으로 9.5-26일간 경찰에서
  합법절차에 의거 조사후 검찰에 송치되어, 현재
  조사중이며 기소되어 공정한 재판을 받을 예정임.

o 10.4일자 동아일보는 김근태에 대한 고문행위를
  운운하고 있으나 상기 조사 과정에서 가혹행위는
  없었으며 수사 절차상 있을수도 없는일임. 끝.

0114

─── 〝拷問·容共 造作 共同對策委〟의 ───

虛構的　主張에　對한　實相

1985. 11. 8 .

0115

虛構的 主張의 背景

最近 當局의 搜査結果

- 問題除籍生들의 集團인 「民靑聯」을 主導한
  金權泰가 李乙鎬 (民靑聯 政策副室長) 의
  〃民族·民主主議革命 (NDR) 〃 理論支援을
  받아 〃民衆聯合政權〃 樹立目標로

- 〃3民鬪〃 〃깃발〃 〃서울大民推委〃
  〃僞裝就業勞鬪〃로 이어지는 學園騷擾 및
  各種 勞動紛争 等 學·勞連帶鬪争의 背後
  操縱者로 判明

0116

○　金槿泰의　「民靑聯」을　背後에서　活動方向提示，
　　資金支援을　하면서　現政權打倒를　窮極的　目標로
　　活動中인　在野運動圈勢力들은

△　前衛鬪爭戰列이　崩壊된데다

△　自身들의　背後追窮에　對한　不安感을　느끼고
　　이를　謀免，自身들의　企図를　隱弊，合理化
　　시키기　爲해

△　分明히　밝혀진　事實마저도　否認하고　〃拷問・
　　容共造作〃이라는　事實無根한　虚構的인
　　主張으로

　　-　拘束者의　鬪爭意識을　鼓吹하는　한편

　　-　對內外의　輿論喚起로　政府를　窮地에　몰아
　　　넣으려는　發悪的인　自救行爲　恣行

0117

○ 또한 金大中·金泳三 等 「民推協」을 中心으로

　　한 在野政治人들은 拷問이라는 政治外的인 人權

　　問題를 잇슈로 在野運動圈団体와 連繋勢力을

　　糾合, 場外 改憲鬪爭의 발판形成을 劃策

※ 所謂 〃拷問 및 容共造作沮止對策委〃라는

　　不法団体를 任意的으로 結成, 11.8.19:00

　　惠化洞 聖堂에서 報告大會를 開催코 世界人權

　　団体에게 보내는 메시지採択 等을 企図하는

　　等 事大主義的인 作態를 露骨化하고 있어 國威

　　損傷 予防 및 社會安定的 次元에서 行事를

　　放置할 수 없는 狀況

0118

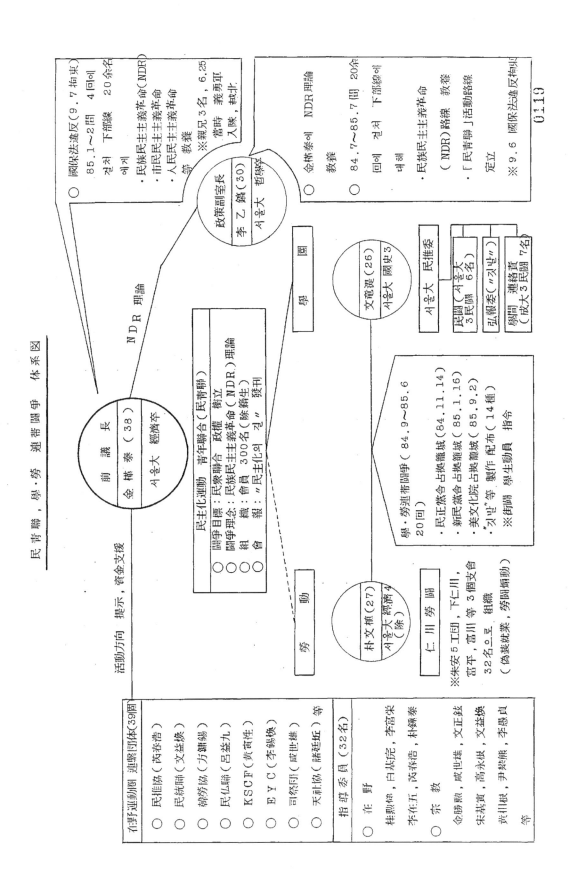

民青聯，學・勞 連帶鬪争 体系図

主張內容別 實相

主張內容	實相
金槿泰 容共造作 및 拷問	
前 民青聯議長 金槿泰의 容共性 罵倒는 當局의 造作	○ 本名은 親兄 3名을 비롯 親姻戚 10名이 越北 또는 處刑된 家庭環境에서 成長 ○ 서울大 卒業後 就業抛棄, 所謂 自身의 一生 目標라고 主張하는 〃社會主義勞動運動〃을 위한 이른바 職業革命家 活動 恣行 ○ 83.9.30 除籍生糾合 民青聯 結成, 北傀의 人民民主主義와 類似한 이른바 〃民族民主主義革命〃主張, 構成員과 問題學生 深層意識化 ○ 그 實踐課業으로 學園街 不純背後組織인 서울大 民推委 背後操縱 △ 學勞連帶鬪爭(84.9~85.9.22) △ 新韓黨舍 占拠籠城(85.1.16 서울大) △ 서울美文化院 占拠籠城(85.5.23 5個大 聯合) △ 〃깃발〃等 不穩油印物 製作 配布(84.8 ~85.6 14種)等 示威 展開 使嗾

0120

主 張 內 容	實 相
事件調査 (9.4～ 9.20間) 過程에서 拷問	○ 金槿泰 拷問主張은 △ 本名이 檢察로 送致될 當時 檢察庁舍 複道에서 妻 印宰根 目擊時 突然 複道에 주저앉아 拷問을 當한것 처럼 四肢를 비틀며 엄살 △ 이를 目擊한 妻 印宰根은 金槿泰가 甚한 拷問을 當한것으로 造作, 意図的으로 國內外에 歪曲 傳播, 本名의 救命과 鬪爭方法의 一環으로 悪用 △ 本名은 拷問主張과는 달리 一切의 痕迹이 없고 얼굴色도 健康, 歩行 및 挙動도 正常 △ 担當辯護人団에서 拷問痕迹 証拠保全申請 (10.2)하였으나 同 事件 担當 김오수 判事는 - 國立医療院에 鑑定人推薦 依頼(10.4) - 同院 整形外科 副科長 조덕연이 鑑定医師로 選定(10.8)까지 되었으나 "證拠保全 必要性을 認定할수 없다"고 判示

主張 內容	實 相
李乙鎬 拷問 李乙鎬(30歲, 民靑聯硏究室 副室長)가 継續 된 拷問捜査로 精神錯乱 ※ 金槿泰에 NDR 理論 敎養, 서울大 "民推委" 事件 背後 操縱・ 國保法違反으로 拘束(9.6)	○ 過去 3 차례에 걸쳐 精神分裂症勢로 入院 加療(75.3 東서울 神經精神科, 77.11 市立精神病院, 81.6 서울大 附屬病院) ○ 捜査過程에서 食事,排泄,잠자리 等 健康狀態 細心한 配慮 ○ 生活環境의 変化 等으로 精神疾患 再發可能性 不無, 10.15∼12.9 間 서울市立精神病院에 鑑定留置中 ※ 調査過程의 拷問暴行主張과는 전혀 無關;本人도 拷問 等 苛酷行爲 當한 事實 없음을 陳述 ○ 国會 安東善(新民黨)議員이 病院을 訪問 11.7.11:00 家族과 同席,面談 한바 " 病院에서 잘해 주어 별일 없다" 고 答弁, 安東善議員도 "실제와 보니 듣던 바와는 事實이 다르다"고 確認

主 張 內 容	實　　相
許仁會拷問 許仁會(前 高大 総學生會長,3民 鬪委全國委員長)는 調査過程(9.8 拘束)에서 拷問 으로 意識不明 狀態였다고 主張	○ 本名은 85.4.17 全學聯傘下 3民鬪 委員長으로 △ 美文化院占拠籠城支持 示威主導 △ 全南大 學生示威 背後操縱 △ 高大 汎國民 時局大討論會 主導 等 各種 學園 不法示威 40余回 主動 ○ 85.9.6 焚身自殺危脅用 석유통 携帯, 高大에 潜入, 學內示威主導와 檢挙된後 警察調查過程에서 犯行一切를 떳떳하게 陳述 ○ 特히 本名은 △ 拘束後 父母들이 거의 毎日 面會, 拷問當했다는 말을 한 事實없고 △ 本名拷問說關聯, 父母가 面會時 身体 異狀없음을 確認 面會온 父母, 高大學生処長(金成福), 高大総學生會副會長(尹永喆, 土木4) 等에게 〃拷問받은 事實없다, 健康하다〃고 強調

主張內容	實　　相
禹宗元死因 禹宗元（서울大, 社會福祉 4 , 民推委 事件關聯　手配者） 自殺事件을　拷問에 依한　他殺, 死体 遺棄라고　主張 （ 85.10.12　10:35 忠北　永同郡　황간面 京釜線下行線　鉄路 辺에서　屍体로 發見）	○　在學中（ 85.1.12 ）　煉炭가스中毒으로 　　4日間　昏睡狀態, 治療後　一部記憶喪失　等 　　腦機能障碍로　平素　悲観 ○　屍体　捜索結果, 本人親筆確認　〃어머니, 兄, 　　누나들, 叔父님　罪悚합니다〃內容의　遺書發見 　　遺族들의　自殺確認下에　屍体引導 ○　屍体檢案醫師（영창醫院　院長　조영호, 50歲） 　　가　墜落에　依한　頭蓋骨骨切死亡으로　確認 ○　屍体　墜落部分이　파여져　있고　革帶빠클이 　　떨어진　狀態로　屍体周辺　情況上　墜落死 　　確認 　　（大田　鉄道庁　미륵駅　線路長　윤석홍 , 35歲）

0124

행－29　83. 8. 1

主張內容	實相
鄭鎭寬 毆打 大邱矯導所에서 鄭鎭寬（仁荷大 除籍生）等 囚人을 無差別 毆打, 치아와 턱뼈損傷 ※ 83.12 國保法 　　違反 拘束（懲役 　　3年 確定）	○ 85.7.31 저녁 食事中 監房이 좁다는 　트집으로 食器쟁반과 汚物을 내던지는 　等 騷亂惹起 ○ 矯導官이 制止하자 意図的으로 高喊과 　亂動을 부리면서 스스로 머리를 　鉄窓에 부딪치는 等 自傷行爲 　（ 2.5 cm 裂傷 ） 　※ 곧 醫務室에 移送 完治 ○ 矯導官의 毆打나 齒芽가 부러지고 　턱뼈가 損傷되었다는 主張은 事實 　無根

0125

主張內容	實 相

東亞日報 編輯陣 苛酷行爲
 	
編輯局長 이채주 等 3名을 8.29 中共機不時着事件 記事關聯 連行, 苛酷行爲 主張
	○ 同事件이 國家安保와 對中共外交關係 等 重要事案으로 公式發表以外의 報道自制 事前(5回) 協調要請
	
	○ 全言論機關이 趣旨를 理解하였으나 東亞日報만이 方針을 無視, 事前報道,
	   △ 中共과의 關係改善을 妨害하려는 北傀策動을 支援한 結果招來
	
	○ 事實 經緯確認을 爲해 任意同行調査 過程에서 本人들이 스스로 잘못을 순순히 是認, 調查가 쉽게 終結
	   △ 苛酷行爲는 事實無根

0126

主 張 內 容	實 相
宋光永 焚身自殺 景園大 學生(法2) 宋光永이 85.9. 17.校庭에서 學園 安定法 反對 焚身 自殺,烈士로 追慕 (9.17 入院, 10.21 死亡)	○ 本名은 平素 不遇한 家庭環境(偏母 行商 極貧者)과 前科關係로 悲観 ───────〈前 科 內 容〉─────── △ 84.11 强姦致傷罪로 懲役 2年6月 執猶 4年 ○ 成績不良으로 學事警告 2回, 特히 2學期 未登錄으로 9.18 除籍措置가 確實하자 하루前 焚身 ○ 平素에도 // 光化門 4거리에서 죽어 버리겠다 //는 等 厭世自殺일 뿐인데 一部 運動圈人士들이 學園安定法 反對 焚身自殺로 美化

0127

─拷問 및 容共造作 沮止 共同對策委 構成員─

0128

区　分		構　成　員
顧　　問 （ 9名 ）		金在俊（ 牧師，基長曾經総會長 ）
		咸錫憲（ 牧師，퀘이커敎　韓國代表 ）　　尹攀熊（ 牧師 ）
		洪南淳（ 辯護士，光州拘束者協會長 ）　　李敏雨（ 新韓黨總裁 ）
		文益煥（ 民統聯議長 ）　　　　　　池學淳（ 原州敎區長 ）
		金大中（ 民推協　共同議長 ）　　金泳三（ 民推協　共同議長 ）
共同代表 （ 14名 ）		桂勳悌（ 民統聯副議長 ）　　　金勝勳（ 神父，民統聯副議長 ）
		朴炯圭（ 基長曾經総會長 ）　　徐敬元（ 가農會長 ）
		楊淳植（ 新韓黨副総裁 ）　　　李愚貞（ 敎授，女神學者協會長 ）
		趙南基（ 牧師，敎社協會長 ）　金命潤（ 民推協副議長 ）
		朴永禄（ 民推協副議長 ）　　　白基琓（ 民統聯서울支部議長 ）
		宋建鎬（ 民言協議長 ）　　　　崔炳佑（ 新韓黨副総裁 ）
		李小仙（ 서勞聯　顧問 ）　　　李貞淑（ 拘束者家族 ）
對策委員 （241名 ）	改新敎 （33名）	姜瑗夏（ 春川人權委員長 ）　　琴栄均（ NCC 木曜礼拜委員長 ）
		金東完（ 牧會者正平協議長 ）　김재열（ NCC 人權委員 ）
		金僑永（ 基監宣敎局総務 ）　　金昌慶（ 忠北人權委員長 ）
		朴尙奕（ 原州人權委員長 ）　　朴鍾基（ 聖公會敎務院長 ）
		高永根（ 牧民宣敎會長 ）　　　김근상（ 牧會者正平協副議長 ）
		金祥根（ 基長総務 ）　　　　　金鍾五（ 城南人權委員長 ）
		김진석（ 牧會者正平協副議長 ）文貞植（ 全南 NCC 人權委員長 ）
		朴永模（ 水原人權委総務 ）　　朴鍾德（ 大田人權委員　）

행－29　83. 8. 1

0129

区　分	構　　成　　員	
〃	卞善奎（天安人權委員長）	辛三錫（全北NCC人權委総務）
	廉容沢（全州NCC人權委員長）	安基重（錦江人權委員長）
	吳忠一（KSCF理事長）	元亨洙（牧會者正平協代弁人）
	이명남（牧會者正平協副議長）	李正學（NCC都農宣教委員長）
	李海學（城南人權委員）	張基天（前KSCF理事長）
	張成竜（牧會者正平協副議長）	趙承赫（基督産業開發院長）
	崔聖黙（釜山NCC人權委総務）	최승렬（牧會者正平協副議長）
	許秉燮（基民研所長）	洪寿夏（大邱人權委総務）
	황규록（仁川人權委員長）	
〃 天主教 (24名)	郭東哲（淸州사직聖堂神父）	金秉相（仁川教区副主教）
	金炳宰（大田도마동聖堂神父）	金成鏞（JOC光州指導神父）
	金英信（全北完州上關聖堂神父）	金沢岩（竜山聖堂神父）
	文正鉉（全北장계聖堂神父）	朴鍾瑾（全北임실聖堂神父）
	孫德万（釜山온천聖堂神父）	申鉉奉（가農原州指導神父）
	楊弘（화곡동聖堂神父）	吳盛栢（점촌聖堂神父）
	吳寿永（釜山초량聖堂神父）	吳泰淳（면목동聖堂神父）
	李啓暢（대사동聖堂神父）	李守鉉（全州正平委會長）
	鄭亨達（光州농성동聖堂神父）	鄭鎬庚（가農指導神父）
	趙喆鉉（大建神大教授）	崔基植（原州教区社會司牧局長）
	咸世雄（서울教区弘報局長）	許淵九（大邱東村聖堂神父）
	扈寅秀（富平聖堂神父）	黄相根（JOC指導神父）

0130

區　分	構　成　員	
仏教 (10名)	境牛（僧侶），木牛（〃），碧牛（〃），性然（〃）， 月雲（〃），智善（〃），真寬（〃），真常（〃），玄基（〃）， 惠照（〃）	
拘束者家族 (12名)	김영희（깃발　박문식　母）	김왕수（大宇어패럴　김준용　父）
	金春玉（美文化院　金敏錫母）	南順子（三民　김봉환　母）
	이숙희（淸溪　김영대　妻）	李次德（三民　이성봉　父）
	李淸子（三民　李　春　母）	민향숙（在日同胞　李　哲　約婚女）
	印宰根（民靑聯　金槿泰　妻）	崔貞順（民靑聯　이을호　妻）
	조아기（효성　김영미　母）	咸貞錫（美文化院　咸雲炅　父）
運動圈團体 (61名)	姜希南（民統聯　中央委員長）	劉雲弼（民統聯　指導委員）
	李斗洙（　〃　指導委員）	全學碩（　　　〃　　）
	李敦明（　　〃　　）	金炳傑（　　　〃　　）
	高　銀（　　〃　　）	李浩哲（　　　〃　　）
	金芝河（　　〃　　）	李昌馥（民統聯　事務處長）
	林采正（民統聯　政策企劃室長）	李富榮（　〃　　民生委員長）
	郭泰栄（　〃　人権委員長）	張琪杓（　〃　　事務次長）
	趙春九（　〃　社會局長）	吳大栄（　〃　　會員）
	李在五（〃　서울支部副議長）	安承吉（　〃　　江原支部長）
	朴武學（〃江原支部　事務局長）	朴炳琪（　〃　　慶北支部長）
	柳康夏（〃　慶北支部副議長）	柳淵昌（〃〃慶北支部　副議長）
	李應碩（〃　慶南支部長）	金英式（〃　慶南支部　事務局長）

區　分	構　成　員	
〃	金奎東（自實顧問）	申庚林（自實顧問）
	千勝世（　〃　）	梁性佑（自實常任運營委員）
	朴泰洵（自實常任運營委員）	李文求（　〃　）
	趙泰一（　〃　）	黃晳暎（　〃　）
	金仁漢（民言協　代表委員）	崔長鶴（民言協　代表委員）
	金泰弘（　〃　）	金承均（　〃　）
	金鍾澈（民文協　共同代表）	元東石（民文協　共同代表）
	趙鏞振（가農　副會長）	裵宗烈（基農　會長）
	李奉九（忠南基農總務）	金英源（基農　副會長）
	方鏞錫（韓勞協委員長）	李英順（韓勞協　幹事）
	朴順姬（韓勞協運營委員）	남상헌（　〃　運營委員）
	李總角（　〃　）	鄭鎭東（基勞協會長）
	李玉順（서勞聯　副委員長）	尹順女（天社協委員長）
	諸廷坵（天社協運營委員）	呂益九（民仏聯議長）
	韓慶南（民靑聯議長）	金永根（서울教區　大學聯幹事）
	文圭鉉（全民協議長）	宣鎭栄（全民協議長）
	金順浩（忠南民協議長）	元亨洙（忠南民協議長）
	朴竜來（忠北民協議長）	宋基寅（釜民協會長）
	李浩雄（仁社聯議長）	
民推協（50名）	金昌槿（副議長）	朴鍾泰（副議長）
	芮春浩（　〃　）	竜南眞（　〃　）
	洪英基（　〃　）	尹奕杓（　〃　） 0132

區　分	構　成　員	
〃	太倫基（副議長）	李相敦（常任運營委員）
	金相賢（常任運營委員）	金德竜（　〃　）
	金道鉉（　〃　）	金炳午（副幹事長）
	金允植（副幹事長）	金忠燮（常任運營委員）
	文富植（常任運營委員）	孫周恒（　〃　）
	辛相佑（　〃　）	安弼洙（　〃　）
	崔泳謹（　〃　）	韓光玉（代　辯　人）
	黃明秀（幹　事　長）	權大福（常任運營委員）
	權斗五（常任運營委員）	金光一（　〃　）
	金吉俊（　〃　）	金鍾完（　〃　）
	金昌煥（　〃　）	宋佐彬（　〃　）
	申鎭旭（　〃　）	李愚兌（　〃　）
	李鍾南（　〃　）	丁采權（　〃　）
	鄭東勳（　〃　）	鄭栈鎬（　〃　）
	李　協（　〃　）	鄭憲柱（　〃　）
	金　守（　〃　）	尹哲夏（　〃　）
	李官炯（　〃　）	李玩衡（　〃　）
	趙昇衡（　〃　）	金殷楫（　〃　）
	李興禄（　〃　）	李基洪（　〃　）
	崔鍾泰（總務局長）	朴熙富（組織局長）
	徐好錫（人権局長）	李珍求（國際局長）
	金壮坤（文教局長）	元聖喜（社會局長）

0133

행－29　83. 8. 1

區　分	構　　　　成　　　　員	
新 韓 黨 (51名)	姜三載（國會議員） 權五台（　〃　） 金東英（院內總務） 金東周（國會議員） 金奉祚（　〃　） 金令培（　〃　） 金正吉（　〃　） 金漢洙（　〃　） 金顥秀（　〃　） 金泰竜（　〃　） 睦堯相（　〃　） 朴寬用（　〃　） 朴容万（中央常務委議長） 朴燦鍾（人權擁護委員長） 潘亨植（　　〃　　） 宋千永（　　〃　　） 愼順範（　　〃　　） 柳成煥（　　〃　　） 李尚玟（　　〃　　） 李重載（副總裁） 李宅敦（國會議員） 趙炳鳳（　〃　） 趙永寿（　〃　） 崔洛道（　〃　） 韓錫奉（　〃　） 洪思德（代辯人）	金東圭（國會議員） 金東旭（　〃　） 金奉旭（　〃　） 金聖植（　〃　） 金完泰（　〃　） 金正秀（　〃　） 金鉉圭（　〃　） 金炯暻（　〃　） 明華燮（　〃　） 文正秀（　〃　） 朴旺植（　〃　） 朴鍾律（　〃　） 朴漢相（　〃　） 徐錫宰（　〃　） 辛基夏（　〃　） 安東善（　〃　） 尹栄卓（　〃　） 李永權（　〃　） 李　哲（　〃　） 張基旭（　〃　） 趙舜衡（黨紀委員長） 趙洪來（國會議員） 崔　薰（　〃　） 許京万（　〃　） 黃珞周（　〃　）

0134

행-29　83. 8. 1

외 무 부

번 호 : USW-2720   일 시 : 606021732   종 별 : 지급

수 신 : 장관 (미북,영사,법무부)

발 신 : 주 미 대사

제 목 : 미국 변호사 협회의 법정방청

1. 미국 변호사 협회 (AMERICAN BAR ASSOCIATION, ABA) 측은 6.5. 및 6.12. 로 예
정된 김근태 사건 항소심에 하기 ABA 소속 변호사 4 명이 방청할수 있도록 당관
에 협조요청하여왔음.

- SAMUEL HEINS (47.5.31.생, 미네아폴리스 거주)

- EUGENE THOMAS

- JEROME COHEN

- JACK GREENBERG

2. ABA 인권담당관실 직원이 당관을 직접방문, 당관직원을 면담하여 본직앞 서한
을 수교하고, 금번 방한계획에 관하여 구체적으로 설명하였는바, 요지 다음과 같음.

가. ABA 측은 INT'L HUMAN RIGHTS TRIAL OBSERVERS PROJECT 에 따라 최근 2
년간 남아공,유고 및 라이베리아등내 정치성이 강한 사건의 재판과정에 변호사들을
참석시켜 ABA 측의 관심을 보여온바 있음.

나. 금번 김근태 공판의 방청도 상기 PROJECT 에 따라 추진하는것이며, 한국이
공개재판을 원칙으로 하는만큼 방청에 문제가 없으리라고 보나 방청허가를 사전에 득
하고 합당한 입국비자를 발급받아서 입국하고저함 (지난 1 월 INT'L HUMAN RIGHTS
LAW GROUP 소속 인사의 방청이 불허된 예를 알고 있었음. : USW-254)

다. 입국 변호사들은 방한중 재판방청, 변호인단 및 검찰측으로부터의 관계자료 입
수등의 활동을 할것임.

라. 그러나 다른 인권단체와는 달리 금번 방한활동을 선전 또는 정치화 하기 위하
여 언론매체를 이용한다든지 하는 경솔한 행위는 자제할것이며, 활동결과의 대외공개

0135

미주국   차관실   1 차보   2 차보   영교국   청와대   안 기   법무부

는 사례별로 엄격히 심사, 처리하겠음. 상기 남아공등의 예에 비추어 보면, 최고심에서 최종판결이 내려질때까지 동 활동 결과를 공개하지 않았음.

3. 당관직원이 방청 제한여부는 법원 결정사항임을 설명하고 동 제한여부 및 방청허가 절차등을 본부에 조회하기에는 시간적으로 거의 불가능하다고 지적하자, ABA 직원은 이번이 안되는 경우에는 차후 재판시 방청이라도 허가될수 있도록 가능한 협조하여 줄것을 요청한다고 하였음.

4. ABA 측은 당초 국무성 한국과를 접촉하였던바, 국무성 한국과는 김근태 사건 일심공판때 주한미대사관 직원의 방청도 허용되지 않아 한국인 고용인이 대신 방청한 사실이 있음을 알려주면서 당관을 직접 접촉토록 권유하 였다함.

5. 당관으로서는 ABA 가 미국내에서 가지고 있는 막대한 영향력등을 감안하여 방청허가 여부에 관계없이 최대한 성의있는 태도로 회보하 는 것이 좋으리라고 사료 되는바, 본건 지급 회시바람. 만일 방청을 불허하는 경우에는 그 불허이유를 가급적 상세히 설명해 주는것이 좋을 것으로 사료 되는바, 법적근거를 포함한 구체적 사유를 회보바람.

6. ABA 측의 본직앞 서한은 명 6.3. 발 파편 발송함.

(대사 김경원-차관)

예고 : 1986.12.31. 일반

외 무 부   착 신 전 보

번 호 : USW-2720   일 시 : 606021732   종 별 : 지급

수 신 : 장관 (미북,영사,법무부)

발 신 : 주 미 대사

제 목 : 미국 변호사 협회의 법정방청

長官報告畢
0314400?

1. 미국 변호사 협회.(AMERICAN BAR ASSOCIATION, ABA) 측은 6,5. 및 6.12. 로 예
정된 김근태 사건 항소심에 하기 ABA 소속 변호사 4 명이 방청할수 있도록 당관
에 협조요청하여왔음. 民靑聯 事件と 拘束 機関? 36式 (法務部と 栒起)

- SAMUEL HEINS (47.5.31.생, 미네아폴리스 거주)

- EUGENE THOMAS

- JEROME COHEN

- JACK GREENBERG

2. ABA 인권담당관실 직원이 당관을 직접방문, 당관직원을 면담하여 본직앞 서한
을 수교하고, 금번 방한계획에 관하여 구체적으로 설명하였는바, 요지 다음과 같음.

㉮. ABA 측은 INT'L HUMAN RIGHTS TRIAL OBSERVERS PROJECT 에 따라 최근 2
년간 남아공,유고 및 라이베리아등내 정치성이 강한 사건의 재판과정에 변호사들을
참석시켜 ABA 측의 관심을 보여온바 있음.

㉯ 금번 김근태 공판의 방청도 상기 PROJECT 에 따라 추진하는것이며, 한국이
공개재판을 원칙으로 하는만큼 방청에 문제가 없으리라고 보나 방청허가를 사전에 득
하고 합당한 입국비자를 발급받아서 입국하고저함 (지난 1 월 INT'L HUMAN RIGHTS
LAW GROUP 소속 인사의 방청이 불허된 예를 알고 있었음. : USW-254)

다. 입국 변호사들은 방한중 재판방청, 변호인단 및 검찰측으로부터의 관계자료 입
수등의 활동을 할것임.

㉰. 그러나 다른 인권단체와는 달리 금번 방한활동을 선전 또는 정치화 하기 위하
여 언론매체를 이용한다든지 하는 경솔한 행위는 자제할것이며, 활동결과의 대외공개

--- --- --- --- --- --- --- --- ---
미주국   자관실   1 차보   2 차보   영교국   청와대   안 기   법무부

김근태 사건 관련 미국 반응, 1985-86   143

는 사례별로 엄격히 심사, 처리하겠음. 상기 남아공등의 예에 비추어 보면, 최고심에 서 최종판결이 내려질때까지 동 활동 결과를 공개하지 않았음.

3. 당관직원이 방청 제한여부는 법원 결정사항임을 설명하고 동 제한여부 및 방청허 가 절차등을 본부에 조회하기에는 시간적으로 거의 불가능하다고 지적하자, ABA 직원은 이번이 안되는 경우에는 차후 재판시 방청이라도 허가될수 있도록 가능한 협 조하여 줄것을 요청한다고 하였음.

④ ABA 측은 당초 국무성 한국과를 접촉하였던바, 국무성 한국과는 김근태 사건 일심공판때 주한미대사관 직원의 방청도 허용되지 않아 한국인 고용인이 대신 방청한 사실이 있음을 알려주면서 당관을 직접 접촉토록 권유하였다함.

⑤ 당관으로서는 ABA 가 미국내에서 가지고 있는 막대한 영향력등을 감안하여 방청허가 여부에 관계없이 최대한 성의있는 태도로 회보하는 것이 좋으리라고 사료 되는바, 본건 지급 회시바람. 만일 방청을 불허하는 경우에는 그 불허이유를 가급적 상세히 설명해 주는것이 좋을 것으로 사료 되는바, 법적근거를 포함한 구체적 사유를 회보바람.

6. ABA 측의 본직앞 서한은 명 6.3. 발 파편 발송함.

(대사 김경원-차관)

예고 : 1986.12.31. 일반
심님

발 신 전 보

번 호 : 6215 - 2227   일 시 : 06003 1840   전보종별 : _____

수 신 : 주   미   대사·총영사

발 신 : 장   관 (미북)

제 목 : 미국 변호사협회 법정 방청

　　　　대 : USW-2720

　　　　1. 미국 변호사협회 (ABA) 의 김근태사건 항소심 방청
요청과 관련하여 법무당국에 알아본 바, 재판은 공개리에 진행될
것이나 외국인의 방청은 억제함이 바람직하다함.

　　　　2. 따라서 ABA 측에 대하여는 다음 요지에 따라 적절히
설명바람.

　　　　　　가. 공판의 공개여부는 재판부가 결정(법원조직법 제 53조)
　　　　　　　　하는 바, 김근태사건의 항소심은 1심과 마찬가지로
　　　　　　　　공개될 예정임.

　　　　　　나. 공개재판시 법정규모에 비하여 방청희망자가 과다할
　　　　　　　　경우 법정질서 유지를 위하여 방청석수에 해당하는
　　　　　　　　방청권을 발행하고 그 소지자에 한하여 방청이 허용
　　　　　　　　되는 바(법정에서의 방청、촬영등에 관한 대법원
　　　　　　　　규칙 제 802호 제 2조 제 1호)、 방청권배부는 재판장
　　　　　　　　(사법부)의 권한이므로 행정부에서 관여할수 없음

　　　　　　　　　　(차관 이상목)

보안
통제

0139

예고문	예고 : '86.12.31.일반.							
앙고재	86년 3월 4일 과	기안자	과 장	심의관	국 장	1차관보	차 관	장 관
		7L						

외신과 접수자 통제

법정에서의 방청、촬영등에 관한 대법원규칙 제 802호

(제 2조) 재판장은 법정질서를 유지하기 위하여 필요하다고 인정한
때에는 방청에 관하여 다음 각호의 조처를 할수 있다.

1. 방청석수에 해당하는 방청권을 발행케하고 그
소지자에 한하여 방청을 허용하는 것

법원 조직법

(제 53조) 재판의 공개

1. 공판은 공개한다. 다만、국가의 안전보장、
안녕질서 또는 선량한 풍속을 해할 염려가
있는 때에는 결정으로써 공개를 정지할수 있다.

2. 제 1항의 결정은 이유를 개시하여 선고한다.

0140

발 신 전 보

번 호 : WUS-2284   일 시 : 6060P 1430   전보종별 : _____

수 신 : 주 미 대사·총영사

발 신 : 장 관 (미북)

제 목 : 미국 변호사협회 (ABA) 인사 방한

    대 : USW-2741, 2808

    연 : WUS-2227

표제건 대응지침을 아래 통보함.

1. 입국사증 발급문제

    가. ABA 측 인사 2인의 입국사증 신청에 대해서는
    "관광 또는 방문사증"(9-4, 90일 체류)를 발급 하여주기 바람.

    나. 다만, 동인들의 사증발급 신청서에 "ABA 대표
    자격으로 김근태 사건 재판 진행절차를 관찰"
    목적으로 기재한데 대해서는, 재판부의 공판 방청
    허가를 받지못한 현상태에서는 9-4에 상응하는 여타
    방문목적 (관광, 대한변호사협회 방문 등)으로 기재
    변경이 불가피함을 설명바람.

2. 공판 방청 허용문제

    가. 공판 방청 허용문제는 재판부의 고유 결정권한이므로
    현지에서 답변할 성질의 문제가 아니라는

보안
통제

앙
고
재
86
년 6
월 9
일
북미
과

기안자	과 장	심의관	국 장	1차관보	차 관	장 관

0141

외
신
과

접수자	통 제

점을 입국 사증 발급시 다시한번 명백히 하기바람.

나. 또한 하기 법무당국의 통보를 참조하여 김근태사건
   공판은 변호인측의 기피 신청으로 현재 공판절차가
   중단된 상태이며 향후 공판기일이 미정인 상태라는
   점도 ~~재차~~ 알려주기 바람.

   ° 현재 공판 진행상황은 6.5 김근태 피고인 및
     변호인이 담당 재판부에 대한 기피신청을 하여
     형사소송법 규정에 따라 재판절차가 중단된
     상태임.

   ° 동 기피신청에 대해서는 그 타당성 여부에 대해
     대법원의 결정이 있을 것이며 만일 기피신청이
     이유 있다고 결정될 경우에는 담당 재판부가
     바뀌는등 현재로서는 담당재판부 및 향후 공판
     기일 지정등이 미정인 상태임.

                                   (차관 이상옥   )

0142

```
┌─────────── 미 변협등 소속 변호사 ───────────┐
│                                              │
│   김 근 태   공 판 방 청   입 국 기 도   관 련    대 책   │
│                                              │
└──────────────────────────────────────────────┘
```

86. 6.

국 가 안 전 기 획 부

0143

1. 개 황

○ 미 변호사협회 (ABA) 소속 유진.토머스 (86.8 차기회장 취임예정) 사뮤엘.헤인스등 변호사 2명은 6.2 주미 한국대사관을 방문

> - 미 변호사협회 대표자격으로 김근태사건 재판진행절차 관찰을 위한 입국비자 발급 (6.6 비자 신청)
> - 입국시 김근태 공판 방청 허용
> - 김근태 사건담당 재판장 성명, 연락처 제공

  등을 요청하면서 이에 대한 회신을 6.9오전중 해줄것을 요망

○ 한편 미 국제 인권법률협회 소속 앤.매리 영 변호사가 주한 미대사관 던롭 참사관에게 "한국 사법제도의 운영실태를 파악코져하니 김근태 공판방청을 주선해달라"고 요청한바 있어

○ 이에 대한 대책협의를 위해 6.7.15:30 ~ 17:30간 검찰, 외무부, 법무부, 당부 (1국, 3국)등 관계기관 실무 대책회의를 개최하였음.

> ──── 토 의 내 용 ────
> - 입국 사증 발급 여부   - 입국시 방청허용 문제
> - 재판장 성명, 연락처 통보 여부
> - 입국후 문제활동과 관련한 당국 대처방안

0144

2. <u>미 변호사 요청 내용</u>

가. 미 변호사 인적사항

> o 미 변호사 협회(A B A)
> - 유진.토머스 (EUGENE.THOMAS, 86.8 차기회장 취임예정)
> - 사뮤엘.헤인즈 (SAMUEL.HEINS , 39세)
> o 미국 제인권법률협회
> - 앤.매리 영 (ANN. MARIE YOUNG, 여, 39세)

나. 요청 내용

> o 미 변호사협회 소속 유진.토머스등 2명
> - 미 변호사협회는 "국제 인권재판 방청계획" 에 따라 최근 2년간 남아프리카 공화국, 유고, 라이베리아등 정치성이 강한 사건의 재판을 방청하여 왔음
> - 금번 김근태 재판 방청계획은 방청에 문제가 없으리라고 보나 사전 방청허가를 득하고 합당한 입국 비자를 발급받고저 함.
> - 공판 방청을 위해 방청권 발급권자인 재판장과 직접 접촉코져하니 재판장의 성명및 연락처를 알려주기 바람
>
> o 국제 인권 법률협회 소속 앤.매리 영
> - 한국의 사법제도가 정치적인 공판에서 어떻게 운영되는가를 파악, 협회소속 변호사들에게 교육할 자료 확보목적으로
> - 입국코져하니 김근태 공판 방청을 주선해 주기 바람
>
> * 동명은 지난 1.31 김근태 공판 방청을 기도타 체류 자격 (9-4) 외 활동으로 출입국 관리법 제6조 위반으로 출국조치당한바있음

3. 대 책

① 입국 사증 발급관계

○ 입국 사증에 대하여는 불허할 명분이 없으므로
ABA회원 "유진.토머스", "사뮤 엘.헤인스"등에 대해
"관광 또는 방문 비자"(9-4, 90일)를 발급 하되

○ 다만 6.6 동인들이 사증 발급 신청서에 "미 변호사협회 대표
자격으로 김근태사건 재판 진행절차를 관찰"목적으로 기재한
사항에 대해서는

- 아국의 출입국 관리법상 체류 자격에 "재판절차 관찰 및
방청"목적등이 없기 때문에 여타 방문목적(관광,
대한변호사협회 방문 등)으로 기재토록 유도

② 공판방청 허용 문제

○ 현재 공판 진행상황은 6.5 김근태 피고인 및 변호인이 담당
재판부에 대한 기피 신청을 하여 형사소송법 규정에
따라 재판절차가 중단된 상태임.

○ 동 기피신청에 대해서는 그 타당성여부에 대해 대법원의
결정이 있을것이며 만일 기피신청이 이유 있다고 결정될
경우에는 담당 재판부가 바뀌는 등 문제로 현재로서는
담당재판부 및 향후 공판기일 지정등이 미정으로 있는
상태임.

- 공판 방청 허용문제에 대해서는 재판부의 고유결정 권한
  이므로 현지에서 답변할 성질의 문제가 아님을
  명백히 하여 통보

* 입국후 공판방청 요청시는 담당 재판부가 방청권 제한을
  이유로 불허, 다만 사법부 접촉 요청시는 법원행정처가
  관련 변호사 접촉 면담.

③ 재판부 성명등 통보 여부

○ 현재 담당재판부는 서울 고등법원 형사 5부 (재판장 한대현)
  이며 사무실위치는 서울 중구 서소문 대법원내 위치
  사실은 알려주되

○ 재판장의 집주소, 전화번호등에 대해서는 불고지

④ 기타 입국후 조사활동에 대한 대처방안

○ "유진.토마스" (차기 ABA 회장)등 입국자는
  미 변협의 유력 인사들이므로
  법무부는 장관 면담을 주선, 동인들의 입국을 계기로
  아국의 재판절차의 공정성등에 대해 설명등
  적극 대처

0147

행-29 83. 8. 1   4

○ 담당검사 면담 요청시에도 같은 방법으로 검찰에서
　사건경위, 범죄사실등을 알려줌으로써 왜곡된 인식교정 및
　아측 재판의 공정성 설명 계기 활용

○ 대한변호사협회 방문 대비, 변협 감독부처인 법무부에서
　사전 조정, 국위손상·국가모독 행위등 없도록 조정

○ 피고인의 처 접촉, NCC인권위 방문등은 방임하되
　경찰 동향감시로 대처

○ 피고인 접촉을 위한 교도소 방문은　　　불허

* 미국 제인권법률협회 소속 앤·매리 영(여, 39세)도
　입국 비자는 발급(9-4)하되 공판방청 문제는 A·B·A 소속
　변호사와 동일차원에서 불허등 대처

0148

미국 변호사협회측의 주미대사관 앞 서한요지 및 아측조치

----

o 5.30 동 협회소속 변호사 4명의 김근태 사건 항소심 방청을
  위한 사증 발급 요청 (실제 참관인은 1-2명 예정)

o 이는 미국 변호사들을 위한 교육 계획의 일환으로 재판
  과정에 불개입하며 단지 참관 및 관찰 보고만 할 것임을
  강조, 아측의 협조 요청

o 동 협회 회장의 상기 4명에 대한 신임각서 및 4인의 VISA
  신청서 첨부 (방문 목적이 '김근태사건 방청'으로 구체적 기재)

o 6.9 주미대사관 사증 신청상 방한목적을 '대한변사 협회 간부
  방문'으로 기재변경후 사증 발급

o 단 재판 방청 허락 문제는 재판부 고유권한인 점을 명백히
  하고 상금 공판일정 미정임도 통보

공람	북미과	86년6월11일	담 당	과 장	심의관	국 장	차관보	차 관	장 관
			조	朽	召				

0149

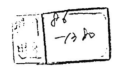

번 호: USW-2829   일 시: 60609 1600

수 신: 장관(미북,영재,법무부)

발 신: 주미대사

제 목: 미국 변호사협회 인사 방한

연: USW-2808

대: WUS-2284

1. 미변호사협회 사무장이 6.9.(월) 오전 당관 영사과에 내방하여
왔기에 연호 2인에게 사증발급 신청서상의 방한목적을 "대한 변호사협회 간
부 방문 및 첨부 메모란덤 참조" (미국(정) 700-160 로 기송부
)로 기재 변경하고 9-4, 90 일 체류 비자를 발급하였음.

2. 동사증 발급시 재판 방청허락 문제는 재판부의 고유권한이라는 점을
명백히 하였고, 아울러 김근태의 공판일정도 미정이라는점을 알려 주었는바,
동사무장은 연호 2인의 방한일정은 재판일정이 확정되는것을 보아가면서 결
정될것이라고 하였음.

3. 동사무장은 상기 2인의 방한이 개인 일정상 어려울경우 MR. WI
LLIAM COBLENTZ (상항거주)가 방한하게될 가능성도 있다고 언급
하였기 첨기함. (대사 김경원-차관)

예고문: 1986.12 (39   일반)

배부처	장관실	의전실	아프리카국	총무과	청와대	재무부	보안사
	차관실	아주국	국기국	감사관	총리실	해협위	문공부
	1차보	미주국	경제국	공보관	안기부	체육부	
	2차보	구주국	정문국	의연원	법무부	SLOOC	
	기획실	중동국	영교국	상황실	상공부	국방부	

- PAGE: 1 -

0150

관리
번호 86
_____-1493

번 호 : USW-3080   일 시 : 606251839   종 별 :

수 신 : 장 관 (미북,영재,법무부)

발 신 : 주 미 대사

제 목 : 미국 변호사협회 인사 방한

대 : WUS-2284

연 : USW-2829

1. 미 변호사협회 사무장 MR.S.G.RAIKIN 은 6.24. 오후 당관 영사과를 방문, 연호
와같은 목적으로 MR.WILLIAM COBLENTZ(연호 3항)의 방한 사증을 신청하였는바, 사증
발급여부 지급 회시바람.

2. 사증신청서 및 같이 접수된 동 사무장 명의 본직앞 서한에 의한 MR.COBLENTZ
의 인적사항 아래보고함.

생년월일 : 1922.7.28

현주소 : 10 FIFTH AVE,SAN FRANSICO

학력 : UNIVERSITY OF CALIFORNIA(A.B.,1943) YALE UNIVERSITY(LL.B.,1947)

경력 : 55-54 DEPUTY ATTORNY GENERAL,STATE OF CALIFORNIA

59-61SPECIAL COUNSEL FOR THE GOVERNOR OF CALIFORNIA

62 CONSULTANT TO THE SECRETARY OF STATE 현직 :

- 변호사

- PACIFIC TELESIS 사 이사 (동사는 아국 86.88 올림픽 통신 자문회사라하며 이사
진에 전 국무차관 MR. CLARK, 전 법무장관 MR. SMITH 등이 포함되어 있다함)

(대사 김경원-국장)

예 고 : 86.12.31. 일반

0151

√ 미주국   차관실   2 차보   영교국   청와대   안 기   법무부

PAGE   1   86.06.26   10:0
                                                            외신 2과   통제

미 변호사 주장내용

o 미변호사 협회는 "국제인권 재판 방청계획"에 따라
  최근 2년간 남아프리카 공화국, 유고, 티베리아등 국가의
  정치성이 강한 재판에 소속변호사를 파견, 방청하여 왔음

o 금번 김근태 공판 방청계획도 위 계획의 일환으로
  한국이 공개재판을 원칙으로 하는 만큼 방청에 문제가
  없으리라고 보나 사전 방청허가를 득하고 합당한 입국비자를
  발급받고져 함.

o 입국변호사들은 방한중 재판방청, 변호인단 및 검찰측으로
  부터 관계자료 입수등 활동을 할것임

o 활동결과에 대해서는 여타 인권단체와 달리 선전 또는
  정치화하지 않고 엄격히 심사, 처리하겠음

   * 남아프리카 공화국 정치사건의 경우 최종판결이
     내려질때까지 활동결과를 공개하지 않았음

o 금번 공판(6.12)을 방청치 못한다면 차기 재판이라도
  방청할 수 있도록 협조해 주기 바람

o 또한 방청권 발급권한자인 재판장과 직접 접촉코져 하니
  재판장의 성명 및 연락처를 알려주기 바람

0152

미 변호사 요청사항

○ 미변호사 협회(ABA : American Bar Association) 소속
  변호사 유진 토마스 (차기 회장 당선), 사뮤 엘 헤인즈등 2명은
  주미 한국 대사관에
   - 김근태 공판(6.12) 방청 및 변호인단, 검찰측으로부터
     관련자료 입수하기 위해 입국하려는 바

   - 김근태 공판방청 허용은 물론 입국비자 발급 허용 밀

   - 방청권 발급 권한자인 담당재판부 재판장 성명,
     연락처를 제공해 줄 것을 요청한바 있고

○ 또한 미변호사 협회 애미.영 변호사는 주한 미대사관
  더롭 참사관에게

   - 한국의 사법제도가 정치적인 공판에서 어떻게 운영되는 가를
     파악, 미변호사 협회 소속 변호사들에게 교육할 자료 확보
     목적으로 입국코자 한다면서

   - 김근태 공판방청을 주선해 달라고 한바 있음.

┌─────────── 관련자 인적사항 ───────────┐
│   │
│ - 유진 토마스 (EUGENE THOMAS   , 차기 미변협회장 당선, │
│   8월 취임 예정)   │
│   │
│ - 사뮤 엘 헤인즈 (SAMUEL HEINS   , 39세)   │
│   │
│ - 앤 매리 영 (ANN MARIE YOUNG   , 여, 39세) 0153 │
│   │
└──────────────────────────────────────┘

행 -29   83. 8. 1

발 신 전 보

관리
번호 86
-150)

번 호 : WUS-2547   일 시 : 6062 1540   전보종별 : 지급

수 신 : 주   미   대사 · 唐영사

발 신 : 장   관 (미북)

제 목 : ABA 인사 방한

대 : USW-3080

연 : WUS-2284

대호 William Coblentz 의 사증 신청에 대해서는

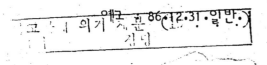

연호 짐청에 따라   사증 발급 바람.
참조 · 방문 사증 (90일 체류) 발급 바람.

(차관 이 상 옥)

0154   보안
통제

앙 고 재	86 년 월 일	북 미 과	기안자		과 장	심의관	국 장	차관보	차 관 전결	장 관		외 신 과	접수자	동 제
			2											

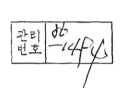

외 무

번 호 : USW-3077   일 시 : 60625 1820   종 별 :

수 신 : 장 관 (미북,영사,법무부)

발 신 : 주 미 대 사

제 목 : ABA 법정 방청

연 : USW-3080

대 : WUS-2284, 2227

1. ABA 측은 주한미대사관측이 김근태 법정방청 문제로 6.17. 한대현 부장판사를 접촉한결과, 한판사는 자신에게 법정방청권 부여권한이 없다고 하였음을 당관에 서한으로 알려오면서 (관련부문 하기) 동 방청권 발급기관을 문의하였음. 동 서한 내용을 국무성 한국과에 확인한바, 주한 미대사관측으로 부터 보고를 받고 ABA 측에 설명해준바 있다함.

THE ABA HAS BEEN INFORMED IN CONFIDENCE BY THE U.S. DEPARTMENT OF STATE VIA THE AMERICAN EMBASSY IN SEOUL THAT JUDGE HAHN INFORMED A U.S. EMBASSY OFFICIAL DURING A MEETING REGARDING OUR REQUEST HELD INSEOUL ON JUNE 17, 1986 THAT HE DID NOT HAVE THE AUTHORITY TO EITHER ADMIT OR DENY ACCESS TO OUR OBSERVER(S) TO HIS COURTROOM. SUBSEQUENTLY, WE WERE INFORMED ON JUNE 19, 1986 THAT MR. EUN HO KIM, THE PRESIDENT OF THE KOREAN FEDERAL BAR ASSOCIATION, HAS REQUESTED THAT THE CHIEF JUSTICE OF THE SUPREME COURT OF THE REPUBLIC OF KOREA AND THE CHIEF JUDGE OF THE SEOUL APPELLATE COURTS (AND THE COURT IN CHARGE OF THE KIM KEUN-TAE CASE) ASSURE US IN AVNANCE THAT OUR REPRESENTATIVES WILL BE ALLOWED TO ATTEND THESE LEGAL PROCEEDINGS ONCE THEY RESUME.

2. 현재 ABA 담당관과 접촉이 되지 않고 있으나, 당관은 대호 지침에 따라 방청권 발급은 재판부 고유결정 권한임을 재차 분명히할 예정인바, 별도지침 있으면 지급 하시바람.

0155

미주국 차관실 1 차보   영고국   청와대   안 기 법무부

PAGE 1   86.06.26 13:26
                                     외신 2과 통제

3. 연이나 주한미대사 보고가 사실인 경우 동일 사안에 관해 사법부측 답변과 대호
지침이 상이하여 대외적으로 혼란을 가져올 우려가 있음을 첨기함.

(대사 김경원-차관)

예고: 1986.12(31. 일반 .)
상님

0156

발 신 전 보

번 호 : WUS-2548 일 시 : 60627 1540 전보종별 : 지 급

수 신 : 주 미 대사 //총영사//

발 신 : 장 관 (미북)

제 목 : ABA 법정 방청

대 : USW-3077

연 : WUS-2284

1. 대호건 확인된 내용은 다음과 같음.

가. 한대현 부장 판사는 6.17, 주한미대사관 직원과의
면담시 동 직원의 ABA 공판 방청허용 신청에 대하여,
재판부가 기피신청을 받고 있는 상태에서 동 판사가
동 사건을 계속 담당하게 될지 모르므로 방청 허용에
관하여 언급할 입장에 있지 않다고 답하였음.

나. 동 사건 피고인측은 6.5, 기피신청 (Challenge) 을
제출하였으며 동 신청은 6.21, 대법원에서 기각되었음.

2. 따라서, 한판사가 재판부에 방청 허용권한이 없다고 하였다
함은 주한미대사관 직원의 오보라는 점을 설명하고, 법정 방청허용이
재판부의 고유권한임은 대법원 규칙에도 명시되어 있는 논란의여지가
없는 사실임을 분명히 하기 바람.

0157

보안
통제

앙고재	86년6월27일	국미과	기안자	과 장	심의관	국 장	차관보	차 관	장 관
			2		후열		후열		

외신과	접수자	통 제

마음년은용판은

3. 김근태 항소심은 6.26. 공판이 열렸으며, 7.3. 10시
선고공판 예정임도 참고로 알려주기 바람.

(차관   이상욱)

일반공개 1986.12.31. 일반.

통 화 요 록
----

*꽃 (Avila) 종이
6.26 항소심의 적법성이
의문을 제기하여,
관계사항 확인하도록
문의하겠다.

1. 통화일시 : 1986. 6.27.(금) 10:20
2. 송 화 자 : 서울고법형사 5부
3. 수 화 자 : 북미과 조백상 사무관
4. 통화내용 :

조 사무관 : 김근태 항소심이 6.26 열렸는데 관련 피고인 및
           변호인측에 적절히 통보되었는지 ?

   5 부 : 6.25 오후 1시 적절한 경로로 피고인 및
           변호인측에 알렸음. 왜 문의하는지 ?

조 사무관 : 동건의 적법성에 이의를 갖는측이 있어 대응
           자료를 찾기위한것임.

   5 부 : 그 점은 적법하게 재판이 열렸으니 그리 알기바람.

조 사무관 : 예정된 7.3 선고공판이 있을런지 ?

   5 부 : 그러함.   끝.

0159

통 화 요 록
----

1. 통화일시 : 1986.6.26(목) 14:30
2. 송 화 자 : 안기부(북미과)
3. 수 화 자 : 북미과 조백상 사무관
4. 통화내용 :

  주미 파견관제보에 따르면, 김근태 재판 방청 관련 VISA 신청을 했던 미국 변호 사협회(ABA) 2명의에 Coblentz 도 재판 방청 목적으로 VISA 신청을 했다함.

  ABA 측은 주한미대사관을 통해 아측 재판부에 방청 허용을 요청했으나 재판부에서 권한이 없다고 답하여 ABA 측이 당황하며 주미대사관에 해명을 요청할것이라함.

  아울러 ABA 측은 어느기관에 재판방청 허용을 요청해야 하는 지 문의하려한다함. 끝.

<table>
<tr><td rowspan="2">공
람</td><td rowspan="2">북
미
과</td><td rowspan="2">86
년
6
월
26
일</td><td>담 당</td><td>과 장</td><td>심의관</td><td>국 장</td></tr>
<tr><td>3</td><td></td><td></td><td></td></tr>
</table>

0160

발 신 전 보

번 호 : WUS-2564　일 시 : 66628 1410　　전보종별 : ___지급___

수 신 : 주　　　미　　　대사·총영사

발 신 : 장　　　관　(미북)

제 목 : ABA 인사 초치

　　　　　대 : USW-3077

　　　　　연 : WUS-2548

　　ABA 측 인사를 조속 초치하여, 연호 아측 입장을
분명히 전달하고 결과 회보 바람.

　~~2. 본부도 오보의 책임자인 Arvizu 서기관을 불러
책임을 물을 예정임을 참고로 전함.~~

　　　　　　　　　　　　　　　　　(미주국장 장선섭)

예고문에
직위　　예한 예후 생략 (12:31)

　　　　　　　　　　　　　0161

외 무 부

번 호 : USW-3134　　　　　일 시 : 606301913　　　　종 별 :

수 신 : 장 관 (미북)

발 신 : 주 미 대사

제 목 : ABA　인사방한

대: WUS-2584

1. 대호건 6.27(금) ABA 및 국무성 측에 설명하였음.

2. 이에 대해 ABA 측은 7.3. 종결되는 항소심 방청을 위한 ABA 측 대표의 방한이 사실상 어렵게 되었다고하면서 그러나 동 재판에 앞서 ABA 측의 입장을 아국정부에제 전달할수 있도록 본직과의 면담을 요청, 명 7.1(화) 오후 면담키로 약속 하였는바, 면담결과는 추가 보고 하겠음

(대사 김경원-국장)

의예고재 86년12.31일반
성림

0162

미주국　차관실　1차보　정문국　청와대　안 기

86.07.01　14:03
외신 2과 통제관

ABA소속 변호사 김근태사건 공판방청

관련 관계기관회의 결과보고

1. 일시.장소

1986.6.28. 10:00-11:30

서울지검 공안 2부 장실

2. 참석자

검찰 : 공안 2부장(회의주재), 김원치, 최연희 검사

외무부 : 북미과장

출입국 관리국 : 입국심사과장

안기부 : 1국, 3국 담당과장

3. 회의내용

0. 방청관련 문제동향

- ABA측은 기히 6.9.자로 입국사증을 발급한 유진 토마스,
사뮤엘 헤인즈 외에, 6.24.자로 동협회 소속 윌리엄 코블렌
츠 에게도 입국사증 발급 요청

- ABA측은 주한 미대사관 2등 서기관 압비조를 통하여 재판

0163

장 면담결과 방청허용 여부를 결정할 입장에 있지 않다는

통보를 받고 이를 오해한 나머지 한국대사관에 방청문제

를 결정할수 있는 기관을 알려달라고 요청

(6.27. 정보보고필, 동보고서 별첨 1)

- 김기섭 변호사의 진술에 의하면, ABA측은 내주중 한국

  정부에 대한 비난성명을 발표할 예정으로 있고, 대한변협

  회장에게도 전문을 보내, 정부에 대한 항의성명서를 발표

  하도록 요구하고 있음

  (대한변협은 6.30. 관련회의 개회예정 — 법무실에 통보필)

0. 토의결과

《입국문제》

- 기히 입국비자를 발급한 사례에 준하여 코블렌츠에게도 사

  증발급, 입국허용

《방청문제》

- 선고공판인 관계로 고문주장, 탄원서 시비등 피고인이 어지

  주장을 펼 기회가 없으며

0164

- 미국 변호사 회장이라는 비중을 고려, 방청허용

《오해 해명 문제》

- 외무부에서 주미대사관을 통하여 ABA 및 국무성에 해명

- 외무부에서 주한미대사관등 압비조를 면담, 진상을 해명
  하는 일방, 사실과 다른 내용의 회신을 한 사실에 대하여
  강력항의

- 동 압비조와 함께 재판장을 면담한 김기섭 변호사로 하여금
  재판장 면담 내용을 사실대로 밝혀 진술서를 작성, ABA 측
  에 발송토록 조치.

《입국후 문제활동시 대처방안》

- 입국후 법무부나 담당검사 면담 요청시 사건경위, 범죄사
  실, 재판절차의 공정성등에 대하여 상세히 설명, 왜곡된
  인식교정

- 대한 변협 방문시 사전에 국위손상, 국가모독등 행위 없도
  록 조치

0165

- 피고인 가족, 문제단체등과 접촉은 허용하되 동향감시 철저

- 피고인 접견요청은 불허

4. 검찰조치

안기부, 외무부등 관계기관에 별첨(2) 해명자료 송부.

0166

서 울 地 方 檢 察 廳

(별첨 1) 정 보 報 告   1986 . 6. 27. 15 : 25
                            공안2 괘 검사 김 원치

김근택에 대한 항소심 공판진행	머구	차 장 검 찰 관 관장	대 검 찰 청 연 구 관 관	수 사 1 과 검 차 사 장	수 사 2 과 장 검사	현 공 안 과 장	응 안 구 과 장	그 검 사 점	저 검 사 점	공 점 결 검 사 장 장
題目: 상황 및 ABA소속 변호사 방청		○○○	○○	○○	○○	○○	○			
관련 조치내용										

內容 :

1. 공판진행 상황

    0. 5.29. 제 1회 공판

        - 검사 변호인 항소요지 진술

        - 탄원서 복사 요구등 시비, 기일 연기

    0. 6.5. 제 2회 공판

        - 재판부 기피신청

            * 소송절차 중단

    0. 6.14. 서울고법에서 기피신청 기각

    0. 6.21. 대법원에서 즉시항고 기각

    0. 6.26. 제 3회 공판

        - 결심

    0. 7.3. 선고 예정

2. 재판장과 미대사관 직원 면담경위 및 내용   0167

    0. 변호인측에서 기피신청을 한 이후인 6.16. 미대사관 2 등 서기관

A. 알비조가 변호사 김기섭을 대동, 재판장을 방문하여 ABA 소

속 변호사의 방청 여부에 관하여 론의

0. 재판장은 자신이 변호인으로 부터 기피신청을 당한 입장이기 때

문에 위 기피신청이 받아들여질 경우 재판을 담당하지 않게 되므

로, 이점에 대한 판단이 내려질때까지는 방청 허용 여부에 대하여

결정할수 있는 입장에 있지 않다라고 설명

0. 위 알비조는 재판장의 답변중 기피신청 부분에 대한 설명은 생략

한채 자신이 이를 결정할 입장에 있지 않다는 부분만 본국에 설명,

ABA 측에 오해를 일으키게 한 것임.

3. 검찰 조치

0. 6.26. 외무부, 안기부로 부터 미국정부 및 ABA 가 한국의 재판

장이 법정 방청허용 여부의 결정도 할수 없는 것으로 오해하여 주

미한국대사관에 대하여 재판방청 문제를 책임있게 조치할수 있는

기관을 알려달라고 요청했다는 통보를 받고

0. 6.27. 검찰은 재판장인 서울고법 한대현 부장을 면담, 위와 같은

0168

진상을 확인하고, 그 사실은 외부부 북미과장 이량에게 통보하여

미국 정부 및 ABA에 진상을 전달, 오해를 해소토록 조치하고, 이

사실을 안기부에도 통보하였음

(주임검사 : 서울고검 정용식, 서울지검 김원치)

(별첨 2)

김근태 공판관련 해명 자료

1. 재판장 한대현 부장판사가 재판방청 허용여부를 독 자적으로 결정권한 이 없다고 말하였다는 점에 관하여

   - 86.6.17. 변호사 김기섭은 대한변협의 요청에 의하여 주한 미대 사관 압비조와 함께 담당 재판장인 서울 고등법원 한대현 부장 판사를 상면하였음

   - 면담결과 재판장은 김근태 피고인이 재판부에 기피신청을 하여 공판절차가 중단되어 있으며 앞으로 위 기피신청이 상급 법원에 의하여 받아들여질 경우, 자신이 재판을 할 수 없고, 위 신청에 대한 결정이 될때까지는 재판을 담당할수 있을지 불투명하며, 만 일 자신이 사건을 계속 담당할수 있게 된다면 누구든지 방청을 허용 하겠으며, 지금 까지 2회공판 과정에서도 방청이 자유롭게 허 용되었다고 설명

   - 위 압비조는 본국에 보고를 하면서 기피신청이 되어 자신이 이 사건을 계속 담당할수 있을지 불투명하다는 재판장의 말을 잘못 알아듣고 재판장이 결정할 수 없다는 취지로 ABA 측에 보고한

0170

것임.

- 한국 형사소송법 규정에 의하면 당사자 및 변호인이 기피신청을 할 경우 기피신청에 대한 상급법원의 결정이 있을때 까지 재판절차가 중단됨.

2. 6.26.심리를 종결한 것은 ABA측의 재판 방청을 회피하기 위한 의도적 조치라는 점에 관하여

- 김근태에 대한 구속기간 만기는 1986.7.6.로서 고등법원의 이 재판도 그 기간 내에 종결되어야 하는바,

- 그동안 피고인측 및 변호인등 기피신청을 하여 소송절차가 중단되는 바람에 자연히 지연되었으며

- 재판 기일은 1주나 2주 뒤에 다음 기일을 지정하는 것이 관례이나, 본건의 경우에는 박두한 구속만기일로 인하여 불가피하게 그 간이 재판 기일이 지정된 것임.

3. 피고인의 처 인재근을 불법연행 하였다는 점에 관하여

- 1986.6.26. 11:30경 서울 형사지법 111호 법정에서 소위 전태일 기념관 시위, 농성 관련자에 대한 재판진행중 방청객 30여명이

0171

피고인의 구호 제창등 소란행위에 동조하여, 욕설 폭행등 소란

행위를 자행하자, 재판이 일시중단 되었는 바,

- 방청인중 관련자를 관할서로 연행하여 법정 모욕죄 여부를 조

사하여 혐의없는자는 즉시 석방 조치하고, 혐의 인정되는 자에

대하여 계속 수사중, 위 인재근이 일행 10여명과 동 경찰서에

내방하여 계속 조사중인 3명중 여자 1명을 석방해 달라고 요청

하다가 그대로 돌아간 사심이 있을뿐 동녀를 경찰에서 연행한

사실은 없으며 경찰서를 방문한 동녀를 보고 연행된 것으로 잘

못 전해진 것임이 확인됨.

0172

(86. 6. 28. 김기섭변호사와의 통화내용)

대한변호사협회(_American Bar Association_) 대표단의 ,

피고인 김근태의 고등법원 재판 관람의 통역을 맡기로 되어

그 이후 이틀이 지나 미국 대사관에서 전화가 와서 통역 준비 및

미국 변호사협회 보고 관계로 본인을 만나고 싶다하여 프라자 호텔

커피숍에서 멕시코계 미국인으로 보이는 2등 서기관을 만났는데,

2등 서기관은 본인에게 피고인 김근태의 재판방청이 1심에서는 허용이

되지 아니하였다고 하며, 고등법원에서 방청이 허용될지 아니할지 모

르겠으며 이러한 상황에서 미국변호사협회에 현재 대사관에서 무엇을

보고하여야 될지 모르겠다. 하여, 본인이 추측의 보고를 하지 말고 직

접 담당재판부를 찾아가 정식 방청의 요청을 하자고 권고하였더니,

담당 재판부를 찾아 갔더니 재판장인 한대현 부장판사께서는 사건의

담당변호인 이외의 제3자는 만날 수 없다고 접견을 거절하여, 본인이

한대현부장과 민사법원에서 같이 판사로 근무한 인연 및 가족끼지 잘

알고 있는 점 그리고, 미국변호사 협회와 미국대사관이 개재되어 있는 점,

- 1 -

0173

재판장과의 접견이 이루어지지 아니하면 방청이 불가능하다고 판단할 것인점을 설명하자, 한 부장판사는 일반적인 이야기만 하자고 하시면서 접견을 허락하여,

미대사관측의 접요한 질문에 대하여 한 부장판사는 급근 태백고인이 기피신청을 하여 자기가 이 사건을 계속 담당할지 현재로서는 불투명하다는 점.

만일 자기가 이 사건을 담당하면 누구든지 방청을 할 수 있으며 지난 2회의 공판도 자유스럽게 방청이 허락되었다는 점을 설명하고,

한 부장판사는 비록 미국이라할지라도 재판과정에 제3국의 대표단이 참석한다는 것은 국가와 국가사이에 유쾌한 일은 아니라고 하여,

본인은 이와 같은 대화를 본인의 최선을 다하여 통역하였고, 국가이익이 훼손되는 것을 원하지 아니하였음

이등서기관은 한국말이 유창하였고, 대화도중 본인의 통역을 거치지 아니하고 직접 이야기도 2, 3회 하였음

1986. 6. 27. 미국변호사협회의 책임자라고 신분을 밝힌 사람과 한국과 미국사이의 장거리 전화를 하였는데, 그 책임자는 본인에게 1986. 6. 26.

- 2 -

0174

45분간의 재판끝에 김근태 사건이 결심되었고 검사의 구형량이 경감 되지 아니하였고, 김근태의 고문조사 요청을 재판부가 거절하였다는 것을 설명하고 한국방문이 사실상 의미가 없어졌다고 이야기 하였음.

미국 변호사 협회는 이와 같은 사태 발전에 대해 한국정부에 대하여 주미대사를 통하여 외교 문제화 삼는 것과 한국정부를 비난하는 성명 (Strong Statement)을 발표하는 것 중 어떠한 것이 효과적 이냐고 본인의 판단을 요구하기에 미국이 한국의 사법제도에 관하여 의견을 발표하는 것은 좋은 일이 아니라고 이야기 하였음.

미국 변호사 협회는 늦어도 내주 월요일까지 김근태사건에 관하여 성명서를 발표하겠다고 하였고 한국변호사 협회도 이와같은 성명서를 발표 하는 것이 좋겠다는 그들의 희망을 한국변호사협회에 전달해 달 라고 하였음.

본인의 판단으로는 미국변호사 협회가 김근태사건의 형량감소에 지대한 관심을 가지고 있는 것으로 보이며, 한국내 다른 정치적인 사건(political Crime)을 방청하겠으니 본인에게 그 와같은 사건을 수집, 보고해 달라고 하였음.

- 3 -

0175

한국 사법제도에 관하여 그들은 불신을 갖고 있는 것으로 보이며,

기피신청 및 기피신청의 재판절차, 그 후의 재판관할권에 관하여 정

확하지 아니하나 일반적인 지식은 갖고 있었음.

- 4 -

0176

발 신 전 보

번 호 : 045-2602   일 시 : 60701 1930   전보종별 : 지급

수 신 : 주   미   대사·총영사

발 신 : 장   관 (미북)

제 목 : ABA 인사 방한

대 : USW-3134

연 : WUS-2548

대호관련
본부는 ABA측에 사실과 다른 통보를 한 주한미대사관
담당직원을 작 6.30 초치, 연호 통보된 바와같이 잘못된 보고로
아국정부와 ABA 측간 불필요한 오해가 야기되었음을 지적하고,
ABA 측에 필요한 해명조치를 취하도록 촉구하였음을 참고 바람.

(미주국장 장선섭)

예고문에 의거 재분류 (16)
예고 : 86.12.31. 일반 :
직위

0177

보안	
통제	

앙고재	86년 7월 1일 북미과	기안자	과 장	국 장	차 관	장 관		외신과	접수자	통 제

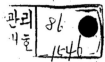

기 안 용 지

분류기호 문서번호	미북 700-215	(전화 :)	시 행 상 특별취급	

보존기간	영구·준영구. 10. 5. 3. 1.	장 관	

수 신 처 보존기간		

시행일자	1986. 7. 2.	

보 조 기 관	국 장	전결	협 조 기 관		문 서 통 제
	심의관	✓			
	과 장				발 송 인
기안책임자		조백상			

경 유 수 신 참 조	서울지방검찰청장 공안 2부장	발신명의	

제 목	자료송부

ABA 소속 변호사의 김근태사건 공판 방청허용 문제에

관련하여 당부는 6.30 주한미대사관 2등 서기관 Arvizu 를 면담

~~재판부의 견해를 ABA 측에 액극 전달한데 대한 해명을 촉구~~

하였는 바, 동 면담~~자료를~~ 별첨 송부하니 귀업무에 참고 바랍니다.

~~요록을~~

첨부 : 동 면담~~자료~~ 사본 1부. 끝.

0178

1505-25(2-1) 일(1)갑
85. 9. 9. 승인   190mm×268mm 인쇄용지 2급 60g /㎡
가 40-41·1985. 10. 29.

184 한국 인권문제 미국 반응 및 동향 2

면 담 요 록

1. 일   시 : 1986년   6 월   30 일(월 요일)15:30 시～16:10 시

2. 장   소 : 외무부 북미과

3. 면 담 자 : 김원수 북미과 사무관

Alexander Arvizu 주한미대사관 정무과 서기관

4. 내   용 :

김원수 : 미 변호사 협회 (ABA) 의 김근태 사건 항소심 방청허가

건과 관련 저간의 사실을 명확히 하고자 함.

최근 ABA 측 인사들은 워싱턴의 아국 대사관을

방문하여, 귀하의 재판장 (한판사) 접촉결과 보고를

인용 "재판장은 외국인의 방청을 허가 또는 불허할

권한을 가지고 있지 않다"고 하면서 재판장이 여사한

권한을 가지고 있다고 한 아측 설명과 상치된다고 주장한

바 있음. 귀하가 이러한 보고를 한것이 사실인지?

Arvizu : 그러함.

김원수 : 여사한 상치되는 진술 내용은 당초 ABA 측에 설명해준
내용을 파악 워싱턴에 알려준 바 있는 본인을 무척
당혹케 하였는 바, 본인은 법무당국을 통해 상기
귀하의 보고 내용 사실 여부를 재판장에게 확인해
보았음.

동 확인결과, 한판사 언급 내용과 귀하의 보고
내용 간에 근본적인 차이점이 있음을 발견하였음.

한판사는 당시 "현재 변호인에 의해 제기된 기피
신청으로 인해 방청 허가 여부에 관해 답변할 위치에
있지 않다"고 한것을 귀하는 "방청허가 여부를 결정할
권한이 없다"고 보고하였기 때문에, 아국 정부와 ABA
간에 심각한 오해와 불신이 야기되었음.

법무당국에 확인한 바, 변호인단이 6.5 기피신청을
제출하여 6.21 대법원에 의해 동 기피신청이 기각될
때까지 재판 절차는 중단되었기 때문에 귀하가 한판사와
면담한 6.17에는 재판장으로서 방청허가 문제에 대해
확실히 답변할 위치에 있지 않았음이 사실임.

- 2 -

0180

　　　　　　귀하의 보고 내용이 사실과 다르다는 점에 대해서는
워싱턴의 아국 대사관을 통해 ABA 측에 통보토록 했음.
이와는 별도로, 귀하의 사실과 다른 보고로 ABA 측이
좋지 않은 오해를 갖게되었음을 감안, 귀하에 의한 해명
조치가 필요하다고 봄.

Arvizu :　본인의 6.17 한판사 면담결과에 대한 보고에는 기피신청
중이므로 답변할 위치에 있지 않다고 한 한판사의 언급
내용도 포함되어 있음.

　　　　　　귀하가 언급한 "재판장이 권한이 없다"고 한 부분은
본인이 한판사와의 면담결과 내린 결론임.

　　　　　　본인은 김근태 사건 공판을 처음서 부터 지켜보았는 바,
동 사건과 관련 한국 정부는 문제를 덮고 지나가려는 듯한
태도를 보여왔음.

　　　　　　한국의 많은 사람들이 김근태 고문에 대해 신빙성
있는 주장을 하고 있고, 고문이 없었음을 의심하고 있음
에도 법정에서 만족할만큼 다투어지지 않았으며, 공개
재판이라고 하면서도 항상 기술적 이유를 내세워 관심있는
외국인의 방청을 교묘히 회피하여 왔음.

　　　　　　동 사건에 있어서 재판부는 완전히 독립적이라고
느껴지지 않았음.

- 3 -

0181

　　　　　본인은 한판사와 상당시간 대화를 나누었으나,
본인이 ABA 측의 방청허가 신청을 전달한데 대해
한판사는 기피신청중이라는 이유를 내세워 명확한 답을
하지 않았음.

　　　　　당시 ABA 측은 방청허가 여부에 관한 재판장의
입장타진을 원하고 있었기 때문에, 본인은 "기피신청중이
아니라면 어떻게 하겠는가"라는 가정법 질문도 하는등
한판사의 답변을 얻으려고 노력하였는 바, 동 판사는
기피신청중이라는 기술적 이유만을 내세워 계속 명확한
답을 회피하였으나 외국인 방청신청 자체에 대해 부정적
견해를 가지고 있다고 감지하였음.

김연수 :　귀하의 판단이 그렇다 하더라도, 귀하의 보고는 너무 멀리
　　　　　나갔다고 봄. 한 판사가 직접 언급하지 않았는데도
　　　　　귀하의 판단으로 재판장은 권한이 없다고 했다고 통보했기
　　　　　때문에 당초 아국 대사관의 ABA 측 통보 내용의 신뢰성에
　　　　　대한 의문이 제기되었음.

Arvizu :　또한가지, 6.26. 항소심 공판 개최 결정이 왜 그렇게
　　　　　급하게 내려졌는지 납득키 어려움. 변호인들이 6.25에도
　　　　　재판부에 6.26 공판개최 여부를 계속 확인했음에도
　　　　　미정이라고 하다가 갑자기 6.25 저녁에야 익일 공판 개최
　　　　　예정임을 통보해 왔음. 이러한 갑작스러운 결정은 ABA
　　　　　측의 재판방청을 회피하기 위한 의도적 조치가 아닌지?

- 4 -

0182

김원수 : 이에 대해서도 법무부를 통해 확인한 바, 박두한 구속
만기일로 인하여 불가피하게 재판기일이 여사하게
지정되었다함. 김근태에 대한 구속기간은 1986.7.6로
만기되기 때문에, 고등법원의 항소심 공판도 이기간내에
종결되어야 하는 바, 그간 기피신청으로 소송 절차중단
으로 지연되었기 때문이라 함.

항소심의 마지막 공판이 7.3로 예정되어 있는 바,
ABA 측이 동 공판의 방청을 원한다면 사정은 아국
대사관이 ABA 측에 최초 통보한 내용 (사증은 발급,
방청허가는 재판부 결정)과 같다는 사실을 유의바람.
이와 함께 귀하의 보고 내용중 사실과 다른 부분에 대해
ABA 측에 적절한 경로를 통해 귀하가 해명조치를 취해
주기 바람.

Arvizu : 알겠음. 7.3 공판은 단순히 선고만 내리고 간단히 끝날
것으로 예상되기 때문에 ABA 측 대표가 오지 않을 것으로
예상되나, 귀하의 언급 사항을 통보토록 하겠음.   끝.

예원 : 1986.12.31. 일반

- 5 -

0183

기 안 용 지

분류기호 문서번호	미북 700-262	(전화 :)	시행상 특별취급	
보존기간	영구·준영구. 10. 5. 3. 1.	장	관	
수신처 보존기간				
시행일자	1986. 7. 4.			

보조기관	국 장	전결	협조기관		문 서 통 제
	심의관				
	과 장				
기안책임자	조 백상			발 송 인	

경유 수신 참조	주미대사	발신명의	

제 목	면담요록 송부

연 : WUS-2602

연호, 주한미대사관의 Arvizu 서기관과의 면담내용을

송부하니 참고 바랍니다.

첨부 : 동 면담요록 사본 1부.   끝.

0184

일반문서로 재분류(1986. 12. 31.)

1505-25(2-1) 일(1)갑
85. 9. 9. 승인

190mm×268mm 인쇄용지 2급 60g/㎡
가 40-41·1985. 10. 29.

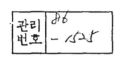

외 무 부

번 호 : USW-3166   일 시 : 607021508   종

수 신 : 장 관(미북)

발 신 : 주 미 대사

제 목 : 미국변호사 협회(ABA) 인사 면담

연: USW-3134

대: WUS-2584

1. ROBERT EVANS (ABA 워싱톤 지부장) 및 CRAIG BAAB (ABA STAFF DIRECTOR FOR GOVERNMENTAL LIASON) 양인이 금 7.1. 본직을 방문, ABA 측이 김근태 항소심을 방청하고자 했던 이유를 설명하는 한편, 방청이 어렵게된 상황하에서 ABA 측이 가지고 있는 재판절차 및 과정에 관한 의문사항을 제기, 이에대한 답변을 요청하였는바, 아래 보고함. (김삼훈 참사관, 이선진서기관 배석)

가. ABA 측은 외국의 TRIAL OBSERVATION PROGRAM 에 따라 최근 2 년간 남아공,유고,라이베리아 재판과정을 방청한바 있음.

나. ABA 는 다른 인권단체와 근본적으로 성격을 달리하며 매우 보수적 단체로서 여사한 재판방청을 어떠한 정치문제화 또는 여론화를 위한 수단으로 사용하는것은 엄격히 자제해 왔음.

다. 상기 PROGRAM 에 따라 그간 갖가지 풍문이 많이있었던 김근태 재판을 방청코자 하였던 것인바, 이는 동사건의 재판 절차 및 과정에 관해 ABA 측이 듣고있는 여러가지 의문점을 알아보려는 것이었으며, 추후도 재판자체에 어떤 영향을 끼치려는것이 아니었음.

라. 연이나 항소심이 이미 개정되어 7.3. 최종판결이 있을 예정이라하브로 동 재판방청은 불가능하게 되었는바, 이와관련 아래 두가지 의문 사항에 대한 한국정부의 답변을 듣고자함.

첫째, 방청허가 여부가 재판장의 권한이라는 설명과 관련한 혼선에 대한 해명 및 일

─────────────────────────

미주국   차관실   1 차보   정문국   청와대   안 기

0185

반인의 방청이 허가되는 공개재판에 ABA 차기회장의 방청이 허가되지 않은점에 대한 설명.

둘째, 또한 동 사건관련, 피고인 고문설, 상당기간 변호사와의 면담이 허용되지 않았다는 소문, 피고인이 자신의 고문주장에 관하여 작성하였다는 113 페이지의 청원서가 법원기록에서 삭제되었다가 항소심 재판시작 이틀전 재기록되었다는 소문등에 대한 한국정부의 설명 (ABA 측은 사실을 알지못하며 여사한 소문이 사실이라면 재판의 공정성이 의문시 되므로 동 절차와 과정에 관심을 가지는것이고 따라서 한국정부의 답변을 요청한다는 설명이었음)

2. 이에대해 본직은 ABA 의 권위와 권능을 인정하며, 솔직한 의견교환을 갖기를 원한다고 전제한 후, 아래와 같이 설명함.

가. 재판권은 주권국가의 독립된 권한으로 어떠한 외부의 간섭이 있어서는 안될것이며, 한국은 공개사회로써 관련법규정에 따라 공개재판을 하는 나라임.

나. 한국의 전통,사회,문화 관습을 잘 모르고 특히 한국어를 모르는 외국인이 단지 몇차례의 방청만으로 진상을 옳게 판단하기 보다는 오히려 왜곡되게 해석할수 있는 위험성이 있음.

다. 재판의 방청허가 여부는 재판장의 권한임이 명문으로 규정되어 있으며, 혼선이 야기된 구체적인 경위는 알수 없으나 주한미대사관 직원이 재판장의 설명을 잘못 이해한데서 비롯된 것이 분명한바, 아국정부는 이점을 주한미대사관 직원에게도 다시 설명하였음.

라. 대사관과 외무부는 ABA 측에 대해 최대한 협조코자 노력하였으나, ABA 회장이라고 해서 재판장에게 방청을 사전 보장하게 할수 없을뿐만 아니라 재판장도 어떤 특정인을 특별 대우할수는 없을 것이라는 점을 법률가인 ABA 측이 더 잘알고 있을 것으로 믿음.,

마. 고문주장 관련, 아국법은 자백을 유일한 증거로 유죄판결을 할수없게 되어있고 변호인 없는 재판이란 법규정상 있을수 없으므로 소문과 같은 일들은 있을수 없다고 보며, 따라서 알려진 소문은 진상과는 거리가 먼 것으로 알고있음.

3. 상기 본직의 설명에 따라 재판장의 방청허가 권한부분 (첫째질문)에 대해서는 이

PAGE 2

0186

해를 표시하였으나, 두번째 질문인 고문 및 재판절차 과정에 관한 부분에 대해서는 구체적인 답변을 원한다고 하였음.

4. ABA 측은 면담서두 상기 1 항 내용이 포함된 장문의 서한초안을 제시 하였는바, 금일 면담결과를 감안한 ABA 측 서한을 재작성 제시하겠다는 반응을 보였음.

5. 관찰 및 건의

가. 면담분위기는 좋았으며, 이들은 ABA 가 여타 인권단체들(AI 및 INTERNATIONAL HUMAN RIGHTS LAW GROUP 등)과는 다르다는 점을 수차 강조, ABA 의 권위에 대한 이해를 촉구하고 있었음.

나. 경위가 어떠 하든 ABA 차기회장이 공개재판의 방청을 시도하였으나 실패하였다는 점에서 ABA 의 권위에 손상을 입었다고 불만스럽게 생각하고 있는듯함. (ABA 회장이 오하이오주 크리브랜드에 거주한다는바, 적절한 기회에 본직이 면담코자함)

다. 재판절차와 과정에 관한 문의 서한을 보내오는 경우 관계기관이 성의있는 답변을 해주는것이 좋을 것으로 사료됨.

(대사 김경원-차관)
예고문: 1986.12.31. 일반

관리 번호	86 -15185		분류번호	보존기간

발 신 전 보

번 호 : WUS-2656   일 시 : 60704 1130   전보종별 : _____

수 신 : 주　미　대사·총영싸

발 신 : 장　관 (미북)

제 목 : 김근태 선고공판

　　　　　연: WUS-2548
　　　　　　　　　　　　항소심
　　7.3 예정되었던 표제공판은 7.4. 13:00에 열려 징역 5년 (1신7년)
　　　　　　　　　　　　　　　　(선서)
자격정지 5년의 선고 되었음. ~~학총 상고 변형 여부 상금 미정임~~
　　　　　(1신6면)

　　　　　　　　　　　　　　　　(미주국장　장선섭)

0188   보안
통제

	86 년 7 월 4 일		기안자	과 장	심의관	국 장		차 관	장 관		접수자	통제
앙 고 재		과	2							외 신 과		

외 무 부 착 신 전 문

번 호 : USW-3182   일 시 : 60702 1821   종 별 :

수 신 : 장 관(미북)

발 신 : 주 미 대사

제 목 : 김근태 건

당지 ASIA WATCH 는 본직앞 서한을 통하여 김근태가 공정한 재판절차를 받지못
하고 있다고 주장하면서 113 페이지의 김근태 청원서의 법정 기록 미비 및 변호인단
의 동 청원서 사본 복제 불허등을 그 예로 들고 있음을 참고로 보고함

(대사 김경원-국장)

0189

미주국   차관실   2 차보   청와대   안 기

PAGE   1

86.07.04 10:26
외신 2과 통제관

趙

주 미 대 사 관

미국(정)700-205   1986. 7. 3.

수 신 : 장 관

참 조 : 미주국장

제 목 : 서한송부

연 : USW - 3182

연호 Asia Watch   의 본직앞 서한을 별첨 송부
합니다.

첨 부 : 동서한 사본 1부. 끝.

주   미   대

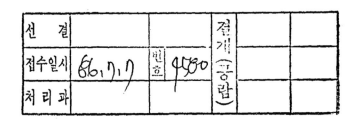

0190

ASIA WATCH

739 Eighth Street SE, Washington DC 20003
(202) 546-9336

시로 ~~ ~~ ~~
~~ July ~~

July 2, 1986

ADRIAN DEWIND
Chairman
▪
ARYEH NEIER
Vice Chairman
▪
ERIC SCHWARTZ
Program Director
▪
HOLLY BURKHALTER
Washington Representative

His Excellency Kim Kyung-won
Ambassador Extraordinary and Plenipotentiary
Embassy of the Republic of Korea
2370 Massachusetts Avenue, NW
Washington, DC 20008

Dear Ambassador Kim:

Asia Watch is concerned about developments in the
Kim Keun-tae case. Available information indicates that
Mr. Kim was tried and convicted at the district court
level for non-violent activities protected in
international law. Moreover, actions taken by
interrogators, prosecutors, and judicial authorities
resulted in effective denial of Mr. Kim's right to a fair
trial. Thus, we believe that an appellate court decision
to confirm the verdict of the district court will
represent a miscarriage of justice.

As you know, several organizations and institutions --
including the Korean Federal Bar Association and the U.S.
State Department -- have expressed concerns about abuses
of due process, and the details in this case have been
reported widely. They include, inter alia, reports that
Mr. Kim was subject to severe torture while in custody,
denied the opportunity to preserve physical evidence of
torture, and denied access to his lawyers until 10 days
before the trial began. We are concerned that there has
been no thorough investigation into these well-documented
allegations, or into reports that persons who provided
evidence against Mr. Kim did so under coercion.

Issues arising during appellate hearings appear to
confirm our fears about the impartiality of the judiciary
in this case. We are concerned about the appellate
court's refusal to investigate the circumstances around
the disappearance of a 113 page petition written by Mr.
Kim and submitted to the district court in March. We

0191

understand that the petition was not included in the district
court records, and appeared just two days before the appeal
began. This raises the question of whether all members of the
district court panel considered the petition before reaching
their verdict. Moreover, we were disturbed to learn that the
appellate court prevented Mr. Kim's lawyers from copying the
document.

We believe that the prosecution of this case has conflicted
with your government's stated commitment to the rule of law and
democratization. We urge that your government thoroughly
investigate these reports of abuses, especially the reports of
Mr. Kim's torture, and bring those responsible to justice.
Furthermore, we respectfully request that President Chun exercise
his authority to review this case and order Mr. Kim's release, as
he has been convicted for non-violent activities protected under
international law.

We would appreciate your relaying our concerns to the
appropriate authorities, and we look forward to hearing from you.

Sincerely yours,

Eric Schwartz
Program Director

0192

외 무 부

번 호 : USW-4450   일 시 : 609261643

수 신 : 장관(미북)

발 신 : 주미대사

제 목 : 김근태 관련서한

1. EDWARD FIEGHAN 하원의원 (민주-오하이오) 은 김근태등에 대한 부당한 처우방지를 요망하는 내용의 별첨 대통령 각하 앞 서한을 작성, 동료의원들의 서명을 받고있는것으로 파악됨.

2. 당관 은 LESTER WOLFF 전하원의원등을 통하여 FEIGHAN 의원측에 동서한발송 계획의 철회를 종용한바 있으나 예정대로 추진하겠다는 반응임. 동서한은 금 9.26.현재 약 40 명정도 하원의원들의 연서를 받았으며, 내주경 발송예정이라함.

첨부: 상기서한 (대사김경원-장관)

예고문: 1987.6.30. 일반

PRESIDENT CHUN DOO HWAN

THE BLUE HOUSE

SEOUL

REPUBLIC OF KOREA

DEAR MR. PRESIDENT:

WE WOULD LIKE TO EXPRESS OUR DEEP CONCERN ABOUT THE CASE OF MR. KIM KUEN-TAE, W

HOM WE BELIEVE HAS BEEN THE VICTIM OF STATE-SANCTIONED TORTURE BY SOUTH KOREAN S

TATE OFFICIALS. KIM KUEN-TAE IS THE FORMER CHAIRMAN OF THE NATIONAL YOUTH ALLIA

NCE FOR DEMOCRACY (NYAD), AN ORGANIZATION WHICH HE FOUNDED IN 1983. HE HAD PREVI

OUSLY BEEN INVOLVED IN NON-VIOLENT, OPPOSITION POLITICS FROM THE EARLY 1970 S ON

WARD AND HAS SPENT A GOOD PART OF THAT DECADE IN HIDING. KIM WAS DETAINED ON SEV

ERAL OCCASIONS PRIOR TO HIS ARREST ON SEPTEMBER 4,1985, BY THE ANTI-COMMUNIST BU

미주국   차관실   1 차보   청와대   총리실   안 기   (서명)   0196

PAGE   1   86.09.27 08:11
                                                      외신 2과 통재관

REAU OF THE NATIONAL POLICE.

FROM SEPTEMBER 4 TO 26, 1985, KIM WAS INTERROGATED AND REPORTEDLY TORTURED BY M
EMBERS OF THE ANTI-COMMUNIST BUREAU BEFORE FINALLY BEING TRANSFERRED TO THE SEOU
L DISTRICT PUBLIC PROSECUTOR S OFFICE ON SEPTEMBER 26. ON OCTOBER 25, HE WAS CHA
RGED UNDER THE LAW ON ASSEMBLIES AND DEMONSTRATIONS ON COUNTS RELATED TO HIS ORG
ANIZATION OF AND/OR PARTICIPATION IN EIGHT MEETINGS QTE FEARED TO CAUSE SOCIAL U
NREST UNQTE AS WELLAS UNDER THE NATIONAL SECURITY LAW WITH MAKING PROPAGAND A FO
R NORTH KOREA. KIM WAS SENTENCED TO TRIAL COURT ON MARCH 6, 1986, TO SEVEN YEARS
IMPRISONMENT AND SIX YEARS LOSS OF CIVIL RIGHTS. ON JULY 4, 1986, THE APPEALS C
OURT AFFIRMED THE LOWER COURT S FINDING OF GUILT, BUT REDUCED THE PRIS ON SENTEN
CE FROM SEVEN TO FIVE YEARS. ON AUGUST 19, 1986, KIM S LAWYERS FILED AN APPEAL W
ITH THE SUPREME COURT OF SOUTH KOREA. A DATE FOR THE HEARING HAS YET TO BE SET.

이하계속

외 무 부 착 신 전 분

번 호 : USW-4454   일 시 : 609261720   종 별 :

수 신 :

발 신 :

제 목 : USW-4450 의 계속

DURING HIS INTERROGATION FROM SEPTEMBER 4 TO 26, MR. KIM WAS BRUTALLY AND PER
SISTENT TORTURED AT THE ANTI-COMMUNIST BUREAU OFFICES OF THE NATIONAL POLICE HE
ADQUARTERS LOCATED AT NAMYOUNG-DONG. TORTURE METHODS INCLUDED ELECTRIC SHOCK, W
ATER TORTURE, AND BEING FORCED TO SWALLOW WATER WHICH HAD BEEN LACED WITH RED PE
PPER AND SALT. HE WAS DEPRIVED OF FOOD PRIOR TO TORTURE SESSIONS AT OTHER TIMES,
AS WELL, AS A FORM OF PSYCHOLOGICAL TORTURE DESIGNED TO MAKE HIM THINK THAT TOR
TURE WAS ABOUT TO BEGIN WHEN, IN FACT, IT WAS NOT. AGAIN, IN AUGUST OF 1986, KIM
ALONG WITH SEVENTEEN STUDENT PRISONERS WERE SEVERELY BEATEN. THE OTHER PRISONER
S WERE PROTESTING THE FACT THAT KIM WAS BEING KEPT IN A CELL SO SMALL THAT HE C
OULD NOT STRETCH OUT THE FULL LENGTH OF HIS BODY TO SLEEP. THEY WERE BEATEN AS A
RESULT OF THEIR PROTESTS, AS WAS KIM, AND YET KIM REPORTEDLY CONTINUES TO BE KE
PT IN THE SAME SMALLCELL.
OUR CONCENTRATION IN THIS LETTER ON THE CASE OF ONE INDIVIDUAL SHOULD NOT BE TA
KEN TO MEAN THAT WE FEEL THAT KIM'S CASE IS AN ISOLATED ONE. ON THE CONTRARY, KI
M'S EXPERIENCES ARE SEEN AS PART OF A DELIBERATE AND PERVASIVE POLICY, WHICH WE
FIND TO BE MOST TROUBLING. WE ARE CONCERNED ABOUT MR. KIM'S PERSONAL WELFARE IN
PRISON AND EARNESTLY HOPE THAT HE IS NO LONGER SUBJECT TO ABUSE DURING THE REMA
INDER OF HIS PRISON SENTENCE. WE HOPE AS WELL THAT YOU WILL BE ABLE TO SEE THAT
MEASURES ARE TAKEN IN THE FUTURE TO INVESTIGATE ALLEGATIONS OF TORTURE AND ABUSE
FULLY WHEN THEY ARISE. MORE IMPORTANTLY, WE URGE YOU TO DO WHAT YOU CAN TO STOP

0195

THIS PRACTICE OF HUMAN RIGHTS VIOLATIONS TAKING PLACE WITHIN YOUR GOVERNMENT.

AS AMERICANS, WE HAVE SHARED AN IMMPORTANT HISTORY WITH THE PEOPLE OF SOUTH KOR

EA DURING THE PAST FORTY YEARS--INCLUDING FIGHTING SIDE-BY-SIDE DURING WARTIME,

A POWERFUL POSTWAR ALLIANCE, AND STRONG AND FRUITFUL ECONOMIC TIES. WITH THE A P

PROACH OF THE OLYMPIC GAMES IN SEOUL AND THE PRESIDENTIAL ELECTIONS IN 1988, WE

SINCERELY HOPE THAT KOREAN-AMERICAN RELATIONS WILL CONTINUE TO BE STRONG AND COR

DIAL, AND THAT THEY WILL SERVE TO STRENGTHEN OUR GREAT, SHARED TRADITION OF DER

MOCRACY AND FREEDOM.

SINCERELY,

END

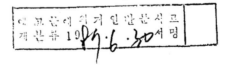

USW(F) - 1342   071509百0

장관 (미북.정문.해신)   발 신 : 주미 대사

미 인권단체, 김근태 석방요구   / 매

The New York Times   TUESDAY, JULY 15, 1986   A3

South Korea Is Urged
To Release 2 Prisoners

Three human rights organizations asked the South Korean Government yesterday to release two opposition political leaders whom the groups call "prisoners of conscience" whose rights to due process have been denied.

In separate statements, the organizations — Asia Watch, Amnesty International and the International Human Rights Law Group — said they were issuing the pleas in response to a ruling on July 3 by an appeals court, which refused to overturn a conviction of a student leader, Kim Keun Tae. The court sentenced Mr. Kim to five years in prison for violating the National Security Act.

One judge on the sentencing panel was reported to have acknowledged that Mr. Kim had been tortured into making a confession, but said that was not enough to overturn the conviction. Mr. Kim, founder of the National Youth Alliance for Democracy, was arrested last September for taking part in meetings- and demonstrations "feared to cause social unrest" and for spreading propaganda on behalf of North Korea.

김경원대사 귀하

- Asia Watch 는 김근태 사건의 전개에 관심을 가지고
있음. 김은 공정한 재판과정을 거치지 않았으므로 1심을 확정한
2심 결정이 법을 잘못 이행한 것으로 봄.

- 적접절차 위반에 대한 우려가 있어왔으며, 특히 김이 구금중
  심한 고문을 당했고 신체상 고문증거 보존기회를 거부당했으며
  재판 개시 10일전까지 변호사와의 접촉이 거부되었음.

- 상기 주장 또는 김근태에 불리한 증거를 제시했던것은 강제에
  의한것이라는 보도에 대한 철저한 조사가 없었음을 우려함.

- 항소 공판중 제기되었던 문제는 이사건에 대한 사법부의 공정성에
  대한 우려를 확인시켜 주었음.

- 김근태가 작성하고 금년 3월 지방법원에 제출했던 113페이지의
  소장이 분실된건에 대해 항소심 재판부가 조사요청을 거절한것에
  우려를 표명함.

- 김의 소장이 지방법원 재판부 기록에 포함되어 있지 않고,
  항소심 공판개시 이틀전에 발견된바, 이는 지방법원 재판부가
  판결내리기전 김의 소장을 고려했는지 여부에 대한 의문을
  제기하는것임.

- 더우기 항소심 재판부가 김의 변호사들이 관련문서를 복사하는
  것을 금지시켰다는 사실에 불쾌감을 느낌.

0198

- 금번 사건은 귀정부가 공약한 법의지배 및 민주화 원칙에 배치된다고 생각함.

- 귀정부가 김근태의 고문등에 대한 보고에 대해 철저히 조사해 줄 것과 관계자를 법적으로 처리할것을 요청함.

- 또한 김이 국제법에 보장된 비폭력행위 때문에 유죄판결을 받았기 때문에 전대통령이 김근태 사건을 재검토하여 김을 석방시켜 줄 것을 요청함.

- 우리의 관심사항을 관련기관에 전달해 준 것에 대해 감사하며 답신을 기대함.

기획국장 Eric SchWartz

0199

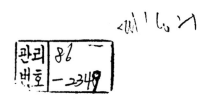

법 무 부

검삼 700- 220   503-7055   1986. 10. 13.

수신 외무부장관

참조 미주국장

제목 자료회신

　　　귀부 미북 700-3483 (86. 10. 6.)과 관련, <u>검근태에 대한 관계</u>

자료를 별첨과 같이 송부합니다.

첨부 관계자료 1부. 끝.

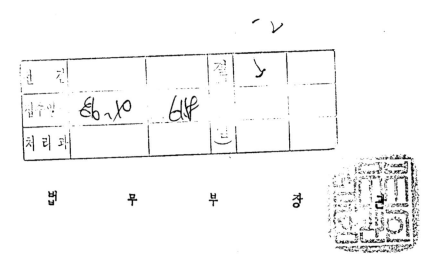

법 무 부 장

0200

근 거 자 료

o 김근태는 85. 1 - 85. 6 간 폭력혁명에 의한 국가전복 및 노동자,

   농민등이 주체가 된 사회주의 국가건설을 목적으로 하는 소위

   "민청련"이란 반국가단체를 조직, 민주, 민족, 인민민주주의

   혁명이란 구호아래 불법집회, 시위등 활동을 하여 북괴의 대남혁명

   노선에 동조한 명백한 반국가적 범죄자로서 86. 9. 23. 대법원에서

   징역 5년, 자격정지 5년의 형이 확정되어 복역중에 있음.

o 고문은 헌법상 금지되어 있고, 관계법률에서 고문등으로 인한 자백은

   유죄의 증거로 사용할 수 없고, 고문을 중한 범죄로 규정하는등

   인권보장에 관한 완벽한 장치를 두고 있고, 나아가 정부는 이와

   같은 법정신에 입각하여 국민의 인권옹호에 최대한 노력을 기울이고

   있음.

o 김근태가 경찰수사과정에서 고문을 당했다고 주장하는 사람들이

   있어 다각도로 확인한 결과,

0201

그문을 당했다고 인정할만한 사실이나 흔적을 발견할 수 없었고,

자신의 형사책임을 모면해 보려는 의도로 재야 운동권 단체등에

경찰수사과정에서 고문을 당했다고 악의적으로 왜곡 전파한데서

비롯된 것으로 밝혀졌음.

o 김근태는 고도소내에서 한때 행형 규정상 인정되지 아니하는

사항을 요구하며, 출입문을 발로 차 부수는등 소란을 피워 이를

수차 설유하여도 듣지 아니하여 부득이 <u>행형법규에 따라 정법</u>

<u>조치를 취한 사실이있을 뿐</u> 폭행을 가한 사실은 없었음.

0202

金槿泰씨 國家상대
손해배상 청구소송

국가보안법등 위반혐의로
징역5년이 확정돼 복역중인
前民靑聯의장 金槿泰씨(39)
가 7일 수사기관의 가혹행
위·불법 장기구속·면금지
등을 이유로 국가를 상대로
5백만1백원의 손해배상청구
소송을 서울민사지법에 냈다.
金씨는 소장에서 『치안본부
에서 조사받으면서 당한 살
인적인 가혹행위등으로 지금
까지 후유증에 시달리고 있
으므로 국가는 관련공무원들
의 불법행위에대한 배상책임
을 져야한다』고 주장했다.

10.7 중앙일보

金槿泰씨 5년刑
大法서 확정

대법원 형사2부(主審 李炳
厚대법원판사)는 23일 前民靑
聯의장 金槿泰(39) 피고인에
대한 국가보안법 위반사건 상
고심선고공판에서 金피고인의
상고를 기각, 징역 5년을
확정했다.
재판부는 판결문에서「피고인
에게 불법수사를 가했다는 주장
은 인정할수없으며 피고인이 내
세운 ZDR이념은 반국가단체
인 북괴를 이롭게할 인식에서
나온것으로 판단된다」고 말
했다.

86.9.23 중앙일보

정 리 보 존 문 서 목 록

기록물종류	일반공문서철	등록번호	21360	등록일자	1994-10-04
분류번호	701	국가코드	US	보존기간	영구
명 칭	부천서 (권인숙) 사건 관련 미국 반응, 1986				
생 산 과	북미과	생산년도	1986~1986	담당그룹	북미국
내용목차					

0001

受信: 外務部 次官

發信: 安企部

0002

부천경찰서 수사시비사건 수사결과

1986. 7. 16

인 천 지 방 검 찰 청

0003

1. 수 사 경 위

0 인천지방검찰청은 타인의 주민등록증을 절취, 자신의 주민

　등록증으로 변조하여 부천시 소재 주식회사 성신에 위장취업

　한 사실과 관련하여 절도죄와 공문서 변조죄 등으로 인천

　소년교도소에 구속되어 있던 권인숙으로부터 자신이 부천

　경찰서에서 조사를 받을당시 부천경찰서 수사과 근무 문귀동

　경장으로부터 폭행과 성적 모욕행위를 당했다고 주장하는

　고소장을 86. 7. 3 접수하고

0 문귀동으로부터도 86.7.3 권인숙이 허위사실을 유포하여

　자신의 명예를 훼손하였다는 내용의 고소장과 7. 5 허위고소

　로 무고하였다는 내용의 고소장을 각각 접수하여

0 86. 7. 3 ~ 7.16까지 동 고소사실들의 진상을 규명하기 위해

　집중수사를 전개하였음.

0004

o 인천지검은 그동안

- 사건 당사자인 위 문귀동을 7회, 권인숙을 8회 소환,

   조사하였고

- 관련 참고인 43명을 소환, 진술을 들었으며

- 또한 사건현장에 대한 면밀한 실황조사를 실시하는

등 가능한 모든 조사를 실시하였음.

0005

2. 수 사 결 과

0 권인숙의 고소 사실중 86. 6. 7 21:00 - 23:00사이 문귀동이

권인숙을 조사하면서 성적 모욕행위를 가했다는 부분은

- 문귀동이 조사를 행한 조사실은 2면벽이 유리창으로 되어

있어 안이 들여다 보이고 조사실 뒷편에 있는 무기고의

전등불빛이 조사실 안으로 비치고 있었을뿐 아니라 당시

바로 옆의 조사실에서도 다른 경찰관들이 날씨가 더워

모두 문을 열어 놓은채 다른 피의자를 조사하면서 문귀동

의 조사실 앞을 왔다갔다한 사실이 있었으며

- 또한 권인숙과 함께 부천경찰서 유치장에 수감되어 있던

최모여인(32세), 박모여인(30세) 등도 참고인진술에서조사받고온

유치장에서

권인숙이 폭행을 당했다는 말은 한 일이 있으나 성적모욕

을 당했다는 말은 한 사실이 없다고 진술하고 있고

옆 조사실에서 조사를 한 경찰관 김해성, 권오성, 박경천

0006

등도 그와같은 사실을 목격하거나 감지한바 없다고 진술한

점 등에 비추어 사실로 인정할 수 없음

o 그러나 권인숙의 고소사실중

- 86. 6. 6 04:00 - 06:30.분 귀동이 부천경찰서 제5조 사실

에서 권인숙을 조사하는 과정에서 인천소요사건 관련

수배자의 소재를 알아내기 위해 아는 사람의 이름과 주소를

대라고 거듭 요구했으나 권인숙이 완강히 아는 사람이 없다

고 말하자 권인숙에게 자켓을 벗게한 후 티샤스를 입은

가슴부위를 손으로 3 - 4회 쥐어박아 폭행을 가한 사실과

- 86. 6. 7 21:00 - 23:00.분 귀동이 부천경찰서 제2조 사실

에서 같은 내용을 조사하던중 권인숙이 전일과 마찬가지로

계속하여 아는 사람이 없다고 말하자 권인숙에게 또 다시

가슴부위를 손으로 3 - 4회 쥐어박아 폭행을 가한 사실등은

- 문귀동이 자백하고 있을뿐 아니라 기타 증거에 의하여 사실로

인정됨.

0007

3. 처   리

o   이상과 같이 권인숙의 고소사실중 성적 모욕행위 부분은

    사실이 아닌 것으로 밝혀졌으나 폭언·폭행부분은 일부

    사실이 인정됨

o   폭언·폭행부분은 문이 조사에 집착한 나머지 저지른 우발적

    인 과오로서 이로인해 이미 파면처분을 받았으며

o   문귀동은 10년 이상 경찰에 봉직하면서 성실하게 근무하여

    왔고,

o   현재 자신의 과오를 깊이 반성하고 있으므로 검찰은 이와같은

    정상을 참작 ·문귀동을 기소유예 처분할 방침임.

0008

4. 사건의 성격

0 . 급진좌경사상에 의한 노학 연계투쟁을 전개해왔던 권인숙의
   "성적모욕"의 허위사실 주장은 운동권세력이 상습적으로
   벌이고 있는 소위 의식화투쟁의 일환으로서

0 폭행사실을 성 모욕행위로 날조, 왜곡함으로써 자신의 구명과
   아울러 일선 수사기관의 위신을 실추시키고 반체제 혁명투쟁
   을 사회일반으로 확산시켜 정부의 공권력을 무력화 시키려는
   의도로 판단됨.

0 이러한 사실은 동 권인숙이 학원 의식화투쟁을 벌이다가
   성적불량으로 대학 4년 제적후 (서울대 가정대 의류학과),
   부모의 권유도 뿌리치고 가출한 후 위장취업으로 노동현장
   으로 뛰어들어 반정부, 반체제 투쟁활동을 전개한 전력을
   볼 때에도 뚜렷하게 나타나고 있음.

0009

검찰발표에 대한 변호인단의 견해와 결의   86. 7/18

1.   검찰의 수사결과발표에 접한 우리들 변호인단은 분노에 앞서서 깊

은 슬픔과 절망을 가늠길이 없다.

      우리가 아는 한 이 사건은 그 동안의 검찰조사과정에서 이미 그

진상이 백일하에 드러났다.   인천지방검찰청의 수사인력이 총동원

되다시피 한 가운데 연일 불철주야로 사건당사자와 참고인 43명에

대한 집중조사가 진행됨에 따라 권양의 모든 주장은 하나하나 진실

과 부합됨이 명백히 입증되어갔고 반면에 범행은폐를 위하여 꾸며댄

문귀등의 모든 주장과 그를 비호하기 위해 조작된 부천서 간부진 및

형사들의 모든 진술내용은 낱낱이 거짓임이 판명되었다.

      한마디로 그동안의 모든 검찰수사결과는 권양측의 일방적이며 완벽

한 승리로 귀결되었다.   우리가 알고 있기로는 검찰은 그 동안 전례

없이 진지하고 성실한 자세로 이 사건 수사에 임하였으며 그 결과

권양의 성고문 주장이 더이상 의심할 여지없는 확고부동한 진실임을

드러내었다.   그러나 검찰은 수사과정에서 고심끝에 찾아낸 진실

을 발표과정에서는 허겁지겁 왜곡하고 은폐해버렸다.

                                                            0010

"폭언·폭행만 있었고 성적모욕은 없었다"는 검찰의 발표내용은 검찰이

그 동안 모든 노고를 기울여 도달한 수사결론을 스스로 뒤엎는 것밖에

되지 않는다.   우리는 대체 어떻게하여 이같은 어처구니없는 일이

일어나게 되었는지 그 경위에 대하여 의혹을 품지 않을 수 없다.

이번 검찰발표과정에 검찰권의 독립적행사를 저해하는 외부세력의

작용이 개입되었던 것이 아닌가 하는 의심을 떨쳐버릴 수가없다.

항간의 소문대로 당초에는 문귀동을 구속할 방침이었다가 급작히 기소

유예방침으로 전환한것이었다면 그 이유는 대체 무엇인가?

검찰의 소신과 명예는 어디로 갔는가?

우리는 검찰의 발표내용을 믿지 않는다.

국민들 중 누구도 검찰의 발표내용을 믿지 않을 것이다.

그리고, 단언하거니와 다른 누구보다도 검찰 자신이 스스로의

발표내용을 믿지않을 것이다.

2. 우리가 검찰의 발표내용을 믿을 수 없는 이유는 다음과 같다.

(1). 문귀동은 당초에 권양을 명예훼손죄로 고소하면서 문귀동 본인이

0011

권양을 6. 7. 저녁 7:45경부터 9:45경까지 이흥기 형사등의

입회 아래 단 한차례 조사한 일 밖에 없다고 주장하였고 또

6. 6.에는 서에는 출근도 하지 않았다고 주장하면서 당일 송추

에 놀러갔다는 알리바이까지 제시하였다. 문귀동은 검찰에서

조사받는 과정에서도 당초에는 완강하게 위 주장을 유지하다가

알리바이가 깨어지고 제반 관계증거에 의하여 위 주장이 거짓

임이 명백히 드러나게 된 후에야 비로소 진술을 번복하여 권양

의 주장대로 자신이 권양을 6.6. 새벽과 6.7. 아침 및 밤중

세 차례에 걸쳐 조사하였으며, 6. 7. 밤중에는 9시경부터

11시경까지 입회형사가 없는 가운데에서 조사하였다는 사실을

자백하였다. 부천서 형사 이흥기는 실제로는 6. 6. 새벽

문귀동이 권양을 조사할 당시("1차 성고문" 당시) 입회하였던

자였고 권양이 누차 그 사실을 지적하였음에도 불구하고 위 문

귀동의 허위진술을 뒷받침해 주기 위한 목적에서 굳이 6. 6. 새

벽에 입회한 사실을 부인하면서 6. 7. 저녁에 자신이 문귀동의

조사현장에 입회하였던 것처럼 허위진술을 하다가 나중에와서야

0012

이를 번복하고 권양의 주장이 진실임을 자백하였다.

사건 당시의 부천서 수사과장이었던 경감 유희수 또한 검찰 조사시 문귀동이 6. 6. 새벽에 출근한 사실이 없는 것처럼 허위진술을 하였고 나아가서는 부천서장 옥봉환이 6. 6. 아침 10시 이후에야 서에 출근한 것처럼 허위진술을 하였다. 그러나 수사결과 위 옥봉환이 권양의 당초 주장대로 6. 6. 새벽에 출근하였던 사실이 판명됨으로써 위 유희수의 진술은 허위였음이 드러났다.

부천서 형사 김해성은 당초에는 위 문귀동의 거짓말을 뒷받침하기 위하여 6. 7. 밤에 문귀동이 권양을 조사할 때 형사 이흥기가 함께 있는것을 보았다고 거짓진술을 하다가 나중에 이흥기가 진술을 번복한 후에야 비로소 당일 이흥기를 본 사실이 없다고 자백하였다.

뿐만아니라 부천서 형사들 중 문귀동이 6. 7. 밤 조사시 옆에 입회했다고 주장한 형사들과 그날 밤 권양을 유치장까지 데려다 주었다고 하는 형사까지 나타나서 위 문귀동의 허위진술내용을

0013

뒷받침하는 진술을 하다가 나중에 모두 조작임이 단명되었다.

요컨대 문귀동의 당초의 허위진술을 뒷받침하기 위하여 부천서 전체가 동원되다시피 하였다고 해도 과언이 아니다.

만약 검찰발표와같이 문귀동이 권양을 조사할 당시 "조사에 열중한 나머지 우발적인 과오로 인하여" 권양의 가슴을 주먹(손등)으로 서너차례 툭툭 건드린 것이 이 사건의 전부라고 한다면, 대체 무엇 때문에 문귀동은 위와같이 조사횟수, 조사시간, 입회형사 유무 등 가장 기초적인 사실에 관해서부터 터무니없는 허위주장을 조작하여 완강하게 버티었으며 더구나 무엇 때문에 부천서 전체가 공모하다시피하여 감히 조직적으로 검찰을 기만하면서까지 집요하게 위 문귀동의 허위주장을 감싸고 돌았겠는가?

이것이 우리가 검찰의 발표내용을 도저히 믿을 수 엇는 첫번째 이유이다.

(2). 검찰이 "성적모욕행위가 없었다"고 단정하는 근거로서 제시한 것은 "양쪽(권양과 문귀동)주장이 크게 대립되고 있을뿐 아니라

0014

구체적인 목격자도 없다" (조선일보 86. 7. 17. 보도)라는
것이다.

원래 강간이나 강제추행, 간통등 성범죄는 목격자가 없는 가
운데에서 일어나는 것이 통례이다.   그러므로 이같은 밀실범죄
로서의 특성을 감안하여 강간 등 성범죄의 경우에는 제3자의
직접 증언이 없더라도 피해자의 진술내용이 제반 정황에 비추어
경험칙상 수긍할 수 있을 정도이면 피해자의 진술만으로써 얼마
든지 유죄를 선고할 수 있다는 것이 우리 법원의 확립된 판례의
태도인 것이다.   그렇다면 이 사건에서 권양과 문귀동 중 어느
쪽의 주장을 믿어야 할 것인가?

43명의 참고인들을 조사한 끝에 모든 세부적인 정황에 이르기
까지 어느것 한 가지도 사실과 다른 점이 없는 것으로 드러난
권양의 시종일관된 진술내용과,   처음부터 알리바이까지 조작해
가며 어느것 하나 사실과 부합하는 점이 없는 허위주장을 내세
우고 거짓말에 거짓말을 거듭하던 끝에 관계증거에 의하여 파탄
에 부딪치자 어쩔수 없이 "약간의 폭언·폭행" 사실만을 자백

0015

하기에 이르렀다는 문귀동의 진술내용 중 어느쪽을 믿고 어느쪽을 배척하여야 할 것인가?

도와줄 사람 하나 없는 고독한 수감생활 속에서 수치심과 굴욕감 때문에 오랜 번민과 망설임을 거쳐 마침내 여성으로서의 전도를 희생하는 결단을 내리고 차마 입으로 옮길 수도 없는 처참한 피해사실을 눈물로써 호소하기에 이른 스물세살의 미혼처녀의 주장과, 후안무치하게도 스스로 기독교인임을 내세우며 "욱이라도 한 마디 했더라면 억을하지나 않겠다"고 범행을 깡그리 부인하고 도리어 피해자를 명예훼손죄로 고소하기까지 하였던 문귀동의 주장 중 어느쪽을 믿고 어느쪽을 배척하여야 할 것인가?

묻지 않아도 알 수 있는 일이다.

검찰발표는 결국 "폭언·폭행" 부분까지는 문귀동이 자백했으니 사실로 인정하고 그 이상의 "성모욕" 행위는 문귀동이 자백하지 않았으니 사실로 인정할 수 없다는 이야기 밖에 안된다.

문귀동에 대한 이같은 절대적 신뢰가 대체 어떻게 하여 형성된

0016

것인지 도저히 이해할 수 없다.

이것이 우리가 검찰발표내용을 믿을 수 없는 두번째 이유이다.

(3). 검찰발표는 6. 7. 밤 9시부터 11시까지 문귀동이 권양을 조사했던 조사실이 "2면벽이 유리창으로 되어있어 안이 들여다 보이고 조사실 뒷편에 있는 무기고의 전등불빛이 조사실 안으로 비치고 있었을 뿐 아니라 당시 … 다른 경찰관들이 문귀동의 조사실 앞을 왔다갔다 한 사실이 있었으며 … 위 경찰관 김 해성, 권오성, 박경천 등도 그와같은 사실(성고문사실)을 목격하였거나 감지한 바 없다고 진술"하였다는 등의 이유를 들 어 성고문사실을 인정할 수 없다고 단정하고 있다.

그러나 우리는 위 조사가 경찰서 내에 대부분이 직원이 퇴근 하고 없는 토요일 깊은 밤중에 밀폐된 조사실 내에서 이루어진 사실, 검찰도 자인하듯이 당시 위 조사실 내에는 불이 꺼져 있었고 바깥마당에 있는 전등의 외광만이 마당쪽에 면한 유리창 을 통하여 겨우 명암을 식별할 수 있을 정도로 희미하게 흘러

0017

들고 있는 가운데에서 문귀동과 권양 단 들만이 대치하고 있었던 사실, 따라서 당시 조사실 바깥으로는 일반인이 왕래할 까닭도 없었거니와 설혹 누가 왕래하였다 하드라도 유리창을 통하여 조사실 내부를 들여다보는 것은 불가능하였던 사실이 은폐되어서는 안 된다는 점을 지적하고자 한다.

또 위 경찰관 김해성 등은 문귀동의 동료이고 검찰조사과정에서 문귀동의 거짓말을 뒷받침 하기 위한 허위진술을 일삼다가 사후에 탄로가 나자 진술을 번복한 사실이 있어 그들의 진술 내용을 도저히 신빙할 수 없을뿐 아니라 설령 그들이 밀폐되어 있는 문귀동의 조사실 바깥을 왔다갔다 했다할지라도 내부를 들여다볼 수 없었던 이상 성고문사실을 목격할수는 없었을 것이 너무나도 당연할 일인데 어떻게 그들의 진술내용을 가지고 성고문이 없었음을 단정하는 근거로 삼을 수 있다는 것인지 실로 이해할 수가 없다.

이것이 우리가 검찰발표내용을 믿을 수 없는 세번째 이유이다.

(4). 검찰발표는 "권양과 함께 부천경찰서 유치장에 수감되어있던

0018

최모여인(32세), 박모여인(30세) 등도 ... 권인숙이 폭행
을 당했다는 말은 유치장에서 한 일이 있으나 성적모욕을 당했
다는 말은 한 사실이 없다고 진술" 하였다고 주장하면서 그것
이 마치 "성적모욕이 없었다"는 검찰의 결론을 뒷받침할 무슨
근거나 되는 것처럼 내세우고 있다.

그러나 권양이 2차성고문을 당한 직후 유치장 내에서 위 두
여인에게 차마 피해사실전부를 이야기할 수가 없어서 일부분
만을 이야기한 일이 있다고 하는 점은 권양이 본 변호인단 접견
시(7. 2.)부터 밝혔을 뿐 아니라 검찰조사과정에서도 당초부터
밝힌 바이고 강제추행을 당한 처녀가 피해사실을 곧바로 타인
에게 전부 이야기하지 아니한다는 것은 경험칙에 부합하는 지극
히 자연스러운 일인 것이다.   그렇다면 어째서 위 두 여인의
진술내용이 권양의 주장을 뒷받침하는 근거가 아니라 도리어
그것을 부인하는 근거로 사용될 수 있는 것인지 우리로서는 도저히
이해할 수가 없다.

뿐더러 우리가 알기로는 위 두 여인은 검찰조사과정에서 자신

0019

"6. 7. 밤 문귀동이 1호조사실에서 권양을 조사할 당시 자신은 맞은편 방에 있었다. 문귀동이 자신에게 수갑을 가져오라고 하여 갖다주었으며 그때 문귀동이 책상의자에 앉고 권양이 그 앞에 꿇어앉아 있는것을 보았다. 그 후 문귀동이 권양을 데리고 단 둘이 2호조사실로 들어가 문을 걸어잠근채 조사를 하였다. 조사가 끝날 무렵 문귀동이 방문을 열고 수갑키를 달라고하여 갖다주었다. 조사시간은 분명히 기억나지 않으나 밤 8시 이후부터 10시반 경까지쯤 되는 것 같다. 조사실 안은 어두웠다. 조사도중 권양의 비명소리를 들었다."

검찰이 발표에서 "성적모욕이 없었다"고 강변하는 것은 이같은 검찰의 조사성과를 스스로 뒤엎는 것밖에 되지 않는다.

6. 6. 새벽 다른 형사가 입회한 자리에서도 "권양의 수치심을 건드리기 위하여" 옷을 벗기고 젖가슴을 "주먹으로 쥐어박았다"고 하는 문귀동이 6. 7. 토요일 깊은 밤 중에 자신의 조사실 안에서 문을 걸어잠그고 불을 끈채 권양에게 수갑을 채워놓고 한시간 반 가량을 권양과 단 둘이 있는 상태에서 아무런 성적

0020

모욕을 가한 일이 없다고 한다면 그것을 대체 누가 믿겠는가?

"이것이 우리가 검찰의 발표내용을 믿을 수 없는 다섯번째 이유이다.

(6). 검찰발표에 의하면 문귀동은 권양의 수치심을 건드리기 위하여 웃옷을 벗게 한 후 "가슴부위"를 주먹으로 몇차례 쥐어박았다고 한다. 처녀의 가슴이란 곧 젖가슴이다. 처녀의 젖가슴을 성적모욕이 아닌 다른 목적으로 구타한다는 일이 있을 수 있겠는가?

권양 자신은 시종일관 문귀동이 유방을 주물렀다고 주장하고 있는데 검찰은 대체 무슨 근거에서 "주물른 것과는 크게 다르고 손등으로 가볍게 툭툭 건드린 것" 이라고 단정하는가? 문귀동이 그렇게 말했기 때문에 그대로 믿는다는 것인가? 만일 검찰이 문귀동의 비행을 은폐하거나 비호할 의사가 없었다면 최소한 "주물른 것인지 손등으로 건드린 것인지는 분명치 않다" 라고는 말하였어야 할 것이다.

0021

이것이 우리가 검찰의 발표내용을 믿을 수 없는 여섯번째

이유이다.

그밖에도 우리가 검찰의 발표내용을 믿을 수 없는 이유는 얼마든지

있으나, 일일이 열거할 수 없으므로 이 정도로 줄인다.

3.   우리는 권양에 대한 비열하고 악의적인 모함과 중상으로 가득찬

"공안당국의 분석자료" 라는 것을 보고

분노를 느끼지 않을 수 없다.   이 정체불명의 "공안당국"

이란 대체 누구인가?   검찰발표문에는 그같은 "분석자료"가 전혀

포함되어있지 않았으니 검찰이 아닌 것만은 확실하다.   그렇다면

권양 사건을 조사한 당사자도 아닌 검찰 이외의 "공안 당국"이란

것이 도대체 어떤 근거에서 권양의 피해사실 주장을 "운동권학생의

상습적인 의식화투쟁의 일환"이라고 단정할 수 있는가?

물거니와 지금까지 "운동권학생들"이 "고문·폭행·추행 사건을 조작"

한 전례라도 있단 말인가?   우리가 아는한 지금껏 양심수들이 제

기한 수사과정에서의 고문 등 가혹행위 주장이 수사당국의 수사기피로

0022

인하여 진위가 가려지지 않은채 묻혀버린 일은 있을 지언정 철저

한 수사 끝에 조작된 허위주장으로 판명된 사례는 단한 건도 없다.

더우기 명문대학까지 다닌 스물세살의 처녀가 어떻게 "의식화투

쟁의 일환"으로 하필이면 추악한 성고문을 당하였다는 허위주장을

조작해 낼 수가 있겠는가?

　　　우리는 이제　　　　　　"공안당국"이

　　　　　　　　　　　　　그 "분석"이라는 것이 대체 어떤 객

관적사실에 기초한 것이고 어떤 논리적근거에 입각한 것인지를 분

명히 밝히기를 요구한다.　　만약 그렇지 않을 경우, 우리는 이

번의 검찰발표가 수사 이전에 이미 결론부터 내려놓은 저 "공안당국"

의 "분석"에 억지로 발을 맞추기 위하여 검찰자체의 수사결론과는

상반되게 왜곡될 수밖에 없었던 것이라고 단정하지 않을 수 없다.

4.　　우리는 7. 1.과 7. 2. 두차례에 걸쳐 권양을 접견하면서부터

이미 권양의 피해사실주장이 진실이라는 확고한 심증을 얻었다.

0023

첫째로 권양의 진술태도로 보아 의심할만한 점이 전혀 없었으며,

들째로 권양의 진술내용이 너무나도 소상하고 구체적이어서 어떤

천재적인 소설가라도   상상만으로는 꾸며낼

래야 꾸며낼 수 없을 정도로 절실한 현실감이 있었으며,

셋째로 권양이 성고문사실을 폭로하게 되기까지에 이른 경위가 지

극히 자연스러운 것이었으며(처음에는 부모에게도 밝히지 아니하다

가 나중에 접견을 온 변호사 앞에서 마치 남의 일인 것처럼 강간

죄의 성립여부를 물었고 망서리던 끝에 성고문사실의 일부를 밝혔으며

그것이 검찰에 보고되어 검사가 묻게되자 비로소 울면서 사건의 전모

를 밝히기 된 것임.)

넷째로 신체의 자유를 박탈당하고 갇혀있는 약자의 처지에서 막강한

국가권력을 상대로 있지도 아니한 사실을 날조해 낸다는 것은 심리

법칙상 상상하기 어려운 일이었으며,

마지막으로 무엇보다도 자존심있는 처녀가 당하지도 아니한 강제추행

을 당했다고 주장한다는 것은 있을 수 없는 일이라고 판단되었기 때

문이었다.   0024

검찰 조사결과는 위와같은 우리의 심증이 적중하였음을 모든 객관적인 증거자료로써 뒷받침하였다. ──── 우리가 검찰의 발표내용을 믿을 수 없는 여섯가지 이유는 동시에 권양의 성고문주장이 진실임을 입증하는 여섯가지 이유이기도 하다.

특히, 6. 7. 밤의 조사상황에 관하여 문귀동이 처음부터 완강하게 조사시간을 밤 7:45 경부터 9:45경까지였다고 속이고 조사실 내에 불이 켜져있었으며 3명의 형사가 입회한 가운데에서 조사하였다고 거짓말하였던 점에 비추어보면 당시 문귀동이 권양의 주장내용과같은 성고문 범죄를 저지른 것이 사실이었음은 경험칙과 논리칙에 비추어 넉넉히 인정되고도 남음이 있다고 하지 않을 수 없다. 도대체 성고문이 없었다면 무엇때문에 한시간 반 동안이나 불을 끄고 입회인도 없이 조사를 했을 것인가, 불문가지이다.

뿐더러 부천경찰서 간부진과 형사들이 공모하여 집요하게 문귀동의 범행을 은폐하기 위한 허위진술을 꾸며내었던 점에 비추어 볼때 이 사건이 문귀동 일개인의 우발범행이 아니라 경찰권력 내부의 성고문계획에 따라 자행된 조직범죄였다는 사실도 명백히 입증되

0025

없다고 확신한다.

이제 우리들 변호인단 일등은 우리의 모든 직업적 및 인간적인 긍지와 명예와 성실성을 걸고 단호하게 선언한다. 권양의 모든 주장은 단 한치의 거짓도 없는 진실이다. 권양은 그 자신이 제출한 고소장과 본 변호인단이 제출한 고발장에 기재된 내용 그대로 부천 경찰서 내에서 필설로 이루 형언할 수 없는 천인공노할 추악한 성고문의 만행을 당하였다.

이 전대미문의 만행의 진상이 백일하에 공개되고 그 관련자들이 남김없이 의법처단되기 전까지는 우리들 변호인단은 물론이요 이 나라의 모든 국민과 산천초목까지도 결코 잠잠하지 아니할 것이다.

두렵고 두렵다.

이 사건 하나에 우리 사회의 법질서와 인권과 인륜도덕의 존폐가 달려있다.

1986. 7. 18.

변호사 고 영구, 김 상철, 박 원순,

이 돈명, 이 상수, 조 영래,

0026 조 준희, 홍 성우, 황 인철.

1986. 7. 18.

변호사 고 영 구

변호사 김 상 철

변호사 박 원 순

변호사 이 돈 명

변호사 이 상 수

변호사 조 영 래

변호사 조 준 희

변호사 홍 성 우

변호사 황 인 철

0027

※ 이 글은 보다 많은 사람들이 볼 수 있도록
되도록 많이 복사하여 나눠 읽읍시다.

2 발 인 : 고영구 / 김상철 / 박연운 / 이돈명 / 이상수 / 조영래 / 조준희 / 홍성우 / 황인철 (이상 전원 변호사)

미고발인 : 문귀동 (부천경찰서 수사과 형사) / 옥봉환 (부천경찰서 서장) / 성명불상 (부천경찰서 수사과장) /
성명불상 3인 (부천경찰서 수사과 형사, 성고문서 입회자)

1. 우리는 공문서위조 피의사건으로 인천소년교도소에 수감중인 권양의 변호인들로서, 권양을 접견한 후 통문으로 전해들은 성
고문 행위가 사실이라는 것을 확인하고, 놀라움과 분노를 금할 길이 없었다. 거 나라쯤하여서나 있었음직한 비인간적인
만행이 이 땅에서도 버젓이 자행되고있다는 사실을 알게 되었을 때, 경악과 공분을 느낌과 아울러 인간에 대한 믿음마저
앗아가는 듯한 암담한 좌절감을 느끼게 되었다. 단순히 충동적인 음욕때문에 일어난 것이 아니고, 성이 고문의 도구로
악용되어 계획적으로 자행되었다는 점에서, 이 사건은 우리에게 더 큰 충격을 불어 일으켰다. 이제 우리는 사건의 실상을
확인하고서도 계속 침묵을 지킨다는 것은 변호인으로서의 최소한의 의무마저 포기하는 것이라고 결론짓고, 이 사건 관련자들
고발하여 처벌을 요구하기에 이르렀다.

2. 고발내용

6·4. 밤 9시경 집에서 형사들에 의해 부천서로 연행되어 4층 공안담당실(?)로 가서 그 다음날인 6·5 새벽 3시경까지
조사를 받았다. 권양의 혐의 사실에 대한 조사 외에도 양승조 등 인천사태 수배자들 중 지면관계가 있거나 소재를
아는 사람이 있는지 여부에 관하여 집요하게 캐물었다.

6·5. 아침 9시경 1층 수사계 수사실로 끌려갔다. 정모 경사가 권양에 대한 수사를 담당키로 되어서 4층 420호실(421호
실인지도 모른다)로 데려갔다. 이때부터 오후 6시경까지 공문서(주민등록증) 위조혐의와 수배자에 관한 조사를 받고
보호실로 가서 하룻밤을 잤다.

6·6. 새벽 4시에 누군가가 데리러 와서 상황실로 데려갔다. 이 때 부천경찰서에 무슨 비상(非常)이 걸린 모양으로 형사
들이 다들 일찍 출근해 있는 상태였다. 서장이 권양을 보더니 "권양이 수사에 너무 협조를 안하는군"하고 확를 내며
밖으로 나갔다. 수사에 너무 협조를 안한다는 것은 형사들이 권양에게 인천사태 수배자들 (대부분 인천노동연합운동
관계자들)의 명단을 대면서 그중에서 아는 사람이 있는지 여부를 묻고 특히 인천노동운동연합 양승조 의원장을 알고 있는
가 또는 양승조를 아는 사람이라고 알고 있는지를 캐물었는데, 권양이 이에 대하여 아는 사람이 있는데도 협조를 하지
않는다는 이야기였다. 서장이 밖으로 나간후 상황실장 (는이 그후 약간 되어나온 듯한 인상, 당시 전투복을 입고 상
환실장"이라는 완장을 두르고 있었다)이 말하기를 권양이 너무 말을 안하는데 아무래도 지금까지 조사과정에서 나온
사람들 (인천사태 수배자들을 지칭한 듯함)과 한 팀이 아니냐고 하면서 형사 문귀동 ("문기동"인지도 모른다). 형사
들이 "문반장"이라고 부르고 있었으며 얼굴은 검은편, 입술이 두껍고 눈이 매서운 험악한 인상, 키는 보통, 나이는 35-
36세 정도로 보이고 말씨는 서울말씨. 스스로 밝힌바에 의하면 예전에 "부평"에 있었다고 함. 이하 이들 "문귀동"이
라고 부른다)을 보고 "문기동- 자네가 맡아서 해 보게"하면서 수사를 지시했다. 이에 문귀동은 권양을 1층 수사계
수사실 ("조사실"인지도 모른다)로 데리고 가서 새벽 4:30부터 6:30분경까지 사이에 걸쳐 아래와 같이 추잡한
성고문 ("1차 성고문"이라 부른다)을 자행하였다.

(1) 우선 문귀동은 권양에게 "너 쇠는 정책변화도 들먹일 죄도 아니고 하니 수배자 중에서 아는 사람을 불어라.
불기만 하면 훈방하겠다"고 강요하였다. 권양이 끝내 모른다고 하자 문귀동은, "이년 안 되겠다"하고 온을 벗으면서
"나는 5·3 사태때 여자만 다뤘다. 그때 들어온 년들도 모두 아랫도리를 발가벗겨서 책상에 올려 놓으니까 다 불더
라. 네 몸(자궁)에 봉 (막대기를 지칭한 듯하나 정확히 무슨 의미인지는 모른다)이 들어가면 안 불겠느냐"고 협박하였다.

(2) 권양이 겁에 질려서 벌벌 떨고 있으니까 문귀동은 권양에게 옷을 벗으라고 강요하였다. 권양이 상의 겉옷 (자켓)
가 남방만을 벗고 티와 브래지어 및 바지를 입은채로 있자 문귀동은 다른형사 1명 (젊고 직급이 낮은 듯함)을 불러들여
옆에 서 있게 한후 스스로 권양의 바지 단추와 지머를 풀어 밑으로 내리면서 "너 처녀냐? 자위행위 한 본적 있느냐?"
고 브래지어를 들추어 밑어 올리면서 "젖가슴 생김으로 보니 처녀가슴 같지가 않다"고 하는등 더러운 수작을 하면서 끌
이어 격발 살려 달라는 권양의 애원을 뿌리치고 권양의 바지를 벗겨 내렸다.

(3) 이에 권양이 극도의 굴욕감과 수치심과 공포를 이기지 못하여 엉겁결에 한 친구 (노동현장취업 과정에서 사귀게
된 이모라는 여성으로 그 이름이 본명인지 여부도 모른다. 인천사태와 관계없는 사람임)의 이름을 대자 문귀동은 권양
에게 그 친구의 인적사항을 자세히 적으로요 요구하였다. 권양이 의 이모양의 인적사항에 대하여 자세히 모른다고
하자 문귀동은 엎에 서 있던 형사에게 "고춧가루 물을 가쳐오라"고 지시한 후 권양에게 "책상의로 올라가라고 하면서
"기억이 자중에 봉을 집어넣어야 말하겠느냐"라고 협박하였다. 권양이 의 이모양이 자취하던 집이라는 곳의 위치를
적어넣자 문귀동은 그제서야 일단 수확을 거두었다는 듯 조사를 중단하고 권양의 바지 지머를 올리게 했으나 그러면서도
다시 "진짜 처녀냐"고 물었다.

(4) 뒤이어 태균과 형사들이 권양에게 수배자들의 사진을 보여 주면서 의 이모양이 수배자들 중의 하나가 아닌지를
확인하였다. 그후 권양은 보호실로 옮겨가서 그곳에서 하룻밤을 잤다.

0028

- 2 -

0029

6.7.(토요일) 아침 7시경 문귀동이 다시 권양을 데리고 가서 "너 망승조 안다고 그랬지?"라고 물어, 모른다고 대답하자 "더 아는 사람이 있으면 얘기하지"고 번번 더구지지며 눌러보냈다. 아침 9시경 누가 권양을 데리러 와서 1층수사과로 갔는데 가보니 상황실에 상황실장, 정오도 경사, 문귀동 등 10여명의 형사들이 모여 있었다. 그들은 권양이 알려준대로 이 모양의 자취하던 집이라는 곳을 방문해 보니 그런 사람이 자취한 일이 없다고 하더라면서 집주인 여자를 권양과 대질시켰다. 대질신문결과 그들은 권양이 이제까지 한말이 거짓말이라고 판단, 경사 정오도가 권양을 한대 후려쳤고 상황실장은 권양에게 "앞으로는 이제까지 대우한 것과는 달라질테니 있다고 오늘 저녁에 두고 보라"고 협박하면서 옆에 있던 문귀동을 보고, "저녁 때 그런 방법으로 조사해"라고 지시하였다. 문귀동이 권양을 다시 보호실로 데려가면서 "네가 이제까지 한 말은 전부 거짓말이니 그냥 안두겠다"고 협박하였다. 그날 낮 내내 권양은 보호실에서 대기하면서 불안과 초조에 떨었고 한시바삐 검찰청으로 송치되기만을 기다리는 심정이었다. 그러나 다른 수감자들에게 물어본 결과 여기서 한 열흘쯤 있어야 검찰청으로 넘어간다는 절망적인 대답을 들었다. 밤 9:00경 문귀동이 다시 권양을 1층 수사과 조사실(문귀동이 조사하는 방의 옆방)로 불러냈다. 당시는 수사과 직원들이 모두 퇴근하였고 청내는 모두 불이 꺼진 상태였으며 조사실 역시 불이 꺼져 있었는데 다만 건물 바깥에 있는 등에서 나오는 외광(外光)에 의해 방안의 물체들을 어렴풋이 식별할 수 있는 정도였다. 문귀동은 토요일 밤에 퇴근도 못하고 "일"을 해야 된 데, 무척 화가 난 듯 권양에게 "독한 년"이라고 하면서 "남들은 다 퇴근했는데 네년때문에 한 밤중에 또 조사를 해야 된다. 위에서 그년 되게 악질이니 족치라고 했다."라고 겁을 주고 나서 다른 (남자)형사 2명을 불러들여 권양의 양팔을 등뒤로 돌려 놓은 상태로 양손목에 수갑 (이른바 "뒷수갑")을 채우게 하고 그 자세로 무릎을 굽혀 앉힌후 안쪽 다리 사이로 각목을 끼워 넣고 넓적다리와 허리부위 등을 계속 짓밟고 때리게 하면서 권양에게 이 모양의 본명과 출신학교, 사는 집 등을 불도록 요구했다. 이로 인하여 권양의 넓적다리는 시퍼렇게 멍이 들고 퉁퉁 부었다. 권양이 고통과 공포를 참지 못하여 비명을 지르자 문귀동은 "이년이 어디서 소리를 꽥꽥 지르느냐, 소리지르면 죽여버리겠다. 너같은 년하나 죽이는 건 아무것도 아니다"라고 윽박 질렀다. 뒤이어 문귀동은 권양에게 수배자 중 아는 사람을 대라고 추궁하다가 계속 모른다고 하니까 옆에 있던 형사에게 고문기구를 가져오라고 소리쳤고, 그 형사가 검은색 가방을 가져오자 불을 켜더니 인천노동운동연합 소속 수배자 20명의 인적사항과 사진 등이 편철되어 있는 서류철을 꺼내어 한장씩 넘기면서 아는 사람을 대라고 다구쳤다. 권양이 모른다고 하자 문귀동은 "이년 안되겠다"고 하면서 형사들을 내보내더니 권양을 조사실 옆에 있는 작기 방(양쪽이 창문으로 되어 있음)으로 데리고 갔다. 이때가 밤 9:30경으로, 이때부터 밤 11:00경까지 약 1시간 반 동안에 걸쳐 문귀동은 인면수심의 실로 천인공노할 야만적 추행을 저지르면서 권양을 고문하였다. 이 한시간 반 동안 방안에는 계속 불이 꺼져 있었고 권양은 계속 뒷수갑을 찬 채로 문귀동과 단 둘이 약 2평정도의 방안에 남아 있었으며 주위에서도 전혀 인기척을 느낄 수 없는 절망적인 상황에 처해 있었다. 문귀동이 저지른 추행의 내용은 다음과 같다.

(1) 먼저 권양에게 아버지가 뭘 하느냐고 물어 권양이 식당을 한다고 거짓 대답하자 (권양의 아버지는 법원서기관인데 권양이 공무원신분에 영향이 있을까봐 걱정이 되어 거짓 대답한 것임) 문귀동은 "비시시 웃더니 "간첩도 고문하면 다 부는데 네년이 독하면 얼마나 독하냐"는 최지의 말을 하면서 권양에게 옷을 벗으라고 명령하였다. 권양이 윗옷만을 벗자 문귀동은 권양에게 다시 뒷수갑을 채운 후 브래지어를 위로 들어올리고 바지를 풀러 지퍼를 내리더니 권양의 국부에 손을 집어넣었다. 권양이 비명을 지르자 소리지르면 죽인다고 하면서 윽박질렀다.

(2) 권양의 팬티마저도 벗겨내리고 의자 두 개를 서로 마주보는 상태로 놓고 권양을 한쪽의자 위에 수갑찬 손을 의자 뒤로 돌린 상태에서 앉게 하고, 문귀동 자신은 맞은편 의자를 바짝 끌어당겨 그 위에 앉아 권양의 몸과 밀착된 자세를 취한 다음 계속 수배자의 소재를 불 것을 강요하였다. 권양이 제발 이러지 말라고 애원하였으나 문귀동은 들은척도 않고 "너 같은년 하나 여기서 죽어도 아무일 없다"고 협박하였다. 이때부터 문귀동은 수시로 권양의 젖가슴을 주무르고 국부를 만지며 권양의 몸에 자신의 몸을 비벼댔다.

(3) 그후 문귀동은 권양을 일으켜 세워 바지를 완전히 발가벗기고 윗도리 브래지어를 밀어올려 젖가슴을 앞으로 드러나게 해놓은 상태에서 뒷수갑을 찬 채로 앞에 놓인 책상 위에 엎드리게 한 후 자신도 아랫도리를 벗고 권양의 뒷쪽에 붙어서서 자신의 성기를 권양의 국부에다 갖다대었다 떼었다 하기를 몇차례에 걸쳐 반복하였다. 이 때 권양이 절망적인 공포와 경악과 굴욕감으로 인하여 거의 실신상태에 들어가자 문귀동은 권양을 다시 의자위에 앉히더니 담배에 불을 붙여 강제로 몇모금을 빨게 하였다.

(4) 잠시후 문귀동은 권양을 의자 밑으로 난폭하게 끌어내려 바닥에 무릎을 꿇게 하고 앉힌후 자신은 의자에 앉아 권양이 자신의 성기를 정면으로 보도록 하는 자세로 조사를 계속하였다. 그러던 중 문귀동은 권양의 얼굴을 앞으로 잡아 당겨 입이 자신의 성기에 닿도록 하면서 자신의 성기를 권양의 입에 넣으려 하다가 권양이 놀라서 고개를 돌리니까 난폭하게 권양의 몸을 일으켜 세운후 강제로 몇차례 키스를 시도하였다. 권양이 입을 벌리지 않고 고개를 돌리니까 문귀동은 입을 권양의 왼쪽 젖가슴쪽으로 가져가더니 유두를 세차게 빨기를 두어차례에 걸쳐 하였다.

(5) 그후 문귀동은 다시 권양을 책상 위에 먼저번과 같은 자세로 엎드리지게 해 놓고 뒤쪽에서 자신의 성기를 권양의 국부에 몇차례 갔다 대었다 떼었다 하는 짐승과 같은 동작을 반복하던 끝에 크리넥스 휴지를 꺼내는 소리가 들리더니 그것으로 권양의 국부를 닦아내고 옷을 입혔다. 이때가 밤 11시경

(6. 위와 같은 짐승과 같은 동작을 계속하는 동안에도 문귀동은 집요하게 권양에게 아는 수배자의 이름을 대라고 강요하였고 권양이 비밀을 지키면 죽이겠다고 하면서 윽박질렀다. 또 위와같은 동작을 하는 중간간에 문귀동은 권양을 서너차례 정도 쉬게 하면서 먹다 남은 술병인 담배를 입속에 밀어넣고 물을 마시게 하였으며, 그리고나서는 다시 같은 협박을 하면서 수배자의 관한 추궁을 계속하였다. 그동안에 권양은 고통을 이기지 못하여 자신의 집에 찾아왔던 어느 여성 한사람의 이름과 동인이 응연핬다니던 회사의 이름을 댔으며 문귀동은 권양이 말한 내용을 종이게 스게 하였다. 위와 같은 추악한 만행을 저지른 후 문귀동은 권양에게 호언하기를 "내가 당한 일을 검사앞에 나가서 얘기해 봤자 아무 소용없다. 검사나 우리나 다 한 동속이다."라고 하였다.

밤11시가 지나 문귀동은 기진맥진해 있는 권양을 으로실로 데리고 가서 권양의 소지품을 챙기더니 유치장으로 끌고갔다. (이때 권양에 대한 구속영장이 발부된 상태였음.) 일반적으로 유치장에 처음 입감될때는 흉수색을 의하여 속옷을 벗게 하는 것이 상례인데, 이때 문귀동은 여교관을 부르더니, "내가 다 봤으니 몸검사는 필요없다. 독방을 주어라"고 지시하고는 돌아갔다. 그후 권양은 검찰에 송치되기까지 유치일여서 열흘간을 보냈는데 한동안은 아무것도 먹지 못하였고 먹으면 계속 토하며 밤에는 악몽에 시달리느라고 잠을 제대로 이루지 못했다. 몇차몇차 자살을 하고 싶은 충동이 엄습해 왔으나, 점차도 자신의 여성으로서의 전도를 희생해서라도 이와같은 끔찍한 일이 다시는 "일어날 수 없도록 하기" 위하여 끝까지 싸우겠다는 결의가 굳어지면서 가까스로 자살충동을 이겨냈었다.

6.16. 교도소로 옮겨진 후 지금에 이르기까지도 권양은 계속 악몽에 시달리고 있다. 인천법원의 서기관으로 재직하던 권양의 부친은 이 사건의 충격으로 사표를 제출하였다. 권양의 소식이 인천교도소내의 재소자들에게 알려지면서 교도소 내 양심수 약 70여명이 문귀동의 구속등을 요구하는 무기한 단식투쟁에 들어갔고 권양자신도 6.28.부터 시작하여 7.2.현재까지 닷새째 단식을 계속하여 건강이 극도로 악화하였다.

3. 이상이 국가권력의 집행자인 경찰에 의하여 저질러진 저 전대 미문의 추악한 성 폭행고문에 관하여 피해당사자인 권양이 변호인들 앞에서 밝힌 내용의 개요이다. 우리는 권양의 진술태도나 기타 보손 정황으로 보아 위 내용이 진실인 것으로 확신한다. 우리는 이 입에 담기에도 더러운 "천인공노할 만행이 다른곳도 아닌 경찰서 안에서 다른 사람도 아닌 경찰관에 의하여 저질러졌다는 사실에 대하여 실로 경악과 전율을 금치 못한다. 더구기 이같은 만행이 인권옹호직무수행자라는 검찰에까지 상세히 알려졌음에도 불구하고 그 범인이 아직까지도 버젓이 경찰관신분을 유지하면서 밝은 세상을 활보하고 있는 데에 이르러서는 이 나라에 과연 법질서라는 것이 형식적으로 나마 존재하고 있는 것인지를 근본적으로 의심하지 않을 수 없다. 최고학부까지 다닌 한 여성이 입에 담기조차 수치스러운 저 끔직한 강제추행을 당한 사실을 스스로 밝힌 이상 그 밖에 도 무슨 "증거"가 필요해서 수사를 못한다는 말인가? 경찰서 안에서는 목격자만 없으면 어떤일이 일어나도 좋다는 것인가? 검찰이 경찰의 인권유린행위에 대하여 이와 같이 수수방관적인 태도를 취한다면, 무고한 시민들이 경찰권력의 횡포아래 희생되는 것을 막을 길도 전혀 없게 된다. 이 사건의 진상이 철저히 규명되고 직접 범행을 저지른 자는 물론 관계책임자들이 모두 엄중히 처단되지 않는 한, 이후 여성들은 경찰서 앞을 지날 때마다 공포에 질리게 될 것이다. 이에 우리는 말설토 이루 형언할 수 없는 분노에 치를 떨면서 먼저 저 인간의 탈을 쓰고서는 차마 상상도 할 수 없는 패륜을 저지른 문귀동을 고발한다. 피고발인 상황실장, 성명불상자와 경찰서장 옥동우는 제반정황으로 보아 문귀동의 범행에 공무 가담하였거나 교사.방조하였거나 또는 적어도 이를 알면서도 묵인.방치하고 단속하지 아니하였음이 명백하다고 인정되므로 아울러 고발한다. 피고발인 형사성명불상자 3명 역시 문귀동의 범행에 공모.가담 또는 방조한 혐의로 고발한다. 이 사건을 그대로 두고서는 실로 인간의 존엄성이니 양심이니 인권이니 법질서니 민주주의니 하는 말들이 입에 올리기조차 낯도 겂다.

우리들 고발인 일동은 문귀동을 비롯한 피고발인들 전원이 지체없이 의법처단되지 않는 한 이 사건에서 한치도 물러나지 않고 모든 합법적수단을 동원하여 기어이 고발의 실을 거두도록 총력을 기울일 결의임을 천명한다.

4. 우리는 귀청이 이 사건을 수사함에 있어서 다음 몇가지 점에 유의하여 줄 것을 촉구한다.

첫째, 이 사건은 문귀동이라는 변태성욕에 사로잡힌 한 개인에 의하여 우발적인 충동으로 저질러진 단독 범행이 아니고 경찰권력조직 내부의 의도적인 성고문계획에 따라 자행된 조직범죄임이 명백하다고 생각된다. 우리는 귀청이 이 끔직한 조직범죄의 전모를 낱낱이 파헤쳐 이 범죄가 어느 선에서부터 계획되었는지를 밝히고 피고발인들 외에도 일체의 관련자들을 남김없이 의법처단하여 주기를 강력히 요청한다.

둘째, 피고발인들의 소행은 강간죄 내지는 강제추행죄로 의률될 수 있음을 물론이나 이 점은 친고죄이므로 이 고발에서는 제외하였고 다만 인신구속에 관한 직무를 행하는 자의 폭행 및 가혹행위에 해당하는 부분만을 들어 고발한다. 그러나 우리는 이사건이 종래에 흔히 볼 수 있던 통상의 고문.가혹행위의수법이 아니라 여성에 대한 인간적 마귀를 노리고 반인륜적인 성고문 수법을 사용한 범행이며 더구기 피의사실에 관한 조사가 아닌 단순한 수배자의 검거를 위한 수단으로 이와 같이 끔직한 범행이 자행되었다는 점을 중시한다. 우리는 1984.9.4.에도 청량리경찰서 형사들로부터 경희대 여학생들이 성욕력을 당한 사실을 기억하고 있다. 인천 5.3사태로 구속된 미의자와 가족이 자기담도 부천경찰서에서 권양과 비슷한 고문을 당했다고 주장한 것들은 바 있다. 이 사건으로 인해 우리는 의 주장도 사실이라는 심증을 굳히게 되었고, 특정서에서 성이 고문의 수단으로 제도도화되어 악용되고 있음을 알게 되었다. 인간의 존엄성을 최고의 이념으로 삼고있는 민주법치국가에서 위와 같은 야만적이고. 비인간적인 만행이, 제도적으로 자행된다는 것은 더 이상 묵과될 수 없다. 이 사건을 최단시일내에 철저히 수사하여 그 진상을 밝힘으로서 검찰이 추후라도 이 사건을 은폐하거나 비호할 의도가 없음을 분명히 하여야 할 것이다. 1986. 7. 5.

-3-

0030

1986년 7월 5일

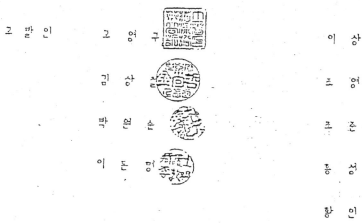

그 말 인   고 영 구

         김 상 철   이 상 수

         박 원 순   조 영 래

         이 돈 명   조 준 희

                         홍 성 우

                         황 인 철

         인천지방검찰청장   귀하.

              - 권양의 심경에 관한 메모 -

    지금 나는 슬프고 착잡한 심정을 금할 수가 없읍니다. 단식 열흘째 스민 배를 움켜 쥐고 어지러운 머리 흔들면서 누워
있는 교도소 동지들이 목숨을 건 외침을 들을 수 있는 지, 이땅 어디에도 들을 수 없는 건지 답답하기만 합니다.
    처녀의 몸으로 강제로 성적 추행을 당하고 그 등분한 현실 앞에 기어코 진실을 밝혀내고자 최후의 생존권마저 포기한 지
이미 열흘이 지났읍니다. 저 추악하고도 가증스러운 문귀동과 부천서는 온갖 허위 증거들 들이대며 오히려 저를 무고죄로 고소
하였읍니다. 검찰에서는 수사를 시작했다는 명목으로 지칠 대로 지친 저에게 아침부터 밤 11시까지 끌려다닌 것을 강요하고
증거법만을 강조하면서 문귀동을 구속시키기 어렵다는 발악을 하고 있읍니다. 저들의 간악한 흉계에 새토운 분노가 치솟아
오릅니다.
    마요정권의 살인적 고문에 수업이 유린당하고 짓밟히면서 심지어 목숨마저 빼앗긴 수많은 민주 영령들은 저들의 증거불충분
이라는 명목으로 한낱 거짓말이라고 묻아부치고 있는 것이 아니고 무엇입니까. 저와 저의 교도소 동지들은 민주 영령들의 신음
소리가 들리는 듯하여 이 분노를 그대로 삭힐 수가 없읍니다. 차가운 교도소 마룻장을 베고 숨이 끊어지는 그 순간까지도 저희
들은 진실을 밝혀내고야 말것입니다.   (86. 7. 7. 제3차 변호인단 접견록 중에서)

0031

同 資料는 所謂 〃拷問 및 容共造作
沮止 共同對策委〃의 明洞聖堂 不法集會
事前 沮止의 不可避性 및 當爲性을
밝히는 說明資料인바 後遺症 極小化에
積極 活用하시기 바랍니다.

安企部 2局長

용공조작, 수사시비 폭로 불법 집회

사 전 저 지 에 따 른 설 명 자 료

o 일부 재야단체와 문제 종교인 및 극렬학생들이 주도하는 소위 '고문 및 용공 조작 저지 공동대책위원회'는 오는 7월 19일 14:00 명동성당에서 용공조작 및 수사시비 폭로 불법집회를 열고, 피의자 수사에 대한 유언비어를 유포하여 국민 오해를 의도적으로 유발, 선동하려 하고 있음

o 좌경 운동권 집회의 성격이 분명한 이같은 모임에 일부 정치인이 가세하는 것은 이해가 가지 않는 일임

o 관계당국은 동 집회가 법적인 요건을 충족하고 있지 못함은 물론, 허위 사실의 유포 확산으로 사회 안정을 해칠 우려가 현저하므로 동 집회의 개최를 허용치 않기로 했음

집회 불허사유

o 동 집회는 대규모 군중 집회를 통해 이미 사실이 규명된 남민전 관련 장기수 사건을 비롯 부천서 수사 시비 사건의 진상을 허위로 날조, 유포함으로써 사회 안정을 파괴하고 불안을 야기할 우려가 지대한 반사회적 모임임
   - 지난 7.16 검찰이 발표한 동 사건 진상과 조치내용은 그동안 엄정한 수사를 통해 밝혀진 극히 객관적인 결과임

o 동 집회는 소위 용공조작 대책위원회 위원으로 일부 종교인이 참여하고 명동성당이라는 종교시설을 이용한다는 점에서 종교집회로 생각할 수 있으나 대회의 성격과 내용을 감안할때 장소를 교회 건물로 이용했을 뿐 순수 종교

행사가 아닌 사회 혼란 선동 집회임

- 동 집회를 준비하는 대책위원들은 일부 종교인외에 정당 정치인, 재야 불순단체와 구속자 가족들로 구성되어 있어 순수 종교인들이 아님

- 당국이 입수한 동 집회의 준비내용과 행사계획은 주로 구속자의 수사 문제에 대한 허위사실 유포와 날조 모략에 국한되고 있음

o 따라서 동 집회를 방치할 경우 그들의 활동 전략과 과거의 불법집회 전례를 감안할때 현저히 사회적 혼란을 야기할 우려가 있으므로 동 불법집회는 집시법 규정에 따라 사회 안정과 질서유지 차원에서 당연히 사전 방지해야 할 것으로 판단함.

o 또한 동 집회는 현재 관계당국에서 수사중이거나 재판에 계류중인 유사한 사건에 대하여 다중이 모여 사실을 왜곡함으로써 좋지않은 영향을 미칠 우려가 큼

- 학원 소요사건 등과 관련하여 수사과정에서 고문을 주장하고 있는 피고(피의자)의 공소사실(혐의사실)도 왜곡시킬 우려가 있음

o 동 집회는 지금 한국에서 진전되고 있는 안정된 분위기 속의 민주정치 발전을 크게 저해할 우려가 있음

- 사회의 전반적이고 점진적인 민주개혁의 실현이 한국이 안고있는 당면과제 이므로 이러한 국가적 목표를 폭력과 선동으로 방해하려는 일부의 책동은 오히려 우리 정부의 일관된 민주화 노력에 부담을 줄 수도 있음

- 이같이 민주발전을 위한 정부의 적극적인 의지와 관용적 자세를 악용하여 사회 불안을 조성, 정치적 이익을 거두려는 이러한 집회는 진정한

0005

민주화를 위해 자제되어야 함

- 동 집회는 안정속에서 개헌과 민주화를 바라는 절대다수 국민의 여망을
  배반하는 것임

0 정부는 지금까지 이러한 민주화 노력과 함께 국민의 기본권 보호와 신장을
   위해 최선의 노력을 기울여 왔고 실제 개선의 실적이 국제적으로도 인정
   받고 있음

- 소위 '권인숙 사건'에 대해서는 엄정한 수사를 통해 관련 경찰관의
  파면, 권인숙의 무고 무혐의 처리 등 공정한 조치를 했음

- 수사관에 대해서도 사전 철저한 교육을 통하여 피의자 폭행 고문 금지
  등 국민 기본권의 보장과 인권의 신장에 각별한 노력을 기울이고 있음.

0036

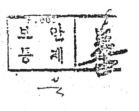

주 미 대 사 관

번호 : USW(F)-1400

수신 : 장관 (미북.정문.해신   ) 발 : 주미대사

제목 : 아주관계 삼략   1매

Drawing Board

"HERE'S A TOUR YOU MIGHT ENJOY, SEN. HELMS... TWELVE POLICE STATES IN FOURTEEN DAYS..."

THE WASHINGTON POST   SATURDAY, JULY 26, 1986 A23

0037

건 호 : USW(F) - 1866

수 신 : 장관 (미북.정문.해선)   발 산 : 주 미 대사

지 목 : 고문반대 불법집회   4 매

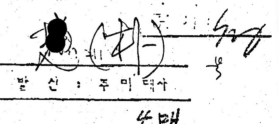

THE SUN

SUNDAY, JULY 20, 1986   1CA

Members of the opposition New Korea Democratic Party clash with police in attempt to reach a Seoul cathedral for planned protest rally.

SOUTH KOREA

Thousands of police fire tear gas to block rally

A massive force of South Korean police fired tear gas yesterday to block dissidents from holding a banned protest rally over the alleged sexual abuse of a young woman during police questioning last month.

Dissident leader Kim Young Sam and lawmakers from the main opposition New Korea Democratic Party tried to force a path through cordons of 2,000 police to the Roman Catholic Myongdong Cathedral in Seoul, where the rally was to be held. Kim Dae Jung, a top dissident, was placed under house arrest yesterday morning to keep him from attending the rally.

The party said its vice president, Yang Sun Jik, was hit in the side by a tear gas shell and badly bruised. Dissident sources said police picked up at least 23 people for questioning.

The New Korea Democratic Party has been campaigning for democratic reforms in the government of President Chun Doo Hwan, who took power in 1980 during the chaos that followed the 1979 assassination of President Park Chung Hee.

0038

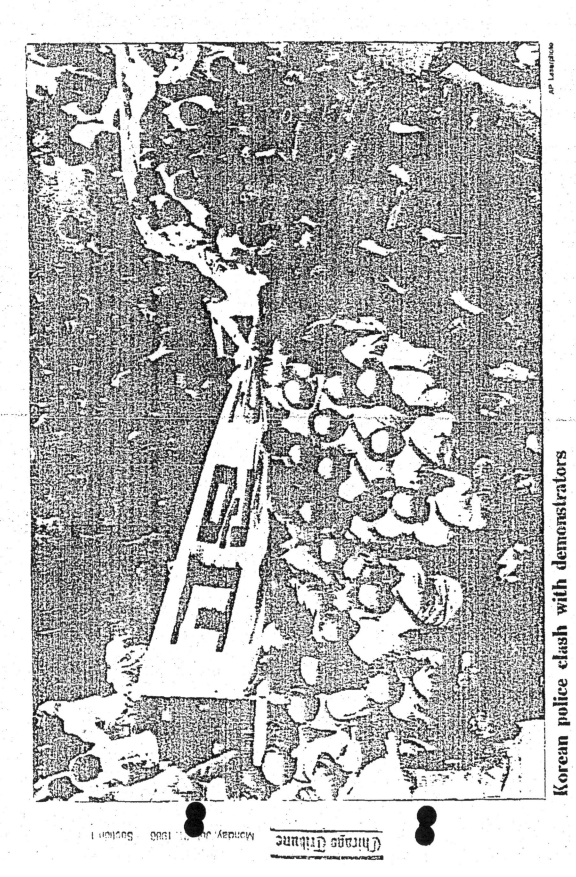

Korean police clash with demonstrators

South Korean riot police battle with members of the opposition New Korea Democratic Party Saturday in Seoul as the protestors tried to attend an anti-government rally called to protest the alleged torturing of jailed dissidents. Police hold opposition leader Kim Dae-jung and other activists under house arrest for several hours earlier Saturday to prevent their taking part in the rally.

AP Laserphoto

Chicago Tribune

Monday July 21, 1986 — Section 1

Police block S. Korean protest

From Herald Wire Services

SEOUL, South Korea — Riot police fired tear gas Saturday to prevent thousands of South Korean opposition activists from holding a rally to demand a new probe into the alleged torture of jailed dissidents.

More than 2,000 security officers ringing the Myongdong Roman Catholic Cathedral blocked the demonstrators, who were led by dissident leader Kim Young Sam.

When some 700 people tried to march to the cathedral from another direction, police fired tear gas to disperse them. Some of the protesters staged street sit-ins and others hurled rocks at police. There were no immediate reports of injuries.

THE CHRISTIAN SCIENCE MONITOR   MONDAY, JULY 21, 1986   2

South Korean dissidents rally against government

Seoul

Riot police fired tear gas Saturday to prevent thousands of opposition activists from holding an anti-

New Korea Democratic Party clashes with Seoul police

government demonstration at a downtown church.

More than 2,000 security officers ringing the Myongdong Roman Catholic cathedral repelled dissident leader Kim Young Sam and others demonstrating against President Chun Doo Hwan. Earlier, about 400 police surrounded the house of opposition leader Kim Dae Jung to prevent him from attending the rally.

136-3

Los Angeles Times 14 Part 1/Saturday, July 12, 1986

Don't Beat Suspects, S. Korean Police Told

From Reuters

SEOUL, South Korea—National police headquarters warned investigators Friday not to beat or otherwise breach the human rights of criminal suspects after four policemen were fired over allegations that a prisoner was sexually abused, police sources said.

State prosecutors said Wednesday that a policeman beat a 21-year-old woman dissident on the breasts, but they denied that she was sexually harassed during questioning last month.

At a news conference Friday, the woman's lawyers accused the prosecution of covering up facts about what they called the "sex torture" of the woman, a former student.

1306-4

0041

외 무 부   착 신 전 보

번 호 : USW-3460   일 시 : 607221606   종 별 :

수 신 : 장 관 (미북,정문)

발 신 : 주 미 대사

제 목 : 명동성당 불법집회 및 권인숙 사건 조사결과--국무성평가

대 : WUS-2836, 2815, AO-45

1. 김삼훈 참사관은 금 7.22.(화)   DAVID BLAKEMORE   국무성 한국과장을 면담, 부천경찰서 수사과정에 대한 정부 조사결과 및 조치내용과 명동성당 불법집회 관련 내용을 설명함.

2. 동 과장은 부천경찰서 수사과정에 대한 <u>정부의 신속한 조치를 평가한다고</u> 하였는 바, 동인 언급요지 아래 보고함.

가. 권인숙 사건

1) 어느나라에나 경찰에 의한 가혹행위나 불법행위는 있을수 있으며, 중요한것은 여사한 가혹행위를 어떻게 조치하는 것인가임.

2) 금번의 경우 한국정부가 문제가 발생하자 신속한 수사를 통해, 관계관 파면, 문책등 필요한 조치를 취한것을 높이 평가하며, 문제의 확대를 방지하는 좋은계기가 되었다고봄.

3) 수사결과를 발표함에 있어서 권인숙은 나쁜사람이므로 다소 부당하게 취급되어도 당연하다는 듯한 느낌을 갖게한점은 <u>좋지 못한 측면</u>이라고 생각함.

4) 미정부로서는 수사결과 발표시 모든 내용이 전부 밝혀진 것인지의 <u>여부에 의구심</u> <u>이 없는 것은 아나나,</u> 한국정부의 신속한 대응조치로 문제를 가라앉힌 것을 평가함.

나. 명동성당 불법집회

1) 사건의 진상과 여사한 사건을 국내정치적 목적으로 악용하려는 명동성당 집회는 별개의 이슈이며, 명동성당 집회와 관련해서는 집회자체나 정부의 불허조치에 대해서 특별한 의견이 없음.

- -

√ 미주국   차관실   1 차보   정문국   청와대 ∘ 총리실   안 기

0042

2) 주한미대사관으로 부터도 상세 내용을 보고받았으나, 평가나 의견이 없었음.

3. 평가

가. 아국정부의 신속한 조치를 평가하는 한편, 과거지사로서 국내적으로 더 이상 문제가 확대 되지 않을 것으로 보고 또 그렇게 기대하는 인상이었음.

나. 명동성당 불법집회가 큰 관심의 대상이라고 하면서도, 국무성의 견해나 평가를 삼가하였는바, 야권에 의한 정치적 악용 및 이로인한 사회혼란을 우려하는 한편, 정부가 취한 조치의 불가피성을 이해하는 것으로 보였음.

다. 미국내적으로 국무성 정오 브리핑시등 문제가 제기될 가능성은 적은 것으로 보았으며 (답변준비도 하지 않는다함) 의회 및 일부 인권단체에 의한 서한문의 가능성이 있을것으로 예상하였음.

(대사 김경원-차관)

예고 : 1986.12.31. 일반
성명

PAGE   2

0043

외 무 부   착 신 전 보

번 호 : CGW-0647   일 시 : 607241715   종 별 :

수 신 : 장 관 (영재,정일,기정동문)

발 신 : 주 시카고 총영사

제 목 : 교민동태 5 (자료응신 제86-20호)

1. 부천경찰서 성적모욕 사건관련 당지 반정부 그룹이 당관에 항의데모를 계획하고 있다는 정보가 있는 가운데 7.22 당관에는 교포로부터 항의 및 폭언 전화가 옴.

2. 당관은 본건 예의주시 대처하고 있음.

(총영사 이승곤-국장)

예고 : 86.12.31.까지

영교국   차관실   2차보   정문국   청와대   안 기   미주국

PAGE 1   86.07.25 15:53
                                       외신 2과 통제관

0044

관리 번호	81 -1641

	분류번호	보존기간

발 신 전 보

번 호 : WUS-2951   일 시 : 60728 1500   전보종별 : _____

수 신 : 주   미   대사 (참여사)

발 신 : 장   관 (미북)

제 목 : 명동성당 집회관련 국무성 논평

                대 : USW-3460

        7.26(토)자 중앙일보 보도에 의하면 McGruder 국무성
동아.태 <del>충</del>당 대변인이 대호 사건에 대해 아래와 같이 논평했다
하는 바,동 사실 여부 및 상세내용 파악 보고 바람.

        1. 평화적 집회를 열 권리에 대한 여하한 침해도 유감으로
           생각하며 모든 당사자들에게 폭력사용을 자제하도록
           촉구함.

        2. 한국에서 진정한 민주주의로의   진전은 오로지 평화적
           대화를 통해 이루어질 수 있으며 가두에서의 대결을
           통해서 이루어질수는 없음.

                                    (미주국장 강신성)

예고문예고의거 1986.12.31..일반.(기)
직위   심병

| | | 보안
통제 | 서명 |

양 고 재	86 년 7 월 26 일	북 미 과	기안자	과 장	심의관	국 장	차 관	장 관		외 신 과	접수자	통제
			조	서명			서명				오	

0075

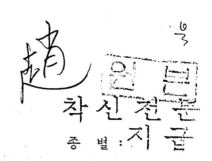

외 무 부   착신전보
지급

번 호 : NYW-0969   일 시 : 60728 1650   종 별 : 지급

수 신 : 장 관(미북,영재)

발 신 : 주 뉴욕 총영사

제 목 : 고문반대 시위

1. 금 7.28. 당지 교민 여성모임중의 하나인 소위 여성청우회(KOREAN AMERICAN WOMEN
FOR ACTION) 주관으로 12:00-13:30간 당관앞에서 소위 부천 성고문 사건에관한
항의 집회를갖고 한국 여성단체 연합 생존권대책 위원회의 공개항의서 채택 및 정부
에대해 동사건에대한 독립적인 수사를 요구하는등 내용의 반정부 유인물을 배포하였
음.

2. 동 집회에는 약 50여명이 참가하였는바 배포된 유인물을 파편 송부하겠음.

3. 여성 청우회는 주로 YMCA 간부 출신들로 구성된 단체로 회원수는 약 4-50명 정
도이고 반정부 성향을 띠고 있는 것으로 알려져있음

(총영사김태지-국장)

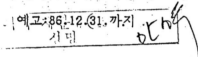

예고:86.12.31 까지
서면

미주국   차관실   2차보   영교국   청와대   안기   총리실

┌─────────────────────────────────────┐
│ ─── ＮＣＣ 關聯團体 ───   │
│   │
│ 富川署捜査是非 糾弾 祈禱會 對備策   │
└─────────────────────────────────────┘

1. 概　　況

○ 新民黨，民推協 等이 加擔한 〝捜査是非

　共同對策委〞（共同代表：朴炯圭 等 14名）

　主管의 明洞聖堂에서의 〝富川署事件

　暴露大會〞（7.19）가 挫折되자

○ ＮＣＣ捜査是非對策委，基督青年協（ＥＹＣ），

　基督學生聯（ＫＳＣＦ），教會女性聯 等

　ＮＣＣ 關聯團体에서는 7.27(日)14：00

　光化門所在 聖公會 서울大聖堂에서

　500余名 參席裡에 〝富川署 捜査是非

　糾弾祈禱會〞開催 企図

0047

2. 關聯 動向

○ 聖公會 朴鍾基 神父 (N C C 副會長),
金在烈 神父 (N C C 人權委員)와 朴準喆
(E Y C 中央委議長) 等은 7.24 08:00
~ 09:40間 聖公會主教舘에서 會同코
同 祈禱會 開催決定

※ N C C 는 祈禱會 說教者를 朴炯圭로
內定했다가 李亭學牧師 (예長統合 楊平
敎會擔任)로 交替

○ 金在烈 神父 (中道性向)는 祈禱會 開催
背景 等과 關聯

- 天主敎女子修道長上聯合會 主催로 開催된
〃祈禱會〃 (7.21)에 刺戟받아
改新敎에서도 推進하게 된 것이라고
말하고

0048

- 豫想되는 在野勢力의 迎合과 基督
  靑年·學生들의 피켓·油印物 搬入
  等 不純策動에 對해 當局에서
  豫防·措置해 줄 것을 要請

3. 對備策

가. 基本方針

"搜査是非" 關聯 不純宗教集會인
點을 勘案, 初動段階에서 强力
沮止

0049

나 . 細 部 對 策

區　分	細　部　對　策	備　考
行事關聯者 事前警告	聖公會　金聖洙主教　및　朴鍾基 主任神父　接触 o　不純集會임을　强調, 場所使用 　　不許토록　誘導 o　行事强行時 -　日曜彌撒　妨害받지　않는 　　範圍內에서　遮斷 -　聖堂內에서　不純活動 　　聖堂側　責任임을　喚起	安 企 部 治安本部
遮斷 沮止	o　非信徒選別　遮斷 ※　11：00彌撒以後　出入者 　　全面遮斷 o　行事場周邊　檢問·檢索　强化 -　06：00부터　聖堂隣接地域 　　檢問·檢索組　運營（私服組）	治安本部

0030

区　分	細　部　對　策	備　考
	－　　學生，勤勞者，在野人物， 　　　　拘束者家族　遠隔　遮断 －　　不純油印物，피켓　等　押收 　　　　및　關聯者　連行　隔離 o　騷擾誘發者　全員　連行　調査	
兵力運用 計劃 別途 樹立施行	o　兵力　遠隔　待期 o　街頭示威　企図　封鎖	治安本部
行事主動者 自家遮斷	EYC，KSCF　核心幹部 ※　朴準喆（EYC），許春中（EYC） 　　鄭海東（EYC），黃仁成（KSCF） 　　等	〃
報道縮小 調整	o　事實報道에　局限（縮小報道） o　捜査是非關聯內容　報道　一切 　　排除	文公部 安企部

0051

區　　分	細　部　對　策	備　　考
外國公舘 事前通報	聖公會　서울大聖堂　周邊에 位置한　美大使舘과　英國大使舘 에　對해　事前　不法集會　遮斷 內容　說明	外務部

0052

7.27(일) 인권관련 성공회 집회 진행 경과 (당시부레고)

- 11:00-12:20 예배, 일부 신민당 의원 참석

- 14:50   신민당의원 부인 합세, 노상기도회 개최시도,
               모두 강제 해산

- 15시 부터 일부 신민당의원 및 민통연 간부등 세문안교회로
  이동

- 15:40 세문안 교회에서 Placard 를 든 200여명의 청년들이
         가두 진출시도, 진압하는 과정에서 산발적 투석전이
         전개

- 16:00 성공회정문이 닫혀지고 상황 종료, 사무실에 10여명
         농성

- 16:10 세문안 교회 계단에서 연좌, 모두 강제 해산

* 13:10 미국 ABC 기자가 당시 상황 취재

0052

"왜 예배까지 막느냐"

〈金錫顯기자〉

性고문 규탄 기도회 무산

議員부인등 連行

86. 7. 29

NCC 고문대책위원회(회장 尹斑雄목사)·NCC여성위원회등 23개 기독교단체가 결성한 「性고문대책위원회」(위원장 朴英淑)·

議員들 폭행규탄

新民黨서 성명

新民黨의 萎三鎬부대변인은 28일 27일의 聖公會기도회사건에 대한 성명을 발표,...

0054

피의자性폭행 美國務省서 논평

[워싱턴=張斗星특파원] 美國

務省은 지난 19일의 明洞사

건에 대해 『평화적 집회를 열

권리에 대한 여하한 침해도

유감으로 생각하며 모든 당

사자들에게 폭력사용을 자제

하도록 촉구한다』고 말했

다.

「매그루더」국무성 東아시아

담당 대변인은 『韓國에서 진

정한 민주주의에로의 진전은

오로지 평화적 대화를 통해

이루어질수 있으며 가두에서

의 대결을 통해서 이루어질

수는 없다』고 논평했다.

외 무 부

번 호 : USW-3535　　　　　일 시 : 607281526

수 신 : 장 관 (미북)

발 신 : 주 미 대사

제 목 : 명동성당 집회관련 국무성 논평

대 : WUS-2951

　대호건 국무성 한국과는 당지 아국특파원들의 질문이 있으므로 지난주 아래와같은
보도지침을 준비하였는바, 대호 중앙일보 보도내용은　MCGRUDER　대변인이 당지 특파
원의 전화 문의에 대하여 동 지침에 따라 답변한것이었음.

KOREA:POLICE BLOCK HUMAN RIGHTS RALLY

Q:DO YOU HAVE IN COMMENT ON KOREAN GOVERNMENT ACTIONS JULY 19 TO PREVENT A RALL
Y AGAINST PURPORTED POLICE MISTREATMENT　OF PRISONERS HUMAN RIGHTS VIOLATIONS?

A:WE UNDERSTAND THE KOREAN GOVERNMENT TOOK STEPS TO BLOCK THE RALLY BECAUSE IT
REGARDED IT AS ILLEGAL UNDER A LAW BANNING GATHERINGS FEARED TO CAUSE SOCIAL UNRE
ST.AS WE HAVE STATED BEFORE,THE US REGRETS ANY INSTANCE OF INFRINGEMENT ON THE R
IGHT OF PEACEFUL ASSEMBLY AND CALLS ON ALL SIDES TO FOREGO THE USE OF VIOLENCE.T
RUE PROGRESS TOWARD DEMOCRACY IN KOREA CAN BE ACHIEVED ONLY THROUGH PEACEFUL DIA
LOGUE,NOT CONFRONTATION IN THE STREETS.

(대사 김경원-국장)

예고 : 86.12.31까지

미주국　차관실　1차보　정문국　청와대　총리실　안 기

PAGE　1

번 호 : USW(F) - 1401　　　　0128 0950

수 신 : 장관 (미북.정문.해신)　　발 신 : 주미대사

제 목 : 아국내정중-성공회서당집회

The New York Times MONDAY, JULY 28, 1986 A4

South Korean Dissidents Detained Before Meeting

SEOUL, South Korea, July 27 (AP) — Riot police detained scores of dissidents today who tried to attend a prayer meeting to protest the reported sexual abuse of a Government opponent while she was in police custody.

Hundreds of police officers turned other protesters away from the meeting site, a downtown Anglican cathedral. One man was reported injured. The exact number of dissidents taken away was not immediately known.

Opposition spokesmen said 19 protesters were later released.

Earlier, the Government ordered the dissident Kim Dae Jung confined to a hotel room to prevent him from attending the meeting, his aides said.

Opposition groups say the Government tried to cover up the case of the woman who was reported molested early last month. The prayer meeting was the latest in a series of protests.

THE CHRISTIAN SCIENCE MONITOR　　MONDAY, JULY 28, 1986　2

S. Korean police detain dissidents at meeting

Seoul

Riot police yesterday detained scores of dissidents who tried to attend a prayer meeting called to protest the alleged sexual abuse of a government opponent in police custody.

Hundreds of police turned other protesters away from the meeting site, a downtown Anglican cathedral. Earlier the government ordered dissident leader Kim Dae Jung confined to a hotel room to prevent him from attending the meeting, his aides said.

0057

The Washington Times

PAGE A / MONDAY, JULY 28, 1986

Korean plainclothes police hustle a protester away from scheduled prayer rally yesterday at an Anglican church in downtown Seoul. The well-drilled riot police contained the rally with no incidents nor injuries reported.

Riot police outsmart protesters in Korea

By Edward Neilan
THE WASHINGTON TIMES

SEOUL — Thousands of South Korean uniformed riot police and plainclothesmen played cat and mouse with several hundred demonstrators yesterday, successfully preventing them for the second straight weekend from holding a prayer meeting to protest alleged police sexual abuse of a female activist.

There was considerable surging against police shields and some brief fighting but no injuries as 50 demonstrators were arrested outside the Anglican cathedral where a 2 p.m. service was scheduled. Those arrested were later released, police said.

Unlike last weekend's attempted service at Myungdong Catholic Cathedral protesting government torture, there was no tear gas fired by police.

A government spokesman said yesterday's service, sponsored by 23 organizations belonging to the National Council of Churches, was "banned because the meeting was not part of the Anglican church's regular Sunday schedule of events and having a large number of opposition political activists on the program would turn the meeting into a non-religious event."

Demonstrators here said the protest was a failure because it did not provoke the police into headline-making retaliation on the eve of a week of political discussions on constitutional revision.

The service was scheduled to protest alleged police torture and sexual abuse of Kwon In Suk, 22, a woman labor activist who is now on a hunger strike. A police interrogator is charged by Miss Kwon with forcing her to disrobe and then beating her on the breasts and using offensive language.

About 2,000 well-disciplined riot police with shields moved first one group of demonstrators, then another, away from the gates of the cathedral in Seoul's downtown Taepyong-no district near the historic Duk-su Palace.

The police then parted ranks while plainclothes "grabbers" picked up demonstrators and hustled them away into waiting buses and vans. The vice presidents of the opposition New Korea Democratic Party, Lee Ki-taek and Kim Hyong-woo, and party Human Rights Committee Chairman Park Chan Jong were pushed away from the gate but not arrested.

Police seemed to have the most problems with some 25 wives of opposition politicians who ran down the middle of the street toward the cathedral. Surrounded by riot police, they sat down in the middle of the 12-lane boulevard, snarling Sunday traffic.

Plainclothes police emerged from buses parked in front of the Seoul Shinmun newspaper and carried away the women, some of whom swung handbags at police and shrieked protests.

Opposition leader Kim Dae-jung checked into the suburban Sheraton Walker Hill Hotel Saturday but found more than 100 plainclothes police blocking his exit from the hotel yesterday. One of Mr. Kim's aides said "a district police chief told Mr. Kim yesterday morning he would not be allowed to attend the service."

Barred from attending the service at the Anglican cathedral, several politicians joined a service a few blocks away at the Saemunan Presbyterian Church. There police also swept away crowds of onlookers and cordoned off the entrance to the church.

1401-2

About 50 radical students taunted police from the church courtyard, and there was some scuffling and rock-throwing by youths. Pleas by church elders calmed the students, and police kept their distance outside the church gates.

Inside the cathedral, an Anglican spokesman told The Washington Times, only one speaker on the service program, Rev. John Kim, was able to lead prayers against torture because of police hindered the entrance of the other participants.

The spokesman, the Rev. Joseph Lee, who is visiting Seoul this summer from his studies at the Virginia Theological Seminary, said the Rev. Oh Chung-il of the Evangelical Church of Korea, delivered an impromptu sermon "citing Koreans' historical example of respect of morality and peace now being shamed by instances of torture."

THE WALL STREET JOURNAL MONDAY, JULY 25, 1986

South Korean riot police detained scores of dissidents, including at least two opposition members of the National Assembly, outside an Anglican cathedral in Seoul. They were arriving for a meeting to protest a policeman's alleged sexual abuse last month of a young woman who had been arrested while working as a labor organizer.

1401-3

0059

외 무 부

번 호 : USW-3580   일 시 : 60730 1133   종 별 : 지급

수 신 : 장 관 (미북)

발 신 : 주 미 대사

제 목 : 불법집회 사건 및 권인숙 사건 국무성 논평

국무성은 7.29 명동성당 및 성공회성당 불법집회 사건 및 성고문 사건에 대한 국무
성 논평을 요구한 기자들의 질의를 접수, 추후 서면답변을 대변인실에 계재하였는바,
동 질의, 답변내용을 별송 (USW(F)-1411) 함.

(대사 김경원-국장)

미주국   차관실   1 차보   2 차보   청와대   안 기   정문국

PAGE   1   86.07.31   11:40
                                                   외신 1과   통재관

0060

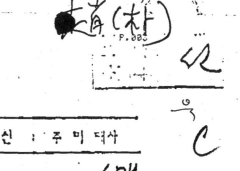

JUL.30 '86 10:28 KOREAN EMBASSY WASHINGTON DC

1412

번 호 : USW(F) - 07301110

수 신 : 장관 (미북.정문.해(L))   발 신 : 주미대사

제 목 : 성고문사건 반응   /매

The Washington Times   PAGE 6A / WEDNESDAY, JULY 30, 1986

U.S. protests Korean's treatment

The United States criticized the South Korean government yesterday over the alleged sexual torture of a woman dissident and expressed regret at the blocking of opposition rallies. In a written answer to journalists' queries, the State Department said it believed the woman, named only as Miss Kwon, was more severely abused than officially acknowledged. A policeman and three of his superiors were fired after a Seoul prosecutor found the policeman had beaten and verbally abused the prisoner.

"There are credible allegations that police mistreatment of Miss Kwon was more severe and harsher than acknowledged," the State Department said. "We find such treatment of prisoners deplorable and appalling. As in all cases involving torture and mistreatment of prisoners, we urge the Korean government to punish as provided by law those responsible."

0061

번 호 : CSW(F) V 072-0950   긴급

주 신 : 장관-(해외공보관장)마북.   발 신 : 주 미 대사

제 목 : 미국무성 논평 (서면)

Posted:

Questions Taken at the July 29, 1986 Daily Press Briefing

Q: A couple of times in the last few weeks the South Korean
authorities have stopped rallies (one was to go from the
Catholic cathedral toward the chief Anglican church in Seoul).
Do you have any reaction to that?

A: WE UNDERSTAND THE KOREAN GOVERNMENT TOOK STEPS TO BLOCK THE

RALLIES BECAUSE IT REGARDED THEM AS ILLEGAL UNDER A LAW BANNING

GATHERINGS THAT COULD LEAD TO SOCIAL UNREST. AS WE HAVE STATED

BEFORE, THE US REGRETS ANY INSTANCE OF INFRINGEMENT ON THE

RIGHT OF PEACEFUL ASSEMBLY AND CALLS ON ALL SIDES TO FOREGO THE

USE OF VIOLENCE. TRUE PROGRESS TOWARD DEMOCRACY IN KOREA CAN

BE ACHIEVED ONLY THROUGH PEACEFUL DIALOGUE, NOT CONFRONTATION

IN THE STREETS.

Q: Do you have anything on the alleged sexual torture of a
Korean trustee?

A: A KOREAN GOVERNMENT PROSECUTOR INVESTIGATING THE CHARGES

HAS FOUND THAT THE POLICEMAN INVOLVED BEAT AND VERBALLY ABUSED

THE PRISONER, A MISS KWON. THE POLICEMAN AND THREE OF HIS

SUPERIORS HAVE BEEN DISMISSED FROM THEIR JOBS. THERE ARE

CREDIBLE ALLEGATIONS THAT POLICE MISTREATMENT OF MISS KWON WAS

MORE SEVERE AND HARSHER THAN ACKNOWLEDGED.

WE FIND SUCH TREATMENT OF PRISONERS DEPLORABLE AND APPALLING.

AS IN ALL CASES INVOLVING TORTURE AND MISTREATMENT OF

PRISONERS, WE URGE THE KOREAN GOVERNMENT TO PUNISH AS PROVIDED

BY LAW THOSE RESPONSIBLE AND TO TAKE STEPS TO ASSURE THAT SUCH

ABUSES ARE NOT REPEATED.

0062

※ 美國務省, 韓國의 性拷問
　　　　　　　　 및 等 糾彈 集会 저지 非難

NNNN
a YK0255

292353 :PM-KOREA-AMERICAN
U.S. SLAMS SEOUL OVER RALLY HALT, SEXUAL TORTURE CHARGE
   WASHINGTON, JULY 29, REUTER - THE UNITED STATES TODAY
CONDEMNED THE SOUTH KOREAN GOVERNMENT OVER THE ALLEGED SEXUAL
TORTURE OF A WOMAN DISSIDENT AND SAID IT REGRETTED THE BLOCKING
OF OPPOSITION RALLIES.
   THE STATE DEPARTMENT, IN A WRITTEN ANSWER TO JOURNALISTS'
QUERIES, SAID IT BELIEVED THE WOMAN, NAMED ONLY AS MISS KWON,
WAS MORE SEVERELY MALTREATED THAN OFFICIALLY ACKNOWLEDGED.
   A POLICEMAN AND THREE OF HIS SUPERIORS WERE DISMISSED FROM
THEIR JOBS AFTER A SEOUL GOVERNMENT PROSECUTOR FOUND THE
POLICEMAN HAD BEATEN AND VERBALLY ABUSED THE PRISONER.
   +THERE ARE CREDIBLE ALLEGATIONS THAT POLICE MISTREATMENT OF
MISS KWON WAS MORE SEVERE AND HARSHER THAN ACKNOWLEDGED,+ THE
STATE DEPARTMENT SAID.
   +WE FIND SUCH TREATMENT OF PRISONERS DEPLORABLE AND
APPALLING. AS IN ALL CASES INVOLVING TORTURE AND MISTREATMENT
OF PRISONERS, WE URGE THE KOREAN GOVERNMENT TO PUNISH AS
PROVIDED BY LAW THOSE RESPONSIBLE AND TO TAKE STEPS TO ASSURE
THAT SUCH ABUSES ARE NOT REPEATED,+ IT ADDED.
   [THE WRITTEN ANSWER] ALSO CONDEMNED THE SEOUL GOVERNMENT FOR
BLOCKING TWO OPPOSITION RALLIES OVER THE PAST TWO WEEKENDS, ONE
AROUND THE CITY'S CATHOLIC CATHEDRAL AND THE OTHER FOCUSED ON
ITS MAIN ANGLICAN CHURCH.
   (3/4)+AS WE HAVE STATED BEFORE, THE U.S. REGRETS ANY INSTANCE OF
INFRINGEMENT ON THE RIGHT OF PEACEFUL ASSEMBLY AND CALLS ON ALL
SIDES TO FORGO THE USE OF VIOLENCE,+ IT SAID.
   REUTER

0063

```
QQ
4021
     R XXX
    US-SOUTH KOREA,0215
    CONCERN OVER HUMAN RIGHTS VOICED BY US
    WASHINGTON (AP) - THE U.S. STATE DEPARTMENT EXPRESSED CONCERN
TUESDAY ABOUT THE HUMAN RIGHTS SITUATION IN SOUTH KOREA, INCLUDING
''CREDIBLE ALLEGATIONS'' THAT AN ARRESTED PROTESTER WAS BEATEN BY
POLICE.
     ''WE FIND SUCH TREATMENT OF PRISONERS DEPLORABLE AND
APPALLING,'' THE DEPARTMENT SAID IN A STATEMENT ISSUED TO
REPORTERS. ''IN ALL CASES INVOLVING TORTURE AND MISTREATMENT OF
PRISONERS, WE URGE THE KOREAN GOVERNMENT TO PUNISH, AS PROVIDED BY
LAW, THOSE RESPONSIBLE AND TO TAKE STEPS TO ASSURE THAT SUCH ABUSES
ARE NOT REPEATED.
     RECENT DEMONSTRATIONS IN SEOUL HAVE BEEN SPARKED BY REPORTS THAT
THE DISSIDENT, A WOMAN, WAS BEATEN AND MOLESTED WHILE IN CUSTODY.
THE DEPARTMENT NOTED THAT A GOVERNMENT PROSECUTOR HAS FOUND THAT
POLICEMEN WERE INVOLVED. FOUR POLICE OFFICIALS HAVE BEEN DISMISSED.
     ''THERE ARE CREDIBLE ALLEGATIONS THAT THE POLICE MISTREATMENT
WAS MORE SEVERE AND HARSHER THAN ACKNOWLEDGED,'' THE DEPARTMENT
SAID.
     THE DEPARTMENT CALLED ON ALL SIDES IN SOUTH KOREA TO ''FOREGO
THE USE OF VIOLENCE,'' BECAUSE ''THE PROGRESS TOWARD DEMOCRACY IN
KOREA CAN BE ACHIEVED ONLY THROUGH PEACEFUL DIALOGUE, NOT
CONFRONTATION IN THE STREETS.''
     AT THE SAME TIME, IT SAID ''THE UNITED STATES REGRETS ANY
INSTANCE OF INFRINGEMENT ON THE RIGHT OF PEACEFUL ASSEMBLY.''
     END

AP-NY-07-30-86 0059GMT
```

0064

韓国関係主要外信報道

1986.7.28(月) 16:00

(第 2 便)

外信名	内　　　　容	페이지
Reuter, AFP,UPI (서울發)	國務總理室　勤務　前公務員，記者會見 -反政府　聲明　發表（권인숙사건 김박비난）	1

0065

NNNN

a YK0385

280607 :PM-KOREA

FORMER CIVIL SERVANT ACCUSES GOVERNMENT OF TORTURE

SEOUL, JULY 28, REUTER - A FORMER CIVIL SERVANT ACCUSED
SOUTH KOREA'S GOVERNMENT TODAY OF TORTURING POLITICAL
DETAINEES AND URGED CIVIL SERVANTS TO DISOBEY WHAT HE TERMED
THE DICTATORIAL REGIME.

KIM HYONG-BAE, 35, TOLD A NEWS CONFERENCE HE WAS DISMISSED
FROM THE PRIME MINISTER'S OFFICE LAST WEEK AFTER SHOUTING
ANTI-GOVERNMENT SLOGANS AT POLICE STOPPING PEOPLE FROM
ATTENDING AN OPPOSITION RALLY HERE EARLIER THIS MONTH.

NO OFFICIAL COMMENT ON HIS STATEMENT WAS AVAILABLE.

IN HIS +DECLARATION OF CONSCIENCE+, WHICH WAS CALLED A
BRAVE ACT BY OFFICIALS OF THE OPPOSITION NEW KOREA DEMOCRATIC
PARTY (NKDP), KIM SAID A 23-YEAR-OLD WOMAN DETAINEE WAS
SEXUALLY TORTURED DURING POLICE QUESTIONING LAST MONTH. THE
GOVERNMENT HAS DENIED THE ALLEGATION.

ACCUSING PRESIDENT CHUN DOO HWAN'S GOVERNMENT OF ILLEGALLY
USING CIVIL SERVANTS TO STAY IN POWER, KIM DECLARED: +CIVIL
SERVANTS ... SHOULD NO LONGER BE THE RUNNING-DOGS OF
DICTATORS.+

HE SAID HE WAS FINALLY DISILLUSIONED WHEN POLICE
RELENTLESSLY FIRED TEAR GAS TO DISPERSE THOUSANDS OF PEOPLE
TRYING TO ATTEND AN OPPOSITION RALLY ON JULY 19 TO PROTEST
AGAINST ALLEGED POLICE TORTURE OF POLITICAL DETAINEES.

THE GOVERNMENT BANNED THE MEETING ORGANISED BY THE NKDP
AND DISSIDENT GROUPS, SAYING IT WOULD INCITE UNREST BY
SPREADING FALSE RUMOURS.

MORE

0066

NNNN
a YK0386

280611 :PM-KOREA =2 SEOUL
    DISSIDENT LEADER KIM YOUNG-SAM, WHO ATTENDED THE NEWS
CONFERENCE AT THE NKDP HEADQUARTERS, SAID THE FORMER
GOVERNMENT OFFICIAL'S MOVE MADE HIM BELIEVE DEMOCRACY WOULD BE
REALISED IN SOUTH KOREA IN THE NEAR FUTURE.
    +IT WILL MOVE THE HEARTS AND MINDS OF THE ONE MILLION
CIVIL SERVANTS (IN SOUTH KOREA) AND THERE WILL BE A SECOND AND
A THIRD KIM HYONG-BAE,+ HE SAID.
    POLITICAL OBSERVERS SAID KIM HYONG-BAE WAS THE FIRST CIVIL
SERVANT TO PUBLICLY CRITICISE THE CHUN GOVERNMENT SINCE IT
CAME TO POWER IN 1980.
    THE NKDP, WHICH HAS DEMANDED THE RESIGNATION OF THE WHOLE
CABINET FOR ALLEGED PERSECUTION OF DISSIDENTS, SAID IT WOULD
TAKE LEGAL STEPS TO REVOKE THE DISMISSAL OF THE OFFICIAL.
    AN NKDP SPOKESMAN SAID IN A STATEMENT TODAY POLICE BEAT
AND DETAINED SOME OPPOSITION MEMBERS OF PARLIAMENT AND THEIR
WIVES TO STOP THEM ATTENDING AN ANTI-TORTURE PRAYER MEETING AT
AN ANGLICAN CHURCH YESTERDAY.
    PRIME MINISTER LHO SHIN-YONG TOLD PARLIAMENT LAST MONTH
THE GOVERNMENT WOULD TRY TO END HUMAN RIGHTS ABUSES AS PART OF
EFFORTS TO BRING GREATER DEMOCRACY TO SOUTH KOREA.
    REUTER

0067

GLGL

EXR0097 4 /AFP-AI89

KOREA

SACKED KOREAN OFFICIAL ISSUES ANTI-GOVERNMENT STATEMENT

SEOUL, JULY 28 (AFP) - A RANKING SOUTH KOREAN OFFICIAL, DISMISSED AFTER TAKING PART IN AN ANTI-GOVERNMENT DEMONSTRATION, ACCUSED THE ADMINISTRATION MONDAY OF ''VIOLATING BASIC HUMAN RIGHTS.''

KIM HYUNG-BAE, 35, A FORMER OFFICIAL IN THE PRIME MINISTER'S OFFICE IN CHARGE OF YOUTH PROBLEMS, MADE HIS STATEMENT IN A ''DECLARATION OF CONSCIENCE'' HE ISSUED AT OPPOSITION PARTY HEADQUARTERS HERE.

HE TOLD A PRESS CONFERENCE AT THE NEW KOREA DEMOCRATIC PARTY HEADQUARTERS THAT HE WAS DISMAYED BY THE ''BRUTAL'' SUPPRESSION NINE DAYS AGO BY POLICE OF A PEACEFUL GATHERING OF SEVERAL THOUSAND PEOPLE AT THE MYONGDONG ROMAN CATHOLIC CHURCH IN DOWNTOWN SEOUL.

THE DEMONSTRATORS WERE PROTESTING AGAINST ALLEGED SEXUAL HARASSMENT DURING POLICE INTERROGATION OF A WOMAN DISSIDENT. THE GOVERNMENT HAS DENIED THE ALLEGATIONS.

MR. KIM SAID HE WAS ARRESTED DURING THE DEMONSTRATION AFTER DEMANDING ''THE WHOLE TRUTH ABOUT ... SEXUAL TORTURE,'' AND WAS FORCED BY HIS SUPERIORS TO RESIGN TWO DAYS LATER.

IN HIS STATEMENT MONDAY, HE ASKED THE NATION'S ONE MILLION CIVIL SERVANTS TO RESIST BECOMING ''RUNNING DOGS OF THE DICTATORIAL REGIME'' AND TO REJECT ALL ''UNJUST OR ILLEGAL INSTRUCTIONS'' FROM THEIR SUPERIORS.

PKM/SF

AFP 280517 GMT JUL 86

0068

SEOUL, JULY 28 (U) -- A MID-RANKING AIDE TO P   ME MINISTER LOH
SHIN-YONG MONDAY DEFECTED TO THE OPPOSITION AND SAID HE WILL FIGHT
AGAINST THE +DICTATORIAL+ GOVERNMENT OF PRESIDENT CHUN DOO HWAN.

IN +A STATEMENT OF CONSCIENCE+ READ AT THE HEADQUARTERS OF THE
MAIN OPPOSITION NEW KOREA DEMOCRATIC PARTY (NKDP), KIM HYONG-BAE,
-35, URGED THE NATION'&S 1 MILLION STATE OFFICIALS TO REVOLT AGAINST
THE CHUN GOVERNMENT.

+I WILL NOT REMAIN SILENT ANY MORE...STATE OFFICIALS CAN NO
LONGER BE THE RUNNING DOGS OF THE DICTATOR,+ KIM SAID IN THE
STATEMENT.

KIM RECEIVED A WARM WELCOME WHEN HE READ THE STATEMENT BEFORE 80
REPORTERS AND OPPOSITION POLITICIANS. NKDP PRESIDENT LEE MIN-WOO AND
PARTY ADVISOR KIM YOUNG-SAM ENCOURAGED HIM BY SHAKING HANDS.

KIM'&S EIGHT-PAGE STATEMENT WAS A SHARP INDICTMENT OF THE CHUN
GOVENRMENT WHICH HAS RECENTLY COME UNDER PUBLIC FIRE FOR ALLEGED
TORTURE OF POLITICAL DISSIDENTS IN JAIL OR UNDER ARREST.

KIM, IDENTIFYING HIMSELF AS AN OFFICIAL WORKING AT PREMIER LOH'&S
ADMINISTRATIVE COORDINATION OFFICE, SAID HE WAS FORCED TO QUIT THE
POST JULY 21 FOR TAKING PART IN AN OPPOSITION RALLY TWO DAYS
EARLIER.

KIM SAID HE WANTED TO ATTEND AN OPPOSITION RALLY AT SEOUL'S
MYUNGDONG ROMAN CATHOLIC CHURCH JULY 19 TO DENOUNCE AN ALLEGED
+SEXUAL TORTURE CASE+ INVOVLING A FEMALE DISSIDENT ACTIVIST.

POLICE BROKE UP THE RALLY BY FIRING TEAR GAS. TURNED BACK BY
POLICE, KIM SAID HE REACHED A NEARBY SUBWAY STATION WHERE HE SHOUTED
ANTI-GOVERNMENT SLOGANS.

+ALL OF A SUDDEN, I REALIZED THAT I SHOULD BE A STATE OFFICIAL
FOR THE PEOPLE, NOT FOR A HANDFUL OF THOSE IN POWER WHO DECEIVE THE
PEOPLE,+ KIM'&S STATEMENT SAID.

THE +SEXUAL TORTURE CASE+ AT ISSUE INVOLVED KWON IN-SUK, 23, A
SEOUL COLLEGE DROPOUT WHO CLAIMS THAT SHE WAS SEXUALLY ABUSED DURING
POLICE QUESTIONING ON TWO OCCASIONS IN EARLY JUNE.

IN A PETITION FILED WITH THE PROSECUTION, KWON ALLEGED THAT
SHE WAS STRIPPED NAKED, HANDCUFFED AND SUBJECT TO +SEXUAL TORTURE+
UNDER A SYSTEMATIC POLICE EFFORT TO GET CONFESSIONS.

THE POLICE OFFICER WHO QUESTIONED KWON TOUCHED HER BREASTS AND
VULVA AND LICKED ONE OF HER NIPPLES DURING INTERROGATION WHICH
LASTED SEVERAL HOURS, THE PETITION SAID.

AFTER TWO WEEKS OF INVESTIGATION, PROSECUTION AUTHORITIES
DISMISSED KWON'&S ALLEGATIONS +UNTRUE+ BUT FIRED THE POLICE OFFICER
AND THREE OF HIS SUPERIORS.

ALTHOUGH AUTHORITIES HAVE NEVER ADMITTED, IT IS NO SECRET THAT
POLITICAL DISSIDENTS ARE COMMONLY SUBJECT TO VARIOUS TORTURE,
INCLUDING BEATING, FORCED DRINKING OF WATER AND ELECTRICAL SHOCKS,

분류번호	보존기간

발 신 전 보

번 호: WUS-2997　일 시: 60730 2020　전보종별: 지급

수 신: 주　미　　대사.총영사.

발 신: 장　　관　(미북)

제 목: 부천 사건 관련 국무성 반응

　　　　대 : USW-3460, 3535

　　　　연 : WUS-2951

1. 7.29자 Reuter, AP 등 외신에 따르면 미국무성은 '부천' 사건과 관련, 기자 질문에 대하여 아래와 같이 서면 답변 하였다고 하는 바 동 사실 여부 파악 보고 바람.

　　가. 권인숙은 공식 발표보다 더 심하게 학대 받았다는 믿을 만한 주장이 있으며, 동 학대에 대해 개탄과 (deplorable) 전율을 금치 못함. (appalling)

　　나. 형사 피고인의 고문 및 학대에 대해서는 법규정에 따른 책임자 처벌과 재발 방지 조치를 한국정부에 요청함.

　　다. 금번 명동 성당 및 성공회 반정부 시위를 한국정부가 방해한 것을 규탄함. (condemn)

/ 계속 /

보안통제

앙고재	86년 7월 30일 북미과	기안자	과 장	심의관	국 장	차관보	차 관	장 관		외신과	접수자	동 제
		3			3	홍00						

0070

2. 상기 국무성 논평이 사실인 경우 아래와 같은 점을 들어
국무성에 대하여 아국 정부의 유감을 표시하고 결과 보고 바람.

　　가. 검찰은 동 사건에 대해서 엄격한 수사를 통해 관련
　　　　사실을 밝혀내고 공정한 조치를 취했음.

　　나. 아울러 정부는 조사과정에서 폭행사실이 드러난
　　　　담당관들에 대해서는 파면등 엄중조치를 취하였으며
　　　　앞으로 어떠한 조사 과정에서든지 고문 · 폭행행위는
　　　　용납않는다는 방침을 재차 분명히 하였음.

　　다. 금번 국무성 논평은, 일부 야권 및 반체제 과격인사들에게
　　　　정치적으로 악용되어 대화와 타협을 통한 현재 정국
　　　　안정에 역행하는 사례가 야기될 우려가 있음.

　　라. 동 사건에 대한 사법절차가 상금 완료되지 않았음.

예고 : 1986.12.31. 일반

(미주국장 정선섭)

0071

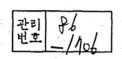

외 무 부   착 신 전 보

번 호 : USW-3594   일 시 : 607301822   종 별 : 지급

수 신 : 장 관 (미북)

발 신 : 주 미 대사

제 목 : 부천사건 관련 국무성 반응

연 : USW-3580

대 : WUS-2997

1. 대호 관련 금 7.30 DAVID BLAKEMORE 국무성 한국과장을 접촉, 아국 검찰이 엄격한 수사를 통하여 공정한 조치를 이미 취한바 있음에도 불구하고 국무성의 여사한 논평이 있었음에 강한 유감을 표명하면서 고문,폭력행위를 근절해 나갈려는 아국정부의 강력한 의지를 재차 설명하고 반체제 과격분자들이 논평을 정치적으로 이용할 가능성이 있음을 지적함.

2. BLAKEMORE 과장은 아국정부의 신속한 조사는 용기있는 조치였으나, 금번 논평은 다음과같은 미측 평가를 토대로 작성하였다고 답변함.

첫째 : 관련 경찰이 파면되었으나 적절히 처벌되었다고 보여지지않으며

둘째 : 권인숙이 아측의 공식발표보다는 훨씬 더 심하게 성적으로 학대되었다고 믿고 있으며

셋째 : 공식발표내용에 직접 명시적으로 언급되지않았으나 마치 권인숙이 나쁜여자같이 묘사되었는바, 이렇게할 필요가 있는지 의문시됨.

3. 동과장은 또한 국무성의 논평이 일부인사들에 의해 악용될 가능성이 있다는 아측 우려를 충분히 이해하겠으며 그러한 일이 없기를 바란다고하면서 그러나 고문문제에 관한한 미국내 여론이 워낙 강력하기 때문에 국무성으로서는 이를 감안하지않을수 없다고 언급함.

4. 이에대해 현재 아국정부가 헌법특위 발족에 즈음하여 대화와 타협을 통한 국내정치 발전을 이룩하기 위하여 모든 노력을 경주하고 있음을 강조하고 이러한 시점에서

미주국   차관실   1 차보   정문국   청와대   총리실   안 기

PAGE   1   86.07.31   10:22
                                                      외신 2과 통제관

0072

국무성의 여사한 논평은 일부 과격분자들에게   AMMUNITION   을 제공하는 것과 다
름이 없음을 인식하여 줄것을 재차 강조하였음

(대사 김경원-국장)

예고:86.12.31일반
      제반
      서명

PAGE   2

분류번호	보존기간

발 신 전 보

번 호: WUS-3027 일 시: 60801 1700   전보종별: _____

수 신: 주   미   대사 /총영사/

발 신: 장   관 (미북)

제 목: 부천사건 관련 미국무성 논평

대 : USW-3594

연 : WUS-3580

1. 대호 국무성 논평과 관련, 금 8.1 미주국장은
Dunlop 주한미 정무참사관을 초치, 다음과 같이 아측 입장을
전달한 바, 동건 처리에 참고 바람.

　　가. 부천사건에 대한 사법절차가 아직 진행중이고
　　　　내주중 국회의 관련 상임위에서도 동 사건에
　　　　대한 문제가 거론될 예정인 바, 국무성의 여사한
　　　　공개적 논평이 나온데 대하여 유감의 뜻과 아울러
　　　　사건처리등에 영향을 미치게 되지 않을까 하는
　　　　우려를 표명하며 이문제에 대하여는 보다 조용하고
　　　　신중하게 대처하는 것이 요망됨.

　　나. 금번과 같은 국무성의 논평은 일부 반체제 세력에
　　　　의해 정치적으로 악용될 우려가 농후하며

보안	
통제	

앙고재	86 년 8 월 1 일	북미과	기안자 경	과 장	심의관 (서명)	국 장	차 관 (서명)	장 관 X	외신과 접수자 어	통제

0074

이와 같은 사태가 야기되는 경우 현 정국 발전에
영향을 미치게 될것이 우려됨.

2. 이에 대하여 Dunlop 참사관은 국무성의 금번
논평은 당초 예정된 초안보 다 공평성을 유지하기 위하여 고심한
바가 있다는 설명을 한후 상기 아측 입장에 대하여 이해를 표명
함과 동시에 본국에 보고하겠다고 하였음.

(차관 이상옥)

예고 예고 의거 1986.12.31. 일반
삭제 선정

0075

부천서(권인숙) 사건 관련 미국 반응, 1986   285

부천사건 관련 미측반응 및 대응조치

86. 7.

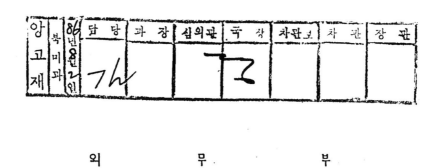

외 무 부

0076

부천 사건 관련 미측 반응 및 대응 조치
----

1. 경   위
   ○ 7.16   검찰, 부천사건 수사결과 발표
   ○ 7.19   재야세력, 소위 '고문 및 용공 조작저지' 명동
             성당 집회 시도
   ○ 7.26   McGruder 미국무성 동아·태국 대변인,
             명동성당 집회관련 유감표명 논평
   ○ 7.27   재야 세력, 성공회 집회 시도
   ○ 7.29   미국무성 대변인, 부천사건 개탄 및 집회 방해
             비난 논평

2. 미국무성 논평 요지
   가. 7.26자 논평

      ○ McGruder 동아태국 대변인, 워싱턴 주재 아국
        특파원의 전화 문의에 다음 요지로 답변

      ○ 논평요지
        - 한국정부는 사회안정을 해칠 우려가 있는 집회를
          금지시키는 법에 의거 동 집회를 불법으로 간주,
          저지 조치를 취했다고 알고 있음.
        - 평화적 집회를 열 권리에 대한 여하한 침해도 유감
          으로 생각하며 모든 당사자들에게 폭력사용을 자제
          하도록 촉구함.

0077

- 한국에 진정한 민주주의로의 진전은 오로지 평화적
대화를 통해 이루어질 수 있으며 가두에서의 대결을
통해서 이루어질 수는 없음.

나. 7.29자 논평

ㅇ 국무성 대변인, 부천사건 및 집회 관련 질문에 대해
추후 게시 답변

- 정오브리핑시 받은 질문에 대한 답변을 추후에
공보국 사무실 게시판에 공고

ㅇ 논평요지

- 동 사건 담당 검사는 수사관의 조사과정에서 권양
구타 및 폭언사실이 있었음을 발견하였고, 동
수사관 및 3명의 상급자는 파면되었음.

- 권양은 공식 발표보다 더 심하게 학대 받았다는
믿을 만한 주장이 있으며, 동 학대에 대해 개탄
(deplorable)과 전율 (appalling) 을 금치 못함.

- 형사 피고인의 고문 및 학대에 대해서는 법규정에
따른 책임자 처벌과 재발 방지 조치를 한국정부에
촉구함.

3. 아측 대응조치

가. 7.30 본부지시에 의거 주미대사관 관계관, Blakemore
국무성 한국과장을 접촉 7.29.자 논평에 대한 아국정부의
유감표시

0078

ㅇ 아측 유감표시 요지

- 검찰은 동 사건에 대해서 엄격한 수사를 통해 관련
  사실을 밝혀내고 공정한 조치를 취했음.

- 아울러 정부는 조사과정에서 폭행사실이 드러난
  담당관들에 대해서는 파면등 엄중조치를 취하였으며
  앞으로 어떠한조사 과정에서든지 고문 · 폭행행위는
  용납않는다는 방침을 재차 분명히 하였음.

- 금번 국무성 논평은, 일부 야권 및 반체제 각계
  인사들에게 정치적으로 악용되어 대화와 타협을
  통한 현재 정국 안정에 역행하는 사태가 야기될
  우려가 있음.

- 동 사건에 대한 사법절차가 상금 완료 되지 않았음.

ㅇ Blakemore 한국과장 국무성 입장 설명 요지

- 관련 경찰이 파면되었으나 적절히 처벌되었다고 보여
  지지 않음.

- 권양이 아측의 공식 발표보다는 훨씬 더 심하게
  성적으로 학대되었다고 믿고 있음.

- 공식 발표 내용에 직접 명시적으로 언급되지
  않았으나 마치 권양이 나쁜 여자 같이 묘사되었는 바,
  이렇게 할 필요가 있는지 의문시됨.

- 국무성 논평이 일부 인사들에 의해 악용될 가능성이
  있다는 한국측 우려를 충분히 이해하겠으며 그러한
  일이 없기를 바람.

0079

다. 8.1 미주국장, Dunlop 주한미 정무참사관을 초치,
아래 아측입장 전달

° 아측입장 요지

- 부천사건에 대한 사법절차가 아직 진행중이고
내주중 국회의 관련 상임위에서도 동 사건에
대한 문제가 거론될 예정인 바, 국무성의여사한
공개적 논평이 나온데 대하여 유감의 뜻과
아울러 사건처리등에 영향을 미치게 되지 않을까
하는 우려를 표명하며 이 문제에 대하여는 보다
조용하고 신중하게 대처하는 것이 요망됨.

- 금번과 같은 국무성의 논평은 일부 반체제 세력에
의해 정치적으로 악용될 우려가 농후하며이와
같은 사태가 야기되는 경우 현 정국 발전에 영향을
미치게 될 것이 우려됨.

° Dunlop 참사관 반응 요지

- 국무성의 금번 논평은 당초 예정된 초안보다 공평성을
유지하기 위하여 고심한 바 있음.

- 상기 한국측 입장 및 우려를 이해하며, 이를 본국
정부에 보고하겠음.

- 특히, 동 사건 조사에 대한 귀측의 노력을 긍정적인
것으로 평가함.

첨 부 : 1. 7.26차 미국무성 논평
2. 7.29차 미국무성 논평

0080

7. 26자 미국무성 논평

Q : Do you have an comment on Korean Government
    actions July 19 to prevent a rally against
    purported police mistreatment of prisoners
    human rights violations?

A : We understand the Korean Government took
    steps to block the rally because it regarded
    it as illegal under a law banning gatherings
    feared to cause social unrest. As we have
    stated before, the US regrets any instance of
    infringement on the right of peaceful assembly
    and calls on all sides to forego the use of
    violence. True progress toward democracy
    in Korea can be achieved only through peaceful
    dialogue, not confrontation in the streets.

7.29자 미국무성 논평

Q : A couple of times in the last few weeks the
South Korean authorities have stopped
rallies (one was to go from the Catholic
cathedral toward the chief Anglican church
in seoul). Do you have any reaction to
that?

A : We understand the Korean Government took
steps to block the rallies because it regarded
them as illegal under a law banning gatherings
that could lead to social unrest. As we
have stated before, the U.S. regrets any
instance of infringement on the right of
peaceful assembly and calls on all sides to
forego the use of violence. True progress
toward democracy in Korea can be achieved
only through peaceful dialogue, not confrontation in the streets.

0082

Q : Do you have anything on the alleged sexual torture of a Korean trustee?

A : A Korean Government prosecutor investigating the charges has found that the policeman involved beat and verbally abused the prisoner, a Miss Kwon. The policeman and three of his superiors have been dismissed from their jobs. There are credible allegations that police mistreatment of Miss Kwon was more severe and harsher than acknowledged. We find such treatment of prisoners deplorable and appalling. As in all cases involving torture and mistreatment of prisoners, we urge the Korean Government to punish as provided by law those responsible and to take steps to assure that such abuses are not repeated.

문 : 피의자 인권유린 같은 경찰 학대에 항의하는 7월 19일자
집회를 한국정부가 저지한 것에 대해 논평해
주기 바람.

답 : 우리는 한국정부가 사회 안정을 해칠 우려가 있는 집회를
금지시키는 법에 의거 동 집회를 불법으로 간주하였기
때문에, 동 집회를 저지시키는 조치를 취했던 것으로
알고 있음.   전에도 언급한 바 같이, 미국은 평화롭게
집회할 권리에 대한 어떠한 침해도 유감으로 여기며, 모든
당사자가 폭력을 사용치 않기를 촉구함. 한국에서의
진정한 민주주의의 발전은 가두에서의 대립이 아닌
평화적 대화에 의해서만 달성될 수 있음.

0084

문 : 피의자 인권유린 같은 경찰 학대에 항의하는
7월 19일자 집회를 한국정부가 저지한것에 대해
논평해 주기 바람.

답 : 우리는 한국정부가 사회안정을 해칠 우려가 있는
집회를 금지시키는 법에 의거 동 집회를 불법으로
간주하였기 때문에, 동 집회를 저지 시키는 조치를
취했던 것으로 알고 있음. 일전에도 언급한 바 같이
미국은 평화롭게 집회할 권리에 대한 어떠한 침해도
유감으로 여기며, 모든 당사자가 폭력을 사용치 않기를
촉구함. 한국에서의 진정한 민주주의로의 발전은
가두에서의 대립이 아닌 평화적 대화에 의해서만
달성될 수 있음.

문 : 소위 성고문 사건에 대한 논평은 무엇인지?

답 : 피의자의 고소를 조사해온 한국 검찰은, 수사관이
권양을 구타하고 폭언을 했다는 점을 밝혀냈음. 수사관
및 3명의 상급자들은 파면 되었음. 권양에 대한 경찰의
학대는 알려진바 보다 더 심하고 거칠었다는 믿을 만한
주장이 있음.

0085

우리는 피의자를 그렇게 취급하는 데 대해 개탄과
전율을 금치 못함.   피의자의 고문및 학대를 포함한
모든 사건에 있어서   우리는 한국정부가 법에 따라
책임자를 처벌하고 그러한 학대행위가 재발되지
않도록 조치를 취할것을 촉구함.

기 안 용 지

분류기호 문서번호	미북 700- 2420	(전화 :)	시행상 특별취급	

보존기간	영구·준영구. 10. 5. 3. 1.	장 관

수 신 처 보존기간	

시행일자	1986. 8. 4.

보 조 기 관	국 장	전결	협 조 기 관			제
	심의관					
	과 장					

기안책임자	김원수

경 유 수 신 참 조	주미대사	발 신 명 의	

제 목	면담요록 송부

연 : WUS-3027

부천사건 미국무성 논평 관련, 미주국장과 Dunlop

주한미 정무참사관간의 면담요록을 별첨 송부하니 참고 바랍니다.

첨부 : 상기 면담요록 사본 1부. 끝.

보고문예고 : 1986. 12. 31. 일반
직원

1505-25(2-1) 일(1)갑
85. 9. 9. 승인

190mm×268mm 인쇄용지 2급 60g/㎡
가 40-41·1985. 10. 29.
0087

면 담 요 록

1. 일   시 : 1986년 8 월 1 일(금 요일) 10:15 시~ 10:45시

2. 장   소 : 미주국장실

3. 면 담 자 : 장선섭 미주국장

   Thomas H..Dunlop 주한미 정무참사관

   (배석 : 김원수 북미과 사무관)

4. 내   용 :

   (랜스 포대 배치)

   미주국장 : 랜스 미사일 포대 배치 관련 관계부처간 협의 예정임.

   본인의 의견으로는   대외발표는 비동맹 정상회담

   1주일후가 적절하다고 봄. 미측이 생각하는 대외발표

   방식은 어떤것인지?

   참 사 관 : 개인적 의견이지만 매우 조용한 방식으로 발표(low key

   announcement) 하게 되기를 바람. 발표 내용은

   오클라호마에서 이동한다는 사실만 언급하고, 발표

   방식도 일상적인 벽보통지문 (posted on the wall)

   정도가 되지 않을까 생각됨.

0088

미주국장 : 발표 내용에 대해서는 계속 협의가 필요하다고 봄.

참사관 : 지난 7.30 면담시 언급한 바와 같이 중공 및 일본에
대해서 적절한 방식으로 사전 협의 또는 통보
(consult or inform) 가 필요하다고 보는 바,
이에도 시간이 소요될 것임.

미주국장 : 여사한 통보는 발표 직전에 하는 것이 바람직 하다고
봄.

참사관 : 동감임.

(부천 사건 관련 국무성 논평)

미주국장 : 동 사건 관련 국무성이 그렇게 강한 내용의 논평을
발표한데 대해 무척 놀랐으며, 우려되는 바 큼.

동 사건에 대해서는 아직도 사법절차가 진행중
이며, 국회에서도 동 사건을 조사키로 여·야간 합의가
이루어져 내주중 내무위에서 다투어 질 것으로 보이는
현상황에서, 국무성의 여사한 공개적 논평이 나온 데
대하여 유감의 뜻과 아울러 사건 처리등에 영향을
미치게 되지 않을까 하는 우려를 표명하며 이 문제에
대하여는 보다 조용하고 신중하게 대처하는 것이
요망됨.

- 2 -

0089

동 사건에 대한 사법절차가 종료될 때까지는
관망 (wait-and-see) 하는 것이 바람직하며, 아국
정부는 사실을 밝히기 위해 최선을 다하고 있음을
다시한번 밝히고자 함.

비록 AP통신 보도와는 달리 'condemn'이
라는 표현을 사용치 않았다고 하나 국무성이 이와
같은 강한 논평을 하게된 배경에 대해서 파악된게
있는지 문의하고자 함. 금번과 같은 국무성의 논평은
일부 반체제 세력에 의해 정치적으로 악용될 우려가
농후하며 이와 같은 사태가 야기되는 경우 현 정국
발전에 영향을 미치게 될 것이 우려됨.

참 사 관 : 상기 귀측 입장 및 우려를 이해하며, 이를 본국정부에
보고하겠음. 특히, 동 사건 조사에 대한 귀측의
노력을 긍정적인 것으로 평가함.

국무성의 금번 논평은 공평성을 유지하기 위해
당초 예정된 초안의 일부 내용을 바꿨음. 예를 들면
당초 초안에는 관계자 파면 및 검사의 과잉행위
(mistreatment) 발견에 대한 언급이 없었음.

- 3 -

0090

(환율 인상 교섭관련 보도)

참 사 관 : 환율 인상 교섭과 관련한 언론 보도에 대해 워커
대사는 강한 불쾌감을 가지고 있음. 양국간에 이견이
존재하더라도 이러한 문제의 교섭 사항에 대해서
여사한 언론 보도는 곤란하다고 봄. 상세한 내용은
알수 없으나, 여사한 방식으로 언론보도가 된 데에는
재무성의 실수가 있었다고 봄. 이러한 교섭은 여사한
언론보도없이 비공개적으로 이루어지는 것이 바람직함
(confidential basis is much better).

본인의 개인적 견해로는, 301조 현안 교섭이
완료되었고, 미의회에 상정되어 있는 각종 부호무역
법안이 채택되지 않는다 하더라도 한국에 대한 보호
무역 압력은 계속 될 것으로 봄.

(Ferraro 여사 방한 취소)

참 사 관 : Ferraro 여사 방한 취소는 모친의 급환등 급한
몇가지 가족문제 때문인 것으로 봄. 동 여사의
아들은 약사인데, 마약불법거래 혐의로 내주경 기소될
것으로 봄.

동 방한 취소에 대해 김상현등은 매우 언짢게
생각하고 있음.

- 4 -

0091

본인의 견해로는 Ferraro 여사가 정치인
으로서의 생명이 거의 끝 났다고 보는데 야당 정치인
들이 왜 그렇게 관심을 갖는지 이해하기 어려움.

동 여사는 뉴욕의 지방정치에 어느 정도
영향력을 행사하고 있다고 보는 것이 그 작일 것임.

끝.

0092

발 신 전 보

번 호 : WUS-3292 일 시 : 60814 1900   전보종별 : _____

수 신 : 주   미   대사·총영사

발 신 : 장   관 (미북)

제 목 : 부천사건 관련 신민당 집회 개최 기도

연 : PIA-0047

1. 금 8.14. 14:00 신민당 중앙당사에서 개최 예정인 소위 '고문 및 용공조작 범국민 폭로 대회'와 관련, 미주국장은 금일 11:00 David Pierce 주한미대사관 정무과 1등 서기관 (참사관대리)를 초치, 다음 아국정부 입장을 설명하였는 바, 귀관에서도 국무성을 접촉, 이를 ~~상세히~~ 설명바람.

가. 신민당의 금번 집회기도는 정당한 정치집회가 아닌 집회 및 시위에 관한 법률에 명백하게 위배되는 불법 집회인 바, 이유는 아래와 같음.

o 신민당 중앙당사는 수용능력이 500명임에도 불구하고 1만여명을 동원코자 하고 있어, 공공의 안녕질서를 저해할 우려가 있음. *실질적으로 옥외집회를 기도하고 있는바* (개최)

o 동 집회는 당국수사로 이미 진상이 밝혀졌고 최근 국회 상임위에서도 다투어진 바 있는 부천서 사건과 고문의 허위사실을 유포하려는 데 그 목적이 있고

보안 등재

앙 고 재	86년 8월 14일 파	기안자	과 장	심의관	국 장	차관보	차 관	장 관

발신시간 :

외 신 과	접수자	과 장
	예	

0093

특히 간첩죄등 아국 안보상 심각한 범죄자를
포함한 수감자의 가족 까지 동원코자 하고 있어
사회안정을 저해할 우려가 있음.

나. 따라서 아국 치안당국은 8.13 신민당 총재에게 동
집회가 불법집회임을 통보하고 계획 취소를 서면으로
요청하였으나, 신민당은 동 요청을 무시하고 집회를
강행할 것으로 예상됨.

다. 신민당이 동 집회를 강행할 경우, 치안당국은 법
질서 유지를 위해 부득이 최소한의 예방조치를 취하게
될 것임.

  ○ 정당의 정상적인 정당활동을 보장하기 위해 현역
    국회의원과 신민당 당직자의 당사출입은 제한하지
    않을 것임.

  ○ 그러나 기타인사, 즉 학생, 구속자 가족등에 대해서는

마. 부천사건과 관련한 지난 2번의 집회후 국무성이 발표한
논평에 대해 아국 ~~정부~~의 유감 표명이 있었는 바, 금번
집회시도에 대해서는 여사한 사례가 재발되지 않도록
아국정부의 입장을 사전에 상세히 통보하는 것이니 이를
국무성에 적절히 ~~협의~~하여 주기 바람.

2. 이에 대해 Pierce 참사관 대리는, 아측의 신속한
사전 정보 제공에 감사하며, 동 내용을 국무성에 지급 보고 하겠다고
언급 하였음을 참고 바람.

(차관 이상옥)

예고예고 목 1986.12.31 일반
직위   상당

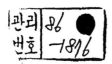

면 담 요 록

1. 일   시 : 1986년   8 월 14 일(목 요일) 11:00 시 ~ 11:30시

2. 장   소 : 미주국장실

3. 면 담 자 : 장선섭 미주국장

  David Pierce   주한미대사관 정무과 1등서기관

                           (참사관 대리)

  (배석 : 김원수 북미과 사무관)

4. 내   용 :

국   장 : 금일 귀하를 초치한 것은 금일 14:00 신민당 중앙당사
            에서 개최키로 예정되어 있는 소위 '고문 및 용공조작
            범국민 폭로 대회'와 관련한 아국 정부의 입장을
            미측에 사전 통보키 위한 것임.

            신민당의 금번 집회기도는 정당한 정치집회가
            아닌 집회 및 시위에 관한 법률에 명백하게 위배되는
            불법 집회인 바, 이유는 아래와 같음.

0096

o 신민당 중앙당사는 수용능력이 500명임에도 불구
   하고 1만여명을 동원코자 하고 있어 실질적으로
   옥외 집회 개최를 기도하고 있는 바, 공공의
   안녕 질서를 저해할 우려가 있음.

o 동 집회는 당국수사로 이미 진상이 밝혀졌고 최근
   국회 상임위에서도 다루어진 바 있는 부천서 사건과
   고문의 허위사실을 유포하려는데 그 목적이 있고
   특히 간첩죄등 아국 안보상 심각한 범죄자를
   포함한 수감자의 가족까지 동원코자 하고 있어
   사회안정을 저해할 우려가 있음.

   따라서 아국 치안당국은 8.13 신민당 총재에게
   동 집회가 불법집회임을 통보하고 계획 취소를 서면
   으로 요청하였으나, 신민당은 동 요청을 무시하고
   집회를 강행할 것으로 예상됨.

   신민당이 동 집회를 강행할 경우, 치안당국은
   법질서 유지를 위해 부득이 아래와 같은 최소한의
   예방조치를 취하게 될 것임.

o 정당의 정상적인 정당활동을 보장하기 위해 현역
   국회의원과 신민당 당직자의 당사출입은 제한하지
   않을 것임.

- 2 -

0097

ㅇ 그러나 기타인사, 즉 학생, 구속자 가족등에 대해
서는 부득이 출입을 일시 제한할 예정임.

부천사건과 관련한 지난 2번의 집회후 국무성이
발표한 논평에 대해 아측의 유감 표명이 있었는 바,
금번 집회시도에 대해서는 여사한 사례가 재발되지
않도록 아국정부의 압장을 사전에 상세히 통보하는
것이니 이를 국무성에 적절히 전달하여 주기 바람.

Pierce : 본인은 여행에서 최근 돌아왔고, Dunlop
참사관의 금일 휴가 출발로 참사관 대리를 금일부터
맡아 아직 본건관련 내용을 완전히 파악치 못하고
있음.

그러나, 귀측의 신속한 정보 제공에 감사하며,
귀측의 통보 내용을 국무성에 지급 보고 하겠음. 끝.

외 무 부 착신전문

번 호 : USW-3840   일 시 : 608141853   종 별 :

수 신 : 장관 (미북)

발 신 : 주 미 대사

제 목 : 신민당 집회 개최기도

대 : WUS-3292

1. 김참사관은 금 8.14.   DAVID BLACKMORE 국무성 한국과장을 면담,대호내용을 상세히 설명하고, 아국내 문제에 대한 미정부의 공개적인 논평은 문제의 해결에 도움이 되지 못할뿐아니라 오히려 문제를 악화시키는경우가 많으므로 한.미 양국정부간의 어떠한 문제도 조용한 방법으로 처리해나가는것이 바람직할것으로 본다고 말함

2. 동과장은 상세한 사전 설명에 감사한다고 하면서 한국정부가 취한 조처를 이행한다고 말한다음 아래와같은 반응을 보였음(동,내용을 알고 있지못하였는바,금일오전 바쁜일정으로 공관보고 전문을 읽지못했다고 하였음)

가. 미 정부로서는 기자의 공개질문이 제기되는경우,공개답변 할수밖에 없으며,답변지침서 작성시 미국내 여론을 의식하지 않을수 없다는 사실을 한국측이 이해해야 할것임.

나. 동 집회를 위요한 사태의 경과 여하에 따라 기자에 의한 질문제기 가능성 여부를 검토,기자브리핑 답변지침서 준비여부를 결정하게되겠지만 일단 금일의 설명내용으로 보아 특별한 관심을 기울여야할 사안은 아니라고 생각함

(대사 김경원-국장)

예고:86.12.31일반

미주국   차관실   1차보   정문국   청와대   총리실   안 기

PAGE   1   86.08.15 12:11
                                                   외신 2과 통제관

수신: 외무부 미주국장

발신: 안기부

신한당 당사 이용 불법 집회 관련 외신 및 공관 설명 자료

1. 신한민주당 중앙당사에서 86.8.14. 14:00 개최 예정인 소위 고문 및

   용공조작 범국민 폭로대회는 정당한 정치집회가 아니라 집회 및

   시위에 관한 법률에 명백하게 위배되는 불법집회임

2. 동 대회가 불법집회인 이유는 아래와 같음

   1) 신한민주당 중앙당사는 수용능력이 약 500명이내 임에도 불구하고

      대회 주최측은 1만여명을 동원하려 하고 있는 바 이것은 실질적인

      옥외집회를 개최하려는 기도로서 공공의 안녕질서를 저해 할

      우려가 있다고 판단되며

   2) 동 집회는 당국수사로 이미 진상이 규명된 부천서 사건과 고문의

      허위사실을 날조 유포하려는데 그 목적이 있으므로 사회안정을

      저해 할 우려가 있고

   3) 특히 '남조선 민족해방전선' 사건에 관련되어 국가보안법 위반죄로
      대법원에서 ~~유죄확정을 받고~~ 확정되어 무기징역을 복역중인자의 가족까지 동원 하려는

      것은 법원의 확정 판결 마저 용공조작으로 역국선전하려는

4-29 83. 5. 1

기도로서 결과적으로 北괴의 대남 비방 선전에 역 이용당할

우려가 있다고 판단됨.

3. 다락서 치안당국은 86.8.13 신한민주당 총재여게 동 대회가

불법집회임을 설명하고 대회 개최 계획을 취소해 줄 것을 공식

요청하는 서한을 보냈는 바 신한민주당이 이 요청을 무시하고

대회를 강행한다면 시민생활을 보호하고 치안질서를 유지하기 위해

부득이 불법집회를 저지하기 위한 예방조치를 취하지 않을 수 없을

것임.

4. 이상과 같이 예방조치를 취한다 하더라도 불법집회를 사전에 예방할 수

있는 최소한에 그칠 것이며 정당의 정상적인 정당 활동을 보장하기

위해 현역국회의원과 신한민주당 중앙당 사무국 요원 등 당직자의

당사 출입은 제한하지 않을 것임

5. 그러나 기타 인사의 당사 출입에 대해서는 불법집회를 계획하려는 기도로

판단되어 사회안정과 공공질서 유지를 위해서 부득이 일시 제한을

가하지 않을 수 없을 것임.

韓国關係主要外信報道

1986.8.7(木) 16:00

(第 2 便)

外 信 名	内　　　　容	페이지
AFP (서울發)	韓國, 美國의 원貨 平價切上 要求 拒否	1
AFP (서울發)	88 서울올림픽 聖火 奉送 計劃	4
AP (서울發)	아시안게임 入場券 販売	5
Reuter (서울發)	"性 拷問" 關聯	6

0102

070420 :BC-TORTURE (FEATURE, PIX HKG01F)

+SEX TORTURE+ ALLEGATIONS STIR SEOUL FROM SUMMER TORPOR

BY ROGER CRABB, REUTERS

SEOUL, AUG 7, REUTER - ONE OF THE MOST TALKED-ABOUT PEOPLE IN SEOUL THIS HOT STEAMY AUGUST IS KWON IN-SOOK, A FORMER STUDENT WHO HAS SPARKED A POLITICAL ROW BY ALLEGING THAT A DETECTIVE SEXUALLY TORTURED HER.

MISS KWON, 23, A DROP-OUT FROM SEOUL NATIONAL UNIVERSITY, SAYS SHE WAS SEXUALLY ABUSED BY THE DETECTIVE WHILE HE QUESTIONED HER AT A POLICE STATION ABOUT CHARGES THAT SHE FALSIFIED AN IDENTITY CARD TO GET WORK AT A FACTORY.

KWON, DESCRIBED BY AUTHORITIES AS A RADICAL LEFTIST TRYING TO INFILTRATE THE LABOUR MOVEMENT AND INCITE UNREST, MADE THE ACCUSATIONS LAST MONTH IN A PETITION FILED WITH THE PROSECUTORS' OFFICE IN THE PORT CITY OF INCHON.

AFTER A TWO-WEEK INVESTIGATION THE OFFICE RULED THAT SERGEANT MOON KWI-DONG HAD BEATEN KWON ABOUT THE BREASTS AND VERBALLY ABUSED HER DURING TWO INTERROGATIONS LASTING A TOTAL OF 4-1/2 HOURS.

BUT IT REJECTED THE SEXUAL ABUSE CLAIM, SAYING THE YOUNG WOMAN HAD FALSELY EXAGGERATED HER ILL-TREATMENT WITH THE AIM OF +DAMAGING THE PRESTIGE OF LAW-ENFORCEMENT AGENCIES AND ABETTING AND ESCALATING REVOLUTIONARY ANTI-ESTABLISHMENT STRUGGLES.+

MORE

0103

NNNN

a YK0941

070423 :BC-TORTURE =1.1
     THESE FINDINGS FAILED TO SATISFY OPPOSITION PARTIES WHO
TOOK UP KWON'S CAUSE AS ANOTHER STICK WITH WHICH TO BEAT THE
GOVERNMENT OF PRESIDENT CHUN DOO HWAN.
     RIOT POLICE TEARGASSED HUNDREDS OF DEMONSTRATORS WHO TRIED
TO HOLD AN +ANTI-TORTURE PRAYER MEETING+ AT SEOUL'S MAIN
ANGLICAN CHURCH AND BROKE UP A PROTEST RALLY AT THE CITY'S
CATHOLIC CATHEDRAL.
     THEN THE U.S. STATE DEPARTMENT IN WASHINGTON JOINED THE
FRAY.
     A DEPARTMENT SPOKESMAN CONDEMNED KWON'S ILL-TREATMENT
WHICH WASHINGTON BELIEVED WAS +MORE SEVERE AND HARSHER THAN
ACKNOWLEDGED.+
     HE ADDED: +WE FIND SUCH TREATMENT OF PRISONERS DEPLORABLE
AND APPALLING.
     +AS IN ALL CASES INVOLVING TORTURE AND MISTREATMENT OF
PRISONERS, WE URGE THE KOREAN GOVERNMENT TO PUNISH AS PROVIDED
BY LAW THOSE RESPONSIBLE AND TO TAKE STEPS TO ASSURE (SIC)
THAT SUCH ABUSES ARE NOT REPEATED.+
     KWON IS ONLY ONE OF AT LEAST 10 WOMEN STUDENTS AND WORKERS
SAID BY WOMEN'S GROUPS TO HAVE BEEN STRIPPED BY INVESTIGATORS
AND SEXUALLY TORTURED AFTER TAKING PART IN RECENT
ANTI-GOVERNMENT PROTESTS.
     THE PROSECUTORS' OFFICIAL REPORT SAID KWON WAS BEATEN
AFTER SHE FAILED TO GIVE DETECTIVE MOON NAMES OF RADICALS WHO
TOOK PART IN BLOODY STREET RIOTS IN INCHON IN MAY.
     MORE

0104

070425 :BC-TORTURE =1.2
     KWON, THE REPORT SAID, DENIED SHE KNEW ANYONE INVOLVED IN
THE DISTURBANCES, THE WORST IN SOUTH KOREA SINCE THE ARMY PUT
DOWN A CIVILIAN INSURRECTION IN THE SOUTHERN CITY OF KWANGJU
IN MAY 1980 WITH HEAVY LOSS OF LIFE.
     +THEREUPON, MOON MADE KWON TAKE HER JACKET OFF, BUT NOT
HER T-SHIRT, AND BEAT HER IN THE BREASTS THREE OR FOUR TIMES.+
     DURING A SECOND INTERROGATION LATE THE FOLLOWING NIGHT
KWON AGAIN DENIED KNOWING ANY OF THE INCHON RIOTERS AND WAS
AGAIN BEATEN, THE REPORT ADDED.
     OFFICIAL NEWSPAPER REPORTS OF KWON'S ALLEGATIONS HAVE BEEN
COUCHED IN EUPHEMISTIC TERMS. BUT LEAFLETS CIRCULATED BY HUMAN
RIGHTS GROUPS AND THE MAIN PARLIAMENTARY OPPOSITION GROUP, THE
NEW KOREA DEMOCRATIC PARTY (NKDP), QUOTED HER AS SAYING SHE
WAS STRIPPED, HER HANDS WERE BOUND AND THAT THE DETECTIVE
HIMSELF PARTIALLY UNDRESSED AND ABUSED HER TO THE VERGE OF
SEXUAL PENETRATION.
     SINCE THE ROW ERUPTED MOON HAS BEEN DISMISSED FROM THE
POLICE FORCE BUT AUTHORITIES REFUSE TO PROSECUTE HIM.
     THIS WEEK, DURING A HEATED DEBATE IN A PARLIAMENTARY
COMMITTEE WHICH THE NKDP CALLED INTO SPECIAL SESSION BECAUSE
OF THE KWON CASE, JUSTICE MINISTER KIM SUNG-KY DENIED THE
YOUNG WOMAN WAS SEXUALLY ASSAULTED AND RESISTED CALLS FOR THE
DETECTIVE'S INDICTMENT, SAYING MOON HAD +MADE A MISTAKE OUT OF
HIS PREOCCUPATION WITH HIS JOB.+
     MORE

070427 :BC-TORTURE =1.3
     SEOUL, FREQUENTLY ACCUSED OF HUMAN RIGHTS ABUSES IN ITS
TREATMENT OF POLITICAL DISSIDENTS, DENIES THAT IT SANCTIONS
THE TORTURE OF DETAINEES.
     PRIME MINISTER LHO SHIN-YONG RESPONDED IN PARLIAMENT AFTER
THE LONDON-BASED HUMAN RIGHTS GROUP AMNESTY INTERNATIONAL
ISSUED A REPORT IN JUNE SAYING SOUTH KOREA JAILED HUNDREDS OF
GOVERNMENT CRITICS EACH YEAR AND TORTURED SOME OF THEM.
     LHO SAID GOVERNMENT POLICY FORBADE HUMAN RIGHTS VIOLATIONS
AND +ACTS OF ATROCITY+ IN CRIMINAL INVESTIGATIONS.
     HE SAID SEOUL COULD NOT BE SURE OF PREVENTING ABUSES AT
GRASSROOTS LEVEL BUT PLEDGED EFFORTS TO HALT ALL SUCH
INCIDENTS WHICH HE SAID OCCURRED +BECAUSE HUMAN BEINGS ARE
EMOTIONAL.+
     THE AMNESTY REPORT SAID SOME DETAINEES WERE GIVEN ELECTRIC
SHOCKS, BEATEN OR DEPRIVED OF SLEEP. OTHERS HAD THEIR HEADS
PLUNGED IN WATER OR WERE SUFFOCATED WITH WET TOWELS, THE
REPORT SAID.
     LAST YEAR A SEOUL CIVIL COURT ORDERED THE GOVERNMENT TO
PAY 28,000 DOLLARS COMPENSATION TO A 49-YEAR-OLD WOMAN AFTER
IT FOUND POLICE HAD TORTURED HER DURING A MURDER CASE PROBE.
     THE WOMAN HAD TOLD THE COURT DETECTIVES STRIPPED HER, BOUND
HER HANDS AND FEET, TRAMPLED ON HER CHEST AND POURED WATER
INTO HER NOSE WHILE SHE HUNG UPSIDE DOWN FROM THE CEILING.
     MORE

0106

NNNN

a YK0944

070430 :BC-TORTURE =1.4

GOVERNMENT OFFICIALS SAY KWON EXAGGERATED WHAT HAPPENED
DURING HER INTERROGATION TO TRY TO SMEAR THE POLICE AND
ADVANCE HER IDEOLOGICAL CAUSE.

ONE SENIOR OFFICIAL TOLD REUTERS KWON SAW HER MOTHER AT
THE POLICE STATION AFTER BEING QUESTIONED AND MADE NO MENTION
OF SEXUAL ABUSE.

+THAT ONLY CAME AFTER SHE WAS BACK AMONGST HER RADICAL
FRIENDS IN THE WOMEN'S PRISON,+ HE SAID.

IN A LETTER TO A PRO-GOVERNMENT NEWSPAPER THIS WEEK KWON'S
PARENTS SAID: +WE HAVE SOME CONSOLATION WITH AN ANNOUNCEMENT
MADE BY THE PROSECUTION AUTHORITIES THAT NO SEXUAL VIOLENCE
HAS BEEN INFLICTED ON OUR DAUGHTER ...+

THEY APPEALED TO CHURCHES, POLITICIANS AND THE MEDIA NOT
TO CONTINUE TALKING ABOUT THE INCIDENT WHICH, THEY SAID, +CAN
ONLY AMOUNT TO KILLING OUR POOR DAUGHTER TWICE.+

REUTER

0107

The Washington Post

WEDNESDAY, AUGUST 6, 1986 **A23**

Seoul Accused of Torture

Woman's Sexual Assault Charge Spurs Protest Campaign

By John Burgess
Washington Post Foreign Service

SEOUL—An emotional campaign launched by dissidents against what they call widespread use of torture by the government has grown in recent weeks following allegations by a labor organizer that a South Korean policeman sexually assaulted her during a station house interrogation two months ago.

The government, which concedes the woman was beaten but not sexually abused, has tried to end further debate on the case.

But many Koreans appear to have latched onto this incident as a means to dramatize their allegations about widespread torture.

Riot police dispersed about 3,000 people who gathered last month for a protest rally on the woman's case at the Myongdong Cathedral and two weeks ago, about 1,000 riot police and plainclothes officers barred entry to Seoul's Anglican cathedral, where another prayer and protest meeting against torture had been scheduled.

Dissidents and human rights activists said the number of torture cases is unknown but that the woman's case is the latest in a series.

Her case is also unusual because Korean women seldom make public accusations of rape or other sexual violence, because society typically blames them for such incidents nearly as much as it does their attackers and because their chances of marriage are threatened. But in this incident, the woman sued the policeman, and the case quietly drew wide public interest.

[In Washington, the State Department, referring to the woman's case, has noted that four police officials were dismissed in connection with it. "There are credible allegations that the police mistreatment was more severe and harsher than acknowledged," a spokesman said. The department also said, "We find such treatment of prisoners deplorable and appalling."]

Dissidents also are questioning circumstances of the deaths in recent months of four men said to be involved in antigovernment activities. The authorities have ruled that they died by suicide or natural causes.

According to an official at the Human Rights Committee of the Korean National Council of Churches, prisoners are manhandled or beaten so often that many of them consider it routine. Less frequent, but still reported regularly, he said, are more elaborate forms of abuse such as electric shock, dripping of water into prisoners' noses and, for women, sexual abuse or harassment.

Last fall, the government was accused of torturing Kim Kun Tae, an organizer at a dissident group called the Democratic Youth League. Two editors of the major Seoul newspaper Dong-a Ilbo were reported to have been beaten while police questioned them over a broken news embargo. The government dismissed both cases as fabrications.

Dissidents also said the military tortured about 15 persons arrested this spring on charges that included participating in illegal labor activity, making false statements about a joint U.S.-Korean military exercise and taking part in rioting at Inchon.

Critics said police rely on coerced confessions to obtain convictions in many cases, but torture during interrogation is rarely proved beyond a doubt. Reluctance to expose failures of Confucian concepts of moral government or to give communist North Korea material for propaganda are said to reinforce the government's unwillingness to investigate reports of torture. The London-based human rights group Amnesty International has said it knows of many credible reports of torture in South Korea but only two cases in which officials have been prosecuted for it.

The government has dismissed most allegations of torture as fabrications intended to discredit it. Abuse is rare, officials said, and determined efforts are under way to stamp out what does exist. They cited the fact that the sexual assault case was investigated and debated publicly as a sign of progress.

"If that type of thing happened in the past, the police would have tried to put it under a rock," said H.C. Hyun, a former senior official in the Korean Central Intelligence Agency and now a spokesman for President Chun Doo Hwan's ruling Democratic Justice Party.

The government also argues that many of today's dissidents are hard-nosed revolutionaries who, while in

0108

The Washington Post

custody, provoke officers by shouting obscenities, destroying government property and, in at least one case, throwing excrement.

The accuser in the sexual assault case is a 22-year-old radical labor organizer who formerly attended the elite Seoul National University. She alleged that during interrogations at a police station in Puchon, west of Seoul, on June 6 and 7, a policeman forced her to remove most of her clothes, beat her, attempted to have oral sex with her and committed other acts of sexual violence. During the ordeal, he repeatedly demanded to know the names of other dissidents, she said.

A committee of nine lawyers formed by the opposition to defend the woman interviewed her in jail and issued a report amplifying her claims. The report circulated in churches and dissident offices, since South Korea's closely supervised newspapers did not print full details.

Under pressure, the government conducted an investigation. It announced afterward that it had found that the policeman had forced her to remove her jacket in order to humiliate her, had hit her on the breast six or eight times during interrogation and had used abusive language.

This, however, did not constitute sexual abuse, it said. Her charges were fabrications aimed at "damaging the prestige of law enforcement agencies and abetting and escalating revolutionary antiestablishment struggles," it said in a formal statement. It also accused her and fellow activists of leading "morally decadent private lives."

The policeman was fired, but prosecutors said they would not indict him because he had a good record until this case and was repentant. The woman remains in jail on the original charge of stealing a resident registration card with the intent of using it to conceal her student background and get a job at a factory.

Dissidents said prosecutors found out the true story but got orders from above to back off.

"The government doesn't want to punish him but protects him," said Kim Dae Jung, an opposition leader. The government is adamant that the full story is out.

0109

부천서(권인숙) 사건 관련 미국 반응, 1986   319

Seoul Accused of Torture

Woman's Sexual Assault Charge Spurs Protest Campaign

By John Burgess
Washington Post Foreign Service

SEOUL—An emotional campaign launched by dissidents against what they call widespread use of torture by the government has grown in recent weeks following allegations by a labor organizer that a South Korean policeman sexually assaulted her during a station house interrogation two months ago.

The government, which concedes the woman was beaten but not sexually abused, has tried to end further debate on the case.

But many Koreans appear to have latched onto this incident as a means to dramatize their allegations about widespread torture.

Riot police dispersed about 3,000 people who gathered last month for a protest rally on the woman's case at the Myongdong Cathedral and two weeks ago, about 1,000 riot police and plainclothes officers barred entry to Seoul's Anglican cathedral, where another prayer and protest meeting against torture had been scheduled.

Dissidents and human rights activists said the number of torture cases is unknown but that the woman's case is the latest in a series.

Her case is also unusual because Korean women seldom make public accusations of rape or other sexual violence because society typically blames them for such incidents nearly as much as it does their attackers and because their chances of marriage are threatened. But in this incident, the woman sued the policeman, and the case quickly drew wide public interest.

[In Washington, the State Department, referring to the woman's case, has noted that four police officials were dismissed in connection with it. "There are credible allegations that the police mistreatment was more severe and harsher than acknowledged," a spokesman said. The department also said, "We find such treatment of prisoners deplorable and appalling."]

Dissidents also are questioning circumstances of the deaths in recent months of four men said to be involved in antigovernment activities. The authorities have ruled that they died by suicide or natural causes.

According to an official at the Human Rights Committee of the Korean National Council of Churches, prisoners are manhandled or beaten so often that many of them consider it routine. Less frequent, but still reported regularly, he said, are more elaborate forms of abuse such as electric shock, dripping of water into prisoners' noses and, for women, sexual abuse or harassment.

Last fall, the government was accused of torturing Kim Kun Tae, an organizer at a dissident group called the Democratic Youth League. Two editors of the major Seoul newspaper Dong-a Ilbo were reported to have been beaten while police questioned them over a broken news embargo. The government dismissed both cases as fabrications.

Dissidents also said the military tortured about 15 persons arrested this spring on charges that included participating in illegal labor activity, making false statements about a joint U.S.-Korean military exercise and taking part in rioting at Inchon.

Critics said police rely on coerced confessions to obtain convictions in many cases, but torture during interrogation is rarely proved beyond a doubt. Reluctance to expose failures of Confucian concepts of moral government or to give communist North Korea material for propaganda are said to reinforce the government's unwillingness to investigate reports of torture. The London-based human rights group Amnesty International has said it knows of many credible reports of torture in South Korea but only two cases in which officials have been prosecuted for it.

The government has dismissed most allegations of torture as fabrications intended to discredit it. Abuse is rare, officials said, and determined efforts are under way to stamp out what does exist. They cited the fact that the sexual assault case was investigated and debated publicly as a sign of progress.

"If that type of thing happened in the past, the police would have tried to put it under a rock," said H.C. Hyun, a former senior official in the Korean Central Intelligence Agency and now a spokesman for President Chun Doo Hwan's ruling Democratic Justice Party.

The government also argues that many of today's dissidents are hardened revolutionaries who, while in custody, provoke officers by shouting obscenities, destroying government property and, in at least one case, throwing excrement.

The accuser in the sexual assault case is a 22-year-old radical labor organizer who formerly attended the elite Seoul National University. She alleged that during interrogations at a police station in Puchon, west of Seoul, on June 6 and 7, a policeman forced her to remove most of her clothes, beat her, attempted to have oral sex with her and committed other acts of sexual violence. During the ordeal, he repeatedly demanded to know the names of other dissidents, she said.

A committee of nine lawyers formed by the opposition to defend the woman interviewed her in jail and issued a report amplifying her claims. The report circulated in churches and dissident offices, since South Korea's closely supervised newspapers did not print full details.

Under pressure, the government conducted an investigation. It announced afterward that it had found that the policeman had forced her to remove her jacket in order to humiliate her, had hit her on the breast six or eight times during interrogation and had used abusive language.

This, however, did not constitute sexual abuse, it said. Her charges were fabrications aimed at "damaging the prestige of law enforcement agencies and abetting and escalating revolutionary antiestablishment struggles," it said in a formal statement. It also accused her and fellow activists of leading "morally decadent private lives."

The policeman was fired, but prosecutors said they would not indict him because he had a good record until this case and was repentant. The woman remains in jail on the original charge of stealing a resident registration card with the intent of using it to conceal her student background and get a job at a factory.

Dissidents said prosecutors found out the true story but got orders from above to back off.

"The government doesn't want to punish him but protects him," said Kim Dae Jung, an opposition leader. The government is adamant that the full story is out.

法制司法委員會

懸 案 報 告

1986.8.5

法 務 部

0111

報 告 順 序

0112

一. 富川警察署事件 搜查結果

1. 事件의 發端

○ 이 事件은 他人의 住民登錄證을 竊取한 후, 이를 變造 行使하여 富川市 所在 株式會社 成信(電氣器具 製造業體)에 僞裝就業한 事實로 86. 6. 7. 拘束된 權仁淑(21歲, 서울大 家政大 衣類學科 4年 除籍)이 檢察에 送致되어 仁川 少年矯導所에 收監되어 있던 중, 自身이 富川警察署에서 調査받을 當時 同 警察署 搜査課 調査係 勤務 警長 文貴童(39歲)으로부터 暴行과 醜行을 당했다고 主張하는 內容의 告訴狀을 .86. 7. 3. 仁川地方檢察廳에 提出하고,

○ 또한 文貴童도 같은날 權仁淑이 虛僞事實을 流布하여 自身의 名譽를 毀損하였다는 內容의 告訴狀과 86. 7. 5. 權仁淑이 虛僞告訴로 自身을 誣告하였다는 告訴狀을 各 提出하고,

18-1

0113

○ 86. 7. 5. 辯護士 高泳耉등 9名이 文貴童과 富川 警察署長 玉鳳煥등 警察官 6名에 대하여 瀆職暴行, 苛酷行爲등을 內容으로 하는 告發狀을 提出한 것이 端緖가 되어 管轄 仁川地方檢察廳이 搜査에 着手하게 된 事件입니다.

2. 權仁淑 및 辯護人들의 告訴·告發要旨

○ 文貴童은,

— 6. 6. 04:00～06:30 富川警察署 搜査課 調査係 第5號 調査室에서 權仁淑에게 仁川事態 手配者中 아는 사람의 이름과 居處를 대라고 追窮하면서 자켓과 남방샤쓰를 벗게하고 바지의 지퍼를 연 다음 티샤쓰 위로 가슴을 만지고 그 무렵 入室한 同 警察署 搜査課 刑事係 巡警 李與基에게 "고추가루물 가져와"라고 말하여 겁을 주는 등으로 脅迫 및 醜行을 하고,

18-2

- 6. 7. 21:00 ～ 23:00 第1號 調査室에서 姓名不祥 警察官 2名과 함께 위와 같은 事實을 追窮하면서 權仁淑의 손을 등뒤로 하여 手匣을 채운채 다리뒤에 木棒을 끼워 무릎을 꿇린후 다리 및 허리를 몇차례 때리고, 다시 文貴童이 혼자 權仁淑을 第2號 調査室로 데리고 가 椅子에 앉혀놓고 調査를 繼續하면서 同女의 가슴등을 만지고 下衣를 무릎 아래로 내린후 性的 侮辱을 加하는 등으로 暴行 및 醜行을 하였다는 內容이었으며,

○ 富川警察署長 玉鳳煥, 同 搜査課 調査係長 朴成龍 등은 文貴童으로 하여금 위와 같이 苛酷行爲를 하도록 敎唆하고,

○ 同 警察署 搜査課 刑事係 巡警 李興基는 文貴童이 6. 6. 04:30頃 第5號 調査室에서 위와 같이 苛酷行爲를 할 때 立會하는 등 文貴童의 犯行을 幇助하였다는 內容이었읍니다.

18-3

3. 搜查經緯

○ 이 事件은 警察搜査過程에서의 女性 被疑者에 대한 性的 苛酷行爲 有無가 爭點으로 浮刻되어 이에 대한 一般國民의 關心이 至大하였고,

○ 關聯 當事者의 主張이 完全히 相反되어 맞告訴에 까지 이르렀으며, 告訴狀에 摘示된 事實이 두사람 사이에 이루어진 行爲를 內容으로 하고 있어 性質上 眞相을 糾明하기가 매우 어려운 事件이었읍니다.

○ 檢察은 이 事件의 重要性에 비추어 기필코 그 眞相을 徹底히 그리고 迅速하게 糾明하여 國民들에게 알려야 한다는 基本方針아래 86. 7. 3. 權仁淑의 告訴狀이 接受된 즉시 檢事 9名을 動員하여 7. 16. 까지 14日間 事件當事者인 文貴童을 7回, 權仁淑을 8回에 걸쳐 召喚 調査하였고 그밖에 富川警察署長 玉鳳煥등 警察官 25名과 富川警察署 留置場에 權仁淑과 같이 收容되어 있었던 崔某女人 등 民間人 25名 計 50名을 召喚 調査하는 한편, 2回에 걸쳐 事件現場인 富川警察署 搜査課 調査係 事務室에 대하여 綿密한 實況調査를 하는등 集中的이고 執拗한 搜査를 展開하였읍니다.

0116

18-4

○ 搜査가 展開된 始初에는 文貴童이 一切의 犯行을 頑强히 否認하고 특히 權仁淑의 告訴狀에 文貴童으로부터 처음 調査를 받았다고 摘示된 86.6.6.에는 出勤조차 하지 않고 親舊들과 함께 松湫에 놀러 갔으며 當日 새벽에 權仁淑을 調査한 事實이 전혀 없다고 하면서 松湫에 같이 놀러 갔다는 民間人 3名으로 하여금 虛僞陳述마저 하게 하여 아리바이를 主張하고 있었읍니다.

○ 그러나 檢察의 多角的인 搜査結果, 文貴童이 造作한 아리바이 主張을 깨는 등으로 搜査의 실마리가 풀려 事件의 眞相을 밝히게 된것입니다.

4. 搜査結果

○ 먼저 文貴童이 6.6. 새벽 權仁淑에게 苛酷行爲를 하였다는 告訴事實中,

- 權仁淑에게 暴行을 하면서 옷을 벗으라고 要求하여 同女로 하여금 上衣中 겉옷인 자켓과 남방샤쓰를 벗게 한 후 티샤쓰 위로 가슴部位를 손으로 서너차례 쥐어박아 暴行한 事實, 調査當時 立會하였던 李興基에게 고추가루 물을 가져

18-5

0117

오라고   말하여   脅迫한   事實은   文貴童의   自白등에   依하여
事實로   認定되었읍니다.

- 그러나   文貴童이   權仁淑의   바지   지퍼를   내렸다는   主張에
  關하여는   文貴童이   이를   極口   否認하고   있을   뿐만   아니라
  調査現場에   立會하였던   李興基도   그런   事實은   보지   못했다고
  陳述하고,   當時   富川警察署에   非常召集이   發令되어   職員들이
  往來하는   등   狀況에   비추어   認定할   수   없었읍니다.

○ 다음으로   文貴童이   6.7.밤   姓名不祥   警察官   2名과   함께
  權仁淑에게   暴行을   加하고,   나아가   文貴童이   同女를   醜行
  하였다는   告訴事實中,

- 文貴童이   第1號   調査室에서   權仁淑에게   暴言을   하면서
  調査를   하던   途中   같은   警察署   搜査課   刑事係   巡警
  韓喜正과   黃炳善이   調査室로   들어와   權仁淑에게   手配者
  寫眞帖을   提示하면서   아는   사람을   대라고   追窮한   事實,   그후
  文貴童이   第2號   調査室로   옮겨   權仁淑에게   手匣을   채운채
  單獨으로   繼續   追窮하면서   가슴部位를   서너차례   쥐어박아
  暴行한   事實은   文貴童의   自白등에   의하여   事實로
  認定되었읍니다.

18-6

0118

- 그러나 韓喜正, 黃炳善등과 함께 權仁淑의 무릎을 꿇게
하고 때렸다는 등의 主張에 대하여는 文貴童이 그런 事實이
전혀 없었다고 否認할 뿐 아니라,
위 韓喜正, 黃炳善등도 權仁淑에게 手配者 寫眞帖을 提示
追窮한 事實은 있으나 同女를 꿇어 앉히거나 때린 事實은
없었다고 主張하고, 權仁淑 自身도 그때 加勢한 사람 2名의
얼굴조차 確實히 記憶하지 못하고 있는 點등에 비추어 이를
認定할 수 없었읍니다.

- 나아가 文貴童이 同日밤 權仁淑의 가슴등을 만지고 下衣를
내린후 性的侮辱을 加하는 등으로 醜行을 하였다는 點에
대하여는,

  · 文貴童이 그러한 事實이 없었다고 犯行을 極口 否認
  하고 있고,

  · 實況調査結果 同 警察署 調査室 사이의 칸막이는 防音
  狀態가 不良하여 옆방에서 말하는 소리와 打字소리까지
  들리는 程度의 施設이고,

0119

18-7

· 當時 權仁淑을 調査하던 第2號 調査室 바로 옆방인 第
7號 調査室에서는 搜查課 調查係 巡警 朴炅天이, 또
5〜8미터 밖에 떨어지지 않은 第3號, 第5號 調査室에는
巡警 權五成, 金海成이 각기 門을 열어놓고 勤務를
하면서 第2號 調査室 앞을 往來한 바 있으나 위와
같은 事實을 目擊하거나 感知하지 못하였다고 陳述하고
있으며,

· 위 第2號 調査室은 外部로 向한 兩面이 유리窓으로 되어
있는 데다가 그 뒷편에 있는 武器庫의 外燈이 켜져있어
밖에서 調査室 內部가 들여다 보일 뿐만 아니라 每
時間마다 2人 1組의 巡察組가 武器庫 周圍를 巡察하면서
異常有無를 確認하고 있는 狀況이었고

· 또한 當時 權仁淑 自身도 調査받는 現場에서 文貴童에게
反抗하거나 소리를 친 事實은 없고 나아가 調査直後
留置場으로 가는 途中에서나 入監 直後에도 이에 대해
抗議한 事實이 없었다고 陳述하고 있읍니다.

0120

18-8

• 위에서 報告드린 바와 같이 이 事件 現場이 警察官署內의 公開된 調査場所일 뿐 아니라, 當時 다른 調査室에서도 同僚 警察官들이 勤務를 하고 있었던 點, 權仁淑이 主張하는 被害當時나 直後에 取한 態度등에 비추어 볼 때 위 告訴 內容과 같은 醜行이 있었다고 보기에는 通常의 常識이나 一般 經驗則上 到底히 納得하기 어렵고 權仁淑의 陳述만으로는 이를 認定할 수 없다 하겠읍니다.

○ 다음으로 富川警察署長 玉鳳煥과 同 調査係長 朴成龍이 文貴童에게 苛酷行爲를 하도록 敎唆하였다는 點에 관하여는, 위 兩人이 文貴童에게 苛酷行爲를 하도록 指示한 事實이 전혀 없다고 陳述하고 文貴童도 그러한 指示를 받은 바 없다고 陳述하고 있어 달리 犯罪嫌疑를 認定할 資料를 發見할 수 없었읍니다.

○ 다음으로 李興基가 文貴童의 苛酷行爲를 幇助하였다는 點에 관하여 同人은 文貴童이 權仁淑을 調査할 때 잠시 立會하였을 뿐 文貴童의 暴行에 加勢한 바 없다고 陳述하고, 權仁淑의 陳述도 이에 符合되므로 犯罪嫌疑를 認定할 수 없었읍니다.

0121

18-9

○ 끝으로 文貴童의 權仁淑에 대한 告訴事實中

- 名譽毁損의 點은 權仁淑이 辯護士와 接見할 때 위와 같은 말을 한 事實은 認定되나 이는 辯護人의 助力을 받기 위하여 相談을 한 것일 뿐 이를 外部에 傳播시킬 意圖는 없었다고 認定되므로 公然性이 없어 그 嫌疑를 認定할 수 없고,

- 誣告의 點은 文貴童에 대한 一部 被疑事實이 認定되어 그 犯意를 認定할 수 없으므로 誣告罪로 處罰할 수 없다 하겠읍니다.

5. 處 理 方 針

檢察은 위에서 報告드린 搜査結果를 土臺로 今明間

○ 被疑者 韓喜正, 黃炳善, 玉鳳煥, 朴成龍, 李興基, 權仁淑에 대한 被疑事實 및 文貴童에 대한 一部 被疑事實에 관하여는 그 嫌疑가 認定되지 아니하여 不起訴 處分할 方針이고,

0122

18-10

○ 文貴童의 被疑事實中 위와 같이 犯罪嫌疑가 認定되는 部分은 瀆職苛酷行爲罪에 該當되나 이는 文貴童이 職務에 過剩執着한 나머지 저지른 過誤로서 이로 인하여 86. 7. 16. 이미 懲戒罷免處分을 받았고 同人은 10年以上 警察官으로 奉職하여 왔을 뿐 아니라, 自身의 잘못을 깊이 反省하고 있는 등의 情狀을 參酌하여 起訴猶豫 處分할 方針입니다.

○ 政府는 앞으로도 捜査過程에서 人權 蹂躪 事例가 있어서는 絶對로 안된다는 確固한 方針아래 이번事件을 敎訓삼아 檢察로 하여금 隷下 司法警察官吏에 대한 指揮監督을 더욱 徹底히 하도록 하는 한편, 萬에 一이라도 如斯한 事例가 再發되는 경우에는 法에 따라 斷乎히 措置하여 이를 根絶하는데 倍前의 努力을 기울이겠읍니다.

二. 公安關聯收容者 騷亂 및 鎭壓經緯

1. 서울拘置所 騷亂 및 鎭壓經緯

○ 서울拘置所에 收容中인 國家保安法 違反 安相鍾(23歲, 延大 4年) 및 集會 및 示威에 관한 法律違反 河東夾(22歲, 서울大 3年 休學)등은 常習的으로 行刑 規律을 違反하여 오던 者들로서,

86. 6. 24. 12:00頃 向後 規律을 遵守 할 것을 促求하는 矯尉 李康龍에 대하여 "왜 通房을 못하게 하느냐"면서 辱說을 하고, 舍棟 複道로 뛰쳐나가 다른 收容者들을 향하여 "여러분 通房하는 것 가지고 뭐라 하는데 같이 鬪爭하자"고 高聲으로 외치므로 이를 制止 還房시킨 바 있으며,

翌日 이들에게 官規違反의 不當性을 指摘하며, 收容秩序 維持를 위하여 諸般 規律을 遵守할 것을 敎育하고, 아울러 所內 有線放送을 通하여 全 在所者에게 行刑 規律 遵守를 當付한 事實이 있읍니다.

0124

18—12

○ 86. 6. 26. 14 : 00 頃 集會 및 示威에 관한 法律違反 金慶愛 (23 歲, 女, 成大 4 年)는 檢察의 召喚에 따라 出房하면서 上衣 背面에 齒藥으로 "欺瞞的 憲特 決死反對"라는 不純 口號를 記載하여 着用하고 나오므로 다른 옷으로 갈아 입을 것을 指示하였으나, 不應하여 矯尉 周衡玉등 女職員 으로 하여금 上衣를 갈아 입도록 한 後, 出廷시킨 事實이 있읍니다. 그후 同日 19 : 00 頃 檢事調査를 마치고 歸所한 위 金慶愛가 "出廷中 集團 毆打"云云하며 虛僞事實을 외치는 것을 信號로 公安關聯 女子收容者 40餘名이 "暴力 行爲 公開謝過"등의 口號를 외치고 騷亂을 피우므로 矯尉 周衡玉등이 暴行事實이 없었음을 積極 說諭하였으나 이에 不應 居室內에서 繼續 騷亂타가 翌日 01 : 00 頃 集會 및 示威에 관한 法律違反 朱道暎 (21 歲, 女, 中卒, 工員)등 6 名이 居室門을 破損하고 無斷 出房, 複道를 占據하여 極烈 騷亂을 恣行하자 在房中인 다른 公安關聯事犯들이 이에 合勢, 食器로 房門을 두드리며, 밤새도록 騷亂을 피우므로 不得已 同日 10 : 00 頃 保安課長등 全 幹部를 動員, 이를 制止 鎭壓하고 極烈騷亂者 崔柄伊 (23 歲, 成大 4 年)등 16 名을 保護室에 隔離收容하였읍니다.

0125

18-13

○ 86. 6. 26. 21：00頃 女舍와 隣接한 第9舍 및 11舍에 收容中인 위 河東夾등 男子 收容者들이 室內燈을 消燈한 後 不純口號를 齊唱하면서 居室門을 발로 차는등, 騷亂을 피우므로 騷亂者 16名을 保護室에 隔離收容하였읍니다.

○ 86. 6. 30. 10：15頃 6舍에 收容中인 集會 및 示威에 관한 法律違反 金秉權（ 22歲, 延大 3年）등 20餘名은 運動을 마치고 還房中 入室을 拒否하고 "同 舍棟入口에 設置된 鐵格子 出入門은 在所者를 彈壓하기 위한 것이다"라고 외치면서 同 鐵格子 出入門을 밀어 넘어뜨리고 "鐵格子 設置 撤回, 懲罰 撤回" 云云하며, 同 舍棟複道를 占據하고 保安課長등 幹部職員들의 强力한 說諭에도 不拘하고 繼續 極烈 騷亂을 恣行하므로 收容秩序 維持를 위하여 不得已 緊急 編成된 職員 60餘名으로 하여금 制止 鎭壓하고 極烈 騷亂者 20名을 保護室에 隔離收容한 바 있읍니다. 그후 서울拘置所에 收容中인 200餘名의 公安關聯事犯들이 散發的으로 口號齊唱, 騷亂등을 繼續하므로 이를 각기 說得 또는 鎭壓하고 極烈 騷亂者는 保護室에 隔離收容한 바 있으나, 이들을 毆打하는등 暴力을 加한 事實은 없읍니다.

18-14   0126

○ 위와 같은 一連의 騷亂으로 保護室에 隔離 收容된 收容者가 延 68名에 達하였으나 職員들의 積極的인 說諭로 本人들이 잘못을 是認하고 向後 規律遵守를 다짐하므로 86. 7. 1.부터 7日 사이에 全員 還房措置 하였으며, 現在 隔離 收容되었거나 懲罰 執行中인 사람은 한 사람도 없을 뿐 아니라 이들 全員이 收容秩序에 順應하고 있읍니다.

2. 永登浦拘置所 騷亂 및 鎭壓經緯

○ 永登浦拘置所에서는 86. 6. 30. 16:50頃 檢察召喚에 不應하는 集會 및 示威에 관한 法律違反 丁海京 (28歲, 女, 서울大 卒業, 無職)을 同行하였다가, 翌日 04:30頃 歸所한 事實이 있는 바,

同人이 들어가면서 "오늘 强制出廷 갔다 왔다. 우리 모두 싸우자" 라고 큰소리로 외치는등 다른 收容者를 煽動하므로 不得已 女舍 2棟 1室에 分離收容하였다가 同日 16:20頃 女舍 1棟 3室로 還房措置한 事實이 있읍니다.

0127

18-15

○ 86. 7. 2. 08：30 頃 위 丁海京등 公安關聯 女子收容者 18名은 "强制出廷 責任지고 拘置所長 물러가라" 는등 口號를 외치며, 居室門을 발로 차고 食器등으로 門을 두드리고 이를 制止 說諭하는 勤務職員에게 殘飯과 汚物 등을 投擲하면서 極烈騷亂을 恣行하였고

○ 同日 13：00 頃 擔當勤務中인 矯導 宋永玉이 殘飯 收去를 위하여 女舍 1棟1室을 開門하는 瞬間 同 室에 收容中이던 集會 및 示威에 관한 法律違反 鄭恩娥(21歲, 女 서울大 4年)가 부서진 螢光燈을 들고 뛰어나와 職員을 威脅, 舍棟밖으로 내쫓고 舍棟 出入門을 안으로 잠근 後 窓門을 부순 角木으로 다른 居室의 자물쇠를 쳐서 破損하여 金賢珠(24歲, 女, 成大卒, 無職)등 18名을 出房케 하여 合勢하고 유리窓을 부수는등 極烈亂動을 恣行, 副所長등의 强力한 說得에도 不應하므로 不得已 이를 制止, 鎭壓하여 保安課 事務室등으로 分散하였다가, 同日 17：30 頃 多少 鎭静되었으므로 還房시킨 바 있읍니다.

0128

18-16

○ 이들은 자기 房으로 돌아간 後에도 一切의 運動, 接見, 出廷등 出房을 拒否하고 同行을 못하도록 옷을 벗고 室內에서 騷亂을 부리며, 繼續的인 說得에도 不應하므로 同月 5日 그中 極烈騷亂者 9名에 대하여 禁置 10~15日의 懲罰에 處하고 反省을 促求한 바, 自身의 過誤를 是認하고 向後 規律遵守할 것을 다짐하므로 同月 12日 全員에 대하여 殘罰 執行을 免除하였으며, 現在 隔離 收容되었거나 懲罰 執行中인 사람은 한 사람도 없을 뿐 아니라, 이들 全員이 收容秩序에 順應하고 있읍니다.

3. 綜 合 意 見

○ 拘置所등에 收容된 公安關聯事犯들은 拘束된 後 裁判을 拒否하거나 收容生活中의 騷亂, 亂動行爲를 鬪爭의 一環으로 생각하고 常習的으로 規律違反 行爲를 恣行하고 이를 制止하는 過程에서 頑强히 反抗하면서 矯導官과의 摩擦을 誘導함으로써 그 鎭壓過程에서 생기는 若干의 傷處를 暴行 또는 拷問 당하였다고 歪曲主張하면서 社會輿論化를 劃策하는 傾向이 있읍니다.

0129

18-17

○ 拘置所는 刑事訴訟節次上의 收容保護 機關이므로 이들이 規律을 遵守하는 한 日常生活을 干涉하는 일이 없으며, 더우기 意思强要를 目的으로 하는 拷問등 暴力行爲는 있을 수 없는 것입니다.

○ 그리고 公安關聯事犯 뿐만 아니라 凶惡犯, 思想犯등 많은 重犯者들을 收容하고 있는 拘置所 當局으로서는 在所者를 保護하고 所內 秩序를 維持하기 위하여 不得已 이를 制止, 法 節次에 따라 隔離收容 하거나 戒具使用 등 最小限의 强制力 行使는 不可避한 것임을 理解하여 주시기 바랍니다.

○ 앞으로 公安關聯收容者들의 騷亂行爲가 再發되지 않도록 幹部職員들로 하여금 持續的인 相談活動을 施行함과 아울러 社會著名人士등의 醇化面談을 通하여 收容生活에 適應토록 積極 善導하는 한편 不純策動이나 常習的인 規律違反行爲가 根絶되도록 嚴正한 收容管理에 最善을 다 하겠읍니다.

感謝합니다.

0130

18-18

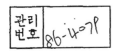

외 무 부

번 호 : AVW-1037   일 시 : 610171700   종 별 :

수 신 : 장관(국기,기정동문)

발 신 : 주오스트리아대사

제 목 : 유엔 여성 당국에대한 부천 권양 사건 진정

1.당지 소재 유엔 사회 개발 및 인도 문제 센타를 관장하는 OPPENHEIMER 유엔
사무차장보는 86.10.9.자 본직앞 비밀 서한(당관 86.10.17.접수)을 통해 이돈명등 9
명의 변호사가 문귀동등 4인의 경찰관을 상대로 86.7.5.인천 지검에 제출한 부천 사
건관련 고발장 영역문이 유엔 EXOSOC 결의들 (304 XI,1983/27,1986/29 등)에 의
거한 아국내 여성 지위관련 비밀 통지문으로 유엔 당국에 접수되었음과 관련,동 고발
장 영역문 사본을 송부하여 오면서 이에대한 아국 정부의 논평등 답신을 87.9월까지
회보하여 줄것을 요청하여왔음.

2.동 서한에의하면,동 통지문의 작성자 성명은 작성자 자신이 성명등을 공개하지 않
는한 ECOSOC 결의들에 따라 공개할수 없다고함.

3.동 통지문 및 아국 정부의 답변은 요약되어 여성 지위관련 LIST OF COMMUNICATIO
NS 에 수록, 1988년 열릴 여성 지위위원회 제32차 정기 회의기간중 WORKING GROUP
ON COMMUNICATIONS 에 의해 심사될것이라함.

4.송부된 통지문 사본은 변호인단의 고발장 영문 번역이 전부이며 그밖의 내용은 포
함하고 있지않음.

5.동 서한 및 통지문 차주 파편 송부 예정임.

(대사 이시용-국장)

예고:87.12.31.일반

국기국   차관실   1 차보   정문국   청와대   총리실   안 기   구주국

PAGE   1   86.10.18   10:16
                                                      외신 2과   통제관

주 오 스 트 리 아 대 사 관

오 지 리(정)743-87

수신 : 외무부 장관

참조 : 국제기구조약국장

제목 : 유엔 여성 당국에 대한 부천 권양 사건 진정

연 : AVW - 1037

표제 관계, Oppenheimer   유엔 사무차장보의 서한 및 동 서한
첨부물(여성지위 관련 통지문) 사본을 별첨 송부합니다.

첨부 : 동 서한(SD 3012/15) 및 첨부물.

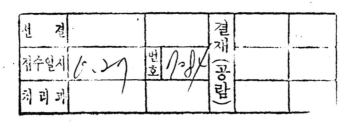

주 오 스 트 리 아

0132

REFERENCE: SD 3012/15   09 October 1986

CONFIDENTIAL

Sir,

    I have the honour to refer to Economic and Social Council resolution 76 (V) of 5 August 1947, as amended by ECOSOC resolution 304 (XI) of 14 and 17 July 1950, ECOSOC resolutions 1983/27 of 26 May 1983 and 1986/29 of 23 May 1986, all regarding "Communications concerning the status of women".

    In keeping with these three resolutions and as specifically stated in ECOSOC resolution 304 (XI), the Secretary-General is requested:

    "... to furnish each Member State concerned with a copy of any communication concerning the status of women which refers explicitly to that State, or to territories under its jurisdiction, without divulging the identity of the author" ... "except in cases where the authors state that they have already divulged or intend to divulge their names or that they have no objection to their names being divulged".

    Accordingly, the attention of the Government of the Republic of Korea is drawn to the enclosed confidential communication received by the United Nations concerning the status of women in the Republic of Korea.

    Pursuant to the above-mentioned resolutions of the Economic and Social Council, the contents of this communication and any reply received from the Government will be summarized for publication in the list of communications concerning the status of women, which will be reviewed by the Working Group on Communications of the United Nations Commission on the Status of Women, at the thirty-second regular session of the Commission to be held in 1988.

H.E. Mr. Sie Yong Lee
Ambassador Extraordinary and Plenipotentiary
Embassy of the Republic of Korea
Kelsenstrasse 2   0132
A-1030 Vienna

In order to ensure inclusion of all relevant information in the summary of communications, it would be appreciated if the comments of the Government regarding this communication could be received by the Branch for the Advancement of Women, Centre for Social Development and Humanitarian Affairs, in Vienna, no later than September 1987.

Accept, Sir, the assurances of my highest consideration.

Tamar Oppenheimer
Assistant Secretary-General
Officer-in-Charge
Centre for Social Development
and
Humanitarian Affairs

0134

<u>A Bill of Indictment</u>

Accusers
1. Ko, Young-gu
   57-9, Seosomun-dong, Chung-gu, Seoul (Hanyoung Bl. Rm.901)

2. Kim, Sang-chul
   360-1 Taepyungro 2 ga, Chung-gu, Seoul (Kwanghack Bl. 905)

3. Park, Won-soon
   57-7, Seosomun-dong, Chung-gu, Seoul (Daegun Bl. 801)

4. Lee, Don-myong
   7-1, Mukyo-dong, Chung-gu, Seoul (Mukyo Bl. 502)

5. Lee, Sang-soo
   55-4, Seosomun-dong, Chung-gu, Seoul (Baejae Bl. 311)

6. Cho, Young-rae
   58-17, Seosomun-dong, Chung-gu, Seoul (Myungjee Bl. 1306)

7. Cho, Jun-hee
   360-1, Taepyungro 2 ga, Chung-gu, Seoul (Kwanghack Bl. 706)

8. Hong, Sung-woo
   55-4, Seosomun-dong, Chung-gu, Seoul (Baejae Bl. 503)

9. Hwang, In-chul
   360-1, Taepyungro 2 ga, Chung-gu, Seoul (Kwanghack Bl. 601)

The Accused
1. Mun, Kwi - dong
   (Police detective of the criminal investigation section
   of Puchon Police Station)

2. Ok, Bong-whan
   (Chief of Puchon Police Station)

3. Unknown
   (Chief of the criminal investigation section of Puchon
   Police Station)

4. 3 unknown
   (Police detectives of criminal investigation section
   of Puchon Police Station; three observers at the time
   of sex torture)

1. We are the lawyers of Miss Kwon who is confined in Inchon Juvenile
Prison under the charge of forgery of an offical document. Having interviewed
her and confirmed that the act of sex torture, which was previously known
to us as a rumor, was actually inflicted upon her by policeman, we cannot
help being shocked and angry. When we recognized that such barbarous cruelty,
which we had thought existed only under Nazi rule, was shamelessly committed
in this land, we felt not only shock and anger but gloomy despair over this
incident which demages one's trust in human beings. In the sense that this
act was not done simply out of impulsive lust but was committed systematically

0135

and abusively as a means of torture, this case was all the more shocking. Now we have concluded that with our recognition of the reality of the case, to keep silence would mean our giving up of our minimum responsibility as lawyers. Therefore, we have decided to indict the persons related to this case and to demand their punishment.

2. The contents of Indictment

June 4.

At about 9:00 p.m. Miss Kwon was taken by the police-detective to the "Room for Investigation of Public Security Offenses" on the 4th floor of Puchon police station. There she was investigated until about 3:00 a.m. on the following day, June 5. Besides the investigation of the charge, they persistently asked whether she knew Yang Seung-cho, and whether she knew the whereabouts of any of those wanted in relation to the Inchon incident, or whether she had seen any of them before.

June 5.

At about 9:00 a.m. she was taken to the investigation room of the police detectives on the first floor. Police Sergeant Chung Oh-do, who was supposed to be in charge of interrogating her, took her to room 420 (or room 421) on the fourth floor. From that time till about 6 p.m., she was interrogated under the charge of forgery of an offical document (a certificate of residence), and questioned about the persons wanted by the police, and then she went to bed in the police custody room.

June 6.

At 4:00 a.m. someone came and took her to the "situation room". At that time there was an atmosphere of emergency in Puchon police station, with all the detectives already present in the office. Looking at Miss Kwon, the chief of the police station said, "Miss Kwon is too uncooperative with us in the investigation", and stalked out angrily. (By non-cooperation with the investigation he meant: When the detectives, showing Miss Kwon the list of the wanted persons related to the Inchon incident, persistently asked if there was anybody she knew among them, and especially if she knew the chairman of Inchon United Labour Movement, Yang Seung-cho, or any other person who knew him, she did not cooperate with the detectives despite their belief that there were persons she knew on the list.) After the chief went out, the 'manager of situation room' (with pop-eyes, wearing combat fatigues and an armband inscribed 'manager of situation room') said that she was too untalkative and seemed to be on the same team as the persons who were mentioned in the process of investigation. (This seemed to indicate the persons wanted in relation to the Inchon Incident). Then, he ordered the investigation to be turned over to Mun,Kwi-dong, saying, "Mun Kwi-Dong, you take charge of her and try to manage it."(It is not clear if the name is 'Mun, Kwi-dong' or 'Mun,Kee-dong'. The detectives called him 'Mun Ban-chang' (section leader). He had a grim look, with a dark complexion, thick lips, and hard eyes. He was of average height, and about 35-36 years old. He spoke with a Seoul accent. According to his own words, he was in Pupyung before. From hereon he will be referred to as 'Mun,Kwi-dong'.) Accordingly, Mun Kwi-dong took Miss Kwon to the police detectives' investigation room on the 1st floor, and conducted the dirty sex torture (called "the 1st sex torture"), from 4:30 a.m. till about 6:30 a.m., as follows:

0136

(1) To begin with, saying "your crime cannot be forgiven even under a changed policy. Neverth[...] if you inform us about anybody whom you know among the wanted, we will release you", Mun,Kwi-dong tried to force Miss Kwon to confess the names of persons she knew. Because she insisted up to the end that she knew nobody, Mun,Kwi-dong threatened her, saying, "You wretched woman! I dealt only with women at the time of the 5.3 Incident (the Inchon Incident). All those bitches brought to the police station at that time, confessed everything after I put them over the desk naked from the waist down. Even if a stick (the exact meaning of this is unclear) enters your body (womb) will you still not confess?"

(2) As she trembled with fear, Mun,Kwi-dong forced Miss Kwon to take off her clothes. When she had taken off only her jacket and one shirt, and was wearing only a T-shirt, a brassiere, and pants, Mun Kwi-Dong called another detective (he looked young and of a lower position) and had him stand beside them. Then, unbuttoning and unzipping her pants by himself, he asked, "Are you a virgin? Have you masturbated?" Uncovering her brassiere, he pushed it up, and saying dirty words such as, "your breasts don't look like a virgin's", in a moment he had pulled off Miss Kwon's pants in spites of her begging, "Please, help me!"

(3) Due to her extreamely unbearable humiliation, disgraceful feeling, and fear, she finally told the name of one friend (whom she had met while looking for work). She did not even know if it was the woman's real name or not. (The friend was not related to the Inchon incident.) Mun,Kwi-dong asked her to write the friend's personal history in detail. When Miss Kwon said she did not know about it, Mun,Kwi-dong ordered the detective standing beside them, "Bring the hot-pepper water" and then, forcing Miss Kwon onto the desk, he threatened her, "Will you tell me that if I really put a 'stick' into your womb?" Only when Miss Kwon wrote the location of the house where the above Miss Lee lived, did Mun, Kwi-dong, somewhat satisfied that he would get some results, stop the investigation and let Miss Kwon put on her pants. Even then, he again asked, "Are you a real virgin?"

(4) Soon, detectives in 'the communism section' showed her pictures of the wanted persons and confirmed that the above Miss Lee was not one of them. After that she was taken into the police custody room and slept there one night.

June 7 (Saturday)

At about 7:00 a.m. Mun,Kwi-dong took Miss Kwon again and asked, "You said you knew Yang,Seung-cho?" When she answered 'No', he questioned her closely again several times, "Tell me if there are more persons you know", and returned her to the other room. At about 9:00 a.m. someone came to take her to the police detective on the first floor. When she got there, she saw about 10 detectives including "manager of situation room", Police Sergeant Chung,Oh-do, Mun,Kwi-dong and others. Telling her that when they had visited Miss Lee's house as Miss Kwon had informed them, the landlady told them nobody like Miss Lee had lived in that house, they brought the landlady face to face with Miss Kwon. As a result of the cross examination, they concluded that Miss Kwon had lied to them all the time. Then Police Sergeant, Chung,Oh-do slapped her once, and "manager of situation room" said intimidatingly, "The treatment from now on will be different from before. You'll see tonight!", and directed Mun,Kwi-dong, "Tonight interrogate her in that way". Taking Miss Kwon to the police custody room again, Mun,Kwi-dong treatened her, "The information that you gave us was a total lie. I will punish you!" While Miss Kwon was in the custody room all

0137

that day, she shivered with fear and anxiety, only hoping for remand to the prosecutor's office as soon as possible. Inquiring of other detainees about how long she would probably be kept there, however, she heard only the hopeless answer that she would be sent to the prosecutor's office after about 10 days, from that day. At about 9:00 p.m. Mun Kwi-Dong called her to the "police detectives' investigation room" (next to the room where Mun,Kwi-dong investigated her) on the 1st floor. At that time, all the staff of that office left, and all the lights in the building were turned off so that it was only by the light from outside the building the objects in the room could be vaguely distinguished. Mun,Kwi-dong angrily said, "I have to work even on Saturday night, you spiteful witch!" and threatened her, "Because of you, I have to remain in the office to interrogate you, even at midnight when everyone else has gone home. The orders from above are to find out the facts using whatever means". Then he called two other detectives into the room and had them handcuff her wrists behind her back. In that position, they forced her to kneel down with a stick inserted in the bend behind her knees. Mun,Kwi-dong had them continuously beat and tramp down on her thighs, waist, etc. At the same time, Mun,Kwi-dong tried to force her to confess the above Miss Lee's real name, her alma mater, her residence, etc. Her thighs became bruised and blue-black, and swelled. When Miss Kwon screamed because of her unbearable pain and fear, Mun,Kwi-dong shouted her down, "You, bitch! How can you shout and yell! I'll kill you if you yell. To kill a wretched woman like you is nothing!" Later on, persistently ordering her to tell the names of persons she knew among the wanted, as Miss Kwon said she did not know any of them, Mun,Kwi-dong shouted at the detective beside him to bring the torture tools. When the detective brought a black bag, he turned on the light and took a file out of the bag, which was filled with personal records and pictures of the 20 wanted persons, and turning the pages of the record one by one, Mun Kwi-Dong stubbornly continued the same line of questioning. As Miss Kwon repeatedly told him she did not know any of them, Mun,Kwi-dong said disgustedly, "You, wretched woman, I cannot endure you anymore!", and he sent the detectives out of the room and took her to his room (both sides of the room had windows), next to the investigation room. It was about 9:30 p.m. For about one and a half hours from that time till about 11:00 p.m., the beast with a human face, Mun,Kwi-dong, committing barbarous acts which were sinful against God and humanity, tortured Miss Kwon. For this one and a half hours, the light was off in the room and Miss Kwon, with her hands handcuffed behind her back, had to remain in this approximately 2 pyung-size room alone with Mun,Kwi-dong. It was a desperate situation for her with no indication of any other person being around. The barbarous acts committed by Mun,Kwi-dong are as follows;

(1) First, Mun,Kwi-dong asked what her father's job was and she lied that her father owned a restaurant.(Actually, her father is a clerk of the court. Worring about the bad effect on his status as a public servant, she told this lie.) He reacted scornfully and threatened,"I will see how hard-headed you are, you bitch! If tortured even spies confess everything to us!, Mun,Kwi-dong ordered her to take off her clothes. As Miss Kwon took off her outer clothes, Mun,Kwi-dong pushed up her brassiere, unzipped her pants, and then put his hand into her private parts. As she screamed, he shouted her into silence threatening that he would kill her if she screamed.

(2) Taking off even Miss Kwon's underwear, and placing two chairs facing each other, Mun, Kwi-dong made Miss Kwon sit on a chair, putting her hand-cuffed hands behind the chair and himself sitting on another chair which he put close to Miss Kwon's so that he could adhere himself to her body. In that pose, he ordered her to tell the whereabouts of the wanted persons. Although Miss Kwon begged him not to do so, Mun, Kwi-dong just ignored her and threatened her, "Nothing will happen even if such a wretched woman as

0138

you dies here." From then, Mun, Kwi-dong frequently fumbled with her breasts, touched her private parts, and rubbed his body on Miss Kwon's repeatedly.

(3) Later, Mun Kwi-dong made Miss Kwon stand, took off her pants completely, and made her breasts naked by pushing up her brassiere. Then, he pushed her face down onto the desk in the same handcuffed position and, standing behind her and taking off his pants, put his penis against Miss Kwon's private parts and took it off several times. Due to her desperate fear and humiliation, Miss Kwon was almost fainting. Mun, Kwi-dong made her sit down on the chair again and forced her to suck a lit cigarette.

(4) A little later, Mun, Kwi-dong pulled Miss Kwon down from the chair violently and made her kneel down on the floor so that he, sitting on the chair, could make her face his penis. In that position, he continued to investigate her. In the meantime, Mun, Kwi-dong pulled her head toward himself, made her lips touch his penis, and tried to put his penis into her mouth. Shocked, Miss Kwon turned her head. Then Mun, Kwi-dong jerked her violently to a standing position and attempted to kiss her by force. As Miss Kwon did not open her lips and turned her head away, Mun, Kwi-dong roughly sucked the nipple of Miss Kwon's left breast two or three times.

(5) Later, Mun, Kwi-dong again pushed her face down onto the desk as before and, standing behind her, repeated his brutal conduct; that is, he put his penis against Miss Kwon's private parts several times. Finally, a little later, she heard the sound of Kleenex tissue being pulled out of a box. With this he washed Miss Kwon's private parts and dressed her.

(6) While he continued the above brutal conduct, Mun, Kwi-dong persistently tried to force Miss Kwon to tell the names of the wanted persons whom she knew and threatened that if she screamed, he would kill her.

Also, while committing the above acts, Mun, Kwi-dong let her rest three or four times, put lit cigarettes into her mouth by force, and had her drink water. Then, he continued to question her closely about the wanted persons, threatening her with various means. Meanwhile, due to the unbearable pain, Miss Kwon told the name of a woman who had visited her house and the name of the company at which the same woman had worked. Mun, Kwi-dong ordered her to write the contents of what she had told him on a paper. After he had committed the above barbarous acts, Mun, Kwi-dong arrogantly proclaimed, "It will be no use for you to tell prosecutor about what you have experienced here. They and we are all in cahoots with each other."

After 11:00 p.m. Mun, Kwi-dong took the completely exhausted Miss Kwon to the police custody room, packed her things, and then took her to a jail cell. (At that time, a warrant of arrest had already been issued to Miss Kwon.)

Generally, when a person is imprisoned in a police jail, his/her clothes are first removed, for the conventional body search. In Miss Kwon's case, Mun, Kwi-dong called and directed a female jailer, "I have already searched her. Therefore, it is not necessary to do a body search. Just give her a single room." And then he went away.

From then, Miss Kwon stayed in the jail cell for 10 days until she was sent to the prosecutor. She could not eat anything for a while; when she did eat, she suffered continuously from indigestion. Also, she could not sleep well at night because of nightmares.

Several times, she was tempted to kill herself. However, she managed with difficulty to overcome this temptation to suicide, gradually coming to the dicision that she would fight to the end in order that such grim violence might not be committed again, even if she had to sacrifice her future as a woman.

0139

June 16

Since her imprisonment in the jail cell, Miss Kwon has continued to suffer
from nightmares, up to the present. Miss Kwon's father, a clerk of Wonju
court, handed in his resignation due to the shock he experienced from her
case.
As Miss Kwon's case became known to the prisoners in Inchon jail, about 70
prisoners of conscience in that jail went on a hunger strike demanding Mun,
Kwi-dong's arrest, etc. Miss Kwon herself also continuously abstained from
eating for 5 days, from June 28 till July 2, causing extreme injury to her
health.

3. The above is the summary of what the victim, Miss Kwon revealed before
her lawyers about the barbarous sex violence-torture that has been unheard of
in our history. We are convinced of the truth of the above contents, based
on Miss Kwon's attitude during her testimony and on the whole surrounding
situation. We find ourselves shocked and trembling in the face of this
commission of acts so unmentionably dirty and barbarously sinful against
God and humanity, especially when these acts were committed by none other
than a policeman in the very police station itself. Moreover, despite the
fact that these barbarous acts have been made known to the so-called protec-
tor of human rights, the prosecutor, the criminal has kept his status as a
policeman and continues to strut shamelessly along the streets; this makes us
doubt whether legal order exists even superficially in this country. When
this young woman, a former student of one of the highest educational institutions, has confessed such a humiliating experience, the fact that she was
inflicted with sex torture, what other possible evidence do they need for
investigation and why have they not investigated this case yet? Inside the
police station, with no witness, is it then possible for anything to happen,
however illegal and inhuman? Thus, if prosecutors only look on without taking
action against human rights violations by the police, there will be no way to
protect the innocent citizens from victimization under the violence of
police power. If the real situation of this case is not thoroughly proved,
and if severe punishment is not imposed, both on the person who directly
committed the crime and on the other responsible persons related to this
crime, then, in the future every woman will be paralyzed with fear whenever
she passes in front of a police station. Accordingly, as we tremble with
indignation beyond our power to describe, first, we indict Mun, Kwi-dong, who
committed this crime which is too immoral to imagine. We indict also the
accused, the manager of the situation room (name unknown) and the chief of
the police station, Ok, Bong-ho, who must have conspired with Mun, Kwi-dong,
aided and abetted the crime, or at least overlooked and left the situation
as it was even as they knew the fact. In addition, we indict the accused
3 unknown detectives under the charge of conspiring with Mun, Kwi-dong or
aiding the crime.

If this case is ignored, it will be too shameful even to mention such words
as human dignity, conscience, human rights, legal order, democracy, etc.

We, all the accusers, will not retreat our step until Mun, Kwi-dong and all
the other accused are punish   by law, which we demand immediately. We
declare that, by using whatever legal means necessary, we are bound and
determined to get real result from this indictment.

4. We call your office's attention to the following points in investigating this case.

0140

First, it is evident that this case is not merely a single offense committed
due to the uncontrolled sex drive of one individual, Mun, Kwi-dong, who
might have been sexually perverted, but rather a systematically executed
crime of deliberate sex torture, planned by the hierarchical police authority.
We strongly demand that your office expose the whole picture of this appalling,
deliberate crime in detail, clarify the facts of the crictial plan of the
crime, and legally punish all the persons who are related to this case including all those accused here.

Second, the acts of the accused deserve to be defined as rape or forced
criminal assault, but they are excluded from this indictment because they are
a crime which can be legally punished by personal accusation only. Therefore,
we indict only the acts which can be defined as violent and cruel, which were
committed by these persons who are legally in charge of human confinement.
However, we take a serious view of this case in the sense that it involved
not only the type of conventional torture or brutality we have often seen,
but was a crime committed by means of immoral sex torture for the purpose of
destroying the humanity of woman, and the brutal crime was committed not in
order to investigate the charge against Miss Kwon but simply for the purpose
of arresting other wanted persons. We also remember the incident in which a
female student of Kyunghee University was the victim of sex violence com-
mitteed by combat police at Chungryangri police station on September 4, 1984.
Moreover, we have been told that the families of suspected persons arrested
in relation to the May 3 (1986) Inchon Incident insisted that their daugh-
ters were victimized by torture similar to that used in Miss Kwon's case.
In the process of checking into Miss Kwon's case, we have been convinced that
the claims of these families were also true, and have realized that sex has
been systematically abused as a means of torture in certain police stations.
We must not overlook the fact that the human atrocities described above are
being systematically committed in a democratic, and constitutional country,
which taken human dignity as its highest ideal. By investigating this case
thoroughly over the shortest possible period, and exposing the real facts to
the public, the prosecutors should make it clear that they have no intention
of concealing and defending this crime.

July 5, 1986

Accusers: Ko, Young-gu
Kim, Sang-chul
Park, Won-soon
Lee, Don-myong
Lee, Sang-soo
Cho, Young-rae
Cho, Jun-hee
Hong, Sung-woo
Hwang, In-chul

To: The Chief of the Inchon Local Prosecution

0141

權양 上告 포기
1년6월 刑확정

사진의 權모양(23·서울大의 뉴4제적)이 2일 변호인단을 통해 상고포기서를 법원에 제출했다. 검찰도 상고를 포기…

공문서변조등혐의로 구속기소돼 1·2심에서 징역 1년6월…

…월을 선고받은 權모양은 징역 1년6월의 실형이 확정됐다.

1,6개월 81.3까지 항소로예정

「靑年동맹」 결성혐의
서울大生 3명 拘束

치안본부는 2일 서울대생 양기철군(23·국제경제3년)과 고대생 정재성군(23·식품공학4년) 김창수군(23·철학4년) 등 3명을 국가보안법위반혐의로 구속했다.

경찰에 따르면 양군들은 지난해부터 NLPDR(민족해방인민민주주의)이론에 입각한 「청년동맹」을 결성하려한 혐의이다.

〈81.4.3 金 한국〉

W172
    R
    SOUTH KOREA-TRIAL
    RA
    SENTENCE CONFIRMED FOR DISSIDENT WHO CLAIMED SEXUAL TORTURE
    SEOUL, SOUTH KOREA (AP) - THE 18-MONTH PRISON SENTENCE FOR A
FORMER STUDENT WHO CLAIMED SHE WAS SEXUALLY TORTURED BY POLICE
DURING INTERROGATION WAS CONFIRMED THURSDAY AS SHE FAILED TO
APPEAL, COURT OFFICIALS SAID.
    THEY SAID KWON IN-SUK, A 24-YEAR-OLD COLLEGE DROPOUT, LET THE
SIX-DAY DEADLINE GO BY WITHOUT APPEALING TO THE SUPREME COURT.
    LAST SATURDAY, AN APPELLATE COURT UPHELD MISS KWON'S CONVICTION
ON CHARGES OF FALSIFYING A DOCUMENT. THE CHARGES SAID THAT IN
APPLYING FOR EMPLOYMENT AT A FACTORY, SHE OMITTED REFERENCE TO THE
FACT THAT SHE HAD BEEN A STUDENT AT AN INSTITUTION OF HIGHER
LEARNING.
    AUTHORITIES HAVE ACCUSED ACTIVIST STUDENTS OF TAKING SUCH STEPS
IN TRYING TO INFILTRATE THE RANKS OF LABOR TO PROMOTE UNIONISM OR
STIR DISSENT.
    AT THE TIME OF HER ARREST LAST JUNE, MISS KWON CLAIMED SHE WAS
MOLESTED BY A POLICE INVESTIGATOR SEEKING A CONFESSION THAT SHE HAD
DISSIDENT BACKING. THE CASE BROUGHT SHARP OUTCRIES FROM DISSIDENTS
AND HUMAN RIGHTS ACTIVISTS.
    THE GOVERNMENT PROSECUTION CALLED HER CHARGE EXAGGERATED BUT
LATER ACKNOWLEDGED THAT SHE HAD BEEN PHYSICALLY ABUSED DURING
POLICE INTERROGATION.
    END
AP-NY-04-02-87 0814GMT

8, 21자. 경향일보

0144

「富川사건」裁定신청

仁川地檢 기각

서울高檢으로 송치

仁川지검은 5일 富川경찰서
권양(22)을 「성고문」사건의 權某양(22)
등 기각, 사건기록을 서울高
검에 제출한 재정신청30여건을 인용않
되니 仁川지검과 의견을 같이
할때는 30일내에 사건을 서울
고검으로 송치했다.

서울고검은 재정신청이 이
유있다고 인정될때는 仁川지
검에 공소제기명령을
서울고검은 재정신청이 「이
사건이 서울고법으로 송
치될경우 그동안 한번도 공개되
지 않았던 이사건의 검찰수
기록을 변호인들이 열람·복사
할수 있게된다.

서울대4년제적)과 張基旭변
호사등 1백66명의 변호인단이
제출한 재정신청을 인용않
고법으로 송치해야한다.

한국일보 9.6자.

0145

재판부-기피신청
"위장就業" 權양

13일 상오10시 인천지법형
사2부 (재판장 尹會漢부장판
사) 심리로 열린 「부천서 성
고문사건」의 權모피고인(여·
22·서울대 의류학과4년제
적)에 대한 위장취업관련부
분 첫공판은 검찰의직접 신문
과 변호인 반대신문을 모두
마친뒤 재판부와 변호인단사
이에 증○채택여부로 논란을
벌인끝에 변호인측이 재판부
기피신청을 내 하오4시30분
쯤 공판이 중단됐었다.

변호
인단은 성고문사건의 결찰수
사기록을 검증할것과 文貴童
당자인 文貴童결찰과 수사담
의 범행사실을 목격했다는
李휴기 巡警성형사등 3명을 재
판부에 신청했다.
증인으로 채택해 줄것을

10.16. 경향신문.

0146

前富川署長 면직

치안본부는 14일 「부천서 성고문사건」과 관련, 지난 7월 16일자로 직위해제했던 玉鳳煥전부천경찰서장의 사표를수리했다. 玉署경의 사표수리는 직위해제 발령후 3개월내 보직 발령을 받지못할 경우 행직되는 인사규정에 따른 것이다.

10. 15. 조선일보

0147

裁判部기피·棄却
富川署사건

인천지법 형사1부(재판장 金元培부장판사)는 25일 부천
서 성고문사건」의 權모양(22,
서울대4년 제적)에 대한 공판에서 변호인
단이 담당재판부(인천지법형
사2부)를 상대로낸 재판부기피
신청에 대해 「공소사실과 판결
없는 증인신청을 재판부가 받
아들이지 않았다는것은 당연하다
는 이유로」기각했다.

변호인단은 지난22일 權모양에
대한 공문서변조사건공판중
증거조사과정에서 文貴童 전부
천경찰서형사들등 3명의 경찰관
을 증인으로 신청했으나 재판
부에의해 받아들여지지않자 재
판부 기피신청을 냈었다.

1986. 10. 26. 조선일보

0148

第6520號　　1986年11月7日　金曜日　　中　

法院 "富川署사건은 수사관의 우발적 犯行"

權양 재정신청 大法에 再抗告

86.11.7. 중앙일보
(印)

0149

富川署 사건 權양

징역 3年刑 구형

담배를 끊읍시다

[仁川=咸永攄기자] 인천 지검 南忠鉉검사는 21일 「부천서 성고문사건」의 權모양 (22·서울대 가정대4년제적)에게 공무집행방해등 「부녀자준강제추행」을 적용, 징역 3년을 구형했다.

검찰은 이날 인천지법 형사 2부 (재판장 尹鍾洙부장판사) 심리로 열린 결심공판에서 「노사분규를 일으킬 목적으로 남의 주민등록증을 변조해 취업한 행위는 전혀 정상을참작할 여지가 없다」고 구형했다.

이어 共生福祉변호사등 변호인단은 「이 시대의 옳스런 성고문사건이 일어난 것만으로도 우리 모두가 참회해야 되는 것이며 『노동자의 비참한 생활을 개선하기 위해 안락한 가정을 버리고 노동계에 뛰어든 權양의 행위는 도덕적·법률적으로 모두 무죄』라고 주장하고 「수사과정에서 權양에게 부도덕한 범죄를 저지른 文貴童 경장은 법정에 서지않고 權양만 재판을 받는것 자체가 잘못된것」이라고 주장했다.

한편 民黨의원, 朴炯圭 金東吉목사등 1백여명이 재판을 지켜봤다.

낮12시40분쯤 재판이 끝날무렵 50여명의 방청객들은 법원구내에, 모여 「고문정권물러가라」고 적힌 머리띠를 두르고 20여분간 농성하다 해산했다.

선고공판은 오는28일 오전9시30분.

5·3인천사태와 관련, 국가보안법위반등 혐의로 구속기소돼 1심에서 징역7년, 자격정지3년을 선고받은 張琪杓 (41·전민통정책연구실장) 피고인의 변호인단은 21일 1심 판결에 불복, 서울형사지법에 항소했다.

民統聯 張琪杓씨 항소

360 한국 인권문제 미국 반응 및 동향 2

0150

정 리 보 존 문 서 목 록				
기록물종류	일반공문서철	등록번호	21349	등록일자	1994-09-29
분류번호	701	국가코드	US	보존기간	영구
명 칭	미국 국무부의 한국 인권문제 보고서, 1985 -87			
생 산 과	북미과	생산년도	1985~1987	담당그룹	북미국
내용목차	1. 1985 (1984 년도) 2. 1986 (1985 년도) 3. 1987 (1986 년도)			

0001

1. 1985 (1984년도)

외 무 부 착 신 전 보

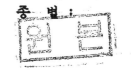

번 호 : USW-748   일 시 : 02131908   종 별 :

수 신 : 장 관 (미북, 정이)

발 신 : 주 미 대 사

제 목 : 국무성인권 보고서

　　84 년도 국무성 인권 보고서를 금 2.13. 한국과로 부터 입수한바, 2.15. 정파편
송부함.

　　(대사 류병현)

미주국　　1차보　　정문국　　청와대　　안 기　　３기３

주 미 대 사 관

미국(정) 700 -   ٦538   1985. 2. 14.

수 신 : 장 관

참 조 : 미주국장, 정보문화국장

제 목 : 국무성 인권보고서

연 :   U S W - 748 (85.2.13), 751 (8

미 국무성이 85.2. 13. 의회에 제출한   및

북한부분을 별첨 보고 합니다.

첨 부 : 1.   아국 인권보고서

2.   북한 인권보고서

3.   국별 인권보고서 (미주국).   끝.

주   미   대

0001

0005

미국 무성의 1984년 인권보고서

1985.2.13 공개된 각국 인권보고서중 한국 및 북괴관련 부분의
주요특징은 다음과 같음.

1. 한국 관계

   ○ 1983년도 인권보고서 내용과 대동소이. 단 하기사항이
     추가 또는 수정되었음.

     - 북한은 수해물자 제공 및 대화제의등 평화적 제스추어
       에도 불구하고 대남 무력도발을 계속 하고 있으며,
       공격적인 무력증강을 강화하고 있음.

     - 1984년중 학원자율화, 교수 및 언론인 복직, 과거
       정치인에 대한 복권 및 정치해금등 적극적인 자유화
       조치가 있었음. 1984년의 정치관련범은 제5공화국
       이후 최저 수준인 110명 가량임.

     - 대통령각하는 1988년 평화적 정권교체 약속을 재확인
       하였음.

2. 북괴관계

   ○ 북한사회는 김일성 족벌체제하에 세계에서 가장 조직화
     되고 통제되었으며, 모든 개인권리가 철저히 당에 종속

0006

되었다고 기술한 점에서 1983년도 보고서와 거의 같으나
하기사항이 특별히 강조됨.

- 84년중 북한은 남한에 수재물자를 제공했고, 경제회담
  및 이산가족 재회를 위한 남한의 회담제의에 긍정적인
  반응을 보이기도 했으나, 남한을 공격목표로 하는
  군사력을 계속 증강시키고 있음.

첨부 : 동 보고서 요지 1부.   끝.

제 1 차 관 보

공 람	북미과	85년 2월 14일	담 당	과 장	심의관	국 장	차 관	장 관
			김	2용	동	보		

ACTION: POL-3 INFO: AMB DCM ADM RSO ECON2 CON/RR ACPUSAN CPRON-//

VZCZCULO186
OO RUEHUL
DE RUEHC #6704/01 0372017
ZNY CCCCC ZZH
O 062003Z FEB 85
FM SECSTATE WASHDC
TO AMEMBASSY SEOUL   IMMEDIATE 4702
BT
C O N F I D E N T I A L   STATE 036704

LOC: 85229   407
06 FEB 85   2017
CN: 45659
CHRG: PROG
DIST: PCLC

IMMEDIATE

EAP ONLY

E.O. 12356: DECL: CADR
TAGS: SHUM, KS, PINS
SUBJECT: 1984 SOUTH KOREAN HUMAN RIGHTS REPORT

1. FOLLOWING IS THE FINAL VERSION OF THE SOUTH KOREAN
HUMAN RIGHTS REPORT FOR 1984. THIS REPORT IS EMBARGOED
BY THE DEPARTMENT AND WILL NOT BE RELEASABLE TO ANY
NON-DEPARTMENT SOURCE UNTIL FURTHER NOTICE.

2. BEGIN TEXT:

IN THE REPUBLIC OF KOREA, PRESIDENT CHUN DOO HWAN, WITH
THE SUPPORT OF THE COUNTRY'S MILITARY ESTABLISHMENT,
DOMINATES THE POLITICAL SCENE. THE ELECTED LEGISLATURE
HAS SOME INFLUENCE BUT CONTINUES TO BE CONTROLLED BY THE
EXECUTIVE BRANCH. THE GOVERNMENT, WHICH ASSUMED POWER
WITH PRIMARILY MILITARY SUPPORT IN 1980, IS ORGANIZED
UNDER A CONSTITUTION ADOPTED BY REFERENDUM IN OCTOBER
1980. BECAUSE OF THE THREAT FROM AN AGGRESSIVE COMMUNIST
REGIME IN NORTH KOREA, ALL KOREAN GOVERNMENTS SINCE THE
REPUBLIC'S FOUNDING IN 1948 HAVE FELT IT NECESSARY TO
GIVE TOP PRIORITY TO MAINTAINING EXTERNAL AND INTERNAL
SECURITY; THEIR POLICIES IN THIS RESPECT, AS IMPLEMENTED

IN PART BY THE LARGE AND WELL-ORGANIZED SECURITY
SERVICES, HAVE BROUGHT CHARGES THAT DISSENT AND PEACEFUL
OPPOSITION POLITICAL ACTIVITY ARE SUPPRESSED, AND TO MANY
KOREANS THE DEGREE OF LEGITIMACY OF THE CHUN GOVERNMENT
IS OPEN TO QUESTION. AT THE TIME OF THE NEXT
PRESIDENTIAL ELECTION, SCHEDULED FOR 1988, PRESIDENT CHUN
HAS PROMISED TO STEP DOWN TO PROVIDE FOR A PEACEFUL AND
CONSTITUTIONAL CHANGE OF POWER.

THE REPUBLIC OF KOREA HAS A MIXED ECONOMY WITH EXTENSIVE
PUBLIC SECTOR INTERVENTION TO STIMULATE AND INFLUENCE THE
DIRECTION OF PRIVATE SECTOR ACTIVITY. SINCE ADOPTING AN
OUTWARD-LOOKING DEVELOPMENT STRATEGY IN THE MID-1960'S,
THE REPUBLIC OF KOREA HAS HAD ONE OF THE HIGHEST REAL
GROWTH RATES IN THE WORLD AND HAS ACHIEVED MIDDLE-INCOME,
"MIDDLE POWER" STATUS. SINCE 1981, THE ECONOMIC
LEADERSHIP HAS MOVED TOWARD A MORE OPEN, FREER MARKET
SYSTEM.

KOREA IS AN ETHNICALLY HOMOGENEOUS NATION. SURROUNDED BY
GREAT POWERS--CHINA, JAPAN, AND IN MODERN TIMES THE
USSR--KOREA HISTORICALLY FOCUSED ITS FOREIGN POLICY ON
THE OBJECTIVE OF AVOIDING SUBJUGATION BY THESE
NEIGHBORS. IN 1910, KOREA WAS ANNEXED BY THE JAPANESE
EMPIRE. LIBERATED IN 1945, IT WAS THEN DIVIDED INTO
TEMPORARY SOVIET AND AMERICAN ZONES OF MILITARY
ADMINISTRATION, ORGANIZED IN 1948 AS, RESPECTIVELY, THE
DEMOCRATIC PEOPLE'S REPUBLIC OF KOREA, OR NORTH KOREA,
AND THE REPUBLIC OF KOREA, OR SOUTH KOREA.

SINCE THE DIVISION OF THE PENINSULA IN 1945,
REUNIFICATION HAS BEEN A MAJOR GOAL OF KOREANS ON BOTH
SIDES OF THE DIVIDING LINE. NORTH KOREA, HOWEVER, HAS
INSISTED ON REUNIFYING THE NATION ON ITS OWN TERMS AND
THROUGH ANY MEANS, INCLUDING USE OF MILITARY FORCE OR
TERRORIST ACTIVITIES. DESPITE NORTH KOREA'S DELIVERY OF
FLOOD RELIEF GOODS TO THE SOUTH IN 1984 AND ITS POSITIVE
RESPONSE TO SOUTH KOREAN PROPOSALS TO HOLD NORTH-SOUTH
TALKS ON ECONOMIC COOPERATION AND FAMILY REUNIFICATION,
MILITARY ACTIVITIES AGAINST THE SOUTH CONTINUED,
INCLUDING CONTINUING FORWARD DEPLOYMENT OF ITS ARMED
FORCES. THE MEMORY OF THE 1983 RANGOON BOMBING AGAINST
SOUTH KOREAN LEADERS, WHICH THE BURMESE GOVERNMENT
DETERMINED WAS CARRIED OUT BY NORTH KOREA, IS STILL FRESH
IN THE MINDS OF SOUTH KOREANS. THE AREA ON EITHER SIDE
OF THE DEMILITARIZED ZONE REMAINS ONE OF THE MOST HEAVILY
ARMED REGIONS IN THE WORLD. DURING THE DEFECTION OF A
SOVIET LANGUAGE STUDENT ACROSS THE DMZ ON NOVEMBER 23,
30-40 NORTH KOREANS SOLDIERS CROSSED THE DMZ AND

EXCHANGED FIRE WITH SOUTH KOREAN AND AMERICAN UN COMMAND
GUARDS IN AN EFFORT TO RETRIEVE THE SOVIET STUDENT.

FURTHERMORE, NORTH KOREA CONTINUES TO STRENGTHEN ITS
OFFENSIVE FORCE STRUCTURE. OVER THE YEARS, UNREMITTING
NORTH KOREAN PROPAGANDA, OVERT AND COVERT, HAS BEEN
DIRECTED AT SOUTH KOREA, CALLING FOR THE DESTRUCTION OF
AMERICAN AND SOUTH KOREAN INSTALLATIONS, VIOLENCE AGAINST
SOUTH KOREAN LEADERS, AND THE OVERTHROW OF THE SOUTH
KOREAN GOVERNMENT.

THUS, FEAR OF ANOTHER INVASION FROM THE NORTH IS A
FUNDAMENTAL FACTOR IN SOUTH KOREAN THINKING, AND
SUCCESSIVE GOVERNMENTS HAVE HELD THAT FOR SECURITY
REASONS THE REPUBLIC CANNOT AFFORD THE UNFETTERED DISSENT
AND DISCORD WHICH WOULD BE PERMITTED IN AN OPEN POLITICAL
SYSTEM. NONETHELESS, MANY KOREANS QUESTION THE RATIONALE
FOR THIS POSITION.

KOREA'S TRADITIONAL SOCIO-POLITICAL IDEOLOGY,
CONFUCIANISM, WITH ITS EMPHASIS ON ORDER, CONFORMITY,

0009

CONSENSUS AND FILIAL PIETY, RETAINS GREAT STRENGTH,
COEXISTING UNEASILY WITH THE WESTERN DEMOCRATIC IDEALS
AND INDUSTRIAL-AGE VALUES TO WHICH KOREANS HAVE BEEN
EXPOSED IN THIS CENTURY.

KOREANS OF BOTH SEXES PARTICIPATE IN POLITICS.
CONSTITUTIONAL SAFEGUARDS AGAINST EX POST FACTO LAWS AND
DOUBLE JEOPARDY ARE GENERALLY OBSERVED. ALTHOUGH THE
CONSTITUTION GUARANTEES FREEDOM OF SPEECH AND THE PRESS,
IN PRACTICE BOTH ARE ABRIDGED. POLITICIANS AND OTHERS
WHO PUBLICLY CRITICIZE THE GOVERNMENT ARE AWARE THAT
THERE ARE LIMITS BEYOND WHICH THEY MAY BE SUBJECT TO SOME
FORM OF GOVERNMENT ACTION. NEWSPAPERS ARE EXPECTED TO
PRACTICE SELF-CENSORSHIP, AND FAILURE TO COMPLY WITH THIS
REQUIREMENT HAS LED TO INTERROGATION AND ON OCCASION
DISMISSALS OF REPORTERS AND EDITORS. THE LAW LIMITS THE
FREEDOM TO ASSEMBLE AND DEMONSTRATE, ALTHOUGH IN 1984, IN
A BREAK WITH PAST PRACTICE, THE GOVERNMENT DID NOT APPLY
THE LAW TO UNIVERSITY CAMPUSES AND ARRESTS HAVE
ACCORDINGLY BEEN SHARPLY REDUCED. RELIGIOUS FREEDOM,
THOUGH OTHERWISE COMP4ETE, DOES NOT EXTEND TO CHURCHES'
INVOLVEMENT IN POLITICAL AND SOME FORMS OF SOCIAL ACTION.
THERE IS FREEDOM OF MOVEMENT WITHIN THE COUNTRY AND
FREEDOM TO TRAVEL ABROAD, EXCEPT THAT PASSPORT
APPLICATIONS FROM PERSONS WITH A HISTORY OF POLITICAL
OPPOSITION ARE CONSIDERED ON A CASE-BY-CASE BASIS AND
SOME ARE NOT ALLOWED TO LEAVE THE COUNTRY.

DURING 1984 THE GOVERNMENT TOOK SEVERAL SIGNIFICANT
POSITIVE STEPS IN THE HUMAN RIGHTS FIELD. MORE THAN 220
STUDENTS JAILED FOR CAMPUS DEMONSTRATIONS WERE RELEASED
FROM PRISON DURING THE YEAR IN THREE SEPARATE AMNESTIES,
AND ABOUT 1,400 STUDENTS PREVIOUSLY EXPELLED FOR
POLITICAL ACTIVISM WERE ALLOWED TO RE-ENROLL AT THEIR OLD
CAMPUSES. ABOUT HALF THIS NUMBER HAD ACTUALLY RETURNED
BY THE FALL TERM. SOME 86 DISSIDENT PROFESSORS, BANNED
FROM TEACHING SINCE 1980, WERE ALSO PERMITTED TO TEACH
AGAIN AT THEIR ORIGINAL CAMPUSES. IN EARLY 1984 THE
GOVERNMENT INITIATED A POLICY OF "CAMPUS AUTONOMY" UNDER
WHICH IT WITHDREW SECURITY FORCES FROM UNIVERSITY
CAMPUSES, A MAJOR STUDENT DEMAND; ALLOWED PEACEFUL
DEMONSTRATIONS ON CAMPUSES; AND STATED THAT HENCEFORTH
UNIVERSITIES WOULD BEAR THE PRIMARY RESPONSIBILITY FOR
ENFORCING CAMPUS DISCIPLINE. IN THE FACE OF INCREASED
STUDENT RESISTANCE MEASURES, THE GOVERNMENT IN NOVEMBER
WARNED THAT IT WAS PREPARED TO HAVE POLICE ENTER CAMPUSES
EVEN WITHOUT INTERVENTION REQUESTS BY SCHOOL OFFICIALS.
IN PRACTICE, HOWEVER, SECURITY FORCES ONLY ENTERED
CAMPUSES ON A FEW OCCASIONS. HOWEVER, STUDENTS HAVE
ACCUSED THE GOVERNMENT OF MAINTAINING CAMPUS NETWORKS OF
POLICE INFORMERS. STUDENT ATTEMPTS TO MOVE
DEMONSTRATIONS OFF CAMPUS WERE MET BY LARGE GOVERNMENT
SECURITY FORCES, WHICH LED TO VIOLENT CONFRONTATIONS AT
UNIVERSITY GATES AND, ON OCCASION, ELSEWHERE IN DOWNTOWN
SEOUL.

IN ANOTHER AMNESTY MOVE, THE GOVERNMENT RESTORED CIVIL
RIGHTS TO MORE THAN THAN 700 FORMER POLITICAL PRISONERS,

0010

INCLUDING SOME PROMINENT INTELLECTUALS AND HUMAN RIGHTS
ACTIVISTS, AND MANY CONVICTED UNDER EMERGENCY DECREES OF
THE PARK CHUNG HEE GOVERNMENT. THE GOVERNMENT ALSO
ANNOUNCED THAT JOURNALISTS WHO HAD BEEN BANNED FROM
EMPLOYMENT SINCE 1980 COULD BE REEMPLOYED AT THE
DISCRETION OF THEIR FORMER EMPLOYERS, AND SOME HAVE GONE
BACK TO WORK. AS A RESULT OF THE LARGE-SCALE AMNESTIES
CARRIED OUT EARLY IN THE YEAR, THE NUMBER OF PRISONERS IN
POLITICALLY-RELATED CASES WAS REDUCED TO ABOUT 110, THE
LOWEST SINCE THE FIFTH REPUBLIC CAME INTO BEING IN 1980.
ABOUT ONE-THIRD THAT NUMBER ARE KOREAN RESIDENTS OF JAPAN
CONVICTED OF ESPIONAGE ON BEHALF OF NORTH KOREA, AND MOST
OF THE REST ARE CONVICTED OF NATIONAL SECURITY LAW
VIOLATIONS OR ACTIVITIES INVOLVING THE USE OR PLANNED USE
OF VIOLENCE. HOWEVER, THE GOVERNMENT'S CURRENT TACTIC OF
HOLDING OFF-CAMPUS DEMONSTRATION LEADERS IN JAIL FOR
BRIEF PERIODS, AFTER SUMMARY CONVICTIONS ON MINOR
CHARGES, MEANS THAT THE TOTAL NUMBER OF PRISONERS AT ANY
ONE TIME MAY BE GREATER THAN THE NUMBER OF ARRESTED AND

CONVICTED PERSONS ON THE "PRISONER OF CONSCIENCE" LIST.

POLITICAL ACTIVITIES OF 551 FORMER POLITICIANS.
FOLLOWING GOVERNMENT ACTION IN 1983 TO LIFT THE BAN ON
250 OF THEM, IN 1984 THE GOVERNMENT LIFTED THE BAN ON 286
MORE, LEAVING A TOTAL OF 15 STILL AFFECTED. THE 15,
HOWEVER, INCLUDED SEVERAL OF KOREA'S MAJOR FORMER
OPPOSITION PARTY LEADERS. ONE OF THE MOST PROMINENT OF
THESE, KIM DAE JUNG, HAS BEEN IN THE UNITED STATES FOR
TWO YEARS FOR MEDICAL TREATMENT. ALTHOUGH HE FACES
POSSIBLE ARREST AND AN UNEXPIRED PRISON SENTENCE IN
KOREA, HE HAS ANNOUNCED PLANS TO RETURN EARLY IN 1985.

TORTURE OR SEVERE PHYSICAL MISTREATMENT BY THE POLICE
OCCURRED IN 1984, BUT THERE WERE NO REPORTS OF THIS ABUSE
OCCURRING IN POLITICALLY SENSITIVE CASES. SOME FEMALE
STUDENT DEMONSTRATORS, HOWEVER, CHARGED THAT THEY WERE
SUBJECTED TO ABUSIVE STRIP SEARCHES BY THE POLICE. THE

0011

GOVERNMENT HAS SAID THAT IT IS TRYING TO ELIMINATE THE
DEEPLY-ROOTED PROBLEM OF ABUSIVE TREATMENT BY POLICE,
ESPECIALLY BEATINGS OF SUSPECTS DURING INTERROGATION.
THIS EFFORT APPARENTLY HAS HIGH-LEVEL SUPPORT WITHIN THE
GOVERNMENT, AS INDICATED BY THE PASSAGE IN DECEMBER 1983
OF A LAW PROVIDING PENALTIES UP TO LIFE IMPRISONMENT FOR
OFFICIALS COMMITTING ACTS OF TORTURE. HOWEVER, THE
PROBLEM, THOUGH DIMINISHED, HAS NOT DISAPPEARED. IN
ADDITION TO THE POLICE, THERE ARE TWO OTHER SECURITY
SERVICES WHOSE AGENTS ARE ALLEGED TO HAVE BEATEN OR
OTHERWISE MISTREATED SUSPECTS AS WELL AS DISSIDENTS,
INCLUDING STUDENTS AND ACTIVIST WORKERS, WHO WERE NOT IN
CUSTODY.

PRISON CONDITIONS REMAIN SPARTAN, AND THERE ARE REPORTS
OF HUNGER STRIKES AND OTHER PROTESTS, ESPECIALLY BY
STUDENTS. THERE WERE NO ALLEGATIONS OF MURDER AGAINST
THE GOVERNMENT IN 1984, THOUGH SOME DISSIDENTS QUESTION
THE CIRCUMSTANCES OF THE DEATH OF ONE DISSIDENT STUDENT
SAID TO HAVE DIED ACCIDENTALLY WHILE SERVING IN THE
MILITARY IN 1983.

STRONG FORCES WITHIN KOREA SEEK IMPROVEMENTS IN HUMAN
RIGHTS AND LIBERALIZATION OF THE GOVERNING STRUCTURE,
NOTABLY SOME CHRISTIAN CHURCHES' LEADERSHIP AND THE
RISING MIDDLE CLASS. FORMIDABLE OBSTACLES TO THESE
FORCES EXIST, PRIMARILY KOREA'S CONFUCIANIST HIERARCHICAL
TRADITIONS AND THE LACK OF ENTHUSIASM ON THE PART OF THE
POWERFUL MILITARY OFFICER CORPS FOR DIRECT PARTICIPATION
BY ALL KOREANS IN THE DEMOCRATIC PROCESS AND FOR FREEDOM

OF EXPRESSION. FURTHERMORE, THE PERCEIVED NEED FOR UNITY
IN THE FACE OF THE NORTH KOREAN THREAT INHIBITS EFFORTS
FOR POLITICAL CHANGE WHICH MIGHT AFFECT STABILITY.

RESPECT FOR HUMAN RIGHTS

SECTION 1 RESPECT FOR THE INTEGRITY OF THE PERSON,
INCLUDING FREEDOM FROM:

-- A. POLITICAL KILLING

THERE WERE NO REPORTS IN 1984 OF POLITICALLY MOTIVATED
KILLINGS BY THE GOVERNMENT.

-- B. DISAPPEARANCE

THERE WERE NO CASES OF PERMANENT DISAPPEARANCE IN 1984,
ALTHOUGH THE POLICE SOMETIMES WAITED FOR MORE THAN THE
LEGAL MAXIMUM OF 40 DAYS BEFORE NOTIFYING THE FAMILIES OF
ARRESTED PERSONS.

--C. TORTURE AND CRUEL, INHUMAN, OR DEGRADING
TREATMENT OR PUNISHMENT

THE CONSTITUTION PROHIBITS TORTURE. CONFESSIONS
DETERMINED TO HAVE BEEN INDUCED BY DURESS ARE
INADMISSIBLE IN THE COURTS, AND A CONFESSION ALONE IS NOT

0012

LEGALLY SUFFICIENT TO SECURE A CONVICTION. THE
GOVERNMENT INSISTS THAT IT HAS ISSUED INJUNCTIONS AGAINST
TORTURE AND THAT THESE ARE STRICTLY ENFORCED AND
VIOLATIONS STERNLY PUNISHED. NEVERTHELESS, WHILE THERE
WERE NO ALLEGATIONS OF TORTURE IN POLITICALLY SENSITIVE
CASES IN 1984, THERE WERE CONTINUING REPORTS OF BEATINGS
BY POLICE DURING INTERROGATIONS OF PRISONERS. TWO FEMALE
STUDENTS WHO HAD BEEN DETAINED FOR PARTICIPATING IN AN
OFF-CAMPUS DEMONSTRATION FILED SUIT AGAINST POLICE WHOM
THEY ACCUSED OF CONDUCTING ABUSIVE STRIP SEARCHES. THE
USE OF EXCESSIVE FORCE BY THE POLICE, DESPITE HIGH-LEVEL
EFFORTS TO REDUCE OR ELIMINATE IT, HAS PROVEN TO BE A
PERVASIVE AND INGRAINED PROBLEM. IN VIOLENT
CONFRONTATIONS WITH STUDENT RIOTERS, POLICE UNITS HAVE
GENERALLY REMAINED WELL-DISCIPLINED BUT RIOTERS HAVE ALSO
BEEN BEATEN ON APPREHENSION. ACCUSATIONS OF POLICE
BEATINGS IN NON-POLITICAL CASES OCCUR FAIRLY FREQUENTLY
AND ARE SOMETIMES REPORTED IN THE PRESS. NO CASE HAS YET

BEEN BROUGHT UNDER THE LAW ADOPTED BY THE NATIONAL
ASSEMBLY IN 1983 TOUGHENING SENTENCES FOR THOSE CONVICTED
OF KILLING OR INJURING THROUGH TORTURE.

HUMAN RIGHTS GROUPS ALLEGE, IN ADDITION, THAT THE POLICE
AND OTHER GOVERNMENT SECURITY AGENCIES HAVE BEEN
R
SPONSIBLE FOR, OR HAVE NOT INTERVENED TO PREVENT, THE
BEATING OF SOME STUDENTS, WORKERS AND OTHER DISSIDENTS
NOT IN CUSTODY. A HUMAN RIGHTS ACTIVIST LEADER WAS
BEATEN AT HIS CHURCH BY MEN THAT SOME CHRISTIAN ACTIVISTS
LINKED TO THE SECURITY SERVICES. THE GOVERNMENT DENIED
THE CONNECTION.

IN EARLY 1984 THE GOVERNMENT ARRESTED A PROMINENT
CLERGYMAN AND TWO PROFESSORS WHO HAD BEEN CONDUCTING A
STUDY OF REUNIFICATION POLICIES AND CHARGED THEM WITH
VIOLATING THE NATIONAL SECURITY LAW. THESE DISSIDENTS
WERE SUBSEQUENTLY RELEASED WITHOUT TRIAL, BUT CHRISTIAN
ACTIVISTS STATE THAT THE GOVERNMENT USED THREATS TO

0013

COERCE THE DEFENDANTS INTO MAKING PUBLIC EXPRESSIONS OF
REGRET AS A CONDITION OF THEIR RELEASE. ACTIVISTS ALSO
ACCUSE POLICE OF FORCING STUDENTS UNDER INVESTIGATION FOR
CONNECTION WITH WORKERS ISSUES INTO SIGNING CONFESSIONS
OF SUBVERSIVE ACTIVITIES. THERE IS NO EVIDENCE ON THE
RECORD TO SUPPORT THESE CHARGES.

CONDITIONS IN KOREAN CORRECTIONAL INSTITUTIONS ARE
SPARTAN, AND DISCIPLINE IS STRICT. WHILE PRISONERS WHO
BREAK RULES OR PROTEST CONDITIONS ARE SOMETIMES BEATEN,
UNDER NORMAL CIRCUMSTANCES CONVICTS ARE NOT SUBJECTED TO
PHYSICAL PUNISHMENT. PRISONERS MAY RECEIVE VISITS ONLY
FROM THEIR LAWYERS AND IMMEDIATE FAMILIES. THERE DOES
NOT SEEM TO BE A DIFFERENCE BETWEEN THE TREATMENT OF
POLITICAL AND NON-POLITICAL PRISONERS, ALTHOUGH THE
AUTHORITIES HAVE OCCASIONALLY ALLOWED SPECIAL PROVISIONS
FOR POLITICAL PRISONERS, SUCH AS HEATERS DURING THE
WINTER OR EXAMINATION BY OUTSIDE PHYSICIANS. THERE IS NO
APPARENT DIFFERENCE IN THE TREATMENT OF PRISONERS ON THE
BASIS OF WEALTH, SOCIAL CLASS, RACE, OR SEX.

--D. ARBITRARY ARREST, DETENTION, OR EXILE

FROM TIME TO TIME, THE SECURITY SERVICES HAVE NOT ONLY
DETAINED PERSONS ACCUSED OF VIOLATING LAWS ON POLITICAL
DISSENT BUT HAVE ALSO INCREASED SURVEILLANCE OF, OR PUT
UNDER HOUSE ARREST, THOSE THEY THINK INTEND TO VIOLATE
THE LAWS. DISSIDENTS WHO OPENLY CRITICIZE THE GOVERNMENT

IN CASE OF ARREST. FOR PERSONS DEEMED "SOCIALLY DANGEROUS"
THE LAW ALLOWS PREVENTIVE DETENTION UNDER PROVISIONS OF THE
SOCIAL PROTECTION AND SOCIAL STABILITY LAWS. PREVENTIVE
DETENTION IS FOR A FIXED TERM, WHICH, HOWEVER, A JUDICIAL
PANEL MAY EXTEND FOR PERIODS OF UP TO 10 YEARS. HUMAN RIGHTS
ACTIVISTS AND FOREIGN OBSERVERS ARE AWARE OF TWO PERSONS NOW
IN PREVENTIVE DETENTION FOR POLITICALLY-RELATED OFFENSES,
THEIR DETENTION HAVING BEEN RENEWED IN 1984 FOR TWO MORE YEARS.

HABEAS CORPUS, NOT TRADITIONAL IN KOREAN LAW, WAS INTRODUCED
AFTER WORLD WAR II, ABOLISHED IN THE 1970'S, AND REINTRODUCED
IN 1980. IT DOES NOT APPLY TO THOSE CHARGED WITH VIOLATIONS
OF THE NATIONAL SECURITY ACT OR LAWS PUNISHABLE BY AT LEAST 5
YEARS IMPRISONMENT, WHICH INCLUDE MOST POLITICAL OFFENSES.

THE GOVERNMENT RELEASED 229 STUDENTS FROM JAIL IN FOUR
AMNESTIES BETWEEN FEBRUARY AND MAY. ALL THE STUDENTS HAD BEEN
ARRESTED FOR ANTI-GOVERNMENT CAMPUS DEMONSTRATIONS, THOUGH
SOME HAD ALSO BEEN CONVICTED OF NATIONAL SECURITY LAW
VIOLATIONS. WITH THESE RELEASES, THE TOTAL OF STUDENT
DEMONSTATORS RELEASED SINCE DECEMBER 1983 GREW TO 360, AND THE
JAILS WERE EMPTY OF STUDENT DEMONSTRATORS FOR THE FIRST TIME
IN YEARS. A SMALL NUMBER OF STUDENTS CONVICTED UNDER THE
NATIONAL SECURITY LAW FOR CARRYING OUT SUBVERSIVE ACTIVITIES
IS STILL IMPRISONED. IN A LIBERATION DAY AMNESTY THE
GOVERNMENT RESTORED CIVIL RIGHTS TO 714 FORMER POLITICAL
OFFENDERS, INCLUDING A NUMBER OF HUMAN RIGHTS LEADERS,
INTELLECTUALS AND FORMER POLITICIANS. THE GOVERNMENT ALSO
ANNOUNCED THAT IT WILL ERASE THE CRIMINAL RECORDS OF ABOUT

0014

5,000 KOREANS FOR WARTIME COLLABORATION WITH NORTH KOREAN
OCCUPATION FORCES, THUS EASING EMPLOYMENT AND OTHER SOCIAL
DIFFICULTIES FOR THOSE AFFECTED.

FOLLOWING THE LAST STUDENT RELEASE IN MAY, A LIST OF
"PRISONERS OF CONSCIENCE" MAINTAINED BY THE HUMAN RIGHTS
COMMITTEE (HRC) OF THE KOREA NATIONAL COUNCIL OF CHURCHES
CONTAINED 52 NAMES, A LOW SINCE THE BEGINNING OF THE PRESENT
GOVERNMENT. (THE HRC DEFINITION OF "PRISONER OF CONSCIENCE"
DOES NOT EXCLUDE THOSE CONVICTED OF CRIMES INVOLVING THE
ADVOCACY OR USE OF VIOLENCE, CONTRARY TO AMNESTY
INTERNATIONAL'S DEFINITION.) THIS FIGURE COMPARES TO 325 AT
THE END OF 1983, 417 IN NOVEMBER 1982, AND 272 IN NOVEMBER
1981. SUBSEQUENT ARRESTS AND THE ADDITION OF NEWLY DISCOVERED
CASES, MAINLY KOREAN RESIDENTS OF JAPAN CONVICTED, IN PRIOR
YEARS, OF ESPIONAGE FOR NORTH KOREA, BROUGHT THE NUMBER ON THE
LIST TO ABOUT 110. HOWEVER, STUDENT-POLICE CONFRONTATIONS
OFF-CAMPUS AND STUDENT VIOLENCE ON AND OFF CAMPUS IN THE FALL
OF 1984 RESULTED IN A LARGE NUMBER OF PERSONS BEING ARRESTED
AND SENTENCED TO BRIEF PERIODS OF DETENTION ON MINOR CHARGES

AFTER SUMMARY CONVICTIONS. THESE DO NOT FIGURE IN THE
POLITICAL PRISONER LIST.

--   E.   DENIAL OF FAIR PUBLIC TRIAL

THE CONSTITUTION GUARANTEES MANY RIGHTS OF DEFENDANTS: THE
RIGHT TO PRESUMPTION OF INNOCENCE; THE RIGHT AGAINST
SELF-INCRIMINATION, EX POST FACTO LAWS, AND DOUBLE JEOPARDY;
THE RIGHT TO A SPEEDY TRIAL; AND THE RIGHT TO LEGAL COUNSEL.
THESE RIGHTS ARE GENERALLY OBSERVED, ALTHOUGH THERE HAVE BEEN
CASES IN THE PAST IN WHICH DEFENDANTS IN POLITICALLY-SENSITIVE
TRIALS HAVE NOT BEEN ABLE TO OBTAIN LAWYERS, REPORTEDLY
BECAUSE OF LAWYERS' RELUCTANCE TO ACCEPT SUCH CASES IN THE
FACT OF ACTUAL OR POTENTIAL GOVERNMENT PRESSURE.

THE PRESIDENT APPOINTS THE MEMBERS OF THE SUPREME COURT, WHOSE
CHIEF JUSTICE IN TURN APPOINTS LOWER-LEVEL JUDGES. THE

4/9   C O N F I D E N T I A L   STATE   036704/04

0015

JUDICIARY IS CONSIDERED INDEPENDENT IN ORDINARY CRIMINAL AND
CIVIL CASES BUT MUCH LESS SO IN POLITICALLY-SENSITIVE CASES.
IT IS GENERALLY ASSUMED, FOR EXAMPLE, THAT THE ORIGINAL AND
APPEAL VERDICTS IN THE CASE OF SIX CHINESE AIRPLANE HIJACKERS
TRIED BEFORE SEOUL COURTS WERE GUIDED BY FOREIGN RELATIONS
CONSIDERATIONS.

TRIALS ARE USUALLY OPEN TO THE PUBLIC, BUT TRIAL DOCUMENTS ARE
NOT PART OF THE PUBLIC RECORD. CHARGES AGAINST DEFENDANTS IN
THE COURTS ARE CLEARLY STATED, WITH THE EXCEPTION THAT, IN
LENGTHY AND COMPLEX INDICTMENTS, THE RELATIONSHIP BETWEEN
SPECIFIC ACTS ALLEGED AND VIOLATIONS OF SPECIFIC SECTIONS OF
THE PENAL CODE MAY NOT ALWAYS BE CLEARLY DRAWN. IN CASES
INVOLVING A MIXTURE OF POLITICAL AND CRIMINAL CHARGES THIS CAN
BRING INTO QUESTION THE FAIRNESS OF PROCEEDINGS.

THE SAME COURTS TRY POLITICAL AND ORDINARY CRIMINAL CASES.
THE MILITARY COURTS DO NOT TRY CIVILIANS. DEFENDANTS HAVE THE
RIGHT OF APPEAL IN FELONY CASES, A RIGHT WHICH IS OFTEN
EXERCISED AND FREQUENTLY RESULTS IN SUBSTANTIAL REDUCTIONS IN
SENTENCES. DEATH SENTENCES ARE AUTOMATICALLY APPEALED.

-    F.   ARBITRARY INTERFERENCE WITH PRIVACY, FAMILY, HOME, OR
--   CORRESPONDENCE

THE SECURITY APPARATUS IS LARGE AND HIGHLY DEVELOPED. MANY
OPPOSITION FIGURES AND POLITICAL AND RELIGIOUS DISSIDENTS ARE
SUBJECTED TO SURVEILLANCE. DURING POLITICALLY SENSITIVE
PERIODS, THIS SURVEILLANCE BY ONE OR MORE SECURITY AGENCIES
MAY INCREASE OR A FORM OF HOUSE ARREST MAY BE IMPOSED. THERE
HAVE ALSO BEEN CHARGES OF TELEPHONE TAPPING AND OPENING OR
INTERCEPTION OF CORRESPONDENCE. KOREANS WHO MEET WITH

FOREIGNERS, PARTICULARLY WITH JOURNALISTS AND EMBASSY
OFFICIALS, ARE OFTEN QUESTIONED AFTERWARDS. WHILE THE
CONSTITUTION REQUIRES A WARRANT, ISSUED BY A JUDGE UPON
REQUEST OF A PROSECUTOR, FOR SEARCH AND SEIZURE IN A
RESIDENCE, THE POLICE HAVE AT TIMES FORCED THEIR WAY INTO
PRIVATE HOMES WITHOUT WARRANTS.

KOREAN POLICE PRACTICE REQUIRES POLICE COMMANDERS TO KNOW A
GOOD DEAL ABOUT THE PERSONAL AND BUSINESS AFFAIRS OF ALL
RESIDENTS IN THEIR JURISDICTIONS. THIS SYSTEM IS EFFECTIVE IN
CRIME CONTROL, AND URBAN RESIDENTS GENERALLY CREDIT IT WITH
KEEPING THEIR STREETS SAFE. BY CONTRAST, THE PRESENCE OF
POLICE INFORMER NETWORKS ON COLLEGE CAMPUSES WITH THE PRIMARY
PURPOSE OF KEEPING TRACK OF POLITICAL ACTIVITIES THERE HAS
BEEN A KEY ISSUE AMONG STUDENTS, INCLUDING THOSE WHO ARE NOT
POLITICALLY ACTIVE. STUDENTS HAVE ACCUSED THE GOVERNMENT OF
MAINTAINING POLICE INFORMERS ON CAMPUS EVEN AFTER UNIFORMED
FORCES WERE WITHDRAWN IN ACCORDANCE WITH THE "CAMPUS AUTONOMY"
POLICY.

IN MOST OTHER RESPECTS THE GOVERNMENT HONORS THE RIGHT OF
PERSONAL PRIVACY AND THE INTEGRITY OF THE HOME AND FAMILY.
PARENTAL RIGHTS TO EDUCATE CHILDREN ARE BROAD, AND
RESTRICTIONS ON STUDY IN FOREIGN-ADMINISTERED SCHOOLS (WHETHER
IN KOREA OR OVERSEAS), ORIGINALLY IMPOSED TO FORCE WEALTHY

0016

KOREANS TO INVOLVE THEMSELVES IN THE NATION'S SOCIAL AND
EDUCATIONAL DEVELOPMENT, HAVE BEEN RELAXED IN RECENT YEARS.
THE STATE RARELY SEEKS TO INTERVENE IN SUCH INHERENTLY
PERSONAL DECISIONS AS MARRIAGE, CHOICE OF VOCATION, AND
FORMATION OF SOCIAL AND FAMILIAL TIES. HOWEVER, THE STATE, BY
SETTING GRADUATION LEVELS AT HIGHER EDUCATION INSTITUTIONS,
DOES SEEK TO GUIDE THE MIXTURE OF GRADUATES ACCORDING TO
PREDICTED FUTURE MANPOWER NEEDS.

SECTION 2 RESPECT FOR CIVIL RIGHTS, INCLUDING:

"-   A. FREEDOM OF SPEECH AND PRESS

ALTHOUGH FREEDOM OF SPEECH AND PRESS ARE GUARANTEED BY THE
CONSTITUTION, IN PRACTICE THE EXPRESSION OF OPPOSITION
VIEWPOINTS IS SEVERELY LIMITED. DISSIDENTS ARE SOMETIMES
RESTRICTED IN THEIR MEETINGS AND MOVEMENTS IN PERIODS JUDGED
VOLATILE BY THE GOVERNMENT. MEMBERS OF THE NATIONAL ASSEMBLY
FREQUENTLY CRITICIZE PARTICULAR GOVERNMENT ACTIONS OR POLICIES
BUT ARE CAREFUL TO STOP SHORT OF FUNDAMENTAL CRITICISM OF THE
GOVERNMENT ITSELF, SUCH AS ATTACKS ON ITS LEGITIMACY OR
PERSONAL ATTACKS ON THE PRESIDENT. HOWEVER, FORMAL PROPOSALS
FOR VOTES OF "NO CONFIDENCE" AT THE ASSEMBLY AND THE STATED
RATIONALE THEREFORE ARE GIVEN FULL PUBLICITY. LIKEWISE,

CRITICISM OF GOVERNMENT POLICIES (FOR EXAMPLE, THE CAMPUS
AUTONOMY POLICY) IS REPORTED BY THE MEDIA. WHILE NO DIRECT
ACTIONS AGAINST ASSEMBLYMEN WERE TAKEN IN DIRECT RESPONSE TO
OPINIONS EXPRESSED IN THE LEGISLATURE, TWO ASSEMBLYMEN WHO
ATTEMPTED TO SWITCH ALLEGIANCE TO A NEW OPPOSITION PARTY WERE
DETAINED FOR THREE DAYS IN DECEMBER. DISCUSSION OF SECURITY,
FORMULAS FOR POLITICAL SETTLEMENT WITH NORTH KOREA, THE
LEGITIMACY OF THE CHUN ADMINISTRATION, AND OTHER SENSITIVE
TOPICS IS SHARPLY CURTAILED. ACADEMIC FREEDOM IS SUBJECT TO
SOME POLITICAL LIMITATIONS, ALTHOUGH 86 PROFESSORS WHO LOST
THEIR JOBS IN THE POLITICAL UPHEAVALS OF 1980 WERE ALLOWED
DURING 1984 TO RETURN TO TEACHING AT THE SCHOOLS AT WHICH THEY
HAD LAST TAUGHT.

0017

ALL STUDENTS ARRESTED IN CONNECTION WITH DEMONSTRATIONS
OFF-CAMPUS HAVE BEEN CHARGED WITH MINOR OFFENSES AGAINST
PUBLIC ORDER AND RELEASED AFTER SHORT PERIODS OF TIME, RATHER
THAN CONVICTED UNDER THIS LAW. ONLY A SMALL NUMBER OF PEOPLE
WERE CONVICTED AND SENTENCED UNDER THIS LAW IN 1984, IN
PARTICULAR TEN TAXI DRIVERS WHO WERE CONVICTED IN CONNECTION
WITH DEMONSTRATIONS IN TAEGU AND PUSAN. THEY WERE SENTENCED
AND RELEASED.

THE SINGLE NATIONAL LABOR FEDERATION, THE FEDERATION OF KOREAN
TRADE UNIONS (FKTU), AND ITS 16 NATIONAL AFFILIATE UNIONS ARE
NOT CONTROLLED BY THE GOVERNMENT. THEIR FREEDOM OF ACTION,
HOWEVER, IS SEVERELY CIRCUMSCRIBED BY LAW. LABOR
ORGANIZATIONS ARE FORBIDDEN TO SUPPORT POLITICIANS OR
POLITICAL PARTIES, THOUGH THE FKTU DOES LOBBY NATIONAL
ASSEMBLYMEN, PARTICULARLY OF THE RULING DEMOCRATIC JUSTICE
PARTY, AND ASSEMBLYMEN OFTEN ATTEND LABOR-ORGANIZED
GATHERINGS. ALL LOCAL UNIONS MUST BE ORGANIZED WITHIN
INDIVIDUAL ENTERPRISES, CREATING A STRUCTURE OF THOUSANDS OF
INDIVIDUAL UNIONS, MOST OF THEM SMALL AND WEAK. DIRECT
PARTICIPATION IN LOCAL UNIONS' BARGAINING ACTIVITIES BY
OUTSIDE AGENCIES SUCH AS THE ASIAN-AMERICAN FREE LABOR
INSTITUTE, WHICH MAINTAINS AN OFFICE IN KOREA, IS FORBIDDEN.
THE ASIAN-AMERICAN FREE LABOR INSTITUTE MAINTAINS AN OFFICE IN
KOREA. THE FKTU AND ITS CONSTITUENT NATIONAL UNIONS CAN AND
SOMETIMES DO BARGAIN ON BEHALF OF THE LOCALS AND CONDUCT
EDUCATION PROGRAMS, BUT ONLY WITH GOVERNMENT AND EMPLOYER

APPROVAL. COLLECTIVE ACTIONS AND STRIKES, THOUGH TECHNICALLY
LEGAL, ARE TO ALL INTENTS AND PURPOSES FORBIDDEN. RELIGIOUS
LABOR MINISTRIES SUCH AS THE CATHOLIC YOUNG CHRISTIAN WORKERS
AND THE PROTESTANT URBAN INDUSTRIAL MISSION ARE ALSO SEVERELY
LIMITED IN THE ASSISTANCE WHICH THEY CAN PROVIDE THE UNIONS.
UNDER THESE CIRCUMSTANCES, GOVERNMENT AND EMPLOYER INFLUENCE
HAS GREATLY EXCEEDED THAT OF UNIONS IN SETTING WAGES AND
RESOLVING OTHER MAJOR LABOR ISSUES.

0018

THE DOMESTIC MEDIA ENGAGE IN SELF-CENSORSHIP. ACCORDING TO
VERBAL OR WRITTEN GUIDELINES THE GOVERNMENT REGULARLY GIVES TO
EDITORS. JOURNALISTS WHO OBJECT TO OR IGNORE THESE GUIDELINES
OR CRITICIZE THE GUIDANCE SYSTEM HAVE, IN THE PAST, BEEN
PICKED UP FOR QUESTIONING, AND ON OCCASION DISMISSED OR SENT
OUT OF THE COUNTRY ON ASSIGNMENT. THERE WAS A RELIABLE REPORT
IN 1984 OF A JOURNALIST WHOSE COLUMNS WERE CRITICAL OF THE
GOVERNMENT BEING SENT ABROAD FOR STUDY.

THE EXTENT OF JOURNALISTIC FREE EXPRESSION VARIES. FOR
EXAMPLE, WHEN THE NATIONAL ASSEMBLY IS IN SESSION, OPPOSITION
VIEWPOINTS HAVE BEEN RATHER FULLY REPORTED IN THE PRESS.
INCREASED REPORTING IN 1984 WAS PERMITTED BY GOVERNMENT
AUTHORITIES ON THE ACTIVITIES OF DISSIDENT POLITICIANS AND
GROUPS, INCLUDING STUDENT MOVEMENTS. REPORTING ON DISSIDENTS
WAS FACTUAL WITHOUT EDITORIAL COMMENT; REPORTING ON STUDENT
DEMONSTRATIONS WAS MARKED BY EDITORIAL COMMENT HIGHLIGHTING
THE SOCIALLY DISRUPTIVE NATURE OF THEIR ACTIVITIES. ALSO,
INCREASED PRESS EXPOSURE WAS GIVEN TO CERTAIN TOPICS
CONSIDERED POLITICALLY SENSITIVE BY THE GOVERNMENT. FOR
EXAMPLE, A PUBLIC SEMINAR ON THE NATURE OF THE POLITICAL
TRANSITION IN 1988 WAS FULLY REPORTED. HOWEVER, A SUBSEQUENT
MAGAZINE ARTICLE CARRYING COMPLETE TEXTS, THOUGH PLANNED,
NEVER APPEARED. ARTICLES BY OPPOSITION AND DISSIDENT
POLITICIANS INCREASED, BOTH IN NUMBER AND DIRECTNESS OF
CRITICISM AGAINST THE GOVERNMENT. A SCANDAL ALLEGEDLY
INVOLVING A LEADING MEMBER OF THE RULING PARTY RECEIVED FULL
COVERAGE IN THE PRESS AND THE PUBLICITY LED TO HIS
RESIGNATION.

MORE BOOKS BY DISSIDENT RELIGIOUS AND POLITICAL FIGURES
APPEARED IN BOOKSTORES THAN IN RECENT YEARS. SOME BOOKS,
HOWEVER, CONTINUE TO BE CONFISCATED OR BANNED FROM SALE.
APPROVED BOOKS ON COMMUNIST AND SOCIALIST THEORY ARE STUDIED
IN UNIVERSITIES AND CAN BE FOUND IN BOOKSTORES, BUT MANY BOOKS

AND ARTISTIC WORKS WITH "SOCIALIST" THEMES ARE BANNED.

-- B. FREEDOM OF PEACEFUL ASSEMBLY AND ASSOCIATION

THERE ARE THOUSANDS OF PRIVATE ORGANIZATIONS IN KOREA. MOST
PEACEFUL NON-POLITICAL ASSEMBLIES TAKE PLACE ENTIRELY WITHOUT
OFFICIAL SUPERVISION OR RESTRICTION.

THE LAW ON ASSEMBLY AND DEMONSTRATIONS PROHIBITS SPECIFIED
CATEGORIES OF ASSEMBLY, INCLUDING THOSE CONSIDERED LIKELY TO
UNDERMINE PUBLIC ORDER OR CAUSE SOCIAL UNREST. THE LAW ALSO
REQUIRES THAT DEMONSTRATIONS OF ALL TYPES AND OUTDOOR
POLITICAL ASSEMBLIES BE REPORTED IN ADVANCE TO THE POLICE.
VIOLATION OF THE LAW CARRIES A MAXIMUM SENTENCE OF SEVEN YEARS
OR A FINE OF ABOUT $3,750. UNDER THIS LAW, POLICE HAVE AT
TIMES INTERVENED AND BROKEN UP MEETINGS.

BEFORE THE RELEASE THIS YEAR AND LAST OF ALL STUDENTS
IMPRISONED FOR TAKING PART IN DEMONSTRATIONS, FAR MORE THAN
HALF OF ALL KOREA'S "PRISONERS OF CONSCIENCE" WERE IMPRISONED
FOR VIOLATION OF THIS LAW. IN 1984 STUDENTS HAVE NOT BEEN
ARRESTED FOR TAKING PART IN ON-CAMPUS DEMONSTRATIONS; ALMOST

0019

THE PRESIDENT IS CHOSEN BY AN ELECTORAL COLLEGE OF ABOUT 5.000
MEMBERS. BY LAW, PRESIDENTIAL CAMPAIGNS ARE BRIEF, AND
CANDIDATES ARE SEVERELY RESTRICTED IN CAMPAIGNING. INCLUDING
BOTH THE AMOUNT THEY MAY SPEND AND THE METHODS THEY MAY USE TO
APPEAL TO VOTERS. IN THE 1981 PRESIDENTIAL ELECTION THESE
RESTRICTIONS, TOGETHER WITH THE AUTHORITIES' CAREFUL SCREENING
OF ELECTORAL COLLEGE CANDIDATES AND THE RELUCTANCE OF SEVERAL
STRONG POTENTIAL PRESIDENTIAL CANDIDATES TO RUN, RESULTED IN
THE VIRTUAL ABSENCE OF EFFECTIVE OPPOSITION TO INCUMBENT
PRESIDENT CHUN DOO HWAN, WHO WON BY A NEARLY UNANIMOUS
ELECTORAL VOTE. THE CONSTITUTION LIMITS THE PRESIDENT TO A
SINGLE SEVEN-YEAR TERM AND CANNOT BE AMENDED TO ALLOW THE
INCUMBENT PRESIDENT TO CONTINUE IN OFFICE.

THE NEXT PRESIDENTIAL ELECTION IS SCHEDULED FOR 1988.
PRESIDENT CHUN HAS REAFFIRMED THAT HE INTENDS TO STEP DOWN AT
THAT TIME TO PROVIDE FOR A PEACEFUL AND CONSTITUTIONAL
TRANSFER OF POWER.

THE NATIONAL ASSEMBLY, ALTHOUGH POLITICALLY WEAK, IS IMPORTANT
AS A FORUM FOR THE EXPRESSION OF DIVERGENT VIEWS OF THE
GOVERNMENT'S PROGRAMS. RECENT CHANGES IN THE ASSEMBLY LAW
HAVE GIVEN THE ASSEMBLY A SOMEWHAT INCREASED ROLE IN EXAMINING.
GOVERNMENT ACTIONS. INTERPELLATIONS OF MINISTERS HAVE BEEN
INCREASINGLY POINTED AND DEBATE AMONG THE PARTIES INCREASINGLY
VIGOROUS. LEGISLATION NORMALLY ORIGINATES WITH THE EXECUTIVE
BRANCH, ALTHOUGH THE ASSEMBLY HAS AT TIMES PASSED OR BLOCKED
LAWS CONTRARY TO THE PRESIDENT'S WISHES. MEMBERS OF THE
ASSEMBLY, WHO SERVE A FOUR-YEAR TERM, ARE KOREA'S ONLY
DIRECTLY-ELECTED PUBLIC OFFICIALS. THE ELECTION LAWS PASSED
IN 1981 PROVIDE FOR A PROPORTIONAL REPRESENTATION SYSTEM THAT
RESERVES 92 OF THE ASSEMBLY'S 276 SEATS FOR MEMBERS APPOINTED

BY THE PARTIES, WITH TWO-THIRDS OF THOSE SEATS AWARDED TO THE
PARTY WHICH GAINS A PLURALITY OF THE POPULAR VOTE. IN THE
ASSEMBLY ELECTIONS OF MARCH 1981, THE AUTHORITIES BROUGHT
VARIOUS FORMS OF PRESSURE TO BEAR TO DISCOURAGE SOME POTENTIAL
CANDIDATES BUT DID NOT INTERFERE IN THE VOTING. OF THE 184

ACCORDING TO FKTU FIGURES, DUES-PAYING UNION MEMBERSHIP IN
1984 INCREASED BY FOUR PERCENT, AFTER FOUR YEARS OF DECLINE.
INTERNATIONAL CONTACTS BY THE UNIONS INCREASED, WITH THE FKTU
AND ITS MEMBER UNIONS HOSTING THREE REGIONAL CONFERENCES,
INCLUDING THE ASIAN MEETING OF THE INTERNATIONAL CONFEDERATION
OF FREE TRADE UNIONS (ICFTU). THE REPUBLIC OF KOREA SENT AN
OBSERVER DELEGATION TO THE ANNUAL CONFERENCE OF THE
INTERNATIONAL LABOR ORGANIZATION IN 1984. THE FKTU IS
AFFILIATED WITH THE ICFTU, AND FKTU MEMBER UNIONS ARE
AFFILIATED WITH RECOGNIZED INTERNATIONAL TRADE UNION
FEDERATIONS.

--   C.   FREEDOM OF RELIGION

THERE IS NO STATE-FAVORED RELIGION IN KOREA. THERE IS
COMPLETE FREEDOM OF PROSELYTIZING, DOCTRINAL TEACHING, AND
CONVERSION. MINORITY SECTS ARE NOT DISCRIMINATED AGAINST, AND
ADHERENCE TO A FAITH CONFERS NEITHER ADVANTAGES NOR
DISADVANTAGES IN CIVIL, MILITARY, OR OFFICIAL LIFE. CHURCHES
AND RELIGIOUS GROUPS ARE SUBJECT TO THE SAME RESTRICTIONS ON
POLITICAL ACTIVITY AND CRITICISM OF THE GOVERNMENT AS ARE ALL
OTHER INSTITUTIONS IN KOREA. CONSCIENTIOUS OBJECTORS ARE
SUBJECT TO ARREST.

--   D.   FREEDOM OF MOVEMENT WITHIN THE COUNTRY, FOREIGN
--   TRAVEL, EMIGRATION, AND REPATRIATION

THERE IS ESSENTIALLY COMPLETE FREEDOM OF MOVEMENT AND FREEDOM
TO CHANGE EMPLOYMENT IN KOREA. BECAUSE KOREA IS ONE OF THE
MOST DENSELY POPULATED AREAS OF THE WORLD, THE GOVERNMENT
ENCOURAGES A MODEST LEVEL OF EMIGRATION. IT DOES NOT
DISCRIMINATE AGAINST PROSPECTIVE EMIGRANTS. MOST PEOPLE CAN
OBTAIN PASSPORTS, EXCEPT FOR CRIMINALS OR, IN SOME CASES,
PERSONS CONSIDERED POLITICALLY SUSPECT. A NUMBER OF
DISSIDENTS, FORMER POLITICAL PRISONERS, AND PERSONS BANNED
FROM POLITICAL ACTIVITY HAVE BEEN ALLOWED TO TRAVEL ABROAD.
FOREIGN EXCHANGE CONSIDERATIONS HAVE CAUSED THE GOVERNMENT TO
LIMIT TO SOME EXTENT THE NUMBER OF TOURIST PASSPORTS ISSUED.
PASSPORTS, WHEN ISSUED, ARE TYPICALLY LIMITED TO ONE YEAR,
ALTHOUGH THERE ARE EXCEPTIONS IN WHICH PASSPORTS ARE ISSUED UP

TO THE LEGALLY MAXIMUM 5-YEAR VALIDITY.

A SMALL CONTINUING INFLUX OF VIETNAMESE BOAT REFUGEES IS
ADMITTED TO FIRST ASYLUM IN KOREA. THEY ARE CARED FOR AT A
CAMP IN PUSAN BY THE KOREAN RED CROSS UNTIL THEY CAN BE
RESETTLED ABROAD. OVER 600 SUCH REFUGEES HAVE PASSED THROUGH
KOREA IN THE LAST SEVERAL YEARS.

SECTION 3 RESPECT FOR POLITICAL RIGHTS: THE RIGHT OF CITIZENS
--   TO CHANGE THEIR GOVERNMENT

KOREA'S CONSTITUTION AND STATUTES, AS WELL AS ITS TRADITIONS,
CONCENTRATE THEIR POLITICAL POWER IN THE PRESIDENT, A
CONCENTRATION FURTHER INTENSIFIED BY THE SUPPORT THE PRESIDENT
ENJOYS FROM THE MILITARY ESTABLISHMENT. THE PRESIDENT AND THE
MEMBERS OF THE NATIONAL ASSEMBLY ARE THE ONLY ELECTED
OFFICIALS IN KOREA. UNDER THE 1980 PRESIDENTIAL ELECTION LAW,

ASSEMBLY SEATS TO BE FILLED BY ELECTIONS, THE GOVERNMENT PARTY
RAN CANDIDATES FOR 92, OF WHICH IT WON 90, ALONG WITH A 36
PERCENT PLURALITY OF THE POPULAR VOTE. THE GOVERNMENT PARTY
WAS ACCORDINGLY AWARDED 6L PROPORTIONAL REPRESENTATION SEATS,
GIVING IT A COMFORTABLE MAJORITY IN THE NATIONAL ASSEMBLY.
OPPOSITION PARTIES DIVIDED THE REMAINING SEATS. DURING 1984
PREPARATIONS WERE BEING MADE FOR THE NEXT ASSEMBLY ELECTIONS,
EXPECTED EARLY IN 1985. KOREAN OBSERVERS EXPECT THESE
ELECTIONS TO PROVIDE A BENCHMARK OF THE EXTENT OF PROGRESS IN
INCREASING FREEDOM OF POLITICAL CHOICE.

WHILE THE CONSTITUTION PROVIDES FOR LOCAL AUTONOMY, THE
GOVERNMENT HAS RESISTED IMPLEMENTATION ON THE GROUNDS THAT THE
FINANCIAL PRECONDITIONS ESTABLISHED BY LAW HAVE NOT BEEN MET.

THE LAWS GOVERNING PARTICIPATION IN THE POLITICAL PROCESS WERE
ENACTED IN 1981 JUST PRIOR TO THE LIFTING OF MARTIAL LAW. ALL
EXISTING PARTIES WERE DISBANDED AND NEW ONES WERE FORMED. AT
THAT TIME, A LAW WAS ENACTED BARRING 551 PERSONS FROM TAKING
PART IN ANY POLITICAL ACTIVITY FOR EIGHT YEARS. THE
GOVERNMENT IN FEBRUARY AND NOVEMBER 1984 REDUCED THE NUMBER OF
BANNED POLITICIANS TO 15. THE MOST PROMINENT PERSONS AFFECTED
BY THIS BAN REMAIN COVERED BY IT, ALTHOUGH DURING 1984 MANY OF
THE BANNED POLITICIANS WERE BEING ALLOWED TO CARRY OUT LIMITED
POLITICAL ACTIVITY.

ONE OF THE MOST PROMINENT OF THOSE STILL BANNED, KIM DAE JUNG,
HAS SAID HE WILL TO RETURN TO KOREA EARLY IN 1985 FROM HIS
TWO-YEAR STAY IN THE UNITED STATES. IN THE 1971 PRESIDENTIAL
ELECTION, HE GARNERED NEARLY HALF THE VOTE. SUBSEQUENTLY, HIS
POLITICAL ACTIVITY IN KOREA AND ABROAD COST HIM TIME IN JAIL
AND A DEATH SENTENCE (LATER COMMUTED TO 20 YEARS'
IMPRISONMENT). HE WAS RELEASED FROM PRISON IN 1982 TO COME TO
THE UNITED STATES FOR MEDICAL TREATMENT. THE GOVERNMENT'S
OFFICIAL POSITION IS THAT IT WILL "TAKE NECESSARY MEASURES IN
ACCORDANCE WITH THE LAW IF HE RETURNS HOME."

KOREANS, OTHER THAN THOSE UNDER THIS POLITICAL BAN, ARE FREE
TO BELONG TO AND PARTICIPATE IN THE ACTIVITIES OF POLITICAL
PARTIES. HOWEVER, THESE PARTIES HAVE HAD DIFFICULTY
ATTRACTING A POPULAR FOLLOWING FOR A NUMBER OF REASONS. THE
GOVERNMENT MAY DISSOLVE ANY PARTY IT DEEMS CONTRARY TO "BASIC
DEMOCRATIC ORDER;" THE ELECTORAL LAWS PUT TIME AND FISCAL
CONSTRAINTS ON CAMPAIGNING WHICH CAUSE ALL PARTIES, AND

PARTICULARLY THE OPPOSITION, SIGNIFICANT DIFFICULTIES IN
PUBLICIZING THEIR PROGRAMS; AND THE GOVERNMENT CAN AND DOES
VETO THEIR CHOICES OF LEADERS, CANDIDATES, AND POLICY
POSITIONS.

IN DECEMBER L984, TWO MEMBERS OF THE OPPOSITION DEMOCRATIC
KOREA PARTY WHO HAD DEFECTED TO A NEW OPPOSITION PARTY WERE
DETAINED FOR THREE DAYS BY A SECURITY SERVICE. THE NEW PARTY
IS BEING FORMED WITH SIGNIFICANT PARTICIPATION BY POLITICIANS
FROM WHOM THE BAN ON POLITICAL ACTIVITY HAD BEEN LIFTED THIS
YEAR. MANY OBSERVERS BELIEVE THAT THE DETENTION WAS A
GOVERNMENT EFFORT TO DISCOURAGE GREATER PARTICIPATION IN THE
NEW OPPOSITION PARTY.

0022

LIMITATIONS ON FREEDOM OF THE PRESS ALSO CAUSE OPPOSITION
PARTIES PARTICULAR DIFFICULTIES. OPPOSITION PARTIES HAVE NOT
SUCCEEDED IN MODIFYING THE ELECTION LAWS SIGNIFICANTLY IN TIME
FOR THE 1985 ELECTIONS.

WOMEN ARE FREE TO VOTE, BECOME GOVERNMENT OFFICIALS AND RUN
FOR THE NATIONAL ASSEMBLY; THEY HOLD SEVEN ASSEMBLY SEATS, ALL
BUT ONE APPOINTED BY THEIR PARTIES. IN PRACTICE, THE POWER
STRUCTURE REMAINS MALE-DOMINATED.

SECTION 4 GOVERNMENTAL ATTITUDE REGARDING INTERNATIONAL AND
NON-GOVERNMENTAL INVESTIGATION OF ALLEGED VIOLATIONS OF HUMAN
RIGHTS

THE REPUBLIC OF KOREA DOES NOT BELONG TO ANY INTERNATIONAL
HUMAN RIGHTS BODIES AND USUALLY DOES NOT WELCOME OUTSIDE
INVOLVEMENT IN THE HUMAN RIGHTS AREA. THE GOVERNMENT
TOLERATES THE EXISTENCE OF DOMESTIC HUMAN RIGHTS GROUPS BUT
CLOSELY MONITORS THEIR OPERATIONS.

THERE ARE NO GOVERNMENT AGENCIES CHARGED WITH THE PROTECTION
OF HUMAN RIGHTS, ALTHOUGH POLITICAL PARTIES AND THE NATIONAL
ASSEMBLY HAVE COMMITTEES WHICH ARE CONCERNED WITH OVERSIGHT OF
SOME ASPECTS OF THE ISSUE. A NUMBER OF PRIVATE ORGANIZATIONS
ARE ALSO ACTIVE IN THIS AREA, CHIEFLY THE HUMAN RIGHTS
COMMITTEE OF THE KOREAN NATIONAL COUNCIL OF CHURCHES, THE
CATHOLIC JUSTICE AND PEACE COMMITTEE, AND THE KOREA LEGAL AID
CENTER IN SEOUL. THE HUMAN RIGHTS COMMITTEE HAS TIES WITH THE
WORLD COUNCIL OF CHURCHES. THE COMMITTEE AND OTHER HUMAN
RIGHTS ORGANIZATIONS SUBMIT PETITIONS TO THE GOVERNMENT AND
MAKE THEIR VIEWS KNOWN BOTH INSIDE AND OUTSIDE KOREA. MOST
OBSERVERS BELIEVE THAT THESE ORGANIZATIONS HAVE BEEN
RELATIVELY EFFECTIVE IN FURTHERING THEIR AIMS, DEPENDING ON
THE ISSUE. PEOPLE WORKING WITH THESE GROUPS ARE SOMETIMES
QUESTIONED AND, ON OCCASION, VISITED OR DETAINED BY THE

SECURITY SERVICES, THOUGH APPARENTLY NONE HAVE BEEN ARRESTED

0023

EMPLOYERS' FEDERATION, THE AVERAGE WAGE OF FEMALE WORKERS IS 46.8 PERCENT OF THAT OF MALE WORKERS. KOREA HAS NOT DEVELOPED A POLITICALLY POWERFUL FEMINIST MOVEMENT, BUT CONSCIOUSNESS OF WOMEN'S ISSUES HAS BEEN INCREASING. DURING 1984 WOMEN'S GROUPS ORGANIZED A FEDERATION TO CAMPAIGN FOR REVISION OF THE FAMILY LAW, INCLUDING PROVISIONS CONCERNING THE HEAD OF FAMILY SYSTEM, AND IN FAVOR OF EQUAL PROPERTY RIGHTS IN CASE OF DIVORCE AND EQUAL RIGHTS IN CHILD CUSTODY. TRADITIONAL CONFUCIAN INFLUENCE REMAINS STRONG, HOWEVER. THE GOVERNMENT ANNOUNCED THAT IT WOULD ASK THE NATIONAL ASSEMBLY TO RATIFY THE U.N. CONVENTION ON THE PREVENTION OF DISCRIMINATION AGAINST WOMEN WITH A RESERVATION ON ARTICLES 9 AND 16, WHICH CONFLICT WITH PRESENT DOMESTIC KOREAN LAW.

IMPROVED HEALTH CARE AND NUTRITION WERE RESPONSIBLE FOR INCREASING KOREAN LIFE EXPECTANCY AT BIRTH TO 68 YEARS IN 1984. BY 1984 INFANT MORTALITY DECLINED TO 30.4 DEATHS PER 1,000 LIVE BIRTHS. ACCESS TO SAFE DRINKING WATER INCREASED TO 71 PERCENT OF THE POPULATION IN 1979. CALORIC INTAKE IN 1981 WAS 126 PERCENT OF MINIMUM NUTRITIONAL REQUIREMENTS.

EDUCATION RECEIVES HIGH PRIORITY IN GOVERNMENT POLICY. THE ADULT LITERACY RATE INCREASED TO 93 PERCENT IN 1978. PRIMARY SCHOOL EDUCATION IS UNIVERSAL FOR BOTH SEXES, AND OVER 90 PERCENT OF ELEMENTARY STUDENTS ENTER SECONDARY SCHOOL. ENTRANCE TO INSTITUTIONS OF HIGHER EDUCATION IS HIGHLY COMPETITIVE. ONLY ABOUT 50 PERCENT OF THOSE WHO WISH TO ATTEND ARE ABLE TO DO SO. THERE IS A SUBSTANTIAL AMOUNT OF SOCIAL MOBILITY BASED ON THE MERIT SYSTEM IN EDUCATION AND EMPLOYMENT. END TEXT. SHULTZ
BT
#6704

NNNN

9/9   C O N F I D E N T I A L   STATE 036704/09

0024

IN THE PAST SEVERAL YEARS.

THE AMNESTY INTERNATIONAL 1984 REPORT EXPRESSED ITS CONCERN
ABOUT THE DETENTION OF PRISONERS OF CONSCIENCE, REPORTS OF
TORTURE AND UNFAIR TRIALS, WIDESPREAD ARREST OF STUDENTS, THE
USE OF SHORT-TERM DETENTION WITHOUT CHARGE, AND HOUSE ARREST
AGAINST STUDENTS AND OTHER CRITICS OF THE GOVERNMENT. FREEDOM
HOUSE LISTS KOREA AS "PARTLY FREE."

ECONOMIC, SOCIAL, AND CULTURAL SITUATION

THE REPUBLIC OF KOREA IS ONE OF THE MOST DENSELY POPULATED
COUNTRIES IN THE WORLD, WITH 7.4 PERSONS PER ACRE OF ARABLE
LAND. ONLY 22 PERCENT OF ITS 24.4 MILLION ACRES ARE ARABLE.
THE NATION'S PHYSICAL WEALTH IS SPARSE; MOST OF THE NATURAL
RESOURCES OF THE KOREAN PENINSULA ARE FOUND IN NORTH KOREA.
THE REPUBLIC'S MAJOR ECONOMIC ASSET IS ITS WELL-EDUCATED AND
PRODUCTIVE WORK FORCE. THE POPULATION REACHED 42 MILLION IN
1984, BUT THE GROWTH RATE HAS DROPPED TO 1.5 PERCENT, DUE IN
PART TO CONCERTED EFFORTS BY THE GOVERNMENT TO POPULARIZE
VOLUNTARY FAMILY PLANNING.

SKILLFUL MANAGEMENT BY KOREAN ECONOMIC TECHNOCRATS, MANY OF
THEM GRADUATES OF LEADING WESTERN UNIVERSITIES, HAS GIVEN
KOREA ONE OF THE WORLD'S MOST DYNAMIC ECONOMIES. SINCE 1965,
ECONOMIC GROWTH IN REAL TERMS HAS AVERAGED ABOUT 9 PERCENT PER
YEAR; IN 1984 IT WAS ABOUT 8 PERCENT. PER CAPITA GROSS
NATIONAL PRODUCT HAS GROWN FROM $100 IN 1965 TO ABOUT $1,900
IN 1982. THE WIDESPREAD DISTRIBUTION OF INCOME GAINS AND THE
APPROXIMATE PARITY BETWEEN RURAL AND URBAN HOUSEHOLD INCOMES
HAS INCREASED DRAMATICALLY THE NUTRITION, HEALTH, LIVING
CONDITIONS, AND ECONOMIC CHOICES OF THE ENTIRE POPULATION.

THE ECONOMY IS A BLEND OF PRIVATE SECTOR FIRMS AND INDIVIDUALS
AND PUBLIC SECTOR ENTERPRISES. AS THE GROSS NATIONAL PRODUCT
HAS GROWN TO ALMOST $75 BILLION IN 1982, THE GOVERNMENT HAS
BEGUN TO RELY INCREASINGLY ON MARKET FORCES TO ALLOCATE
RESOURCES AND IS GRADUALLY LIBERALIZING ITS CONTROL OVER
IMPORTS, FOREIGN INVESTMENT, AND THE DOMESTIC FINANCIAL SECTOR.

PARTICIPATION IN THE ECONOMY AND A SHARE OF ITS BENEFITS ARE
EFFECTIVELY OPEN TO ALL. THE RIGHT TO OWN PROPERTY, ALONE AND
IN ASSOCIATION WITH OTHERS, IS RECOGNIZED IN LAW AND
PRACTICE. THERE IS NO ECONOMIC DISCRIMINATION BASED ON RACE
OR RELIGION. DISCRIMINATION AGAINST WOMEN IS DECLINING,
ALTHOUGH AS IN MOST TRADITIONAL ASIAN SOCIETIES MEN STILL TEND
TO BE THE PRIMARY INCOME EARNERS AND PROPERTY OWNERS.

A SERIES OF MAJOR REVISIONS TO THE LEGAL CODE IN RECENT YEARS
HAS GIVEN WOMEN RIGHTS IN INHERITANCE, CHILD CUSTODY, FAMILY
HEADSHIP, AND OTHER AREAS WHICH LAW AND CONFUCIAN TRADITION
HAD LONG DENIED THEM. WOMEN ENJOY FULL ACCESS TO EDUCATIONAL
OPPORTUNITIES AT ALL LEVELS. THEY ARE INCREASINGLY
REPRESENTED, THOUGH STILL LARGELY AT ENTRY LEVELS, IN THE
MILITARY, THE POLICE, THE CIVIL SERVICE, THE PROFESSIONS, AND
PRIVATE INDUSTRY. THEY ARE NOT LEGALLY PROTECTED AGAINST
DISCRIMINATION IN HIRING, PAY, OR ADVANCEMENT, AND THESE
REMAIN PROBLEM AREAS. FOR EXAMPLE, ACCORDING TO THE KOREA

0025

ACTION: POL-3 INFO: AMB DCM *ADM RSO* ECON2 CON/RR ACPUSAN CHRON-//

VZCZCULC213
OO RUEHUL
DE RUEHC #6703/01 0372009
ZNY CCCCC ZZH
O 061957Z FEB 85
FM SECSTATE WASHDC
TO AMEMBASSY SEOUL IMMEDIATE 4696
BT
C O N F I D E N T I A L STATE 036703

LOC: 85029   586
06 FEB 85   2156
CN: 45685
CHRG: PROG
DIST: POLC

IMMEDIATE

EAP ONLY

E.O. 12356: DECL: OADR
TAGS: SHUM, PINS, KN
SUBJECT: NORTH KOREA HUMAN RIGHTS REPORT

1.   FOLLOWING IS THE FINAL VERSION OF THE NORTH KOREAN
HUMAN RIGHTS REPORT FOR 1984.   THIS REPORT IS EMBARGOED
BY THE DEPARTMENT AND WILL NOT BE RELEASABLE TO ANY
NON-DEPARTMENT SOURCE UNTIL FURTHER NOTICE.

BEGIN TEXT:

DEMOCRATIC PEOPLE'S REPUBLIC OF KOREA (SEE FOOTNOTE)

THE DEMOCRATIC PEOPLE'S REPUBLIC OF KOREA, FORMED IN 1948
DURING THE SOVIET ADMINISTRATION OF THE NORTHERN HALF OF
THE KOREAN PENINSULA, IS A RIGID COMMUNIST DICTATORSHIP,
STRICTLY DOMINATED BY ONE MAN, KIM IL-SUNG, AND HIS
FAMILY.   ALTHOUGH SOME INTERNATIONALLY RESPECTED HUMAN
RIGHTS ARE ACKNOWLEDGED BY THE CONSTITUTION AND LAWS,
INDIVIDUAL RIGHTS ARE ENTIRELY SUBORDINATED IN PRACTICE
TO THE RULING KOREAN WORKERS' (COMMUNIST) PARTY, WITH ITS
OVERRIDING AIM OF IMPOSING A SOCIAL REVOLUTION AND
ENFORCING UNANIMOUS POPULAR SUPPORT FOR THE COUNTRY'S

GOVERNING SYSTEM AND ITS LEADERS.

THE LATEST CONSTITUTION, PROMULGATED IN 1972, PURPORTS TO
GUARANTEE A WIDE RANGE OF RIGHTS, INCLUDING: FREEDOM OF
THE PRESS, RELIGION, WORK, AND ASSOCIATION, AND FREEDOM
FROM SEX DISCRIMINATION. OTHER PROVISIONS OF THAT
CONSTITUTION, AS WELL AS THE FACT OF COMMUNIST PARTY
CONTROL, RENDER MEANINGLESS MOST OF THESE GUARANTEES.
WHILE THERE WERE PRO FORMA ELECTIONS TO THE SUPREME
PEOPLE'S ASSEMBLY IN FEBRUARY 1982, FREE ELECTIONS DO NOT
EXIST IN NORTH KOREA SINCE CITIZENS HAVE NO CHOICE AMONG
CANDIDATES.

KIM IL-SUNG IS COMMITTED TO REUNIFICATION OF THE DIVIDED
PENINSULA, BY WHATEVER MEANS IS NECESSARY. TO THIS END,
HIS GOVERNMENT HAS PERIODICALLY ATTEMPTED TO DESTABILIZE
THE REPUBLIC OF KOREA, FOR EXAMPLE BY THE ATTEMPT TO
ASSASSINATE THE PRESIDENT OF THE REPUBLIC OF KOREA IN A
BOMBING ATTACK IN RANGOON, BURMA, ON OCTOBER 9, 1983.

0026

FOUR BURMESE AND 17 SOUTH KOREANS, INCLUDING FOUR CABINET
MINISTERS AND A NUMBER OF SENIOR ADVISERS AND OFFICIALS,
WERE KILLED IN THIS NORTH KOREAN ACTION. DESPITE NORTH
KOREA'S DELIVERY OF FLOOD RELIEF GOODS TO THE SOUTH IN
1984 AND THE POSITIVE RESPONSE TO SOUTH KOREAN PROPOSALS
FOR BILATERAL TALKS ON ECONOMIC COOPERATION AND FAMILY
REUNIFICATION, IT CONTINUES TO IMPROVE ITS MILITARY
FORCES TARGETED AGAINST THE SOUTH.

NORTH KOREAN LEADERS JUSTIFY REGIMENTATION AND
MILITARIZATION OF SOCIETY IN THE NAME OF REUNIFICATION.
THE NORTH KOREAN PEOPLE ARE SUBJECT TO RIGID CONTROLS.
PERSONS WHO FAIL TO COOPERATE WITH THE REGIME FACE
IMPRISONMENT, CONFISCATION OF PROPERTY, OR ENFORCED
REMOVAL TO REMOTE VILLAGES. SURVEILLANCE BY INFORMERS IS
PREVALENT. MOVEMENT OUTSIDE ONE'S OWN VILLAGE REQUIRES
DOCUMENTED PERMISSION. PUNISHMENT FOR "POLITICAL CRIMES"
AGAINST THE STATE IS SEVERE. AVAILABLE INFORMATION
INDICATES THAT THE PRACTICES OF FORCED RELOCATION OF
FAMILIES AND IDEOLOGICAL INDOCTRINATION HAVE INTENSIFIED
IN RECENT YEARS.

THE STATE'S INTERVENTION IN THE INDIVIDUAL'S ACTIVITIES
IN NORTH KOREA GOES WELL BEYOND CURTAILING ASSEMBLY AND
EXPRESSION. THE AUTHORITIES ATTEMPT TO SHAPE THE

FOOTNOTE: THE UNITED STATES DOES NOT HAVE DIPLOMATIC
RELATIONS WITH THE DEMOCRATIC PEOPLE'S REPUBLIC OF KOREA;
EVEN REPRESENTATIVES OF GOVERNMENTS THAT DO, AS WELL AS
JOURNALISTS AND OTHER OCCASIONAL INVITED VISITORS TO

NORTH KOREA, ARE NOT PERMITTED THE FREEDOM OF MOVEMENT
THAT WOULD ENABLE THEM EFFECTIVELY TO ASSESS HUMAN RIGHTS
OBSERVANCE THERE. MOST OF THIS REPORT, THEREFORE, IS A
REPEAT OF PREVIOUS HUMAN RIGHTS REPORTS BASED ON
INFORMATION OBTAINED OVER A PERIOD OF TIME EXTENDING FROM
WELL BEFORE 1984. WHILE LIMITED IN SCOPE AND DETAIL, THE
INFORMATION IS INDICATIVE OF THE HUMAN RIGHTS SITUATION
IN NORTH KOREA TODAY.

CONSCIOUSNESS OF THE POPULACE. PRESCHOOL CHILDREN ARE
DRILLED IN HOMAGE TO KIM IL-SUNG AND HIS FAMILY, WHILE
YOUTHS AND ADULTS ARE REQUIRED TO PARTICIPATE IN DAILY
IDEOLOGICAL TRAINING CONDUCTED BY YOUTH ORGANIZATIONS OR
AT PLACES OF EMPLOYMENT. THE PROPAGANDA REQUIRES ROTE
RECITATION OF PARTY MAXIMS AND POSITIONS AND STRIVES FOR
IDEOLOGICAL PURITY. THE RESULT IS THAT NORT4 KOREA'S
SOCIETY IS ONE OF THE MOST HIGHLY REGIMENTED AND
CONTROLLED IN THE WORLD TODAY. AT LEAST TWO NORTH KOREAN
SECURITY ORGANIZATIONS ENFORCE THESE CONTROLS.

VIRTUALLY NO OUTSIDE INFORMATION OTHER THAN THAT APPROVED

미국 국무부의 한국 인권문제 보고서, 1985-87 **387**

AND DISSEMINATED BY THE NORTH KOREAN AUTHORITIES IS
ALLOWED TO REACH THE NORTH KOREAN PUBLIC. FOREIGNERS WHO
HAVE TRAVELED TO PYONGYANG, THE CAPITAL CITY, HAVE BEEN
SURPRISED TO LEARN HOW LITTLE THE NORTH KOREAN POPULACE
KNOWS OF THE OUTSIDE WORLD. SENIOR GOVERNMENT OFFICIALS,
HOWEVER, SEEM TO BE SOMEWHAT BETTER INFORMED.

SECURITY RATINGS FOR EACH PERSON ARE BASED ON SUCH
CONSIDERATIONS AS CLASS ORIGIN, IDEOLOGICAL FERVOR, AND
RELIABILITY, AND WHETHER ANY OF THE INDIVIDUAL'S
RELATIVES OR ASSOCIATES COLLABORATED WITH JAPANESE
OCCUPATION AUTHORITIES (1910-1945) OR HAVE ATTEMPTED TO
DEFECT TO OTHER COUNTRIES. THESE RATINGS DETERMINE
ACCESS TO THE BETTER JOBS, SCHOOLS, MEDICAL FACILITIES,
AND STORES, AS WELL AS ADMISSION TO THE KOREAN WORKERS'
PARTY, THE ROUTE TO THE HIGHEST LEVELS AND PRIVILEGES OF
THE SOCIETY. ANY INDIVIDUAL WHOSE RELATIVE OR CLOSE
FAMILY ASSOCIATE HAS SETTLED IN SOUTH KOREA IS TREATED AS
SUSPECT BY THE NORTH KOREAN AUTHORITIES.

IN 1984, FOR THE FIRST TIME, NORTH KOREA'S GOVERNMENT-
CONTROLLED RADIO EXPLICITLY REFERRED TO KIM IL-SUNG'S
SON, KIM CHONG-IL, AS HIS FATHER'S EVENTUAL "SUCCESSOR."
THE YOUNGER KIM, WHO WAS ELEVATED TO SEVERAL SENIOR
LEADERSHIP POSITIONS IN 1980, IS REPORTEDLY ASSUMING
INCREASING CONTROL OF THE GOVERNMENT AND PARTY. THAT KIM
IL-SUNG APPEARS THUS FAR TO BE ABLE TO ENSURE HIS
SUCCESSION BY HIS SON, A FIRST FOR ANY COMMUNIST COUNTRY,

INDICATES THE ENORMOUS POWER HE HAS ASSUMED IN 36 YEARS
OF RULE. THE ABSENCE OF ANY EVIDENCE OF PUBLIC DEBATE
ABOUT THE SUCCESSION IS ALSO INDICATIVE OF THE LACK OF
REAL POPULAR PARTICIPATION IN THE POLITICAL PROCESS.

RESPECT FOR HUMAN RIGHTS

SECTION 1 RESPECT FOR THE INTEGRITY OF THE PERSON,
--   INCLUDING FREEDOM FROM:

--   A. POLITICAL KILLING

NO RELIABLE INFORMATION IS AVAILABLE ON POLITICALLY
MOTIVATED KILLING IN NORTH KOREA. HOWEVER, THE NORTH
KOREAN ATTITUDE TOWARD POLITICAL KILLING WAS CLEARLY
DEMONSTRATED IN THE RANGOON BOMBING AND THE NOVEMBER 23,
1984 SHOOTING IN THE JOINT SECURITY AREA OF THE
DEMILITARIZED ZONE (DMZ) DIVIDING NORTH AND SOUTH KOREA.

AFTER A CAREFUL INVESTIGATION, THE GOVERNMENT OF BURMA
DETERMINED THAT THE DEMOCRATIC PEOPLE'S REPUBLIC OF KOREA
WAS RESPONSIBLE FOR THE OCTOBER 9, 1983, ATTEMPT TO
ASSASSINATE REPUBLIC OF KOREA PRESIDENT CHUN DOO HWAN
DURING HIS VISIT TO BURMA. THE BOMB KILLED FOUR CABINET
MINISTERS AND A NUMBER OF SENIOR ADVISERS AND OFFICIALS.
TWO NORTH KOREAN ARMY OFFICERS WERE BROUGHT TO TRIAL IN
RANGOON FOR THE ATTACK, AND ON DECEMBER 9, 1983, WERE
FOUND GUILTY AND SENTENCED TO DEATH. IN THE DMZ INCIDENT A
YOUNG SOVIET STUDENT WHO WANTED TO DEFECT BROKE AWAY FROM

0028

A TOUR GROUP AND RAN ACROSS THE MILITARY DEMARCATION LINE
INTO THE AREA CONTROLLED BY THE U.N. COMMAND. THE NORTH
KOREAN SECURITY GUARDS OPENED FIRE ON THE FLEEING SOVIET.
TRIGGERING AN EXCHANGE OF FIRE IN WHICH SEVERAL LIVES
WERE LOST, AND UNSUCCESSFULLY PURSUED THE DEFECTOR ACROSS
THE LINE WITH GUNS BLAZING.

--   B.   DISAPPEARANCE

THERE IS NO INFORMATION AVAILABLE ON DISAPPEARANCE.

--   C.   TORTURE AND CRUEL, INHUMAN, OR DEGRADING
TREATMENT OR PUNISHMENT

FREEDOM HOUSE'S 1983-84 REPORT STATES THAT "TORTURE IS
REPORTEDLY COMMON" IN NORTH KOREA. THE ACCOUNTS OF
TORTURE AND BEATINGS OF CREW MEMBERS OF THE USS PUEBLO
AFTER THEIR CAPTURE IN 1968 ARE WELL-KNOWN AND
DOCUMENTED. THE ONLY OTHER RELIABLE SOURCE ON PRISON
CONDITIONS AND TREATMENT OF PRISONERS IN NORTH KOREA IS

VENEZUELAN POET ALI LAMEDA, WHO WAS DETAINED IN NORTH
KOREA FROM SEPTEMBER 1967 THROUGH 1974,
ALLEGEDLY FOR ATTEMPTED SABOTAGE AND ESPIONAGE. WHILE
PHYSICAL TORTURE WAS NOT USED ON MR. LAMEDA, HE STATED THAT
KOREAN PRISONERS WERE ROUTINELY BEATEN. LAMEDA NOTED THAT
"BEATING WAS ALSO USED AS A MEANS OF PERSUASION DURING
INTERROGATION."

LAMEDA REPORTED THE USE OF DEPRIVATION OF FOOD TO FORCE
"CONFESSIONS," AS WELL AS SOLITARY CONFINEMENT. CONTINUOUS
INTERROGATION, ENFORCED WAKING PERIODS, POOR OR NONEXISTENT
MEDICAL TREATMENT, AND 12 HOURS OF FORCED LABOR PER DAY. IN
ADDITION. PRISONERS WERE DENIED FAMILY VISITS, PARCELS,
CORRESPONDENCE, WRITING MATERIALS, NEWSPAPERS, AND CLOTHING
CHANGES. PRISONERS APPEARED TO BE REGARDED AS PERSONS WITHOUT
ANY RIGHTS.

2/6   C O N F I D E N T I A L   STATE 036703/02

0029

--   D.   ARBITRARY ARREST, DETENTION, OR EXILE

INFORMATION ON SPECIFIC CRIMINAL JUSTICE PROCEDURES AND
PRACTICES IN NORTH KOREA IS EXTREMELY SCARCE. NORTH KOREA HAS
REFUSED TO PERMIT OUTSIDE OBSERVATION OF ITS LEGAL SYSTEM AND
PRACTICES. THE ACCOUNTS PROVIDED BY THE CREW MEMBERS OF THE
USS PUEBLO AND BY VENEZUELAN POET ALI LAMEDA, WHILE CLEARLY
FROM AN EARLIER PERIOD, COMPRISE VIRTUALLY ALL THE SPECIFIC
INFORMATION AVAILABLE ON THE OPERATION OF THE CRIMINAL JUSTICE
SYSTEM IN NORTH KOREA.

NORTH KOREAN LAW PROVIDES THAT THE PERIOD PRISONERS MAY BE
HELD FOR INTERROGATION SHALL NOT EXCEED TWO MONTHS. THIS
PERIOD MAY BE EXTENDED INDEFINITELY, HOWEVER, IF THE
INTERROGATION DEPARTMENT OBTAINS APPROVAL OF THE CHIEF
PROSECUTOR. LAMEDA, HIMSELF, WAS DETAINED FOR 12 MONTHS
WITHOUT TRIAL OR CHARGE. HIS REQUEST FOR A LAWYER OF HIS
CHOICE AND AN OPEN TRIAL WERE RIDICULED AS "BOURGEOIS."
HABEAS CORPUS OR ITS EQUIVALENT DOES NOT EXIST IN PRACTICE.

ACCORDING TO NEWSPAPER REPORTS, NORTH KOREAN DEFECTORS IN
SOUTH KOREA ESTIMATED IN APRIL 1982 THAT AT LEAST 105.000
"IDEOLOGICAL OFFENDERS" WERE BEING HELD IN EIGHT MAJOR CAMPS
IN THE NORTH. AMNESTY INTERNATIONAL HAS RECEIVED UNCONFIRMED
REPORTS OF ARRESTS OF THOSE OPPOSED TO HEIR APPARENT KIM
CHONG-IL.

--   E.   DENIAL OF FAIR PUBLIC TRIAL

THE NORTH KOREAN CONSTITUTION STATES THAT COURTS ARE
INDEPENDENT, AND JUDICIAL PROCEEDINGS ARE TO BE CARRIED OUT IN
STRICT ACCORDANCE WITH LAW. ALL COURTS, HOWEVER, ARE

RESPONSIBLE TO THE PEOPLE'S ASSEMBLIES, WHICH EFFECTIVELY
MEANS TOTAL GOVERNMENTAL CONTROL OF THE JUDICIARY. ARTICLE
138 STATES THAT "CASES ARE HEARD IN PUBLIC, AND THE ACCUSED IS
GUARANTEED THE RIGHT TO DEFENSE; HEARINGS MAY BE CLOSED TO THE
PUBLIC AS STIPULATED BY LAW." LAMEDA WAS TWICE DENIED PUBLIC
TRIAL. AFTER HIS FIRST ARREST HE WAS IMPRISONED FOR A YEAR
WITHOUT A HEARING; AFTER HIS SECOND ARREST, HE WAS PUT THROUGH
A CLOSED SESSION WITHOUT BENEFIT OF COUNSEL OF HIS CHOICE, OR
EVEN KNOWLEDGE OF THE CHARGES. HIS TRIBUNAL WAS UNDER THE
DIRECTION OF THE MINISTRY OF INTERNAL SECURITY, WITH ONE
PERSON SERVING AS BOTH JUDGE AND PROSECUTOR.

LAMEDA STATED THAT, OTHER THAN TO ADMIT GUILT, HE WAS REFUSED
THE RIGHT TO SPEAK OUT OR DEFEND HIMSELF AT HIS TRIAL. HIS
"DEFENSE COUNSEL" REPRESENTED HIM BY MAKING A LENGTHY SPEECH
PRAISING KIM IL-SUNG AND THEN REQUESTING A 20-YEAR SENTENCE,
WHICH THE TRIBUNAL IMPOSED AFTER FIVE MINUTES OF DELIBERATION.

IN A 1979 INTERVIEW WITH AMERICAN JOURNALIST JOHN WALLACH,
NORTH KOREAN SUPREME COURT JUSTICE LI CHUN-UK NOTED THAT THE
DEFENSE COUNSEL'S JOB IS "TO GIVE THE SUSPECT DUE
PUNISHMENT." OPEN COURT APPEARS TO CONSIST OF AN ANNOUNCEMENT
OF THE TERM OF IMPRISONMENT, WHICH HAS ALREADY BEEN DETERMINED
BY THE PROVINCIAL SAFETY BUREAU.

0030

--   F. ARBITRARY INTERFERENCE WITH PRIVACY, FAMILY, HOME, OR
--   CORRESPONDENCE

THE POPULACE IS SUBJECTED TO CONTINUOUS INDOCTRINATION,
DESIGNED TO SHAPE INDIVIDUAL CONSCIOUSNESS. PRESCHOOL
CHILDREN ARE DRILLED IN HOMAGE TO KIM IL-SUNG AND HIS FAMILY,
WHILE YOUTHS AND ADULTS ARE REQUIRED TO PARTICIPATE IN DAILY
IDEOLOGICAL TRAINING CONDUCTED BY YOUTH ORGANIZATIONS OR AT
PLACES OF EMPLOYMENT. THE PROPAGANDA REQUIRES ROTE RECITATION
OF PARTY MAXIMS AND POSITIONS AND STRIVES FOR IDEOLOGICAL
PURITY. AT LEAST TWO NORTH KOREAN SECURITY ORGANIZATIONS
ENFORCE THESE CONTROLS.

REPORTS, PRIMARILY FROM DEFECTORS, INDICATE THAT FORCED
RESETTLEMENT, PARTICULARLY FOR THOSE DEEMED POLITICALLY
UNRELIABLE, IS COMMON. PERMISSION TO RESIDE IN, OR EVEN
ENTER, PYONGYANG IS STRICTLY CONTROLLED.

ACCORDING TO REPORTS IN SOUTH KOREAN JOURNALS, JAPANESE WIVES
OF KOREANS REPATRIATED FROM JAPAN SINCE 1959 HAVE NOT BEEN
PERMITTED TO VISIT JAPAN AND, BECAUSE THEIR LETTERS ARE
SUBJECT TO STRICT CENSORSHIP, MANY HAVE LOST CONTACT WITH
THEIR FAMILIES.

THE CONSTITUTION STATES THAT "CITIZENS ARE GUARANTEED THE
INVIOLABILITY OF PERSON AND RESIDENCE AND THE PRIVACY OF
CORRESPONDENCE." LAMEDA REPORTED, HOWEVER, THAT HIS RESIDENCE
WAS NOT RESPECTED AND THAT LISTENING DEVICES WERE USED AGAINST
HIM. HE WAS ARRESTED AND HIS COLLECTED PAPERS AND POETRY
DESTROYED WITHOUT WARRANT.

SECTION 2 RESPECT FOR CIVIL RIGHTS, INCLUDING:

--   A. FREEDOM OF SPEECH AND PRESS

THE CONSTITUTION STATES THAT "CITIZENS HAVE THE FREEDOMS OF
SPEECH, THE PRESS, ASSEMBLY, ASSOCIATION, AND DEMONSTRATION."
IN FACT, NORTH KOREANS ENJOY NONE OF THESE RIGHTS. SUCH

0031

ACTIVITIES ARE PERMITTED ONLY IN SUPPORT OF GOVERNMENT
OBJECTIVES. OTHER ARTICLES OF THE CONSTITUTION THAT REQUIRE
CITIZENS TO FOLLOW THE "SOCIALIST NORMS OF LIFE" AND TO OBEY A
"COLLECTIVE SPIRIT" TAKE PRECEDENCE OVER INDIVIDUAL POLITICAL
OR CIVIL LIBERTIES. CENSORSHIP OF FOREIGN AND DOMESTIC MEDIA
IS ENFORCED, AND NO DEVIATION FROM THE OFFICIAL GOVERNMENT
LINE IS TOLERATED. LISTENING TO FOREIGN MEDIA BROADCASTS IS
PROHIBITED, AND VIOLATORS REPORTEDLY ARE SUBJECT TO SEVERE
PUNISHMENT. MOST NORTH KOREANS DO NOT POSSESS RADIOS BUT MUST
LISTEN TO GOVERNMENT MEDIA THROUGH LOUDSPEAKERS INSTALLED IN
THEIR APARTMENTS. ARTISTIC AND ACADEMIC WORKS ARE CONTROLLED
BY THE GOVERNMENT, AND VISITORS REPORT THAT A PRIMARY FUNCTION
OF PLAYS, MOVIES, OPERAS, AND BOOKS IS TO CONTRIBUTE TO THE
CULT OF PERSONALITY SURROUNDING "THE GREAT LEADER," KIM
IL-SUNG, AND HIS SON, "THE BELOVED LEADER," KIM CHONG-IL.

-- B. FREEDOM OF PEACEFUL ASSEMBLY AND ASSOCIATION

THE GOVERNMENT HAS DEVELOPED A PERVASIVE SYSTEM OF INFORMERS
THROUGHOUT THE SOCIETY. NO PUBLIC MEETINGS CAN BE HELD
WITHOUT GOVERNMENTAL AUTHORIZATION. TRADE UNIONS AND
PROFESSIONAL ASSOCIATIONS APPEAR TO EXIST SOLELY AS ANOTHER
METHOD OF GOVERNMENTAL CONTROL OVER THEIR MEMBERS. THEY HAVE
NO EFFECTIVE RIGHTS TO ORGANIZE, NEGOTIATE, OR STRIKE.

-- C. FREEDOM OF RELIGION

ALTHOUGH THE CONSTITUTION GUARANTEES THAT "CITIZENS HAVE
RELIGIOUS LIBERTY AND THE FREEDOM OF ANTIRELIGIOUS
PROPAGANDA," NORTH KOREA, IN FACT, HAS SEVERELY PERSECUTED
CHRISTIANS AND BUDDHISTS SINCE THE LATE 1940'S. NO CHURCHES
HAVE BEEN REBUILT SINCE THE KOREAN WAR. THE REGIME USES
RELIGIOUS ORGANIZATIONAL FACADES TO PROCLAIM THE PRACTICE OF
RELIGIOUS FREEDOM BUT APPEARS TO HAVE LONG SINCE PURGED THE
MEMBERSHIP OUT OF EXISTENCE. PERSONS WHOSE FAMILY OR

RELATIVES ONCE HAD A STRONG RELIGIOUS INVOLVEMENT ARE
DISCRIMINATED AGAINST. THOUGH RELIGIOUS PRACTICE APPEARS
IMPOSSIBLE, SOME FOREIGN VISITORS TO NORTH KOREA BELIEVE THAT
THE GOVERNMENT DOES NOT CURRENTLY PERSECUTE THE SMALL NUMBER
OF CHRISTIANS WHO CONTINUE TO WORSHIP AT HOME.

-- D. FREEDOM OF MOVEMENT WITHIN THE COUNTRY, FOREIGN
--   TRAVEL, EMIGRATION, AND REPATRIATION

INTERNAL TRAVEL IN NORTH KOREA IS STRICTLY CONTROLLED. A
TRAVEL PASS IS REQUIRED FOR ANY MOVEMENT OUTSIDE ONE'S HOME
VILLAGE AND IS GRANTED ONLY FOR REQUIRED OFFICIAL OR PERSONAL
TRAVEL. THIS REQUIREMENT IS STRICTLY ENFORCED. FOREIGN
TRAVEL IS LIMITED TO OFFICIALS OR TRUSTED ARTISTS AND
PERFORMERS. EMIGRATION IS NOT ALLOWED, AND FEW REFUGEES OR
DEFECTORS SUCCEED IN FLEEING THE COUNTRY. RETALIATION
REPORTEDLY IS TAKEN AGAINST THE RELATIVES OF THOSE FEW PERSONS
WHO MANAGE TO ESCAPE. ACCORDING TO FREEDOM HOUSE, "RIGHTS TO
TRAVEL INTERNALLY AND EXTERNALLY ARE PERHAPS THE MOST
RESTRICTED IN THE WORLD: TOURISM IS UNKNOWN--EVEN TO
COMMUNIST COUNTRIES."

0032

IN 1959 NORTH KOREA BEGAN ACTIVELY ENCCURAGING KORFAN
RESIDENTS OVERSEAS TO REPATRIATE TO "THE FATHERLAND." SCME
OBSERVERS ESTIMATE THAT DURING THE NEXT SEVERAL YEARS OVER
100,000 OVERSEAS KOREANS, ALMOST ALL FRCM JAPAN, VOLUNTARILY
REPATRIATED TO NORTH KOREA. SINCE THEN, HOWEVER, REPORTS OF
THE HARSH TREATMENT GIVEN REPATRIATES REACHED OVERSEAS
KOREANS. REDUCING THE FLOW TO NORTH KOREA TO A TRICKLE.
(BECAUSE OF THEIR "CORRUPTION" BY EXPOSURE TO FCREIGN
INFLUENCES. REPATRIATES ARE ISOLATED FROM NORTH KOREAN SOCIETY
AFTER THEIR ARRIVAL UNTIL THEY CAN BE INDCCTRINATED AND THEIR
IDEOLOGICAL RELIABILITY GAUGED.)

NORTH KOREA HAS PERMITTED SOME OVERSEAS KCREAN RESIDENTS TO
ENTER ITS TERRITCRY TO VISIT THEIR RELATIVES, AND SEVERAL HAVE
MADE REPEAT VISITS.

SECTION 3 RESPECT FOR PCLITICAL RIGHTS: THE RIGHT OF CITIZENS
--   TO CHANGE THEIR GOVERNMENT

POLITICAL PROCESSES IN NORTH KOREA ARE DOMINATED BY KIM
IL-SUNG, WHO LEADS THE KCREAN WORKERS' PARTY, AND ALSO HEADS
THE GOVERNMENT. KIM HAS GROOMED HIS SON KIM CHONG-IL TO
SUCCEED HIM, AND THERE ARE REPORTS THAT KIM CHCNG-IL HAS BEEN
ACQUIRING INCREASING POWER AND INFLUENCE. THE LEGISLATURE,
THE SUPREME PEOPLE'S ASSEMBLY, HAS NEVER TAKEN ANY ACTICN
OTHER THAN UNANIMOUS PASSAGE OF RESOLUTICNS PRESENTED TO IT EY
THE LEADERSHIP. IN AN EFFORT TO CREATE AN APPEARANCE OF

DEMOCRACY, NCRTH KOREA HAS CREATED SEVERAL "MINORITY
PARTIES." THEY EXIST CNLY AS ROSTERS CF CFFICIALS WHO HAVE
TOKEN REPRESENTATION IN THE PEOPLE'S ASSEMBLY AND COMPLETELY
SUPPORT THE GOVERNMENT LINE.

FREE ELECTIONS DO NOT EXIST IN NORTH KOREA. ALTHOUGH
ELECTIONS TO THE SUPREME PEOPLE'S ASSEMBLY WERE HELD IN
FEBRUARY 1982, AND TO CITY AND COUNTY ASSEMBLIES IN MARCH
1983. IN ALL CASES CNLY ONE CANDIDATE WAS APPROVED BY THE
GOVERNMENT PARTY IN EACH ELECTCRAL DISTRICT. AND. ACCORDING TC

0033

THE GOVERNMENT-CONTROLLED MEDIA. 100 PERCENT OF THE VOTERS
TURNED OUT TO ELECT 100 PERCENT OF THE APPROVED CANDIDATES.
SUCH "ELECTIONS" IN REALITY ARE A MANDATORY EXERCISE IN WHICH
VOTERS ARE REQUIRED TO PARTICIPATE AND TO APPROVE THE PARTY'S
CANDIDATES.

THE AVERAGE CITIZEN IS COMPLETELY EXCLUDED FROM ANY REAL
PARTICIPATION IN THE POLITICAL PROCESS. TO ACHIEVE EVEN A
SEMBLANCE OF REAL PARTICIPATION, ONE MUST BECOME A MEMBER OF
THE KOREAN WORKER'S PARTY. THE SELECTION PROCESS FOR ENTRANCE
TO THE PARTY IS LONG AND RIGOROUS. INDIVIDUALS FROM "BAD
SOCIAL BACKGROUNDS," I.E., THOSE WHO HAVE RELATIVES WHO FLED
SOUTH DURING THE KOREAN WAR, THOSE WHOSE FAMILIES HAD STRONG
RELIGIOUS INVOLVEMENT OR WERE ONCE PROPERTY OWNERS OR MEMBERS
OF THE BOURGEOISIE, AND THOSE WHO HAVE RELATIVES WHO ARE
POLITICAL PRISONERS, EFFECTIVELY ARE DENIED ENTRY INTO THE
PARTY AND ARE DISCRIMINATED AGAINST. MOST LEVELS OF THE PARTY
HAVE NO VOICE, SERVING ONLY TO CARRY OUT THE DECREES AND "ON
THE SPOT GUIDANCE" PROMULGATED BY PARTY LEADER KIM IL-SUNG AND
HIS TOP SUBORDINATES.

SECTION 4   GOVERNMENTAL ATTITUDE REGARDING INTERNATIONAL AND
  --   NON-GOVERNMENTAL INVESTIGATION OF ALLEGED VIOLATIONS
  --   OF HUMAN RIGHTS

NO ORGANIZATIONS EXIST WITHIN NORTH KOREA TO REPORT ON OR
OBSERVE HUMAN RIGHTS VIOLATIONS. NORTH KOREA DOES NOT
PARTICIPATE IN ANY INTERNATIONAL OR REGIONAL HUMAN RIGHTS
ORGANIZATIONS. ON SEPTEMBER 14, 1981, NORTH KOREA ACCEDED TO
THE INTERNATIONAL COVENANT ON CIVIL AND POLITICAL RIGHTS
(ICCPR) AND THE INTERNATIONAL CONVENANT ON ECONOMIC, SOCIAL
AND CULTURAL RIGHTS. AT THE MARCH-APRIL 1984 SESSION OF THE
HUMAN RIGHTS COMMITTEE, AN EXPERT BODY CONSISTING OF MEMBERS
ELECTED BY STATE PARTIES TO THE ICCPR, MEMBERS CRITICIZED A
REPORT SUBMITTED BY NORTH KOREA ON ITS HUMAN RIGHTS PRACTICES
AS TOO SHORT AND INADEQUATE. THE NORTH KOREAN REPRESENTATIVE
DENIED THAT HIS COUNTRY HAD ANY PROBLEMS AT ALL, PROMPTING AN
EXPERT MEMBER TO URGE THAT THE NORTH KOREAN'S ASSURANCES OF
FREEDOM OF RELIGION, POLITICAL ACTIVITY, AND TRAVEL OUTSIDE

KOREA BE MADE KNOWN TO THE NORTH KOREAN PEOPLE.

AMNESTY INTERNATIONAL HAS REQUESTED A VISIT TO NORTH KOREA
THE GOVERNMENT HAS NOT RESPONDED TO OR ACKNOWLEDGED THIS
REQUEST. A DECEMBER 1982 REQUEST BY AMNESTY INTERNATIONAL FOR
INFORMATION ON NORTH KOREAN LAWS, ON USE OF THE DEATH PENALTY,
AND ON REPORTS OF ARRESTS AND LONG-TERM IMPRISONMENT OF
POLITICAL FIGURES ALSO RECEIVED NO REPLY.

THE AMNESTY INTERNATIONAL 1984 REPORT NOTED THAT ITS WORK
CONTINUED TO BE SERIOUSLY IMPAIRED BY THE ABSENCE OF ANY
OFFICIAL INFORMATION DURING THE YEAR CONCERNING ANY ARRESTS,
TRIALS, OR DEATH SENTENCES, THAT IT CONTINUED TO INVESTIGATE
REPORTS THAT FOUR PROMINENT POLITICAL FIGURES HAD BEEN
DETAINED FOR SEVERAL YEARS, AND THAT IT DID NOT RECEIVE ANY
REPLIES TO CORRESPONDENCE DIRECTED TO THE GOVERNMENT. FREEDOM
HOUSE, IN ITS 1984-85 REPORT, LISTS NORTH KOREA AS "NOT FREE."

0034

ECONOMIC, SOCIAL, AND CULTURAL SITUATION

NORTH KOREA IS A LESS-DEVELOPED COUNTRY WITH A HIGHLY
CENTRALIZED, PLANNED ECONOMY. MANY OBSERVERS BELIEVE THAT,
AFTER A SHORT PERIOD OF RAPID GROWTH IN THE EARLY 1970'S, THE
ECONOMY EXPERIENCED DIFFICULTIES IN SUBSEQUENT YEARS DUE
LARGELY TO ECONOMIC POLICIES THAT OVEREMPHASIZED MILITARY
EXPENDITURES, STRESSED ATTAINMENT OF SELF-SUFFICIENCY, AND
PUSHED FOR RAPID GROWTH OF HEAVY INDUSTRY. MORE THAN TWENTY
PERCENT OF NORTH KOREA'S GROSS NATIONAL PRODUCT IS COMMITTED
TO MILITARY EXPENDITURES, THE SECOND HIGHEST SUCH RATE IN THE
WORLD.

IN THE EARLY 1980'S THE GOVERNMENT GRADUALLY HAS SHIFTED ITS
POLICY EMPHASIS TOWARD EXPANDING TRADE. IN SEPTEMBER 1984,
NORTH KOREA PROMULGATED A JOINT VENTURES LAW TO ATTRACT
FOREIGN CAPITAL AND TECHNOLOGY. AS YET THERE IS LITTLE
EVIDENCE OF FOREIGN INVESTOR INTEREST OR ANY SHIFT IN INTERNAL
ECONOMIC PRIORITIES AWAY FROM SUPPORT OF MILITARY INDUSTRY.
THE APPARENT SHIFT IN ECONOMIC POLICY IS ALSO SHOWN BY NORTH
KOREA'S APPARENT WILLINGNESS TO DISCUSS ECONOMIC TRADE AND
COOPERATION WITH THE REPUBLIC OF KOREA.

THE POPULATION OF NORTH KOREA IS ESTIMATED TO BE ABOUT 19
MILLION, WITH AN ANNUAL GROWTH RATE OF 2.3 PERCENT. THE 1984
INFANT MORTALITY RATE WAS 30 PER 1,000 LIVE BIRTHS. LIFE
EXPECTANCY AT BIRTH WAS 65.8 YEARS IN 1984. THE WORLD BANK
ESTIMATED IN 1981 THAT THE CALORIE SUPPLY AVAILABLE FOR
CONSUMPTION WAS 129 PERCENT OF NUTRITIONAL REQUIREMENTS.

NORTH KOREA APPEARS TO HAVE INVESTED CONSIDERABLE EFFORT AND
MONEY IN DEVELOPING A COMPREHENSIVE HEALTH CARE SYSTEM. BOTH
PRE- AND POST-WORKING AGE CITIZENS ARE CARED FOR BY THE
STATE. BASIC FOOD SUPPLIES ARE HEAVILY SUBSIDIZED
ANDRATIONED. THERE WERE SOME REPORTS OF REDUCED RATIONS AND
FOOD SHORTAGES IN 1983; THE PROPORTION OF RICE IN THE GRAIN
RATION HAS BEEN STEADILY REDUCED WITH GRAINS CONSIDERED LESS
DESIRABLE, SUCH AS MILLET OR BARLEY, BEING SUBSTITUTED.
REPORTEDLY, BECAUSE QUALITY FOODS ARE DIFFICULT TO OBTAIN,
JOBS IN FOOD-HANDLING INDUSTRIES ARE HIGHLY PRIZED. FOREIGN

0035

VISITORS HAVE NOTED THAT NORTH KOREANS THEY OBSERVED APPEARED
ADEQUATELY FED. PER CAPITA INCOME WAS ESTIMATED TO BE $968 IN
1982.

THE PARTY, GOVERNMENT, AND MILITARY ELITE ENJOY SIGNIFICANT
ECONOMIC PRIVILEGES, SUCH AS ACCESS TO SPECIAL STORES AND
MEDICAL FACILITIES, BETTER HOUSING, AND BETTER EDUCATION,
WHICH ARE NOT AVAILABLE TO ORDINARY CITIZENS.

THE NORTH KOREAN GOVERNMENT PROVIDES 11 YEARS OF COMPULSORY
FREE EDUCATION TO ITS CITIZENS AND CLAIMS TO HAVE ELIMINATED
ILLITERACY. THE ADJUSTED PRIMARY SCHOOL ENROLLMENT RATIOS FOR
1976 WERE 96.6 FOR FEMALES AND 101 FOR MALES, FOR A COMBINED
RATIO OF 98.7.

THE CONSTITUTION STATES THAT "WOMEN HOLD EQUAL SOCIAL STATUS
AND RIGHTS WITH MEN." DESPITE THIS PROVISION, FEW WOMEN REACH
HIGH LEVELS OF THE PARTY OR THE GOVERNMENT. WOMEN ARE
REPRESENTED PROPORTIONALLY IN THE LABOR FORCE, AND PERSONNEL
IN SMALL FACTORIES ARE PREDOMINATELY WOMEN. REPORTEDLY, WOMEN
ARE OFTEN PAID LESS THAN MEN FOR SIMILAR WORK. SHULTZ
BT
#6703
NNNN

6/6 C O N F I D E N T I A L STATE 036703/06

0036

2. 1986 (1985년도)

외 무 부

착 신 전 보

번 호 : USW-5249   일 시 : 511221840   종 별 :

수 신 : 장 관 (미북)

발 신 : 주 미 대사

제 목 : 국무성 인권과장 면담

1. 국무성은 매년 1월말 미의회에 세계 각국의 인권 상황에 대한 인권보고서를 제출하며, 2월초에는 동 인권 보고서가 유인물로 발간됨 국무성 인권과의 THOMAS MURPHY 담당관은 지난 10월초 4일간 방한한바 있으며 국무성 동아태국측은 이미 수차에 걸쳐 내년도 인권보고서가 전보다 나빠질 가능성에 대한 우려를 표명해 온바 있음

2. 김삼훈 참사관은 금 11.22(금) JAMES THYDEN 인권과장을 오찬에 초청, 아국의 안보현실, 정치발전 상황등을 종합적으로 설명, 올바른 인식을 갖도록 노력한바 아래보고함, 동 오찬에는 이선진 서기관과 MURPHY 담당관이 동석함

가. 아국은 88년의 평화적 정권교체의 실현, 올림픽의 성공적 개최등 중요한 일을 앞두고 민주화를 위한 올바른 방향으로 착실하게 전진하고 있음.

나. 남북대화가 진행중에 있으나 북한은 결코 적화통일 야욕을 포기하지 않고 있으며 88년의 중대사를 앞두고 북한의 사회적 혼란 야기 기도와 침략 위협을 항상 우려하지 않을수 없는 실정임

다. 북한의 위협하에 있는 한국으로서는 법과질서를 파괴하려는 기도에 대해 강력히 대치 이를 지키고 조용한 다수를 보호해야할 의무가 있음. 법과 질서 수호과정에서 다소간 과잉 행동이 있을수도 있으나 만약 있었다면 우발적인 것이었을것임

라. 80년 마아아미 폭동시 미국경찰이 질서수호를 위해 취한 조치를 가지고 잠시 미국을 여행하던 여행자가 미국이 비민주적인 나라라고 한다면 아무도 이를 올바른 견해라고 인정하지는 않을것임

마. 다른 나라의 인권과 자유를 오로지 미국적 시각의 차를 가지고 평가할수는 없으며 올바른 방향으로 노력하고 있는 우방국 정부에 대해서는 공개적인 언급이나 비난

미주국   차관실   1차보   청와대   안 기 [[handwritten]]

85.11.23 11:07
외신 2과 통제관

0038

보다는 조용한 방법으로 충고하고 협의하는것이 바람직함.

바. 아국의 경우 국내문제에 다한 우방 미국의 공개적인 관심표명은 민주화를 위한 정부의 노력에 부담이되고 오히려 일을 악화시키는 경우가 많았다는 것이 과거의 경험임

사. 안보위협에 직면하고 450억불의 외채 부담을 안고 있으면서 매년 7푸로 이상의 경제 성장을 달성하므로써 신규창출 노동력에 대한 취업의 기회를 제공해 주어야하는 아국으로서는 무엇보다도 정치적, 사회적 안정이 가장 중요한바, 이를 위한 우방국의 이해와 협조가 필요함

3.   THYDEN 과장은 면담초 강경한 의견개진이 있었으나 약 2시간에 걸친 대화를 통해 부분적으로 상당한 이해를 표시하였음. 그러나 인권국으로서는 정책 방향을 운위하는것이 아니라 있었던 일을 사실대로 의회에 보고해야하는 의무가 있다는 점과 어떠한 인권상호이 의무적으로 문제가 되었을때 이를 조용한 방법으로만 다룰수 없다는 미행정부로서의 애로가 있다는 점을 강조하였음.

(대사 김경원)

예고: 86.6.30.일반

PAGE   2

0039

발 신 전 보

번 호: WUS-421   일 시: 120330   전보종별: _____

수 신: 주 미   대사·총영사

발 신: 장   관   (미북)

제 목: 국무성 인권보고서

대 : USW-5249

1. 대호 국무성 인권보고서 작성건에 대해서는 계속 유념하기 바라며 85년도 인권보고서의 아국관련 부분내용을 자연스럽게 사전파악 할수있을 경우 동 내용을 보고바람.

2. 인권상황 설명자료는 근간 발려중에 오편송에 있음.

예고 : 85.12.31. 일반.

(차관 - 이상옥)

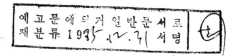

예고문에 의거 일반문서로
재분류 1985.12.31 서명 ㅇ

보안
통제

앙 고 재	85년 11월 3일 미과	기안자	과 장	국 장	차 관	장 관		
		ㅇ			전결		외신과	접수자 / 통제

0040

기 안 용 지

분류기호 문서번호	미북 700-	(전화번호)	전결규정	조 항
				전결사항

처리기간	3/25	장 관
시행일자	1985. 11. 30.	
보존연한		

보 조 기 관	차 관	전결	제 1 차관보	협	
	국 장		심 의 관		
	과 장			조	
기 안 책 임 자	박인국		북 미 각		

경 유		발		통
수 신	법무부장관			
참 조		신		제
제 목	85년도 미국무성 인권보고서			

발 / 송
1985. 12.
외무부

검열
1985.

검 토 필 (1985. 12. 11)

연 : 미북 700-3256

1. 미국무성은 매년 1월말 미의회에 세계각국의 인권상황에
대한 보고서를 제출하며, 2월초에는 동 인권보고서를 유인물로
발간, 배포하고 있는 바, 동 인권보고서 작성을 위하여 국무성
인권과의 Thomas Murphy 담당관이 지난 10월초 방한하여
귀부를 방문한바도 있읍니다.

2. 최근 미국무성측은 수차에 걸쳐 86.2 발간 예정인
85년도 인권보고서의 아국 관계 내용이 전년도 보다 제약될 가능성에
대한 우려를 주미대사관에 표명하여 온 바 있읍니다. ※ 비판적이 될

3. 미국무성의 상기입장 표명에 대해 주미대사관은 국무성

/ 계속 /

정서
관인
발송

1205 - 25 (2 - 1) A (갑)
1981. 12. 18승인

정직 질서 창조

190mm×268mm (인쇄용지 2급 60g./㎡)
강 40-41 1985. 8. 7.
0041

관계자들을 다각적으로 접촉하여 아국의 안보현실, 정치발전 상황

등을 종합적으로 설명, 올바른 인식을 갖도록 노력하고 있는바,

향후 보다 설득력 있는 홍보활동을 위한 자료, 특히 1984년에 비하여

인권보장 부분에서 개선된 사항등이 있을 경우 관련자료를 당부로

송부하여 주시기 바랍니다.

첨 부 : 84년도 미국무성 인권보고서.   끝.

예 고 : 86.6.30.일반.

0042

미국무성의 1984년 인권보고서(1985.2.13 발간)

----

1. 한국 및 북괴관련 부분 주요특징

　가. 한국관계

　　o 1983년도 인권보고서 내용과 대동소이, 단 하기
　　　사항이 추가 또는 수정되었음.

　　　- 북한은 수재물자 제공 및 대화제의등 평화적
　　　　제스추어에도 불구하고 대남 무력도발을 계속
　　　　하고 있으며, 공격적인 무력증강을 강화하고
　　　　있음.

　　　- 1984년중 학원자율화, 교수 및 언론인 복직,
　　　　과거 정치인에 대한 복권 및 정치해금등 적극
　　　　적인 자유화 조치가 있었음. 1984년의 정치
　　　　관련범은 제5공화국 이후 최저 수준인 110명
　　　　가량임.

　　　- 대통령각하는 1988년 평화적 정권교체 약속을
　　　　재확인 하였음.

　나. 북괴관계

　　o 북한사회는 김일성 독벌체제제하에 세계에서 가장
　　　조직화되고 통제 되었으며, 모든 개인 권리가
　　　철저히 당에 종속 되었다고 기술한 점에서 1983년도

0043

보고서와 거의 같으나 하기 사항이 특별히 강조됨.

- 84년중 북한은 남한에 수재물자를 제공했고,
  경제회담 및 이산가족 재회를 위한 남한의
  회담 제의에 긍정적인 반응을 보이기도 했으나,
  남한을 공격목표로 하는 군사력을 계속 증강
  시키고 있음.

0044

2. 인권보고서 주요 내용

　가. 한국 관계

　　1) 개　　관

　　　　o 대통령이 대부분의 권력을 장악하고 있으며、국회는
　　　　　다소의 영향력이 있으나 행정부 권한에는 훨씬 못미침·

　　　　o 역대 한국정부는 북한의 위협에 직면하여 국내외 안정
　　　　　문제를 최우선 과제로 삼고 있으며、이로 인하여 반대
　　　　　파의 정치활동을 억압하고 있다는 비난받고 있음·

　　　　o 한국경제는 정부주도와 자유경제 체제의 혼합형이며、
　　　　　1981년 이후 더욱 자유로운 경제체제를 추구하고 있음·
　　　　　지난 20여년간 세계에서 가장 급속한 경제성장을 시현
　　　　　하고 있음·

　　　　o 휴전선은 세계에서 가장 심각히 무장화된 지역이며
　　　　　북한은 무력통일을 포함하여 자신의 조건과 방식에
　　　　　의한 통일방안을 주장하고 있음·

　　　　o 북한은 특히 수재물자 제공 및 대화를 제의하는 등
　　　　　평화적 제스추어도 불구하고 대남 무력도발을 계속하고
　　　　　있음· 한국 국민들은 랑군사건을 여전히 생생히 기억
　　　　　하고 있음·

0045

○ 북한은 궁격적인 무력증강을 강화하고 있으며 한국
국민들 사이에는 북한의 남침위협에 대한 우려가
상존하고 있음. 역대 한국정부는 이를 이유로
무제한의 반대의견을 용납할수 없다는 조치를 취해
왔음.

○ 언론·출판의 자유는 헌법상 보장에도 불구 실제로
제한되고 있으며 결사 및 시위권도 한계가 있으나
비정치적 신앙의 자유는 완전함.

○ (1984년의 학원자율화, 교수 및 언론인 복직, 과거
정치인에 대한 복권, 정치해금등을 상세 설명) 한국
에는 제5공화국 이후 최저 수준인 110명 가량의
정치관련범이 있으나 1/3 가량은 간첩행위, 나머지는
폭력을 사용한 보안법 위규 사건 관련자임.

○ 정치적으로 민감한 사건에는 고문사례 보도 없었음.
한국정부는 경찰고문 근절을 위하여 노력하고 있음.

○ 지도자 인권개선 및 정치체제 자유화를 위한 강한
움직임에도 불구, 유교적인 계급사상, 군부의 서구형
민주주의 열의 부족, 그리고 북한의 위협에 대처키
위한 국민적 화합의 필요성등이 자유화 움직임에 큰
장애요소 임.

0046

2) 개인의 기본권

○ 정치적 살인
- 정치적 살해 무

○ 행방불명 : 전무

○ 고 문
- 헌법상 고문이 금지되어 있으며, 1983년 고문 상해 사건의 처벌 강화법 제정
- 그러나 경찰의 학생데모 진압에 구타 및 과격한 폭력사용이 문제화 되기도 하였으나 관련 경찰 처벌 사례는 전무

○ 임의체포 및 구속
- 반정부인사 구금 및 감시증가, 사회혼란 방지를 위한 예비 검속 가능
- 학원자율화 조치로 학원사태 관련한 구속학생수의 현저한 감소

○ 공개재판 거부
- 헌법상 피의자 권리보장 공개재판 규정
- 사법부의 독립은 일반적으로 유지되고 있으나, 정치적으로 민감한 경우 독립성이 다소 감소

0047

o 개인의 사생활권 침해

  - 야당인사 및 반정부인사에 대한 감시、도청 및
    가택연금 사례 상존

  - 일반시민의 사생활은 보호

3) 시 민 권

o 언론출판의 자유

  - 반대의견일 경우 표현의 자유 제한

  - 국회내에서도 체제 논쟁등 민감한 문제에 대한
    비판에는 신중

  - 그러나 정부정책 비판은 언론 게재

  - 언론은 자율규제、그러나 정부가 보도지침 시달

o 집회결사의 자유

  - 일반적인 집회의 자유에도 불구、특정부류의 집회
    금지

  - 노조관계법 및 노조활동 상세설명

o 종교의 자유

  - 비정치적 종교활동의 자유 완전보장

o 거주이전의 자유

  - 국내거주 이전의 자유 완전 보장

  - 반정부인사 정치활동 금지 정치인 다수 해외여행
    허용

0048

4) 정치적 권리

    o 대통령이 정치권력의 핵심

    o 전대통령은 헌법규정에 따라 88년에 물러날것임을
      재확인

    o 국회가 정치적으로 약하나 정부시책에 대한 다양한
      견해 개진의 광장으로 중요

    o 정치활동 규제조치로 다수 정치인 활동이 상금
      금지 상태

    o 해금자들로 구성된 신당 창립

5) 국제기구 또는 비정부기구의 인권위반 사례조사에 대한
   정부입장

    o 한국은 국제인권단체에 가입치 않고있으며、외국
      인권단체의 개입을 환영치 않음·

    o 인권관계 정부기관은 없으나 국제인권단체와 연관되어
      있는 사설단체는 존재

6) 경제사회 문화 정세

    o 주요 경제적 자산은 교육수준 높은 노동력

    o 84년도 성장율 8%

    o 여권신장、사회복지 조건 개선

0049

나. 북괴관계

1) 개 관

- 북한은 엄격한 공산독재국가로서 개인의 권리는
  김일성 및 그의 가족 지배하에 있는 노동당에 철저히
  종속되어 있음.

- 김일성은 어떠한 수단방법을 다해서라도 한반도
  통일을 해야한다고 하면서, 랑군사건의 예에서 보는
  바와같이 한국내에 불안정을 획책하고 있음.
  - 84년중 북한은 남한에 수재물자를 제공하고 경제
    회담 및 이산가족 재회를 위한 한국의 회담제의에
    긍정적인 반응을 보이기도 했으나, 남한을 공격
    목표로 하는 군사력을 계속 증강시키고 있음.

- 북한 지도자들은 또한 통일 명목하에 북한을 조직화,
  군사화하고 있으며 이에 불응하는 자는 구금, 재산
  압수, 유배됨.

- 북한은 주민들에 대한 사상교육을 강력히 시행하고
  있으며 그결과 북한은 오늘날 세계에서 가장 조직화
  되고 통제된 사회임.
  - 북한의 일반주민은 외부와 정보를 거의 접할수
    없음.

0050

o 북한 주민들은 출신계급·당성·그 가족의 과거
  친일행동 여부등을 근거로 하여 분류되는 성분에
  따라 차별적 대우를 받고 있음.

o 북한의 국영라디오 방송은 84년에 처음으로 김정일이
  김일성의 후계자임을 명백히 언급했는바, 김일성은
  자신의 사후에도 현체제가 유지되도록 시도하고 있음.

2) 개인적 기본권

  o 정치적 살해
    - 북한내의 정치적 동기에 의한 살인에 관한 정보는
      없으나 랑군 폭발사건과 84·11·23 발생한 비무장
      지대에서의 총격사건은 북한의 태도를 잘 나타내
      주고 있음.

  o 행방불명 : 정보부족

  o 고 문
    - 1983-1984 Freedom House 보고서는 북한에서
      고문이 보통 있는 일이라고 지적
    - 푸에블로호 선원과 베네수엘라 시인의 경험담

  o 임의체포
    - 영장이나 유사한 제도가 없으며 자의적인 구금이나
      체포 가능

0051

- 북한에는 현재 약 105,000명의 사상범이 8개
  수용소에 수용되어 있음.

o 공개재판 거부
  - 사법부는 전적으로 정부통제하에 있음.

o 가택 및 통신에 대한 무단 침범
  - 일반주민은 계속적으로 사상교육을 받아야함.
  - 북한으로 송환된 일본인 부인 일본 방문 불허,
    서신교환 금지
  - 외국방송 청취 불허
  - 개인주택 도청

3) 시민권

o 언론출판의 자유
  - 정부시책에 대한 지지를 제외하고는 언론, 집회,
    시위의 자유 불안정

o 집회 결사의 자유
  - 조동조합 및 각종협회등은 주민에 대한 효과적인
    지배 및 통제의 수단으로 이용

o 종교의 자유
  - 40년대 후반이후 지속적인 종교박해
  - 종교기관이란 주민의 효과적인 통제 및 대외 선전용

0052

ο 거주 이전의 자유

 - 북한내의 여행 엄격 통제

4) 정치적 권리

ο 정치과정은 김일성 노동당의 독점물

 - 입법기관인 최고 인민회의는 지도부가 제출한
   법안을 만장일치로 통과시키는 역할만 수행

ο 자유선거는 없으며 선거구 별로 당이 지명한 인사가
  단독출마

 - 노동 당원외에는 참정권 불안정

5) 국제기구로부터의 인권위반 비난에 대한입장

ο 국제적 또는 지역적 인권기구에 전혀 불참

 - 1981.9 민권 및 참정권에 관한 국제협약에 가입
   했으나, 1984년 동 협약 인권위원회는 북한측의
   보고서가 부적절하다고 비난

ο Amnesty International   의 북한 방문요청
  및 82.12월 사형에 관한 법률, 정치적 인물 체포,
  구금에 대한 문의에 무응답

 - 1984년도   Amnesty International 보고서는
   북한내의 체포, 재판, 사형선고등에 대한 정보가
   없어 동 기구의 작업이 손상되고 있다고 지적

0053

    °   Freedom House   1984-85년도 보고서는 북한을

      자유가 없는 국가로 분류

6) 경제사회 문화 정세

    °   과도한 군사비 지출로 경제발전에 지장

       - 80년대 초부터 대외교역 다소 증대

       - 84.9 합영법 발표

       - 83년도에 식량부족 및 배급량 감소설

       - 82년도 개인소득 968불 추정

0054

REPUBLIC OF KOREA

Korea, calling for the destruction of American and South Korean installations, violence against South Korean leaders, and the overthrow of the South Korean Government.

Thus, fear of another invasion from the North is a fundamental factor in South Korean thinking, and successive governments have held that for security reasons the Republic cannot afford the unfettered dissent and discord which would be permitted in an open political system. Nonetheless, many Koreans question the rationale for this position.

Korea's traditional sociopolitical ideology, Confucianism, with its emphasis on order, conformity, consensus and filial piety, retains great strength, coexisting uneasily with the Western democratic ideals and industrial-age values to which Koreans have been exposed in this century.

Koreans of both sexes participate in politics. Constitutional safeguards against ex post facto laws and double jeopardy are generally observed. Although the Constitution guarantees freedom of speech and the press, in practice both are abridged. Politicians and others who publicly criticize the Government are aware that there are limits beyond which they may be subject to some form of government action. Newspapers are expected to practice self-censorship, and failure to comply with this requirement has led to interrogation and, on occasion, dismissals of reporters and editors. The law limits the freedom to assemble and demonstrate, although in 1984, in a break with past practice, the Government did not apply the law to university campuses and arrests have accordingly been sharply reduced. Religious freedom, though otherwise complete, does not extend to churches' involvement in political and some forms of social action. There is freedom of movement within the country and freedom to travel abroad, except that passport applications from persons with a history of political opposition are considered on a case-by-case basis and some are not allowed to leave the country.

During 1984 the Government took several significant positive steps in the human rights field. More than 220 students jailed for campus demonstrations were released from prison during the year in three separate amnesties, and about 1,400 students previously expelled for political activism were allowed to reenroll at their old campuses. About half this number had actually returned by the fall term. Some 86 dissident professors, banned from teaching since 1980, were also permitted to teach again at their original campuses. In early 1984 the Government initiated a policy of "campus autonomy" under which it withdrew security forces from university campuses, a major student demand; allowed peaceful demonstrations on campuses; and stated that henceforth universities would bear the primary responsibility for enforcing campus discipline. In the face of increased student resistance measures, the Government in November warned that it was prepared to have police enter campuses even without intervention requests by school officials. In practice, however, security forces only entered campuses on a few occasions. However, students have accused the Government of maintaining campus networks of police informers. Student attempts to move demonstrations off campus were met by large government security forces, which led to violent confrontations at university gates and, on occasion, elsewhere in downtown Seoul.

0055

REPUBLIC OF KOREA

In the Republic of Korea, President Chun Doo Hwan, with the support of the country's military establishment, dominates the political scene. The elected legislature has some influence but continues to be controlled by the executive branch. The Government, which assumed power with primarily military support in 1980, is organized under a Constitution adopted by referendum in October 1980. Because of the threat from an aggressive Communist regime in North Korea, all Korean governments since the Republic's founding in 1948 have felt it necessary to give top priority to maintaining external and internal security; their policies in this respect, as implemented in part by the large and well-organized security services, have brought charges that dissent and peaceful opposition political activity are suppressed, and to many Koreans the degree of legitimacy of the Chun Government is open to question. At the time of the next presidential election, scheduled for 1988, President Chun has promised to step down to provide for a peaceful and constitutional change of power.

The Republic of Korea has a mixed economy with extensive public sector intervention to stimulate and influence the direction of private sector activity. Since adopting an outward-looking development strategy in the mid-1960's, the Republic of Korea has had one of the highest real growth rates in the world and has achieved middle-income, "middle power" status. Since 1981, the economic leadership has moved toward a more open, freer market system.

Korea is an ethnically homogeneous nation. Surrounded by great powers--China, Japan, and in modern times the USSR--Korea historically focused its foreign policy on the objective of avoiding subjugation by these neighbors. In 1910, Korea was annexed by the Japanese Empire. Liberated in 1945, it was then divided into temporary Soviet and American zones of military administration, organized in 1948 as, respectively, the Democratic People's Republic of Korea, or North Korea, and the Republic of Korea, or South Korea.

Since the division of the peninsula in 1945, reunification has been a major goal of Koreans on both sides of the dividing line. North Korea, however, has insisted on reunifying the nation on its own terms and through any means, including use of military force or terrorist activities. Despite North Korea's delivery of flood relief goods to the South in 1984 and its positive response to South Korean proposals to hold North-South talks on economic cooperation and family reunification, military activities against the South continued, including continuing forward deployment of its armed forces. The memory of the 1983 Rangoon bombing against South Korean leaders, which the Burmese government determined was carried out by North Korea, is still fresh in the minds of South Koreans. The area on either side of the Demilitarized Zone remains one of the most heavily armed regions in the world. During the defection of a Soviet language student across the DMZ on November 23, 30-40 North Koreans soldiers crossed the DMZ and exchanged fire with South Korean and American UN Command guards in an effort to retrieve the Soviet student.

Furthermore, North Korea continues to strengthen its offensive force structure. Over the years, unremitting North Korean propaganda, overt and covert, has been directed at South

In another amnesty move, the Government restored civil rights to more than 700 former political prisoners, including some prominent intellectuals and human rights activists, and many convicted under emergency decrees of the Park Chung Hee government. The Government also announced that journalists who had been banned from employment since 1980 could be reemployed at the discretion of their former employers, and some have gone back to work. As a result of the large-scale amnesties carried out early in the year, the number of prisoners in politically-related cases was reduced to about 110, the lowest since the Fifth Republic came into being in 1980. About one-third that number are Korean residents of Japan convicted of espionage on behalf of North Korea, and most of the rest are convicted of National Security Law violations or activities involving the use or planned use of violence. However, the Government's current tactic of holding off-campus demonstration leaders in jail for brief periods, after summary convictions on minor charges, means that the total number of prisoners at any one time may be greater than the number of arrested and convicted persons on the "prisoner of conscience" list.

In 1980, the Government imposed an eight-year ban on political activities of 551 former politicians. Following Government action in 1983 to lift the ban on 250 of them, in 1984 the Government lifted the ban on 286 more, leaving a total of 15 still affected. The 15, however, included several of Korea's major former opposition party leaders. One of the most prominent of these, Kim Dae Jung, has been in the United States for two years for medical treatment. Although he faces possible arrest and an unexpired prison sentence in Korea, he has announced plans to return early in 1985.

Torture or severe physical mistreatment by the police occurred in 1984, but there were no reports of this abuse occurring in politically sensitive cases. Some female student demonstrators, however, charged that they were subjected to abusive strip searches by the police. The Government has said that it is trying to eliminate the deeply-rooted problem of abusive treatment by police, especially beatings of suspects during interrogation. This effort apparently has high-level support within the Government, as indicated by the passage in December 1983 of a law providing penalties up to life imprisonment for officials committing acts of torture. However, the problem, though diminished, has not disappeared. In addition to the police, there are two other security services whose agents are alleged to have beaten or otherwise mistreated suspects as well as dissidents, including students and activist workers, who were not in custody.

Prison conditions remain spartan, and there are reports of hunger strikes and other protests, especially by students. There were no allegations of murder against the Government in 1984.

Strong forces within Korea seek improvements in human rights and liberalization of the Governing structure, notably some Christian churches' leadership and the rising middle class. Formidable obstacles to these forces exist, primarily Korea's Confucianist hierarchical traditions and the lack of enthusiasm on the part of the powerful military officer corps for direct participation by all Koreans in the democratic process and for freedom of expression. Furthermore, the

perceived need for unity in the face of the North Korean threat inhibits efforts for political change which might affect stability.

RESPECT FOR HUMAN RIGHTS

Section 1 Respect for the Integrity of the Person, Including Freedom from:

a. Political Killing

There were no reports in 1984 of politically motivated killings by the Government.

b. Disappearance

There were no cases of permanent disappearance in 1984, although the police sometimes waited for more than the legal maximum of 40 days before notifying the families of arrested persons.

c. Torture and Cruel, Inhuman, or Degrading Treatment or Punishment

The Constitution prohibits torture. Confessions determined to have been induced by duress are inadmissible in the courts, and a confession alone is not legally sufficient to secure a conviction. The Government insists that it has issued injunctions against torture and that these are strictly enforced and violations sternly punished. Nevertheless, while there were no allegations of torture in politically sensitive cases in 1984, there were continuing reports of beatings by police during interrogations of prisoners. Two female students who had been detained for participating in an off-campus demonstration filed suit against police whom they accused of conducting abusive strip searches. The use of excessive force by the police, despite high-level efforts to reduce or eliminate it, has proven to be a pervasive and ingrained problem. In violent confrontations with student rioters, police units have generally remained well-disciplined but rioters have also been beaten on apprehension. Accusations of police beatings in non-political cases occur fairly frequently and are sometimes reported in the press. No case has yet been brought under the law adopted by the National Assembly in 1983 toughening sentences for those convicted of killing or injuring through torture.

Human rights groups allege, in addition, that the police and other government security agencies have been responsible for, or have not intervened to prevent, the beating of some students, workers and other dissidents not in custody. A human rights activist leader was beaten at his church by men that some Christian activists state that the Government denied the connection.

In early 1984 the Government arrested a prominent clergyman and two professors who had been conducting a study of reunification policies and charged them with violating the National Security Law. These dissidents were subsequently released without trial, but Christian activists state that the Government used threats to coerce the defendants into making public expressions of regret as a condition of their release. Activists also accuse police of forcing students into signing investigation for connection with workers issues into signing

0056

confessions of subversive activities. There is no evidence on the record to support these charges.

Conditions in Korean correctional institutions are spartan, and discipline is strict. While prisoners who break rules or protest conditions are sometimes beaten, under normal circumstances convicts are not subjected to physical punishment. Prisoners may receive visits only from their lawyers and immediate families. There does not seem to be a difference between the treatment of political and non-political prisoners, although the authorities have occasionally allowed special provisions for political prisoners, such as heaters during the winter or examination by outside physicians. There is no apparent difference in the treatment of prisoners on the basis of wealth, social class, race, or sex.

d. Arbitrary Arrest, Detention, or Exile

From time to time, the security services have not only detained persons accused of violating laws on political dissent but have also increased surveillance of, or put under house arrest, those who they think intend to violate the laws. Dissidents who openly criticize the Government are sometimes picked up for short periods and then released. Arrest warrants are required by law but are sometimes not produced at the time of arrest in politically-related cases.

Korean law requires that, within 40 days after making an arrest, the police notify an arrested person's family of his detention and whereabouts. The police normally wait at least several days, and occasionally more than 40 days, before making notification. The Constitution guarantees the right of prompt legal assistance and the right to request court review in case of arrest. For persons deemed "socially dangerous" the law allows preventive detention under provisions of the Social Protection and Social Stability Laws. Preventive detention is for a fixed term, which, however, a judicial panel may extend for periods of up to 10 years. Human rights activists and foreign observers are aware of two persons now in preventive detention for politically-related offenses, their detention having been renewed in 1984 for two more years.

Habeas corpus, not traditional in Korean law, was introduced after World War II, abolished in the 1970's, and reintroduced in 1980. It does not apply to those charged with violations of the National Security Act or laws punishable by at least 5 years imprisonment, which include most political offenses.

The Government released 229 students from jail in four amnesties between February and May. All the students had been arrested for anti-government campus demonstrations, though some had also been convicted of National Security Law violations. With these releases, the total of student demonstrators released since December 1983 grew to 360, and the jails were empty of student demonstrators for the first time in years. A small number of students convicted under the National Security Law for carrying out subversive activities is still imprisoned. In a Liberation Day amnesty the Government restored civil rights to 714 former political offenders, including a number of human rights leaders, intellectuals and former politicians. The Government also announced that it will erase the criminal records of about 5,000 Koreans for wartime collaboration with North Korean

occupation forces, thus easing employment and other social difficulties for those affected.

Following the last student release in May, a list of "prisoners of conscience" maintained by the Human Rights Committee (HRC) of the Korea National Council of Churches contained 52 names, a low since the beginning of the present Government. (The HRC definition of "prisoner of conscience" does not exclude those convicted of crimes involving the advocacy or use of violence, contrary to Amnesty International's definition.) This figure compares to 325 at the end of 1983, 417 in November 1982, and 272 in November 1981. Subsequent arrests and the addition of newly discovered cases, mainly Korean residents of Japan convicted, in prior years, of espionage for North Korea, brought the number on the list to about 110. However, student-police confrontations off-campus and student violence on-and off-campus in the fall of 1984 resulted in a large number of persons being arrested and sentenced to brief periods of detention on minor charges after summary convictions. These do not figure in the political prisoner list.

e. Denial of Fair Public Trial

The Constitution guarantees many rights of defendants: the right to presumption of innocence; the right against self-incrimination, ex post facto laws, and double jeopardy; the right to a speedy trial; and the right to legal counsel. These rights are generally observed, although there have been cases in the past in which defendants in politically-sensitive trials have not been able to obtain lawyers, reportedly because of lawyers' reluctance to accept such cases in the fact of actual or potential government pressure.

The President appoints the members of the Supreme Court, whose Chief Justice in turn appoints lower-level judges. The judiciary is considered independent in ordinary criminal and civil cases but much less so in politically-sensitive cases. It is generally assumed, for example, that the original and appeal verdicts in the case of six Chinese airplane hijackers tried before Seoul courts were guided by foreign relations considerations.

Trials are usually open to the public, but trial documents are not part of the public record. Charges against defendants in the courts are clearly stated, with the exception that, in lengthy and complex indictments, the relationship between specific acts alleged and violations of specific sections of the penal code may not always be clearly drawn. In cases involving a mixture of political and criminal charges this can bring into question the fairness of proceedings.

The same courts try political and ordinary criminal cases. The military courts do not try civilians. Defendants have the right of appeal in felony cases, a right which is often exercised and frequently results in substantial reductions in sentences. Death sentences are automatically appealed.

f. Arbitrary Interference with Privacy, Family, Home, or Correspondence

The security apparatus is large and highly developed. Many opposition figures and political and religious dissidents are subjected to surveillance. During politically sensitive periods, this surveillance by one or more security agencies may increase or a form of house arrest may be imposed. There have also been charges of telephone tapping and opening or interception of correspondence. Koreans who meet with foreigners, particularly with journalists and embassy officials, are often questioned afterwards. While the Constitution requires a warrant, issued by a judge upon request of a prosecutor, for search and seizure in a residence, the police have at times forced their way into private homes without warrants.

Korean police practice requires police commanders to know a good deal about the personal and business affairs of all residents in their jurisdictions. This system is effective in crime control, and urban residents generally credit it with keeping their streets safe. By contrast, the presence of police informer networks on college campuses with the primary purpose of keeping track of political activities there has been a key issue among students, including those who are not politically active. Students have accused the Government of maintaining police informers on-campus even after uniformed forces were withdrawn in accordance with the "campus autonomy" policy.

In most other respects the Government honors the right of personal privacy and the integrity of the home and family. Parental rights to educate children are broad, and restrictions on study in foreign-administered schools (whether in Korea or overseas), originally imposed to force wealthy Koreans to involve themselves in the nation's social and educational development, have been relaxed in recent years. The state rarely seeks to intervene in such inherently personal decisions as marriage, choice of vocation, and formation of social and familial ties. However, the state, by setting graduation levels at higher education institutions, does seek to guide the mixture of graduates according to predicted future manpower needs.

Section 2 Respect for Civil Rights, Including:

a. Freedom of Speech and Press

Although freedom of speech and press are guaranteed by the Constitution, in practice the expression of opposition viewpoints is severely limited. Dissidents are sometimes restricted in their meetings and movements in periods judged volatile by the Government. Members of the National Assembly frequently criticize particular government actions or policies but are careful to stop short of fundamental criticism of the Government itself, such as attacks on its legitimacy or personal attacks on the President. However, formal proposals for votes of "no confidence" at the Assembly and the stated rationale therefore are given full publicity. Likewise, criticism of government policies (for example, the campus autonomy policy) is reported by the media. While no direct actions against Assemblymen were taken in direct response to opinions expressed in the legislature, two Assemblymen who attempted to switch allegiance to a new opposition party were detained for three days in December. Discussion of security, formulas for political settlement with North Korea, the legitimacy of the Chun administration, and other sensitive topics is sharply curtailed. Academic freedom is subject to some political limitations, although 86 professors who lost their jobs in the political upheavals of 1980 were allowed

during 1984 to return to teaching at the schools at which they had last taught.

The domestic media engage in self-censorship, according to verbal or written guidelines the Government regularly gives to editors. Journalists who object to or ignore these guidelines or criticize the guidance system have, in the past, been picked up for questioning, and on occasion dismissed or sent out of the country on assignment. There was a reliable report in 1984 of a journalist whose columns were critical of the Government being sent abroad for study.

The extent of journalistic free expression varies. For example, when the National Assembly is in session, opposition viewpoints have been rather fully reported in the press. Increased reporting in 1984 was permitted by government authorities on the activities of dissident politicians and groups, including student movements. Reporting on dissidents was factual without editorial comment; reporting on student demonstrations was marked by editorial comment highlighting the socially disruptive nature of their activities. Also, increased press exposure was given to certain topics considered politically sensitive by the Government. For example, a public seminar on the nature of the political transition in 1988 was fully reported. However, a subsequent magazine article carrying complete texts, though planned, never appeared. Articles by opposition and dissident politicians increased, both in number and directness of criticism against the Government. A scandal allegedly involving a leading member of the ruling party received full coverage in the press and the publicity led to his resignation.

More books by dissident religious and political figures appeared in bookstores than in recent years. Some books, however, continue to be confiscated or banned from sale. Approved books on Communist and socialist theory are studied in universities and can be found in bookstores, but many books and artistic works with "socialist" themes are banned.

b. Freedom of Peaceful Assembly and Association

There are thousands of private organizations in Korea. Most peaceful non-political assemblies take place entirely without official supervision or restriction.

The Law on Assembly and Demonstrations prohibits specified categories of assembly, including those considered likely to undermine public order or cause social unrest. The law also requires that demonstrations of all types and outdoor political assemblies be reported in advance to the police. Violation of the law carries a maximum sentence of seven years or a fine of about $3,750. Under this law, police have at times intervened and broken up meetings.

Before the release this year and last of all students imprisoned for taking part in demonstrations, far more than half of all Korea's "prisoners of conscience" were imprisoned for violation of this law. In 1984 students have not been arrested for taking part in on-campus demonstrations; almost all students arrested in connection with demonstrations off-campus have been charged with minor offenses against public order and released after short periods of time, rather than convicted under this law. Only a small number of people

0058

dissidents, former political prisoners, and persons banned from political activity have been allowed to travel abroad. Foreign exchange considerations have caused the Government to limit to some extent the number of tourist passports issued. Passports, when issued, are typically limited to one year, although there are exceptions in which passports are issued up to the legally maximum 5-year validity.

A small continuing influx of Vietnamese boat refugees is admitted to first asylum in Korea. They are cared for at a camp in Pusan by the Korean Red Cross until they can be resettled abroad. Over 600 such refugees have passed through Korea in the last several years.

Section 3   Respect for Political Rights: The Right of Citizens
.   to Change Their Government

Korea's Constitution and statutes, as well as its traditions, concentrate their political power in the President, a concentration further intensified by the support the President enjoys from the military establishment. The President and the members of the National Assembly are the only elected officials in Korea. Under the 1980 Presidential Election Law, the President is chosen by an electoral college of about 5,000 members. By law, presidential campaigns are brief, and candidates are severely restricted in campaigning, including both the amount they may spend and the methods they may use to appeal to voters. In the 1981 Presidential election these restrictions, together with the authorities' careful screening of electoral college candidates and the reluctance of several strong potential presidential candidates to run, resulted in the virtual absence of effective opposition to incumbent President Chun Doo Hwan, who won by a nearly unanimous electoral vote. The Constitution limits the President to a single seven-year term and cannot be amended to allow the incumbent President to continue in office.

The next presidential election is scheduled for 1988. President Chun has reaffirmed that he intends to step down at that time to provide for a peaceful and constitutional transfer of power.

The National Assembly, although politically weak, is important as a forum for the expression of divergent views of the Government's programs. Recent changes in the Assembly Law have given the Assembly a somewhat increased role in examining government actions. Interpellations of Ministers have been increasingly pointed and debate among the parties increasingly vigorous. Legislation normally originates with the executive branch, although the Assembly has at times passed or blocked laws contrary to the President's wishes. Members of the Assembly, who serve a four-year term, are Korea's only directly-elected public officials. The election laws passed in 1981 provide for a proportional representation system that reserves 92 of the Assembly's 276 seats for members appointed by the parties, with two-thirds of those seats awarded to the party which gains a plurality of the popular vote. In the Assembly elections of March 1981, the authorities brought various forms of pressure to bear to discourage some potential candidates but did not interfere in the voting. Of the 184 Assembly seats to be filled by elections, the government party ran candidates for 92, of which it won 90, along with a 36 percent plurality of the popular vote. The government party was accordingly awarded 61 proportional representation seats,

were convicted and sentenced under this law in 1984, in particular ten taxi drivers who were convicted in connection with demonstrations in Taegu and Pusan. They were sentenced and released.

The single national labor federation, the Federation of Korean Trade Unions (FKTU), and its 16 national affiliate unions are not controlled by the government. Their freedom of action, however, is severely circumscribed by law. Labor organizations are forbidden to support politicians or political parties, though the FKTU does lobby national assemblymen, particularly of the ruling Democratic Justice Party, and assemblymen often attend labor-organized gatherings. All local unions must be organized within individual enterprises, creating a structure of thousands of individual unions, most of them small and weak. Direct participation in local unions' bargaining activities by outside agencies such as the Asian-American Free Labor Institute, which maintains an office in Korea, is forbidden. The Asian-American Free Labor Institute maintains an office in Korea. The FKTU and its constituent national unions can and sometimes do bargain on behalf of the locals and conduct education programs, but only with government and employer approval. Collective actions and strikes, though technically legal, are to all intents and purposes forbidden. Religious labor ministries such as the Catholic Young Christian Workers and the Protestant Urban Industrial Mission are also severely limited in the assistance which they can provide the unions. Under these circumstances, government and employer influence has greatly exceeded that of unions in setting wages and resolving other major labor issues.

According to FKTU figures, dues-paying union membership in 1984 increased by four percent, after four years of decline. International contacts by the unions increased, with the FKTU and its member unions hosting three regional conferences, including the Asian meeting of the International Confederation of Free Trade Unions (ICFTU). The Republic of Korea sent an observer delegation to the annual conference of the International Labor Organization in 1984. The FKTU is affiliated with the ICFTU, and FKTU member unions are affiliated with recognized international trade union federations.

c. Freedom of Religion

There is no state-favored religion in Korea. There is complete freedom of proselytizing, doctrinal teaching, and conversion. Minority sects are not discriminated against, and adherence to a faith confers neither advantages nor disadvantages in civil, military, or official life. Churches and religious groups are subject to the same restrictions on political activity and criticism of the Government as are all other institutions in Korea. Conscientious objectors are subject to arrest.

d. Freedom of Movement within the Country, Foreign Travel, Emigration, and Repatriation

There is essentially complete freedom of movement and freedom to change employment in Korea. Because Korea is one of the most densely populated areas of the world, the Government encourages a modest level of emigration. It does not discriminate against prospective emigrants. Most people can obtain passports, except for criminals or, in some cases, persons considered politically suspect. A number of

Section 4 Governmental Attitude Regarding International and Non-governmental Investigation of Alleged Violations of Human Rights

The Republic of Korea does not belong to any international human rights bodies and usually does not welcome outside involvement in the human rights area. The Government tolerates the existence of domestic human rights groups but closely monitors their operations.

There are no government agencies charged with the protection of human rights, although political parties and the National Assembly have committees which are concerned with oversight of some aspects of the issue. A number of private organizations are also active in this area, chiefly the Human Rights Committee of the Korean National Council of Churches, the Catholic Justice and Peace Committee, and the Korea Legal Aid Center in Seoul. The Human Rights Committee has ties with the World Council of Churches. The Committee and other human rights organizations submit petitions to the Government and make their views known both inside and outside Korea. Most observers believe that these organizations have been relatively effective in furthering their aims, depending on the issue. People working with these groups are sometimes questioned and, on occasion, visited or detained by the security services, though apparently none have been arrested in the past several years.

The Amnesty International 1984 Report expressed its concern about the detention of prisoners of conscience, reports of torture and unfair trials, widespread arrest of students, the use of short-term detention without charge, and house arrest against students and other critics of the Government. Freedom House lists Korea as "Partly free."

ECONOMIC, SOCIAL, AND CULTURAL SITUATION

The Republic of Korea is one of the most densely populated countries in the world, with 7.4 persons per acre of arable land. Only 22 percent of its 24.4 million acres are arable. The nation's physical wealth is sparse; most of the natural resources of the Korean peninsula are found in North Korea. The Republic's major economic asset is its well-educated and productive work force. The population reached 42 million in 1984, but the growth rate has dropped to 1.5 percent, due in part to concerted efforts by the Government to popularize voluntary family planning.

Skillful management by Korean economic technocrats, many of them graduates of leading Western universities, has given Korea one of the world's most dynamic economies. Since 1965, economic growth in real terms has averaged about 9 percent per year; in 1984 it was about 8 percent. Per capita gross national product has grown from $100 in 1965 to about $1,900 in 1982. The widespread distribution of income gains and the approximate parity between rural and urban household incomes have increased dramatically the nutrition, health, living conditions, and economic choices of the entire population.

The economy is a blend of private sector firms and individuals and public sector enterprises. As the gross national product has grown to almost $75 billion in 1982, the Government has begun to rely increasingly on market forces to allocate

0060

giving it a comfortable majority in the National Assembly. Opposition parties divided the remaining seats. During 1984 preparations were being made for the next Assembly elections, expected early in 1985. Korean observers expect these elections to provide a benchmark of the extent of progress in increasing freedom of political choice.

While the Constitution provides for local autonomy, the Government has resisted implementation on the grounds that the financial preconditions established by law have not been met.

The laws governing participation in the political process were enacted in 1981 just prior to the lifting of martial law. All existing parties were disbanded and new ones were formed. At that time, a law was enacted barring 551 persons from taking part in any political activity for eight years. The Government in February and November 1984 reduced the number of banned politicians to 15. The most prominent persons affected by this ban remain covered by it, although during 1984 many of the banned politicians were being allowed to carry out limited political activity.

One of the most prominent of those still banned, Kim Dae Jung, has said he will to return to Korea early in 1985 from his two-year stay in the United States. In the 1971 presidential election, he garnered nearly half the vote. Subsequently, his political activity in Korea and abroad cost him time in jail and a death sentence (later commuted to 20 years' imprisonment). He was released from prison in 1982 to come to the United States for medical treatment. The Government's official position is that it will "take necessary measures in accordance with the law if he returns home."

Koreans, other than those under this political ban, are free to belong to and participate in the activities of political parties. However, these parties have had difficulty attracting a popular following for a number of reasons. The Government may dissolve any party it deems contrary to "basic democratic order;" the electoral laws put time and fiscal constraints on campaigning which cause all parties, and particularly the opposition, significant difficulties in publicizing their programs; and the Government can and does veto their choices of leaders, candidates, and policy positions.

In December 1984, two members of the opposition Democratic Korea Party who had defected to a new opposition party were detained for three days by a security service. The new party is being formed with significant participation by politicians from whom the ban on political activity had been lifted this year. Many observers believe that the detention was a government effort to discourage greater participation in the new opposition party.

Limitations on freedom of the press also cause opposition parties particular difficulties. Opposition parties have not succeeded in modifying the election laws significantly in time for the 1985 elections.

Women are free to vote, become government officials and run for the National Assembly; they hold seven Assembly seats, all but one appointed by their parties. In practice, the power structure remains male-dominated.

REPUBLIC OF KOREA

resources and is gradually liberalizing its control over imports, foreign investment, and the domestic financial sector.

Participation in the economy and a share of its benefits are effectively open to all. The right to own property, alone and in association with others, is recognized in law and practice. There is no economic discrimination based on race or religion. Discrimination against women is declining, although as in most traditional Asian societies men still tend to be the primary income earners and property owners.

A series of major revisions to the legal code in recent years has given women rights in inheritance, child custody, family headship, and other areas which law and Confucian tradition had long denied them. Women enjoy full access to educational opportunities at all levels. They are increasingly represented, though still largely at entry levels, in the military, the police, the civil service, the professions, and private industry. They are not legally protected against discrimination in hiring, pay, or advancement, and these remain problem areas. For example, according to the Korea Employers' Federation, the average wage of female workers is 46.8 percent of that of male workers. Korea has not developed a politically powerful feminist movement, but consciousness of women's issues has been increasing. During 1984 women's groups organized a federation to campaign for revision of the Family Law, including provisions concerning the head of family system, and in favor of equal property rights in case of divorce and equal rights in child custody. Traditional Confucian influence remains strong, however. The Government announced that it would ask the National Assembly to ratify the U.N. Convention on the Prevention of Discrimination Against Women with a reservation on Articles 9 and 16, which conflict with present domestic Korean law.

Improved health care and nutrition were responsible for increasing Korean life expectancy at birth to 68 years in 1984. By 1984 infant mortality declined to 30.4 deaths per 1,000 live births. Access to safe drinking water increased to 71 percent of the population in 1979. Caloric intake in 1981 was .126 percent of minimum nutritional requirements.

Education receives high priority in government policy. The adult literacy rate increased to 93 percent in 1978. Primary school education is universal for both sexes, and over 90 percent of elementary students enter secondary school. Entrance to institutions of higher education is highly competitive. Only about 50 percent of those who wish to attend are able to do so. There is a substantial amount of social mobility based on the merit system in education and employment.

U.S.OVERSEAS -LOANS AND GRANTS- OBLIGATIONS AND LOAN AUTHORIZATIONS
(U.S.FISCAL YEARS - MILLIONS OF DOLLARS)

COUNTRY: KOREA, REPUBLIC OF

	1982	1983	1984
I.ECON. ASSIST.-TOTAL...	0.0	0.0	0.0
LOANS...............	0.0	0.0	0.0
GRANTS..............	0.0	0.0	0.0
A.AID	0.0	0.0	0.0
LOANS...............	0.0	0.0	0.0
GRANTS..............	0.0	0.0	0.0
(SEC.SUPP.ASSIST.)...	0.0	0.0	0.0
B.FOOD FOR PEACE.......	0.0	0.0	0.0
LOANS...............	0.0	0.0	0.0
GRANTS..............	0.0	0.0	0.0
TITLE I-TOTAL..........	0.0	0.0	0.0
REPAY. IN $-LOANS.....	0.0	0.0	0.0
PAY. IN FOR. CURR.....	0.0	0.0	0.0
TITLE II-TOTAL.........	0.0	0.0	0.0
E.RELIEF.EC.DEV & WFP.	0.0	0.0	0.0
VOL.RELIEF AGENCY.....	0.0	0.0	0.0
C.OTHER ECON. ASSIST...	0.0	0.0	0.0
LOANS...............	0.0	0.0	0.0
GRANTS..............	0.0	0.0	0.0
PEACE CORPS......	0.0	0.0	0.0
NARCOTICS.......	0.0	0.0	0.0
OTHER...........	0.0	0.0	0.0
II.MIL. ASSIST.-TOTAL...	167.4	186.7	231.8
LOANS...............	166.0	185.0	230.0
GRANTS..............	1.4	1.7	1.8
A.MAP GRANTS..........	0.0	0.0	0.0
B.CREDIT FINANCING....	166.0	185.0	230.0
C.INTL MIL.ED.TRNG....	1.4	1.7	1.8
D.TRAN-EXCESS STOCK...	0.0	0.0	0.0
E.OTHER GRANTS........	0.0	0.0	0.0
III.TOTAL ECON. & MIL...	167.4	186.7	231.8
LOANS...............	166.0	185.0	230.0
GRANTS..............	1.4	1.7	1.8
OTHER US LOANS.........	58.7	9.0	0.0
EX-IM BANK LOANS......	58.7	9.0	0.0
ALL OTHER.............	0.0	0.0	0.0

ASSISTANCE FROM INTERNATIONAL AGENCIES

	1982	1983	1984	1946-84
TOTAL.........	607.1	942.4	975.9	7394.5
IBRD	470.0	672.0	768.5	5269.3
IFC	1.7	2.2	34.6	164.1
IDA	0.0	0.0	0.0	106.9
IDB	0.0	0.0	0.0	0.0
ADB	132.2	265.5	172.8	1804.3
AFDB	0.0	0.0	0.0	0.0
UNDP	0.5	2.7	0.0	34.5
OTHER-UN	2.7	0.0	0.0	15.4
EEC	0.0	0.0	0.0	0.0

1900

DEMOCRATIC PEOPLE'S REPUBLIC OF KOREA*

The Democratic People's Republic of Korea, formed in 1948 during the Soviet administration of the northern half of the Korean peninsula, is a rigid Communist dictatorship, strictly dominated by one man, Kim Il-sung, and his family. Although some internationally respected human rights are acknowledged by the Constitution and laws, individual rights are entirely subordinated in practice to the ruling Korean Workers' (Communist) Party, with its overriding aim of imposing a social revolution and enforcing unanimous popular support for the country's governing system and its leaders.

The latest Constitution, promulgated in 1972, purports to guarantee a wide range of rights, including: freedom of the press, religion, work, and association, and freedom from sex discrimination. Other provisions of that Constitution, as well as the fact of Communist Party control, render meaningless most of these guarantees. While there were pro forma elections to the Supreme People's Assembly in February 1982, free elections do not exist in North Korea since citizens have no choice among candidates.

Kim Il-sung is committed to reunification of the divided peninsula, by whatever means is necessary. To this end, his Government has periodically attempted to destabilize the Republic of Korea, for example by the attempt to assassinate the President of the Republic of Korea in a bombing attack in Rangoon, Burma, on October 9, 1983. Four Burmese and 17 South Koreans, including four cabinet ministers and a number of senior advisers and officials, were killed in this North Korean action. Despite North Korea's delivery of flood relief goods to the South in 1984 and the positive response to South Korean proposals for bilateral talks on economic cooperation and family reunification, it continues to improve its military forces targeted against the South.

North Korean leaders justify regimentation and militarization of society in the name of reunification. The North Korean people are subject to rigid controls. Persons who fail to cooperate with the regime face imprisonment, confiscation of property, or enforced removal to remote villages. Movement outside one's own village requires documented permission. Punishment for "political crimes" against the state is severe. Available information indicates that the practices of forced relocation of families and ideological indoctrination have intensified in recent years.

The state's intervention in the individual's activities in North Korea goes well beyond curtailing assembly and expression. The authorities attempt to shape the

*The United States does not have diplomatic relations with the Democratic People's Republic of Korea; even representatives of governments that do, as well as journalists and other occasional invited visitors to North Korea, are not permitted the freedom of movement that would enable them effectively to assess human rights observance there. Most of this report, therefore, is a repeat of previous human rights reports based on information obtained over a period of time extending from well before 1984. While limited in scope and detail, the information is indicative of the human rights situation in North Korea today.

JAPAN

and members of the Burakumin community (descendants of feudal era "outcasts" who practiced so-called "unclean" professions such as hide tanning) restricts the access of both groups to private housing, employment, and marriage opportunities. The Government has extended until 1987 a Special Measures Law (first issued in 1969) designed to help assimilate Burakumin into mainstream society through a number of social, economic, and legal programs.

Japan's population in 1984 was 119,996,000, growing at an annual rate of 0.6 percent. The infant mortality rate was 6 per 1,000 live births in 1984, while life expectancy at birth in 1980 was 75.5 years. With a highly competitive education system that provides nine years of free, compulsory schooling, Japan has a primary school enrollment ratio of 106 percent and has long had nearly total adult literacy. The ratio of calorie supply available for consumption relative to nutritional requirements was 126 percent in 1977. The GNP per capita in 1982 was $10,075.

DEMOCRATIC PEOPLE'S REPUBLIC OF KOREA

consciousness of the populace. Preschool children are drilled in homage to Kim Il-sung and his family, while youths and adults are required to participate in daily ideological training conducted by youth organizations or at places of employment. The propaganda requires rote recitation of party maxims and positions and strives for ideological purity. The result is that North Korea's society is one of the most highly regimented and controlled in the world today. At least two North Korean security organizations enforce these controls.

Virtually no outside information other than that approved and disseminated by the North Korean authorities is allowed to reach the North Korean public. Foreigners who have traveled to Pyongyang, the capital city, have been surprised to learn how little the North Korean populace knows of the outside world. Senior government officials, however, seem to be somewhat better informed.

Security ratings for each person are based on such considerations as class origin, ideological fervor, and reliability, and whether any of the individual's relatives or associates collaborated with Japanese occupation authorities (1910-1945) or have attempted to defect to other countries. These ratings determine access to the better jobs, schools, medical facilities, and stores, as well as admission to the Korean Workers' Party, the route to the highest levels and privileges of the society. Any individual whose relative or close family associate has settled in South Korea is treated as suspect by the North Korean authorities.

In 1984, for the first time, North Korea's government-controlled radio explicitly referred to Kim Il-sung's son, Kim Chong-il, as his father's eventual "successor." The younger Kim, who was elevated to several senior leadership positions in 1980, is reportedly assuming increasing control of the Government and party. That Kim Il-sung appears thus far to be able to ensure his succession by his son, a first for any Communist country, indicates the enormous power he has assumed in 36 years of rule. The absence of any evidence of public debate about the succession is also indicative of the lack of real popular participation in the political process.

RESPECT FOR HUMAN RIGHTS

Section 1 Respect for the Integrity of the Person, Including Freedom from:

a. Political Killing

No reliable information is available on politically motivated killing in North Korea. However, the North Korean attitude toward political killing was clearly demonstrated in the Rangoon bombing and the November 23, 1984 shooting in the Joint Security Area of the Demilitarized Zone(DMZ) dividing North and South Korea.

After a careful investigation, the Government of Burma determined that the Democratic People's Republic of Korea was responsible for the October 9, 1983, attempt to assassinate Republic of Korea President Chun Doo Hwan during his visit to Burma. The bomb killed four cabinet ministers and a number of senior advisers and officials. Two North Korean army officers were brought to trial in Rangoon for the attack, and on December 9, 1983, were found guilty and sentenced to death.

DEMOCRATIC PEOPLE'S REPUBLIC OF KOREA

In the DMZ incident a young Soviet student who wanted to defect broke away from a tour group and ran across the military demarcation line into the area controlled by the U.N. Command. The North Korean security guards opened fire on the fleeing Soviet, triggering an exchange of fire in which several lives were lost, and unsuccessfully pursued the defector across the line with guns blazing.

b. Disappearance

There is no information available on disappearance.

c. Torture and Cruel, Inhuman, or Degrading Treatment or Punishment

Freedom House's 1983-84 report states that "torture is reportedly common" in North Korea. The accounts of torture and beatings of crew members of the USS Pueblo after their capture in 1968 are well-known and documented. The only other reliable source on prison conditions and treatment of prisoners in North Korea is Venezuelan poet Ali Lameda, who was detained in North Korea from September 1967 through 1974, allegedly for attempted sabotage and espionage. While physical torture was not used on Mr. Lameda, he stated that Korean prisoners were routinely beaten. Lameda noted that "beating was also used as a means of persuasion during interrogation."

Lameda reported the use of deprivation of food to force "confessions," as well as solitary confinement, continuous interrogation, enforced waking periods, poor or nonexistent medical treatment, and 12 hours of forced labor per day. In addition, prisoners were denied family visits, parcels, correspondence, writing materials, newspapers, and clothing changes. Prisoners appeared to be regarded as persons without any rights.

d. Arbitrary Arrest, Detention, or Exile

Information on specific criminal justice procedures and practices in North Korea is extremely scarce. North Korea has refused to permit outside observation of its legal system and practices. The accounts provided by the crew members of the USS Pueblo and by Venezuelan poet Ali Lameda, while clearly from an earlier period, comprise virtually all the specific information available on the operation of the criminal justice system in North Korea.

North Korean law provides that the period prisoners may be held for interrogation shall not exceed two months. This period may be extended indefinitely, however, if the Interrogation Department obtains approval of the Chief Prosecutor. Lameda, himself, was detained for 12 months without trial or charge. His request for a lawyer of his choice and an open trial were ridiculed as "bourgeois." Habeas corpus or its equivalent does not exist in practice.

According to newspaper reports, North Korean defectors in South Korea estimated in April 1982 that at least 105,000 "ideological offenders" were being held in eight major camps in the North. Amnesty International has received unconfirmed reports of arrests of those opposed to heir apparent Kim Chong-il.

0063

DEMOCRATIC PEOPLE'S REPUBLIC OF KOREA

e. Denial of Fair Public Trial

The North Korean Constitution states that courts are independent, and judicial proceedings are to be carried out in strict accordance with law. All courts, however, are responsible to the people's assemblies, which effectively means total governmental control of the judiciary. Article 138 states that "cases are heard in public, and the accused is guaranteed the right to defense; hearings may be closed to the public as stipulated by law." Lameda was twice denied public trial. After his first arrest he was imprisoned for a year without a hearing; after his second arrest, he was put through a closed session without benefit of counsel of his choice, or even knowledge of the charges. His tribunal was under the direction of the Ministry of Internal Security, with one person serving as both judge and prosecutor.

Lameda stated that, other than to admit guilt, he was refused the right to speak out or defend himself at his trial. His "defense counsel" represented him by making a lengthy speech praising Kim Il-sung and then requesting a 20-year sentence, which the tribunal imposed after five minutes of deliberation.

In a 1979 interview with American journalist John Wallach, North Korean Supreme Court Justice Li Chun-uk noted that the defense counsel's job is "to give the suspect due punishment." Open court appears to consist of an announcement of the term of imprisonment, which has already been determined by the Provincial Safety Bureau.

f. Arbitrary Interference with Privacy, Family, Home, or Correspondence

The populace is subjected to continuous indoctrination, designed to shape individual consciousness. Preschool children are drilled in homage to Kim Il-sung and his family, while youths and adults are required to participate in daily ideological training conducted by youth organizations or at places of employment. The propaganda requires rote recitation of party maxims and positions and strives for ideological purity. At least two North Korean security organizations enforce these controls.

Reports, primarily from defectors, indicate that forced resettlement, particularly for those deemed politically unreliable, is common. Permission to reside in, or even enter, Pyongyang is strictly controlled.

According to reports in South Korean journals, Japanese wives of Koreans repatriated from Japan since 1959 have not been permitted to visit Japan and, because their letters are subject to strict censorship, many have lost contact with their families.

The Constitution states that "citizens are guaranteed the inviolability of person and residence and the privacy of correspondence." Lameda reported, however, that his residence was not respected and that listening devices were used against him. He was arrested and his collected papers and poetry destroyed without warrant.

DEMOCRATIC PEOPLE'S REPUBLIC OF KOREA

Section 2 Respect for Civil Rights, Including:

a. Freedom of Speech and Press

The Constitution states that "citizens have the freedoms of speech, the press, assembly, association, and demonstration." In fact, North Koreans enjoy none of these rights. Such activities are permitted only in support of government objectives. Other articles of the Constitution that require citizens to follow the "socialist norms of life" and to obey a "collective spirit" take precedence over individual political or civil liberties. Censorship of foreign and domestic media is enforced and no deviation from the official government line is tolerated. Listening to foreign media broadcasts is prohibited, and violators reportedly are subject to severe punishment. Most North Koreans do not possess radios but must listen to government media through loudspeakers installed in their apartments. Artistic and academic works are controlled by the Government, and visitors report that a primary function of plays, movies, operas, and books is to contribute to the cult of personality surrounding "the great leader," Kim Il-sung, and his son, "the beloved leader," Kim Chong-il.

b. Freedom of Peaceful Assembly and Association

The Government has developed a pervasive system of informers throughout the society. No public meetings can be held without governmental authorization. Trade unions and professional associations appear to exist solely as another method of governmental control over their members. They have no effective rights to organize, negotiate, or strike.

c. Freedom of Religion

Although the Constitution guarantees that "citizens have religious liberty and the freedom of antireligious propaganda," North Korea, in fact, has severely persecuted Christians and Buddhists since the late 1940's. No churches have been rebuilt since the Korean War. The regime uses religious organizational facades to proclaim the practice of religious freedom but appears to have long since purged the membership out of existence. Persons whose family or relatives once had a strong religious involvement are discriminated against. Though religious practice appears impossible, some foreign visitors to North Korea believe that the Government does not currently persecute the small number of Christians who continue to worship at home.

d. Freedom of Movement Within the Country, Foreign Travel, Emigration, and Repatriation

Internal travel in North Korea is strictly controlled. A travel pass is required for any movement outside one's home village and is granted only for required official or personal travel. This requirement is strictly enforced. Foreign travel is limited to officials or trusted artists and performers. Emigration is not allowed, and few refugees or defectors succeed in fleeing the country. Retaliation reportedly is taken against the relatives of those few persons who manage to escape. According to Freedom House, "rights to travel internally and externally are perhaps the most restricted in the world: tourism is unknown—even to communist countries."

DEMOCRATIC PEOPLE'S REPUBLIC OF KOREA

In 1959 North Korea began actively encouraging Korean residents overseas to repatriate to "the Fatherland." Some observers estimate that during the next several years over 100,000 overseas Koreans, almost all from Japan, voluntarily repatriated to North Korea. Since then, however, reports of the harsh treatment given repatriates reached overseas Koreans, reducing the flow to North Korea to a trickle. (Because of their "corruption" by exposure to foreign influences, repatriates are isolated from North Korean society after their arrival until they can be indoctrinated and their ideological reliability gauged.)

North Korea has permitted some overseas Korean residents to enter its territory to visit their relatives, and several have made repeat visits.

Section 3 Respect for Political Rights: The Right of Citizens to Change Their Government

Political processes in North Korea are dominated by Kim Il-sung, who leads the Korean Workers' Party, and also heads the Government. Kim has groomed his son Kim Chong-il to succeed him, and there are reports that Kim Chong-il has been acquiring increasing power and influence. The legislature, the Supreme People's Assembly, has never taken any action other than unanimous passage of resolutions presented to it by the leadership. In an effort to create an appearance of democracy, North Korea has created several "minority parties." They exist only as rosters of officials who have token representation in the People's Assembly and completely support the government line.

Free elections do not exist in North Korea. Although elections to the Supreme People's Assembly were held in February 1982, and to city and county assemblies in March 1983, in all cases only one candidate was approved by the government party in each electoral district, and, according to the government-controlled media, 100 percent of the voters turned out to elect 100 percent of the approved candidates. Such "elections" in reality are a mandatory exercise in which voters are required to participate and to approve the party's candidates.

The average citizen is completely excluded from any real participation in the political process. To achieve even a semblance of real participation, one must become a member of the Korean Worker's Party. The selection process for entrance to the party is long and rigorous. Individuals from "bad" social backgrounds, i.e., those who have relatives who fled south during the Korean War, those whose families had strong religious involvement or were once property owners or members of the bourgeoisie, and those who have relatives who are political prisoners, effectively are denied entry into the party and are discriminated against. Most levels of the party have no voice, serving only to carry out the decrees and "on the spot guidance" promulgated by party leader Kim Il-sung and his top subordinates.

Section 4 Governmental Attitude Regarding International and Non-governmental Investigation of Alleged Violations of Human Rights

No organizations exist within North Korea to report on or observe human rights violations. North Korea does not

DEMOCRATIC PEOPLE'S REPUBLIC OF KOREA

participate in any international or regional human rights organizations. On September 14, 1981, North Korea acceded to the International Covenant on Civil and Political Rights (ICCPR) and the International Covenant on Economic, Social and Cultural Rights. At the March-April 1984 session of the Human Rights Committee, an expert body consisting of members elected by state parties to the ICCPR, members criticized a report submitted by North Korea on its human rights practices as too short and inadequate. The North Korean representative denied that his country had any problems at all, prompting an expert member to urge that the North Korean's assurances of freedom of religion, political activity, and travel outside Korea be made known to the North Korean people.

Amnesty International has requested a visit to North Korea; the Government has not responded to or acknowledged this request. A December 1982 request by Amnesty International for information on North Korean laws, on use of the death penalty, and on reports of arrests and long-term imprisonment of political figures also received no reply.

The Amnesty International 1984 Report noted that its work continued to be seriously impaired by the absence of any official information during the year concerning any arrests, trials, or death sentences, that it continued to investigate reports that four prominent political figures had been detained for several years, and that it did not receive any replies to correspondence directed to the Government. Freedom House, in its 1984-85 report, lists North Korea as "not free."

ECONOMIC, SOCIAL, AND CULTURAL SITUATION

North Korea is a less-developed country with a highly centralized, planned economy. Many observers believe that, after a short period of rapid growth in the early 1970's, the economy experienced difficulties in subsequent years due largely to economic policies that overemphasized military expenditures, stressed attainment of self-sufficiency, and pushed for rapid growth of heavy industry. More than twenty percent of North Korea's Gross National Product is committed to military expenditures, the second highest such rate in the world.

In the early 1980's the Government gradually has shifted its policy emphasis toward expanding trade. In September 1984, North Korea promulgated a joint ventures law to attract foreign capital and technology. As yet there is little evidence of foreign investor interest or any shift in internal economic priorities away from support of military industry. The apparent shift in economic policy is also shown by North Korea's apparent willingness to discuss economic trade and cooperation with the Republic of Korea.

The population of North Korea is estimated to be about 19 million, with an annual growth rate of 2.3 percent. The 1984 infant mortality rate was 30 per 1,000 live births. Life expectancy at birth was 65.8 years in 1984. The World Bank estimated in 1981 that the calorie supply available for consumption was 129 percent of nutritional requirements.

North Korea appears to have invested considerable effort and money in developing a comprehensive health care system. Both pre- and post-working age citizens are cared for by the state. Basic food supplies are heavily subsidized and rationed. There were some reports of reduced rations and food shortages in 1983; the proportion of rice in the grain ration has been steadily reduced with grains considered less desirable, such as millet or barley, being substituted. Reportedly, because quality foods are difficult to obtain, jobs in food-handling industries are highly prized. Foreign visitors have noted that North Koreans they observed appeared adequately fed. Per capita income was estimated to be $968 in 1982.

The party, government, and military elite enjoy significant economic privileges, such as access to special stores and medical facilities, better housing, and better education, which are not available to ordinary citizens.

The North Korean Government provides 11 years of compulsory free education to its citizens and claims to have eliminated illiteracy. The adjusted primary school enrollment ratios for 1976 were 96.6 for females and 101 for males, for a combined ratio of 98.7.

The Constitution states that "women hold equal social status and rights with men." Despite this provision, few women reach high levels of the party or the Government. Women are represented proportionally in the labor force, and personnel in small factories are predominantly women. Reportedly, women are often paid less than men for similar work.

U.S.OVERSEAS -LOANS AND GRANTS- OBLIGATIONS AND LOAN AUTHORIZATIONS
(U.S.FISCAL YEARS - MILLIONS OF DOLLARS)

COUNTRY: KOREA, NORTH

	1982	1983	1984
I.ECON. ASSIST.-TOTAL...	0.0	0.0	0.0
LOANS...	0.0	0.0	0.0
GRANTS...	0.0	0.0	0.0
A.AID ...	0.0	0.0	0.0
LOANS...	0.0	0.0	0.0
GRANTS...	0.0	0.0	0.0
(SEC.SUPP.ASSIST.)...	0.0	0.0	0.0
B.FOOD FOR PEACE...	0.0	0.0	0.0
LOANS...	0.0	0.0	0.0
GRANTS...	0.0	0.0	0.0
TITLE I-TOTAL...	0.0	0.0	0.0
REPAY. IN $-LOANS...	0.0	0.0	0.0
PAY. IN FOR. CURR...	0.0	0.0	0.0
TITLE II-TOTAL...	0.0	0.0	0.0
E.RELIEF.EC.DEV & WFP.	0.0	0.0	0.0
VOL.RELIEF AGENCY...	0.0	0.0	0.0
C.OTHER ECON. ASSIST...	0.0	0.0	0.0
LOANS...	0.0	0.0	0.0
GRANTS...	0.0	0.0	0.0
PEACE CORPS...	0.0	0.0	0.0
NARCOTICS...	0.0	0.0	0.0
OTHER...	0.0	0.0	0.0
II.MIL. ASSIST.-TOTAL...	0.0	0.0	0.0
LOANS...	0.0	0.0	0.0
GRANTS...	0.0	0.0	0.0
A.MAP GRANTS...	0.0	0.0	0.0
B.CREDIT FINANCING...	0.0	0.0	0.0
C.INTL MIL.ED.TRNG...	0.0	0.0	0.0
D.TRAN-EXCESS STOCK...	0.0	0.0	0.0
E.OTHER GRANTS...	0.0	0.0	0.0
III.TOTAL ECON. & MIL...	0.0	0.0	0.0
LOANS...	0.0	0.0	0.0
GRANTS...	0.0	0.0	0.0
OTHER US LOANS...	0.0	0.0	0.0
EX-IM BANK LOANS...	0.0	0.0	0.0
ALL OTHER...	0.0	0.0	0.0

ASSISTANCE FROM INTERNATIONAL AGENCIES

	1982	1983	1984	1946-84
TOTAL...	3.6	0.2	0.0	4.1
IBRD	0.0	0.0	0.0	0.0
IFC	0.0	0.0	0.0	0.0
IDA	0.0	0.0	0.0	0.0
IDB	0.0	0.0	0.0	0.0
ADB	0.0	0.0	0.0	0.0
AFDB	0.0	0.0	0.0	0.0
UNDP	3.6	0.2	0.0	4.1
OTHER-UN	0.0	0.0	0.0	0.0
EEC	0.0	0.0	0.0	0.0

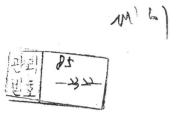

朴 (인)
-후라지

법　무　부

검삼 700-255　　　　503-7056　　　　1985. 12. 23.

수신　외무부장관

참조　미주국장

제목　85년도 미국무성 인권보고서에 관한 회신

　　귀부 미북 700-3925(85. 12. 3.)과 관련, 인권개선사항에 대한

자료를 별첨과 같이 회신합니다.

첨부　인권개선사항 1부.　끝.

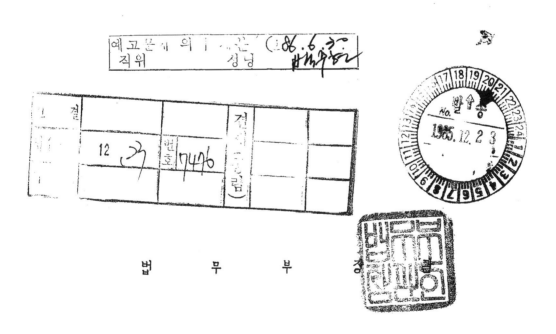

법　무　부

0067

우리 정부에서는 인권문제에 관하여 지대한 관심을 가지고
그 개선향상을 위하여 부단한 노력을 경주하고 있는 데, 최근에
이루어진 몇가지 예를 들면 다음과 같음.

○ 금년도에 우리 정부는 국제인권규약에 가입키로 결정하고,
   현재 국회에 그 동의안을 제출해 두고 있는 데, 그중 A 규약은
   아무런 유보없이 가입하고, B 규약은 국내법에 저촉되는
   일부 조항을 유보하고 가입키로 하였음. 그러나 규약에 가입
   한다는 사실자체보다 얼마나 성실히 이를 준수하는가가 더
   중요하므로 가입후에도 동 규약의 준수에 최선을 다할 것임.

○ 금년부터 수사기관에서 구속되었다가 검사의 수사결과 무혐의
   석방된 피의자에 대한 보상제도를 실시하고 있음.

○ 금년 5.27. 국가보안법 위반죄로 복역중이던 오송회사건 관련자
   3명을 포함하여 상당수의 수감자를 가석방 하였음.

○ 금년초 정치풍토 쇄신을 위한 특별조치법에 따라 정치활동이
   금지되고 있던 정치활동 피규제자중 일부 미해금자를 전원
   해금조치하여 현재 동법에 따른 정치활동 규제자는 한 사람도
   없음.

0068

발 신 전 보

번 호 : WUS-4459 일 시 : 51230 1800   전보종별 : _____

수 신 : 주   미   대사·총영사

발 신 : 장   관 (미북)

제 목 : 미국무성 인권보고서

대 : USW-5249

대호 미국무성 인권보고서의 아국 관계부분이 전년도보다
비판적이될 가능성이 있다는 국무성 관계관의 우려표명과 관련,
작년도보다 개선된 인권상황에 관한 하기 관계부처 설명자료를
국무성측에 전달하고 동 내용이 1985년도 인권보고서에 반영될수
있도록 국무성측~~과 접촉, 선처~~ 과 접촉, 선처 바람.

~~에 난민의 지위에 관한 의정서~~

1. 금년도에 우리정부는 국제인권규약에 가입키로 결정하고, 현재
국회에고 동의안을 제출해 두고 있는데, 그중 A 규약은
아무런 유보없이 가입하고, B규약은 국내법에 저촉되는
일부 조항을 유보하고 가입키로 하였음.

2. 금년부터 수사기관에서 구속되었다가 검사의 수사결과 무혐의
석방된 피의자에 대한 보상제도를 실시하고 있음.

3. 금년 5.27 국가보안법 위반죄로 복역중이던 오송회사건 관련자
3명을 포함하여 상당수의 수감자를 가석방하였음.

앙고고재	85년12월8일 북미과	기안자	과 장 심의관	국 장 제1차관보	차 관 전결	장 관		발신시간 :		
							외신과	접수자	과 장	

0069

4.
나. 금년초 정치풍토 쇄신을 위한 특별조치법에 따라 정치활동이
   금지되고 있던 정치활동 피규제자중 일부 미해금자를 전원
   해금조치하여 현재 동법에 따른 정치활동 규제자는 한사람도
   없음.   (차관)

예고 : 86. 6. 30. 일반.

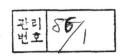

외 무 부   착 신 전

번 호 : USW-0014   일 시 : 601021820   종 별 : 지급

수 신 : 장 관(미북)

발 신 : 주미대사

제 목 : 국무성 인권보고서

대 : WUS-4459

1. 김삼훈참사관은 금 1.2 오후 ISOM 국무성 한국과장을 면담,대호 내용을 설명하고 아국의 개선된 인권상황이 인권 보고서에 반영되도록 협조를 당부하였음.

2. 동과장은 대호 4항은 이미 내용이 반영된것으로 안다고 하면서,관련사항을 인권국에 전달하겠다고 하였음.

3. 본직은 현재 휴가중인 인권 차관보를 1월 중순이후 신임인사차 면담예정임을 첨언함.

(대사 김경원)

예고 : 86.6.30일반
성립

미주국   차관실   1 차보   청와대   안 기

PAGE   1

외 무 부　　　　착 신 전 보

번 호 : USW-0511　　　일 시 : 601312000　　　종 별 :

원 본

수 신 : 장 관 (미북)

발 신 : 주 미 대사

제 목 : 국무성 인권 브고서

대 : WUS-4121

1. 국무성 인권보고서는 금 1.31 의회에 제출되었는바 의회는 이를 2.13. 경 대의발표할 예정인것으로 확인됨.

2. 당관은 그간 국무성 인권국 및 한국과를 등하여 아국관계부군을 사전 입수크자 노력하였으나 행정부측이 의회발포전 이를 외부에 제공하는것은 금지되어있다함 가능한 빠른시일내 입수, 송부하겠음.

(대사 김경원)

예고 : 86.6.30일반

───

미주국　차관실　1 차브　정군국　청와대　안 기

번　호 : USW-0746　　　　　일 시 : 60213 1852　　　종 별 :

수　신 : 장 관 (미북,정이)

발　신 : 주 미 대사

제　목 : 국무성 인권 보고서 발표

연: USW-0710

연호 1985년도 각국 인권 보고서는 예정대로 금 2.13. 16:00 대외 공개되었는바, 총
1440 페이지의 동 보고서는 명 2.14 발송 파편 송부하겠음

(대사 김경원)

미주국　1 차보　정문국　청와대　안 기

외　무　부　착　신　전　보

번　호 : USW-0710　　　　일　시 : 60212 1824　　　　종　별 :

수　신 : 장　관 (미북,정이)

발　신 : 주　미　대사

제　목 : 국무성 인권보고서

1. 85 년도 국무성 인권보고서중 아국 및 북한관계를 별전 송부함.

2. 동 보고서는 명 2.13. 16:00 대외 공개 예정임.

　　첨부: 1). 15 매　　　2). 7 매

(대사 김경원)

미주국　1 차보　정문국　청와대　안 기

PAGE　1　　　　　　　　　　　　　　　　　　86.02.13　09:46
　　　　　　　　　　　　　　　　　　　　　　외신 1과　통제관

0074

주　미　대　사　관

미국(정)700-　0505　　　　　　　　　　　1986.　2.　14.

수신 : 장　관

참조 : 미주국장

제목 : 국무성 인권보고서 '85

　　　　　연 : USW - 710

　　　당관에서 우선 구득한 국무성 인권보고서 2부를 별첨 송부하며,

추가 구득 송부위계입니다.

　　　첨부 : 동 책자 2부. 끝.

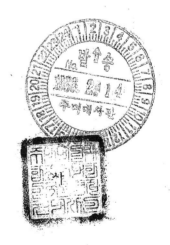

　　　　　　주　　　미　　　대

선결				결재(공람)		
접수일시	1986.2.17	번호				
처리과			11664			

0075

첨부)

REPUBLIC OF KOREA

President Chun Doo Hwan dominates the political scene in the Republic of Korea. The elected legislature has limited power but considerable influence on public opinion. President Chun, a former army general, assumed power with military support in 1980, at which time martial law was declared and civil disturbances in Kwangju were harshly confronted. The Constitution was adopted by referendum in October 1980 under strict martial law conditions, leading many Koreans to question the referendum's fairness. At the time of the next presidential election, in late 1987 or early 1988, President Chun has promised to step down to provide for a peaceful and constitutional change of power.

Korea's traditional sociopolitical ideology, Confucianism, emphasizes order and conformity, as well as a subordinate role for women. This thinking retains great strength, coexisting uneasily with Western democratic ideals.

Citing this tradition and faced with a heavily armed Communist North Korea that once invaded the South and that remains extremely hostile to it, successive South Korean governments have given top priority to maintaining external and internal security, implemented in part by the large and well-organized security forces. Many Koreans have charged throughout the years that the very real threat from the North was also used as a pretext to suppress internal opposition politics, despite the democratic ideals professed by all South Korean leaders.

Koreans enjoy considerable personal freedom, including economic and religious freedom and broad rights to pursue private interests. Although the Constitution guarantees freedom of speech and press, in practice both are abridged.

During the past 20 years, Korea's export-oriented, mixed economy has achieved one of the world's highest growth rates and a twentyfold increase in per capita gross national product (GNP). The population is urbanized and well educated. Abject poverty has been largely eliminated. The rapid growth of the economy has created a growing middle class with increasing access to education and wealth. They have joined with other groups to become a strong voice for fuller political participation and greater freedom to express political views.

Human rights issues as well as "democratization" issues were the focus of greater public discussion and debate than in recent years. There was some progress in the human rights field in the early months of 1985, continuing the trend of 1984. The National Assembly election held on February 12 was widely regarded as among the most democratic in the Republic's history, with candidates freely criticizing the Government at large rallies. Press coverage was frank and lively. The election resulted in a new party, supported by leading opposition politicians, becoming the largest opposition party in the Assembly since the Republic's founding.

In March a statutory political ban originally applied to 567 politicians was lifted on the remaining 14 persons affected, including prominent dissident leaders Kim Young Sam and Kim Dae Jung. (The political activities of Kim Dae Jung and some other politicians remained restricted, however, by other legal provisions.) At the same time, Kim Dae Jung was freed from the house arrest imposed on him on his return to Korea one month earlier. Nine political prisoners were released in an amnesty on May 27. Under the Government's "campus autonomy" policy,

15-1

0076

REPUBLIC OF KOREA

the formation of independent student councils was permitted and
police stayed off campus as students began the most active
semester of student protest since 1980.

The Government soon responded heavily to the newly assertive
opposition and the increased student activism, initiating a new
wave of repression of dissent. Political tension remained high
throughout the remainder of the year. On several occasions
journalists were detained for writing politically sensitive
articles. There were credible reports of torture or physical
intimidation of several journalists and dissidents. After the
May 23-26 student sit-in at the U S. Information Service
library in Seoul, the Government returned to its pre-1984
practice of arresting and trying student protest leaders, and
police entered campuses readily to stop demonstrations. During
the fall semester, student protests became increasingly
violent. The Government reacted by arresting some or all of
those involved in the more violent protests, raising the number
of students in prison at the end of the year to over 400, the
largest number since 1980. The Government announced that it
was considering a plan to send activist students to
6-month-long ideological reeducation centers, but it backed off
because of widespread opposition.

RESPECT FOR HUMAN RIGHTS

Section 1   Respect for the Integrity of the Person, Including
            Freedom from:

   a.   Political Killing

There were no reports of politically motivated killings in 1985.

   b.   Disappearance

There were no reports of disappearances in 1985.

   c.   Torture and Cruel, Inhuman, or Degrading Treatment or
        Punishment

Reports of torture or cruel treatment in 1985 increased
significantly over 1984. The Constitution prohibits torture,
and the Government insists that it has issued injunctions
against it and that those are strictly enforced and violations
sternly punished. Nonetheless, there were credible reports of
torture, such as that of an antigovernment youth activist who
was subjected to torture while under police detention in
September, and reliable reports of three senior Korean
journalists who were detained and beaten by security officials
for breaking a government embargo on a news story. Korean
human rights groups and political opposition leaders also made
plausible charges that a number of students and other prisoners
in politically related cases were subjected to various degrees
of physical maltreatment including beatings, sleep and food
deprivation, electric shock, and forced water intake during
police interrogations in the latter half of 1985. The
Government publicly denied that any of these prisoners had been
mistreated.

On February 26, 1985, the Supreme Court upheld a lower court's
acquittal of a woman whose conviction for murder had been based
on a confession which she later said had been made as a result
of police torture. She was awarded the equivalent of about
$29,500 in compensation from the state. Court sources say some

15-2

REPUBLIC OF KOREA

cases were prosecuted in 1985 under a law adopted by the
National Assembly in 1983 increasing sentences for those
convicted of killing or injuring through torture.

The use of excessive force by the police has proven to be a
pervasive and ingrained problem, despite some high-level
efforts to reduce or eliminate it. Rioters have been beaten on
apprehension, often by plainclothes police. Charges of police
beatings in nonpolitical cases occur fairly frequently and are
sometimes reported in the press. There were reports in 1985
that police were using a stronger form of tear gas to break up
student and other unauthorized demonstrations which caused skin
blisters on those who came into direct contact with it.

Conditions in Korean correctional institutions are austere,
especially in winter as cells are not heated. Discipline is
strict. Under normal circumstances, convicts are not subjected
to physical punishment, but prisoners who break rules or
protest conditions are sometimes beaten. There were reports
that 19 political prisoners transferred to Taegu Prison in July
were beaten severely when they protested overcrowded conditions.

Prisoners may receive visits only from their lawyers and
immediate families. Their mail is monitored and sometimes
censored. There does not seem to be a difference between the
treatment of political and non-political prisoners.

   d. Arbitrary Arrest, Detention, or Exile

Arrest warrants are required by law but are sometimes not
produced at the time of arrest in politically related cases.
In 1985 the Supreme Court ruled that police may not detain
persons for more than 48 hours without arrest warrants. An
indictment must be issued within 30 days after arrest. Within
40 days after making an arrest, the police must notify an
arrested person's family of his detention and whereabouts. The
police normally wait at least several days, and occasionally
more than 40 days, before making notification The
Constitution guarantees the right of prompt legal assistance
and the right to request court review in case of arrest.

Habeas corpus, not traditional in Korean law, was introduced
after World War II, abolished in the 1970's, and reintroduced
in 1980. It does not apply to those charged with violations of
the National Security Act or laws punishable by at least 5
years' imprisonment, which includes most politically related
offenses. There is a system of bail, but it does not apply to
offenses punishable by 10 or more years' imprisonment. In 1985
the Government adopted a new policy to compensate persons held
for questioning but who are subsequently found to be innocent
by prosecutors. .

Dissidents who openly criticize the Government are sometimes
picked up and detained for short periods and then released.
There were several instances in 1985 of journalists who had
written politically sensitive articles being detained for short
periods, usually overnight, by security forces.

From time to time, the security services have not only detained
persons accused of violating laws on political dissent but have
also increased surveillance of, or put under various forms of
house arrest, those they think intend to violate the laws. In
the longest continuous application of such restrictions in
1985, opposition politician Kim Dae Jung was not permitted to

15 - 3

REPUBLIC OF KOREA

leave his home for about 1 month after his return to Korea from
the United States in February 1985. Kim and others were also
confined to their homes on several other occasions for briefer
periods. In the latter half of 1985 the Government arrested
and charged with National Security Law violations about 80
students and other Koreans associated with student and youth
organizations the Government characterized as pro-Communist
and/or pro-North Korean. About 60 of these had been convicted
or remained under detention awaiting trial at the end of 1985.
Government critics claim that, in many of these cases, the
National Security Law was misused to suppress domestic,
particularly student, dissent.

For persons deemed "socially dangerous," the law allows
preventive detention under provisions of the Social Protection
and Social Stability Laws. Neither provision affords the
accused the benefit of legal counsel or appeal. Under the
Social Protection Law, a judicial panel may order preventive
detention for a fixed term of 2 years, which can be extended by
the panel for additional 2-year periods. The Social Stability
Law allows for a preventive detention term of 7 to 10 years.
In the city of Chongju there exists a "preventive custody
center" where prisoners judged to be insufficiently repentant
are held following the completion of their original prison
sentences. Soh Joon Shik, whose original 7-year sentence ran
out in 1978, is one of two political prisoners believed to be
held in this facility. The Government has not released figures
on the total number of persons under preventive detention.

There were no reports in 1985 of forced labor as defined by the
International Labor Organization (ILO).

    c. Denial of Fair Public Trial

The Constitution guarantees many rights to defendants: The
right to presumption of innocence, the right against
self-incrimination, freedom from ex-post facto laws and double
jeopardy, the right to a speedy trial, and the right to legal
counsel. These rights are generally observed. Trials, with
some exceptions, must be held within 6 months of arrest. In
Seoul, trials usually begin within a month after indictment.

The President appoints the members of the Supreme Court, whose
Chief Justice in turn appoints lower-level judges. The Chief
Justice serves a 5-year term. The judiciary is considered
independent in ordinary criminal and civil cases but much less
so in politically sensitive cases. In 1985 the Chief Justice
was criticized in opposition and legal circles for transferring
several judges to less desirable positions, allegedly because
they had ruled in favor of defendants in cases involving
student protesters or had complained about the treatment of
their colleagues who were accused of being too lenient toward
student defendants. The Korean Bar Association called for the
Chief Justice's resignation; an impeachment sponsored by the
opposition was voted down in the National Assembly.

In several politically sensitive trials in 1985, as in the
trial of students who seized the U.S. Information Service
(USIS) Library in May, public attendance was limited, and the
defendants sometimes were removed from the courtroom for
attempting to disrupt the proceedings by shouting slogans and
singing. Judges generally allowed great scope for examination
of witnesses by both prosecution and defense, but they often
denied defense requests to call witnesses to discuss the

15 - 4

REPUBLIC OF KOREA

political or ideological leanings of the defendants, even when
the prosecution had introduced evidence on such topics.

Trials are usually open to the public, but trial documents are
not part of the public record. Charges against defendants in
the courts are clearly stated, with the exception that, in
lengthy and complex indictments, the relationship between
specific acts alleged and violations of specific sections of
the penal code may not always be clearly drawn. In cases
involving a mixture of political and criminal charges this can
bring into question the fairness of the proceedings.
The same courts try political and ordinary criminal cases. The
military courts do not try civilians. Defendants have the
right of appeal in felony cases, a right which is often
exercised and frequently results in substantial reductions in
sentences. Death sentences are automatically appealed. The
list of political prisoners maintained by the Human Rights
Committee (HRC) of the National Council of Churches hovered
around 100 names throughout the first 5 months of 1985. The
list grew to around 700 names by November as the Government
continued its crackdown on activist students begun in the
aftermath of the USIS Library seizure, but the number had
dropped to around 600 by the end of December. The HRC includes
on its list persons indicted but not yet tried for
politically-related offenses as well as those already
convicted; this list contains the names of some persons who
have advocated or used violence. The Minister of Justice
reported to the National Assembly in October 1985 that there
are no prisoners of conscience in the Republic of Korea.

Of the 600 names on the HRC list, more than 400 are university
students. About 30 people on the HRC's list were charged with
illegal labor actions; several were farmers charged with
illegal assembly and demonstration. The list also includes 40
or so persons, many of whom were Korean residents in Japan,
accused of espionage for North Korea.

Not included in the HRC political prisoner list are students
and others briefly detained but not indicted in connection with
student and labor demonstrations during 1985. According to
government statistics, between May and October police referred
over 1,000 students to summary court where they were charged
with minor offenses and sentenced to a maximum of 29 days'
detention. Some students receiving summary judgments chose to
exercise their right to formal trials.

   f. Arbitrary Interference with Privacy, Family, Home, or
       Correspondence

Many political and religious dissidents are subjected to
surveillance by the security forces. During politically
sensitive periods, this surveillance by one or more security
agencies may increase or a form of house arrest may be
imposed. There have also been charges of telephone tapping and
opening or interception of correspondence. Koreans who meet
with foreigners, particularly with journalists and foreign
diplomats, are sometimes questioned afterwards. In the
aftermath of the seizure by students of the USIS library in
May, police tried to stop relatives of the students involved
and others from meeting U.S. Embassy officials.

While the Constitution requires a warrant issued by a judge
upon request of prosecutor for search and seizure in a
residence, the police at times force their way into private

15-5

REPUBLIC OF KOREA

homes without warrants. During politically sensitive periods,
the police and security force presence in city centers and near
university campuses is very heavy. Citizens, particularly
students, are frequently stopped, questioned, and searched.

Traditional Korean police practice requires police commanders
to know a good deal about the personal and business affairs of
all residents in their jurisdictions. This system is effective
in crime control, and urban residents generally credit it with
keeping their streets safe. By contrast, the presence of
police informer networks on college campuses with the primary
purpose of keeping track of political activities has been a key
complaint among students, including those who are not
politically active.

In most other respects the Government honors the right of
personal privacy and the integrity of the home and family.
Parental rights to educate children are broad, and restrictions
on study in foreign-administered schools (whether in Korea or
overseas), originally imposed to force wealthy Koreans to
involve themselves in the nation's social and educational
development, have been relaxed in recent years. The State
rarely seeks to intervene in such inherently personal decisions
as marriage, choice of vocation, and formation of social and
familial ties. However, persons thought to have politically
suspect backgrounds are denied some forms of employment and
advancement, particularly in government, press, and education.
In 1985, Korean newspapers reported that a number of teachers
and college graduates had been denied jobs in public schools
solely because of their past involvement in student protest
activities.

Section 2 Respect for Civil Rights, Including:

    a. Freedom of Speech and Press

Although freedom of speech and press are guaranteed by the
Constitution, in practice the expression of opposition
viewpoints is limited, sometimes severely. Government critics
say that laws such as the Basic Press Law, under which media
organizations are licensed and permitted to operate, and
criminal code provisions against the spreading of "rumors which
eventually disturb peace and order" and "defiling the state"
are used to muzzle and punish dissident views. Opposition
political parties have called for the repeal or reform of the
Basic Press Law.

During the February 1985 National Assembly election campaign,
opposition candidates made speeches before large crowds in
which they were highly critical of the Government. Most Korean
and foreign observers alike agreed the campaign was
characterized by the most outspoken political debate permitted
in the Republic of Korea in many years. Print media coverage
was extensive, although television reporting reflected much
more government influence. When the new National Assembly was
inaugurated, it continued to be characterized by a breaking of
old taboos on speaking out on sensitive political topics,
including thinly-veiled challenges to the Government's
legitimacy stemming from the serious civil disturbance in
Kwangju in 1980, policy toward South-North Korean dialogue, and
constitutional revision, all of which received print media
coverage. The government party, concerned about increasingly
sharp opposition criticism, sought with limited success to
precensor opposition politicians' remarks. After several

15 - 6

REPUBLIC OF KOREA

opposition politicians complained of government intimidation
when they or their aides were summoned for questioning about
critical remarks made on the Assembly floor, the Government
promised it would respect Assemblymen's rights to free speech.
Details of the most critical speeches were generally not
reported in the press, and government party speeches received
heavier coverage. Nonetheless, newspapers did report in
greater detail than in many years about opposition views on
previously taboo political subjects.

The domestic media engage in self-censorship, according to
verbal or written guidelines the Government regularly gives to
editors. Journalists who object to or ignore these guidelines
or criticize the guidance system have been picked up for
questioning and on occasion dismissed or sent out of the
country on assignment; in one case in 1985 journalists were
beaten. Nonetheless, the domestic media, notably newspapers
and magazines, became noticeably more outspoken during and in
the aftermath of the February National Assembly election. An
edition of a prestigious monthly magazine carrying an article
on the 1980 civil disturbances in Kwangju was confiscated by
the Government shortly after its publication, and the article's
author was interrogated by security officials. In late 1985
about 30 reporters, mostly from provincial papers, were fired
for corruption on orders from the Ministry of Culture and
Information. There were reports that at least some were in
fact fired for holding views critical of the Government. In
December a visiting U.S. Washington Times journalist was
ordered out of the country temporarily, reportedly for writing
an article on an alleged meeting between North and South Korean
leaders.

The early months of 1985 saw the publication of an increasing
number of books and magazines by dissident religious,
political, and cultural figures. In May police confiscated
books they considered dangerous on the grounds of being
"leftist" or "encouraging revolution." According to the
Minister of Culture and Information, in October 11,000 copies
of 395 books were confiscated.

Twenty teachers who contributed to a magazine criticizing the
Government's education policy were arrested or fired, and the
magazine's publishing company was closed under the Basic Press
Law. The Basic Press Law was also used against a student
charged with editing a "seditious" publication; at least seven
other students were charged with National Security Law
violations in connection with publications said to be
"sympathetic to Communism and serving the interests of the
enemy." In July police raided an art exhibition and jailed
five artists for a week, saying the paintings and prints there
were objectionable on ideological grounds. A Christian youth
activist received a suspended sentence for "defiling the state"
by distributing dissident leaflets to foreign journalists.

Academic freedom is subject to some political limitations. In
fall 1985 a group of professors who signed a petition opposing
the proposed campus stabilization law came under official
pressure to retract their views.

     b. Freedom of Peaceful Assembly and Association

A number of specified categories of assembly, including those
considered likely to undermine public order or cause social
unrest, are prohibited by the Law on Assembly and

15-7

0082

REPUBLIC OF KOREA

Demonstrations. The law also requires that demonstrations of all types and outdoor political assemblies be reported in advance to the police. Violation of the law carries a maximum sentence of 7 years' imprisonment or a fine of about $3,750. Under this law, police have at times intervened and broken up meetings. Most peaceful nonpolitical assemblies take place entirely without official supervision or restriction. However, meetings of dissidents are monitored and sometimes prevented, often by placing the scheduled speaker under some form of house arrest.

The Law on Assembly and Demonstrations was most often used in 1985 against student demonstrators. According to a government report submitted to the National Assembly in late October, a total of 1,923 students had been taken to police stations for involvement in demonstrations on and off campus since the May USIS Library seizure. Of that number, 305 were charged with violating the Law on Assembly and Demonstrations and/or laws punishing violent acts. Another 104 were booked without physical detention. About 1,000 were summarily tried on minor charges, and the remainder were released with warnings.

In September two opposition National Assemblymen and several other oppositionists were indicted under the Law on Assembly and Demonstration after they were stopped by police for shouting protest slogans against the Government at the gates of a Seoul campus on the day of a scheduled protest meeting. In October the lawyers for some of the students charged under the Law on Assembly and Demonstration requested a review by the Constitution Committee of the legitimacy part of the law, asserting that the vagueness of one clause rendered it unconstitutional. The Supreme Court ruled against the claim, stating that the right to assembly and protest is limited.

Under the Constitution, workers are guaranteed the right to independent association, to bargain collectively, and to collective action. These rights are circumscribed by law and practice and do not extend to workers employed by the Government, public utilities, defense-related industries, or firms "that exercise great influence on the national economy." In the past the last category has applied primarily to heavy industry.

The single national labor federation, the Federation of Korean Trade Unions (FKTU), and its 16 national affiliate unions are not controlled by the Government, but their activities are limited by law and subject to government interference. In 1985, five ranking FKTU officials were forced to resign under government pressure, reportedly because they were either held responsible for or did not agree with the Government's tough policy on recent labor disputes. Labor organizations are forbidden by law to support politicians or political parties, though the FKTU does lobby National Assemblymen, and Assemblymen often attend labor gatherings.

According to the FKTU, after an increase in 1984, dues-paying union membership in 1985 remained at about 800,000 workers, about 10 percent of the full-time work force. Ministry of Labor figures, based on reports submitted by individual unions, place total union membership at slightly over 1 million.

Some FKTU-supported revisions to labor regulations, approved in 1985, permitted a larger role for the Federation in local

15-8

0083

REPUBLIC OF KOREA

affairs. The FKTU continued to press for broader revision of the labor law, as did the main opposition party.

The FKTU is affiliated with the International Confederation of Free Trade Unions, and its constituent unions are affiliated with recognized international trade union federations. The Republic of Korea has observer status at the International Labor Organization.

All local unions must be organized within individual enterprises, creating a structure of thousands of individual unions, most of them small and weak. Direct participation in local unions' bargaining activities by outside agencies is forbidden. The FKTU and its constituent national unions can and sometimes do bargain on behalf of the locals and conduct education programs, but only with government and employer approval. Religious labor ministries such as the Catholic Young Christian Workers and the Protestant Urban Industrial Mission are also severely limited in the assistance which they can provide the unions. Under these circumstances, government and employer influence has greatly exceeded that of unions in setting wages and resolving other major labor issues.

Collective actions and strikes, though technically legal, are strongly discouraged. The Government used the Law on Assembly and Demonstration on a number of occasions in connection with workers' and farmers' rallies. Despite the legal restrictions and other obstacles, collective actions by workers, including strikes, increased in 1985. The Government charged radical student involvement in many of the disputes, saying it had identified at least 277 "disguised workers" through the end of September who had hidden their university credentials in order to "infiltrate" the workforce and "instigate" the workers to strike. Of these, 160 were fired by their employers, 97 "voluntarily" quit their jobs, and 20 are still working. In a few strikes, groups of nonstriking workers wielded pipes and stormed their workplaces to end worker sit-in's forcibly. They were not prevented by police from doing so, and many Koreans charged that the attacks were government-sponsored.

According to government statistics, the government committee charged with investigating unfair labor practices heard 227 cases in the first eight months of 1985, 205 of which involved problems with union organization and alleged employer obstructionism. The committee decided in favor of the workers in 64 cases.

c. Freedom of Religion

There is no state-favored religion in Korea. There is generally complete freedom of proselytizing, doctrinal teaching, and conversion. Korea both sends and receives missionaries of various faiths. Many religious groups in Korea maintain active links with coreligionists in other countries. Minority sects are not discriminated against, and adherence to a faith confers neither advantages nor disadvantages in civil, military, or official life. Churches and religious groups are subject to many of the restrictions on political activity and criticism of the Government that apply to all other institutions. On those occasions where pastors are harassed by the authorities, it is usually for religiously motivated social or political activism. One Protestant minister active in human rights issues has made plausible charges that a government security agency has sponsored efforts to disrupt his church

15-9

0084

444 한국 인권문제 미국 반응 및 동향 2

REPUBLIC OF KOREA

services; other ministers have joined with him to protest what
they term government infringement on religious freedom. The
Government denied the charges and says the church's troubles
are an internal problem. Conscientious objectors are subject
to arrest.

    d. Freedom of Movement Within the Country, Foreign
       Travel, Emigration, and Repatriation

There is almost universal freedom of movement and freedom to
change employment in Korea. Because Korea is one of the most
densely populated countries in the world, the Government does
not discourage emigration or discriminate against prospective
emigrants. Most people can obtain passports, except for
criminals and some persons considered politically suspect. A
number of dissidents, former political prisoners, and persons
banned from political activity have been allowed to travel
abroad. The Government limits the number of passports issued
to tourists and prospective students, citing foreign exchange
considerations and the problem of unqualified students going
abroad. Passports, when issued, are typically limited to 1
year, although there are exceptions in which passports are
issued up to the legally maximum 5-year period of validity.

A small continuing influx of Vietnamese boat refugees is
admitted to first asylum in Korea. They are cared for at a
camp in Pusan by the Korean Red Cross until they can be
resettled abroad. Over 700 displaced persons from Vietnam have
passed through Korea in the last several years. Very few have
been permanently resettled in Korea.

Section 3 Respect for Political Rights: The Right of Citizens
          to Change Their Government

Korea's Constitution and statutes, as well as its traditions,
concentrate political power in the President, a concentration
further intensified by the support the President enjoys from
the military. The President and the members of the National
Assembly are the only elected officials in Korea. Under the
1980 Presidential Election Law, the President is chosen by a
popularly elected electoral college of at least 5,000 members.
By law, presidential campaigns are brief and candidates
severely restricted in campaigning, including the amount they
may spend, the number of speeches they may deliver, and the
number of publications they may distribute. In the 1981
presidential election these restrictions, together with the
authorities' screening of electoral college candidates,
resulted in the absence of effective opposition to incumbent
President Chun Doo Hwan, who won nearly unanimously. In the
1985 National Assembly election, two of the most prominent
opposition politicians, Kim Dae Jung and Kim Young Sam, were
not allowed to participate.

The Constitution limits the President to a single 7-year term
and may not be amended to allow the incumbent president to run
for another term. The next presidential election will be held
in late 1987 or early 1988. President Chun continued to
reaffirm throughout 1985 that he intends to step down in 1988
to provide for a peaceful and constitutional transfer of
power. His party, the Democratic Justice Party (DJP), has
announced that it will convene in early 1987 to choose a
presidential candidate. However, the main opposition party and
most dissident groups are calling for a revision of the
Constitution to allow for direct popular election of the

15-10   0085

REPUBLIC OF KOREA

president, contending that it would be less susceptible to
government manipulation than the current system.

The National Assembly, although institutionally weak, acquired
new importance in 1985 with the holding of elections and the
emergence of a new, more outspoken opposition party. Members
are directly elected and serve a 4-year term. The election law
passed in 1981 provides for a proportional representation
system that reserves 92 of the Assembly's 276 seats for members
designated by the parties, with two-thirds of those seats
awarded to the party gaining a plurality of the popular vote.
The government party faced a strong challenge in the February
1985 Assembly election from a new opposition party, the New
Korea Democratic Party (NKDP), formed only weeks before the
election and led largely by politicians recently freed from the
political ban. The government party, the Democratic Justice
Party (DJP), garnered a plurality of 35.3 percent and, with its
proportional representation seats, maintained a comfortable
majority of 148 out of 276 Assembly seats. However, the NKDP
obtained a surprising 29.2 percent of the popular vote. The
former main opposition party, the Democratic Korea Party (DKP),
received only 19.5 percent. Almost all of its members defected
to the NKDP after the elections, boosting the NKDP's Assembly
seats to 102 and making it the largest opposition party in the
Republic's parliamentary history in terms of Assembly seats
held. The campaign included outspoken criticism of the
Government and its leaders by the opposition at large rallies
and calls for constitutional revision to allow for direct
presidential elections. Voter turnout was 84 percent, the
highest since 1958. Press coverage was extensive, television
less so.

In the aftermath of the election, the DJP pledged to practice
the politics of "dialogue" and to "reflect the people's wishes
as expressed in the election." The NKDP took a more aggressive
stance than that adopted by other opposition parties since
1980, taking the Government to task on sensitive issues
including the handling of the 1980 civil disturbances in
Kwangju and constitutional reform.

On March 6, 1985, the Government lifted the political ban on
the 14 people still affected by it. However, several persons,
including prominent opposition figure Kim Dae Jung, although
freed from the political ban, were still prohibited from
joining a political party or running for office because they
were under suspended sentences from prior convictions.

Women are free to vote, become government officials, and run
for the National Assembly. Women hold seven Assembly seats,
all but two appointed by their parties. In practice, however,
the power structure remains male-dominated, and in many
significant respects the legal system and social custom
strongly discriminate against women. There is some pressure to
address women's rights; in recognition of this, the ruling
party has formed an ad hoc committee to study the issue.

Section 4   Governmental Attitude Regarding International and
            Nongovernmental Investigation of Alleged Violations
            of Human Rights

The Republic of Korea does not belong to any international
human rights bodies and usually does not welcome outside
involvement in the human rights area, although government
officials have allowed the visits of and met with

15-11   0086

809

REPUBLIC OF KOREA

representatives of international human rights bodies, including
Amnesty International and Asia Watch. Prison authorities
rebuffed attempts by human rights groups and opposition
politicians to investigate conditions in prisons.

There are no government agencies charged with the protection of
human rights, although political parties and the National
Assembly have committees which are concerned with oversight of
some aspects of the issue. In March 1985 opposition party
leaders held up the convening of the National Assembly to
negotiate the release of prisoners convicted on political and
security charges. While the negotiations did not result in the
release of many prisoners, they did represent the most open
discussion of the issue in several years and received extensive
press coverage in Korea. The autumn session of the National
Assembly saw opposition interpellation of government ministers
on human rights issues including torture and arbitrary arrest.
Although the Government rejected calls for a special Assembly
committee to investigate human rights abuses, especially
torture, the opposition party and other opposition groups
dispatched investigative teams, held press conferences, formed
special committees, and provided legal defense in connection
with numerous human rights issues.

A number of politically nonaffiliated private organizations
have long been active in human rights, chiefly the Human Rights
Committee of the Korean National Council of Churches, the
Catholic Justice and Peace Committee, and the Korea Legal Aid
Center in Seoul. The Committees and other human rights
organizations submit petitions to the Government and make their
views known both inside and outside Korea. People working with
these groups are frequently questioned and sometimes detained
by the security services, though apparently none have been
arrested in the past several years.
Amnesty International temporarily closed its office in Seoul in
1985, over the objections of its Korean chapter, on the grounds
that the group's independent activities were not possible under
present conditions. In its 1985 Report, Amnesty International
remained concerned about the imprisonment of people for
peaceful expression of their views. While it welcomed the
release in the early part of 1984 of over 200 students, it was
concerned about an increase in the use of short-term detention
for people participating in public protests and about several
well-known critics of the Government being placed under house
arrest. It noted that it had received fewer reports of torture
during interrogation, but that there were numerous reports of
police violence against demonstrators both before and after
arrest. Freedom House rated South Korea "partly free."

ECONOMIC, SOCIAL, AND CULTURAL SITUATION

The Republic of Korea's population in 1985 was 42.6 million.
Over the last 20 years the population growth rate has decreased
from 2.6 to 1.5 percent, due in part to concerted efforts by
the Government to encourage voluntary family planning. During
the past 20 years, Korea's export-oriented, mixed economy has
achieved one of the highest growth rates in the world, with per
capita GNP rising from $100 in 1963 to $2,010 in 1983. A
notable feature of this rapid growth has been the relative
evenness of income distribution, though many Koreans
characterize the gap between rich and poor as worsening. The
percentage of the population below absolute poverty was
estimated to be 16 percent in urban areas and 11 percent in
rural areas. There is no economic discrimination based on race

15-12

0087

REPUBLIC OF KOREA

or religion. The right to own property, both alone and in association with others, is recognized in law and practice.

Improved health care and nutrition have increased life expectancy to 68.2 years, while infant mortality has declined to 29.6 per 1,000 live births. In 1980, an estimated 78 percent of the population had access to safe drinking water, and caloric supply per person was 126 percent of minimum nutritional requirements.

Education is highly valued in Korean society. Ninety-six percent of the population was estimated to be literate in 1980-82. Primary school education is universal for both sexes, and over 90 percent of elementary school students enter secondary school. About 34 percent of all high school graduates pass competitive entrance exams and enter college. There is great social mobility based on merit in education and employment.

Chapter V of the Labor Standards Law governs the employment of minor and female workers. Under this provision, minors under age 13 must have a special permit issued by the Ministry of Labor to be employed. Minors under age 18 must have a parent's or guardian's written approval in order to work, and they are prohibited from night work without special permission from the Ministry of Labor. The law requires that employers of 30 or more minors provide educational facilities or arrange scholarship funds for them. Employment of minors is widespread, particularly in family-operated enterprises and in some labor-intensive industries, and abuses of legal protections are common.

The Constitution states that the Government "shall endeavor to promote the employment of workers and to guarantee optimum wages through social and economic means." Standards of working conditions are to be "determined by law in such a way as to guarantee human dignity." The Labor Standards Law provides for a maximum workweek of 60 hours with mutual consent of employer and employee, a paid day of rest during the workweek, compensation for overtime and holiday work, paid holidays, and annual leave. There are no exceptions to working conditions standards for industries established in export-processing zones. Recent statistics indicate that the average full-time worker spends 54.4 hours per week on the job. Korea has no minimum wage system, but the Government has pledged to institute one as part of the 5-year economic plan beginning in 1987. Meanwhile, the Government is attempting to persuade the employers of the 300,000 workers earning less than 100,000 won ($112) per month to raise wages. The Government announced in late 1985 that its efforts had resulted in a decrease of 112,000 workers in the below 100,000 won per month category.

Responding to a series of labor disputes highlighting criticism of its labor policy, the Government promised in 1985 to use stronger measures, including fines and imprisonment, to curb employer abuses such as delayed wage payments, illegal firings, and violations of regulations on working conditions. The Minister of Labor reported in late 1985 that 24 employers were arrested in the first half of 1985 for failure to pay wages and for physical abuse of employees. During that period, the Government reported uncovering 16,000 cases of employer wrongdoing, including nearly 2,500 cases of non-payment of wages, about 150 cases of unfair dismissal, and 40 violations of safety and health standards.

15-13

0088

811

REPUBLIC OF KOREA

In the first half of 1985, 605 job-related deaths and 64,000 injuries were reported by government sources. In 1984 there were 1,667 deaths and 156,133 injuries reported in connection with industrial accidents. A government study cited lack of adequate safety precautions as a major cause of industrial casualties in about 10 percent of all cases. The Government has mandated insurance to cover industrial accidents at places of business employing 10 or more workers. The 1981 revision of the Industrial Accident Compensation Law covers job-related medical costs, sick leave benefits, disability benefits, and other costs.

Women's rights constitute a problem area. Some progress has been made--the family law was revised in 1960 and 1979--but critics contend that the law is still inconsistent with Korean constitutional guarantees of sexual equality. Women do not have equal rights with men in passing nationality to their children, nor do they have equal rights with regard to child custody in divorce cases. Women's rights groups are campaigning for changes in these and some other points of the family law.

Women do enjoy full access to educational opportunities. They are increasingly represented, though still largely at entry levels, in the military, the police, and in private industry. Other areas are more problematic. As of 1985, only 34 women had ever passed the bar examination. Five had passed the National Administration Examination, given for higher level civil service jobs. In general, women are not protected against discrimination in hiring, pay, or advancement. Some members of the National Assembly, however, are trying to focus more attention on women's rights.

15-14

0089

U.S.OVERSEAS -LOANS AND GRANTS- OBLIGATIONS AND LOAN AUTHORIZATIONS
(U.S.FISCAL YEARS - MILLIONS OF DOLLARS)

COUNTRY: KOREA, REPUBLIC OF

	1983	1984	1985
I.ECON. ASSIST.-TOTAL...	0.0	0.0	0.0
LOANS...............	0.0	0.0	0.0
GRANTS.............	0.0	0.0	0.0
A.AID	0.0	0.0	0.0
LOANS..............	0.0	0.0	0.0
GRANTS............	0.0	0.0	0.0
(SEC.SUPP.ASSIST.)...	0.0	0.0	0.0
B.FOOD FOR PEACE.......	0.0	0.0	0.0
LOANS..............	0.0	0.0	0.0
GRANTS............	0.0	0.0	0.0
TITLE I-TOTAL..........	0.0	0.0	0.0
REPAY. IN $-LOANS.....	0.0	0.0	0.0
PAY. IN FOR. CURR.....	0.0	0.0	0.0
TITLE II-TOTAL.........	0.0	0.0	0.0
E.RELIEF.EC.DEV & WFP.	0.0	0.0	0.0
VOL.RELIEF AGENCY.....	0.0	0.0	0.0
C.OTHER ECON. ASSIST...	0.0	0.0	0.0
LOANS..............	0.0	0.0	0.0
GRANTS............	0.0	0.0	0.0
PEACE CORPS......	0.0	0.0	0.0
NARCOTICS.........	0.0	0.0	0.0
OTHER............	0.0	0.0	0.0
II.MIL. ASSIST.-TOTAL...	186.7	231.8	231.9
LOANS.............	185.0	230.0	230.0
GRANTS...........	1.7	1.8	1.9
A.MAP GRANTS..........	0.0	0.0	0.0
B.CREDIT FINANCING....	185.0	230.0	230.0
C.INTL MIL.ED.TRNG....	1.7	1.8	1.9
D.TRAN-EXCESS STOCK...	0.0	0.0	0.0
E.OTHER GRANTS........	0.0	0.0	0.0
III.TOTAL ECON. & MIL...	186.7	231.8	231.9
LOANS.............	185.0	230.0	230.0
GRANTS...........	1.7	1.8	1.9
OTHER US LOANS..........	9.0	0.0	0.0
EX-IM BANK LOANS........	9.0	0.0	0.0
ALL OTHER..............	0.0	0.0	0.0

ASSISTANCE FROM INTERNATIONAL AGENCIES

	1983	1984	1985	1946-85
TOTAL.........	942.4	977.5	697.2	8093.4
IBRD	672.0	768.5	556.0	5825.3
IFC	2.2	34.6	7.2	171.4
IDA	0.0	0.0	0.0	106.9
IDB	0.0	0.0	0.0	0.0
ADB	265.5	172.8	134.0	1938.3
AFDB	0.0	0.0	0.0	0.0
UNDP	2.7	1.6	0.0	36.1
OTHER-UN	0.0	0.0	0.0	15.4
EEC	0.0	0.0	0.0	0.0

15-15

0090

책부)

DEMOCRATIC PEOPLE'S REPUBLIC OF KOREA*

The Democratic People's Republic of Korea, formed in 1948
during the Soviet administration of the northern half of the
Korean peninsula, is a rigid Communist dictatorship, strictly
dominated by one man, Kim Il Sung, and his family. Although
some internationally respected human rights are acknowledged by
the 1972 Constitution and laws, individual rights are entirely
subordinated in practice to the ruling Korean Workers'
(Communist) Party (KWP), with its overriding aim of imposing a
social revolution and enforcing unanimous popular support for
the country's governing system and its leaders. While there
were pro forma elections to the Supreme People's Assembly in
February 1982, free elections do not exist in North Korea
because citizens have no choice among candidates.

The North Korean people are subject to rigid controls. The
State establishes security ratings for each person, and these
ratings determine access to jobs, schools, medical facilities,
and stores, as well as admission to the Korean Workers' Party,
the route to the highest levels and privileges of the society.
Persons who fail to cooperate face imprisonment, confiscation
of property, or enforced removal to remote villages.
Surveillance by informers is prevalent. Punishment for
"political crimes" against the State is severe. Virtually no
outside information other than that approved and disseminated
by the North Korean authorities is allowed to reach the
public. However, senior government officials seem to be
somewhat better informed.

President Kim Il Sung's 13-year effort to groom his son, Kim
Chong Il, as successor is testimony to the enormous power the
elder Kim has amassed during 37 years of rule. The younger Kim
was elevated to several senior party positions in 1980. The
absence of any evidence of public debate about the succession
is also indicative of the lack of real popular participation in
the political process.

North Korea has not been successful through its command economy
in producing the desired economic development. It remains a
less-developed country with a low standard of living and a
severe balance of payments problem.

Kim Il Sung's commitment to reunification on his own terms has
led to periodic attempts to destabilize the Republic of Korea.
More recently, North Korea has engaged in talks with South
Korea. These have addressed possibilities for cooperation in
the economic, parliamentary, sports, and humanitarian fields.
This last area of discussion has focused on the plight of
families separated during the postwar division of the peninsula

---

*The United States does not have diplomatic relations with the
Democratic People's Republic of Korea; even representatives of
governments that do, as well as journalists and other
occasional invited visitors to North Korea, are not permitted
the freedom of movement that would enable them effectively to
assess human rights conditions there. Nor does North Korea
publish socioeconomic statistics. Most of this report,
therefore, is a repeat of previous human rights reports based
on information obtained over a period of time extending from
well before 1985. While limited in scope and detail, the
information is indicative of the human rights situation in
North Korea today.

7-1   0091

DEMOCRATIC PEOPLE'S REPUBLIC OF KOREA

and the Korean War (1950-53). During September 20-23, 1985, both sides arranged historically unprecedented exchange visits by separated family members.

However, there is little evidence to suggest that North Korea has improved its dismal performance in the human rights area. Both short- and long-term trends indicate continued one-family rule with scant respect for basic human rights.

RESPECT FOR HUMAN RIGHTS

Section 1   Respect for the Integrity of the Person, Including Freedom from:

a. Political Killing

No reliable information is available on politically motivated killing in North Korea. However, the North Korean attitude toward political killing was clearly demonstrated in the October 9, 1983, Rangoon bombing and the November 23, 1984, shooting in the Joint Security Area of the Demilitarized Zone (DMZ) dividing North and South Korea.

After a careful investigation, the Government of Burma determined that the Democratic People's Republic of Korea was responsible for the attempt to assassinate Republic of Korea President Chun Doo Hwan during his 1983 visit to Burma. Two North Korean army officers brought to trial in Rangoon were convicted and sentenced to death for the attack, in which four cabinet ministers and a number of officials were killed. In the DMZ incident, North Korean security guards opened fire on a Soviet student trying to defect from a tour group, triggering an exchange of fire in which several lives were lost.

b. Disappearance

There is no information available on disappearance.

c. Torture and Cruel, Inhuman, or Degrading Treatment or Punishment

According to the Freedom House 1984-85 report, "torture is reportedly common" in North Korea. The accounts of torture and beatings of crew members of the USS Pueblo after their capture in 1968 are well-known and documented. The only other reliable source on prison conditions and treatment of prisoners in North Korea is Venezuelan poet Ali Lameda, who was detained in North Korea from September 1967 through 1974, allegedly for attempted sabotage and espionage. While physical torture was not used on Mr. Lameda, he stated that Korean prisoners were routinely beaten. Lameda noted that "beating was also used as a means of persuasion during interrogation."

Lameda reported the use of deprivation of food to force "confessions," as well as solitary confinement, continuous interrogation, enforced waking periods, poor or nonexistent medical treatment, and 12 hours of forced labor per day. In addition, prisoners were denied family visits, parcels, correspondence, writing materials, newspapers, and clothing changes. Prisoners appeared to be regarded as persons without any rights.

1-2

0092

DEMOCRATIC PEOPLE'S REPUBLIC OF KOREA

d.   Arbitrary Arrest, Detention, or Exile

Information on specific criminal justice procedures and
practices in North Korea is extremely scarce. North Korea has
refused to permit outside observation of its legal system and
practices. The accounts provided by the crew members of the
USS Pueblo and by Lameda, while clearly from an earlier period,
comprise virtually all the specific information available on
the operation of the criminal justice system in North Korea.

North Korean law states that no prisoner may be held for
interrogation over 2 months. This period may be extended
indefinitely, however, if the Interrogation Department obtains
approval of the Chief Prosecutor. Lameda states that he was
detained for 12 months without trial or charge. His request
for a lawyer of his choice and an open trial were ridiculed as
"bourgeois." Habeas corpus or its equivalent does not exist in
law or practice.

According to newspaper reports, North Korean defectors in South
Korea estimated in April 1982 that at least 105,000
"ideological offenders" were being held in eight major labor
camps in the North. Amnesty International has received
unconfirmed reports of arrests of those opposed to heir
apparent Kim Chong Il.

There is no prohibition on the use of forced or compulsory
labor. Information as to whether it is practiced is not
available.

e.   Denial of Fair Public Trial

The North Korean Constitution states that courts are
independent and that judicial proceedings are to be carried out
in strict accordance with law. All courts, however, are
responsible to the people's assemblies, which effectively means
government control of the judiciary. Article 138 states that
"cases are heard in public, and the accused is guaranteed the
right to defense; hearings may be closed to the public as
stipulated by law." Lameda claims that he was twice denied
public trial. He reports that after his first arrest he was
imprisoned for a year without a hearing; after his second
arrest, he was put through a closed session without benefit of
counsel of his choice or even knowledge of the charges. His
tribunal was under the direction of the Ministry of Internal
Security, with one person serving as both judge and prosecutor.

Lameda stated that, other than to admit guilt, he was refused
the right to speak out or defend himself at his trial. His
"defense counsel" represented him by making a lengthy speech
praising Kim Il Sung and then requesting a 20-year sentence,
which the tribunal imposed after 5 minutes of deliberation.

In a 1979 interview with American journalist John Wallach,
North Korean Supreme Court Justice Li Chun Uk noted that the
defense counsel's job is "to give the suspect due punishment."
Open court appears to consist of an announcement of the term of
imprisonment, which has already been determined by the
Provincial Safety Bureau.

7-3

0093

DEMOCRATIC PEOPLE'S REPUBLIC OF KOREA

f. Arbitrary Interference with Privacy, Family, Home, or
Correspondence

The populace is subjected to regular indoctrination, designed
to shape individual consciousness. Preschool children are
drilled in homage to Kim Il Sung and his family, while youths
and adults are required to participate in daily ideological
training conducted by youth organizations or at places of
employment. The propaganda requires rote recitation of party
maxims and positions and strives for ideological purity.
Multiple North Korean security organizations enforce these
controls.

Reports, primarily from defectors, indicate that forced
resettlement is common, particularly for those deemed
politically unreliable. Permission to reside in, or even
enter, Pyongyang, the capital, is strictly controlled.

According to reports in South Korean journals, Japanese wives
of Koreans repatriated from Japan since 1959 have not been
permitted to visit Japan and many have lost contact with their
families because their letters are subject to strict censorship.

The Constitution states that "citizens are guaranteed the
inviolability of person and residence and the privacy of
correspondence." Lameda reported, however, that the privacy of
his residence was not respected and that listening devices were
used against him. He was arrested and his collected papers and
poetry seized and destroyed without warrant.

Section 2   Respect for Civil Rights, Including:

a. Freedom of Speech and Press

The Constitution states that "citizens have the freedoms of
speech, the press, assembly, association, and demonstration."
In fact, North Koreans enjoy none of these rights. Such
activities are permitted only in support of government
objectives. Other articles of the Constitution that require
citizens to follow the "socialist norms of life" and to obey a
"collective spirit" take precedence over individual political
or civil liberties. Foreign media are excluded, domestic media
censorship is enforced, and no deviation from the official
government line is tolerated. Listening to foreign media
broadcasts is prohibited, and violators reportedly are subject
to severe punishment. Most urban households have a radio and
some have television, but reception is limited to domestic
programming. Artistic and academic works are controlled by the
Government, and visitors report that a primary function of
plays, movies, operas, and books is to contribute to the cult
of personality surrounding "the great leader," Kim Il Sung, and
his son, "the beloved leader," Kim Chong Il.

b. Freedom of Peaceful Assembly and Association

The Government has developed a pervasive system of informers
throughout the society. No public meetings can be held without
government authorization. There appear to be no organizations
other than those created by the Government.

Trade unions and professional associations appear to exist
solely as another method of government control over their
members. There are no effective rights to organize, bargain
collectively, or strike.

7-4

0094

795

DEMOCRATIC PEOPLE'S REPUBLIC OF KOREA

c.   Freedom of Religion

Although the Constitution guarantees that "citizens have
religious liberty and the freedom of antireligious propaganda,"
North Korea, in fact, has severely persecuted Christians and
Buddhists since the late 1940's. No churches have been rebuilt
since the Korean War. The regime uses religious organizational
facades to proclaim the practice of religious freedom but
appears to have long since purged the membership out of
existence. Persons whose family or relatives once had a strong
religious involvement are discriminated against. Though
religious practice appears impossible, some foreign visitors to
North Korea believe that the Government does not currently
persecute the very small number of Christians who continue to
worship at home.

d.   Freedom of Movement Within the Country, Foreign
      Travel, Emigration, and Repatriation

Internal travel in North Korea is strictly controlled. A
travel pass is required for any movement outside one's home
village and is granted only for required official or personal
travel. This requirement is strictly enforced. Foreign travel
is limited to officials or trusted artists and performers.
Emigration is not allowed, and few refugees or defectors
succeed in fleeing the country. Retaliation reportedly is
taken against the relatives of those few persons who manage to
escape. According to Freedom House, "rights to travel
internally and externally are perhaps the most restricted in
the world; tourism is unknown--even to Communist countries."

In 1959 North Korea began actively encouraging Korean residents
overseas to repatriate to "the Fatherland." Some observers
estimate that during the next several years over 100,000
overseas Koreans, almost all from Japan, voluntarily
repatriated to North Korea. Since then, however, reports of
the harsh treatment given repatriates have reached overseas
Koreans, reducing the flow to North Korea to a trickle.
(Because of their "corruption" by exposure to foreign
influences, repatriates are isolated from North Korean society
after their arrival until they can be indoctrinated and their
ideological reliability gauged.)

North Korea has permitted entry to some overseas Korean
residents to visit their relatives, and several have made
repeat visits.

Section 3   Respect for Political Rights: The Right of Citizens
             to Change Their Government

The political system in North Korea is dominated by Kim Il Sung,
who leads the Korean Workers' Party, and also heads the
Government. Kim has groomed his son Kim Chong Il to succeed
him, and there are reports that Kim Chong Il has been acquiring
increasing power and influence. The legislature, the Supreme
People's Assembly, has never taken any action other than
unanimous passage of resolutions presented to it by the
leadership. In an effort to create an appearance of democracy,
North Korea has created several "minority parties." They exist
only as rosters of officials who have taken representation in
the People's Assembly and completely support the government line.

7 - 5

DEMOCRATIC PEOPLE'S REPUBLIC OF KOREA

Free elections do not exist in North Korea. Although elections to the Supreme People's Assembly were held in February 1982, and to city and county assemblies in March 1983, in all cases only one candidate was approved by the government party in each electoral district, and, according to the government-controlled media, 100 percent of the voters turned out to elect 100 percent of the approved candidates. Such "elections" in reality are a mandatory exercise in which voters are required to participate and to approve the party's candidates

Most citizens are completely excluded from any real participation in the political process. To achieve even a semblance of real participation, one must become a member of the Korean Worker's Party. The selection process for entrance to the party is long and rigorous. Individuals from "bad social backgrounds," i.e., those who have relatives who fled south during the Korean War, those whose families had strong religious involvement or were once property owners or members of the middle class, and those who have relatives who are political prisoners, effectively are denied entry into the party and are discriminated against. Most levels of the party have no voice, serving only to carry out the decrees and "on the spot guidance" promulgated by party leader Kim Il Sung and his top subordinates.

Section 4   Governmental Attitude Regarding International and
             Nongovernmental Investigation of Alleged Violations
             of Human Rights

No organizations exist within North Korea to report on or observe human rights violations. North Korea does not participate in any international or regional human rights organizations.

Amnesty International has requested a visit to North Korea; the Government has not responded to or acknowledged this request. A December 1982 request by Amnesty International for information on North Korean laws, on use of the death penalty, and on reports of arrests and long-term imprisonment of political figures also received no reply.

The Amnesty International 1985 Report noted that its work continued to be seriously impaired by the virtual absence of any official information during the year concerning any arrests, trials, or death sentences, that it continued to investigate reports that four prominent political figures had been detained for several years, and that it did not receive any replies to correspondence directed to the Government. Freedom House rates North Korea as "not free."

ECONOMIC, SOCIAL, AND CULTURAL SITUATION

The population of North Korea is estimated to be about 19.6 million, with an annual growth rate of 2.3 percent. It is a less-developed country that has a low standard of living by most measures. It has a highly centralized, planned economy, with a gross national product (GNP) of $23 billion (1984), or $1,175 per capita (1984 dollars).

Many observers believe that, after a short period of rapid growth in the early 1970's, the economy experienced difficulties due largely to policies that overemphasized military expenditures, stressed attainment of self-sufficiency, and pushed for rapid growth of heavy industry. During that period,

7-6

0096

DEMOCRATIC PEOPLE'S REPUBLIC OF KOREA

North Korea imported large quantities of industrial equipment from the West for which it was unable to pay. It remains in default to Western creditors on an estimated $1.5 billion. More than 20 percent of North Korea's GNP is committed to military expenditures, the second highest such rate in the world.

There have been recent signs of a shift in policy emphasis toward expanding trade. In September 1984 North Korea promulgated a joint venture law to attract foreign capital and technology. The apparent shift in economic policy was also suggested by North Korean willingness to discuss economic trade and cooperation with South Korea. North Korea's default on its foreign debt is in large measure responsible for scant foreign interest in joint ventures. The only such ventures North Korea has publicized involve a project with a French company to build a hotel in Pyongyang and one with overseas Koreans in Japan to build a department store that has recently opened in Pyongyang. The new emphasis on expanding trade has not produced any shift in internal economic priorities away from support of military industry. North Korea receives assistance from the Soviet Union and China, but actual levels are difficult to estimate.

The 1985 infant mortality rate was 30 per 1,000 live births. Life expectancy at birth was 65.6 years in 1985. North Korea appears to have invested considerable effort and money in developing a health care system. It includes care for nonworking-age citizens. Basic food supplies are heavily subsidized and rationed. The proportion of rice in the grain ration has been steadily reduced, with grains considered less desirable, such as millet or barley, being substituted. Reportedly because quality foods are difficult to obtain, jobs in food-handling industries are highly prized. Foreign visitors have noted that North Koreans appear adequately fed. The World Bank estimated in 1981 that the calorie supply available for consumption was 129 percent of nutritional requirements.

The party, government, and military elite enjoy significant economic privileges, such as access to special stores and medical facilities, better housing, and better education, which are not available to ordinary citizens.

The North Korean Government provides 11 years of compulsory free education to its citizens and claims to have eliminated illiteracy. The primary school enrollment ratios for 1975 were 96.3 percent for females and 101 percent for males, for a combined ratio of 98.5 percent.

There is no data available on minimum age for employment of children, minimum wages, maximum hours of work, or occupational safety and health.

The Constitution states that "women hold equal social status and rights with men." Few women have reached high levels of the party or the Government. Women are represented proportionally in the labor force, and personnel in small factories are predominantly women.

7-7

0097

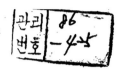

외 무 부
보 고 사 항

외 미북 700-60호

1986 . 2 . 15 .

수 신 : 대 통 령 각 하

제 목 : <u>1985년도 미국무성 인권보고서 발행</u>

다음과 같이 보고 합니다.

1. 미국무성은 2.13, 1985년도 각국 인권보고서를 발간 하였읍니다.

2. 국무성 인권국에서 작성된 보고서는 아국을 비롯한 세계각국의 인권상황을 국무성이 설정한 일정한 항목별로 기술하고 있는바, 동 보고서의 아국 및 북한 부분내용 및 전년도 보고서와의 차이점 등을 별첨과 같이 보고드립니다.

첨부 : 1. 상기 인권보고서 아국부분 내용 보고
2. 상기 인권보고서 북한부분 내용 보고.   끝.

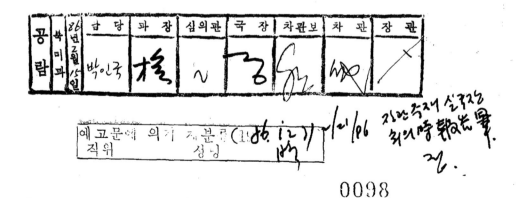

0098

1986.   2.

외   무   부

1. 주요 내용

가. 개 관

o 대통령이 정치를 장악하고 있으며, 국회는 제한된
힘만을 가지고 있으나 여론에 대해서는 상당한
영향력을 행사하고 있음.

o 역대 한국정부는 북한의 위협에 직면하여 국내외
안전문제를 최우선 과제로 삼고 있으며, 이를 이유로
반대파의 정치활동을 억압하고 있다는 비난받고 있음.

o 한국경제는 지난 20년간 1인당 국민소득이 20배나
성장함으로써 고도의 성장을 이룩하였으며, 이러한
경제성장의 결과 보다많은 정치적 자유를 원하는
중산계층을 증가시켰음.

o 한국인들은 경제, 종교 및 개인적 관심을 추구할수
있는 광범위한 자유를 누리고 있으나, 언론, 출판의
자유는 억압 당하고 있음.

o 최근 한국에서는 인권문제와 함께 '민주화' 문제가
일반 국민들의 가장 큰 관심사로 등장하고 있으며,
85.2.12 국회의원 선거는 한국 역사상 가장 민주적인
선거로 평가되고 있음.

o 85.3 김영삼, 김대중을 포함한 정치활동 피규제자
전원이 해금 되었으며, 김대중은 귀국 당시 가택
연금에서 해제되었음. 곧이어 학생 자치조직 허용

- 1 -

0100

및 대학내 경찰 철수등으로 1980년이후 최대의 학원
자율화 분위기가 조성되었음.

ο 그러나 5.23 미문화원 점거사건 이후 한국정부는 1984년
이전의 강경 정책으로 선회하였으며, 비판적 인사들과
언론인에 대해 고문과 물리적 협박을 가했다는 신뢰할수
있는 보고가 있음.

ο 85년도 가을학기 이후 학생 저항운동은 보다 과격해졌고, 85년말
현재 수감된 학생수는 1980년 이후 최대인 400명을 상회했음.

ο 반정부운동권 학생의 재교육 실시계획은 광범위한 반대에
부딪혀 철회되었음.

나. 개인의 기본권

　ο 정치적 살인

　　- 없음.

　ο 행방불명

　　- 없음.

　ο 고　문

　　- 헌법상 고문이 금지되어 있으나, 정부의 고문금지
　　조치에도 불구하고 1984년에 비해 고문 및 잔혹
　　행위가 크게 증가하고 있음.

　　- 반정부 운동 청년이 경찰에서 고문을 받았으며,
　　보도관제를 어겼다는 이유로 3명의 중진언론인이

- 2 -

0101

보안 요원으로 부터 감금과 구타를 당하였다는
신뢰할수 있는 보고가 있음.

- 비판적 인사들은 1985년 후반에 정부가 시위학생 및
반체제 인사에 대해 구타、 수면 박탈、 음식공급
중단、 전기쇼크、 물먹이기등 가혹행위를 하였다는
주장을 하고 있음.

- 85.2 대법원은 한 노파 살인사건에서 고문에 의한
자백을 인정하지 않고 피고인에게 무죄를 선고한바
있으며、 이로인해 국가는 보상금을 지불한바 있음.

○ 임의체포 및 구속
- 정치관련 사건에서 영장없이 체포하는 경우가 있음.
- 김대중등 반정부인사에 대한 가택연금이 늘어나고 있음.
- 1985년 후반 국가보안법에 의해 60여명이 구속되었음.
- 서준식등이 보호감호를 이유로 형기종료 이후에도
계속 수감중이며、 보호감호자 명단이 공개되지
않고 있음.

○ 공개재판 거부
- 사법부의 독립은 일반적으로 유지되고 있으나、 정치
적으로 민감한 사건의 경우 독립성이 감소되고 있음.

- 대법원장은 시위학생에 대해 관대한 판결을 내린
법관에 대한 인사처분과 관련、 야당과 대한 변호사
협회로부터 탄핵소추와 사임권고를 받았음.

- 3 -

0102

- 미문학원 점거사건등 정치적 사건에서 피고인의
  정치 및사상 성향을 검토하기 위한 피고인측의
  증언 출석요구가 묵살되었음.

- NCC 는 85.5 현재 약 100명의 정치범이 수감
  되었으나, 12월말에는 600명으로 증가되었으며
  그중 400명이상이 대학생인 것으로 보고하고 있음.

○ 개인의 사생활권 침해

- 야당인사 및 반정부 인사에 대한 감시, 도청 및
  가택연금 사례가 상존함.

- 미문학원 점거사건 이후 관련 학생가족들의
  미대사관 접근이 금지되었음.

- 거리에서의 검문, 검색이 강화되고 있고 사상과 관련한
  연좌제가 취업등에 영향을 미치고 있음.

다. 시민적 권리
  ○ 언론출판의 자유

- 1985.2 국회의원 선거시와 국회개원후 종래 타부시
  되던 사항에 대한 활발한 의견발표가 허용되었음.

- 그러나 5월이후 395종의 '좌경'서적 압수 사건을 비롯하여
  선동기사 게재 교사 면직, '좌경' 작가 전시회 해산등
  규제가 강화되었음.

- 4 -

0103

○ 집회 결사의 자유

- 미문학원 점거사건 이후 1923명의 학생이 연행
  되었고, 그 때 시위선동 혐의로 2명의 국회의원이
  기소됨.

- 정부의 노동정책을 비판한 노조간부가 면직되었음.

라. 정치적 권리

○ 85.2 국회의원 선거에서 야당이 29.2%의 득표율과
  102석을 차지 함으로써 한국의회 역사상 최대의
  야당으로 등장하였음.

○ 전대통령은 헌법규정에 따라 88년에 퇴진할것임을
  거듭 확약하고 있으며, 차기선거는 87년 후반부 또는
  88년 전반부에 거행될 예정임.

○ 85.3.6 정치활동 피규제자의 전면해금 조치가 있었
  으나, 김대중등 일부 야당인사는 아직 복권되지 않고
  있음.

마. 국제기구 또는 비정부 기구의 인권위반 사례조사에 대한
   정부입장

○ 한국은 국제인권단체에 가입치 않고 있으며, 외국 인권
  단체의 개입을 환영치 않음.

○ 국제사면위는 현상황하에서는 독립적인 활동이 불가
  하다는 이유로 한국지부를 잠정 폐쇄하였음.

- 5 -

0104

바. 경제, 사회, 문화정세

　　o 지난 20년간 20배의 경제성장에도 불구하고 절대 빈곤층이

　　　도시인구의 18%, 농촌인구의 11%를 차지하고 있음.

　　o 정부는 약 30만명의 월소득 100,000원 이하 저소득

　　　근로자에 대한 지위향상을 위해 노력하고 있음.

2. 84년도 보고서와의 차이점

　가. 1984년도 인권보고서는 학원자율화, 교수 및 언론인 복직,

　　　구 정치인에 대한 복권 및 정치해금등 적극적인 자유화

　　　조치가 있었고, 정치 관련범이 제 5공화국 이후 최저수준인

　　　110명 가량으로 감소되었음을 기술하는 등 아국 인권문제에

　　　대해 비교적 온건한 입장을 취한바 있음.

　나. 금번 85학년도 보고서에서도 85.2 실시된 국회의원 선거와

　　　이에따른 신민당의 출현을 한국 민주주의 역사에서 가장

　　　획기적인 사건중의 하나로 평가하면서 정치활동

　　　피규제자의 전면해금과 학원자율화 조치등 아국

　　　정부의 제반 자유화 조치에 대하여는 긍정적인 평가를 내리고

　　　내리고 있음.

　다. 그러나, 85.5 미문화원 점거사건이후 한국정부는 1984년

　　　이전의 강경정책으로 선회하였으며, 이에따른 수감자수가

　　　80년이후 최대에 달하고 있으며, 이 과정에서 고문 및

　　　가혹행위가 증대되고 있음을 새로운 변화로 특기하고 있음.

- 6 -

3. 검토 및 대책

가. 그간 당부는 85년도 인권보고서가 작년에 비해 나쁘게될
   가능성이 있다는 공관보고에 따라 전면해금 조치등 아국
   정부의 제반 민주화조치를 국무성측에 적극 설명하고 이의
   반영을 촉구한바 있음.

나. 국무성측은 아측입장에 대해 이해를 표시하면서도 국무성이
   해당년도에 일어난 일을 사실대로 의회에 보고해야하는
   의무가 있으며, 대외적으로 널리 알려진 신체적 가혹행위에
   관해서는 미국내 여론의 공격에 대해 미정부로서 이를
   방어하고 옹호할 형편에 있지 못함을 설명한바 있음.

다. 금번 국무성 인권보고서는 Kerry 결의안등 향후 미의회의
   아국 인권문제 논의시 기초자료로 활용될 가능성이 있음에
   비추어 관계부처와 동 보고서에 대한 면밀한 검토와 아울러
   향후 대책을 협의토록 함.

라. 금번 국무성 보고서는 Amnesty Int'l, Asia Watch
   및 Freedom House 등 아국 국내문제에 관심을 가지고
   있는 국제 민간 인권단체의 활동 및 보고에도 영향을
   받은것으로 짐작되는바, 동 민간인권단체의 대아국 관련
   활동에 대해서도 적절한 대책을 강구토록 함.

- 7 -

0106

1. 주요 내용

가. 개 관

o 북한은 엄격한 공산독재 국가로서 개인의 권리는
김일성 및 그의 가족 지배하에 있는 노동당에 철저히
종속되어 있음.

o 1982년 형식상의 최고 인민회의 선거가 있었으나,
후보자 선택의 자유가 없으면 자유선거가 존재하지
않음.

o 당의 지도노선에 협조하지 않는 주민들은 구금, 재산
압수, 유배를 겪어야 함.

o 김정일을 후계자로 만든 사실자체가 김일성이 지난
37년간 축적한 독재의 표현이 될것임.

o 자신의 생전에 한반도 통일을 달성하려는 김일성의
야망으로 인해 한국내 불안정을 주기적으로 획책하고
있음.

o 최근 북한은 남한과의 대화를 추구하고 있는데, 이는
경제, 국회, 스포츠 및 인도적 분야에서의 협력
가능성을 나타내는 것임. 85.9 양측은 전례없는
이산가족 상면을 주선하였음.

o 그러나 아직도 북한이 현재의 암담한 인권현실을
개선할 어떤조짐도 보이지 않고 있음.

- 8 -

0107

나. 개인적 기본권

　ㅇ 정치적 살해

　　- 북한내의 정치적 동기에 의한 살인에 관한
　　　정보는 없으나 랑군 폭발사건과 84·11·23 발생한
　　　비무장 지대에서의 총격사건은 북한의 태도를 잘
　　　나타내 주고 있음.

　ㅇ 행방불명

　　- 정보 부족

　ㅇ 고　문

　　- 금년도 Freedom House 보고서는 북한에서
　　　고문이 일상적인 일이라고 지적하였음.

　　- 푸에블로호 선원과 베네수엘라 시인의 경험담 인용

　ㅇ 임의체포

　　- 영장이나 유사한 제도가 없으며 자의적인 구금이나
　　　체포가 가능함.

　　- 북한에는 현재 약 105,000명의 사상범이 8개
　　　수용소에 수용되어 있는 것으로 추정됨.

　ㅇ 공개재판 거부

　　- 사법부는 전적으로 정부 통제하에 있음.

　ㅇ 가택 및 통신에 대한 무단침범

　　- 일반주민은 계속적으로 사상교육을 받아야 함.

　　- 북한으로 송환된 일본인 부인 일본방문 불허,
　　　서신교환 금지

- 9 -

0108

- 외국방송 청취 불허

- 개인주택 도청

다. 시민적 권리

   o 언론출판의 자유

   - 정부시책에 대한 지지를 제외하고는 언론,
     집회, 시위의 자유 불안정

   o 집회결사의 자유

   - 노동조합 및 각종 협회등은 주민에 대한 효과적인
     지배 및 통제의 수단으로 이용

   o 종교의 자유

   - 40년대 후반이후 지속적인 종교 박해

   - 종교기관이란 주민의 효과적인 통제 및
     대외선전용

   o 거주이전의 자유

   - 북한내의 여행 엄격 통제

라. 정치적 권리

   o 정치과정은 김일성 노동당의 독점물

   - 입법기관인 최고 인민회의는 지도부가 제출한
     법안을 만장일치로 통과시키는 역할만 수행

   o 자유선거는 없으며 선거구 별로 당이 지명한 인사가
     단독 출마

   - 노동 당원외에는 참정권 불안정

- 10 -

0109

마. 국제기구로 부터의 인권위반 비난에 대한 입장

  ○ Amnesty International의 북한 방문 요청 및
    각종 인권관련 자료 제공 요청에 무응답

  ○ Freedom House 금년도 보고서는 북한을 '자유가
    없는 국가'로 분류

바. 경제, 사회, 문화 정세

  ○ GNP 의 20%를 국방비에 지출함으로 써 세계 제 2위의
    국방비 지출 비율을 기록하였음.

  ○ 최근 합영법 발표등 대외무역 중시경향을 보이고
    있으며, 이는 남한과의 경제교류 희망태도 에서도
    나타나고 있음.

  ○ 그러나 새로운 대외 통상정책 추진에도 불구하고
    국방우선 정책에는 변화가 없음.

2. 84년도 보고서와의 차이점

  ○ 금번 보고서는 84년도 보고서와 대동소이한 내용이나
    북한의 남·북 대화 대응 차세를 비교적 긍정적인 것으로
    평가하고 85.9 이산가족 상봉을 그 구체적인 성과로
    간주하고 있음.

- 11 -

0110

기 안 용 지

분류기호 문서번호	미북 700-*145*	(전화 :)		시 행 상 특별취급		
보존기간	영구·준영구. 10. 5. 3. 1.		장		관	
수 신 처 보존기간						
시행일자	1986. 3. 10.					
보조기관	국 장	전결	협조기관		문 서 통 제	
	심의관	~				
	과 장	扎음				
기안책임자	이기철				발	

경유 수신 참조	법무부장관	발신명의	

제 목	1985년도 미국무성 인권보고서

　　1. 1985년도 미국무성 발간 인권보고서중 아국 및 북한

부분을 별첨과같이 송부하오니 동/보고서에 대한 귀부의 의견을

당부로 송부하여 주시기 바랍니다.

　　2. 아울러 동 보고서에 관해 당부가 작성한 대통령각하앞

보고서를 첨부하오니 참고하시기 바랍니다.

상담　86.12.7.1

　　첨 부 : 1. 상기 인권보고서 1부

　　　　　 2. 상기 대통령각하앞 보고서 1부.　　끝.

1505-25(2-1) 일(1)갑
85. 9. 9. 승인

0111

190mm×268mm 인쇄용지 2급 60g/㎡
가 40-41·1985. 10. 29.

미국 국무부의 한국 인권문제 보고서, 1985-87　471

DEMOCRATIC PEOPLE'S REPUBLIC OF KOREA*

The Democratic People's Republic of Korea, formed in 1948 during the Soviet administration of the northern half of the Korean peninsula, is a rigid Communist dictatorship, strictly dominated by one man, Kim Il Sung, and his family. Although some internationally respected human rights are acknowledged by the 1972 Constitution and laws, individual rights are entirely subordinated in practice to the ruling Korean Workers' (Communist) Party (KWP), with its overriding aim of imposing a social revolution and enforcing unanimous popular support for the country's governing system and its leaders. While there were proforma elections to the Supreme People's Assembly in February 1982, free elections do not exist in North Korea because citizens have no choice among candidates.

The North Korean people are subject to rigid controls. The State establishes security ratings for each person, and these ratings determine access to jobs, schools, medical facilities, and stores, as well as admission to the Korean Workers' Party, the route to the highest levels and privileges of the society. Persons who fail to cooperate face imprisonment, confiscation of property, or enforced removal to remote villages. Surveillance by informers is prevalent. Punishment for "political crimes" against the state is severe. Virtually no outside information other than that approved and disseminated by the North Korean authorities is allowed to reach the public. However, senior government officials seem to be somewhat better informed.

President Kim Il Sung's 12-year effort to groom his son, Kim Chong Il, as successor is testimony to the enormous power the elder Kim has amassed during 37 years of rule. The younger Kim was elevated to several senior party positions in 1980. The absence of any evidence of public debate about the succession is also indicative of the lack of real popular participation in the political process.

North Korea has not been successful through its command economy in producing the desired economic development. It remains a less-developed country with a low standard of living and a severe balance of payments problem.

Kim Il Sung's commitment to reunification on his own terms has led to periodic attempts to destabilize the Republic of Korea. More recently, North Korea has engaged in talks with South Korea. These have addressed possibilities for cooperation in the economic, parliamentary, sports, and humanitarian fields. This last area of discussion has focused on the plight of families separated during the postwar division of the peninsula.

*The United States does not have diplomatic relations with the Democratic People's Republic of Korea; even representatives of governments that do, as well as journalists and other occasional invited visitors to North Korea, are not permitted the freedom of movement that would enable them effectively to assess human rights conditions there. Nor does North Korea publish socioeconomic statistics. Most of this report, therefore, is a repeat of previous human rights reports based on information obtained over a period of time exter... from well before 1985. While limited in scope and detail information is indicative of the human rights situ... North Korea today.

JAPAN

Women comprise approximately 36 percent of the employed population. Social pressures discouraging involvement of women in positions of managerial and professional responsibility remain strong. Discrimination by private employers against women continues despite its prohibition by the Constitution and by legislative measures adopted over the past 30 years to accord women the same legal status as men. In a recent government survey, around 60 percent of responding corporations indicated they have job categories that exclude females, and more than 65 percent hire only men as executive recruits. Another recent survey indicated nearly 86 percent of women workers said they had no interest in management positions and preferred marriage and motherhood to careers.

In May 1985, the Diet passed the Equal Employment Opportunity Law which will take effect in April, 1986. This law prohibits discrimination based on sex in such areas as recruitment and hiring, pay inequality, and the number of night or overtime hours that can be worked. The law has been criticized, however, as containing no concrete measures, such as penalties for violators, to ensure equality for women workers.

In recent years the Government has enacted several laws and regulations extending to permanent resident aliens, 82 percent of whom are Koreans, the benefits of equal access to public housing and loans, social security pensions for those who otherwise qualify, and certain public employment rights. The Foreign Ministry now pronounces Korean names according to the Korean, rather than the Japanese, reading of name characters. The Government has also extended, until 1987, a Special Measures Law (first issued in 1969) designed to help assimilate Burakumin (descendants of Feudal Era "outcasts" who practiced so-called "unclean" professions such as hide tanning) into mainstream society through a number of social, economic, and legal programs. Nevertheless, entrenched social prejudice against both Koreans and Burakumin restricts the access of both groups to private housing, employment, and marriage opportunities. There is a growing conflict between alien residents, primarily Koreans (although some Americans are also involved), and the Government over the requirement that foreign residents be fingerprinted every five years. Korean rights activists have recently been arrested and fined for refusing to be fingerprinted. They argue that it harms the individual dignity of foreign residents (Japanese citizens are not routinely fingerprinted) and is in violation of the International Human Rights Covenant as well as the Equal Protection Article of the Japanese Constitution. The Government asserts that it is a reasonable way to confirm the identity of foreign residents and justified on the basis of public welfare.

DEMOCRATIC PEOPLE'S REPUBLIC OF KOREA

and the Korean War (1950-53). During September 20-23, 1985, both sides arranged historically unprecedented exchange visits by separated family members.

However, there is little evidence to suggest that North Korea has improved its dismal performance in the human rights area. Both short- and long-term trends indicate continued one-family rule with scant respect for basic human rights.

RESPECT FOR HUMAN RIGHTS

Section 1   Respect for the Integrity of the Person, Including Freedom from:

a.   Political Killing

No reliable information is available on politically motivated killing in North Korea. However, the North Korean attitude toward political killing was clearly demonstrated in the October 9, 1983, Rangoon bombing and the November 23, 1984, shooting in the Joint Security Area of the Demilitarized Zone (DMZ) dividing North and South Korea.

After a careful investigation, the Government of Burma determined that the Democratic People's Republic of Korea was responsible for the attempt to assassinate Republic of Korea President Chun Doo Hwan during his 1983 visit to Burma. Two North Korean army officers brought to trial in Rangoon were convicted and sentenced to death for the attack, in which four cabinet ministers and a number of officials were killed. In the DMZ incident, North Korean security guards opened fire on a Soviet student trying to defect from a tour group, triggering an exchange of fire in which several lives were lost.

b.   Disappearance

There is no information available on disappearance.

c.   Torture and Cruel, Inhuman, or Degrading Treatment or Punishment

According to the Freedom House 1984-85 report, "torture is reportedly common" in North Korea. The accounts of torture and beatings of crew members of the USS Pueblo after their capture in 1968 are well-known and documented. The only other reliable source on prison conditions and treatment of prisoners in North Korea is Venezuelan poet Ali Lameda, who was detained in North Korea from September 1967 through 1974, allegedly for attempted sabotage and espionage. While physical torture was routinely used on Mr. Lameda, he stated that Korean prisoners were routinely beaten. Lameda noted that "beating was also used as a means of persuasion during interrogation."

Lameda reported the use of deprivation of food to force "confessions," as well as solitary confinement, continuous interrogation, enforced waking periods, poor or nonexistent medical treatment, and 12 hours of forced labor per day. In addition, prisoners were denied family visits, parcels, correspondence, writing materials, newspapers, and clothing changes. Prisoners appeared to be regarded as persons without any rights.

DEMOCRATIC PEOPLE'S REPUBLIC OF KOREA

d.   Arbitrary Arrest, Detention, or Exile

Information on specific criminal justice procedures and practices in North Korea is extremely scarce. North Korea has refused to permit outside observation of its legal system and practices. The accounts provided by the crew members of the USS Pueblo and by Lameda, while clearly from an earlier period, comprise virtually all the specific information available on the operation of the criminal justice system in North Korea.

North Korean law states that no prisoner may be held for interrogation over 2 months. This period may be extended indefinitely, however, if the Interrogation Department obtains approval of the Chief Prosecutor. Lameda states that he was detained for 12 months without trial or charge. His request for a lawyer of his choice and an open trial were ridiculed as "bourgeois." Habeas corpus or its equivalent does not exist in law or practice.

According to newspaper reports, North Korean defectors in South Korea estimated in April 1982 that at least 105,000 "ideological offenders" were being held in eight major labor camps in the North. Amnesty International has received unconfirmed reports of arrests of those opposed to heir apparent Kim Chong Il.

There is no prohibition on the use of forced or compulsory labor. Information as to whether it is practiced is not available.

e.   Denial of Fair Public Trial

The North Korean Constitution states that courts are independent and that judicial proceedings are to be carried out in strict accordance with law. All courts, however, are responsible to the people's assemblies, which effectively means government control of the judiciary. Article 138 states that "cases are heard in public, and the accused is guaranteed the right to defense; hearings may be closed to the public as stipulated by law." Lameda claims that he was twice denied public trial. He reports that after his first arrest he was imprisoned for a year without a hearing; after his second arrest, he was put through a closed session without benefit of counsel of his choice or even knowledge of the charges. His trial was under the direction of the Ministry of Internal Security, with one person serving as both judge and prosecutor.

Lameda stated that, other than to admit guilt, he was refused the right to speak out or defend himself at his trial. His "defense counsel" represented him by making a lengthy speech praising Kim Il Sung and then requesting a 20-year sentence, which the tribunal imposed after 5 minutes of deliberation.

In a 1979 interview with American journalist John Wallach, North Korean Supreme Court Justice Li Chun Uk noted that the defense counsel's job is "to give the suspect due punishment." Open court appears to consist of an announcement of the term of imprisonment, which has already been determined by the Provincial Safety Bureau.

0113

c. Freedom of Religion

Although the Constitution guarantees that "citizens have religious liberty and the freedom of antireligious propaganda," North Korea, in fact, has severely persecuted Christians and Buddhists since the late 1940's. No churches have been rebuilt since the Korean War. The regime uses religious organizational facades to proclaim the practice of religious freedom but appears to have long since purged the membership out of existence. Persons whose family or relatives once had a strong religious involvement are discriminated against. Though religious practice appears impossible, some foreign visitors to North Korea believe that the Government does not currently persecute the very small number of Christians who continue to worship at home.

d. Freedom of Movement Within the Country, Foreign Travel, Emigration, and Repatriation

Internal travel in North Korea is strictly controlled. A travel pass is required for any movement outside one's home village and is granted only for required official or personal travel. This requirement is strictly enforced. Foreign travel is limited to officials or trusted artists and performers. Emigration is not allowed, and few refugees or defectors succeed in fleeing the country. Retaliation reportedly is taken against the relatives of those few persons who manage to escape. According to Freedom House, "rights to travel internally and externally are perhaps the most restricted in the world: tourism is unknown--even to Communist countries."

In 1959 North Korea began actively encouraging Korean residents overseas to repatriate to "the Fatherland." Some observers estimate that during the next several years over 100,000 overseas Koreans, almost all from Japan, voluntarily repatriated to North Korea. Since then, however, reports of the harsh treatment given repatriates have reached overseas Koreans, reducing the flow to North Korea to a trickle. (Because of their "corruption" by exposure to foreign influences, repatriates are isolated from North Korean society after their arrival until they can be indoctrinated and their ideological reliability gauged.)

North Korea has permitted entry to some overseas Korean residents to visit their relatives, and several have made repeat visits.

Section 3   Respect for Political Rights: The Right of Citizens to Change Their Government

The political system in North Korea is dominated by Kim Il Sung, who leads the Korean Workers' Party, and also heads the Government. Kim has groomed his son Kim Chong Il to succeed him, and there are reports that Kim Chong Il has been acquiring increasing power and influence. The legislature, the Supreme People's Assembly, has never taken any action other than unanimous passage of resolutions presented to it by the leadership. In an effort to create an appearance of democracy, North Korea has created several "minority parties." They exist only as rosters of officials who have token representation in the People's Assembly and completely support the government line.

---

f. Arbitrary Interference with Privacy, Family, Home, or Correspondence

The populace is subjected to regular indoctrination, designed to shape individual consciousness. Preschool children are drilled in homage to Kim Il Sung and his family, while youths and adults are required to participate in daily ideological training conducted by youth organizations or at places of employment. The propaganda requires rote recitation of party maxims and positions and strives for ideological purity. Multiple North Korean security organizations enforce these controls.

Reports, primarily from defectors, indicate that forced resettlement is common, particularly for those deemed politically unreliable. Permission to reside in, or even enter, Pyongyang, the capital, is strictly controlled.

According to reports in South Korean journals, Japanese wives of Koreans repatriated from Japan since 1959 have not been permitted to visit Japan and many have lost contact with their families because their letters are subject to strict censorship.

The Constitution states that "citizens are guaranteed the inviolability of person and residence and the privacy of correspondence." Lameda reported, however, that the privacy of his residence was not respected and that listening devices were used against him. He was arrested and his collected papers and poetry seized and destroyed without warrant.

Section 2   Respect for Civil Rights, Including:

a. Freedom of Speech and Press

The Constitution states that "citizens have the freedoms of speech, the press, assembly, association, and demonstration." In fact, North Koreans enjoy none of these rights. Such activities are permitted only in support of government objectives. Other articles of the Constitution that require citizens to follow the "socialist norms of life" and to obey a "collective spirit" take precedence over individual political or civil liberties. Foreign media are excluded, domestic media censorship is enforced, and no deviation from the official government line is tolerated. Listening to foreign media broadcasts is prohibited, and violators reportedly are subject to severe punishment. Most urban households have a radio and some have television, but reception is limited to domestic programming. Artistic and academic works are controlled by the Government, and visitors report that a primary function of plays, movies, operas, and books is to contribute to the cult of personality surrounding "the great leader," Kim Il Sung, and his son, "the beloved leader," Kim Chong Il.

b. Freedom of Peaceful Assembly and Association

The Government has developed a pervasive system of informers throughout the society. No public meetings can be held without government authorization. There appear to be no organizations other than those created by the Government.

Trade unions and professional associations appear to exist solely as another method of government control over their members. There are no effective rights to organize, bargain collectively, or strike.

DEMOCRATIC PEOPLE'S REPUBLIC OF KOREA

Free elections do not exist in North Korea. Although elections to the Supreme People's Assembly were held in February 1982, and to city and county assemblies in March 1983, in all cases only one candidate was approved by the government party in each electoral district, and, according to the government-controlled media, 100 percent of the voters turned out to elect 100 percent of the approved candidates. Such "elections" in reality are a mandatory exercise in which voters are required to participate and to approve the party's candidates.

Most citizens are completely excluded from any real participation in the political process. To achieve even a semblance of real participation, one must become a member of the Korean Worker's Party. The selection process for entrance to the party is long and rigorous. Individuals from "bad social backgrounds," i.e., those who have relatives who fled south during the Korean War, those whose families had strong religious involvement or were once property owners or members of the middle class, and those who have relatives who are political prisoners, effectively are denied entry into the party and are discriminated against. Most levels of the party have no voice, serving only to carry out the decrees and "on the spot guidance" promulgated by party leader Kim Il Sung and his top subordinates.

Section 4   Governmental Attitude Regarding International and Nongovernmental Investigation of Alleged Violations of Human Rights

No organizations exist within North Korea to report on or observe human rights violations. North Korea does not participate in any international or regional human rights organizations.

Amnesty International has requested a visit to North Korea; the Government has not responded to or acknowledged this request. A December 1982 request by Amnesty International for information on North Korean laws, on use of the death penalty, and on reports of arrests and long-term imprisonment of political figures also received no reply.

The Amnesty International 1985 Report noted that its work continued to be seriously impaired by the virtual absence of any official information during the year concerning any arrests, trials, or death sentences, that it continued to investigate reports that four prominent political figures had been detained for several years, and that it did not receive any replies to correspondence directed to the Government. Freedom House rates North Korea as "not free."

ECONOMIC, SOCIAL, AND CULTURAL SITUATION

The population of North Korea is estimated to be about 19.6 million, with an annual growth rate of 2.3 percent. It is a less-developed country that has a low standard of living by most measures. It has a highly centralized, planned economy, with a gross national product (GNP) of $23 billion (1984), or $1,175 per capita (1984 dollars).

Many observers believe that, after a short period of rapid growth in the early 1970's, the economy experienced difficulties due largely to policies that overemphasized military expenditures, stressed attainment of self-sufficiency, and pushed for rapid growth of heavy industry. During that period,

DEMOCRATIC PEOPLE'S REPUBLIC OF KOREA

North Korea imported large quantities of industrial equipment from the West for which it was unable to pay. It remains in default to Western creditors on an estimated $1.5 billion. More than 20 percent of North Korea's GNP is committed to military expenditures, the second highest such rate in the world.

There have been recent signs of a shift in policy emphasis toward expanding trade. In September 1984 North Korea promulgated a joint venture law to attract foreign capital and technology. The apparent shift in economic policy was also suggested by North Korean willingness to discuss economic trade and cooperation with South Korea. North Korea's default on its foreign debt is in large measure responsible for scant foreign interest in joint ventures. The only such ventures North Korea has publicized involve a project with a French company to build a hotel in Pyongyang and one with overseas Koreans in Japan to build a department store that has recently opened in Pyongyang. The new emphasis on expanding trade has not produced any shift in internal economic priorities away from support of military industry. North Korea receives assistance from the Soviet Union and China, but actual levels are difficult to estimate.

The 1985 infant mortality rate was 30 per 1,000 live births. Life expectancy at birth was 65.6 years in 1985. North Korea appears to have invested considerable effort and money in developing a health care system. It includes care for nonworking-age citizens. Basic food supplies are heavily subsidized and rationed. The proportion of rice in the grain ration has been steadily reduced, with grains considered less desirable, such as millet or barley, being substituted. Reportedly because quality foods are difficult to obtain, jobs in food-handling industries are highly prized. Foreign visitors have noted that North Koreans appear adequately fed. The World Bank estimated in 1981 that the calorie supply available for consumption was 129 percent of nutritional requirements.

The party, government, and military elite enjoy significant economic privileges, such as access to special stores and medical facilities, better housing, and better education, which are not available to ordinary citizens.

The North Korean Government provides 11 years of compulsory free education to its citizens and claims to have eliminated illiteracy. The primary school enrollment ratios for 1976 were 96.3 percent for females and 101 percent for males, for a combined ratio of 98.5 percent.

There is no data available on minimum age for employment of children, minimum wages, maximum hours of work, or occupational safety and health.

The Constitution states that "women hold equal social status and rights with men." Few women have reached high levels of the party or the Government. Women are represented proportionally in the labor force, and personnel in small factories are predominantly women.

President Chun Doo Hwan dominates the political scene in the Republic of Korea. The elected legislature has limited power but considerable influence on public opinion. President Chun, a former army general, assumed power with military support in 1980, at which time martial law was declared and civil disturbances in Kwangju were harshly confronted. The new Constitution was adopted by referendum in October 1980 under strict martial law conditions, leading many Koreans to question the referendum's fairness. At the time of the next presidential election, in late 1987 or early 1988, President Chun has promised to step down to provide for a peaceful and constitutional change of power.

Korea's traditional sociopolitical ideology, Confucianism, emphasizes order and conformity, as well as a subordinate role for women. This thinking retains great strength, coexisting uneasily with Western democratic ideals.

Citing this tradition and faced with a heavily armed Communist North Korea that once invaded the South and that remains extremely hostile to it, successive South Korean governments have given top priority to maintaining external and internal security, implemented in part by the large and well-organized security forces. Many Koreans have charged throughout the years that the very real threat from the North was also used as a pretext to suppress internal opposition politics, despite the democratic ideals professed by all South Korean leaders.

Koreans enjoy considerable personal freedom, including economic and religious freedom and broad rights to pursue private interests. Although the Constitution guarantees freedom of speech and press, in practice both are abridged.

During the past 20 years, Korea's export-oriented, mixed economy has achieved one of the world's highest growth rates and a twentyfold increase in per capita gross national product (GNP). The population is urbanized and well educated. Abject poverty has been largely eliminated. The rapid growth of the economy has created a growing middle class with increasing access to education and wealth. They have joined with other groups to become a strong voice for fuller political participation and greater freedom to express political views.

Human rights issues, as well as "democratization" issues were the focus of greater public discussion and debate than in recent years. There was some progress in the human rights field in the early months of 1985, continuing the trend of 1984. The National Assembly election held on February 12 was widely regarded as among the most democratic in the Republic's history, with candidates freely criticizing the Government at large rallies. Press coverage was frank and lively. The election resulted in a new party, supported by leading opposition politicians, becoming the largest opposition party in the Assembly since the Republic's founding.

In March a statutory political ban originally applied to 567 politicians was lifted on the remaining 14 persons affected, including prominent dissident leaders Kim Young Sam and Kim Dae Jung. (The political activities of Kim Dae Jung and some other politicians remained restricted, however, by other legal provisions.) At the same time, Kim Dae Jung was freed from the house arrest imposed on him on his return to Korea one month earlier. Nine political prisoners were released in an amnesty on May 27. Under the Government's "campus autonomy" policy,

the formation of independent student councils was permitted and police stayed off campus as students began the most active semester of student protest since 1980.

The Government soon responded heavily to the newly assertive opposition and the increased student activism, initiating a new wave of repression of dissent. Political tension remained high throughout the remainder of the year. On several occasions journalists were detained for writing politically sensitive articles. There were credible reports of torture or physical intimidation of several journalists and dissidents. After the May 23-26 student sit-in at the U.S. Information Service library in Seoul, the Government returned to its pre-1984 practice of arresting and trying student protest leaders, and police entered campuses readily to stop demonstrations. During the fall semester, student protests became increasingly violent. The Government reacted by arresting some or all of those involved in the more violent protests, raising the number of students in prison at the end of the year to over 400, the largest number since 1980. The Government announced that it was considering a plan to send activist students to 6-month-long ideological reeducation centers, but it backed off because of widespread opposition.

RESPECT FOR HUMAN RIGHTS

Section 1 Respect for the Integrity of the Person, Including Freedom from:

a. Political Killing

There were no reports of politically motivated killings in 1985.

b. Disappearance

There were no reports of disappearances in 1985.

c. Torture and Cruel, Inhuman, or Degrading Treatment or Punishment

Reports of torture or cruel treatment in 1985 increased significantly over 1984. The Constitution prohibits torture, and the Government insists that it has issued injunctions against it and that these are strictly enforced and violations sternly punished. Nonetheless, there were credible reports of torture, such as that of an antigovernment youth activist who was subjected to torture while under police detention in September, and reliable reports of three senior Korean journalists who were detained and beaten by security officials for breaking a government embargo on a news story. Korean human rights groups and political opposition leaders also made plausible charges that a number of students and other prisoners in politically related cases were subjected to various degrees of physical maltreatment including beatings, sleep and food deprivation, electric shock, and forced water intake during police interrogations in the latter half of 1985. The Government publicly denied that any of these prisoners had been mistreated.

On February 26, 1985, the Supreme Court upheld a lower court's acquittal of a woman whose conviction for murder had been based on a confession which she later said had been made as a result of police torture. She was awarded the equivalent of about $29,500 in compensation from the State. Court sources say some

0116

cases were prosecuted in 1985 under a law adopted by the National Assembly in 1983 increasing sentences for those convicted of killing or injuring through torture.

The use of excessive force by the police has proven to be a pervasive and ingrained problem, despite some high-level efforts to reduce or eliminate it. Rioters have been beaten on apprehension, often by plainclothes police. Charges of police beatings in nonpolitical cases occur fairly frequently and are sometimes reported in the press. There were reports in 1985 that police were using a stronger form of tear gas to break up student and other unauthorized demonstrations which caused skin blisters on those who came into direct contact with it.

Conditions in Korean correctional institutions are austere, especially in winter as cells are not heated. Discipline is strict. Under normal circumstances, convicts are not subjected to physical punishment, but prisoners who break rules or protest conditions are sometimes beaten. There were reports that 19 political prisoners transferred to Taegu Prison in July were beaten severely when they protested overcrowded conditions.

Prisoners may receive visits only from their lawyers and immediate families. Their mail is monitored and sometimes censored. There does not seem to be a difference between the treatment of political and non-political prisoners.

d. Arbitrary Arrest, Detention, or Exile

Arrest warrants are required by law but are sometimes not produced at the time of arrest in politically related cases. In 1985 the Supreme Court ruled that police may not detain persons for more than 48 hours without arrest warrants. An indictment must be issued within 30 days after arrest. Within 40 days after making an arrest, the police must notify an arrested person's family of his detention and whereabouts. The police normally wait at least several days, and occasionally more than 40 days, before making notification. The Constitution guarantees the right of prompt legal assistance and the right to request court review in case of arrest.

Habeas corpus, not traditional in Korean law, was introduced after World War II, abolished in the 1970's, and reintroduced in 1980. It does not apply to those charged with violations of the National Security Act or laws punishable by at least 5 years' imprisonment, which includes most politically related offenses. There is a system of bail, but it does not apply to offenses punishable by 10 or more years' imprisonment. In 1985 the Government adopted a new policy to compensate persons held for questioning but who are subsequently found to be innocent by prosecutors.

Dissidents who openly criticize the Government are sometimes picked up and detained for short periods and then released. There were several instances in 1985 of journalists who had written politically sensitive articles being detained for short periods, usually overnight, by security forces.

From time to time, the security services have not only detained persons accused of violating laws on political dissent but have also increased surveillance of, or put under various forms of house arrest, those they think, intend to violate the laws. In the longest continuous application of such restrictions in 1985, opposition politician Kim Dae Jung was not permitted to

leave his home for about 1 month after his return to Korea from the United States in February 1985. Kim and others were also confined to their homes on several other occasions for briefer periods. In the latter half of 1985 the Government arrested and charged with National Security Law violations about 80 students and other Koreans associated with student and youth organizations the Government characterized as pro-Communist and/or pro-North Korean; about 60 of these had been convicted or remained under detention awaiting trial at the end of 1985. Government critics claim that, in many of these cases, the National Security Law was misused to suppress domestic, particularly student, dissent.

For persons deemed "socially dangerous," the law allows preventive detention under provisions of the Social Protection and Social Stability Laws. Neither provision affords the accused the benefit of legal counsel or appeal. Under the Social Protection Law, a judicial panel may order preventive detention for a fixed term of 2 years, which can be extended by the panel for additional 2-year periods. The Social Stability Law allows for a preventive detention term of 7 to 10 years. In the city of Chongju there exists a "preventive custody center" where prisoners judged to be insufficiently repentant are held following the completion of their original prison sentences. Son Joon Shik, whose original 7-year sentence ran out in 1978, is one of two political prisoners believed to be held in this facility. The Government has not released figures on the total number of persons under preventive detention.

There were no reports in 1985 of forced labor as defined by the International Labor Organization (ILO).

e. Denial of Fair Public Trial

The Constitution guarantees many rights to defendants: The right to presumption of innocence, the right against self-incrimination, freedom from ex-post facto laws and double jeopardy, the right to a speedy trial, and the right to legal counsel. These rights are generally observed. Trials, with some exceptions, must be held within 6 months of arrest. In Seoul, trials usually begin within a month after indictment.

The President appoints the members of the Supreme Court, whose Chief Justice in turn appoints lower-level judges. The Chief Justice serves a 5-year term. The judiciary is considered independent in ordinary criminal and civil cases but much less so in politically sensitive cases. In 1985 the Chief Justice was criticized in opposition and legal circles for transferring several judges to less desirable positions, allegedly because they had ruled in favor of defendants in cases involving student protesters or had complained about the treatment of their colleagues who were accused of being too lenient toward student defendants. The Korean Bar Association called for the Chief Justice's resignation; an impeachment sponsored by the opposition was voted down in the National Assembly.

In several politically sensitive trials in 1985, as in the trial of students who seized the U.S. Information Service (USIS) Library in May, public attendance was limited, and defendants sometimes were removed from the courtroom for attempting to disrupt the proceedings by shouting slogans and singing. Judges generally allowed great scope for examination of witnesses by both prosecution and defense, but they often denied defense requests to call witnesses to discuss the homes without warrants. During politically sensitive periods, the police and security force presence in city centers and near university campuses is very heavy. Citizens, particularly students, are frequently stopped, questioned, and searched.

Traditional Korean police practice requires police commanders to know a good deal about the personal and business affairs of all residents in their jurisdictions. This system is effective in crime control, and urban residents generally credit it with keeping their streets safe. By contrast, the presence of police informer networks on college campuses with the primary purpose of keeping track of political activities has been a key complaint among students, including those who are not politically active.

In most other respects the Government honors the right of personal privacy and the integrity of the home and family. Parental rights to educate children are broad, and restrictions on study in foreign-administered schools (whether in Korea or overseas), originally imposed to force wealthy Koreans to involve themselves in the nation's social and educational development, have been relaxed in recent years. The State rarely seeks to intervene in such inherently personal decisions as marriage, choice of vocation, and formation of social and familial ties. However, persons thought to have politically suspect backgrounds are denied some forms of employment and advancement, particularly in government, press, and education. In 1985, Korean newspapers reported that a number of teachers and college graduates had been denied jobs in public schools solely because of their past involvement in student protest activities.

Section 2 Respect for Civil Rights, Including:

a. Freedom of Speech and Press

Although freedom of speech and press are guaranteed by the Constitution, in practice the expression of opposition viewpoints is limited, sometimes severely. Government critics say that laws such as the Basic Press Law, under which media organizations are licensed and permitted to operate, and criminal code provisions against the spreading of "rumors which eventually disturb peace and order" and "defiling the state" are used to muzzle and punish dissident views. Opposition political parties have called for the repeal or reform of the Basic Press Law.

During the February 1985 National Assembly election campaign, opposition candidates made speeches before large crowds in which they were highly critical of the Government. Most Korean and foreign observers alike agreed the campaign was characterized by the most outspoken political debate permitted in the Republic of Korea in many years. Print media coverage was extensive, although television reporting reflected much more government influence. When the new National Assembly was inaugurated, it continued to be characterized by a breaking of old taboos on speaking out on sensitive political topics, including thinly-veiled challenges to the Government's legitimacy stemming from the serious civil disturbance in Kwangju in 1980, policy toward South-North Korean dialogue, and constitutional revision, all of which received print media coverage. The government party, concerned about increasingly sharp opposition criticism, sought with limited success to precensor opposition politicians' remarks. After several

political or ideological leanings of the defendants, even when the prosecution had introduced evidence on such topics.

Trials are usually open to the public, but trial documents are not part of the public record. Charges against defendants in the courts are clearly stated, with the exception that, in lengthy and complex indictments, the relationship between specific acts alleged and violations of specific sections of the penal code may not always be clearly drawn. In cases involving a mixture of political and criminal charges this can bring into question the fairness of the proceedings. The same courts try political and ordinary criminal cases. The military courts do not try civilians. Defendants have the right of appeal in felony cases, a right which is often exercised and frequently results in substantial reductions in sentences. Death sentences are automatically appealed. The list of political prisoners maintained by the Human Rights Committee (HRC) of the National Council of Churches hovered around 100 names throughout the first 5 months of 1985. The list grew to around 700 names by November as the Government continued its crackdown on activist students begun in the aftermath of the USIS Library seizure, but the number had dropped to around 600 by the end of December. The HRC includes on its list persons indicted but not yet tried for politically-related offenses as well as those already convicted; this list contains the names of some persons who have advocated or used violence. The Minister of Justice reported to the National Assembly in October 1985 that there are no prisoners of conscience in the Republic of Korea.

Of the 600 names on the HRC list, more than 400 are university students. About 30 people on the HRC's list were charged with illegal labor actions; several were farmers charged with illegal assembly and demonstration. The list also includes 40 or so persons, many of whom were Korean residents in Japan, accused of espionage for North Korea.

Not included in the HRC political prisoner list are students and others briefly detained but not indicted in connection with student and labor demonstrations during 1985. According to government statistics, between May and October police referred over 1,000 students to summary court where they were charged with minor offenses, and sentenced to a maximum of 29 days' detention. Some students receiving summary judgments chose to exercise their right to formal trials.

f. Arbitrary Interference with Privacy, Family, Home, or Correspondence

Many political and religious dissidents are subjected to surveillance by the security forces. During politically sensitive periods, this surveillance by one or more security agencies may increase or a form of house arrest may be imposed. There have also been charges of telephone tapping and opening or interception of correspondence. Koreans who meet with foreigners, particularly with journalists and foreign diplomats, are sometimes questioned afterwards. In the aftermath of the seizure by students of the USIS library in May, police tried to stop relatives of the students involved and others from meeting U.S. Embassy officials.

While the Constitution requires a warrant issued by a judge upon request of prosecutor for search and seizure in a residence, the police at times force their way into private

opposition politicians complained of government intimidation when they or their aides were summoned for questioning about critical remarks made on the Assembly floor, the Government promised it would respect Assemblymen's rights to free speech. Details of the most critical speeches were generally not reported in the press, and government party speeches received heavier coverage. Nonetheless, newspapers did report in greater detail than in many years about opposition views on previously taboo political subjects.

The domestic media engage in self-censorship, according to verbal or written guidelines the Government regularly gives to editors. Journalists who object to or ignore these guidelines or criticize the guidance system have been picked up for questioning and on occasion dismissed or sent out of the country on assignment; in one case in 1985 journalists were beaten. Nonetheless, the domestic media, notably newspapers and magazines, became noticeably more outspoken during and in the aftermath of the February National Assembly election. An edition of a prestigious monthly magazine carrying an article on the 1980 civil disturbances in Kwangju was confiscated by the Government shortly after its publication, and the article's author was interrogated by security officials. In late 1985 about 30 reporters, mostly from provincial papers, were fired for corruption on orders from the Ministry of Culture and Information. There were reports that at least some were in fact fired for holding views critical of the Government. In December a visiting U.S. Washington Times journalist was ordered out of the country temporarily, reportedly for writing an article on an alleged meeting between North and South Korean leaders.

The early months of 1985 saw the publication of an increasing number of books and magazines by dissident religious, political, and cultural figures. In May police confiscated books they considered dangerous on the grounds of being "leftist" or "encouraging revolution." According to the Minister of Culture and Information, in October 11,000 copies of 395 books were confiscated.

Twenty teachers who contributed to a magazine criticizing the Government's education policy were arrested or fired, and the magazine's publishing company was closed under the Basic Press Law. The Basic Press Law was also used against a student charged with editing a "seditious" publication; at least seven other students were charged with National Security Law violations in connection with publications said to be "sympathetic to Communism and serving the interests of the enemy." In July police raided an art exhibition and jailed five artists for a week, saying the paintings and prints there were objectionable on ideological grounds. A Christian youth activist received a suspended sentence for "defiling the state" by distributing dissident leaflets to foreign journalists.

Academic freedom is subject to some political limitations. In fall 1985 a group of professors who signed a petition opposing the proposed campus stabilization law came under official pressure to retract their views.

b. Freedom of Peaceful Assembly and Association

A number of specified categories of assembly, including those considered likely to undermine public order or cause social unrest, are prohibited by the Law on Assembly and

Demonstrations. The law also requires that demonstrations of all types and outdoor political assemblies be reported in advance to the police. Violation of the law carries a maximum sentence of 7 years' imprisonment or a fine of about $3,750. Under this law, police have at times intervened and broken up meetings. Most peaceful nonpolitical assemblies take place entirely without official supervision or restriction. However, meetings of dissidents are monitored and sometimes prevented, often by placing the scheduled speaker under some form of house arrest.

The Law on Assembly and Demonstrations was most often used in 1985 against student demonstrators. According to a government report submitted to the National Assembly in late October, a total of 1,923 students had been taken to police stations for involvement in demonstrations on and off campus since the May USIS Library seizure. Of that number, 309 were charged with violating the Law on Assembly and Demonstrations and/or laws punishing violent acts. Another 104 were booked without physical detention. About 1,000 were summarily tried on minor charges, and the remainder were released with warnings.

In September two opposition National Assemblymen and several other oppositionists were indicted under the Law on Assembly and Demonstration after they were stopped by police for shouting protest slogans against the Government at the gates of a Seoul campus on the day of a scheduled protest meeting. In October the lawyers for some of the students charged under the Law on Assembly and Demonstration requested a review by the Constitution Committee of the legitimacy part of the law, asserting that the vagueness of one clause rendered it unconstitutional. The Supreme Court ruled against the claim, stating that the right to assembly and protest is limited.

Under the Constitution, workers are guaranteed the right to independent association, to bargain collectively, and to collective action. These rights are circumscribed by law and practice and do not extend to workers employed by the Government, public utilities, defense-related industries, or firms "that exercise great influence on the national economy." In the past the last category has applied primarily to heavy industry.

The single national labor federation, the Federation of Korean Trade Unions (FKTU), and its 16 national affiliate unions are not controlled by the Government, but their activities are limited by law and subject to government interference. In 1985, five ranking FKTU officials were forced to resign under government pressure, reportedly because they were either held responsible for or did not agree with the Government's tough policy on recent labor disputes. Labor organizations are forbidden by law to support politicians or political parties, though the FKTU does lobby National Assemblymen, and Assemblymen often attend labor gatherings.

According to the FKTU, after an increase in 1984, dues-paying union membership in 1985 remained at about 800,000 workers, about 10 percent of the full-time work force. Ministry of Labor figures, based on reports submitted by individual unions, place total union membership at slightly over 1 million.

Some FKTU-supported revisions to labor regulations, approved in 1985, permitted a larger role for the Federation in local

0119

affairs. The FKTU continued to press for broader revision of the labor law, as did the main opposition party.

The FKTU is affiliated with the International Confederation of Free Trade Unions, and its constituent unions are affiliated with recognized international trade union federations. The Republic of Korea has observer status at the International Labor Organization.

All local unions must be organized within individual enterprises, creating a structure of thousands of individual unions, most of them small and weak. Direct participation in local unions' bargaining activities by outside agencies is forbidden. The FKTU and its constituent national unions can and sometimes do bargain on behalf of the locals and conduct education programs, but only with government and employer approval. Religious labor ministries such as the Catholic Young Christian Workers and the Protestant Urban Industrial Mission are also severely limited in the assistance which they can provide the unions. Under these circumstances, government and employer influence has greatly exceeded that of unions in setting wages and resolving other major labor issues.

Collective actions and strikes, though technically legal, are strongly discouraged. The Government used the Law on Assembly and Demonstration on a number of occasions in connection with workers' and farmers' rallies. Despite the legal restrictions and other obstacles, collective actions by workers, including strikes, increased in 1985. The Government charged radical student involvement in many of the disputes, saying it had identified at least 277 "disguised workers" through the end of September who had hidden their university credentials in order to "infiltrate" the workforce and "instigate" the workers to strike. Of these, 160 were fired by their employers, 97 "voluntarily" quit their jobs, and 20 are still working. In a few strikes, groups of nonstriking workers wielded pipes and stormed their workplaces to end worker sit-in's forcibly. They were not prevented by police from doing so, and many Koreans charged that the attacks were government-sponsored.

According to government statistics, the government committee charged with investigating unfair labor practices heard 227 cases in the first eight months of 1985, 205 of which involved problems with union organization and alleged employer obstructionism. The committee decided in favor of the workers in 64 cases.

c. Freedom of Religion

There is no state-favored religion in Korea. There is generally complete freedom of proselytizing, doctrinal teaching, and conversion. Korea both sends and receives missionaries of various faiths. Many religious groups in Korea maintain active links with coreligionists in other countries. Minority sects are not discriminated against, and adherence to a faith confers neither advantages nor disadvantages in civil, military, or official life. Churches and religious groups are subject to many of the restrictions on political activity and criticism of the Government that apply to all other institutions. On those occasions where pastors are harassed by the authorities, it is usually for religiously motivated social or political activism. One Protestant minister active in human rights issues has made plausible charges that a government security agency has sponsored efforts to disrupt his church

services; other ministers have joined with him to protest what they term government infringement on religious freedom. The Government denied the charges and says the church's troubles are an internal problem. Conscientious objectors are subject to arrest.

d. Freedom of Movement Within the Country, Foreign Travel, Emigration, and Repatriation

There is almost universal freedom of movement and freedom to change employment in Korea. Because Korea is one of the most densely populated countries in the world, the Government does not discourage emigration or discriminate against prospective emigrants. Most people can obtain passports, except for criminals and some persons considered politically suspect. A number of dissidents, former political prisoners, and persons banned from political activity have been allowed to travel abroad. The Government limits the number of passports issued to tourists and prospective students, citing foreign exchange considerations and the problem of unqualified students going abroad. Passports, when issued, are typically limited to 1 year, although there are exceptions in which passports are issued up to the legally maximum 5-year period of validity.

A small continuing influx of Vietnamese boat refugees is admitted to first asylum in Korea. They are cared for at a camp in Pusan by the Korean Red Cross until they can be resettled abroad. Over 700 displaced persons from Vietnam have passed through Korea in the last several years. Very few have been permanently resettled in Korea.

Section 3   Respect for Political Rights: The Right of Citizens to Change Their Government

Korea's Constitution and statutes, as well as its traditions, concentrate political power in the President, a concentration further intensified by the support the President enjoys from the military. The President and the members of the National Assembly are the only elected officials in Korea. Under the 1980 Presidential Election Law, the President is chosen by a popularly elected electoral college of at least 5,000 members. By law, presidential campaigns are brief and candidates severely restricted in campaigning, including the amount they may spend, the number of speeches they may deliver, and the number of publications they may distribute. In the 1981 presidential election these restrictions, together with the authorities' screening of electoral college candidates, resulted in the absence of effective opposition to incumbent President Chun Doo Hwan, who won nearly unanimously. In the 1985 National Assembly election, two of the most prominent opposition politicians, Kim Dae Jung and Kim Young Sam, were not allowed to participate.

The Constitution limits the President to a single 7-year term and may not be amended to allow the incumbent President to run for another term. The next presidential election will be held in late 1987 or early 1988. President Chun continued to reaffirm throughout 1985 that he intends to step down in 1988 to provide for a peaceful and constitutional transfer of power. His party, the Democratic Justice Party (DJP), has announced that it will convene in early 1987 to choose a presidential candidate. However, the main opposition party and most dissident groups are calling for a revision of the Constitution to allow for direct popular election of the president, contending that it would be less susceptible to government manipulation than the current system.

The National Assembly, although institutionally weak, acquired new importance in 1985 with the holding of elections and the emergence of a new, more outspoken opposition party. Members are directly elected and serve a 4-year term. The election law passed in 1981 provides for a proportional representation system that reserves 92 of the Assembly's 276 seats for members designated by the parties, with two-thirds of those seats awarded to the party gaining a plurality of the popular vote. The government party faced a strong challenge in the February 1985 Assembly election from a new opposition party, the New Korea Democratic Party (NKDP), formed only weeks before the election and led largely by politicians recently freed from the political ban. The government party, the Democratic Justice Party (DJP), garnered a plurality of 35.3 percent and, with its proportional representation seats, maintained a comfortable majority of 148 out of 276 Assembly seats. However, the NKDP obtained a surprising 29.2 percent of the popular vote. The former main opposition party, the Democratic Korea Party (DKP), received only 19.5 percent. Almost all of its members defected to the NKDP after the elections, boosting the NKDP's Assembly seats to 102 and making it the largest opposition party in the Republic's parliamentary history in terms of Assembly seats held. The campaign included outspoken criticism of the Government and its leaders by the opposition at large rallies and calls for constitutional revision to allow for direct presidential elections. Voter turnout was 84 percent, the highest since 1958. Press coverage was extensive, television less so.

In the aftermath of the election, the DJP pledged to practice the politics of "dialogue" and to "reflect the people's wishes as expressed in the election." The NKDP took a more aggressive stance than that adopted by other opposition parties since 1980, taking the Government to task on sensitive issues including the handling of the 1980 civil disturbances in Kwangju and constitutional reform.

On March 6, 1985, the Government lifted the political ban on the 14 people still affected by it. However, several persons, including prominent opposition figure Kim Dae Jung, although freed from the political ban, were still prohibited from joining a political party or running for office because they were under suspended sentences from prior convictions.

Women are free to vote, become government officials, and run for the National Assembly. Women hold seven Assembly seats, all but two appointed by their parties. In practice, however, the power structure remains male-dominated, and in many significant respects the legal system and social custom strongly discriminate against women. There is some pressure to address women's rights; in recognition of this, the ruling party has formed an ad hoc committee to study the issue.

Section 4 Governmental Attitude Regarding International and Nongovernmental Investigation of Alleged Violations of Human Rights

The Republic of Korea does not belong to any international human rights bodies and usually does not welcome outside involvement in the human rights area, although government officials have allowed the visits of and met with

representatives of international human rights bodies, including Amnesty International and Asia Watch. Prison authorities rebuffed attempts by human rights groups and opposition politicians to investigate conditions in prisons.

There are no government agencies charged with the protection of human rights, although political parties and the National Assembly have committees which are concerned with oversight of some aspects of the issue. In March 1985 opposition party leaders held up the convening of the National Assembly to negotiate the release of prisoners convicted on political and security charges. While the negotiations did not result in the release of many prisoners, they did represent the most open discussion of the issue in several years and received extensive press coverage in Korea. The autumn session of the National Assembly saw opposition interpellation of government ministers on human rights issues including torture and arbitrary arrest. Although the Government rejected calls for a special Assembly committee to investigate human rights abuses, especially torture, the opposition party and other opposition groups dispatched investigative teams, held press conferences, formed special committees, and provided legal defense in connection with numerous human rights issues.

A number of politically nonaffiliated private organizations have long been active in human rights, chiefly the Human Rights Committee of the Korean National Council of Churches, the Catholic Justice and Peace Committee, and the Korea Legal Aid Center in Seoul. The Committees and other human rights organizations submit petitions to the Government and make their views known both inside and outside Korea. People working with these groups are frequently questioned and sometimes detained by the security services, though apparently none have been arrested in the past several years. Amnesty International temporarily closed its office in Seoul in 1985, over the objections of its Korean chapter, on the grounds that the group's independent activities were not possible under present conditions. In its 1985 Report, Amnesty International remained concerned about the imprisonment of people for peaceful expression of their views. While it welcomed the release in the early part of 1984 of over 200 students, it was concerned about an increase in the use of short-term detention for people participating in public protests and about several well-known critics of the Government being placed under house arrest. It noted that it had received fewer reports of torture during interrogation, but that there were numerous reports of police violence against demonstrators both before and after arrest. Freedom House rated South Korea "partly free."

ECONOMIC, SOCIAL, AND CULTURAL SITUATION

The Republic of Korea's population in 1985 was 42.6 million. Over the last 20 years the population growth rate has decreased from 2.6 to 1.5 percent, due in part to concerted efforts by the Government to encourage voluntary family planning. During the past 20 years, Korea's export-oriented, mixed economy has achieved one of the highest growth rates in the world, with per capita GNP rising from $100 in 1965 to $2,010 in 1983. A notable feature of this rapid growth has been the relative evenness of income distribution, though many Koreans characterize the gap between rich and poor as worsening. The percentage of the population below absolute poverty was estimated to be 18 percent in urban areas and 11 percent in rural areas. There is no economic discrimination based on race or religion. The right to own property, both alone and in association with others, is recognized in law and practice.

Improved health care and nutrition have increased life expectancy to 68.2 years, while infant mortality has declined to 29.6 per 1,000 live births. In 1980, an estimated 78 percent of the population had access to safe drinking water, and caloric supply per person was 126 percent of minimum nutritional requirements.

Education is highly valued in Korean society. Ninety-six percent of the population was estimated to be literate in 1980-82. Primary school education is universal for both sexes, and over 90 percent of elementary school students enter secondary school. About 34 percent of all high school graduates pass competitive entrance exams and enter college. There is great social mobility based on merit in education and employment.

Chapter V of the Labor Standards Law governs the employment of minor and female workers. Under this provision, minors under age 13 must have a special permit issued by the Ministry of Labor to be employed. Minors under age 18 must have a parent's or guardian's written approval in order to work, and they are prohibited from night work without special permission from the Ministry of Labor. The law requires that employers of 30 or more minors provide educational facilities or arrange scholarship funds for them. Employment of minors is widespread, particularly in family-operated enterprises and in some labor-intensive industries, and abuses of legal protections are common.

The Constitution states that the Government "shall endeavor to promote the employment of workers and to guarantee optimum wages through social and economic means." Standards of working conditions are to be "determined by law in such a way as to guarantee human dignity." The Labor Standards Law provides for a maximum workweek of 60 hours with mutual consent of employer and employee, a paid day of rest during the workweek, compensation for overtime and holiday work, paid holidays, and annual leave. There are no exceptions to working conditions standards for industries established in export-processing zones. Recent statistics indicate that the average full-time worker spends 54.4 hours per week on the job. Korea has no minimum wage system, but the Government has pledged to institute one as part of the 5-year economic plan beginning in 1987. Meanwhile, the Government is attempting to persuade the employers of the 300,000 workers earning less than 100,000 won ($112) per month to raise wages. The Government announced in late 1985 that its efforts had resulted in a decrease of 112,000 workers in the below 100,000 won per month category.

Responding to a series of labor disputes highlighting criticism of its labor policy, the Government promised in 1985 to use stronger measures, including fines and imprisonment, to curb employer abuses such as delayed wage payments, illegal firings, and violations of regulations on working conditions. The Minister of Labor reported in late 1985 that 24 employers were arrested in the first half of 1985 for failure to pay wages and for physical abuse of employees. During that period, the Government reported uncovering 16,000 cases of employer wrongdoing, including nearly 2,500 cases of non-payment of wages, about 150 cases of unfair dismissal, and 40 violations of safety and health standards.

In the first half of 1985, 685 job-related deaths and 64,000 injuries were reported by government sources. In 1984 there were 1,667 deaths and 156,133 injuries reported in connection with industrial accidents. A government study cited lack of adequate safety precautions as a major cause of industrial casualties in about 10 percent of all cases. The Government has mandated insurance to cover industrial accidents at places of business employing 10 or more workers. The 1981 revision of the Industrial Accident Compensation Law covers job-related medical costs, sick leave benefits, disability benefits, and other costs.

Women's rights constitute a problem area. Some progress has been made—the family law was revised in 1960 and 1979—but critics contend that the law is still inconsistent with Korean constitutional guarantees of sexual equality. Women do not have equal rights with men in passing nationality to their children, nor do they have equal rights with regard to child custody in divorce cases. Women's rights groups are campaigning for changes in these and some other points of the family law.

Women do enjoy full access to educational opportunities. They are increasingly represented, though still largely at entry levels, in the military, the police, and in private industry. Other areas are more problematic. As of 1985, only 24 women had ever passed the bar examination. Five had passed the National Administration Examination, given for higher level civil service jobs. In general, women are not protected against discrimination in hiring, pay, or advancement. Some members of the National Assembly, however, are trying to focus more attention on women's rights.

```
U.S.OVERSEAS -LOANS AND GRANTS- OBLIGATIONS AND LOAN AUTHORIZATIONS
                  (U.S.FISCAL YEARS - MILLIONS OF DOLLARS)

COUNTRY: KOREA, REPUBLIC OF

                           1983      1984      1985
-----------------------------------------------------
I.ECON. ASSIST.-TOTAL...    0.0       0.0       0.0
   LOANS................    0.0       0.0       0.0
   GRANTS...............    0.0       0.0       0.0
  A.AID ................    0.0       0.0       0.0
   LOANS................    0.0       0.0       0.0
   GRANTS...............    0.0       0.0       0.0
  (SEC.SUPP.ASSIST.)....    0.0       0.0       0.0
  B.FOOD FOR PEACE......    0.0       0.0       0.0
   LOANS................    0.0       0.0       0.0
   GRANTS...............    0.0       0.0       0.0
  TITLE I-TOTAL.........    0.0       0.0       0.0
   REPAY. IN $-LOANS....    0.0       0.0       0.0
   PAY. IN FOR. CURR....    0.0       0.0       0.0
  TITLE II-TOTAL........    0.0       0.0       0.0
   E.RELIEF.EC.DEV & WFP    0.0       0.0       0.0
   VOL.RELIEF AGENCY....    0.0       0.0       0.0
  C.OTHER ECON. ASSIST..    0.0       0.0       0.0
   LOANS................    0.0       0.0       0.0
   GRANTS...............    0.0       0.0       0.0
   PEACE CORPS.........    0.0       0.0       0.0
   NARCOTICS...........    0.0       0.0       0.0
   OTHER..............    0.0       0.0       0.0
II.MIL. ASSIST.-TOTAL...  186.7     231.8     231.9
   LOANS................  185.0     230.0     230.0
   GRANTS...............    1.7       1.8       1.9
  A.MAP GRANTS.........    0.0       0.0       0.0
  B.CREDIT FINANCING....  185.0     230.0     230.0
  C.INTL MIL.ED.TRNG....    1.7       1.8       1.9
  D.TRAN-EXCESS STOCK...    0.0       0.0       0.0
  E.OTHER GRANTS.......    0.0       0.0       0.0
III.TOTAL ECON. & MIL...  186.7     231.8     231.9
   LOANS................  185.0     230.0     230.0
   GRANTS...............    1.7       1.8       1.9
-----------------------------------------------------
OTHER US LOANS.........    9.0       0.0       0.0
   EX-IM BANK LOANS.....    9.0       0.0       0.0
   ALL OTHER..........    0.0       0.0       0.0
-----------------------------------------------------
ASSISTANCE FROM INTERNATIONAL AGENCIES
                1983      1984      1985    1946-85
TOTAL......    242.4     977.5     697.2    8093.4
IBRD           672.0     768.5     556.5    5825.3
IFC              2.2      34.6       7.2     171.4
IDA              0.0       0.0       0.0     106.9
IDB              0.0       0.0       0.0       0.0
ADB            265.5     172.8     134.0    1938.3
AFDB             0.0       0.0       0.0       0.0
UNDP             2.7       1.6       0.0      36.1
OTHER-UN         0.0       0.0       0.0      15.4
EEC              0.0       0.0       0.0       0.0
```

The Lao People's Democratic Republic (LPDR) is ruled by a Communist Government established in December 1975 after an insurgency of 20 years supported by North Vietnam. The sole political party, the Lao People's Revolutionary Party, takes its political ideology from Marx, Lenin, and Ho Chi Minh. It is dependent on Vietnamese and Soviet military and economic support to retain power. Laos' approximately 3.6 million ethnically diverse people, scattered over more than 91,000 square miles of rugged terrain, have no common national history and share few common traditions. National institutions remain weak. There is no constitution or codified body of law. No national elections have been held since the establishment of the regime.

The Government's insecurity and efforts to establish a Communist political and economic structure based on the Soviet and Vietnamese models have resulted in numerous human rights violations. Regional and domestic political tension, scattered anti-government resistance activity, and poor economic conditions continue, contributing to a siege mentality on the part of the narrowly-based Lao leadership. The Government is faced with a number of resistance groups which field as many as several thousand fighters seeking its overthrow. The approximately 50,000 Vietnamese troops in Laos regularly conduct operations with the Lao People's Army (LPA) against resistance groups and serve as the ultimate guarantor of the Government's survival. The state security apparatus, which reinforces central control through threats, fear, intimidation, and imprisonment, is a primary source of human rights abuses. Its power over the lives of Lao citizens is legally unrestricted.

Laos is an extremely poor and underdeveloped country. Although Laos apparently met its food needs with a successful 1984/85 crop year, nutritional levels remain barely adequate. Most large businesses were nationalized after 1975 and efforts during 1985 to reduce further the scope of private trade have disrupted supplies.

Human rights violations continued in 1985, and the individual remained subject to the arbitrary control of the state and the Communist Party. Compared with the period just after the Communist takeover, there have been a few limited improvements in the human rights situation since 1983. In 1985, few people were apparently sent to "re-education camps," some were released, and the conditions of some who remain under detention reportedly improved. However, serious abuses such as arbitrary arrests and detention without trial still exist. Government pressures against private economic activity increased. The totalitarian nature of the regime is mitigated somewhat by the importance of humane values in traditional Lao culture.

RESPECT FOR HUMAN RIGHTS

Section 1 Respect for the Integrity of the Person, Including Freedom from:

a. Political Killing

Refugee reports continued in 1985 of villagers, particularly Hmong tribespeople, being killed or made ill by government and/or Vietnamese forces using toxic weapons. However, such

0123

산리 번호 86 -252

법 무 부

검삼 700-85   503-7055   1986. 3. 28.

수신 외무부장관
참조 미주국장
제목 1985년도 미국무성 인권보고서에 대한의견

　　귀부 미북 700-745 (86. 3. 10.) 와 관련, 1985년도 미국무성 인권
보고서에 대한 당부의 의견을 별첨과 같이 송부합니다.

첨부 미국무성 한국관계 인권보고서에 대한 반박자료 1부. 끝.

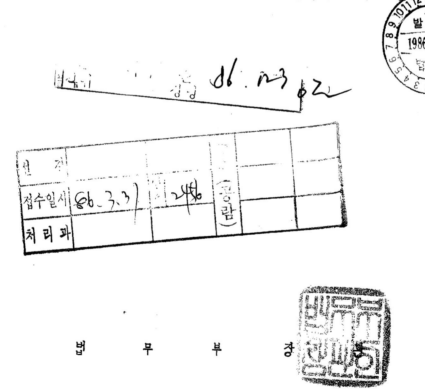

법 무 부 장

0124

미국무성 한국관계 인권보고서에 대한 반박자료

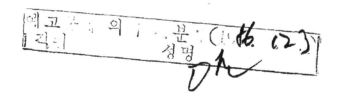

0125

I. 개인의 기본권

o 고문.기타 가혹행위

> '85년 후반에 시위학생 및 반체제 인사에 대해
> 구타, 수면박탈, 음식공급 중단, 전기쇼크, 물먹이기등
> 가혹행위를 했다는 주장에 관하여

o 간혹 수사기관에서 불법구금, 고문등 가혹행위를
   당하였다고 주장하는 사례가 없지 않았음.

o 그러나 이는 당사자 또는 그 가족등이 형사책임을
   면해 보거나 또는 국내외의 여론을 오도하여
   정치적으로 악용하려는 의도하에 왜곡, 과장전파
   시킨 것이 대부분임.

o 또한 그러한 경우에도 공판과정에서 허위주장임이
   입증되어 모두 유죄판결을 받고 있음.

0126

'85. 7경 대구고도소로 이감된 19명의 정치범이
수용시설이 복잡함을 항의했다는 이유로 심하게
구타당했다는 주장에 관하여

o 당시 대구고도소에 이감된 정진관등은 일부 인권
   단체에서 주장하는 것과 같이 정치범이 아니라
   좌익사상을 포지하고 현 정부의 전복을 기도하는등
   실정법을 위반하여 유죄판결이 확정된 자들임.

o 또한 그 시경 고도관이 동 고도소의 수용사정관계로
   방을 옮길 것을 지시하자 동인을 포함한 일부 수감자
   등이 이에 불복, 고도관에게 식기와 오물을 던지는등
   집단난동을 부렸음.

o 직원들이 이를 진압하는 과정에서 동인이 스스로
   복도에 뒹굴며 턱을 복도 바닥에 부딪쳐 가벼운
   찰과상을 입은 것일 뿐 고도관으로부터 구타당하였다는
   주장은 전혁 근거없음.

0127

o   자의적 연행 및 구금등

> 체포후 40일 이내에 가족에게 구금사실과 장소등을
> 알리도록 되어 있으나, 그 기간을 경과하는 경우가
> 간혹 있다는 주장에 관하여

o   형사소송법상 피의자를 구속할 때에는 구속한
    날로부터 40일이 아닌 3일이내에 변호인 또는
    가족등 변호인 선임권자에게 구속일시, 장소와
    변호인을 선임할 수 있는 취지를 서면으로 알리도록
    규정되어 있으며,

o   그 기간내에 통지가 제대로 이루어지고 있음.

0128

> 반정부 인사들이 정부를 비방했다는 이유로 연행되어
> 단기구금 되었다가 석방되곤 한다는 주장에 관하여

o 반정부 인사들이 단지 정부를 비방하였다는 이유로
   수사당국이 그들을 연행 또는 구금한 사실은 전혀 없음.

o 다만 그들은 경범죄처벌법등 실정법을 위반하여
   법관에 의한 즉결심판으로 구류형을 선고받고
   그 형이 집행된 자들임.

> '85 후반기에 60여명이 국가보안법위반으로 판결을
> 받거나 재판중에 있는등 국가보안법 적용이 남용되고
> 있다는 주장에 관하여

o 외국의 일부 인권단체에는 간혹 우리나라의 몇몇
   국가보안법위반사건 수감자등을 소위 양심범이나
   정치범으로 간주하는 듯한 일이 없지 않으나,

0129

○ 그들은 남북이 대치된 우리 현실하에서 북괴의
지령을 받아 간첩활동을 하거나, 우리 자유민주주의
체제를 전복하려는 목적하에 반국가 단체를 구성하여
암암리에 활동하는 등으로 반국가 단체를 이롭게
하는 행위를 한 좌익사범이 대부분이고,

○ 그밖에 우방의 문화기관, 기타 공공건물을 점거하여
파괴, 방화를 하고 인명을 살상하는등 중대 범법자
들이라는 점을 이해하지 못한데서 기인하는 것이라
하겠음.

0130

사회적으로 위험하다고 간주되는 자에 대하여
사회보호법 또는 사회안전법에 의거 2년 또는 7년,
10년의 감호결정을 할 수 있고 변호인의 조력을 받을
권리와 불복할 권리가 인정되지 않는다는 주장에
관하여

○ 사회보호법은 고질적 상습범과 정신질환 범법자로
부터 사회를 보호하고 그들을 교화, 치료하기 위하여
제정된 법률로서, 동 법률에 의거 법원의 판결로써
재범의 위험성이 있는 상습범에 대하여는 7년 또는
10년, 정신질환 범법자에 대하여는 그 완치시까지
감호결정을 할 수 있음.

○ 사회보호법에 의한 보호감호 결정은 법원의 재판을
통해 이루어지므로 변호인의 조력을 받을 권리 및
상소권이 인정되고,

0131

o 사회안전법에 의한 보안감호 결정도 행정소송의

   대상이 되므로 이에 불복시 행정소송을 제기할 수

   있고 변호인의 조력을 받을 권리도 당연히 인정됨.

.0132

o 공정하고 공개된 재판을 받을 권리의 불인정

┌───┐
│   │
│ 미문화원 난입점거사건과 관련하여 부당하게 방청권을   │
│   │
│ 제한하였다는 주장에 관하여   │
│   │
└───┘

o 법정은 그 수용규모에 한계가 있어 방청하고자
   하는 자가 과다한 경우 법정의 공간적 제약으로 인해
   법원이 부득이 방청권을 발행하는 경우가 있음.

o 또한 법원조직법 제51조 제2항은 재판장은 법정의
   존엄과 질서를 해할 우려가 있는 자의 입정을 금지
   또는 퇴정을 명하며 기타 법정의 질서유지에 필요한
   명령을 발할 수 있다고 규정하고 있는 바,

o 공판시 피고인들이 법정에서 반정부 구호를 외치면서
   재판을 거부하였을 때 방청객이 이에 가담하여
   난동행위를 하여 인정신문조차 못하고 연기되는등
   법정의 질서를 유지할 수 없어 재판부로서는 법정질서

0133

유지를 위해 부득이 일부 방청을 제한한 사례가

한 두번 있었으나 이 경우에도 피고인 개개인의

가족방청은 허용하였던 것으로 그들의 공개재판을

받을 권리를 부당하게 제한한 것은 아님.

0134

> 정치적인 사건의 경우 법원의 독립성이 보장되어 있지
> 않으며, 피고인의 증거신청을 일방적으로 받아들이지
> 않는다는 주장에 관하여

o   정치적인 사건의 경우에도 일반사건과 마찬가지로
    법관은 양심과 법률에 따라 판결을 할 수 있도록
    제도적으로 보장되어 있음.

o   간혹 재판을 자기들의 구호주장이나 정치적 투쟁
    수단으로 악용하거나, 기소내용과는 전혀 관계가
    없는 사실에 관한 증거신청등으로 재판을 지연시키려는
    사례가 있어 재판부에서 이를 받아들이지 않는
    것일 뿐, 피고인의 방어권을 제한하려는 것은
    결코 아님.

0135

o   개인의 사생활권 침해

야당인사.반정부인사에 대한 감시.도청 및 가택연금
사례가 상존한다는 주장에 관하여

---

o   일부에서 주장하는 바와 같이 치안당국이 특정인사를
    물리적으로 가택에 연금하거나 하는 사례는 없음.

o   다만 범법행위가 자행될 것이 명백히 예상되어 사전
    예방조치가 필요하거나 특정인의 신변을 보호해야 할
    급박한 사정이 있을 경우에는 관계법규에 따라
    치안당국에 그 가택주변을 보호하는 일은 있을 수
    있음.

o   그러한 경우에도 반드시 사전에 본인의 양해를
    구하며 범죄나 위해야기에 관계없는 외부인사들의
    출입은 자유스럽게 이루어 지도록 주의를 기울이고
    있음.

0136

Ⅱ. 시민권

○ 집회 및 결사의 자유

┌───┐
│   │
│ 파업시 파업을 반대하는 근로자들이 정부의 사주를   │
│ 받고 파이프를 휘두르며 농성현장에 처들어가 파업   │
│ 중이던 근로자를 집단폭행 했다는 주장에 관하여   │
│   │
└───┘

○ 일부 사건의 경우 그러한 주장이 있었으나,
   수사결과, 그 당시 폭행을 가한 근로자들은
   노사분규 발생시 회사나 근로자와는 아무런
   관계없는 제3자가 노사분규에 개입하는데 격분한
   나머지 범행에 이르게 된 것일 뿐, 정부나 회사의
   사주를 받았다는 주장은 전혀 근거없는 것으로
   판명되었음.

0137

o   종교의 자유

정부내 정보기관에서 인권관계 활동에 적극 참여하고
있는 계신교 목사의 교회에 대한 분규를 조장하고
있다는 주장에 관하여

o   동 교회에서는 수년전부터 일부 신도들간의
    내부적인 불만으로 상호 분규가 있어 왔던 것으로,

o   정부내 정보기관이 이를 조장하고 있다는 주장은
    전혀 근거가 없는 것임.

0138

Ⅲ. 국제적 민간단체의 인권조사에 관한 한국정부의 입장

한국정부는 국제인권단체에 가입치 않고 있으며 외국 인권단체의 개입을 환영치 않고 있다는 보고서 내용에 관하여

---

o 현재 한국정부는 국제인권규약 가운데 **A**규약 및 **B**규약중 일부 국내법과 저촉되는 부분을 제외한 나머지 모두에 대하여 가입하기로 방침을 정하고 그 동의안을 국회에 제출하고 있음.

o 동 규약은 유엔인권선언의 이념을 구체화 하기 위한 것으로서 단순한 가입문제 보다는 이를 얼마나 충실히 준수하는가가 더 중요하다고 생각함.

o 또한 한국정부는 평소 인권상황의 개선을 위해 부단한 노력을 하고 있는 만큼, 세계 각국의 인권 향상을 위해 어느 외국 인권단체와도 기꺼이 공동 협력을 할 준비가 되어 있음.

0139

> 인권보호의 책무를 맡고 있는 정부내 기관이 없다는
> 보고서 내용에 관하여

o 검사는 공익의 대표자로서 인권옹호에 관한
   직무수행을 하고 있음.

o 검사는 불법구속의 유무를 조사하기 위하여
   매월 1회이상 경찰서의 유치장소를 감찰하여야
   할 뿐 아니라, (형사소송법 제 198조의 2)

o 이러한 검사의 인권옹호 직무를 방해하는 자에
   대하여는 5년이하의 징역에 처하도록 규정하고
   있음. (형법 제139조)

o 또한 법무부내에 인권옹호사업의 종합계획을
   수립하고, 인권침해 사례에 대한 조사등 업무를
   담당하는 인권과라는 별개의 부서를 두고 있음.

0140

기 안 용 지

분류기호 문서번호	미북 700- 1148	(전화 :)	시 행 상 특별취급	
보존기간	영구·준영구. 10. 5. 3. 1.	장 관		
수 신 처 보존기간				
시행일자	1986.4.3.			

보 조 기 관	국 장	전결	협 조 기 관		문	
	심의관	_N_				
	과 장					
기안책임자		이기철			발 송 인	

경 유 수 신 참 조	주미대사	발 신 명 의	북미과

제 목	미국무성 인권보고서에 대한 의견 송부

대 : 미국(정) 700-0505 (86.2.14)

대호   미국무성 인권 보고서중 한국관련 부분에

대한 법무부의 의견을 별첨 송부하니 업무에 참고하시기 바랍니다.

첨 부 : 동 의견서 사본 1부.   끝.

검 토 필 (1986.12.기)

성 명

1505 - 25 (2 - 1) 일 (1)갑
85. 9. 9. 승인

0141

190mm×268mm 인쇄용지 2급 60g /㎡
가 40 - 41 · 1985. 10. 29.

미국 국무부의 한국 인권문제 보고서, 1985-87   501

85년도 미국무성 한국관계 인권보고서에 대한 법무부의 반박자료

I. 개인의 기본권

○ 고문, 기타 가혹행위 - 정치적 악용을 위해 사실을 <u>왜곡,</u>
<u>과장</u> 전파한것

○ 자의적 연행, 구금 - 명백한 실정법의 위반행위에 한함

적법연행, 구금

○ 공정하고 공개된 재판을 받을권리 불인정

- 방청 희망인이 과다한 경우 방청권 발행 가능

- 법정질서 해할 우려가 있는자, 입정금지가능

(법조법 51조 2항)

○ 반정부인사에 대한 감시, 도청, 가택연금

- 범법행위가 명백히 예상될 경우에 가택주변 보호

II. 시민권

○ 정부의 사주를 받은 근로자의 농성 근로자에 대한 폭행

- 자발적인 행위로 정부와는 무관

○ 정부가 개신교 교회 분규조장 - 교회의 내부적인 문제로
정부와는 무관

III. 기   타

○ 인권단체 가입문제 - 현재 진행중   0142

○ 인권보호를 담당하는 정부기관 부재 - 검사가 하고있음.

3. 1987 (1986년도)

0143

외 무 부   착 신 전 보

번 호 : USW-5704   일 시 : 8612181729   종 별 :

수 신 : 장관(미북,정이)

발 신 : 주미대사

제 목 : 국무성 인권 보고서

연 : USW-1584,2784

1. 86 년도 국무성 인권보고서 발간계획과 관련, 국무성 인권과와 접촉 타악한바,
ROBERT RACKMALES 인권과장 및 THOMAS MURPHY 동아태담당관은 아래요지르 금년
도 보고서에 관해 언급하였음

가. 86년도 보고서는 85년도 보고서와 전체적인 구성은 유사하나 전반적으로는 한국
의 인권상황이 진전되고 있다는 어조를 띄게될것임

나. 특히 대통령각하의 단임의지 재천명과 여야간의 헌정문제 대화 개시가 전반적
인 정치상황을 호전시키고있다는점과, 데모진압 경찰이 무력수단을 가능한 자제크자
노력하고 있다는 점이 보고서에서 지적될것임

다. 금년도 인권보고서 작성에 있어 그간 한국대사의 SCHIFTER 인권차관보와의
면담을 통한 의견교화내용(연호 참조), 박수길 제1차관보 (86.11. SCHIFTER 차관
보)등 한국정부 인사들의 국무성 방문시 설명등이 이해의 폭을 넓히는데 도움이 되었
음

2. 국무성은 금년도 보고서중 북한 인권상황과 관련, 그간 아측의 자료협즈는 물론,
신상옥,최은희와 직접인터뷰를 통해 상세정브를 입수하므로써 전년도 보다 구체적이
고 현장감이 있는 보고가 될것이라고 하면서, 남.북한 인권 상화이 커다란 대즈를 이
루게 될것이라고할

3. 86년도 보고서는 87.1.31 의회에 제출되어, 2월증순 공개발간될 예정이라함
(대사 김경원)

의거 재분류(19 .
예고 : 87.12성명일반

미주국   차관실   1차보   정문국   정와대   총리실   안기

PAGE 1   86.12.19 09:55
                                                외신 2과 통제관

0144

외 무 부 착 신 전 문

번 호 : USW-0691   일 시 : 702131644   종 별 : 조

수 신 : 장관(미북,김경원주미대사)

발 신 : 주미대사대리

제 목 : 하원 인권소위 수석전문위원 접촉

당관 장재룡 참사관은 금 2.12. MARK TAVLARIDES 하원 외무위 인권소위 수석전
문위원을 오찬에 초청,인권 소위내 아국 관련 동향을 탐문하고 최근 국내정국 움직임
등에 관하여 설명한바 동 내용을 아래 보고함.

1. TAVLARIDES 보좌관은 인권소위가 2.19(목) SHIFTER 국무성 인권담당차관보를
출석시켜 국무성 인권보고서와 관련한 청문회를 개최할예정이라고 밝힘.동 청문회에
서 YATRON 인권 및 국제기구 소위원장은 이란,칠레,쏘련,엘살바돌의 인권 문제를
언급할것이며 한국문제는 거론하지 않을예정이나, 여타의원이 한국문제를 제기할 가능
성은 배제할수 없다함.

2. 한편 인권소위는 아태소위와 합동으로 한국의 인권문제에 관한 청문회를 4월경 개
최할 예정이라함.이와관련 장참사 관은 최근 정부의 인권보호를 위한 적극적 조치내
용을 상세히 설명한바,동 보좌관은 청문회가 균형된 입장을 취하도록 자기로서는 최
선을 다할것을 약속함.동 보좌관은 대학생 사망사건후 정부가 취한 즉각적인 조치들
을 매우 긍정적으로 평가함.

3. YATRON 소위원장은 또한 올림픽에 관한 청문회를 금년 가을 경 개최할것을 검
토중에 있다함.동 청문회는 올림픽의 발전에 관한 전반적 사항을 다루게될것이나 서
울 올림픽의 성공적 개최에 관한 내용도 포함 될것이라함.

4. 장참사관은 북한의 금강산 댐 건설이 아국 안보에 미칠 영향등에 관하여 설명하고,
YATRON 위원장등 한국의 친구들이 적절한 방법으로 북한의 댐 건설을 규탄하는
방안에 대하여 의견교환함.이에 대해 동 보좌관은 긍정적 반응을 보이면서 구체적 내
용을 계속 협의 하자고 말함. (공사 한택채)

미주국 차관실 1 차보 정문국 청와대 총리실 안기 대사

외 무 부   착 신 전 문

번 호 : USW-0694   일 시 : 702131741   종 별 :

수 신 : 장관(미북,김경원 주미대사)

발 신 : 주 미 대사대리

제 목 : 국무성 인권 보고서

연: USW-5704

1. 국무성 인권과에 의하면 금년도 국무성 각국 인권보고서는 2.19(목) 발표될 예정이라함.

2. THOMAS MURPHY 동아태 담당관은 금년도 아국관계 보고서는 아국인권 상황의 변화에 대해 오전 또는 악화등 전체적인 상황 설명을 하지않고 주로 사례를 열거하는 형식으로 작성되었다함.

3. 동 담당관에 의하면 금년 보고서중 대통령각하의 평화적 정권교체의지,경제사회,종교등 분 야에서의 언론 상황진전을 긍정적인 부분으로 들수 있고, 부정적인 측면으로 반정부 인사들에 대한 강경조치,학생운동의 극렬화, TV 및 라디오 방송의 통제계속 등이 지적되고 있다하며 박종철사건은 금번 보고서에서 언급되지 않았다함.

4. 국무성은 2.19. 발표이전 관계국 주재 미국대사관으로 하여금 주재국 측에 금년도 보고서 내용을 사전 설명토록하였다함.

(공사 한탁채)

예고:87.제 분류(19

성명

미주국   차관실   1차보   정보국   청와대   총리실   안기   대사

 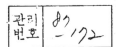

외 무 부 착신전문

번 호 : USW-0742   일 시 : 702172214   종 별 :

수 신 : 장관(미북,김경원주미대사)

발 신 : 주 미 대사대리

제 목 : 국무성 인권보고서

연 : USW-694

2.19(목) 의회에서 발표된 86년도 각국인권보고서를 입수한바, 이중 한국관계(15 페이지) 및 북한관계(7 페이지) 부분 주요내용은 다음과 같으며, 텍스트는 발표당일 훼시 송부하겠음.

1. 한국관계 부분

가. 대통령 각하의 평화적 정권교체를 위한 의지, 여론형성에 있어 국회의 상당한 영향력

나. 한국의 안보상황과 국내정치와의 연관성

다. 경제, 종교적 자유를 포함한 개인의 자유신장

라. 급속한 경제발전과 상응하는 정치적 욕구상승

마. 헌법개정을 위요한 여야간 대립과 협상교착 상태

바. 학생운동의 극렬, 폭력화 및 정부의 강경조치

사. 경찰고문, 임의구속 및 연행, 공개공정 재판, 언론자유, 집회결사의 자유, 노동권문제등 각 문제별 설명

2. 북한관계부분

가. 북한 공산당 지배에 의한 완전통제 사회

나. 당에 대한 개인의 충성도에 의해 계급화, 상층개급의 특권 향유

다. 정치범에 대한 가혹한 처벌

라. 외부정보의 완전차단

마. 김일성의 38 년간 통치로 세습체제 구축시도

- -
미주국   차관실   1 차보   정문국   청와대   총리실   안 기   대사

바. 북한의 한반도 안정 파괴기도 및 86.1 월 남북대화 중지

사. 기타 인권 각분야 거의 최악상태(신상옥, 최은희의 증언부분 포함)

(공사 한탁채-국장)

예고 분: 고문에 의지 재분류 (9)
1987.6.30정 깔지

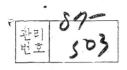

외 무 부 착 신 전 보

번 호 : USW-0759   일 시 : 8702181627   종 별 :

수 신 : 장 관(미북,김경원 주미대사, 해신)

발 신 : 주 미 대사대리

제 목 : 국무성 인권 보고서

연   USW-742

1. 연호 86년도 인권보고서의 한국관계 부분중 각분야별 기술 요지는 다음과 같음

가. 신체의 자유 존중

1) 정치적 이유로 인한 사망

-반정부인사 사망 보도수건(미확인)

-야당 및 인권단체는 경찰의 관련성 주장

2)실종

-86년중 실종사건 보도없음

3) 고문,잔혹행위,또는 형벌

-고문 및 잔혹행위에 대해 신빙성 있는 보도 계속

-권인숙,김근태사건

-경찰의 과도한 무력 사용 문제상존, 그러나 데모진압 경찰은 규율이 잘되어 있음

-교정행정의 미흡

라. 임의구속 및 연행

-정치적 사건에 있어 영장없이 연행되는 경우 상존

-야당인사에 대한 감시 및 가택연금 계속

-아시안 게임중 보안강화 위해 263,564명 조사

-국가보안법의 남용사례

-서준식,강종건사건

마. 공개 공정재판 문제

미주국   차관실   1 차보   청와대   총리실   안 기   대 사   문공부

PAGE   1

87.02.19 10:11
외신 2과 통제관

0149

-사법부의 독립과 3심제도 운용, 그러나 정치적 사건의 경우 독립성에 의문

-야당과 인권단체는 약 1,000 내지 3,000명의 정치범이 수감되고 있으며 이중 다수가 학생이라고 주장

-정부는 정치범 부재를 주장하면서도 86.12월 검찰당국은 86년중 3,405명이 정치적 상황과 관련하여 구속되었다고 발표, 이중 대부분은 집시법 위반.

4)사생활의 침해

-다수의 정치,종교 인사가 감시대상

-헌법규정에도 불구 경우에 따라 경찰이 영장없이 가택수색

-그외의 경우 사생활의 자유 존중되고 있음

나. 시민적 자유의 존중

1)언론자유

-헌법의 언론자유 보장에도 불구 반대 의견 표현 제약

-야당 및 언론계의 언론 기본법 폐지 또는 개정 주장

-정부당국에 의한 보도지침 어길 경우 조사 또는 해고

-전반적으로 개방적 보도성향, 그러나 텔레비존과 라디오 방송은 아직 엄격한 통제

-유성환의원 사건

2) 평화적 집회 결사의 자유

-집시법에 의해 공공질서 저해 및 사회불안 조성이 우려 되는 집회금지(야당 및 학생시위 저지로 이용)

-대부분의 비정치적 평화적 집회는 감시 및 제한없이 개최

-신민당의 헌법개정 추진위한 옥외집회 개최, 인천사건 및 11월 서울집회 사건

-노동3권의 제약

3)종교의 자유

-거의 완전한 종교의 자유향유, 그러나 종교인사의 반정부 활동등 정치행위는 제약

-86년 승려들의 사찰관계법 반대시위 사건

4) 국내외 거주이전의 자유

-거의 완전한 거주이전의 자유보장

PAGE   2

0150

-정치적 집회자와 범죄인을 제외하고는 정해진 범위내에서 해외여행자유

다. 정치적 권리의 존중

1) 권력집중 현상

-대통령과 국회의원만 선거에 의해 선출

-선거운동의 법적제약

-85년 국회의원선거시 야당세력의 증가

2) 헌법절차에 의한 88년 평화적 정권 이양

-헌법개정 절차

-정부 형태결정을 위요한 여야간 대립

3) 좌경세력 활동

-86년중 제도권밖의 정치종교 활동에 대해 압력가중

-용공세력의 색출 및 관련단체 해체

-정부는 신민당에 대해 용공세력과의 관계를 명백히 할것을 요구

라. 인권위반 주장에대한 정부의 입장

1) 인권기구

-한국의 어떠한 국제인권 기구에도 미가입

-인권문제에 대한 외부의 관여를 반대하면서도, 정부관리의 국제사면협회등 인권단

체 대표와의 접촉은 허용

2) 국내인권 관계기관

-법무부가 인권보호 및 위반조사 책임기관

-각 정당의 인권 위원회

3) 독립 인권단체

- KNCC 의 인권위, 기독교 정의평화위원회,변호사 협회등

-정부의 인권단체에 대한 감시, 수색등 압력

마. 인종,성별,종교,언어등에 의한 차별

1)인종차별

-소수인종 그룹 없음

PAGE   3

0151

-지역간 차별대우 문제

2) 남녀차별

-전통적 남성우위 사회

-여권신장 운동계속

바. 노동조건

1)미성년자의 취업

-미성년자 취업시 보호자의 동의 필요.

-미성년자 고용사례 많음

2) 근로기준법

-근로시간 최대주 60시간

-최저임금제 미실시, 그러나 88년까지는 제도화계획

-근로자 연금제도 실시계획

3) 노사분규

-임금 체불등 노사분규 해결위한 정부의 강력조치

-산재보상법으로 근로자 보호노력

2. 국무성의 RICHARD SCHIFTER 인권차관보는 2.19(목) 09:00 금년도 각국 인권
보고서를 토대로 기자 브리핑을 가질예정이며 , 동일 오후 하원 인권소위에서 동 보
고서와 관련한 청문회가 개최될 예정임.

(공사 한탁채)

재 고 예후 :87.7.36가지

직 의

외 무 부   착 신 전 보

번 호 : USW-0788   일 시 : 70219 1800   종 별 :

수 신 : 장 관 (미북,김경원주미대사)

발 신 : 주 미 대사대리

제 목 : 국무성 인권차관보 브리핑

금 2.19(목) 국무성 인권차관보의 86년도 인권보고에 대한 브리핑시 아국 및 북한에
관해 아래와 같은 질의응답이 있었음

Q. CAN I SWITCH TO A DIFFERENT PART OF THE WORLD ?

YOU MENTIONED THE PHILIPPINES AS ENCOURAGING IN ASIA. WHAT ABOUT SOUTH KOREA ? Y
OU SEEM TO HAVE GIVE IT A SLAP ON THE WRIST BUT NOT MUCH SERIOUS CRITICISM. DON'
T YOU FIND THE SITUATION THERE SOMEWHAT DISCOURAGING ?

AMB. SCGIFTER: IF YOU LOOK AT OUR REPORT, IT'S MORS THAN A SLAP ON THE WRIST. WE
INDICATE OUR CONCERNS ABOUT SOUTH KOREA VERY, CLEARLY.

Q. CAN YOU RESTATE THEM ?

AMB. SCHIFTER: BASICALLY, OUR FUNDAMENTAL CONCERN THERE IS WITH THE CONTINUING R
EPORTS ON TORTURE. WE HAVE NOT ONLY MADE THISPOINT CLEAR IN OUR DISCUSSION IN OU
R REPORT, BUT HAVE ALSO SPOKEN TO THAT SUBJECT IN PRES GUIDANCE AND IN SOME OF O
UR BRIEFINGS.

Q. HOW WOULD YOU ASSESS THE SITUATION AS COMPARED TO SAY A YEAR AGO ?

AMB. SCHIFTER: UNFORTUNATELY, WE ARE DEALING WITH A PROBLEM THAT HAS BEEN A PROB
LEM FOR SOME TIME, OF TORTURE BY THE POLICE, AND ALSO UNDULY HEAVY SENTENCES FOR
POLITICALLY MOTIVATED, MINOR OFFENSES, OVER-REACTION BY THE POLICE IN DEALING W
ITH DEMONSTRATIONS. WHILE WE'RE ON THAT SUBJECT, LET ME ALOS SAY THAT IF YOU JUS
T GO NORTH OF THAT BORDER YOU'RE DEALING WITH PROBABLY THE WORST HUMAN RIGHTS OF
FENDER IN THE WORLD. NORTH KOREA IS THE ONE COUNTRY THAT COMES CLOSEST, I WOULD

미주국   차관실   1차보   청와대   안 기   정문국   외연원   대 사   문공부

SAY, TO GEORGE ORWELL'S MODEL OF A 1984 STATE. YES ?

(공사 한탁채)

0154

기 안 용 지

분류기호 문서번호	미북 202-608	(전화 :)	시 행 상 특별취급	
보존기간	영구·준영구. 10. 5. 3. 1.	장 관		
수 신 처 보존기간				
시행일자	1987. 2. 20.			

보 조 기 관	국 장		협 조 기 관		문 서 통 제
	심의관				검 열 1987. 2. 23 통제관
	과 장				
기안책임자	조 백상			발 송 인

경 유		발 신 명 의	
수 신	법무부장관		
참 조			

제 목	1986년도 미국무성 인권 보고서

미국무성은 2.19. 1986년도 인권보고서를 발간 하였는 바, 아국

및 북한관련 부분을 별첨 송부하오니 동 보고서를 검토하여 주시고

귀부의 의견이 있으면 관련자료와 함께 당부로 송부하여 주시기

바랍니다. 검토필 (1987. 6. 20.)

예고문에 의거 재분류(1987.12.2)

첨 부 : 동 보고서 1부. 끝.

0155

ACTION POL3   INFO AMB DCM SAA3 USIS ECON2 CON/RR FCS AGAF CUST ACPUSAN 16

18-FEB-87   TOR: 03:02
CN: 07971
CHRG: PROG
DIST: POLC

VZCZCUL0290
OO RUEHUL
DE RUEHC #7058/01 0490256
ZNY CCCCC ZZH
O 182245Z FEB 87
FM SECSTATE WASHDC
TO AMEMBASSY SEOUL IMMEDIATE 7186
BT
C O N F I D E N T I A L STATE 047058

ACTION COPY

IMMEDIATE

KS

TAGS: PHUM, KS, US
SUBJECT: 1986 REPUBLIC OF KOREA HUMAN RIGHTS REPORT

1. (C) - ENTIRE TEXT.

2. THE FINAL TEXT OF THE 1986 HUMAN RIGHTS REPORT FOR
THE REPUBLIC OF KOREA IS TRANSMITTED HEREWITH. IT
REMAINS CONFIDENTIAL AND EMBARGOED UNTIL RELEASE BY THE
CONGRESS. YOU WILL RECEIVE AN INSTRUCTION NOTIFYING YOU
OF THE RELEASE DATE, CURRENTLY EXPECTED TO BE 2/19. AT
THAT TIME YOU WILL BE AUTHORIZED TO PROVIDE A COPY TO THE
ROKG ON A CONFIDENTIAL BASIS, 24 HOURS BEFORE RELEASE.

3. BEGIN TEXT:

PRESIDENT CHUN DOO HWAN DOMINATES THE POLITICAL SCENE IN
THE REPUBLIC OF KOREA. THE ELECTED LEGISLATURE HAS
LIMITED POWER BUT CONSIDERABLE INFLUENCE ON PUBLIC
OPINION. PRESIDENT CHUN, A FORMER ARMY GENERAL, ASSUMED
POWER WITH MILITARY SUPPORT IN 1980, WHEN MARTIAL LAW WAS
DECLARED AND CIVIL DISTURBANCES IN KWANGJU HARSHLY
CONFRONTED. THE CONSTITUTION WAS ADOPTED BY REFERENDUM
IN OCTOBER 1980 UNDER STRICT MARTIAL LAW CONDITIONS,

LEADING MANY KOREANS TO QUESTION THE REFERENDUM'S
FAIRNESS. PRESIDENT CHUN HAS PROMISED TO STEP DOWN IN
EARLY 1988, WHEN HIS TERM OF OFFICE ENDS, TO PROVIDE FOR
A PEACEFUL AND CONSTITUTIONAL CHANGE OF POWER.

KOREA'S SOCIOPOLITICAL TRADITION EMPHASIZES ORDER,
CONFORMITY, AND A SUBORDINATE ROLE FOR WOMEN. THESE
ATTITUDES RETAIN GREAT STRENGTH, COEXISTING UNEASILY WITH
WESTERN DEMOCRATIC IDEALS. CITING THIS TRADITION AND
FACED WITH A HEAVILY ARMED COMMUNIST NORTH KOREA THAT
INVADED THE SOUTH IN 1950 AND THAT REMAINS COMMITTED TO
BRINGING THE ENTIRE PENINSULA UNDER ITS CONTROL,
SUCCESSIVE SOUTH KOREAN GOVERNMENTS HAVE GIVEN TOP
PRIORITY TO MAINTAINING EXTERNAL AND INTERNAL SECURITY.
THE SUCCESSIVE REGIMES HAVE IMPLEMENTED THEIR POLICIES IN
PART BY EMPLOYING LARGE, WELL-ORGANIZED SECURITY FORCES.

MANY KOREANS HAVE CHARGED THROUGHOUT THE YEARS THAT THE
VERY REAL THREAT FROM THE NORTH HAS BEEN USED AS A
PRETEXT TO SUPPRESS INTERNAL OPPOSITION, DESPITE THE
DEMOCRATIC IDEALS PROFESSED BY ALL SOUTH KOREAN LEADERS.

KOREANS ENJOY CONSIDERABLE PERSONAL FREEDOM, INCLUDING
ECONOMIC AND RELIGIOUS FREEDOM, AND BROAD RIGHTS TO
PURSUE PRIVATE INTERESTS. ALTHOUGH THE CONSTITUTION
GUARANTEES FREEDOM OF SPEECH AND PRESS, IN PRACTICE BOTH
ARE ABRIDGED.

DURING THE PAST 2Ø YEARS, KOREA'S EXPORT-ORIENTED ECONOMY
HAS ACHIEVED ONE OF THE WORLD'S HIGHEST GROWTH RATES AND
A TWENTY-FOLD INCREASE IN PER CAPITA GROSS NATIONAL
PRODUCT. THE POPULATION IS URBANIZED AND WELL EDUCATED.
ABJECT POVERTY HAS BEEN LARGELY ELIMINATED. THE RAPID
GROWTH OF THE ECONOMY HAS CREATED A GROWING MIDDLE CLASS
WITH INCREASING ACCESS TO EDUCATION AND WEALTH. THE
UNIVERSITY STUDENT POPULATION HAS INCREASED SHARPLY OVER
THE PAST DECADE. STUDENTS HAVE JOINED WITH OTHER GROUPS
TO BECOME A STRONG VOICE FOR FULLER POLITICAL
PARTICIPATION AND GREATER FREEDOM TO EXPRESS POLITICAL
VIEWS.

THE ISSUE OF CONSTITUTIONAL REFORM DOMINATED KOREAN
POLITICS IN 1986. IN FEBRUARY THE OPPOSITION LAUNCHED A
PETITION CAMPAIGN IN SUPPORT OF ITS DEMAND THAT THE
CONSTITUTION BE AMENDED TO PROVIDE FOR DIRECT POPULAR
ELECTION OF THE NEXT PRESIDENT. THE GOVERNMENT INITIALLY
DECLARED THE CAMPAIGN ILLEGAL AND SOUGHT TO BLOCK IT,
PLACING SOME OPPOSITION LEADERS UNDER HOUSE ARREST. THE
GOVERNMENT SUBSEQUENTLY MODERATED ITS POSITION, BUT THE
OPPOSITION PARTY CONTINUED TO APPLY PRESSURE BY STAGING A

SERIES OF LARGE PUBLIC RALLIES THROUGHOUT THE NATION. IN
LATE SPRING PRESIDENT CHUN RESPONDED BY AGREEING TO
NEGOTIATIONS BETWEEN THE POLITICAL PARTIES IN THE
NATIONAL ASSEMBLY TO AMEND THE CONSTITUTION. THE
GOVERNMENT PARTY PROPOSED CREATING A PARLIAMENTARY SYSTEM
OF GOVERNMENT WHILE THE MAIN OPPOSITION PARTY INSISTS ON
A DIRECTLY ELECTED PRESIDENT. AT THE END OF THE YEAR THE
DEBATE REMAINED STALEMATED WITH BOTH SIDES SEEKING TO
BOLSTER POPULAR SUPPORT FOR THEIR POSITIONS.

THE GOVERNMENT CONTINUED TO TAKE A HARD LINE TOWARDS
DISSIDENT, PARTICULARLY STUDENT DISSIDENT, POLITICAL
ACTIVISMIN 1986, CITING INCREASING RADICALISM AND
VIOLENCE. AS THE YEAR PROGRESSED, STUDENT PROTEST
SLOGANS BECAME INCREASINGLY REVOLUTIONARY AND IN SOME
INSTANCES CLOSELY PARALLELED NORTH KOREAN PROPAGANDA.
APPROXIMATELY 3,4ØØ PERSONS WERE JAILED IN CONNECTION
WITH POLITICAL ACTIVITIES, SOME OF THEM VIOLENT. IN
DECEMBER WELL OVER 1,ØØØ PERSONS REMAINED IN CUSTODY FOR
POLITICALLY RELATED OFFENSES. FOR THE FIRST TIME UNDER
THE PRESENT GOVERNMENT, AN OPPOSITION ASSEMBLYMAN WAS

INDICTED AND JAILED IN CONNECTION WITH THE DISTRIBUTION
OF THE TEXT OF AN ASSEMBLY SPEECH THE GOVERNMENT CLAIMED
VIOLATED THE NATIONAL SECURITY LAW IN ITS CRITICISM OF
THE GOVERNMENT'S UNIFICATION AND ANTI-COMMUNIST
POLICIES. IN 1986 THERE CONTINUED TO BE NUMEROUS CHARGES
OF POLICE MISTREATMENT OF PRISONERS INCLUDING CREDIBLE
ALLEGATIONS OF TORTURE IN SOME CASES.

RESPECT FOR HUMAN RIGHTS

SECTION 1 RESPECT FOR THE INTEGRITY OF THE PERSON,
INCLUDING FREEDOM FROM:

A. POLITICAL KILLING

THERE WERE UNCONFIRMED REPORTS THAT THE DEATHS OF SEVERAL
PERSONS SAID TO BE CRITICAL OF THE GOVERNMENT OR ENGAGED
IN OPPOSITION POLITICAL ACTIVITY MAY HAVE BEEN AT THE
HANDS OF THE POLICE OR OTHER GOVERNMENT SECURITY
AGENCIES. IN ONE CASE INVOLVING THE DEATH OF A MILITARY
RESERVIST IN POLICE CUSTODY, THERE WERE CHARGES THAT HE
DIED AS A RESULT OF BEATINGS BY POLICE OR MILITARY
OFFICIALS AFTER MAKING REMARKS CRITICAL OF THE
GOVERNMENT. THE MINISTER OF HOME AFFAIRS TOLD THE
NATIONAL ASSEMBLY THAT THE RESERVIST DIED OF ACUTE RENAL
PARALYSIS WHILE IN$POLICE CUSTODY ON CHARGES OF VIOLATING
THE LAW ON ASSEMBLY AND DEMONSTRATIONS. IN THE OTHER
CASES, INCLUDING THE DEATHS OF A UNIVERSITY STUDENT AND A

WORKER, WHICH THE POLICE ANNOUNCED WERE SUICIDES, SOME
OPPOSITION AND HUMAN RIGHTS GROUPS EXPRESSED SUSPICIONS
OF OFFICIAL CULPABILITY.

B. DISAPPEARANCE

THERE WERE NO REPORTS OF DISAPPEARANCES IN 1986.

C. TORTURE AND CRUEL, INHUMAN, OR DEGRADING TREATMENT O
PUNISHMENT

IN 1986 THERE CONTINUED TO BE CREDIBLE REPORTS OF TORTURE AND
CRUEL TREATMENT. THE CONSTITUTION PROHIBITS TORTURE, AND THE
GOVERNMENT INSISTS THAT IT HAS ISSUED AND STRIC LY ENFORCES
INJUNCTIONS AGAINST IT. IN ADDITION, IN 1983 THE NATIONAL
ASSEMBLY PASSED A LAW INCREASING SENTENCES FOR THOSE CONVICTE
OF KILLING OR INJURING THROUGH TORTURE.

NONETHELESS, DURING 1986 THERE WERE PLAUSIBLE CHARGES OF
SERIOUS PRISONER MISTREATMENT. IN ONE SUCH CASE, A FEMALE
DISSIDENT, MS. KWON IN SOOK, CLAIMED THAT HE WAS SEXUALLY
ASSAULTED BY A POLICEMAN DURING INTERROGATION. THE GOVERNMEN
DENIED THE SEXUAL ASSAULT CHARGES BUT DISMISSED THE POLICEMAN
FROM HIS POST FOR IMPROPER AND "EXCESSIVE" CONDUCT. KOREAN
HUMAN RIGHTS GROUPS AND POLITICAL OPPOSITION LEADERS ALSO MAD
PLAUSIBLE CHARGES THAT A NUMBER OF STUDENTS, WORKERS, AND
OTHERS IN POLITICALLY RELATED CASES WERE SUBJECTED TO VARIOUS
DEGREES OF PHYSICAL MALTREATMENT. THESE GROUPS CHARGED THAT
SOME 15 LABOR ACTIVISTS WERE INTERROGATED AND TORTURED BY THE

KOREAN MILITARY SECURITY AGENCY. ANOTHER GROUP OF DISSIDENTS
CHARGED WITH PUBLISHING SEDITIOUS LITERATURE ALLEGEDLY WAS
BEATEN BY POLICE. THE GOVERNMENT DENIED THESE ALLEGATIONS.
YET ANOTHER DISSIDENT ACTIVIST, KIM KEUN TAE, MADE CREDIBLE
CHARGES THAT HE HAD BEEN SEVERELY TORTURED IN 1985, BUT THE
KOREAN SUPREME COURT UPHELD HIS CONVICTION ON APPEAL AND
REFUSED TO "RECOGNIZE" HIS CLAIM THAT HE HAD BEEN UNLAWFULLY
MISTREATED BY POLICE.

THE USE OF EXCESSIVE FORCE BY THE POLICE CONTINUES TO BE A
PERVASIVE AND INGRAINED PROBLEM. DEMONSTRATORS HAVE BEEN
BEATEN ON APPREHENSION, OFTEN BY PLAINCLOTHES POLICE. ON THE
OTHER HAND, RIOT POLICE GENERALLY WERE WELL DISCIPLINED WHEN
CONFRONTING PROTESTERS WHO WERE THEMSELVES OFTEN EXTREMELY
VIOLENT. POLICE ACTED PROFESSIONALLY IN 1985 WHEN U.S.
OFFICIALS REQUESTED THAT OFFICERS PHYSICALLY REMOVE STUDENTS
WHO HAD INVADED A U.S. FACILITY.

CHARGES OF POLICE BEATINGS OCCUR FAIRLY FREQUENTLY IN
NONPOLITICAL CASES AND ARE SOMETIMES EPORTED IN THE PRESS.

FOR EXAMPLE, IN LATE 1986 THE MEDIA REPORTED THE ACQUITTAL OF
A MURDER SUSPECT WHO CLAIMED HE HAD BEEN TORTURED INTO MAKING
A FALSE CONFESSION.

CONDITIONS IN KOREAN CORRECTIONAL INSTITUTIONS ARE AUSTERE,
ESPECIALLY IN WINTER BECAUSE CELLS ARE UNHEATED. DISCIPLINE
IS STRICT. PRISONERS OF WHATEVER SO T WHO BREAK RULES OR
PROTEST CONDITIONS ARE SOMETIMES BEATEN. PRISONERS MAY
RECEIVE VISITS ONLY FROM THEIR LAWYERS AND IMMEDIATE
FAMILIES. THEIR MAIL IS MONITORED AND AT TIMES CENSORED.
THERE DOES NOT SEEM TO BE A DIFFERENCE BETWEEN THE OVERALL
TREATMENT OF POLITICAL AND NONPOLITICAL PRISONERS, BUT IN 198
REPORTS OF CONFLICT BETWEEN PRISONERS JAILED FOR
ANTIGOVERNMENT ACTIVITIES AND PRISON AUTHORITIES INCREASED.
OPPOSITION AND PRISONER FAMILY GROUPS HAVE CLAIMED THAT
PRISONERS HAD BEEN BEATEN AND SUBJECTED TO OTHER MISTREATMENT
BECAUSE OF THEIR POLITICAL VIEWS. THE GOVERNMENT DENIED THIS
AND INSISTED THAT PRISON AUTHORITIES WERE ONLY EXERCISING

NECESSARY MINIMAL FORCE TO DEAL WITH PRISONER DEFIANCE OF
AUTHORITY.

D.   ARBITRARY ARREST, DETENTION, OR EXILE

ARREST WARRANTS ARE REQUIRED BY LAW BUT SOMETIMES ARE NOT
PRODUCED AT THE TIME OF ARREST IN POLITICALLY RELATED CASES.
IN ONE CASE, A DEFENDANT CHARGED WITH "PRAISING NORTH KOREA"
WAS ACQUITTED ON THE GROUNDS THAT HIS CONFESSION HAD BEEN MAD
WHILE HE WAS DETAINED WITHOUT AN ARREST WARRANT. IN 1985 THE
SUPREME COURT RULED THAT POLICE MAY NOT DETAIN PERSONS FOR
MORE THAN 48 HOURS WITHOUT WARRANTS. AN INDICTMENT IS
SUPPOSED TO BE ISSUED WITHIN 30 DAYS AFTER ARREST. WITHIN 3
DAYS AFTER MAKING AN ARREST, THE POLICE ARE SUPPOSED TO NOTIF
AN ARRESTED PERSON'S FAMILY OR LAWYER OF HIS DETENTION AND
WHEREABOUTS. THIS REQUIREMENT IS NOT ALWAYS OBSERVED,
PARTICULARLY IN CASES OF DETENTION BY SECURITY AGENCIES OTHER
THAN THE NATIONAL POLICE. FOR EXAMP E, IN THE CASE OF A GROU
OF LABOR ACTIVISTS WHO WERE INTERROGATED AND ALLEGEDLY BEATEN
BY THE DEFENSE SECURITY COMMAND, THERE ARE CREDIBLE REPORTS
THAT THE SUSPECTS' FAMILIES WERE NOT INFORMED OF THE
DETENTIONS FOR OVER A WEEK. THE CONSTITUTION ALSO GUARANTEES
THE RIGHT TO PROMPT LEGAL ASSISTANCE AND TO A REVIEW OF AN
ARREST BY A COURT.

HABEAS CORPUS, NOT TRADITIONAL IN KOREAN LAW, WAS INTRODUCED
AFTER WORLD WAR II, ABOLISHED IN THE 1970'S, AND REINTRODUCED
IN 1980. IT DOES NOT APPLY TO THOSE CHARGED WITH VIOLATIONS
OF THE NATIONAL SECURITY LAW OR LAWS GOVERNING CRIMES
PUNISHABLE BY AT LEAST 5 YEARS' IMPRISONMENT. MOST POLITICAL
OFFENSES ARE, THEREFORE, EXCLUDED. THERE IS A SYSTEM OF BAIL

BUT IT DOES NOT APPLY TO OFFENSES PUNISHABLE BY 10 OR MORE
YEARS' IMPRISONMENT. IN 1985 THE GOVERNMENT ADOPTED A NEW
POLICY TO COMPENSATE PERSONS HELD FOR QUESTIONING WHO ARE
SUBSEQUENTLY FOUND INNOCENT BY PROSECUTORS, AND THE COURTS
HAVE STARTED TO APPLY THIS PROVISION. IN 1986 A KOREAN COURT
AWARDED DAMAGES TO A MAN WHO WAS INJURED WEEN HE REFUSED A
POLICEMAN'S REQUEST THAT HE "VOLUNTARILY" ACCOMPANY THE
POLICEMAN TO THE POLICE STATION FOR QUESTIONING. THERE WAS
CRITICISM FROM THE PRESS AND LEGAL GROUPS OF EXCESSIVE NU BER
OF FALSE OR UNJUSTIFIED ARRESTS.

DISSIDENTS WHO OPENLY CRITICIZE THE GOVERNMENT ARE SOMETIMES
PICKED UP AND DETAINED FOR SHORT PERIODS AND THEN RELEASED.
IN 1986 THERE WERE INSTANCES OF DISSIDENTS RETURNING FROM
OVERSEAS TRIPS BEING DETAINED IN SUCH FASHION, AS WERE SEVERA
JOURNALISTS WHO HAD WRITTEN POLITICALLY SENSITIVE ARTICLES.

FROM TIME TO TIME THE SECURITY SERVICES HAVE NOT ONLY DETAINE
PERSONS ACCUSED OF VIOLATION OF LAWS ON POLITICAL DISSENT BUT
HAVE ALSO INCREASED SURVEILLANCE OF OR PUT UNDER VARIOUS FORM
OF HOUSE ARREST THOSE THEY THINK "INTEND TO VIOLATE THE LAW."
KOREA'S PUBLIC SECURITY LAW PERMITS MEASURES INCLUDING
"PROTECTIVE SURVEILLANCE," "RESIDENTIAL RESTRICTION," AND
"PREVENTIVE CUSTODY" OF CERTAIN PERSONS CONSIDERED LIKELY
LAWBREAKERS. SUCH RESTRICTIONS WERE USED AGAINST OPPOSITION
POLITICAL FIGURES, INCLUDING THE LEADERS OF THE MAIN

0160

OPPOSITION, THE NEW KOREA DEMOCRATIC PARTY (NKDP), IN EARLY
1986 IN AN EFFORT TO STOP THE PETITION CAMPAIGN FOR
CONSTITUTIONAL REVISION. DURING THIS PERIOD, OPPOSITION
POLITICIAN KIM DAE JUNG WAS NOT PERMITTED TO LEAVE HIS HOME
FOR 12 DAYS. KIM AND OTHERS ALSO WERE CONFINED TO THEIR HOME
FOR BRIEFER PERIODS ON NUMEROUS OTHER OCCASIONS.

THE GOVERNMENT ALSO TAKES A SWEEPING APPROACH TO CRIME
PREVENTION IN INSTANCES WHERE ITS IMAGE IS INVOLVED. KOREAN
POLICE INVESTIGATED 283,564 SUSPECTED CRIMINALS IN A 3-MONTH
DRIVE TO TIGHTEN SECURITY FOR THE SEPTEMBER ASIAN GAMES HELD
IN SEOUL. SOME 43,000 PERSONS WERE FORMALLY CHARGED, AND MORE
THAN 76,000 SUMMARILY SENTENCED TO UP TO 29 DAYS IN JAIL.
MOST OTHERS WERE RELEASED.

IN 1986 THE GOVERNMENT CONTINUED TO INVESTIGATE DISSIDENT AND
STUDENT ORGANIZATIONS AND TO MAKE ARRESTS FOR NATIONAL
SECURITY LAW VIOLATIONS FOR ACTIVITIES CHARACTERIZED AS
PRO-COMMUNIST, PRO-NORTH KOREA, OR ANTI-STATE. GOVERNMENT
CRITICS CLAIM THAT IN MANY OF THESE CASES THE NATIONAL
SECURITY LAW WAS MISUSED TO SUPPRESS DOMESTIC, PARTICULARLY
STUDENT, DISSENT. THERE WERE ALSO CHARGES THAT THE GOVERNMENT
WAS IDENTIFYING STUDENT ACTIVISTS FOR IMMEDIATE CONSCRIPTION

INTO THE ARMED FORCES. (MILITARY SERVICE IS REQUIRED OF ALL
KOREAN MALES, BUT STUDENTS NORMALLY ARE GIVEN DEFERMENTS TO
COMPLETE THEIR EDUCATIONS.) OTHER STUDENTS PICKED UP FOR
PARTICIPATING IN ANTIGOVERNMENT DEMONSTRATIONS WERE REQUIRED
TO COMPLETE "REORIENTATION PROGRAMS" BEFORE BEING RELEASED.
SOME 1,200 STUDENT UNDERWENT SUCH PROGRAMS IN THE FIRST HALF
OF 1986. MORE THAN 900 WERE JUDGED TO HAVE SUCCESSFULLY
COMPLETED THE PROGRAM AND WERE RELEASED.

FOR PERSONS DEEMED "SOCIALLY DANGEROUS," THE LAW ALLOWS
PREVENTIVE DETENTION UNDER PROVISIONS OF THE SOCIAL PROTECTION
AND SOCIAL STABILITY LAWS. UNDER THE SOCIAL PROTECTION LAW,
JUDICIAL PANEL MAY ORDER PREVENTIVE DETENTION FOR A FIXED TERM
OF 2 YEARS, WHICH CAN BE EXTENDED BY THE PANEL FOR ADDITIONAL
2-YEAR PERIODS. THE SOCIAL STABILITY LAW ALLOWS FOR A

C O N F I D E N T I A L — STATE 047055/03

C O N F I D E N T I A L   STATE 04706 /03

OPPOSITION, THE NEW KOREA DEMOCRATIC PARTY (NKDP), IN EARLY
1986 IN AN EFFORT TO STOP THE PETITION CAMPAIGN FOR
CONSTITUTIONAL REVISION. DURING THIS PERIOD, OPPOSITION
POLITICIAN KIM DAE JUNG WAS NOT PERMITTED TO LEAVE HIS HOME
FOR 12 DAYS. KIM AND OTHERS ALSO WERE CONFINED TO THEIR HOME
FOR BRIEFER PERIODS ON NUMEROUS OTHER OCCASIONS.

THE GOVERNMENT ALSO TAKES A SWEEPING APPROACH TO CRIME
PREVENTION IN INSTANCES WHERE ITS IMAGE IS INVOLVED. KOREAN
POLICE INVESTIGATED 263,564 SUSPECTED CRIMINALS IN A 3-MONTH
DRIVE TO TIGHTEN SECURITY FOR THE SEPTEMBER ASIAN GAMES HELD
IN SEOUL. SOME 43,000 PERSONS WERE FORMALLY CHARGED, AND MOR
THAN 76,000 SUMMARILY SENTENCED TO UP TO 29 DAYS IN JAIL.
MOST OTHERS WERE RELEASED.

IN 1986 THE GOVERNMENT CONTINUED TO INVESTIGATE DISSIDENT AND
STUDENT ORGANIZATIONS AND TO MAKE ARRESTS FOR NATIONAL
SECURITY LAW VIOLATIONS FOR ACTIVITIES CHARACTERIZED AS
PRO-COMMUNIST, PRO-NORTH KOREA, OR ANTI-STATE. GOVERNMENT
CRITICS CLAIM THAT IN MANY OF THESE CASES THE NATIONAL
SECURITY LAW WAS MISUSED TO SUPPRESS DOMESTIC, PARTICULARLY
STUDENT, DISSENT. THERE WERE ALSO CHARGES THAT THE GOVERNMENN
WAS IDENTIFYING STUDENT ACTIVISTS FOR IMMEDIATE CONSCRIPTION

INTO THE ARMED FORCES. (MILITARY SERVICE IS REQUIRED OF ALL
KOREAN MALES, BUT STUDENTS NORMALLY ARE GIVEN DEFERMENTS TO
COMPLETE THEIR EDUCATIONS.) OTHER STUDENTS PICKED UP FOR
PARTICIPATING IN ANTIGOVERNMENT DEMONSTRATIONS WERE REQUIRED
TO COMPLETE "REORIENTATION PROGRAMS" BEFORE BEING RELEASED.
SOME 1,200 STUDENT UNDERWENT SUCH PROGRAMS IN THE FIRST HALF
OF 1986. MORE THAN 900 WERE JUDGED TO HAVE SUCCESSFULLY
COMPLETED THE PROGRAM AND WERE RELEASED.

FOR PERSONS DEEMED "SOCIALLY DANGEROUS," THE LAW ALLOWS
PREVENTIVE DETENTION UNDER PROVISIONS OF THE SOCIAL PROTECTIO
AND SOCIAL STABILITY LAWS. UNDER THE SOCIAL PROTECTION LAW,
JUDICIAL PANEL MAY ORDER PREVENTIVE DETENTION FOR A FIXED TER
OF 2 YEARS, WHICH CAN BE EXTENDED BY THE PANEL FOR ADDITIONAL
2-YEAR PERIODS. THE SOCIAL STABILITY LAW ALLOWS FOR A

C O N F I D E N T I A L   STATE 047058/03

0162

522 한국 인권문제 미국 반응 및 동향 2

PREVENTIVE DETENTION T⌴ . OF 7 TO 1Ø YEARS THROUGH
ADMINISTRATIVE LITIGATION. THE GOVERNMENT MAINTAINS THAT
THESE LAWS ARE AIMED AT CHRONIC OFFENDERS AND PRISONERS WHO
ARE MENTALLY ILL.

THERE IS A "PREVENTIVE CUSTODY CENTER" IN THE CITY OF CHONGJU
WHERE PRISONERS JUDGED TO BE INSUFFICIENTLY REPENTANT ARE HEL
FOLLOWING THE COMPLETION OF THEIR ORIGINAL PRISON
SENTENCES.   SOH JOON SHIK, WHOSE ORIGINAL 7-YEAR SENTENCE
RAN OUT IN 1978, AND KANG JONG-KON, WHOSE ORIGINAL 5-YEAR
SENTENCE WAS COMPLETED IN 1981, ARE TWO POLITICAL PRISONERS
BELIEVED TO BE HELD IN CHONGJU. ALTHOUGH THE GOVERNMENT HAS
NOT RELEASED FIGURES ON THE TOTAL NU BER OF PERSONS UNDER
PREVENTIVE DETENTION, SOME HUMAN RIGHTS GROUPS ASSERT THAT AS
MANY AS 38Ø PRISONERS ARE BEING HELD UNDER SOCIAL STABILITY
LAW PROVISIONS.

THERE WERE NO REPORTS IN 1985 OF FORCED LABOR AS DEFINED BY
THE INTERNATIONAL LABOR ORGANIZATION (ILO).

E. DENIAL OF FAIR PUBLIC TRIAL

THE CONSTITUTION GUARANTEES MANY RIGHTS TO DEFENDANTS:
PRESUMPTION OF INNOCENCE, PROTECTION AGAINST
SELF-INCRIMINATION, FREEDOM FROM EX POST FACTO LAWS AND DOUBL
JEOPARDY, THE RIGHT TO A SPEEDY TRIAL, AND THE RIGHT TO LEGAL
COUNSEL. THESE RIGHTS GENERALLY ARE OBSERVED. TRIALS, WITH
SOME EXCEPTIONS, MUST BE HELD WITHIN 6 MONTHS OF ARREST. IN
SEOUL, TRIALS USUALLY BEGIN WITHIN A MONTH AFTER INDICTMENT,
ALTHOUGH IN 1986 THE LARGE NUMBER OF STUDENT PROTESTERS
AWAITING TRIAL SLOWED THE PROCESS SOMEWHAT.

THE PRESIDENT APPOINTS THE MEMBERS OF THE SUPREME COURT, WHOS
CHIEF JUSTICE IN TURN APPOINTS LOWER-COURT JUDGES. THERE IS

THREE-TIER SYSTEM FOR CRIMINAL CASES: DIST ICT COURT,
APPELLATE (HIGH) COURT, AND THE SUPREME COURT. THE JUDICIARY
IS CONSIDERED INDEPENDENT IN ORDINARY CRIMINAL AND CIVIL CASE
BUT MUCH LESS SO IN POLITICALLY SENSITIVE CASES. A NEW CHIEF
JUSTICE WAS APPOINTED IN 1986. UPON ASSUMING HIS POST, HE
EMPHASIZED HIS INTENTION TO STRENGTHEN THE PROTECTION OF HUMA
RIGHTS.

IN SEVERAL POLITICALLY SENSITIVE TRIALS IN 1986, PUBLIC
ATTENDANCE WAS RESTRICTED. THE DEFENDANTS SOMETIMES WERE
REMOVED FROM THE COURTROOM FOR ATTEMPTING TO DISRUPT THE
PROCEEDINGS. IN OTHER CASES, THE DEFENDANTS ATTEMPTED TO
BOYCOTT THE TRIAL PROCEEDINGS, STATING THAT THEY DID NOT
RECOGNIZE THE COURT'S AUTHORITY OR IMPARTIALITY. JUDGES
GENERALLY ALLOW GREAT SCOPE FOR EXAMINATION OF WITNESSES BY
BOTH PROSECUTION AND DEFENSE, BUT THEY OFTEN DENY DEFENSE
REQUESTS TO CALL WITNESSES TO DISCUSS THE POLITICAL OR
IDEOLOGICAL LEANINGS OF THE DEFENDANTS, EVEN WHEN THE
PROSECUTION HAS INTRODUCED EVIDENCE ON SUCH TOPICS.

TRIALS USUALLY ARE OPEN TO THE PUBLIC, BUT TRIAL DOCUMENTS AR
NOT PART OF THE PUBLIC RECORD. CHARGES AGAINST DEFENDANTS IN
THE COURTS ARE CLEARLY STATED. IN LENGTHY AND COMP EX

INDICTMENTS, HOWEVER, THE RELATIONSHIP BETWEEN SPECIFIC ACTS
ALLEGED AND VIOLATIONS OF PARTICULAR SECTIONS OF THE PENAL
CODE IS NOT ALWAYS CLEARLY DRAWN. IN CASES INVOLVING A
MIXTURE OF POLITICAL AND CRIMINAL CHARGES, THIS LACK OF
CLARITY CAN BRING INTO QUESTION THE FAIRNESS OF THE
PROCEEDINGS. THE SAME COURTS TRY POLITICAL AND ORDINARY
CRIMINAL CASES. MILITARY COURTS DO NOT TRY CIVILIANS.
DEFENDANTS HAVE THE RIGHT OF APPEAL IN FELONY CASES, A RIGHT
OFTEN EXERCISED AND FREQUENTLY RESULTING IN SUBSTANTIAL
REDUCTIONS IN SENTENCES. DEATH SENTENCES ARE AUTOMATICALLY
APPEALED, AND THE ENTENCES OFTEN NOT CARRIED OUT.

THE LIST OF POLITICAL PRISONERS MAINTAINED BY THE HUMAN RIGHT
COMMITTEE OF THE NATIONAL COUNCIL OF CHURCHES OF KOREA AND TH
OPPOSITION NEW KOREA DEMOCRATIC PARTY (NKDP) INCLUDED FROM
1,000 TO NEARLY 3,000 NAMES THROUGHOUT 1986. IT REACHED A
HIGH FOLLOWING THE ARREST OF 1,287 PARTICIPANTS IN THE VIOLEN
SEIZURE OF BUILDINGS ON A SEOUL CAMPUS IN OCTOBER; 395 OF
THESE STUDENTS WERE SUBSEQUENTLY INDICTED AND THE REST
RELEASED. IN DECEMBER THE NKDP PUT THE NUMBER OF POLITICAL
PRISONERS IN KOREA AT 1,843. THIS NUMBER INCLUDED PERSONS
INDICTED, BUT NOT YET TRIED AS WELL AS THOSE ALREADY
CONVICTED. THE MAJORITY OF THESE PERSONS ARE STUDENTS
ARRESTED SINCE 1985, INCLUDING SOME WHO ADVOCATED OR USED
VIOLENCE.

WHILE CONTINUING TO DENY THAT IT HOLDS ANY "POLITICAL
PISONERS," HE GOVERNMENT DID MAKE PUBLIC SEVERAL TIMES
DURING THE YEAR THE NUMBER OF PERSONS BEING HELD IN CONNECTIO
WITH THE "POLITICAL SITUATION." IN DECEMBER, GOVERNMENT
PROSECUTORS ANNOUNCED THAT 3,405 PERSONS HAD BEEN ARRESTED IN
1986 IN CONNECTION WITH POLITICAL ACTIVITIES, INCLUDING CAMPU
DEMONSTRATIONS SUCH AS THE SEIZURE OF BUILDINGS AT KONKUK
UNIVERSITY IN OCTOBER. THE TOTAL INCLUDED 2,919 STUDENTS, 91
WORKERS, 146 "DISSIDENTS," AND 240 "ORDINARY CITIZENS."
PROSECUTION SOURCES SAID THAT AS OF MID-DECEMBER, 1,480
PERSONS, INCLUDING STUDENTS, REMAINED UNDER ARREST, AND POLIC
WERE SEARCHING FOR ANOTHER 150 PERSONS SUSPECTED OF
POLITICALLY RELATED OFFENSES. THE RELEASE OF POLITICAL

C O N F I D E N T I A L   STATE 047058/04

0164

PRISONERS WAS THE SUBJECT OF DEBATE AND NEGOTIATION IN THE
NATIONAL ASSEMBLY. ACCORDING TO THE GOVERNMENT, 36 PERSONS
CONVICTED OF POLITICALLY RELATED OFFENSES WERE RELEASED IN A
SPECIAL CLEMENCY IN AUGUST, AND INDICTMENTS AGAINST A NUMBER
OF OTHERS WERE SUSPENDED OVER THE COURSE OF THE YEAR.

ACCORDING TO GOVERNMENT STATISTICS, MOST POLITICAL OFFENDERS
IN 1986 WERE CHARGED WITH VIOLATING THE LAW ON ASSEMBLY AND
DEMONSTRATIONS IN CONNECTION WITH PR TESTS RANGING ROM
PEACEFUL PARTICIPATION IN THE OPPOSITION'S PETITION DRIVE FOR
CONSTITUTIONAL REVISION TO ENGAGING IN VIOLENT ACTIVITIES,
NOTABLY THE SERIOUS CIVIL DISTURBANCE IN THE CITY OF INCHON I
MAY AND THE PROLONGED OCCUPATION OF KONKUK UNIVERSITY
BUILDINGS IN OCTOBER. MOS WERE DETAINED FOR ACTS OF VIOLENC
WHICH, THE ARRESTEES ARGUED, WERE POLITICALLY MOTIVATED.
GOVERNMENT STATISTICS SHOW THA , AS OF OCTOBER, 207 PERSONS
HAD BEEN CHARGED UNDER OR CONVICTED OF VIOLATING THE NATIONAL
SECURITY LAW FOR ACTIVITIES CONSIDERED PRO-COMMUNIST OR ANTI-
STATE, INCLUDING LISTENING TO NORTH KOREAN RADIO BROADCASTS
AND PUBLISHING OR DISTRIBUTING "SUBVERSIVE" LITERATURE. THAT
NUMBER CONTINUED TO RISE THROUGH THE END OF THE YEAR AS THE
GOVERNMENT STEPPED UP ITS CAMPAIGN AGAINST PERSONS AND GROUPS
IT CHARGED WERE VIOLA ING THE NATIONAL SECURITY LAW WHICH
PROHIBITS ACTIVITIES, INCLUDING SPEECH, DEEMED "SUPPORTIVE OF
NORTH KOREA."

F. ARBITRARY INTERFERENCE WITH PRIVACY, FAMILY, HOME, OR
CORRESPONDENCE

MANY POLITICAL AND RELIGIOUS DISSIDENTS ARE SUBJECTED TO
SURVEILLANCE BY THE SECURITY FORCES. DURING POLITICALLY
SENSITIVE PERIODS, THIS SURVEILLANCE BY ONE OR MORE SECURITY
AGENCIES MAY INCREASE, OR A FORM OF HOUSE ARREST MAY BE
IMPOSED. TELEPHONE TAPPING AND OPENING OR INTERCEPTION OF
CORRESPONDENCE IS BELIEVED TO BE PREVALENT. KOREANS WHO MEET
WITH FOREIGNERS, PARTICULARLY WITH JOURNALISTS AND FOREIGN

DIPLOMATS, ARE SOMETIMES QUESTIONED AFTERWARDS. LISTENING TO
NORTH KOREAN RADIO BROADCASTS AND READING OR PURVEYING BOOKS
CONSIDERED SUBVERSIVE, PRO-COMMUNIST, OR PRO-NORTH KOREA ARE
ILLEGAL. SEVERAL PEOPLE WERE ARRESTED AND BHARGED WITH
VIOLATING THE NATIONAL SECURITY LAW FOR SUCH OFFENSES.

WHILE THE CONSTITUTION REQUIRES A WARRANT ISSUED BY A JUDGE
UPON REQUEST OF A PROSECUTOR FOR SEARCH AND SEIZURE IN A
RESIDENCE, THE POLICE AT TIMES FORCE THEIR WAY INTO PRIVATE
HOMES OR OFFICES WITHOUT WARRANTS. THE POLICE AND SECURITY
FORCE PRESENCE IN CITY CENTERS AND NEAR UNIVERSITY CAMPUSES I
FREQUENTLY HEAVY BECAUSE OF FEAR OF ANTIGOVERNMENT
DEMONSTRATIONS. CITIZENS, PARTICULARLY STUDENTS, OFTEN ARE
STOPPED, QUESTIONED, AND SEARCHED. TRADITIONAL KOREAN POLICE
PRACTICE REQUIRES POLICE COMMANDERS TO BE FAMILIAR WITH THE
PERSONAL AND BUSINESS AFFAIRS OF ALL RESIDENTS IN THEIR
JURISDICTIONS. THIS SYSTEM IS EFFECTIVE IN CRIME CONTROL, AN
URBAN RESIDENTS GENERALLY CREDIT IT WIT KEEPING THEIR STREET
SAFE. BUT THE LARGE POLICE PRESENCE NEAR COLLEGE CAMPUSES HA
THE PRIMARY PURPOSE OF KEEPING TRACK OF POLITICAL ACTIVITIES
AND HAS BEEN A KEY COMPLAINT OF STUDENTS, INCLUDING THOSE WHO

ARE NOT POLITICALLY ACTIVE.

IN MOST OTHER RESPECTS, THE GOVERNMENT HONORS THE RIGHT OF
PERSONAL PRIVACY AND THE INTEGRITY OF THE HOME AND FAMILY.
PARENTAL RIGHTS TO EDUCATE CHILDREN ARE BROAD. THE STATE
RARELY SEEKS TO INTERVENE IN SUCH INHERENTLY PERSONAL
DECISIONS AS MARRIAGE, CHOICE OF VOCATION, AND FORMATION OF
SOCIAL AND FAMILIAL TIES. PERSONS THOUGHT TO HAVE POLITICALL
SUSPECT BACKGROUNDS, HOWEVER, ARE DENIED SOME FORMS OF
EMPLOYMENT AND ADVANCEMENT, PARTICULARLY IN GOVERNMENT, PRESS
AND EDUCATION. IN 1986 THE MINISTRY OF EDUCATION REVISED ITS
TEACHER QUALIFICATION REGULATIONS TO EXCLUDE FROM OBTAINING
TEACHING POSITIONS THOSE WHO HAVE RECORDS OF CAMPUS ACTIVISM.

SECTION 2 RESPECT FOR CIVIL LIBERTIES, INCLUDING:

A. FREEDOM OF SPEECH AND PRESS

ALTHOUGH FREEDOM OF SPEECH AND PRESS IS GUARANTEED BY THE
CONSTITUTION, IN PRACTICE THE EXPRESSION OF OPPOSITION
VIEWPOINTS IS LIMITED, SOMETIMES SEVERELY. IN 1930 THE NEW
CHUN GOVERNMENT ENACTED A PRESS LAW, MERGED BROADCASTING
NETWORKS AND NEWSPAPERS, ESTABLISHED A GOVERNMENT-OWNED PUBLI
TELEVISION CORPORATION, AND PROHIBITED THE STATIONING OF
REPORTERS BY NATIONAL NEWSPAPERS IN PROVINCIAL CITIES.

GOVERNMENT CRITICS SAY THAT STATUTES SUCH AS THE BASIC PRESS
LAW, UNDER WHICH MEDIA ORGANIZATIONS ARE LICENSED AND

PERMITTED TO OPERATE, AND CRIMINAL CODE PR VISIONS AGAINST TH
SPREADING OF "RUMORS WHICH EVENTUALLY DISTURB PEACE AND ORDER
AND "DEFILING THE STATE" ARE USED TO MUZZLE AND PUNISH
DISSIDENT VIEWS. OPPOSITION POLITICAL PARTIES AND SEVERAL
MAJOR KOREAN NEWSPAPER EDITORIAL WRITERS HAVE CALLED FOR THE
REPEAL OR REFORM OF THIS BASIC PRESS LAW. THE DOMESTIC MEDIA
ALSO ENGAGE IN "SELF-CENSORSHIP," ACCORDING TO GUIDELINES THE
GOVERNMENT REGULARLY GIVES ORALLY OR IN WRITING TO EDITORS.
JOURNALISTS WHO OBJECT TO OR IGNORE THESE GUIDELINES OR WHO
PRINT CRITICAL STORIES ON POLITICALLY SENSITIVE TOPICS HAVE

C O N F I D E N T I A L   STATE 047058/05

0166

BEEN PICKED UP FOR QUESTIONING AND ON OCCASION DISMISSED OR
SENT OUT OF THE COUNTRY.
IN 1986 SUCH INSTANCES INCLUDED A NEWSPAPER CARTOONIST
QUESTIONED BY SECURITY INVESTIGATORS IN CONNECTION WITH
EDITORIAL CARTOONS DEEMED TO BE INSULTING TO THE STATE AND TH
PRESIDENT. SEVERAL MAGAZINE WRITERS WERE QUESTIONED AND, IN
AT LEAST ONE CASE, DISMISSED FOR WRITING ARTICLES ON SUCH
TOPICS AS THE ACTIVITIES OF THE SECURITY AGENCIES DURING THE
1970'S. ON A NUMBER OF OCCASIONS, ARTICLES OBJECTIONABLE TO
THE GOVERNMENT WERE WITHDRAWN FROM LATER EDITIONS AND EARLIER
EDITIONS CONFISCATED.

NONETHELESS, THE GENERAL TREND OF GREATER OUTSPOKENNESS IN
NEWSPAPERS AND MAGAZINES CONTINUED IN 1986, ALTHOUGH
TELEVISION AND RADIO BROADCASTING WAS STILL RIGIDLY
CONTROLLED. A NUMBER OF OPPOSITION GROUPS, INCLUDING THE
NKDP, PROMOTED A CAMPAIGN TO BOYCOTT THE PAYING OF TELEVISION
VIEWER FEES ON THE GROUNDS THAT THE PUBLIC NETWORK WAS NOT
PROVIDING UNBIASED NEWS COVERAGE AND WAS TOO COMMERCIALIZED.
SOME NEWSPAPERS JOINED IN THE CRITICISM OF THE PUBLIC
TELEVISION CORPORATION. THERE WERE ALSO CALLS FROM POLITICAL
AND RELIGIOUS ACTIVISTS FOR THE RESTORATION OF THE RIGHT OF
THE CHRISTIAN BROADCASTING RADIO STATION TO REPORT OTHER THAN
RELIGIOUS NEWS. THE GOVERNMENT REFUSED THIS DEMAND AND DID
NOT REVOKE THE TELEVISION VIEWER FEE BUT PROMISED TO TAKE INT
ACCOUNT COMPLAINTS ABOUT THE STATION'S PROGRAMING.

IN LATE 1985 A SCREENING COMMITTEE WAS SET UP WITH THE POWER
TO BAN FROM SALE LITERATURE DEEMED HARMFUL TO THE PUBLIC
INCLUDING "ANTISOCIAL OR ANTISTATE IDEOLOGY-ORIENTED"
PUBLICATIONS. IN 1986 THE AUTHORITIES INVOKED THE NATIONAL
SECURITY LAW A NUMBER OF TIMES AGAINST PERSONS ACCUSED OF
PRODUCING, SELLING, OR READING SUBVERSIVE OR PRO-COMMUNIST
LITERATURE. ON SEVERAL OCCASIONS POLICE SEARCHED BOOKSTORES,
DISSIDENT OFFICES, AND CAMPUSES, SEIZING BANNED "LEFTIST"
BOOKS AND DISSIDENT AND STUDENT PUBLICATIONS CARRYING MATERIA
OBJECTIONABLE TO THE GOVERNMENT. GOVERNMENT AUTHORITIES
HALTED THE PUBLICATION OF THE NKDP'S NEWSPAPER ON AT LEAST TW
OCCASIONS IN 1986.

ALTHOUGH NATIONAL ASSEMBLYMEN ENJOY IMMUNITY FROM PROSECUTION
FOR REMARKS MADE WITHIN THE ASSEMBLY, THEY ARE NOT IMMUNE FRO
PROSECUTION FOR WHAT THEY WRITE OR SAY OUTSIDE THE CHAMBER.
ONE OPPOSITION ASSEMBLYMAN WAS QUESTIONED BY AUTHORITIES IN
1986 FOR DISTRIBUTING A LEAFLET WHICH "DENIGRATED THE STATE."
AS NOTED EARLIER, ANOTHER, YOO SUNG HWAN, WAS JAILED FOR
DISTRIBUTING AN ADVANCE TEXT OF A SPEECH HE WAS TO GIVE IN TH
ASSEMBLY.

ACADEMIC FREEDOM IS SUBJECT TO SOME POLITICAL LIMITATIONS.
DURING 1986 OVER 720 UNIVERSITY PROFESSORS SIGNED VARIOUS
STATEMENTS CALLING FOR DEMOCRATIZATION OR CONSTITUTIONAL
REVISION. MANY WERE SUBSEQUENTLY SUBJECTED TO VARIOUS
PRESSURES AND PUNISHMENTS INCLUDING DENIAL OF RESEARCH FUNDS,
WITHHOLDING OF PROMOTIONS, DEMANDS FOR WRITTEN APOLOGIES, AND
PRESSURE TO RESIGN FROM ADMINISTRATIVE POSITIONS. MANY
RESISTED THESE PRESSURES, WITH THE SUPPORT OF THEIR
COLLEAGUES, AND THE GOVERNMENT'S CAMPAIGN AGAINST THEM WAS NO

C O N F I D   N T I A L   STATE 0470 /06

PRESSED AS FAR AS ARRESTS.

PROFESSORS ARE EXPECTED TO PLAY AN ACTIVE ROLE IN PREVENTING
CAMPUS DEMONSTRATIONS, A TASK MANY FIND OBJECTIONABLE. MIDDL
AND HIGH SCHOOL TEACHERS SOMETIMES ARE ALSO PUNISHED FOR
ANTIGOVERNMENT POLITICAL ACTIVITIES. IN 1986 THERE WERE
REPORTS OF TEACHERS BEING DISMISSED, HAVING THEIR PAY REDUCED
AND RECEIVING UNDESIRABLE TRANSFERS BECAUSE OF HAVING
PARTICIPATED IN ANTIGOVERNMENT ACTIVITIES. A CIVIL SERVANT I
THE PRIME MINISTER'S OFFICE REPORTEDLY WAS FORCED TO RESIGN
AFTER HE MADE A PUBLIC STATEMENT CRITICAL OF THE GOVERNMENT.

B. FREEDOM OF PEACEFUL ASSEMBLY AND ASSOCIATION

A NUMBER OF SPECIFIED CATEGORIES OF ASSEMBLY, INCLUDING THOSE
CONSIDERED LIKELY TO UNDERMINE PUBLIC ORDER OR CAUSE SOCIAL
UNREST, ARE PROHIBITED BY THE LAW ON ASSEMBLY AND
DEMONSTRATIONS. THE LAW ALSO REQUIRES THAT DEMONSTRATIONS OF
ALL TYPES, INCLUDING OUTDOOR POLITICAL ASSEMBLIES, BE REPORTE
IN ADVANCE TO THE POLICE. VIOLATION OF THE LAW CARRIES A
MAXIMUM SENTENCE OF 7 YEARS' IMPRISONMENT OR A FINE OF ABOUT
$3,750. UNDER THIS LAW, POLICE HAVE AT TIMES INTERVENED AND
BROKEN UP MEETINGS. MOST PEACEFUL NONPOLITICAL ASSEMBLIES
TAKE PLACE ENTIRELY WITHOUT OFFICIAL SUPERVISION OR
RESTRICTION. MEETINGS OF DISSIDENTS ARE MONITORED AND
SOMETIMES PREVENTED, OFTEN BY PLACING THE SCHEDULED SPEAKER
UNDER SOME FORM OF HOUSE ARREST. IN THE FALL OF 1986, THE
GOVERNMENT DEMANDED THE "VOLUNTARY" DISBANDMENT OF A DISSIDEN
COALITION GROUP; THE ORGANIZATION'S OFFICES WERE SUBSEQUENTLY
SEARCHED AND MANY OF ITS OFFICIALS ARRESTED.

IN 1986 THE NKDP HELD A SERIES OF RALLIES IN SUPPORT OF
CONSTITUTIONAL REVISION THROUGHOUT THE COUNTRY. POLICE
PERMITTED A NUMBER OF EVENTS OUTSIDE THE CAPITAL REGION BUT
ONLY ONE (IN MARCH) IN SEOUL. IN LATE SPRING OPPOSITION
RALLIES DREW CROWDS OF TENS OF THOUSANDS IN PUSAN AND
KWANGJU. BUT AN NKDP RALLY IN INCHON DEGENERATED INTO
VIOLENCE, WITH THE GOVERNMENT BLAMING RADI AL DISSIDENTS AND
THE NKDP BLAMING POLICE FOR INSTIGATING THE CONFRONTATION.

C O N F I D E N T I A L   STATE 047058/06

0168

SUBSEQUENT RALLIES IN THE PROVINCIAL CITIES OF PUSAN AND
KUNSAN ATTRACTED LARGE CROWDS. SOME VIOLENCE ATTENDED THESE
EVENTS AS WELL, BUT THEY WERE ON THE WHOLE WELL-MANAGED. IN
LATE NOVEMBER, HOWEVER, THE GOVERNMENT USED A MASSIVE NUMBER
OF POLICE TO PREVENT AN OPPOSITION MASS MEETING IN SEOUL.

THE LAW ON ASSEMBLY AND DEMONSTRATIONS WAS USED MOST OFTEN IN
1986 AGAINST STUDENT DEMONSTRATORS, WITH GOVERNMENT STATI TIC
SHOWING 813 PERSONS BOOKED FOR INVOLVEMENT IN CAMPUS
DISTURBANCES IN THE FIRST HALF OF 1986. DURING THE SAME
PERIOD, 116 PERSONS, INCLUDING SEVERAL NKDP AND OTHER
OPPOSITION ORGANIZATION FIGURES, WERE CHARGED WIT VIOLATION
OF THE LAW IN CONNECTION WITH THE NKDP RALLIES,.

UNDER THE CONSTITUTION, WORKERS ARE GUARANTEED THE RIGHTS OF
INDEPENDENT ASSOCIATION, COLLECTIVE BARGAINING, AND COLLECTIV
ACTION. THESE RIGHTS, HOWEVER, ARE CIRCUMSCRIBED BY BOTH
LABOR-RELATED LAWS AND PRACTICE AND DO NOT EXTEND TO WORKERS
EMPLOYED BY THE GOVERNMENT, PUBLIC UTILITIES, DEFENSE-RELATED
INDUSTRIES, OR FIRMS THAT "EXERCISE GREAT INFLUENCE ON THE
NATIONAL ECONOMY."

THE SINGLE NATIONAL LABOR FEDERATION, THE FEDERATION OF KOREA
TRADE UNIONS (FKTU), AND ITS 16 NATIONAL AFFILIATE FEDERATION
AND UNIONS ARE NOT DIRECTLY CONTROLLED BY THE GOVERNMENT.
THEIR ACTIVITIES ARE, HOWEVER, LIMITED BY LAW AND SUBJECT TO
GOVERNMENT INTERFERENCE. LABOR ORGANIZATIONS ARE PRECLUDED B
LAW FROM ENDORSING A PARTICULAR POLITICAL PARTY OR POLITICIAN
ALTHOUGH THE FKTU DOES LOBBY NATIONAL ASSEMBLYMEN IN
CONNECTION WITH LABOR AND WELFARE-RELATED LEGISLATION.
ACCORDING TO THE FKTU, NATIONWIDE DUES-PAYING FKTU MEMBERSHIP
AT THE END OF SEPTEMBER WAS 89Ø,472. MINISTRY OF LABOR
FIGURES, BASED ON REPORTS SUBMITTED BY INDIVIDUAL UNIONS,
PLACED TOTAL UNION MEMBERSHIP AT 1,Ø24,27Ø AT THE END OF JUNE
THE FKTU IS AFFILIATED WITH THE INTERNATIONAL CONFEDERATION O
FREE TRADE UNIONS, AND ITS CONSTITUENT FEDERATIONS AND UNIONS
ARE AFFILIATED WITH RECOGNIZED INTERNATIONAL TRADE
SECRETARIATS. THE REPUBLIC OF KOREA HAS OBSERVER STATUS AT
THE ILO AND ASPIRES TO BECOME A FULL-FLEDGED MEMBER.

UNDER EXISTING LABOR LAWS, ALL LOCAL UNIONS MAY BE ORGANIZED
ONLY UP TO THE LEVEL OF INDIVIDUAL ENTERPRISES, CREATING A
STRUC URE OF THOUSANDS OF SHOP UNIONS, MOST OF THEM SMALL AND
WEAK. RECENT AMENDMENTS TO THE LABOR LAWS REMOVED THE FKTU
AND ITS 16 AFFILIATED NATIONAL INDUSTRIAL FEDERATIONS FROM TH
CATEGORY OF "THIRD PARTIES" HERETOFORE ENJOINED FROM ENTERING
INTO LABOR DISPUTES. RELIGIOUS LABOR ORGANIZATIONS SUCH AS
THE CATHOLIC YOUNG CHRISTIAN WORKERS AND THE PROTESTANT URBAN
INDUSTRIAL MISSION ARE SEVERELY LIMITED IN THE ASSISTANCE
WHICH THEY CAN PROVIDE LEGALLY ESTABLISHED UNIONS.

UNDER THESE CIRCUMSTANCES, THE INFLUENCE OF THE GOVERNMENT AN
EMPLOYERS HAS GREATLY EXCEEDED THAT OF UNIONS IN SETTING WAGE
AND RESOLVING OTHER LABOR ISSUES. COLLECTIVE ACTIONS AND
STRIKES, ALTHOUGH TECHNICALLY LEGAL, ARE STRONGLY DISCOURAGED
BY THE GOVERNMENT AND BY EMPLOYERS.

AS PART OF THE OVERALL CRACKDOWN ON DISSIDENT ACTIVITIES IN

LATE 1986, THE MINISTER OF LABOR IN NOVEMBER ORDERED THE
"VOLUNTARY" DISBANDMENT OF FOURTEEN "LEFTIST-ORIENTED" LABOR
ORGANIZATIONS, INCLUDING THE CHONGGYE GARMENT WORKERS' UNION,
WHICH THE MINISTER CLAIMED WAS RESPONSIBLE FOR MANY LABOR
PROBLEMS. GOVERNMENT AUTHORITIES ALSO ANNOUNCED THAT THEY HA
UNCOVERED SEVERAL "CLANDESTINE" LABOR NETWORKS THAT WERE
PURPORTEDLY ENGAGED IN ATTEMPTS TO INDOCTRINATE WORKERS WITH
LEFTIST IDEOLOGY. HUMAN RIGHTS GROUPS ESTIMATED THAT AS MANY
AS 150 PEOPLE, INCLUDING SOME STUDENTS, WERE IN PRISON IN LAT
1986 BECAUSE OF INVOLVEMENT IN VARIOUS LABOR-RELATED
ACTIVITIES. THIS IN PART REFLECTS CONTINUING EFFORTS BY
STUDENT DISSIDENTS TO CONTACT AND INFLUENCE LABOR GROUPS.

IN 1986 THE GOVERNMENT CONTINUED TO USE THE LAW ON ASSEMB Y
AND DEMONSTRATIONS TO DETAIN WORKERS IN CONNECTION WITH LABOR
DISPUTES. DESPITE THE LEGAL RESTRICTIONS AND OTHER OBSTACLES
COLLECTIVE ACTIONS BY WORKERS INCREASED IN 1986. AS OF THE
END OF OCTOBER, 249 LABOR DISPUTES WERE RECORDED BY THE
MINISTRY OF LABOR, COMPARED TO 230 DURING THE CORRESPONDING
PERIOD IN 1985. MOST OF THESE DISPUTES WERE ATTRIBUTED TO
DELAYED OR NONPAYMENT OF WAGES OR TO WORKER COMPLAINTS OVER
WORKING CONDITIONS. THE GOVERNMENT CHARGED THAT STUDENT
ACTIVISTS HAD "INFILTRATED" WORKPLACES, WITH THE INTENTION OF
AGITATING BLUE-COLLAR WORKERS, AND WERE RESPONSIBLE FOR MUCH
OF THE REPORTED LABOR UNREST.

C.   FREEDOM OF RELIGION

THERE IS NO STATE-FAVORED RELIGION IN KOREA. THERE IS
GENERALLY COMPLETE FREEDOM FOR PROSELYTIZING, DOCTRINAL
TEACHING, AND CONVERSION. KOREA BOTH SENDS AND RECEIVES

MISSIONARIES OF VARIOUS FAITHS. MANY RELIGIOUS GROUPS IN
KOREA MAINTAIN ACTIVE LINKS WITH CORELIGIONISTS IN OTHER
COUNTRIES. THE GOVERNMENT AND PEOPLE DO NOT DISCRIMINATE
AGAINST MINORITY SECTS. ADHERENCE TO A PARTICULAR FAITH
CONFERS NEITHER ADVANTAGES NOR DISADVANTAGES IN CIVIL,
MILITARY, OR OFFICIAL LIFE.

C O N F I D E N T I A L   STATE 047058/07

0170

IN 1986 SOME BUDDHIST ADHERENTS DEMONSTRATED AGAINST LAWS
GOVERNING STATE REGULATION OF TEMPLES WHICH THEY CLAIMED
CONSTITUTED DISCRIMINATION.   THESE PROTESTS WERE PUT DOWN BY
POLICE.   CHURCHES AND RELIGIOUS GROUPS ARE SUBJECT TO MANY OF
THE RESTRICTIONS ON POLITICAL ACTIVITIES AND CRITICISM OF THE
GOVERNMENT THAT APPLY TO ALL OTHER INSTITUTIONS.   ON THOSE
OCCASIONS WHERE PASTORS ARE HARASSED BY THE AUTHORITIES, IT I
USUALLY FOR RELIGIOUSLY MOTIVATED SOCIAL OR POLITICAL
ACTIVISM.   CONSCIENTIOUS OBJECTORS ARE SUBJECT TO ARREST.

D.   FREEDOM OF MOVEMENT WITHIN THE COUNTRY, FOREIGN
TRAVEL, EMIGRATION, AND REPATRIATION

EXCEPT FOR CRIMINALS AND PERSONS CONSIDERED POLITICALLY
SUSPECT, MOST PEOPLE CAN OBT IN PASSPORTS FOR TRAVEL IN THE
OFFICIALLY APPROVED CATEGORIES SUCH AS BUSINESS.   A NUMBER OF
DISSIDENTS AND FORMER POLITICAL PRISONERS HAVE BEEN ALLOWED T
TRAVEL ABROAD, ALTHOUGH IN 1986 THE GOVERNMENT BANNED FOREIGN
TRAVEL BY SEVEN OPPOSITION ASSEMBLYMEN WHO HAD BEEN INDICTED
FOR DISRUPTIVE BEHAVIOR IN THE ASSEMBLY.   IN SEPARATE
INCIDENTS, SEVERAL RELIGIOUS DISSIDENTS WERE PREVENTED BY
AUTHORITIES FROM ATTENDING CHURCH CONFERENCES ABROAD AT WHICH
POLITICAL TOPICS WERE TO BE DISCUSSED.   THERE IS ALMOST
UNIVERSAL FREEDOM OF MOVEMENT AND FREEDOM TO CHANGE EMPLOYMEN
IN KOREA.   BECAUSE KOREA IS ONE OF THE MOST DENSELY POPULATED
COUNTRIES IN THE WORLD, THE GOVERNMENT ENCOURAGES EMIGRATION
AND DOES NOT DISCRIMINATE AGAINST PR SPECTIVE EMIGRANTS.

THE GOVERNMENT LIMITS THE NUMBER OF PASSPORTS ISSUED TO
TOURISTS AND PROSPECTIVE STUDENTS, CITING OREIGN EXCHANGE
CONSIDERATIONS AND THE PROBLEM OF UNQUALIFIED STUDENTS GOING
ABROAD.   PASSPORTS, WHEN ISSUED, ARE TYPICALLY LIMITED TO 1
YEAR, ALTHOUGH THERE ARE EXCEPTIONS IN WHICH PASSPORTS ARE
ISSUED UP TO THE LEGALLY MAXIMUM 5-YEAR PERIOD OF VALIDITY.

A SMALL CONTINUING INFLUX OF VIETNAMESE BO T PEOPLE IS
ADMITTED TO TEMPORARY FIRST ASYLUM IN KOREA.   THEY ARE CARED
FOR AT A CAMP IN PUSAN BY THE KOREAN RED CROSS UNTIL THEY CAN
BE RESETTLED ABROAD.   OVER 700 DISPLACED PERSONS FROM VIETNAM
HAVE PASSED THROUGH KOREA IN THE LAST SEVERAL YEARS.   VERY FE
HAVE BEEN PERMANENTLY RESETTLED IN KOREA.

SECTION 3   RESPECT FOR POLITICAL RIGHTS: THE RIG T OF CITIZE
TO CHANGE THEIR GOVERNMENT.

KOREA'S CONSTITUTION AND STATUTES AS WELL AS ITS TRADITIONS
CONCENTRATE POLITICAL POWER IN THE PRESIDENT, A CONCENTRATION
FURTHER INTENSIFIED BY THE SUPPORT THE PRESIDENT ENJOYS FROM
THE MILITARY AND SECURITY AGENCIES.   THE PRESIDENT AND THE
MEMBERS OF THE NATIONAL ASSEMBLY ARE THE ONLY ELECTED
OFFICIALS IN KOREA.   UNDER THE 1980 PRESIDENTIAL ELECTION LAW
THE PRESIDENT IS CHOSEN BY A POPULARLY ELECTED ELECTORAL
COLLEGE OF AT LEAST 5,000 MEMBERS.   BY LAW, PRESIDENTIAL
CAMPAIGNS ARE BRIEF AND CANDIDATES SEVERELY RESTRICTED IN
CAMPAIGNING.   THERE ARE LIMITS ON THE AMOUNT OF MONEY THEY MA
SPEND, THE NUMBER OF SPEECHES THEY MAY DELIVER, AND THE NUMBE
OF PUBLICATIONS THEY MAY DISTRIBUTE.   IN THE 1981 PRESIDENTIA
ELECTION, THESE RESTRICTIONS, TOGETHER WITH THE AUTHORITIES'

CONFID NTIAL   STATE 0470 '09

SCREENING OF ELECTORAL COLLEGE CANDIDATES, RESULTED IN THE
ABSENCE OF EFFECTIVE OPPOSITION TO INCUMBENT PRESIDENT CHUN
DOO HWAN, WHO WON ALMOST UNANIMOUSLY. IN THE 1985 NATIONAL
ASSEMBLY ELECTION, TWO OF THE MOST PROMINENT OPPOSITION
POLITICIANS, KIM DAE JUNG AND KIM YOUNG SAM, WERE NOT ALLOWED
TO PARTICIPATE. THAT ELECTION WAS, HOWEVER, FI RCELY
CONTESTED, AND THE OPPOSITION PARTY SCORED SOME STUNNING
SUCCESSES.
THE CONSTITUTION LIMITS THE PRESIDENT TO A SINGLE 7-YEAR TERM
AND MAY NOT BE AMENDED TO ALLOW THE INCUMBENT PRESIDENT TO RU
FOR ANOTHER TERM. PRESIDENT CHUN CONTINUED TO REAFFIRM THAT
HE INTENDS TO STEP DOWN IN 1988 TO PROVIDE FOR A PEACEFUL,
CONSTITUTIONAL TRANSFER OF POWER. FACED WITH OPPOSITION
DEMANDS TO AMEND THE CONSTITUTION BEFORE 1988, CHUN AGREED TO
REVISE IT IF AGREEMENT CAN BE REACHED BETWEEN POLITICAL
PARTIES IN THE NATIONAL ASSEMBLY. UNDER PRESENT LAW THE
CONSTITUTION CAN BE AMENDED WHEN APPROVED BY A TWO-THIRDS
MAJORITY IN THE NATIONAL ASSEMBLY AND THEN AFFIRMED BY A
SIMPLE MAJORITY OF VOTERS IN A NATIONAL REFERENDUM.

THE GOVERNMENT PARTY PROPOSED INSTITUTING A PARLIAMENTARY
SYSTEM WITH A STRONG PRIME MINISTER ELECTED BY THE NATIONAL
ASSEMBLY, ARGUING THAT SUCH A SYSTEM WOULD HELP CORRECT HE
CONCENTRATION OF POWER IN THE PRESIDENCY. THE OPPOSITION
CONTINUED TO PUSH FOR A DIRECT ELECTION PRESIDENTIAL SYSTEM,
WHICH IT SAID IS MOST COMPATIBLE WITH KOREA'S POLITICAL
CULTURE AND THE WISHES OF THE PEOPLE. BOTH PARTIES EXPRESSED
SUPPORT FOR MORE RAPID DEMOCRATIZATION OF KOREA INCLUDING THE
IMPLEMENTATION OF LOCAL AUTONOMY, BUT AT HE YEAR'S END
NEGOTIATIONS ON CONSTITUTIONAL REVISION WERE STALEMATED.

THE NATIONAL ASSEMBLY, ALTHOUGH INSTITUTIONALLY WEAK, ACQUIRED
NEW IMPORTANCE IN 1985 WITH THE HOLDING OF ELECTIONS AND THE

EMERGENCE OF A NEW AND MORE OUTSPOKEN OPPOSITION PARTY, THE
NKDP, FORMED ONLY WEEKS BEFORE THE ELECTION AND LED LARGELY B
POLITICIANS RECENTLY FREED FROM THE POLITICAL BAN. MEMBERS
ARE DIRECTLY ELECTED AND SERVE A 4-YEAR TERM. THE ELECTION
LAW PASSED IN 1981 PROVIDES FOR A PROPORTIONAL REPRESENTATION

CONFIDENTIAL STATE 047058/08

0172

SYSTEM THAT RESERVES 9. OF THE ASSEMBLY'S 276 SEAT FOR
MEMBERS DESIGNATED BY THE PARTIES, WITH TWO-THIRDS OF THESE
SEATS AWARDED TO THE PARTY GAINING A PLURALITY OF THE POPULAR
VOTE. THE GOVERNMENT PARTY, THE DEMOCRATIC JUSTICE PARTY
(DJP), GARNERED A PLURALITY OF 35.3 PERCENT IN THE 1985
ELECTIONS AND, WITH ITS PROPORTIONAL REPRESENTATION SEATS,
MAINTAINED A COMFORTABLE MAJORITY OF 148 OUT OF 276 ASSEMBLY
SEATS. THE NKDP OBTAINED A SURPRISING 29.2 PERCENT OF THE
POPULAR VOTE, AND, WITH THE POST-ELECTION DEFECTION TO IT OF
ASSEMBLYMEN FROM OTHER OPPOSITION PARTIES, BECAME THE LARGEST
OPPOSITION PARTY IN THE REPUBLIC'S PARLIAMENTARY HISTORY IN
TERMS OF ASSEMBLY SEATS HELD. IN 1986 THE NKDP AND OTHER
OPPOSITIONISTS DEMANDED THE REVISION OF THE ASSEMBLY ELECTION
LAW AS WELL AS CONSTITUTIONAL REVISION.

POLITICAL AND RELIGIOUS ACTIVISTS INVOLVED IN OPPOSITION
GROUPS OUTSIDE THE RECOGNIZED POLITICAL PARTIES CONTINUED TO
COME UNDER INTENSE GOVERNMENT PRESSURE IN 1986. EXPRESSING
WORRIES ABOUT GROWING LEFTIST TRENDS, THE GOVERNMENT
INVESTIGATED A NUMBER OF DISSIDENT GROUPS TO DISCERN WHETHER
THEY INCLUDED PRO-COMMUNISTS AND ORDERED THE "VOLUNTARY"
DISBANDMENT OF SOME OF THEM. AT THE END OF THE YEAR, A NUMBE
OF SUCH DISSIDENTS WERE UNDER INVESTIGATION OR INDICTMENT FOR
NATIONAL SECURITY LAW AND OTHER VIOLATIONS. THE GOVERNMENT
PARTY WARNED THE NKDP AGAINST IDENTIFICATION WITH OR TIES TO
SUCH GROUPS.

SECTION 4 GOVERNMENTAL ATTITUDE REGARDING INTERNATIONAL AND
NONGOVERNMENTAL INVESTIGATION OF ALLEGED VIOLATIONS
OF HUMAN RIGHTS

THE REPUBLIC OF KOREA DOES NOT BELONG TO ANY INTERNATIONAL
HUMAN RIGHTS BODIES AND USUALLY DOES NOT WELCOME OUTSIDE
INVOLVEMENT IN THE HUMAN RIGHTS AREA, ALTHOUGH OVERNMENT
OFFICIALS HAVE ALLOWED THE VISITS OF AND MET WITH
REPRESENTATIVES OF INTERNATIONAL HUMAN RIG TS BODIES,
INCLUDING AMNESTY INTERNATIONAL AND ASIA WATCH.

ACCORDING TO THE GOVERNMENT, PUBLIC PROSECUTORS AND THE HUMAN
RIGHTS DIVISION OF THE MINISTRY OF JUSTICE ARE RESPONSIBLE FO
PROTECTING HUMAN RIGHTS AND INVESTIGATING VIOLATIONS. THE
NATIONAL ASSEMBLY AND POLITICAL PARTIES ALSO HAVE COMMITTEES
WHICH ARE CONCERNED WITH SOME ASPECTS OF HUMAN RIGHTS ISSUES.
THE RELEASE OF POLITICAL PRISONERS AND ALLEGATIONS OF PRISONE

MISTREATMENT WERE THE SUBJECT OF SHARP DEBATE IN THE NATIONAL
ASSEMBLY IN 1986. THE HUMAN RIGHTS COMMITTEE OF THE NKDP WAS
ACTIVE IN INVESTIGATING ALLEGATIONS OF HUMAN RIGHTS ABUSES,
VISITING PRISONS, MEETING WITH PRISONERS AND THEIR FAMILIES,
AND PROVIDING LEGAL DEFENSE IN CONNECTION WITH NUMEROUS HUMAN
RIGHTS ISSUES.

A NUMBER OF POLITICALLY NONAFFILIATED PRIVATE ORGANIZATIONS
ARE ACTIVE IN HUMAN RIGHTS, CHIEFLY THE HUMAN RIGHTS COMMITTE
OF THE NATIONAL COUNCIL OF CHURCHES OF KOREA (KNCC), THE
CATHOLIC JUSTICE AND PEACE COMMITTEE, THE KOREAN BAR
ASSOCIATION, AND THE KOREA LEGAL AID CENTER IN SEOUL. THE
COMMITTEES AND OTHER HUMAN RIGHTS ORGANIZATIONS SUBMIT

PETITIONS TO THE GOVERNMENT, PUBLISH REPORTS ON THE HUMAN
RIGHTS SITUATION IN KOREA, AND MAKE THEIR VIEWS KNOWN BOTH
INSIDE AND OUTSIDE KOREA. PEOPLE WORKING WITH THESE GROUPS
FREQUENTLY ARE QUESTIONED AND SOMETIMES DETAINED BY THE
SECURITY SERVICES. THE CHAIRMAN OF THE CATHOLIC JUSTICE AND
PEACE COMMITTEE WAS ARRESTED IN OCTOBER FOR HIDING A WANTED
DISSIDENT, AND THE HEAD OF THE KNCC HUMAN RIGHTS COMMITTEE WA
PLACED ON THE POLICE WANTED LIST AFTER HE SIGNED A STATEMENT
IN SUPPORT OF A DISSIDENT DEEMED SUBVERSIVE BY THE
GOVERNMENT. IN NOVEMBER POLICE ARMED WITH A SEARCH WARRANT
ENTERED THE KNCC HUMAN RIGHTS COMMITTEE OFFICE AND SEIZED SOM
DOCUMENTS.

SECTION 5 DISCRIMINATION BASED ON RACE, SEX, RELIGION,
LANGUAGE, OR SOCIAL STATUS

THE REPUBLIC OF KOREA WITH ITS 40 MILLION PLUS POPULATION IS
DENSELY INHABITED AND RACIALLY AND CUL URALLY HOMOGENOUS.
THERE ARE NO ETHNIC MINORITIES OF SIGNIFICANT SIZE.

DESPITE THE CULTURAL HOMOGENEITY OF ITS PEOPLE, REGIONAL
RIVALRIES EXIST IN KOREA. MANY KOREANS BELIEVE THAT PERSONS
FROM THE SOUTHWESTERN PROVINCES OF NORTH AND SOUTH CHOLLA FAC
SOME DISCRIMINATION, AND THAT SUCCESSIVE GOVERNMENTS LED
PREDOMINANTLY BY MEN FROM SOUTHEAST KOREA AND OTHER AREAS HAV
NEGLECTED THE ECONOMIC DEVELOPMENT OF THE CHOLLA PROVINCES.
THE PRESENT GOVERNMENT CLAIMS THAT IT IS MAKING PARTICULAR
EFFORTS TO ENCOURAGE THE DEVELOPMENT OF THE CHOLLA REGION.

IN KOREA, WITH ITS CONSERVATIVE CONFUCIAN TRADITION, WOMEN
REMAIN SUBORDINATE TO MEN SOCIALLY, ECONOMICALLY, AND
LEGALLY. SOME PROGRESS HAS BEEN MADE. THE FAMILY LAW WAS
REVISED IN 1960 AND 1979, BUT CRITICS CONTEND THAT THE LAW IS
STILL INCONSISTENT WITH KOREAN CONSTITUTIONAL GUARANTEES OF
SEXUAL EQUALITY. FOR EXAMPLE, WOMEN DO NOT HAVE EQUAL RIGHTS
WITH MEN IN PASSING NATIONALITY, NOR DO THEY HAVE EQUAL RIGHT

WITH REGARD TO CHILD CUSTODY IN DIVORCE CASES. WOMEN'S RIGHT
GROUPS ARE CAMPAIGNING FOR CHANGES IN THESE AND OTHER POI TS

C O N F I D E N T I A L   STATE 047058/09

0174

결 번

넘버링 오류

OF THE FAMILY LAW.

WOMEN ARE FREE TO VOTE, BECOME GOVERNMENT OFFICIALS, AND RUN
FOR THE NATIONAL ASSEMBLY. WOMEN HOLD SEVEN ASSEMBLY SEATS,
ALL BUT TWO APPOINTED BY THEIR PARTIES. HOWEVER, THE POWER
STRUCTURE REMAINS MALE-DOMINATED, AND IN MANY IGNIFICANT
RESPECTS THE LEGAL SYSTEM AND SOCIAL CUSTOM STRONGLY
DISCRIMINATE AGAINST WOMEN.

WOMEN ENJOY FULL ACCESS TO EDUCATIONAL OPP RTUNITIES. THEY
ARE INCREASINGLY REPRESENTED, THOUGH STILL LARGELY AT ENTRY
LEVEL, IN GOVERNMENT AND THE PRIVATE SECTOR. AS OF 1985, ONL
24 WOMEN HAD EVER PASSED THE BAR EXAMINATION. ONLY FIVE HAVE
PASSED THE NATIONAL ADMINISTRATION EXAMINATION GIVEN FOR
HIGHER LEVEL CIVIL SERVICE JOBS. IN GENERAL, WOMEN ARE NOT
PROTECTED AGAINST DISCRIMINATION IN HIRING, PAY, OR
ADVANCEMENT. THEY ARE COMMONLY EXPECTED TO RESIGN UPON
MARRIAGE OR PREGNANCY. WOMEN'S ORGANIZATIONS AND MEMBERS OF
THE NATIONAL ASSEMBLY ARE TRYING TO FOCUS MORE ATTENTION ON
WOMEN'S RIGHTS.

CONDITIONS OF LABOR

CHAPTER V OF THE LABOR STANDARDS LAW GOVERNS THE EMPLOYMENT O
MINOR AND FEMALE WORKERS. UNDER THIS PROVISION, MINORS UNDER
AGE 13 MUST HAVE A SPECIAL PERMIT ISSUED BY THE MINISTRY OF
LABOR TO BE EMPLOYED. MINORS UNDER AGE 18 MUST HAVE A
PARENT'S OR GUARDIAN'S WRITTEN APPROVAL IN ORDER TO WORK, AND
THEY ARE PROHIBITED FROM NIGHT WORK WITHOUT SPECIAL PERMISSIO
FROM HE MINISTRY OF LABOR. IN ADDITION, THE LAW REQUIRES
THAT EMPLOYERS OF 30 OR MORE MINORS PROVIDE EDUCATIONAL
FACILITIES OR ARRANGE SCHOLARSHIP FUNDS FOR THEM. THE
EMPLOYMENT OF MINORS IS WIDESPREAD, PARTICULARLY IN
LABOR-INTENSIVE INDUSTRIES SUCH AS TEXTILES, FOOTWEAR, AND
SMALL ELECTRONICS ASSEMBLY, AND ABUSES OF LEGAL PROTECTIONS
ARE COMMON.

THE LABOR STANDARDS LAW PROVIDES FOR A MAXIMUM WORKWEEK OF 60
HOURS WITH THE MUTUAL CONSENT OF EMPLOYER AND EMPLOYEE, A PAI
DAY OF REST DURING THE WORKWEEK, COMPENSATION FOR OVERTIME AN
HOLIDAY WORK, PAID HOLIDAYS, AND ANNUAL LEAVE. RECENT
STATISTICS INDICATE THAT THE AVERAGE FULL-TIME INDUSTRIAL
WORKER SPENDS CLOSE TO 55 HOURS PER WEEK ON THE JOB. KOREA
HAS NO MINIMUM WAGE SYSTEM, BUT THE GOVERNMENT HAS PLEDGED TO
INSTITUTE ONE, POSSIBLY AS EARLY AS 1988, AS PART OF THE
5 YEAR SOCIOECONOMIC PLAN BEGINNING IN 1987. THE GOVERNMENT
ALSO PLANS TO IMPLEMENT AN AMBITIOUS PENSION SYSTEM--STILL IN

THE DESIGN STAGES--WHICH WOULD EXPAND CONSIDERABLY ELIGIBILIT
FOR RETIREMENT PENSION PLANS BY INDUSTRIAL WORKERS.

IN RESPONSE TO RECURRING CRITICISM OF ITS HANDLING OF LABOR
DISPUTES, THE GOVERNMENT UNDERTOOK IN 1985, AND CONTINUED IN
1986, TO TAKE STRONGER MEASU ES, INCLUDING FINES AND
IMPRISONMENT, TO CURB EMPLOYER ABUSES. DURING THE FIRST 9
MONTHS OF 1986, 39,111 CASES OF EMPLOYER VIOLATIONS OF THE
LABOR STANDARDS LAW WERE RECORDED, AN INCREASE FROM 31,419
DURING THE CORRESPONDING PERIOD IN 1985. MOST OF THE

VIOLATIONS INVOLVED DELAYED PAYMENT OF WAGES.

AS OF AUGUST 1986, THERE WERE 1,07З JOB-RELATED DEATHS AND
92,387 WORK-RELATED INJURIES RECORDED BY GOVERNMENT SOURCES.
IN 1985, THERE WERE 1,718 INDUSTRIAL FATALITIES AND 139,56З
REPORTS OF INJURY. MANUFACTURING, CONSTRUCTION, AND MINING
INDUSTRIES CONTINUED TO BE THE MOST HAZARDOUS. THE GOVERNMENT
HAS MANDATED INSURANCE TO COVER INDUSTRIAL ACCIDENTS AT PLACE
OF BUSINESS EMPLOYING 1З OR MORE WORKERS. THE 1981 REVISION
OF HE INDUSTRIAL ACCIDENT COMPENSATION LAW COVERS JOB-RELATE
MEDICAL COSTS, SICK LEAVE BENEFITS, DISABILITY BENEFITS, AND
OTHER COSTS. END TEXT.   SHULTZ
BT
#7058

NNNN

C O N F I D E N T I A L   STATE 047058/10

ACTION POL3   INFO AMB DCM SAA3 USIS ECON2 CON/RR FCS AGAF CUST ACFUSAN 16

VZCZCULO179   25-FEB-87   TOR: 20:43
PP RUEHUL   CN: 05859
DE RUEHC #4001/01 0362042   CHRG: PROG
ZNY CCCCC ZZH   DIST: POLC
P 052036Z FEB 87
FM SECSTATE WASHDC
TO AMEMBASSY SEOUL PRIORITY 6926
BT
C O N F I D E N T I A L   STATE 034001

TAGS: PHUM, KN, US
SUBJECT: FINAL TEXT OF KN HUMAN RIGHTS REPORT

1. (CONFIDENTIAL ENTIRE TEXT).

2. WE ARE TRANSMITTING HEREWITH THE FINAL VERSION OF THE
HUMAN RIGHTS REPORT FOR NORTH KOREA. THE REPORT REMAINS
CONFIDENTIAL AND EMBARGOED UNTIL RELEASED BY THE
CONGRESS.   AN INSTRUCTION IS FORTHCOMING CONCERNING THE
RELEASE DATE AND DISCRETION TO HAND AN ADVANCE COPY TO
YOUR HOST GOVERNMENT, ON A CONFIDENTIAL BASIS, 24 HOURS
PRIOR TO PUBLIC RELEASE.

3. BEGIN TEXT:

DEMOCRATIC PEOPLE'S REPUBLIC OF KOREA

THE DEMOCRATIC PEOPLE'S REPUBLIC OF KOREA, FORMED IN 1948
DURING THE SOVIET ADMINISTRATION OF THE NORTHERN HALF OF
THE KOREAN PENINSULA, IS A RIGID COMMUNIST DICTATORSHIP
MAINTAINED BY THE RULING KOREAN WORKERS' (COMMUNIST)
PARTY (KWP), WITH ITS OVERRIDING AIM OF IMPOSING A SOCIAL

REVOLUTION AND ENFORCING UNANIMOUS POPULAR SUPPORT FOR
THE COUNTRY'S GOVERNING SYSTEM AND ITS LEADER, KIM IL
SUNG. INDIVIDUAL RIGHTS ARE ENTIRELY SUBORDINATED TO THE
KWP. ALTHOUGH THERE WERE PRO FORMA ELECTIONS TO THE
SUPREME PEOPLE'S ASSEMBLY IN NOVEMBER, FREE ELECTIONS DO
NOT EXIST SINCE CITIZENS HAVE NO CHOICE AMONG CANDIDATES.

THE NORTH KOREAN PEOPLE ARE SUBJECT TO RIGID CONTROLS.
THE STATE ESTABLISHES SECURITY RATINGS FOR EACH PERSON,
AND THESE RATINGS DETERMINE ACCESS TO JOBS, SCHOOLS,
MEDICAL FACILITIES, AND STORES AS WELL AS ADMISSION TO
THE KWP, THE ROUTE TO THE HIGHEST LEVELS AND PRIVILEGES
OF THE SOCIETY. THE PARTY, GOVERNMENT, AND MILITARY ELITE
ENJOY SIGNIFICANT ECONOMIC PRIVILEGES SUCH AS ACCESS TO
SPECIAL STORES AND MEDICAL FACILITIES, BETTER HOUSING,
AND BETTER EDUCATION, WHICH ARE NOT AVAILABLE TO ORDINARY
CITIZENS.

PERSONS WHO FAIL TO CONFORM TO THE RIGID DICTATES OF THE
STATE FACE IMPRISONMENT OR, MORE OFTEN, ENFORCED REMOVAL
TO REMOTE VILLAGES. SURVEILLANCE BY INFORMERS IS

PREVALENT. PUNISHMENT FOR "POLITICAL CRIMES" AGAINST THE
STATE IS SEVERE. NO OUTSIDE INFORMATION OTHER THAN THAT
APPROVED AND DISSEMINATED BY THE NORTH KOREAN AUTHORITIES
IS ALLOWED TO REACH THE GENERAL PUBLIC, ALTHOUGH SENIOR
GOVERNMENT OFFICIALS ARE SOMEWHAT BETTER INFORMED.

PRESIDENT KIM IL SUNG'S 13-YEAR EFFORT TO GROOM HIS SON,
KIM CHONG IL, AS SUCCESSOR IS TESTIMONY TO THE ENORMOUS
POWER THE ELDER KIM HAS AMASSED DURING 38 YEARS OF RULE.
THE YOUNGER KIM HAS BEEN ELEVATED TO SEVERAL SENIOR PARTY
POSITIONS DURING THE LAST FEW YEARS. THE ABSENCE OF ANY
EVIDENCE OF PUBLIC DEBATE ABOUT THE SUCCESSION IS ALSO
INDICATIVE OF THE LACK OF REAL POPULAR PARTICIPATION IN
THE POLITICAL PROCESS.

NORTH KOREA HAS NOT BEEN SUCCESSFUL IN PRODUCING THROUGH
ITS COMMAND ECONOMY THE DESIRED ECONOMIC DEVELOPMENT. IT
REMAINS A LESS-DEVELOPED COUNTRY WITH A STAGNANT STANDARD
OF LIVING AND A BALANCE OF PAYMENTS PROBLEM THAT IS
STEADILY WORSENING.

BEGIN FOOTNOTE:
THE UNITED STATES DOES NOT HAVE DIPLOMATIC RELATIONS
WITH THE DEMOCRATIC PEOPLE'S REPUBLIC OF KOREA.
REPRESENTATIVES OF GOVERNMENTS THAT DO HAVE RELATIONS
WITH THE DPRK, AS WELL AS JOURNALISTS AND OTHER INVITED
VISITORS TO NORTH KOREA, ARE NOT PERMITTED THE FREEDOM OF

MOVEMENT THAT WOULD ENABLE THEM TO ASSESS EFFECTIVELY
HUMAN RIGHTS CONDITIONS THERE. MOST OF THIS REPORT,
THEREFORE, IS A REPEAT OF PREVIOUS HUMAN RIGHTS REPORTS
BASED ON INFORMATION OBTAINED OVER A PERIOD OF IM
EXTENDING FROM WELL BEFORE 1986. WHILE LIMITED IN SCOPE
AND DETAIL, THE INFORMATION IS INDICATIVE OF THE HUMAN
RIGHTS SITUATION IN NORTH KOREA TODAY.
END FOOTNOTE
KIM IL SUNG'S COMMITMENT TO BRING THE ENTIRE KOREAN PENINSULA
UNDER HIS CONTROL HAS LED TO PERIODIC ATTEMPTS TO DESTABILIZE
THE REPUBLIC OF KOREA. NORTH KOREA HAS ENGAGED IN TALKS WITH
SOUTH KOREA, BUT THESE RECENT TALKS WERE SUSPENDED BY NORTH
KOREA IN JANUARY 1986 AND PROSPECTS FOR THEIR RESUMPTION ARE
POOR.

THERE IS NO EVIDENCE TO SUGGEST THAT NORTH KOREA HAS IMPROVED
ITS EXTREMELY POOR PERFORMANCE IN THE HUMAN RIGHTS AREA. BOT
SHORT-AND LONG-TERM TRENDS INDICATE CONTINUED ONE-FAMILY RULE
WITH SCANT RESPECT FOR BASIC HUMAN RIGHTS.

RESPECT FOR HUMAN RIGHTS

SECTION 1 RESPECT FOR THE INTEGRITY OF THE PERSON, INCLUDING

0179

FREEDOM FROM:

A. POLITICAL KILLING

LITTLE INFORMATION IS AVAILABLE ON POLITICALLY MOTIVATED
KILLING IN NORTH KOREA. SEVERAL NORTH KOREAN DEFECTORS REPOR
THAT CERTAIN POLITICAL CRIMINALS HAVE BEEN EXECUTED PUBLICLY
BY FIRING SQUAD. ONE SUCH "CRIMINAL" WHO REPORTEDLY WAS
EXECUTED BY FIRING SQUAD WAS A SCIENTIST WHO USED A PEJORATIV
WORD IN REFERRING TO KIM IL SUNG. THE NORTH KOREAN ATTITUDE
TOWARD POLITICAL KILLING ALSO IS CLEARLY DEMONSTRATED BY THE
NOVEMBER 23, 1984 SHOOTING IN THE JOINT SECURITY AREA OF THE
DEMILITARIZED ZONE (DMZ) DIVIDING NORTH AND SOUTH KOREA. IN
THAT INCIDENT, NORTH KOREAN SECURITY GUARDS OPENED FIRE ON A
SOVIET STUDENT TRYING TO DEFECT FROM A TOUR GROUP, TRIGGERING
AN EXCHANGE OF FIRE IN WHICH SEVERAL LIVES ON BOTH SIDES WERE
LOST.

B. DISAPPEARANCE

THERE IS NO INFORMATION AVAILABLE ON DISAPPEARANCE.

C. TORTURE AND CRUEL, INHUMAN, OR DEGRADING TREATMENT OR
PUNISHMENT

ACCORDING TO THE FREEDOM HOUSE 1985-86 REPORT, "TORTURE IS
REPORTEDLY COMMON" IN NORTH KOREA. THE ACCOUNTS OF TORTURE
AND BEATINGS OF CREW MEMBERS OF THE USS PUEBLO AFTER THEIR
CAPTURE IN 1968 ARE WELL-KNOWN AND DOCUMENTED. ANOTHER
RELIABLE SOURCE ON PRISON CONDITIONS AND TREATMENT OF
PRISONERS IN NORTH KOREA IS VENEZUELAN POET ALI LAMEDA, WHO
WAS DETAINED IN NORTH KOREA FROM SEPTEMBER 1967 THROUGH 1974,
ALLEGEDLY FOR ATTEMPTED SABOTAGE AND ESPIONAGE. WHILE
PHYSICAL TORTURE WAS NOT USED ON MR. LAMEDA, HE STATES THAT
KOREAN PRISONERS WERE ROUTINELY BEATEN. LAMEDA NOTES THAT
"BEATING WAS ALSO USED AS A MEANS OF PERSUASION DURING
INTERROGATION."

LAMEDA REPORTS THE USE OF DEPRIVATION OF FOOD TO FORCE
"CONFESSIONS," AS WELL AS SOLITARY CONFINEMENT, CONTINUOUS
INTERROGATION, ENFORCED WAKING PERIODS, POOR OR NONEXISTENT
MEDICAL TREATMENT, AND 12 HOURS OF FORCED LABOR PER DAY. IN
ADDITION, PRISONERS WERE DENIED FAMILY VISITS, PARCELS,
CORRESPONDENCE, WRITING MATERIALS, NEWSPAPERS, AND CLOTHING
CHANGES. PRISONERS WERE REGARDED AS HAVING NO RIGHTS.

MUCH OF WHAT LAMEDA HAS REPORTED HAS BEEN CORROBORATED BY CHO
UN-WUI AND HER HUSBAND SHIN SANG-OK (HEREINAFTER REFERRED TO
AS THE SHINS), THE FAMOUS KOREAN FILM PRODUCER AND ACTRESS,
WHO REPORTEDLY WERE KIDNAPED BY THE NORTH KOREAN REGIME.
ALTHOUGH SHIN DID NOT WITNESS ANY BEATINGS DURING HIS
INCARCERATION, HE HEARD REPEATED STORIES OF SUCH TREATMENT.
SHIN PERSONALLY EXPERIENCED MANY OF THE OTHER FORMS OF TORTUR
MENTIONED BY LAMEDA, INCLUDING DENIAL OF SLEEP, STARVATION
RATIONS, SOLITARY CONFINEMENT, AS WELL AS BEING REQUIRED TO
SIT MOTIONLESS FOR LONG PERIODS OF TIME.

D. ARBITRARY ARREST, DETENTION, OR EXILE

INFORMATION ON SPECIFIC CRIMINAL JUSTICE PROCEDURES AND
PRACTICES IN NORTH KOREA IS EXTREMELY SCARCE. NORTH KORPA HA
REFUSED TO PERMIT OUTSIDE OBSERVATION OF ITS LEGAL SYSTEM AND
PRACTICES. THE ACCOUNTS PROVIDED BY THE CREW MEMPERS OF THE
USS PUEBLO, LAMEDA, AND THE SHINS COMPRISE VIRTUALLY ALL THE
SPECIFIC INFORMATION AVAILABLE ON THE OPERATION OF THE
CRIMINAL JUSTICE SYSTEM IN NORTH KOREA.

NORTH KOREAN LAW PROVIDES THAT PRISONERS MAY BE HELD FOR
INTERROGATION FOR A PERIOD NOT TO EXCEED 2 MONTHS. THIS
PERIOD MAY BE EXTENDED INDEFINITELY, HOWEVER, IF THE
INTERROGATION DEPARTMENT OBTAINS APPROVAL OF THE CHIEF
PROSECUTOR. LAMEDA STATES THAT HE WAS DETAINED FOR 12 MONTHS
WITHOUT TRIAL OR CHARGE. HIS REQUEST FOR A LAWYER OF HIS

CHOICE AND AN OPEN TRIAL WAS RIDICULED AS "BOURGEOIS." SHIN
NOTES THAT IT IS VERY DIFFICULT FOR FAMILY MEMBERS OR OTHER
CONCERNED INDIVIDUALS TO OBTAIN INFORMATION REGARDING CHARGES
BEING LEVELED AGAINST AN ACCUSED PERSON OR EVEN WHERE AN
ACCUSED PERSON IS BEING DETAINED. HABEAS CORPUS OR ITS
EQUIVALENT DOES NOT EXIST IN LAW OR IN PRACTICE.

ACCORDING TO NEWSPAPER REPORTS, NORTH KOREAN DEFECTORS IN
SOUTH KOREA ESTIMATED IN APRIL 1982 THAT AT LEAST 125,000
"IDEOLOGICAL OFFENDERS" WERE BEING HELD IN 9 MAJOR L BOR CAMP
IN NORTH KOREA. THE SHINS BELIEVE THIS ESTIMATE TO BE
UNDERSTATED AND ADD THAT THE PLIGHT OF POLITICAL PRISONERS HA
WORSENED OVER THE LAST FEW YEARS. AS ONE EXAMPLE, THE SHINS
STATE THAT 10 YEARS AGO POLITICAL PRISONERS WERE ALLOWED
FAMILY VISITORS AND GIFTS BUT NOW ARE ALLOWED NEITHER. THE
SHINS FURTHER REPORT THAT THE FAMILIES OF POLITICAL DETAINEES
ARE PUNISHED FOR THE POLITICAL BELIEFS OF THEIR RELATIVES. I
IS NOT UNUSUAL, ACCORDING TO THE SHINS, FOR ENTIRE FAMILIES T
BE BANISHED TO OUTLYING RURAL REGIONS. AMNESTY INTERNATIONAL
HAS RECEIVED UNCONFIRMED REPORTS OF ARRESTS OF THOSE OPPOSED
TO HEIR APPARENT KIM CHONG IL.

THERE IS NO PROHIBITION ON THE USE OF FORCED OR COMPULSORY

0181

LABOR. MILITARY CONSCR..TS ARE ROUTINELY USED FOR .ORCED
LABOR. ACCORDING TO THE SHINS, CONSCRIPTS NEVER KNOW WHERE
THEY WILL SERVE OR FOR HOW LONG.

E. DENIAL OF FAIR PUBLIC TRIAL

THE NORTH KOREAN CONSTITUTION STATES THAT COURTS
AREINDEPENDENT AND THAT JUDICIAL PROCEEDINGS ARE TO BE CARRIE
OUT IN STRICT ACCORDANCE WITH LAW. ALL COURTS, HOWEVER, ARE
RESPONSIBLE TO THE PEOPLE'S ASSEMBLIES, WHICH EFF CTIVELY
MEANS GOVERNMENT CONTROL OF THE JUDIBIARI. ARTICLE 138 STATE
THAT "CASES ARE HEARD IN PUBLIC, AND THE ACCUSED IS GUARANTEE
THE RIGHT TO DEFENSE; HEARINGS MAY BE CLOSED TO THE PUBLIC AS
STIPULATED BY LAW." LAMEDA CLAIMS THAT HE WAS DENIED A PUBLI
TRIAL, AS DOES SHIN. LAMEDA REPORTS THAT AFTER HIS FIRST
ARREST HE WAS IMPRISONED FOR A YEAR WITHOUT A HEARING; AFTER
HIS SECOND ARREST, HE WAS PUT THROUGH A CLOSED SESSION WITHOU
BENEFIT OF COUNSEL OF HIS CHOICE, OR EVEN KNOWLEDGE OF THE
CHARGES. HIS TRIBUNAL WAS UNDER THE DIRECTION OF THE MINISTR
OF INTERNAL SECURITY, WITH ONE PERSON SERVING AS BOTH JUDGE
AND PROSECUTOR.

LAMEDA STATED THAT AT HIS TRIAL HE WAS REFUSED THE RIGHT TO
SPEAK OUT, OTHER THAN TO ADMIT GUILT, OR TO DEFEND HIMSELF.
HIS "DEFENSE COUNSEL" REPRESENTED HIM BY MAKING A LENGTHY

SPEECH PRAISING KIM IL SUNG AND THEN REQUESTING A 20-YEAR
SENTENCE, WHICH THE TRIBUNAL IMPOSED AFTER 5 MINUTES OF
DELIBERATION.

IN A 1979 INTERVIEW WITH AMERICAN JOURNALIST JOHN WALLACH,
NORTH KOREAN SUPREME COURT JUSTICE LI CHUN UK NOTED THAT THE
DEFENSE COUNSEL'S JOB IS "TO GIVE THE SUSPECT DUE
PUNISHMENT." OPEN COURT APPEARS TO CONSIST OF AN ANNOUNCEMEN
OF THE TERM OF IMPRISONMENT, WHICH HAS ALREADY BEEN DETERMINE
BY THE PROVINCIAL SAFETY BUREAU.

THE SHINS NOTE A DISTINCTION BETWEEN POLITICAL AND COMMON
CRIMINALS, ASSERTING THAT ONLY THE LATTER ARE AFFORDED
TRIALS. THE DPRK EQUATES "POLITICAL CRIMINALS" WITH THOSE WH
CRITICIZE THE REGIME.

F. ARBITRARY INTERFERENCE WITH PRIVACY, FAMILY, HOME, OR
CORRESPONDENCE

THE POPULACE IS SUBJECTED TO REGULAR INDOCTRINATION, DESIGNED
TO SHAPE INDIVIDUAL CONSCIOUSNESS. PRESCHOOL CHILDREN ARE
DRILLED IN HOMAGE TO KIM IL SUNG AND HIS FAMILY, WHILE YOUTHS
AND ADULTS ARE REQUIRED TO PARTICIPATE IN DAILY IDEOLOGICAL
TRAINING CONDUCTED DURING SCHOOL OR AT PLACES OF EMPLOYMENT.
APPROXIMATELY HALF THE SCHOOL DAY IS DEVOTED TO
INDOCTRINATION. NEIGHBORHOOD UNITS HAVE BEEN ORGANIZED TO
PROVIDE INDOCTRINATION SERVICES FOR PERSONS WHO NEITHER WORK
NOR GO TO SCHOOL. THE DAILY INDOCTRINATION REQUIRES ROTE
RECITATION OF PARTY MAXIMS AND POLICIES AND STRIVES FOR
IDEOLOGICAL PURITY. MULTIPLE NORTH KOREAN SECURITY
ORGANIZATIONS ENFORCE THESE CONTROLS.

REPORTS, PRIMARILY FROM DEFECTORS, INDICATE THAT FORCED
RESETTLEMENT, PARTICULARLY FOR THOSE DEEMED POLITICALLY
UNRELIABLE, IS COMMON. PERMISSION TO RESIDE IN, OR EVEN
ENTER, PYONGYANG, THE CAPITAL, IS STRICTLY CONTROLLED.

ACCORDING TO REPORTS IN SOUTH KOREAN JOURNALS, JAPANESE WIVES
OF KOREANS REPATRIATED FROM JAPAN SINCE 1959 HAVE NOT BEEN
PERMITTED TO VISIT JAPAN AND MANY HAVE LOST CONTACT WITH THEI
FAMILIES BECAUSE THEIR LETTERS ARE SUBJECT TO STRICT
CENSORSHIP.

ALTHOUGH THE CONSTITUTION STATES THAT "CITIZENS ARE GUARANTEE
THE INVIOLABILITY OF PERSON AND RESIDENCE AND THE PRIVACY OF
CORRESPONDENCE," PRACTICE SEEMS TO BE OTHERWISE. LAMEDA
REPORTS THAT THE PRIVACY OF HIS RESIDENCE WAS NOT RESPECTED
AND THAT LISTENING DEVICES WERE USED AGAINST HIM. HE WAS

ARRESTED AND HIS COLLECTED PAPERS AND POETRY SEIZED AND
DESTROYED WITHOUT WARRANT.

ACCORDING TO THE SHINS, ELECTRONIC SURVEILLANCE OF RESIDENCES
IS PERVASIVE AND IT IS COMMON PRACTICE FOR NEIGHBORS TO REPOR
ON ONE ANOTHER. IN SCHOOL, CHILDREN ARE ENCOURAGED TO DISCUS
WHAT THEIR PARENTS HAVE SAID AT HOME. THE GOVERNMENT CONDUCT
MONTHLY "SANITATION" INSPECTIONS TO CHECK ON HOUSEHOLD
ACTIVITIES. EACH HOUSE IS REQUIRED TO HAVE PORTRAITS OF KIM
IL SUNG AND KIM CHONG IL, HIS SON AND EXPECTED SUCCESSOR.

SECTION 2 RESPECT FOR CIVIL LIBERTIES, INCLUDING:

A. FREEDOM OF SPEECH AND PRESS

ALTHOUGH THE CONSTITUTION STATES THAT "CITIZENS HAVE THE
FREEDOMS OF SPEECH, THE PRESS, ASSEMBLY, ASSOCIATION, AND
DEMONSTRATION," SUCH ACTIVITIES ARE PERMITTED ONLY IN SUPPORT
OF GOVERNMENT OBJECTIVES. OTHER ARTICLES OF THE CONSTITUTION
THAT REQUIRE CITIZENS TO FOLLOW THE "SOCIALIST NORMS OF LIFE"
AND TO OBEY A "COLLECTIVE SPIRIT" TAKE PRECEDENCE OVER
INDIVIDUAL POLITICAL OR CIVIL LIBERTIES.

C O N F I D E N T I A L   STATE 034001/23

0183

FOREIGN MEDIA ARE EXCLUDED, DOMESTIC MEDIA CENSORSHIP IS
ENFORCED, AND NO DEVIATION FROM THE OFFICIAL GOVERNMENT LINE
IS TOLERATED. LISTENING TO FOREIGN MEDIA BROADCASTS IS
PROHIBITED EXCEPT TO HIGH GOVERNMENT OFFICIALS, AND VIOLATORS
REPORTEDLY ARE SUBJECT TO SEVERE PUNISHMENT. MOST URBAN
HOUSEHOLDS HAVE A RADIO AND SOME HAVE TELEVISION, BUT
RECEPTION IS LIMITED TO DOMESTIC PROGRAMMING. ARTISTIC AND
ACADEMIC WORKS ARE CONTROLLED BY THE GOVERNMENT, AND VISITORS
REPORT THAT A PRIMARY FUNCTION OF PLAYS, MOVIES, OPERAS, AND
BOOKS IS TO CONTRIBUTE TO THE CULT OF PERSONALITY SURROUNDING
"THE GREAT LEADER," KIM IL SUNG, AND "THE BELOVED LEADER," KI
CHONG IL.

THE SHINS, WHO MADE A NUMBER OF MOVIES AT THE BEHEST OF THE
DPRK LEADERSHIP, STATE THAT MOVIE PRODUCERS HAVE POLITICAL
ADVISERS WHO ENSURE THE IDEOLOGICAL PURITY OF THE FINAL
PRODUCT. ACTORS MUST UNDERGO BACKGROUND INVESTIGATIONS PRIOR
TO OBTAINING A ROLE. THEY ALSO UNDERGO CONSTANT
INDOCTRINATION.

B. FREEDOM OF PEACEFUL ASSEMBLY AND ASSOCIATION

THE GOVERNMENT HAS DEVELOPED A PERVASIVE SYSTEM OF INFORMERS
THROUGHOUT THE SOCIETY. NO PUBLIC MEETINGS CAN BE HELD
WITHOUT GOVERNMENT AUTHORIZATION. THERE APPEAR TO BE NO

ORGANIZATIONS OTHER THAN THOSE CREATED BY THE GOVERNMENT.
EVEN APOLITICAL GROUPS SUCH AS NEIGHBORHOOD OR ALUMNI
ORGANIZATIONS ARE PROHIBITED.TRADE UNIONS AND PROFESSIONAL
ASSOCIATIONS APPEAR TO EXIST SOLELY AS ANOTHER METHOD OF
GOVERNMENT CONTROL OVER THEIR MEMBERS. THERE ARE NO EFFECTIV
RIGHTS TO ORGANIZE, BARGAIN COLLECTIVELY, OR STRIKE.

C. FREEDOM OF RELIGION

ALTHOUGH THE CONSTITUTION PROVIDES THAT "CITIZENS HAVE
RELIGIOUS LIBERTY AND THE FREEDOM OF ANTI-RELIGIOUS
PROPAGANDA," NORTH KOREA, IN FACT, HAS SEVERELY PERSECUTED
CHRISTIANS AND BUDDHISTS SINCE THE LATE 1940'S. NO CHURCHES
HAVE BEEN REBUILT SINCE THE KOREAN WAR. THE REGIME USES
RELIGIOUS ORGANIZATIONAL FACADES TO PROCLAIM THE PRACTICE OF
RELIGIOUS FREEDOM BUT APPEARS TO HAVE LONG SINCE PURGED THE
ORIGINAL MEMBERSHIP. PERSONS WHOSE FAMILY OR RELATIVES ONCE
HAD A STRONG RELIGIOUS INVOLVEMENT ARE DISCRIMINATED AGAINST.
NUMEROUS REPORTS SUGGEST THAT THE GOVERNMENT DOES NOT
CURRENTLY PERSECUTE THE VERY SMALL NUMBER OF CHRISTIANS WHO
CONTINUE TO WORSHIP AT HOME, ALTHOUGH PUBLIC WORSHIP IS
STRICTLY PROHIBITED. THE SHINS, HOWEVER, HAVE STATED THAT TH
GOVERNMENT HAS BEEN VERY SUCCESSFUL IN CONVINCING VARIOUS
FOREIGN CHURCH ORGANIZATIONS THAT RELIGION IS TOLERATED.

D. FREEDOM OF MOVEMENT WITHIN THE COUNTRY, FOREIGN
TRAVEL, EMIGRATION, AND REPATRIATION

INTERNAL TRAVEL IN NORTH KOREA IS STRICTLY CONTROLLED. A
TRAVEL PASS IS REQUIRED FOR ANY MOVEMENT OUTSIDE ONE'S HOME
VILLAGE AND IS GRANTED ONLY FOR REQUIRED OFFICIAL OR CERTAIN

C O N F I D E N T I A L   STATE 034001/04

0184

PERSONAL TRAVEL.   PERSONAL TRAVEL IS USUALLY LIMITED TO
ATTENDING THE WEDDING OR FUNERAL OF A CLOSE RELATIVE.   LONG
DELAYS IN OBTAINING THE NECESSARY PERMIT OFTEN RESULT IN
DENIAL OF THE RIGHT TO TRAVEL EVEN FOR THESE LIMITED
PURPOSES.   STATE CONTROL OF INTERNAL TRAVEL IS ALSO ENSURED B
A RATION SYSTEM THAT DISTRIBUTES COUPONS VALID ONLY IN THE
REGION ISSUED.

FOREIGN TRAVEL IS LIMITED TO OFFICIALS OR TRUSTED ARTISTS AND
PERFORMERS.   EMIGRATION IS NOT ALLOWED, AND FEW REFUGEES OR
DEFECTORS SUCCEED IN FLEEING THE COUNTRY.   RETALIATION IS
TAKEN AGAINST THE RELATIVES OF THOSE FEW PERSONS WHO MANAGE T
ESCAPE.   ACCORDING TO FREEDOM HOUSE, "RIGHTS TO TRAVEL
INTERNALLY AND EXTERNALLY ARE PERHAPS THE MOST RESTRICTED IN
THE WORLD: TOURISM IS UNKNOWN--EVEN TO COMMUNIST COUNTRIES."

IN 1959 NORTH KOREA BEGAN ACTIVELY ENCOURAGING KOREAN

RESIDENTS OVERSEAS TO REPATRIATE TO "THE FATHERLAND."   SOME
OBSERVERS ESTIMATE THAT DURING THE NEXT SEVERAL YEARS OVER
100,000 OVERSEAS KOREANS, ALMOST ALL FROM JAPAN, VOLUNTARILY
REPATRIATED TO NORTH KOREA.   SINCE THEN, HOWEVER, REPORTS OF
THE HARSH TREATMENT GIVEN REPATRIATES REACHED OVERSEAS
KOREANS, REDUCING THE FLOW TO NORTH KOREA TO A TRICKLE.
BECAUSE OF THEIR "CORRUPTION" BY EXPOSURE TO FOREIGN
INFLUENCES, AFTER THEIR RETURN REPATRIATES ARE ISOLATED FROM
NORTH KOREAN SOCIETY UNTIL THEY CAN BE INDOCTRINATED AND THEI
IDEOLOGICAL RELIABILITY GAUGED.

NORTH KOREA HAS PERMITTED ENTRY TO SOME OVERSEAS KOREAN
RESIDENTS TO VISIT THEIR RELATIVES, AND SEVERAL HAVE MADE
REPEAT VISITS.

SECTION 3 RESPECT FOR POLITICAL RIGHTS: THE RIG T OF CITIZE
TO CHANGE THEIR GOVERNMENT

THE POLITICAL SYSTEM IN NORTH KOREA IS DOMINATED BY KIM IL
SUNG, WHO LEADS THE KWP AND ALSO HEA S THE GOVERNMENT.   KIM
HAS GROOMED HIS SON KIM CHONG IL TO SUCCEED HIM, AND THERE AR

0185

5/5   C O N F I D E N T I A L   STATE 034001

REPORTS THAT KIM CHONG IL HAS BEEN ACQUIRING INCREASING POWER
AND INFLUENCE. THE LEGISLATURE, THE SUPREME PEOPLE'S
ASSEMBLY, HAS NEVER TAKEN ANY ACTION OTHER THAN UNANIMOUS
PASSAGE OF RESOLUTIONS PRESENTED TO IT BY THE LEADERSHIP. IN
AN EFFORT TO CREATE AN APPEARANCE OF DEMOCRACY, NORTH KOREA
HAS CREATED SEVERAL "MINORITY PARTIES." THEY EXIST ONLY AS
ROSTERS OF OFFICIALS WHO HAVE TOKEN REPRESENTATION IN THE
PEOPLE'S ASSEMBLY AND COMPLETELY SUPPORT THE GOVERNMENT LINE.

FREE ELECTIONS DO NOT EXIST IN NORTH KOREA. ALTHOUGH
ELECTIONS TO THE SUPREME PEOPLE'S ASSEMBLY WERE HELD IN
NOVEMBER 1986, AND TO CITY AND COUNTY ASSEMBLIES IN MARCH
1983, IN ALL CASES ONLY ONE CANDIDATE IN EACH ELECTORAL
DISTRICT WAS APPROVED BY THE GOVERNMENT PARTY AND, ACCORDING
TO THE GOVERNMENT- CONTROLLED MEDIA, 100 PERCENT OF THE VOTER
TURNED OUT TO ELECT 100 PERCENT OF THE APPROVED CANDIDATES.
SUCH "ELECTIONS" IN REALITY ARE AN EXERCISE IN WHICH VOTERS
ARE REQUIRED TO PARTICIPATE AND TO APPROVE THE PARTY'S
CANDIDATES.

MOST CITIZENS ARE COMPLETELY EXCLUDED FROM ANY REAL
PARTICIPATION IN THE POLITICAL PROCESS. TO ACHIEVE EVEN A
SEMBLANCE OF REAL PARTICIPATION, ONE MUST BECOME A MEMBER OF
THE KWP. THE SELECTION PROCESS FOR ENTRANCE TO THE PARTY IS
LONG AND RIGOROUS. PERSONS FROM "BAD SOCIAL BACKGROUNDS,"
I.E., THOSE WHO HAVE RELATIVES WHO FLED SOUTH DURING THE
KOREAN WAR, THOSE WHOSE FAMILIES HAD STRONG RELIGIOUS

INVOLVEMENT OR WERE ONCE PROPERTY OWNERS OR MEMBERS OF THE
MIDDLE CLASS, AND THOSE WHO HAVE RELATIVES WHO ARE POLITICAL
PRISONERS, EFFECTIVELY ARE DENIED ENTRY INTO THE PARTY AND AR
DISCRIMINATED AGAINST. MOST LEVELS OF THE PARTY HAVE NO
VOICE, SERVING ONLY TO CARRY OUT THE DECREES AND "ON THE SPOT
GUIDANCE" PROMULGATED BY PARTY LEADER KIM IL SUNG AND HIS TOP
SUBORDINATES.

SECTION 4 GOVERNMENTAL ATTITUDE REGARDING INTERNATIONAL AND
NONGOVERNMENTAL INVESTIGATION OF ALLEGED VIOLATIONS
OF HUMAN RIGHTS

NO ORGANIZATIONS EXIST WITHIN NORTH KOREA TO REPORT ON OR
OBSERVE HUMAN RIGHTS VIOLATIONS. NORTH KOREA DOES NOT
PARTICIPATE IN ANY INTERNATIONAL OR REGIONAL HUMAN RIGHTS
ORGANIZATIONS.

AMNESTY INTERNATIONAL HAS REQUESTED A VISIT TO NORTH KOREA.
THE GOVERNMENT HAS NOT RESPONDED TO OR ACKNOWLEDGED THIS
REQUEST. A DECEMBER 1982 REQUEST BY AMNESTY INTERNATIONAL FO
INFORMATION ON NORTH KOREAN LAWS, ON USE OF THE DEATH PENALTY
AND ON REPORTS OF ARRESTS AND LONG-TERM IMPRISONMENT OF
POLITICAL FIGURES ALSO RECEIVED NO REPLY.
THE AMNESTY INTERNATIONAL 1986 REPORT NOTES THAT ITS WORK
CONTINUED TO BE SERIOUSLY HAMPERED BY THE AUTHORITIES' REFUSA
TO DIVULGE INFORMATION ABOUT ARRESTS, POLITICAL IMPRISONMENT,
ARRESTS, TRIALS, OR THE DEATH SENTENCES, AND THAT IT CONTINUE
TO RECEIVE REPORTS FROM A WIDE RANGE OF SOURCES ABOUT HUMAN
RIGHTS VIOLATIONS OF POTENTIAL CONCERN TO IT. FREEDOM HOUSE
RATES NORTH KOREA AS "NOT FREE."

C O N F I D E N T I A L   STATE 034001/05

0186

SECTION 5 DISCRIMINATION BASED UPON RACE, SEX, RELIGION,
LANGUAGE, OR SOCIAL STATUS

THE CONSTITUTION STATES THAT "WOMEN HOLD EQUAL SOCIAL STATUS
AND RIGHTS WITH MEN." HOWEVER, FEW WOMEN HAVE REACHED HIGH
LEVELS OF THE PARTY OR THE GOVERNMENT. WOMEN ARE REPRESENTED
PROPORTIONALLY IN THE LABOR FORCE, AND PERSONNEL IN SMALL
FACTORIES ARE PREDOMINANTLY WOMEN.

THE PHYSICALLY HANDICAPPED ARE DISCRIMINATED AGAINST.
HANDICAPPED PERSONS, OTHER THAN WAR VETERANS, ARE REPORTEDLY
NOT ALLOWED WITHIN THE CITY LIMITS OF PYONGYANG. THE DWARF
COMMUNITY HAS BEEN SPECIFICALLY SINGLED OUT FOR HARSH
TREATMENT AND ALL HAVE BEEN BANISHED TO A REMOTE, RURAL REGIO

NORTH KOREA IS A HOMOGENEOUS COUNTRY AND RELATIVELY DEVOID OF
MINORITY GROUPS.

CONDITIONS OF LABOR

TH5RE IS NO DATA AVAILABLE ON MINIMUM AGE FOR EMPLOYMENT OF
CHILDREN, MINIMUM WAGES, OR OCCUPATIONAL SAFETY AND HEALTH.
ALL JOBS ARE ASSIGNED BY THE STATE AND IDEOLOGICAL PURITY,
RATHER THAN PROFESSIONAL COMPETENCE, IS THE STANDARD USED IN
DECIDING WHO RECIEVES A PARTICULAR JOB. LABORERS HAVE NO
INPUT INTO MANAGEMENT DECISIONS AND FREE LABOR UNIONS DO NOT
EXIST. ABSENCE FROM WORK WITHOUT A DOCTOR'S CERTIFICATE
RESULTS IN A REDUCTION IN A WORKER'S RATIONS. THE
CONSTITUTION STIPULATES THAT THE WORKDAY IS LIMITED TO 8 HOUR
BUT SEVERAL SOURCES REPORT THAT MOST LABORERS WORK 12-15 HOUR
DAYS. THE EXTRA HOURS ARE EUPHEMISTICALLY REFERRED TO AS
"PATRIOTIC LABOR" DONE ON A "VOLUNTARY" BASIS BY THE WORKERS.

END TEXT. SHULTZ
BT
#4001

NNNN

C O N F I D E N T I A L   STATE 034001/05

| 국무성 인권보고서 남북한 부분 내용 |

1987. 2.

외 무 부

0188

1 주요 내용

가. 개　관

o 대통령이 정치를 장악하고 있으며, 국회는 제한된 힘만을
가지고 있으나 여론에 대해서는 상당한 영향력을 행사하고
있음.

o 전대통령은 1988년초 평화적 정부이양을 위해 자발적으로
물러날 것을 약속 하였음.

o 역대 한국정부는 북한의 위협에 직면하여 국내외 안전
문제를 최우선 과제로 삼고있으며, 이를 이유로 반대파의
정치활동을 억압하고 있다는 비난받고 있음.

o 한국경제는 지난 20년간 1인당 국민소득이 20배나 성장
함으로써 고도의 성장을 이룩하였으며, 이러한 경제성장의
결과 보다많은 정치적 자유를 원하는 중산계층과 대학생
층을 증가시켰음.

o 한국인들은 경제, 종교 및 개인적 관심을 추구할 수 있는
광범위한 자유를 누리고 있으나, 언론, 출판의 자유는
억압 당하고 있음.

o 1986년은 개헌 문제가 한국정치를 지배하였음.
   - 야당의 개헌 요구에 전대통령은 합의 개헌에 합의
   - 1986년말 현재 정부여당의 내각 책임제와 야당의 직선
     대통령제 협상은 고착 상태

0189

o   정부는 반체제인사, 특히 반체제 학생에 대해 강력 대응
    하였음.

    - 학생의 반정부운동은 1986년 격화되고 구호도 점차
      혁명적, 북한동조 성향 표출

    - 3,000명이 투옥되었으며 86.12월말 1,000명 이상이
      구금중

    - 현정부하에 최초로 야당의원이 국가 보안법 위반혐의로
      구속 기소

o   1986년 동안 정치범에 대한 고문을 비롯한 학대가 지속적으로
    있어왔음.

나. 개인의 기본권

o   정치적 살인

    - 장이기사방, 학생, 노동자등 몇건의 의문의 자살에 대한
      정부의 해명에 대해 야당 및 인권단체에서는 강력한
      의문을 제기

o   행방불명

    - 없 음

o   고   문

    - 헌법상 고문이 금지되어 있으나, 정부의 고문 금지
      조치에도 불구하고 고문 및 잔혹행위가 계속되고 있음.

    - 권인숙에 대한 경찰의 성적학대, 노동운동가 15명에
      대한 보안사의 고문에 대한 보고가 있었으며, 김근태에
      대한 고문여부는 대법원에서 인정되지 않았음.

0190

- 경찰의 과잉 진압이 계속 문제되고 있으나 미문화원을
  점거한 학생들을 퇴각시키는데 효율적으로 대처 하였음.
- 경찰 폭력에 대해 신문에 보도가 되기도 하며,고문에
  의한 자백을 이유로 살인 혐의자에게 무죄 선고를 한
  바 있음.
- 감옥생활 여건은 열악한 편이며 정치범과 비정치범에
  대한 차별 대우는 심하지 않은 편이나 점차 정치범에
  대한 학대가 심하다는 주장이 있음.
ㅇ 임의 체포 및 구속
- 정치적 사건에 있어 영장없는 연행이 계속되고 있으며
  야당인사에 대한 감시 및 가택연금이 계속되고 있음.
- 아시안 게임중 보안강화를 위해 263, 564명을 조사한
  바 있음.
- 서준식, 강종곤등이 형기종료 이후에도 보안감호 처분을
  받고 있으며 380명이 사회안전법으로 수감중임
ㅇ 공개재판 거부
- 사법부의 독립은 일반적으로 유지되고 있으나, 정치적
  으로 민감한 사건의 경우 독립성이 감소되고 있음.
- 야당은 1,000-3,000 여명의 정치범이 있다고 주장하고
  있음.
- 인천 소요사태와 건국대 점거로 학생 구속이 증가
  하였음.

0191

o   개인의 사생활권 침해

  -    야당 및 반정부인사에 대한 감시, 도청 및 가택여금
       사례가 상존함

  -    외국기자나 외교관과 만난 한국사람은 치안당국에 의해
       조사를 받는 경우가 많음.

  -    학생시위에 적극적인 사람의 교사직 취업을 제한 하도록
       문고부 규정이 개정되었음.

다.   시민적 권리

o   언론출판의 자유

  -    언론기본법에 의해 상당한 제약을 받음.

  -    신문. 잡지는 점차 활발한 의사 표시를 하고 있으나
       TV와 라디오는 여전히 심한 통제를 받음.

  -    야당과 종교단체에서는 TV시청료 납부거부로 이에
       항의 하였음.

  -    현역국회의원도 표현의 제한으로 구속 되었음.

  -    중고등학교 교사와 공무원이 반정부 표현을 이유로
       직위 해제 되었음.

o   집회 결사의 자유

  -    집회 및 시위에 관한 기본법에 의해 통제 되고있음.

  -    야당의 개헌 추진 집회를 다수 허용했으나 서울 집회는
       저지 하였음.

  -    86.11. 노동부는 14개 노동단체를 좌익성향을 이유로
       자진 해산할 것을 명령 하였음.

o   종교의 자유

  -    거의 완전한 종교자유 향유

  -    종교인사의 반정부 활동은 제한

0192

o   거주이전의 자유

    -   일반적으로 보장되나 일부 국회의원, 종교인의 회의
        참석을 위한 출국이 제한되기도 하였음.

라. 정치적 권리

o   대통령과 국회의원단 선거에 의해 선출되고 있음.
    -   85년 국회의원선거로 야당세력이 강화되었음.

o   헌법개정 절차 및 정부 형태 결정을 위요한 여야간 대립이
    지속되고있음.

o   86년중 제도권밖의 정치종교 활동에 대해 압력이 가중
    되었으며 용공세력의 색출과 관련, 민통련등 정치 단체가
    해체 되었음.

o   정부는 신민당에 대해 용공세력과의 관계를 명백히 할
    것을 요구한 바 있음.

마. 인권위반 주장에 대한 정부의 입장

o   한국은 어떠한 국제인권 기구에도 가입치 않고 있음.

o   인권문제에 대한 외부의 관여를 반대하면서도, 정부관리의
    국제사면협회등 인권단체 대표와의 접촉은 허용하고 있음.

o   법무부가 인권보호 및 위반조사 책임기관이며 각 정당의
    인권 위원회가 인권보호에 관여하고 있음.

o   한국기독교 협의회 (KNCC)의 인권위, 기독교 정의평화
    위원회, 변호사 협회등이 대표적 독립 인권단체임.

o   정부의 인권단체에 대한 감시, 수색등 압력 사례가 있었음.

0193

바. 인종. 성별. 종교. 언어등에 의한 차별

o 전반적으로는 차별이 없으나 성별 지역별 차별대우는 계속
   문제가 되고 있음.

o 전통적 남성우위 사회이나 여권신장 운동이 계속되고 있음.

사. 노동조건

o 규정상 미성년자 취업시 보호자의 동의가 필요하나 실제로는
   미성년자에 대한 고용사례 많음

o 규정상 근로시간은 60시간을 초과할 수 없으며 평균 근로
   시간은 55시간임.

o 최저임금제는 실시 되고있지 않으나, 88년까지는 제도화,
   시행할 계획이며 근로자 연금제도도 실시 계획임.

o 임금체불 기업주 처벌등 노사분규 해결을 위해 정부가
   강력한 조치를 취하였으며 산재보상법으로 근로자 보호를
   위해 노력하고 있음

2. 85년도 보고서와의 차이점

가. 85년도 보고서에서는 85.2 실시된 국회의원 선거와 이에 따른
    신민당의 출현을 한국 민주주의 역사에서 가장 획기적인 사건
    중의 하나로 평가하면서 정치활동 피규제자의 전면해금과 학원
    자율화 조치등 아국 정부의 제반 자유화 조치에 대하여는
    긍정적인 평가를 내리고 85.5 미문화원 점거사건을 계기로 한국
    정부는 이전의 강경 정책으로 선회하였으며 이에따른 수감자수가
    80년이후에 최대에 달하고 있으며, 이 과정에서 고문 및 가혹
    행위가 증대되고 있음을 새로운 변화로 특기한 바 있음.

0194

나. 금번 86년도 보고서에는 개헌문제가 한국정치를 지배하고
   있다고 개관하고, 개헌현상은 여야의 대립으로 교착상태에
   빠졌으나 야당의 개헌추진 집회를 허용 (서울 집회는 예외)
   한 점, 신문. 잡지가 이전보다 공공연한 정부비판을 한점을
   긍정적으로 평가하고 있음.

다. 그러나, 유성한의원 구속, 권인숙에 대한 성적 학대, 노동
   운동가 15명 고문, 예비군 교육훈련중 숨진 장이기 사건등
   정부의 반정부 인사에 대한 탄압이 심화 되었으며 인천사태와
   건국대 접거사태로 투옥자 수가 증가 한점에 우려를 표명하고
   있음.

라. 한편 노사분규해결을 위한 정부의 임금체불 기업주 처벌,
   최저임금제 실시 결정등 노동조건 개선을 위한 정부의
   노력에 대해서도 긍정적으로 평가하고 있음.

0195

1. 주요 내용

   가. 개 관

   - o 북한은 엄격한 공산독재 국가로서 개인의 권리는 김일성
     및 그의 가족 지배하에 있는 노동당에 철저히 종속되어
     있음.

   - o 1982년 형식상의 최고인민회의 선거가 있었으나, 후보자
     선택의 자유가 없는등 자유선거가 존재하지 않음.

   - o 당의 지도노선에 협조하지 않는 주민들은 구금, 재산
     압수, 유배를 겪어야 함.

   - o 김정일을 후계자로 만든 사실 자체가 김일성이 지난 38년간
     축적한 독재의 표현이 될 것임.

   - o 자신의 생전에 한반도 통일을 달성하려는 김일성의 야망으로
     인해 한국내 불안정을 주기적으로 획책하고 있음

   - o 북한은 한국과 대화를 추구한 바 있으나 86.1북한측에 의해
     동 대화는 정지되었으며 대화가 재개될 가능성은 희박함.

   나. 개인적 기본권

   - o 정치적 살해
     - 북한내의 정치적 동기에 의한 살인에 관한 정보는
       없으나 랑군 폭발사건과 84.11.23. 발생한 비무장
       지대에서의 총격사건 및 김일성에 대한 불경한 말을
       한 어느 과학자의 처형등은 북한의 태도를 잘 나타내
       주고 있음.

0196

o 행발불명

  - 정보 부족

o 고 문

  - 금년도 Freedom House 보고서는 북한에서 고문이
    일상적인 일이라고 지적하였음.

  - 푸에블로호 선원과 베네수엘라 시인의 경험담 인용

  - 신상옥, 최은희의 증언을 통해 고문등 북한의 인권
    탄압 사례가 확인됨.

o 임의 체포

  - 영장이나 유사한 제도가 없으며 자의적인 구금이나
    체포가 가능함.

  - 북한에는 현재 약 105,000명의 사상범이 8개 수용소에
    수용되어 있는 것으로 추정됨.

  - 신상옥씨의 증언에 따르면, 실제 숫자는 그이상일
    것이며 이들에게 가족 면회 및 물품 반입이 금지되어
    있음.

o 공개재판 거부

  - 사법부는 전적으로 정부 통제하에 있음.

o 가택 및 통신에 대한 무단침범

  - 일반주민은 계속적으로 사상교육을 받아야 함.

  - 북한으로 송환된 일본인 부인 일본 방문 불허,
    서신교환 금지

  - 신상옥씨의 증언에 따르면 가택에 대한 전자감시,
    가족상호 감시, 일반주택에 대한 당국의 검사등으로
    인해 개인생활이 철저히 통제되고 있음.

0197

다. 시민적 권리

o 언론 출판의 자유

  - 정부시책에 대한 지지를 제외하고는 언론, 집회,
    시위의 자유 불인정

  - 외국 보도물은 배제되어 있고, 국내보도는 철저한
    검열제임.

  - 신상옥씨는 영화등 예술물 제작에 정치고문이 철저히
    관여하고 있음을 폭로

o 집회 결사의 자유

  - 노동조합 및 각종협회등은 주민에 대한 효과적인
    지배 및 통제의 수단으로 이용

o 종교의 자유

  - 40년대 후반이후 지속적인 종교박해

  - 종교 기관이란 주민의 효과적인 통제 및 대외
    선전용

o 거주이전의 자유

  - 북한내의 여행 엄격 통제

  - 1959년 이후 재일교포의 북송을 추진, 현재 10만명이
    있으나 이들의 일본방문은 금지되어 있으며 철저한
    통제하에 있음.

0198

라. 정치적 권리

　　o　정치과정은 김일성 노동당의 독점물이며 점차 김정일의
　　　　권한이 강화

　　　　-　입법기관인 최고 인민회의는 지도부가 제출한
　　　　　　법안을 만장일치로 통과시키는 역할만 수행

　　o　자유선거는 없으며 선거구 별로 당이 지명한 인사가
　　　　단독 출마

　　　　-　노동 당원외에는 참정권 불인정

마. 국제기구로 부터의 인권 위반 비난에 대한 입장

　　o　Amnesty International 의 북한 방문 요청 및 각종 인권
　　　　관련 자료 제공 요청에 무응답

　　o　Freedom House 금년도 보고서는 북한을 ' 자유가 없는
　　　　국가 '로 분류

바. 노동조건

　　o　하루 8시간 노동 규정에도 불구 대부분 노동자가 하루
　　　　12-16시간 일하고 있으며 이를 자발적, 애국적 근로라고
　　　　합리화함.

2. 85년도 보고서와의 차이점

　　o　금번 보고서는 85년도 보고서와 대동소이한 내용이나 남.북
　　　　대화가 북한에 의해 일방적으로 중단된 점, 신상옥,최은희씨
　　　　탈출로 인한 북한사회 실상이 폭로된 점이 특기할 만함.

0199

長 官 님 報 告 事 項

1987. 2. 20.

美洲局 北美課

題 目 : 1986년 미국무성 인권보고서

개 요

미국무성은 2.19, 1986년도 각국 인권보고서를 발간하였는 바, 동 보고서의
아국 및 북한 관계 요지 및 전년도 보고서와의 차이점등을 아래 보고함.

86년도 보고서 요지

o 86년도에는 개헌문제가 한국정치를 지배하고 있으며 개헌협상은
  여야의 대립으로 교착상태에 빠졌으나 야당의 개헌추진 집회를 허용
  (서울 집회는 예외)한 것과 신문. 잡지가 이전보다 공공연한 정부 비판을
  한점을 긍정적으로 평가

o 그러나, 유성환 의원 구속, 권인숙에 대한 성적 학대, 노동운동가 15명 고문,
  예비군 교육 훈련중 숨진 장이기 사건등 정부의 반정부 인사에 대한 탄압이
  심화되었으며 인천사태와 건국대 점거사태로 투옥자 수가 증가한 점에 우려를
  표명

o 한편 노사분규 해결을 위한 정부의 임금체불 기업주 처벌, 최저임금제 실시
  결정등 노동 조건 개선을 위한 정부의 노력에 대해서도 긍정적으로 평가

0200

| 85년도 보고서 요지 |

ㅇ 85.2 실시된 국회의원 선거와 이에 따른 신민당의 출현을 한국 민주주의
  , 역사에서 가장 획기적인 사건중의 하나로 평가하면서 정치활동 피규제자의
  전면 해금과 학원자율화 조치등 아국정부의 제반 자유화 조치에 대하여
  긍정적인 평가

ㅇ 그러나 85.5 미문화원 점거사건을 계기로 한국정부는 이전의 강경정책
  으로 선회하였으며, 이에 따른 수감자수가 80년이후 최대에 달하고 있으며,
  이 과정에서 고문 및 가혹행위가 증대되고 있음을 새로운 변화로 파악

| 북한관련 내용 |

ㅇ 86년도 보고서는 김일성과 김정일에 의해 철저히 통제되는 북한 사회의
  실상을 예년과 대동소이하게 기술

ㅇ 남북대화가 북한에 의해 일방적으로 중단된점, 신상옥.최은희씨 탈출로
  인한 북한사회 실상이 폭로된 점이 특기할 사항

| 조치 사항 |

ㅇ 법무부 및 관계부처에 동 보고서에 관한 의견 요청
  - 반박자료가 수집되는 대로 주한미대사관과 주미대사관측에 아측의
    입장을 전달할 예정

ㅇ 현재 미의회에서 진행중인 국무성 인권보고서와 관련한 청문회 예의 주시
  - 아국문제 거론시, 최근 박종철 사건이후 한국정부가 취한 고문방지 및
    인권보호를 위한 노력을 설명, 미측의 이해를 촉구

0201

기 안 용 지

분류기호 문서번호	미북 2024-762 (전화:)		시행상 특별취급	

보존기간	영구·준영구. 10. 5. 3. 1	장 관
수신처 보존기간		(서명)
시행일자	1987. 3. 3.	

보조 기관	국 장	전결	협조 기관		문 서 통 제
	심의관				검열 1987.3. 5 외무부 교안담당관
	과 장	(서명) 8/4			
	기안책임자	조백상			발 인 발송 1987. 3. 5 외무부

경유 수신 참조	국 가안전기획부 장	발신명의	

제 목	미국무성 인권보고서 관련대책

　　1. 미국무성은 세계각국의 인권상황에 관한 자료를 정리하여

매년 연초에 인권보고서를 발간해오고 있으며 한국 및 북한의 인권

상황에 대해서도 설명하고 있읍니다.

　　2. 지난 2.19 발간된 86년도 미국무성 인권보서에는 한국

관계가 15페이지, 북한관계가 7페이지 분량을 차지하고 있는 바,

이는 한국이 미국의 인권단체등의 자유로운 방한 및 자료수집을

허용하는 것에 비해 북한은 여사한 국제인권단체에 입국을 불허하고

있기 때문에 북한의 극심한 인권탄압 실태가 서방세계에 잘 알려져

있지 않기 때문인 것으로 판단됩니다.

3. 그간 당부는 귀부에서 제공한 북한의 인권탄압

실태 및 북한문제연구소가 제공한 관련자료를 주미대사관을 통해

미국무성측에 전달하여 북한의 인권 탄압상이 객관적으로 기술될

수 있도록 조치를 취한 바 있으며, 금번 86년도 인권보고서의 북한

부분은 최근 북한을 탈출한 신상옥·최은희씨의 증언이 반영되어

북한의 인권탄압상이 어느정도 서방세계에 폭로된 바 있으나 아직도

북한의 혹심한 인권탄압실태에 대한 인권보고서의 내용은 우리의

기대에 미치지 못하는 실정입니다.

4. 이와관련, 주미대사는 87년도 인권보고서 대책의

일환으로 금년초 북한을 탈출한 김만철씨 가족이 밝힌 북한의

생활상 및 북한의 인권탄압 실태에 대한 자료를 요청하여 왔는 바

미국무성의 87년도 인권보고서 작성시 반영될 수 있도록 김만철씨

가족의 북한실상 폭로 자료를 포함 북한의 인권 탄압 실태에 관한

자료를 당부로 송부하여 주시기 바랍니다.

첨 부 : 86년도 미국무성 인권보고서 남북한 관계. 끝.

0203

분류번호	보존기간

발 신 전 보

번 호 : WUS-1088 일 시 : 70316 1250 전보종별 : _____

수 신 : 주 미 대사·병영사 (마북)

발 신 : 장 관

제 목 : 인권보고서 대책

　　1. 국무성 인권보고서에 대한 대책의 일환으로 김만철씨 일가의 북한의 탄압상 폭로 내용이 87년도 인권 보고서에 반영되도록 관계부처에 협조를 요청한 바 있으나 동 자료는 금년 6월 이후에야 정리가 완성 될 것이라함.

　　2. 동 자료는 입수되는 대로 송부할 예정임.

　　　　　　　　　　　　　　　　　　（미주국장 장선섭）

보안 통제

0204

앙고재	87년3월16일	기안자	과 장	국 장	차 관	장 관	외신과	접수자	통 제
	북미과	3		전결					

BACKGROUNDER

Press Office
United States Information Service (USIS)
United States Embassy, Seoul, Korea

駐韓美國公報院 公報室
Tel. 732-2601 Ext. 4368, 4389

배 경 설 명

1987년 3월 18일

美國外交政策에서의 人權의 역할

美國政府는 韓國에 人權문제가 존재한다고 믿고 있지만 한국정부가 인권 침해 사건을 조사하기 위해서 취하고 있는 구체적인 행동을 보고 고무되었다고 미국의 한 고위 관리가 말했다.

제임스 몽고메리 美國務省 人權 및 人道的 문제 담당 首席 副次官補는 1987년 3월 17일 美國海外公報處(USIA)가 마련한, 한국 기자들과의 국제전화인터뷰에서 질문에 응답하면서 이렇게 말했다.

美國務省이 최근에 발표한 "人權報告書"는 한국의 인권 상황에 관한 부분에서, 1986년에 "고문과 가혹한 취급이 있었다는 신빙성 있는 보고가 계속 있었다"고 말하고 있다.

몽고메리副次官補는 기자들에게, "우리는 고문 문제가 한국 당국의 행동으로 해서 발생한 것이라는 점을 아주 분명히 하고 있다고 생각한다"고 상기시켰다.

그는 이어, "한국정부가 최근 박종철군의 사망에 대해서 취한 행동은 고무적인 것이며, 우리는 그 관계 당국의 어느 구성원이 고문행위를 했을 때 이를 조사하여, 잘못을 범한 자를 처벌하는 것은 그 政府当局이 마땅히 취해야 할 대응책이라고 생각한다"라고 덧붙였다.

최근의 항의 사건에서 체포되었던 학생인 박종철군은 경찰에 감호되어 있는 동안에 사망했다.

勞動權 침해 문제에 대해 그는, "노동자의 권리의 구체적인 문제에 대해서는 美國政府는, 한국이 노동 문제에 관한 限 그 권리에 관계되는 기록을 개선하기 위한 조치를 취한 것으로 최근에 단정했다"고 말했다.

최근 발표된 미국무성 人權報告書는, "한국정부의 노동분규처리에 대한 빈발하는 비난에 대응하여 한국정부는 1985년에 고용주의 횡포를 막기 위해 벌금 및 구금을 포함한, 보다 강경한 조치를 취했으며, 1986년에도 계속 취했다"고 지적했다.

미국이 人權침해자에 대해 사용할 수 있는 "견제수단"에 관한 질문에 답하여 그는, "우리는 盟邦인 한국과의 관계에서 經濟的 제재 조치를 취할 수는 없다고 생각한다"고 말했다.

그는, "韓美간에는 貿易문제가 존재하지만 우리 양국은 우리들 나름대로 그것을 해결할 수 있다고 생각한다. 궁극적으로는 양국간의 通商과 상호접촉이 政治발전과 인권 상황개선에 도움을 주리라고 생각한다"고 지적해서 말했다.

"국민을 학대하고, 국민에게 정치적 권리를 부여하기를 거부하는 政府들에게 가할 수 있는 최선의 압력은 첫째로 그런 나라들에서 행해지고 있는 일들에 온 세계가 일관성 있게 주의를 집중하는 일이다"라고 그는 설명한다.

"우리의 安保上의 이해관계와 우리의 人權政策간에 相衝이 있을 필요가 없다고 생각한다"고 말하고나서 몽고메리 副次官補는 미국이 中華人民共和國에 대해서 추구해온 정책은 "양국간에 다년간 존재해온 긴장을 완화하기 위해 案出된"것이라고 말했다.

0205

(다음은 제임스 몽고메리 美國務副次官補가 3월 17일에 있은 미국 외교정책에서의 人權문제의 역할에
관한 국제전화 인터뷰를 위해 미리 녹음해 둔 성명 全文이다.)

여기는 워싱턴, 나는 人權담당 國務副次官補 짐 몽고메리이다. 1987년 3월 5일   미국의
외교정책에서 차지하는 人權문제의 역할에 관해 이야기할 수 있게 된 것을 기쁘게 생각한
다. 인권문제가 미국 정부 뿐아니라 미국 국민의 토의사항으로 오르게 된 연유에 대해 말하
고자 한다.

外交政策에 관해 미국민의 정치적 관심을 불러일으키는 것에 근본적으로 세 가지가 있다.
물론 여러 가지가 있으나 가장 큰 중요성을 가지고 있는 것은 세 가지이다.

첫째는 核戰爭에서 살아남는 일이다. 우리와 소련이 제각기 상대방을 核공격하여 아마도
여타 세계까지 함께 파멸시킬 것인가 하는 것이 첫번째 문제이다.

세번째는 대외 통상과 이 여러 문제에서 나오는 전반적인 경제문제들로서, 이 문제는 미
국에서도 지역에 따라 사정이 다르다. 노드 캘로라이나州에서는 섬유에 대해 걱정을 하는가
하면, 디트로이트市 사람들은 자동차에 대해 걱정하고, 캘리포니아州 사람들은 실리콘 칩에
대해 걱정하는 따위로서, 이 모든 일들이 하나의 큰 문제를 이룬다.

두번째 문제가 人權 문제이다. 우리가 외교적으로 상대하는 다른 나라 정부들이 그 나라
국민을 어떻게 다루고 있는가 하는 문제이다. 여기서 두번째 문제라고 말하고 있지만 때로
는 첫번째가 되기도 하고, 사실 첫번째 쪽으로 더 가까울 것이다. 미국의 직업외교관들로
하여금 이 문제를 외교적 議題로 올려놓도록 미국 국민이 요구하게 된데 대해서는 여러 가
지 이유가 있다.

첫째 이유는 근본적으로는 제2차 대전이다. 2차대전은 적어도 人權문제를 이유로 하여 치
루어진 전쟁으로서 끝났다. 우리 모두 그리고 우리 가운데 많은 사람들은 부켄발트나 아우
슈비츠, 트레블린카, 또는 그밖의 비슷한 강제수용소에서 나온 영화들을 본 일을 기억하고
있고, 우리의 정부들이 이같은 일을 국민이나 이웃 국민들에 저지르게 되는 것을 다시는 허
용해서는 안되겠다는 결의를 낳게 하는 가운데 전세계인의 의식에 가해졌던 충격을 우리는
기억할 수 있을 것이다.

둘째는 2차대전 이후의 미국의 納稅者들이다. 즉 미국은 납세자들의 많은 돈으로 처음에
는 '마셜 플랜'과 이어 전세계에 걸친 여러 계획을 통해 다른 나라 정부들을 지원하여 이
원조사업들은 매우 고무적인 성공 사례로 열매를 맺었다. 그러나 이 과정에서 미국 국민은
우리의 자원으로 지원해 주고 있는 정부들이 어떤 성격의 정부들인지에 관해 자연히 관심을
갖기 시작했다.

이에 대한 또다른 이유는 2차대전후 미국이 군사 행동을 벌여왔다는데 있다. 다른 나라
에서 전쟁을 하고 돌아온 사람들 또는 非戰鬪的 사명을 띠고 다른 나라에 파견되었다 돌
아온 사람들은 그 후 거기서 일이 어떻게 되어가는가에 대해 지속적으로 관심을 가지게 되
었으며, 한국이나 베트남, 유럽들이 이같은 현상의 으뜸가는 예에 속한다. 아마 미국의 거
의 모든 사람들이 미국 이외의 다른 곳에서 온 사람들이다. 자기가 그렇지 않다 해도 그의
부모나 또는 조부모들이 그랬을 것이고, 자연히 그들은 자기나 또는 부모가 태어난 곳에서
무엇이 벌어지고 있는가에 관심을 계속 갖게 되는 것이다. 이것이 미국 정치에서의 중요한
요소이며, 이는 우리 민주 제도를 통해 選擧로 선출된 정치인들에게 가해지는 압력으로서 나
타나는 것이다.

미국 국민의 입장으로서도 미국 정부의 기반이 되는 命題에 대한 일반적인 믿음이 깔려
있는 것으로 생각된다. 즉 政府란 人權을 보장하기 위해 존재하는 것이지, 人權을 국민에게

0206

부여하기 위해 존재하는 것이 아니라는 것은 전세계적으로 상당한 정도로 전반적으로 받아들여지고 있는 命題로서, 다른 나라 국민들도 아마 이에 동의할 것이고, 이를 자기 나라에서 실현시키려 할 때 주어지는 약간의 원조라도 고맙게 여길 그러한 命題이다.

後者의 경우에 관해서는 전세계적으로 일고 있는 通信革命 현상을 볼 필요가 있을 것이다. 전화를 들고 아주 간단히 약 10초 내에 지구 반대쪽에 있는 누구하고나 통화하는 것이 가능하다. TV인공위성은 다른 나라에서 일어난 사건들을 미국 뿐 아니라 전세계의 안방으로 전달해 준다. 이는 정치인들에 대한 압력을 조성하고, 국가들 사이를 오고가는 감정과 관심의 격렬한 흐름을 조성하기도 한다. 예컨대, 필리핀 사태가 그 완전한 본보기일 것이다. 마르코스는 세계가 보는 앞에서 선거 결과를 가로채려고 했는데, 그것은 TV덕분이었다. 통신혁명이 없었던 25년 전이라면 그가 성공했을지 모르나, 오늘날의 시대에서 이제 그런 일은 제대로 통용되지 않는다.

그리고 우리의 관점에서 볼 때 人權問題를 議題로 오르게 하는 진정한 地政學的인 이유가 있다. 그것은 우리가 전세계의 많은 나라들에 대한 관심을 가지고 있으며, 그 나라의 정부들이 국민의 진정한 욕구를 충족시켜줄 체제를 갖고 있지 않기 때문에 안정되어 있지 않거나, 아니면 국민을 욕되게 하는 체제를 가지고 있을 때 그 나라 체제는 불안정해질 수 밖에 없다는 것으로서, 불안정스런 정권이란 솔직히 말해 매우 현실적인 면에서 우리의 이익에 위협을 가하는 것이다.

그러므로 人權문제가 議題로 올라야 하는 이유는 여러 가지가 된다. 人權문제가 외교의 전통적인 요건이 아니었다는 것을 인식하는 것이 현실적일 것으로 생각된다. 얼마 멀지않은 과거에는 이는 다른 나라 문제에 대한 간섭으로 간주되었었다. 다른 나라 정부가 자기 국민에 고문을 가하거나, 학대를 하거나, 또는 정치적인 권리를 주지 않으려 한다해도 그것은 유감스러운 일이 될 수 있을지언정 전통적인 방식에 따른 外交官들이라면 서로 이야기를 나누려 하지 않을 그런 일이었다.

미국 국민과 미국 議숲는 1970년대에 이러한 일이 시정되기를 요구했고, 미국의 외교계가 다른 나라 정부와 일상적으로 교섭할 때 人權문제에도 관심을 기울이도록 강요하는 여러 조치들을 취했다. 많은 법률이 통과되었으며, 일례로 多國 開發銀行에서 미국이 던지는 표는 자금을 받게 될 나라가 깨끗한 人權記錄을 가지고 있는지의 여부에 따른다는 것 등이다.

이같은 관심사가 조직적이고도 제도적인 발언권을 가질 수 있도록 美國務省 안에 人權・人道的問題局이 설치되었다. 전세계에 나가 있는 미국의 모든 외교관들이 적어도 1년에 한번 人權問題에 관심을 기울이도록 하기 위해 취해진 그밖의 다른 조치 가운데의 하나가 국무성으로 하여금 미국과 교섭하는 모든 나라의 人權에 관한 실태보고서를 해마다 議會에 제출토록 요구하는 것을 입법화한 것이다. 이는 바꾸어 말해 근본적으로 세계에 있는 모든 나라에 해당된다. 미국은 올해에 人權에 관한 우리의 國家別 報告書 작성을 방금 마쳤다. 그것을 읽어보도록 권하는 바이며, 전세계의 美國文化院 도서실에서 얻어볼 수 있다. 그것을 읽어본다면 우리가 이 문제에 대한 고려에서 일관성과 객관성의 유지를 위해 노력하고 있음을 알게 될 것이다.

일관성이란 우리의 人權政策에서 아주 중요한 부문이다. 미국인은 선거로 선출된 그들 대표들을 통해 이 문제를 전면으로 내세움에 있어 미국이 어느 쪽에 편들기를 원치 않고 있다. 미국이 어떤 나라와는 동맹 관계에 있고, 다른 나라와는 아마도 적대적 관계에 있다는 이유로 해서 어떤 나라를 달리 다루거나 또는 B라는 나라보다는 A라는 나라의 人權 남용에 더 많은 우려를 하는 일은 없다. 미국민은 우리가 파라과이의 문제를 폴란드나 南아프리카, 소련, 한국, 칠레 또는 어떤 나라든 그러한 나라를 대하듯 다루기를 기대하고 있다. 미국민은 일관성을 기대한다. 일관성이 없다면 우리에게는 人權政策은 없는 것이나 다름이 없다.

0207

우리는 미국이 갖고 있는 여러 雙務的 관계에 관련하여 정치적 태도 표명을 하는 정책을 가지고 있을 따름이다.

명백한 일이지만 人權問題는 미국과 大韓民國 사이의 外交的 議題에 올라 있다. 이에는 그럴만한 여러 가지 이유가 있다. 첫째 미국이 한국을 볼 때 韓半島의 半은 세계에서 人權의 가장 터무니 없는 침해자의 하나가 될 政權, 즉 북한에 의해 점거당하고 있다는 사실을 인식해야 한다. 北韓에 관한 정보를 얻기는 매우 어렵다. 그러나 우리가 입수하는 모든 정보는 우리가 아무리 상상력의 날개를 펴본다해도 北韓은 우리가 기본 인권이라고 신봉하고 있는 바를 존경하는 나라가 아니라는 것을 명백히 밝혀주고 있다. 人權問題가 外交 議題에 오르는 또하나의 이유는 한국의 미래를 말해주게 될 발전적 정치적 상황이 한국에서 전개되고 있기 때문이다. 이 문제를 다루고 이 문제에 관련하여 이 시점에서 지적하고 싶은 것은 미국은 한국내에서나 해외에서 반대 세력과 긴밀한 접촉을 유지하고 있으며, 이는 우리가 앞으로 유지해 나갈 정책이라는 사실이다.

人權問題의 議題는 한국에 관한 限 두가지의 근본적 문제로 귀착된다고 볼 수 있다. 첫째 우리는 고문에 대해 우려하고 있다. 고문이 미국과 한국정부 사이의 주요 문제이다. 한국 당국이 고문을 행한다는 사실은 큰 문제이다. 우리는 이를 전적으로 부당한 것으로 간주한다. 우리는 20세기의 현실적인 경제 세계로 그토록 극적으로 진입한 한국같은 나라로서는 고문이란 전혀 격에 맞지 않는 일이라고 생각한다. 어느날 밤 TV에서 한국의 '現代'의 광고를 보면서 이 생각이 문득 떠올랐다. 미국에 자동차를 팔고 있는 나라에서 고문의 문제도 안고 있다니 하는 생각이었다. 이는 단적으로 시대에 맞지 않는 일이다. 한국은 現代的 經濟를 가지고 있는데 고문은 암흑시대에 속하는 일이다. 이는 우리가 공개적으로 계속 외치는 문제이고, 우리는 일관성에 기초해서 해당 政府와 논의를 하는 그런 어조로 거리낌없이 이야기 하는 것이다. 우리는 이에 대한 모종 대책의 결의를 표명하면서, 최근 문제에 대해 보인 全斗煥大統領의 반응을 보고 매우 고무되었다. 올림픽을 위해 나아가고 있는 나라로서 이 (고문 문제)는 처리되어야 할 성질의 일이다.

그밖에도 한국 정치제도의 발전과 관련되지 않을 수 없는, 보다 큰 문제—우리가 매우 활발한 관심을 가지는 문제가 있다. 이는 앞에서 언급했던 바로 되돌아가는 것으로 우리의 우방들이 국민에게 스스로를 표현하고 창의력을 발휘하며, 자유를 누리고 국가생활에 공헌할 수 있는 기회를 부여하는 안정된 정부를 갖게 되는데 대한 우리의 관심이다. 한국에서 어떤 해결에 도달하든 간에 그것은 한국 국민으로부터 나올 문제이다. 우리는 해결책을 생각해 낼 수 없고, 해결책을 강요하려 시도할 수도 없다. 그것은 한국 국민으로부터 나와야 하며, 한국의 政体에 받아들여질 수 있는 해결책이어야 한다. 우리는 그것이 평화적이기를 희망한다. 그렇지 못할 경우 잃어버릴 것은 너무나 많다. 우리는 모든 사람들에게 그 목표로 향하도록 촉구하고 있다. 이는 우리의 東아시아·太平洋문제 담당 國務次官補 개스틴 시거가 최근에 행한 연설 속에 가장 잘 요약되어 있다고 생각된다. 질문을 받기 전 그 연설 가운데 몇 구절을 인용하는 것으로 나의 발언을 마치고자 한다. 지금 그 귀절들을 읽어보겠다.

시거 國務次官補는, "大韓民國의 미래와 우리의 雙務관계의 미래를 위해서는 代議정부를 지지하는 어떤 새 憲法이나 법률들이 나오더라도 보다 정통성이 있는 정치체제를 창출해 내는 것이 불가결한 일이다"라고 말했다. 이제 질문을 받겠다.

0208

다음은 1987년 3월 17일, 위성중계 "電話 인터뷰"(Electronic Dialogue) 프로그램을 통해 제임스 몽고메리 美國務省 人權담당次官補와 가진 질의 응답의 내용이다.

문 : 韓國을 포함한 전세계에 걸친 人權상황을 향상시키려는 귀하의 계속적인 노력에 대해 크게 감사를 드리고자 한다.

전통적으로 美國의 인권정책은 전세계의 右翼專制政府들과 매우 크게 제휴해왔다고 나는 생각한다. 하지만, 전세계에 걸쳐 인권상황을 향상시키려는 美國의 노력은 긍정적 조처이다.

전세계에 걸친 美國의 정책을 살펴볼 때, 전통적으로 美國은 스페인의 프랑코政權, 포르투갈 및 그리스의 기타 우익전제政權들을 지지했다. 美國은 비록 이들이 우익전제政權이지만 장차 민주적인 사회를 실현할지도 모른다는데에 얼마간 비관적이었다.

이는 美國이 역사적으로 이같은 우익 전제政府들을 지지했다는 인상을 우리에게 주었다. 바꿔 말하자면, 美國은 전세계에 걸쳐 인권침해를 시정하지 않았다.

1973년에 발표된 국제사면위원회(Amnesty International)의 보고에 따르면, 당시 그리스에 가서 이 나라에서 자행된 拷問사례들을 조사하던 미국인들이 이 고문사례들의 (그리스側) 조사에 관해 서로 협동적으로 물어보지 않았다.

인권문제, 특히 고문문제는 오로지 인권의 시각에서만으로는 해결될 수 없다고 생각한다. 美國의 인권정책에 어떤 변화가 있는가를 묻고자 한다.

답(몽고메리) : 이 특정한 질문에 대한 답변으로서 나는 다만 이렇게 말하고자 한다. 즉, 프랑코政權, 포르투갈과 그리스의 專制政府들을 재론함에 있어서는, 한 나라로서 美國이 정기적으로 또 제도화된 바탕에서 自國의 외교노력의 일환으로 인권문제를 포함시키기로 결정한 것은 약 10년 내지 12년전의 일이라는 것을 우리는 인식해야만 하는데, 어쩌면 이 점을 내가 충분히 밝히지 않았다. 이같은 노력은 美國으로서는 새로운 접근방법이다.

때문에 스페인, 포르투갈 및 그리스의 專制정권을 논하는 것은 약간 시대에 뒤진 감이 있다. 여러 관점에서, 美國이 지금 제도화된 (인권)정책을 추구하고 있는 이유는 부분적으로는 스페인, 포르투갈, 그리스 및 기타 국가의 우익 전제政權들에 대한 美國民들의 반응 때문인것이다.

나는 또한 스페인, 포르투갈 및 그리스가 전제정치에서 벗어나 번영하는 민주국가로 발전하고 있음을 지적하는 바이고, 우리는 그것이 고무적인 전진이라고 생각한다.

고문을 인권문제와 분리시켜 별개문제로 생각할 수 없다는 귀하의 견해에 찬동한다. 우리는 고문과 학대로부터의 市民의 자유에 대한 최선의 보장이 민주적 政体라고 생각한다. (시민의 자유와 민주적 정체) 이들 둘은 서로 손을 맞잡고 간다.

문 : 美國은, 특히 발전도상세계에서 자행되는 인권침해를 시정하기 위한 어떤 견제 수단을 갖고 있는가? 만약 美國이 견제수단을 갖고 있다면 그것이 무엇이며 또 그것을 사용하겠는가?

둘째 질문으로서, 美國은 자유와 민주주의를 신장시키기 위해 니카라과 문제에 개입하고 있다. 美國은 자유와 민주주의의 증진을 위해 칠레 문제에 개입하려는가?

답 : 견제수단의 작용력은 우리가 거론하는 나라에 달려 있다. 그 견제수단이 과장되는 일이 자주 있고, 美國은 실제로 갖고 있는 것보다 더 많은 견제수단을 갖고 있는 것으로 믿어지고 있다. 견제수단 작용력이라 함은 우리가 행하는 것과 실제로 성취할 수 있는 것 사이의 거의 기계적인 관계를 의미한다. 그것은 결코 단순한 것이 아니다.

국민을 학대하고, 국민의 정치적 권리를 거부하는 政府들에게 가할 수 있는 최선의 압력은, 무엇보다도 먼저 전세계가 그같은 나라들에서 일어나고 있는 일에 대해 시종 일관하게 주의를 집중시키는 일—美國과 기타 관계국의 국민들이 인권을 침해하는 나라들의 市民과

0209

政府와 더불어 시종 일관하게 상호작용을 갖는 일이라고 생각한다.

우리는 또한 비공개 외교가 이들 인권침해국을 다루는 데에 매우 중요하고, 매우 有用하다고 생각한다. 우리가 갖고 있는 견제수단의 영역 중의 하나에는 여러 모로 그 성격이 노골적인 것이 있는데, 그것은 경제적인 견제수단이다. 이는 우리가 그 사용을 매우 꺼리는 그러한 성격의 수단이다. 이는 우리가 매우 조심스럽게 접근하고, 극단적인 상황에서만 사용하는 그러한 성격의 수단인데, 이를 사용할 경우 (인권을 침해하는) 政府와 문제를 저지르는 가해자들을 훨씬 넘어 영향을 미치기 때문이다. 그 영향은 결국에는 온 국민이 참고 견디도록 만드는 대가를 치르게 한다.

美國은 니카라과事態에 대한 美國의 입장을 분명히 밝혔다. 우리는 니카라과의 사태를 바꾸고자 시도하고 있는 사람들을 지원하고 있다.

나는 칠레에 대한 美國의 입장도 이와 마찬가지로 명백하다고 생각한다. 작년에 美國은 유엔人權위원회에서, 칠레의 인권상황에 매우 유익한 영향을 미친, 칠레의 인권상황에 관한 한 결의안을 발의했고, 이를 뒷받침했다.

美國은 제네바의 유엔人權위원회에서 방금 또한번 다시 똑같은 일을 했다. 칠레에 관해서는 이 나라가 과거 오랫동안 민주적 정부를 가졌다는 점을 우리가 인식해야만 한다고 나는 생각한다. 그러나 칠레가 근래에 와서 다년간 민주적 정부를 갖지 못해왔는데, 우리는 이 나라가 그 민주적 전통으로 복귀하는 데에 진지한 관심을 갖고 있다. 美國은 이같은 관심을 비공개적 및 공개적 방식으로, 또 칠레政府 뿐만 아니라 역시 칠레와 관계를 맺고 있는 다른 政府들도 다루는 기타의 조처들을 통해 충분할 정도로 명백히 밝혀 왔다.

문: 첫째 질문인데, 귀하는 그같은 고문행위가 韓國정부의 정책과 어느 모로 관련되어 있다고 생각하는가? 귀하는 (미국무성) 年例인권보고서에서 그것에 언급했다.

답: 우리는 고문문제가 韓國의 當局이 취하는 조치에서 생긴다는 것을 꽤 명백히 밝혔다고 생각한다. 韓國헌법은 고문을 불법화하고 있다. 韓國정부는 고문에 반대하는 입장을 천명했는데, 나는 박종철군의 죽음에 대해 韓國정부가 취한 최근의 조치가 고무적이라고 말해야만 하겠다. 그리고 그 조치가 어느 政府이든 그 정부내의 當局이 고문행위를 저지를 때 보이는 옳은 반응이라고 생각하는데—그 반응이란, 진상을 조사하고 범법자를 처벌하는 조치인 것이다.

문: 다음 질문인데, 美國정부는 지금까지 우리의 人權신장을 고무해 왔다. 귀하는 美國이 人權정책으로 그 어떤 진전을 이룩해 왔다고 생각하는가?

답: 韓國의 인권 문제에 대해서 말하고 있는가, 아니면 전세계의 인권문제에 대해 말하고 있는가?

문: 韓國의 경우에 대해 말하고 있다.

답: 美國의 인권정책은 韓國의 전체 상황을 다루는 정책의 매우 작은 부분에 불과하다. 만약 韓國에서 人權분야의 항구적인 향상이 있게 된다면, 이는 韓國정부가 취하는 또 韓國이라는 政体가 취하는 조치 때문일 것이다.

우리는 확실히 인권분야에서 고무적인 역할을 수행할 용의를 갖추고 있다. 우리는 우리가 도움이 될 수 있다면 그 어떤 도움이라도 제공할 용의를 갖추고 있다. 우리는 韓國이 국제 사회의 활동적인 일원임을 믿는다. 韓國은 세계 경제에서 주요 활동국으로서의 책임을 떠맡았고, 내년에 개최되는 올림픽대회에서 주요 역할을 수행하게 될 것이다.

우리는 韓國이 20세기의 현대적 세계로 나아간 이 모든 움직임이 韓國에서 현재 진행중

0210

인 정치 발전의 과정에서 중요한 역할을 수행해 왔고, 또 美國이 지금까지 그 과정에서 일부 역할을 수행해 올 수 있었던 한에서는 우리가 그같은 역할을 한 것이 다행이었다고 생각한다.

문: 귀하도 알다시피 美國대통령은 対美 무역흑자를 낳고, 또한 근로자의 권리를 침해하는 나라들에 대해 보복조치를 취할 수 있다.

나는 근로자의 권리가 인권문제의 하나가 되어 있는 것으로 안다. 귀하는 韓國의 근로자의 상황을 어떻게 생각하는가? (韓國의)근로자의 상황이 韓美間의 무역관계를 증대시킴에 있어 방해물이 될 것인가?

답: 우리 두 나라 사이에서는 정치문제와 경제문제는 어느 정도 분리된 별개의 문제가 되어 있다고 나는 생각한다. 지난 수년간 韓美間의 교역은 크게 증대해 왔다는 것은 분명하다. 근로자의 권리라는 특정한 문제에 관해서는, 美國정부는 최근에 일반특혜관세(GSP)의 측면에서, 또 미국통상법상의 관점에서 韓國이 노동문제에 관한 한 근로자의 권리 행사를 향상시키려는 조치를 취해 왔다고 결론지었다. 이들 조치는 단계별 조치들이다. 앞으로 이루어져야 할 일이 상당히 많으나, 이들 조치는 옳은 방향으로 취해지고 있다.

문: 安保문제와 같은 문제들이 제기될 때의 美國의 전통적인 인권정책 수행 양상을 살펴볼 때, 안보문제에 제1우선순위가 부여되고 인권 문제에 대해서는 보다 낮은 중요성이 부여되는 것이 전통이다.

韓國의 경우 안보 및 경제문제가 보다 중요하다. 美國은 안보 및 경제문제를 균형있게 다루는 어떤 조화된 인권정책을 갖고 있는가?

답: 인권은 美國정책에서 하나의 중요한 부분이 되어 있다. 인권은 美國이 그 어느 나라이든 이와 맺은 관계에서 美國정책의 한 부분이 되어 있다. 분명히 우리에게 기타의 관심사가 있을 때가 자주 있다. 美國에게는 경제적 관심사가 있다. 우리에게는 안보적 관심사, 상업적 관심사, 정치적 및 문화적 관심사가 있다.

우리는 이들 제분야에 대한 정책들이 상호간에 보완적 (청취 불능)인 것이 될 수 있도록 시도하고 있다. 우리는 안보문제와 인권문제 중에서 반드시 하나를 선택해야만 된다고는 생각치 않는다.

만약 귀하가, 美국무성이 가장 최근에 발표한 책자 (국가별인권보고서)를 살펴본다면--이 인권보고서는 주한미국공보원으로부터 입수할 수 있다고 믿는데--우리가 세계 각국의 인권상황을 살피고 있으며 또 그같은 많은 나라들과 우리가 중요한 안보적 및 경제적 관계를 맺고 있는 것을 알게 될 것이다.

우리는, 美國과 아무런 관계를 맺고 있지 않은 나라들의 인권상황을 살필 때와 똑같은 정도로 솔직하게 또 객관적으로 (美國과 안보 및 경제관계를 맺고 있는) 이들 나라의 인권상황을 살피고 있다.

조화된 인권정책이란 美國의 외교가 균형 잡아야만 하는, 美國의 외교가 조정해야만 하는 문제임이 분명하고, 美國의 외교는 쉬운 해답이란 없다는 것을, 그리고 일관성 있게 조화된 정책을 위한 특정한 공식이 없다는 것을 깨달아야만 한다. 조화된 정책이란 상황에 따라 대응책이 강구되어야만 하는, 또 계속 연구되어야만 하는 성질의 것이다.

그러나 나는 이 말은 할 수 있다. 즉, 美國의 일반대중은, 商去來의 종류가 무엇이든 간에, 美國이 상거래 관계를 맺고 있는 나라라면 그 나라에서의 인권고려 사항에 등을 돌리지 않을 것이라는 결심을 했다.

0211

문 : 인권정책과 관련하여 취해진 경제적 제재의 예들에 대해 묻고자 한다. 또한 韓國이 美國의 인권정책과 어떻게 관련되어 있는가를 묻고 싶다.

세째 질문인데, 귀하도 알다시피 韓國에서는 오늘날 학생들과 일반대중 사이에 反美감정이 높아가고 있다. 귀하는 이 반미감정을 美國의 인권정책과 관련하여 어떻게 다루고 있는가?

답 : 매우 좋은 질문들이다. 경제적 제재란 내가 말했다시피 노골적이고도 어려운 수단이다. 제재조치에 대해서보다는 (제재와 인권상황 사이의) 관련성에 대해 더 논하기로 하자. 美國議会는 법률을 통해, 어떤 상황에서는 美國의 경제적 행동과 특정한 나라의 인권상황 사이에는 어떤 연관성이 있을 것이라고 밝혔다. 議会는 매우 구체적으로, 예를 들면 그같은 연관성은 美國의 対南아프리카공화국 関係에 관한 제재형식을 취하게 될 것이라고 밝혔다.

議会는, 국제기구와 국제借款제공기관에서의 美國의 수많은 투표가 그 특정한 나라의 인권 상황에 대한 美國의 견해의 영향을 받는다고 천명했다. 그렇다. 世界 국민들의 인권 면에서의 성취와 한 나라로서 美國이 이의 경제관계 면에서 기꺼이 행하고자 하는 것들 사이에는 연관성이 있다. 美國의 소聯 및 그 위성국가들과의 관계에 관한, 또 중화인민공화국과의 관계에 관한 그 (인권)분야에서, 우리는 매우 구체적인 법률을 갖고 있다.

우리는 美國의 법률과 관행에 존재하는 그같은 모든 갖가지 연관성을 꽤 장시간에 걸쳐 일일이 열거할 수 있다. 우리는 경제적 제재가 美國의 맹방인 韓國과 맺은 우리의 관계를 다루는 수단의 일부분이어야 한다고는 생각치 않는다. 우리는 美國의 견해를 알리기 위해서는 수많은 방법이 있다고 생각한다. 우리는 韓國民들에게 뿐만 아니라 韓國정부에게 미국의 관심사를 알릴 수 있는 여러가지 방도가 있다고 생각한다.

이 정도로 답변하고 귀하의 다음 질문, 즉 反美감정에 관한 질문에 답변하겠다. 우리가 韓國의 모든 사람들이 모든 문제에서 美國 정부의 정책에 찬동하는 것을 기대할 수 없다는 것은 분명하다. 美國에서도 그같은 일은 일어나지 않으며, 다른 어떤 곳에서도 그같은 일이 일어나기를 기대한다는 것은 비현실적인 것이다.

우리는, 韓國에 와있는 美國人들, 주한미국대사관과 미국공보원의 美國관리들이 美國의 정책에 찬동하지 않는 사람들과 또 찬동하는 사람들과의 대화와 토의에 허심탄회하게 임해야 한다는 것이 가장 중요한 일이라고 생각한다.

우리는, 그것이 문제를 다루고, 美國의 견해가 무엇인가를 명백히 밝히는 최선의 길이라고 생각한다. 美國에 대한 반대와 美國에 대한 빈정댐이 오해의 결과일 수 있는 한, 우리는 이 오해를 다루기 위해 계속 노력할 수 있고, 이해의 폭을 넓히고, 오해의 폭을 줄이도록 시도할 수 있다.

문 : 귀하는 지금까지 韓國정부에 대해 野圈 지도자 김대중씨의 복권문제를 제기한 일이 있는가?

답 : 정치 지도자들은 우리가 관심을 갖는 존재들이다. 우리는 美國이 이들 모든 (韓國의) 정치지도자에 대해 갖고 있는 관심을 韓國정부에게 알렸다. 귀하의 질문에 대해서는 "그렇다".(제기했다)가 나의 답변이다.

문 : 그 반응은 어떠했는가? 귀하의 요청에 대한 韓國정부측의 답변은 무엇이었는가?

답 : 그 반응은 우리가 거론하고 있는 개인들을 (韓國정부가) 다루는 방법에서 앞으로 나타날 것이다. 이 문제에 대해서는 美國정부와 韓國정부 사이에 아직도 의견 불일치가 남아 있음이 분명하다.

0212

- 9 -

문 : 사하로프博士가 최근 어느 회의에서 초강대국 간의 군비 증강과 人權侵害는 긴밀하게 연관되어 있다고 말했는데, 이에 개인적으로 동감한다. 유럽에서의 초강대국 軍備 対決은 많이 호전되었다. 군비 통제에 관한 東西相互均衡減軍(MBFR)회의와 같은 것이 그 例이다.

東아시아에서, 美國은 솔선해서 군사 대결을 줄이려고 노력해 왔다. 이 점에서, 東아시아 지역의 安保 때문에 人權은 제2의 우선순위로 간주되어 왔다. 이러한 정책을 변경하거나, 安保를 위해 이렇게 人權이 제2 우선순위로 내려가는 일을 없게할 의도를 가지고 있는가?

답 : 앞서의 질문에 대한 답변에서 말했듯이, 우리의 安保이익과 人權정책 간에 상충이 있어야 할 필요는 없다고 생각한다. 예컨대, 우리는 여러 해 동안 美國과 中國 간에 있었던 긴장을 감소시키기 위해 안출된 対中華人民共和國 정책을 추구해 왔다.

우리는 그 정책에서 어느 정도 성공을 거두었다고 생각한다. 나는 그것이 中國社会와 中國의 정책에 어느 정도의 開放性을 초래했으며, 이러한 현상은 세계에 뿐만 아니라 中國 자체와 그 국민들 및 그들의 経済的 福祉에 이익이 되어왔다고 생각한다.

예컨대, 이 政策이 가져온 결과 중의 하나는 오늘날 1만명을 웃도는 中國학생들이 美國에서 留學하고 있다는 사실이다. 이런 일은 우리의 정책이 시작되기 전에는 일어나지 않았을 사실이다. 그렇게 해서 中國 인구의 중요한 부분이 어느 정도 開放되고, 어느 정도의 탐구 및 研究활동을 할 수 있게 된 것이다. 그전 같으면 있을 수 없는 일이다.

우리가 東아시아에서 군사적 긴장을 감소시키는 방향의 어떠한 정책을 가지고 있건, 그 정책이 北韓住民들에게 가장 큰 관심사인 軍事情勢에 두드러진 영향을 주어오지 않았음은 분명하다.

北韓은 여전히 매우 매우 심각한 위협이며, 그래서 우리는 한 국가로서, 그 위협을 다루는데 있어서 韓國 편에서기로 작정하고 있다. 그 때문에, 우리는 韓國에 수 많은 美軍을 주둔시키고 있다.

다시 말하겠는데, 나는 安保와 人權간에 선택을 해야 할 필요가 없다고 생각한다. 우리는 韓國, 즉 大韓民國은 経済분야에서 발전해 왔다고 생각한다. 이제 韓國은 政治 분야에서도 발전해야 할 때라고 생각한다. 韓國은 이웃 北韓 때문에 주요한 군사적 위협과 高度의 군사적 긴장에 맞서 있다는 사실에도 불구하고 政治 분야에서 전진을 하고 있다고 우리는 생각한다.

문 : 귀하는, 序頭에서, 전통적으로 人權外交는 다른 나라의 内政에 대한 간섭으로 간주되었다고 말했는데, 그렇게 말할 때의 귀하의 판단 기준은 무엇이었는가? 美國의 人權外交를 적용할 때에, 韓國, 蘇聯, 南美 등과 같은 나라들에서 어떠한 반응이 있었는가?

답 : 나는 그 진술에 대한 판단 기준이라는 것은 특별히 가지고 있지 않았다. 나는 歷史的인 考察을 했다고 생각한다. 우리가 美國에서 즐겨 사용하는 逸話중의 하나가 있다. 그것은 디어도어 루스벨트氏가 美國대통령이던 世紀의 전환기에, 우리(美國)가 러시아 내의 유태인들에 대한 대우에 관해서 러시아皇帝에게 항의 각서를 보낸 적이 있는데, 그 항의는 러시아 内政에 대한 간섭이라고 거절되었으며, 그 후 그 문제는 집어치워졌다는 것이다. 오늘날, 蘇聯의 유태인 대우는 蘇聯과 美國간, 그리고 蘇聯과 세계의 餘他 국가들 간에서 언제나 外交面에서 협의되는 문제이다.

그것은 外交的인 協議 사항에서 중요하고도 常存하는 문제이다. 우리가 制度的으로 人權을 다루는, 이러한 과정을 시작했을 때에, 初期에는 그것이 거절되었다고 나는 생각한다. 그것은 저항을 받았지만, 국가 간의 즉각적인 交信 시대, 즉 다른 나라 事情을 잘 알고 있

0213

는 사람들이 있는 시대에, 사람들이 다른 나라에 가족을 두고서 美國에서 생활하고 있는 사람들이 있음을 알게 되자, 세계는 너무나 작고, 뉴스는 너무나 신속히 전달되어, 한 정부가 自國民을 다루는 방법은 세계의 여타 국가들이 염려하지 않아도 되는 문제라는 命題는 이미 유지될 수 없게 되었다고 나는 생각한다. 그것은 지탱될 수 없는 命題이다. 아마도 그것은 50년 전에 지지를 받은 것이었지만, 1987년에는 지지될 수 없는 命題이다.

문 : 최근에 蘇聯의 크레믈린当局이 人權 지도자인 사하로프와 많은 다른 政治犯들을 석방했는데, 蘇聯은 美國外交政策에 어떻게 대응한 것인가?

또 하나 질문하겠는데, 中國 지도자들과 蘇聯 지도자들이 만난 후에, 美國外交政策에 무슨 변화가 있다고 보는가?

답 : 첫째 질문에 관해서, 나는 蘇聯 내에서 발생한 일이 중요하지만, 그것에는 制約이 있다고 생각한다. 蘇聯은 주로 그들 자신의 이유로 해서 그런 일을 했다고 나는 생각한다. 蘇聯은 또한 외부의 압력 때문에도 그런 일을 했다고 나는 생각한다.

지난 수개월 동안에 중요한 政治犯이 석방될 때마다, 그것을 발표하는 것은 蘇聯內務省이 아니라 蘇聯外務省이라는 사실은 매우 흥미있는 일이라고 나는 생각한다.

그것은 蘇聯이 상대로 잡고 있는 청중이 누구인가를 명백히 밝혀주는 것이라고 생각한다. 西方세계와 세계의 여타 국가들은 蘇聯이 自國民들에게 강요하는 유형의 行動이 현대 세계에 참여하기를 원하는 나라에게는 적당치 않은 것이라는 사실을 여러 해 동안 시종일관 蘇聯에게 명백히 밝혀왔다고 나는 생각한다.

나는 계속된 압력, 즉 反復은 효과가 있었다고 생각한다. 그것은 겉으로 보아서도 명백하다고 나는 생각한다. 美國은 아시아에서 우리의 緊張 減少 정책을 계속할 것이라고 나는 생각한다.

蘇聯의 対베트남관계는 어려운 문제이다. 예컨대, 베트남의 캄푸치아占領 계속은 美國과 베트남 사이 뿐만 아니라, 美國과 蘇聯 사이에서 의견이 일치되어 있지 않은 분야이다.

韓半島 문제에 좀더 접근해서 생각해 보자면, 최근 수년 동안 우리가 해온 가장 중요한 일들 중의 하나는 중요한 安保 문제에 대해서 中國과 合意에 도달하려는 우리의 노력이었다고 나는 또다시 생각한다.

나는 그러한 노력에서 현재 변화가 곧 있으리라고는 보지 않는다. 우리는 그것이 우리에게 利로운 것이라고 생각하고 있기 때문에, 우리가 그것을 계속할 것이라고 생각한다. 우리는 그것이 우리 동맹국들을 위해서도 이로운 것이라고 생각한다.

문 : 韓國政府는 최근에 고문을 근절시키기 위해 特別委員会를 구성했다. 귀하는 韓國에서 고문행위를 감소 또는 예방하기 위해서 特別委員会를 발족시키는 韓國의 태도를 환영한다고 말했는데, 귀하는 그것을 人權 문제를 해결하기 위한 이 나라(韓國)의 최종적인 해결책으로 보는가?

둘째 질문을 하겠다. 만약--이것은 매우 큰 假定이지만--그런 종류의 비슷한 행동이 韓國에서 또다시 발생하게 된다면, 미래의 이러한 종류의 행동에 대해서 美國政府가 어떤 행동을 취하리라고 생각하는가?

답 : 우리는 그런 일이 더 이상 일어나지 않기를 바란다. 우리는 그것이 하나의 現実로 발생하는 일이 아니라 하나의 "假定"으로서 남아 있기를 바란다. 내가 앞서 말한 진술로 되돌아가서 이야기해 보자. 즉, 고문 행위가 있었다는 주장이 나왔을 때에, 이에 신속히 대응하여 그러한 주장들을 조사하고, 그 罪를 범한 자들을 처벌하는 것은 政府의 책임이다. 그것이 고문을 종식시킬 수 있는 최선의 방법이라고 우리는 생각한다. 물론 그것은 그밖의 모든

0214

政治 문제와 韓國內에서 여러분이 안고 있는 表現의 自由의 문제를 해결할 수 있는 방법은 아니다.

그것에 대한 최선의 해결책은 全韓國 국민의 폭넓은 지지를 받는 政治的 妥協쪽으로 움직여 가는 것이라고 우리는 생각한다. 그러나, 우리는 고문 문제에 관해서는 정부가 신속히 움직여야 할 뿐 아니라 그것에 대해서 효과적으로 움직여야 한다고 생각한다. 그렇게 됨으로써 아마도 그 "假定"은 現実로 나타나지 않게 될 것이다.

문 : 나의 생애 중에 두 가지 주요한 경험을 했다. 나는 10년 전에 대학교에 입학했으며, 5년 전에 신문사의 記者가 되었다. 이 두 경험을 바탕으로 하여 생각해 보건대, 대학교에서는 많은 학생들이 마르크스主義에 관한 것을 읽고, 마르크스主義 理論을 신봉했는데, 마르크스主義에 관한 것을 읽은 사람들이 요즘 法院에서 재판을 받고 있다. 귀하는 이러한 현상에 찬동하는지, 그리고 찬동한다면, 무슨 이유로 찬동하는가?

답 : 나는 사람들이 책을 읽은 탓으로 구금되고, 재판에 회부되어야 한다는 생각에는 찬동하지 않는다. 나는 그 책들이 무슨 책이든 상관 없다고 생각한다. 사람들은 그들의 思想이 아니라, 그들의 行動으로 해서 재판에 회부되어야 하는 것이다.

문 : 우리의 対美輸出은 우리의 生存을 위해서 절대 중요한 것인데, 귀하는 人權 문제와 (韓·美)양국간의 貿易增進 문제를 어떻게 다룰 것인가?

답 : 내가 앞서 말했듯이, 經濟関係와 人權문제 간에는 몇 가지 関聯性이 있다. 우리는 그것들 (經濟관계와 인권 문제) 사이에 반드시 상충이 있을 수밖에 없다고는 생각하지 않는다. 대부분이 貿易으로 나타난 韓美간의 대폭적인 접촉은 韓國에게 그 국민 소득을 증대시키고, 中産層을 증가시키고 그리고 세계 최고 수준의 교육중의 하나를 제공하는데 필요한 자금 및 財源을 공급함에 있어서 하나의 요긴한 要素가 되어 왔다고 말할 수 있다고 나는 생각한다. 韓國에는 거의 文盲이 없다.

그러한 유형의 발전과 이러한 교육의 이용과 더불어, 韓國은 바야흐로 그 經濟活動을 계속할 뿐 아니라, 政治發展이 곁들여진 經濟發展을 하려는 단계에 들어가게 되며, 그럼으로써 兩面 (경제 발전과 정치 발전)에서 韓國은 현대 세계의 하나의 어엿한 참가국이 되는 것이라고 나는 생각한다.

이러한 일이 가능하게 되는 이유중의 하나는 이룩해놓은 經濟발전 때문이라고 나는 생각한다. 그러한 발전을 하게 된 이유 중의 하나는 韓美간의 대폭적인 交易이었다. 韓國은 우리가 輸入을 많이 하는 나라일 뿐만 아니라, 또한 우리의 상품들을 많이 輸出하는 対象國이라고 理解할 필요가 있다고 나는 생각한다.

韓美간에는 貿易 문제가 있다. 美國과 기타 국가들 간에도 貿易 문제가 있다. 우리는 韓美 간의 貿易 문제들을 각기 나름대로 해결할 수 있다고 나는 생각한다. 결국에 가서 通商 및 접촉은 政治發展과 人權狀況에 도움을 준다고 나는 생각한다.

문 : 韓國에서 우리는 美國이 北韓에 비해서 大韓民國을 (더) 비판하고 있는 것으로 가끔 느끼는데, 이것은 美國이 人權侵害의 情報를 北韓으로부터 얻을 수 있는 것보다 韓國에서 더 많이 얻을 수 있기 때문에 그런 것인가? 귀하는 北韓으로부터 情報를 입수하는데 곤란을 겪은 적이 있는지, 그리고 大韓民國이 이 분야의 불공정한 추세로 해서 고통을 받아왔다고 생각하는가?

둘째 질문을 하겠다. 귀하는 韓國에서의 인권침해에 언급했다. 韓國의 일부 人士들은 美國이 우리의 内政에 간섭하고 있다는 말을 들었는데, 그것은 外交界에서 뿐 아니라, 일반

0215

국민들간에서도 그런 소문이 있다. 그래서 그것은 反美感情을 악화시킬 것이라고 믿는데, 귀하는 어떻게 생각하는가?

답 : 北韓에 관한 情報를 입수하는 것이 곤란하다는 것은 분명하다. 그것은 제일차적으로 北韓이 이루 말할 수 없이 극심한 人權侵害國이기 때문이다. 나는 美國 國務省의 人權報告書를 권하고 싶으며, 北韓의 実情에 관해서 우리가 할 수 있는 最善을 다한 사실을 보아주기를 바란다.

그러나, 또 다른 면에서, 우리가 韓國을 비판하는 이유는 우리가 韓國과 매우 좋은 관계를 맺고 있기 때문이라고 나는 생각한다. 韓國은 우리가 여러 해동안 아주 좋은 관계를 맺어온 나라이다. 韓國은 그 자유를 우리가 지지해 온 나라이며, 韓國은 그 땅에 美軍의 피가 얼룩져 있는 나라이다. 韓國은 우리가 중요하다고 생각하는 나라이다.

이러한 狀況에서, 우리는 분명히 人權 문제에 관심을 갖게 되어 있다. 우리는, 韓國과의 政治 関係를 유지할 수 있는 우리의 능력, 즉 餘他 美國 국민들로 하여금 그 関係를 지지하도록 만들 수 있는 능력이, 人權문제에 의한 영향을 분명하게 그리고 직접적으로 받기 때문에, 人權문제에 대해서 이야기하려는 것이다.

北韓內의 人權 상황이 얼마나 나쁜가는 중요하지 않으며, 韓美 간의 関係에 관한 現實은 계속 우리가 注視하지 않으면 안되는 것이 되어가고 있다. 이제 우리는 우리의 韓國 批判이 內政 干涉인가의 여부에 관해서 모든 종류의 学問的 및 理論的 토의를 해볼 수 있다. 그것은 하나의 現實이다.

그 現實은 美國 국민들과 美國 議会의 현실이다. 왜냐하면 美國은 美國의 국가적인 에너지를 韓國에서 너무나도 많이 소모시켰으며, 美國은 (韓國과) 매우 중요한 貿易 관계를 가지고 있으며, 美國내에서 수많은 韓國人들이 생활하고 있으며, 美國은 韓國을 알고 있으며, 또한 韓國政府가 韓國民을 어떻게 다루는가는 하나의 政治 문제이기 때문이다.

그것은 우리가 하나의 政府로서 다루지 않을 수 없는 힘들고도 엄연한 政治的인 사실이다. 우리는, 그것을 다룰 수 있는 최선의 방법은 韓國政府와 더불어 솔직하고도 허심탄회한 자세가 되고, 그리고 그렇게 함으로써 韓國 국민들과도 그렇게 되는데에 있다고 느낀다. ◆

0216

미국국민은 정부가 인권
을 부여하는 것이 아니라, 인
권보장을 위해 정부가 존재한
다는 哲學을 갖고있다. 이는 모
든 국가의 국민이 동의하고
있는 大前提다.

인권문제와 관련해 국민의
진정한 기대에 부응하지 못하
는 체제나, 권한을 남용하는체
제는 불안정한 체제다. 그리고
이런 체제는 솔직이말해 미
국의 이익도위협한다고믿고있다.

美국무성의 외교적 현안이 되어
있다. 그 이유는 미국의 한국
의 정치상황발전을 위해 노력
하고 있기 때문이다. 미국은
한국정부가 취한 조치는 앞
으로 나라로서는 고무적정을 유
지하고 있고, 앞으로도 이같
은 정책을 견지할 것이다.

한국의 인권제3부가지로
나누어있다. 첫째는 고문문제
로 韓国政府가 고문에 의해

美국무성 人權副次官補 인터뷰內容

一問一答

─미국의 인권 이문제는 기계적이거나
단순한것이 아니다. 우리는 인권
관심는 한국과의 관계에서이
러한것이 인권신장의 방향이
돼야한다고 생각지 않는다.

─미국은 인권문제와 상관있
경제적이해관계와 상관된다는
데대한 비중을 상대적으로
낮추었다. 이러한 이해관계의
수준는 그 깊이에따라 천수만별로
하는 그 깊이에따라 천수만별로

▲몽고메리=미국의 인권정
책은 제도화됐다. 장기적으로
상대국에 어떻게 진화시키는가.

─金大中씨의 사면·복권문제

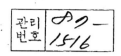

외 무 부

착 신 전 보

번 호 : USW-3334   일 시 : 706231759   종 별 : 지 급

수 신 : 장관(미북)

발 신 : 주 미 대사

제 목 : 국무성 인권 부차관보 면담

연 : USW-1609

대 : WUS-2063

1. 금 6.23(화) 당관 정태익 참사관은 지난 6.16 자로 국무성 인사국 부국장에서 인권국 부차관보로 부임한 ROBERT FAIRAND 와 면담, 여.야간의 대화와 타협전망등 최근 국내정국 상황과 제반 인권개선 조치등에 관해 설명하고 아국정부의 정치발전 및 인권개선 노력에 대한 이해와 협조를 당부하였음.

2. 동 부차관보는 아국 정국이 타협분위기를 조성해 나가고 있는것을 매우 다행으로 생각하고 있다고하면서, 자신은 정치발전과 함께 인권상황도 개선되어 나갈것이라는 희망을 갖고있으며, 내년도 국무성 인권보고서는 금년도 보고서와는 크게 다른 각도 에서 작성될수 있기를 기대한다고 언급하였음

(대사 협결인채 분류(19 . : .)
. 07. 12. 31 설료

검토필 (18).

미주국   차관실   1 차보   2 차보   청와대   총리실   안 기

PAGE 1   87.06.24 19:26

외신 2과 통제관

0218

외교문서 비밀해제: 한국 인권문제 10
한국 인권문제 미국 반응 및 동향 2

초판인쇄 2024년 03월 15일
초판발행 2024년 03월 15일

지은이 한국학술정보(주)
펴낸이 채종준
펴낸곳 한국학술정보(주)
주 소 경기도 파주시 회동길 230(문발동)
전 화 031-908-3181(대표)
팩 스 031-908-3189
홈페이지 http://ebook.kstudy.com
E-mail 출판사업부 publish@kstudy.com
등 록 제일산-115호(2000. 6. 19)

ISBN 979-11-7217-064-6 94340
       979-11-7217-054-7 94340 (set)